AF352665

JNĀNESHVARI

JNĀNESHVARI

[BHĀVĀRTHADIPIKĀ]

Written
by
Shri Jnāneshvar

Translated from the Marāthi
by
V. G. PRADHĀN

Edited and with an Introduction
by
H. M. LAMBERT

State University of New York Press

First published in Great Britain by George
Allen & Unwin Ltd. in 1948

This translation © UNESCO 1969

Published by
State University of New York Press, Albany

Copyright 1987 State University of New York

For information, address State University of New York
Press, State University Plaza, Albany, N.Y., 12246

Library of Congress Cataloging-in-Publication Data

__________, fl. 1290
   Jnaneshvari : Bhāvārthadipikā.

   Translation of Jñānesvarī.
   1. Bhagavadgītā—Commentaries.   I. Pradhan, V. G.
(Vitthal Ganesh), d. 1950.   II. Lambert, H. M. (Hester
Marjorie)   III. Title.
BL1138.66.J5713   1987   294.5′924   86-23069
ISBN 0-88706-487-6
ISBN 0-88706-488-4 (pbk.)

CONTENTS

In the transcription of Sanskrit words it is, unfortunately, necessary to use two systems. It is hoped, however, that this may prove to be of interest to some readers. In the text of the *Bhagavadgitā* it is necessary to employ the standard transcription for Sanskrit used by the author of *The Bhagavadgitā* incorporated in the text. On the other hand, with a view to facility in reading the text of the translation of the *Jnāneshvari*, a conventional system of transcription omitting all diacritical marks except the long mark distinguishing the vowel 'a' from 'ā' is used in transcribing Sanskrit names and Sanskrit terms of Hindu philosophy and religion occurring in the text. The quality of these two distinct vowels may be illustrated by these English examples: 'a' as in '*a*go', or 'er*a*' and '*ā*' as in '*ā*h', or '*ā*fter'. The necessity for using this long mark in transcribing Sanskrit words is illustrated by the following examples: the two words 'bala' and 'bāla' (VI, note 14) have different meanings and are distinguished only by the use of the long mark; in the two names 'Nārāyana' and 'Janārdana' the proper pronunciation of the vowels and therefore the rhythm of the syllables, is indicated only by using this mark. Similarly, it is important to distinguish the two words 'Brahma(n)', 'the Absolute' and 'brāhman', the name of the priestly caste, by the use of this long mark.

As, however, the text of the *Bhagavadgitā* incorporated in the text is that given in S. Rādhākrishnan's work, it is necessary to transcribe this with the full diacritics used by Sanskrit scholars. But comparison with the translation of the *Jnāneshvari* English text will frequently help readers in understanding the Sanskrit system alongside of the Marāthi simplified system.

PREFACE

The work of which the English translation is presented here has been selected by the Indian National Commission to be included as a contribution from Marāthi literature in the UNESCO Collection of Representative Works. Although the *Jnāneshvari* is a mediaeval text, it is widely recognized as the most notable work of Marāthi literature. In modern times it is known not only by scholars but to the common people of Mahārāshtra, who are familiar with it as the revered scripture of a particular religious sect in Western India.

There are many manuscripts of this work, some of which have come to light in relatively recent years. According to an entry at the end of the last chapter of the work it was completed in the year AD 1290, but no recognized contemporary manuscript has become available. The earliest text which was for long considered to be an authentic version, is a manuscript belonging to the late sixteenth century in which the claim is made by an important Marāthi poet, Eknāth, born in 1549, that he had restored the *Jnāneshvari* to its original form. Claims have been made by more recent scholars that manuscripts found by them are nearest to the original, but the matter has for many years been a subject of considerable controversy. Among the most important texts available in recent years are those published by R. V. Mādgāvkar in 1907, by V. K. Rājvāde in 1909, and by A. M. Kunte in 1910. During the last ten years a special committee of the Bombay State Education Department has been trying to determine, as nearly as possible, which version could be established as the oldest manuscript available, and accepted as a standard text. As a result of combined research by scholars, the version published by V. K. Rājvāde in 1909 is now accepted as a standard text and was published as such in 1959.[1]

Until the year 1953 no complete English translation of the *Jnāneshvari* had been published. In that year a society known as the Dnyāneshwari English Rendering Association supported the publication of an English version written by the late Shri B. R. Bhāgavat under the original title, *Bhāvārthadīpikā.*

---

[1] Dāndekar, Śankar Vāman, and others (Ed.). *Jnāneśvarī*, 1st ed. (Bombay, Education Department, 1959).

A*viii

The style is somewhat too free to accompany the standard version of the Marāthi work. The best translation available is an unpublished manuscript by the late Shri Vitthal Ganesh Pradhān, who died in 1950; it was brought to the notice of the Indian National Commission by his daughter in 1955. This version was considered a suitable basis, after appropriate editing, for an English translation to accompany the now established standard Marāthi edition of the *Jnāneshvari* and has been duly collated with the Rājvāde version at the request of the Indian Commission.

The *Jnāneshvari* Marāthi text includes the eighteen chapters of the Sanskrit work known as the *Bhagavadgitā*, which serves as a basis for the author's 'commentary', or greatly extended 'song-sermon'. The English translation of the *Bhagavadgitā* which has been incorporated in these volumes is the one made by Dr Sarvepalli Rādhākrishnan,[1] who has kindly given permission to reproduce it. Thanks are due to Miss Lila Pradhān for her gracious permission to publish her father's work.

The Editor wishes to express here her thanks to her colleagues at the School of Oriental and African Studies, University of London, for assistance given to her in many ways in the preparation of these volumes, in particular to Dr I. M. P. Raeside, Lecturer in Marathi at the School; and to members of the Literature Division of UNESCO for their continued advice and support.

H. M. LAMBERT

Editor.

London, July 1966

[1] Sir S. Radhakrishnan, *The Bhagavadgītā*: London, George Allen and Unwin, 1948.

INTRODUCTION

The historical and religious setting of the *Jnaneshvari*,[1] of which this is the first of two volumes, is of great importance for the understanding and appreciation of its literary and religious merits. The date of its completion, definitely stated at the end of the work as AD 1290,[2] or, in the Indian system of dating used at the time and still in use in many contexts, Shaka 1212, places it historically in the medieval period of Marāthi literature. This language, of Sanskritic origin, is spoken in the region of Western India known as Mahārāshtra (Bombay Province) since the early centuries of this era and today is the mother-tongue of 30,000,000 people in modern Mahārāshtra and elsewhere.[3]

The historical background of this mediaeval period is centred in the upper reaches of the Godāvari river, which rises in the western coastal range of the Sahyādri mountains and flows across the great central plain of India towards the eastern coast south of the Bay of Bengal. Situated at the head of this valley was the ancient city of Devagiri, known since the Moghul invasion at the end of the thirteenth century as Daulatabad, some 150 miles west of Bombay. Here the Yādava kings, coming from the northern part of the region, established their capital, which became the centre from which culture and learning spread throughout the region. The Yādava ruler at the time of Jnāneshvar, the author of the *Jnāneshvari* and also known as Jnānadeva, was Rāmadevarāva, who reigned at Devagiri from 1271 to 1309 and whose name is mentioned in the text.[4] Under the Yādavas peace and prosperity prevailed in the kingdom and this period has been described as the 'golden age' of Mahārāshtra. This kingdom lasted for well over a hundred years, but it eventually succumbed to the Moghul invasion from the north of India in the year 1318 and remained in subjection for more than three centuries.

---

[1] See p. 18 note 1.
[2] See *Jnāneshvari*, Chapter XVIII, v. 1792. Rājvāde edition. (Vol. II.)
[3] Indian Census, 1961.
[4] See Chapter XVIII, v. 1783. Fuller information concerning this period of history in Western India, and the general historical, religious, literary and linguistic background of the *Jnāneshvari* may be found in the works given in the short bibliography at the end of this Introduction.

In the region of Mahārāshtra, during the thirteenth century a widespread revival of religious devotion developed which lasted until the seventeenth; its influence continues, in certain religious sects, till the present day. This revival was not restricted to Mahārāshtra but was active also in other regions of India, notably in northern India and Bengal; parallel movements developed also in some regions in the south. The distinguishing feature of this movement, in contrast to previous trends of mysticism which were philosophical and remote from the everyday life of the common people, is a practical and devotional mysticism intimately interwoven with the daily activities and the spiritual needs of all classes of men and women. Identified with the Hindu god Vishnu was his incarnation in Krishna, whose devotees worshipped him with the 'loving devotion' which was the mainspring of simple religious fervour, satisfying the emotional needs of those for whom philosophical systems and elaborate orthodox ritual would have little meaning. Unlike the traditional Hindu rites, the religious training and the theory and practice of yoga, which were restricted to the brāhman, or priestly, caste, the devotional worship of the Bhakti movement[1] was open to all men. Among the followers of this movement, or 'path' (which leads from the simplest expression of deep devotion to the highest level of religious experience in the realization of oneness with the supreme Spirit, the Absolute), were to be found the learned and the ignorant, the rich and the poor, the great and the humble. Moreover, this form of mysticism was embedded in the community life of the village and religious practice brought about unifying social influences which had an important political value in the building of the Marātha kingdom.

Religious expression among those who followed the path of this movement took the form of individual and group singing of devotional hymns, in the temple courtyards, in roadside gatherings after the day's work was done, and in regular pilgrimages to holy places, usually to the sites of great saints and shrines connected with the worship of Krishna. The medium for the religious instruction and exhortation of the devotees was the rhythmic recitation, often accompanied by simple musical percussion instruments, of ancient myths of the Hindu gods and legendary stories of those who worshipped and

[1] The term Bhakti, in this connection, connotes worship, faithfulness, devotion, and is one of the recognized 'paths' to religious fulfilment.

served them, along with practical expositions and exhortations to simple loving devotion to Krishna. The form in which this was conveyed to groups of worshippers was known as the *kirtana* or 'song-sermon', and these recitations made a powerful appeal to the people of less sophisticated levels.

The central focus of pilgrimage connected with the Bhakti movement was, and still is, the town of Pandharapur, especially the shrine of the god Vitthal, or Vithobā.[1] This town is situated about 150 miles south-east of Bombay on the river Bhima, with its wide and picturesque banks on which many fine temples are visible. At the time of the regular great pilgrimages, which take place twice yearly, hundreds of pilgrim bands converge on this town singing songs of devotion to Krishna and expressing their religious fervour in many ways, including wayside dancing which often induces states of ecstacy. Pandharapur has a long history reaching back into the earliest centuries, and at the time of Jnāneshvar, that is, in the second half of the thirteenth century, had long been the most famous pilgrimage place in Mahārāshtra. Other well-known centres of pilgrimage in this region, though of rather less importance, are the villages of Dehu, about fifty miles from Bombay, and Alandi, site of the shrine and tomb of Jnāneshvar, about twelve miles south of Poona.[2] These three centres were often visited in a continuous cycle of pilgrimage by the devotees of the god Vitthal and the disciples of the great Bhakti saints.

The general influence of this movement on the life of the people of Mahārāshtra was twofold. In the first place it brought into prominence a number of men, and not a few women, of outstanding gifts and saintly devotion who contributed to Marāthi literature some of the greatest treasures of its earlier period. In the second place, the Bhakti movement gave a powerful impetus to the development of the Marāthi language as a medium for the expression of religious thought and devotional worship, while, under the cultural influence of Devagiri, Marāthi was becoming established as a literary language capable of expressing scholarly works. Hitherto, Sanskrit had been the only medium through which the religious and cultural heritage of the Hindus could be passed on and it was therefore accessible only to the learned; but now the

---

[1] For a detailed history of Pandharapur, see G. A. Defleury, *The Cult of Vithobā*.

[2] See below, p. 19.

everyday language of the common people began to be used both to convey the teachings of religion and to express popular devotion in various forms of worship.

Though much of the earliest literature in Marāthi still remains without established date, some works are assumed to have been written in the early or middle thirteenth century. The lack of contemporary manuscripts presents great difficulty in this matter. Among these early works are the philosophical and mystical writings of Mukundarāj, who was said to have been the spiritual teacher of one of the early Yādava kings and who was the author of two important religious works in verse. Other works in both prose and verse by authors belonging to the religious sect of the Mahānubhāvas[1] are said to belong to the end of the thirteenth and beginning of the fourteenth centuries, though the major verse work among these is still under the influence of Sanskrit.

The earliest among these authors had already made some considerable contribution to the development of Marāthi as a literary language, mainly as a medium of religious and philosophical thought and biographical narrative, before the *Jnāneshvari* was composed. The outstanding contribution of the author of this work was that he wrote freely in the mother tongue of his own people in a form which was both acceptable to the learned and easily understood by the unsophisticated; he was thus able to widen the scope of the conventional literary language by enriching it from various sources. The subjects treated by him range from Hindu philosophy and detailed descriptions of the practice of yoga and sacrificial rituals, to practical illustrations culled from everyday village life and the beauties of nature, from exhortations to devotional life in the way of Bhakti to mythology and popular legend. His command of both Sanskrit and Marāthi enabled him to blend the two languages in a flexible and poetic style which meets the needs of both the learned scholar and men of the simple level of the tradesman, the artisan and the peasant.

A word should be said concerning the three most important religious sects existing during this period in Mahārāshtra. The first of these, the *Māhānubhāva* sect,[2] Hindu but though

---

[1] See below, note on religious sects.

[2] For further details concerning this sect, see Raeside, I. M. P.: A Bibliographical Index of Mahānubhāva works in Marāthi', *Bulletin of the School of Oriental and African Studies*, Vol. XXIII, part 3.

unorthodox in some respects, exclusively devoted to the worship of Krishna, was founded towards the end of the thirteen century; they have left a body of literature propounding their special teaching and containing biographical works on their leading teachers. They were considered to have had some influence on the literary style of the period, but they constitute a competitive sect, having no great influence on the development of the *Bhakti* movement. The second sect, of considerable importance in the religious background of the period of Jnāneshvar, is that of the *Nātha* tradition which had been handed down from generation to generation, through the initiation of disciples; its beginning is beyond the possibility of being traced. This was an orthodox Hindu sect practising yogic discipline and rituals within the caste system and, as will be seen later,[1] had a great influence upon Jnāneshvar's family line. The influence of this sect spread widely beyond the boundaries of Mahārāshtra and it has continued as an active religious body in its traditional form, until the present day. The third and most significant of the sects which were active during the period with which we are mainly concerned is that of the *Vārkaris*. The sect is known by this name because of the regular pilgrimages to the great Bhakti centre at Pandharapur; it was thriving in the thirteenth century and is still very active in contemporary Mahārāshtra. The annual pilgrimages to Pandharapur are a prominent feature of popular religious life (as, for instance, in Poona), and people of every caste and calling participate in them. Jnāneshvar himself is revered as the greatest leader, though he was not actually the founder, of the sect. The devotees of the *Vārkari* sect were responsible for much of the religious literature of the following three to four centuries, and the authors of the popular devotional poems of the form known as the *abhanga* are now referred to as the poet-saints of Mahārāshtra;[2] they include men and women of all castes from the highest to the lowest, and the use of this genre for religious poetry continued even beyond the time of the most celebrated of them all, Tukārām—a simple cultivator, who lived during the late sixteenth and early seventeenth centuries.[3]

---

[1] See below, p. 19.

[2] Cf. *Psalms of the Marātha Saints*, Nicol Macnicol. See bibliography.

[3] *Ibid.*, section on Tukāram, with poems. The actual dates of this poet are not established.

This, in general, is the religious and literary background against which the text of the present work is to be understood. Towards the end of the thirteenth century there emerged Jnāneshvar, or Jnānadeva,[1] one who is not only the most renowned figure of mediaeval Marāthi literature but one who has never been surpassed in achievement throughout the whole of Marāthi literary history. His poetic work, the *Bhāvārtha-dipikā*,[2] more widely known as the *Jnāneshvari*, stands out among works of the mediaeval period as marking the dawn of Marāthi literature. In relation to the *Bhakti* movement, Jnānadeva is the most notable and the most deeply revered of its leaders.

Biographical material of an authentic nature regarding the birth of Jnāneshvar, his life and works, and his death through the attainment of the highest level of religious experience in self-immolation, varies considerably in the degree of its authenticity. Inevitably, a figure of such stature becomes surrounded with legend and stories of miraculous achievements. However, in recent years much careful research has established sufficient grounds for giving the main facts of his life and work; accepted tradition is usually relied on to fill out a more detailed picture.

The most reliable of these facts are the two already referred to:[3] the completion date of the composition, giving the name of its scribe, and the reference to the Yādava king Rāmadeva, which confirms the period of composition.

The first biographer of Jnāneshvar is said to have been one of his contemporaries, Nāmadeva, author of many devotional works. According to tradition, Nāmadeva accompanied Jnānadeva on many pilgrimages and it is thought that these two had a considerable mutual influence. Nāmadeva outlived Jnānessvar by some years and would have been in a good position to preserve information about his life, though almost inevitably his biography would be based on an interweaving of fact and legend. The second important source of biographical material is found in the works of Ekanātha (born in 1549), author of religious works which are part of the wealth of *Bhakti* literature. He produced a version of the *Jnāneshvari* which he claimed was an authentic version in which neither

---

[1] The name is based on the Sanskrit word *jnāna*, 'knowledge'; *ishvar*, used here in the sense of 'lord', and *deva*, 'god'. Hence the alternative names.

[2] *The Light of the Meaning of Faith.*

[3] Notes 2 and 4, p. 13.

change nor addition should be permitted. Finally, much information, though varying in reliability, can be found in the works of Mahipati, the eighteenth century poet, which include the lives of various saints of the Bhakti movement in Mahārāshtra. Manuscripts of the *Jnāneshvari* have continued to be found in more recent years, of various degrees of authenticity. References to Jnānadeva's work throughout the history of Marāthi literature and the fact that the *Jnāneshvari* is the most widely read religious book among the faithful worshippers of the Vārkari sect, as well as a large number of his devotional lyrics, bear witness to the deep and lasting influence of the author.

The generally accepted date of Jnāneshvar's birth is AD 1271, but tradition varies concerning the place. According to the most popular tradition, he was born at Ālandi, where his parents lived, and which is also the site of his shrine; another tradition claims that he was born at the village of Apegāo in the Godāvari valley. He came from a long line of spiritual teachers of the Nātha sect and was initiated into the sect by his elder brother, Nivrittinātha. His father, Vitthalpant by name, was a deeply religious man whose wife, Rakhumābāi, belonged to the village of Ālandi. No children were born from their marriage for some years and meanwhile Vitthalpant, deeply drawn towards the religious life of renunciation, left his wife and made a pilgrimage to Benares where he became initiated as a member of a religious community. Thus he abandoned his obligations as a householder, one of the essential stages of the life of an orthodox brāhman, without having reared a family.[1] However, his *guru* (that is, his spiritual director), on discovering that he was a married man who had left his wife without her consent and without giving her children, made him return and fulfil his family obligations. The necessary withdrawal from his initiation in Benares was regarded as a serious deviation from the requirements of his caste and therefore, on his return to Ālandi, he and his family were rejected from association with his fellow brāhmans and they were obliged to live on the outskirts of the village. In course of time his wife bore four children, the eldest son was Nivritti; two years later was born Jnānadeva, and Sopānadeva, the third son, after another two years; lastly comes a daughter, Muktābāi. As the sons grew to the age at which they should

[1] See Note 7 in Chapter VII in the text, giving these stages of brāhman life.

go through the ceremony of full admission to the brāhman
caste, permission was withheld owing to the severe disapproval
of the brāhman elders; and the father, Vitthalpant, undertook
to expiate his sin by throwing himself into the river Ganges.

In course of time, however, the four children came to be
recognized as having saintly qualities, and, in the case of
Jnānadeva, as being endowed with miraculous powers; whether
they were re-admitted to the brāhman caste is not known, but
they were revered as true saints, and subsequently made their
contribution to *Vākari* literature. Nivritti initiated his brother
Jnānadeva into the Nātha sect and is frequently referred to in
the *Jnāneshvari*; Sopānadeva followed a similar path, and
Muktābāi became one of the best known women Bhakti poets.
The family settled for some time at Nevāsā, not far from
Paithan, on the Godāvari river, and it was here that Jnānadeva
composed the *Bhāvārthadipikā*—and, later, his more philosophical work, the *Amritānubhāva*,[1] a work still held in high
esteem. He also composed many religious songs and devotional
hymns. After the completion of his two major works the family
returned to Ālandi and it was here, in his early twenties, that
he took the final step to the highest level of religious experience,
known as samādhi, in committing himself to live entombment
whilst in a state of ecstasy.

The main narrative theme of the *Jnāneshvari* is based on one
of the most widely known of the poetical works of Sanskrit
literature, the *Bhagavadgitā*, sometimes given the name of
'Song of the Lord', in English translations, and frequently
referred to by the shortened form of the title, the *Gitā*. This
work is the most highly treasured of the religious scriptures of
the Hindus, and its eighteen chapters form the core of one of
the sections of the great epic of the Mahābhārata, that is, the
Bhishmaparva, in which the famous deeds of the warrior
Bhishma are narrated.[2] This epic is the legendary history of
the descendants of Bharata, the 'universal monarch' of ancient
India.[3] The two great families descended from Bharata were
that of the king Pāndu, known as the *Pāndavas*, and that of

---

[1] For a study of this work, see Bahirat, B. P., *The Philosophy of Jnānadeva*,
noted in the Bibliography.

[2] The names and relationships of the principal persons taking part in the
battle drama are given in the notes accompanying Chapter I of the text.

[3] The ancient name of India was *Bharatavarsha*, the 'country of Bharata'.
The descendants of Bharata are the *Bhāratas*; hence the name of the epic,
'The Great Bhārata'.

the king Kuru, known as the *Kauravas*; the inclusive name of these descendants is the *Bhāratas*. Between these two families, or clans, a great feud had arisen connected with the inheritance of the kingship. The king Dhritarāshtra, of the *Kuru* line, wished his kingdom to be inherited by Yudhishthira, the eldest son of the *Pāndava* line, a plan which had been interfered with by Duryodhana, son of Kuru, who secured it for himself. This treachery brought about the threat of war between the two clans, cousins by relationship; Arjuna the son of Pāndu (also called Pārtha) being the leader of the *Pāndavas* and Duryodhana being the leader of the *Kauravas*. The battlefield on which this conflict is about to be fought out provides the dramatic setting in which a deep philosophical problem is the subject of a discourse between Arjuna and the god Krishna, incarnation of Vishnu, in the guise of Arjuna's charioteer. Arjuna's dilemma is the cause of his deep depression, vividly portrayed in the first chapter of the *Jnāneshvari*; it involves the choice between shedding the blood of his own kinsmen for the sake of inheriting a worldly kingdom, and his obligation to fulfil his own appointed role as a warrior by caste to enter into battle. As the two armies stand arrayed face to face, we are shown the blind old king Dhritarāshtra seated in his chariot within sight of the battlefield and accompanied by his charioteer, Sanjaya, who describes the scene to his master. Arjuna's dilemma provides the opportunity for an exposition by Krishna of the religious and philosophical tenets of Hindu teaching concerning the goal of life in this world as being a process of attaining salvation through becoming one with the Absolute.[1]

The *Jnāneshvari* is often referred to as a 'commentary' on the *Bhagavadgitā*. In the actual text it is referred to both as a *dharmakirtan* or religious 'song-sermon'[2] and as a *tikā* or commentary.[3] The former of these terms would perhaps be the more accurate, as it combines an exposition of Hindu philosophical principles, set forth in the dialogue between Arjuna and Krishna, with a popular sermon in which Jnāneshvar

---

[1] Throughout the text of the poem its author places great emphasis on this religious philosophy, known as *advaita*, non-duality, or identity, in contrast to the teaching of the opposite principle of *dvaita*, duality, or the essential separateness of the individual soul from the Supreme Spirit, Brahma, upheld by certain of his predecessors if not his contemporaries. A full discussion of the philosophy expounded in the Bhagavadgitā, on which Jnāneshvar bases his teaching may be found in the Introductory Essay of *The Bhagavadgitā* of S. Rādhākrishnan, noted in the bibliography.

[2] See Chapter XVIII, v. 1771. [3] *Ibid.*, v. 1792.

himself is preaching in simpler terms to his audience of disciples. It is this combination which results in the expansion of the seven hundred verses of the *Bhagavadgitā* to, roughly, nine thousand verses of the *Jnāneshvari*. The reader should remember that though the *Jnāneshvari* appears in the form of a written work, it should be read in the imagined context of Jnānadeva preaching to his audience who, from time to time interrupt him, even growing impatient with his long digressions, so that he feels a need to appease them. He expounds to them, in terms of the religious paths of knowledge, Action, Renunciation of Action, Devotion and others,[1] the ways in which salvation may be attained; he appeals to the intellects of the learned and exhorts the simple to piety by drawing his material from many sources, including the whole range of Sanskrit literature. In the opening verses of the first chapter, references are made to the *Upanishads*, mystical writings of the ancient teachers designed to discover and expound the secrets of the sacred texts of the *Vedas*, to the traditions and codes of established law, and to the *Purānas* which contain the legends and mythological stories of the Hindu gods and their followers. The *Purānas*, especially, supply him with an unlimited wealth of material with which to illustrate his teachings and he draws on his intimate knowledge of village life to provide simile and metaphor to drive home his points.

The poem is written in a form of rhythmic prose peculiar to the verse forms of Marāthi, and especially suitable for recitation, or chanting; it is in the form of a *kirtan*, accompanied by percussion instruments. Each verse consists of four lines or quarters, constituting an *ovi*, the name given to the metre; the first three lines are rhymed and are formed from a varying number of syllables ranging from five to fifteen, the fourth line consisting of between three and thirteen syllables, not related by rhyme to the first three. This scheme has a wide range of variety in length of line allowing for many irregularities; but this freedom makes it possible to convey different types of subject matter without the restriction which would be imposed by a more fixed type of versification.

The translation of the work has been done in a simple English prose style as, apart from the problem presented by the magnitude of the work, it would prove impossible to combine a faithful rendering with any kind of poetic form which might

---

[1] Cf. titles of chapters under Contents.

interfere with the clear expression of philosophical principles, or the description of yogic practices.

A short bibliography is given below of the main works in English and French which have been the sources of reference in this Introduction, in which any readers who wish to follow up particular aspects of the *Jnāneshvari* will find further information.

BIBLIOGRAPHY

Abbott, Justin. *The Poet Saints of Mahārāshtra*, a series of volumes of translations from mediaeval and later Marāthi poets, Vol. I. Office of the Poet-Saints of Mahārāshtra, United Theological College, Poona, 1926.

Bahirat, B. P. *The Philosophy of Jnānadeva*, Pandharapur Research Society, 1956.

Deleury, G. A. *Les Psaumes du Pélerin*, UNESCO, Paris, 1954. The Cult of Vithobā, Deccan College Research Institute, Poona, 1960.

Edwards, J. F. *Dnyāneshvar, the Outcaste Brāhman*, Āryabhushan Press, Poona, 1941.

Macnicol, Nicol. *Psalms of the Marātha Saints*, Heritage of India series, Associated Press, Calcutta, and Oxford University Press, London, 1919.

Master, Alfred. *A Grammar of Old Marāthi*, Clarendon Press, Oxford, 1964.

Mokashi, D.B. *Palkhi* Translated by Philip C. Engblom, SUNY Press, Albany, 1987

Ranade, R. D. *Mysticism in India: The Poet Saints of Maharashtra*, SUNY Press, Albany, 1983.

Sargeant, Winthrop. *The Bhagavad Gita*, SUNY Press, Albany, 1984.

THE JNĀNESHVARI

CHAPTER I

Salutation to Shri Ganesha!

1. Om! Salutation to the Supreme Being, described in the Vedas! Victory to that Self-known One, Pure Nature of the Self![1]

2. O God! Thou art Ganesha, the illuminator of all intelligence. The servant of Nivritti says, Attend to my story.

3. The Vedas in their perfection are as the beautiful image of the god, of which the flawless words are the resplendent body.

4. The Smritis are the limbs thereof, the marking of verses shows their structure, and in the meaning lies a veritable treasure-house of beauty.[2]

5. The eighteen Purānas are the rich ornaments, and the theories propounded in them are the gems, for which the rhythmic style provides the settings.[3]

6. The fine metrical form is his many-coloured garment of which the composition is the fine shining texture.

7. So the epic poems and dramas in it, read with delight, are as jingling bells giving out the music of the sense.

8. The various principles carefully considered in them and the aptness of the words expressing them appear as precious jewels set in the bells.

9. The wisdom of Vyāsa and others is as the waist-cloth, its tassled end gleaming with purity.[4]

10. The six systems of philosophy are as the six arms, and the different theories expounded in them are the six weapons held in the hands.[5]

11. The art of reasoning is the hatchet, logic is the goad, the Vedānta philosophy is the luscious sweetmeat [held in the hand].[6]

1

12. In one hand is held the broken tooth, symbolizing the rejection of the teaching of Buddha, refuted by the Vedānta commentaries.

13. Then the doctrine of the Universal Spirit is the lotus-like hand of blessing; the establishment of religion is the hand of reassurance.[7]

14. Pure discrimination is the straight trunk, wherein dwells the highest joy of supreme bliss.

15. Impartial discussion is the pure white tusk; [Ganesh is] the small-eyed elephant-god, remover of obstacles, [representing the subtle eye of wisdom].

16. I regard the two systems as his two ears, and the bees [hovering over his temples] as the sages who taste of the nectar of their teaching.[8]

17. The themes of duality and non-duality come together on the temples of his elephant-head as lustrous corals.

18. The fragrant flowers adorning the crown of the head are the ten Upanishads, containing in full the honey of knowledge.[9]

19. The A of the Om is the legs, U is the large belly, and the M is the great circle of the head.[10]

20. When these three are united, the sacred word is formed. Through the grace of my preceptor, I salute this, the primal cause of all being, the Om.

21. Now I salute Shāradā, whose delight is in speech, lover of wisdom, sense, and skill, enchantress of the world.[11]

22. In my heart dwells my spiritual teacher, by whose grace I have been rescued from the ocean of this wordly existence and have become devoted to the way of discrimination.

23. As when a pigment is applied to the eyes, the sight gains in clarity, so that one finds one's way to the store of great treasure;

24. or when the stone of desire has been found, all one's wishes are fulfilled, Jnānadeva says that all his desires have been satisfied through the grace of Shri Nivritti.[12]

25. So also those men who wisely serve their spiritual teachers thereby attain the object of their lives, just as when the roots of a tree are watered the branches begin to sprout.

26. As bathing in the sea confers the same benefits [that are obtained from bathing] in the holy places of the three worlds, or in the taste of nectar all essences may be experienced,[13]

27. so have I again and again saluted my Preceptor, for he is the gratifier of all my wishes.

28. Now listen to the great mystic story, the source of all wonderful stories, which is as a beautiful garden, full of the trees of discrimination.

29. It is the origin of all bliss, the great store of truth, the ocean of nectar of the nine sentiments.[14]

30. It is the revealed place of beatitude, the primal abode of learning and the everlasting seat of all the sciences;

31. the home of all religion, the heart of all good men, the treasure-house of the beauty of Shāradā.

32. In this work through the medium of Vyāsa's intellect, the goddess Bhārati has, by means of different episodes, revealed herself throughout the three worlds.[15]

33. Therefore is this poem the king of all epics, the store-house of the greatness of all writings, and from it do all the sentiments derive their beauty.

34. Hear also another of its merits. The wealth of language has been related to science, and the tenderness of the highest knowledge increased.

35. Through the medium of this story, wisdom itself has become wise, love is added to delight, and owing to it the blessedness of joy has been increased.

36. Through it sweetness is added to the quality of sweetness, beauty to the sentiment of love, and by it dignity is imparted to all that is good.

37. The artistic quality in all art is due to this; righteousness owes its power to it, and by means of it all the sins of Janmejaya were miraculously annulled.[16]

38. And if we reflect for a moment [we will understand that] all colour derives its beauty from this, and even goodness its quality of goodness.

39. As when the sun shines the whole world becomes illuminated, so has the whole universe derived from this its spiritual light through the intellect of Vyāsa.

40. As when seeds planted in good soil multiply freely, so has all meaning found its fullest expression in the Bhārata;[17]

41. or as a man becomes civilized from living in a city, so everything reflects the light of Vyāsa's speech;

42. or as the charm of beauty reaches its perfection in woman in the prime of her youth,

43. or as when spring appears in a garden, a wealth of beauty is brought forth greater than before;

44. or while gold in the mass looks dull, it assumes a special glory [when made into] ornaments.

45. So, knowing that the words of Vyāsa impart a charm to any episode, they are reflected in all history.

46. The Purānas, feeling that they would thus be raised to eminence, have with humility turned to the Mahābhārata [for inspiration] in all forms of stories and episodes.

47. Thus it is said that what is not found in the Mahābhārata does not exist in all the three worlds, and that everything else is but remnants of the work of Vyāsa.

48. The Sage narrated to the King Janmejaya this story, the sweetest in the world and the source of the highest truths.

49. Listen therefore to this story which is unequalled, matchless, most pure, and the source of all auspiciousness.

50. So the Mahābhārata is like a lotus, while the episode called the Gitā in which Shri Krishna converses with Arjuna is like the pollen of it.[18]

51. This Gitā is the divine butter churned by Vyāsa from the ocean of the Vedas with the churning rod of his intellect.[19]

52. When the butter was heated in the fire of wisdom and boiled to perfection by discrimination it became the delicious ghi of the Gitā.[20]

53. It is sought after by the dispassionate and saints desire to experience it. Those who have realized their oneness with the Divine take delight in it.

54. Devotees long to listen to it. It is the most to be worshipped in the three worlds and is expounded in the chapter called 'Bhishma Parva'.[21]

55. It is called the Song of the Lord; the creator Brahma extolled it, so also did the god Shiva; Sanaka and other sages treated it with great reverence.[22]

56. As the young of the chakora bird picks up the tender and luscious drops of nectar falling from the moon of the sharada season,[23]

57. so should hearers enjoy this story with dispassionate and gentle minds.

58. It should be pondered over silently, enjoyed apart from any action of the senses, and thus its truths may be grasped [by the inner self].

59. Just as a bee may carry away pollen and the lotus be entirely unaware of it, so is the method of understanding this work.

60. As the lotus, remaining in its place, embraces the rising moon, and thus experiences the joy of it,

61. so only he who approaches it with seriousness and with a tranquil heart, can understand this matter.

62. Now, all those who like Arjuna are qualified to listen to this, such sages do I beseech to listen to my words.

63. I say this with affection, and touching your feet, O Sirs, I call upon you, for [I know] you feel reverence in your hearts.

64. As it is the nature of parents to be all the more pleased when their child lisps out his words,

65. so have you good men accepted me as your own; why then should I beseech you when I know you will overlook my shortcomings?

66. But there is another fault, in that I claim to understand the Gitā and I have asked you to listen to me.

67. In my eagerness I have thoughtlessly undertaken this work; would a glow-worm show its light in the presence of the sun?

68. As the titibha bird tries to sound the depth of the sea with its tiny beak, so with little knowledge I am setting out on this task.

69. Listen! In order to encompass the sky one must be greater than it; so, really speaking, to expound the Gitā is beyond my capacity.

70. So deep in meaning is it, that even the god Shambhu explained it to Bhavāni, as with wonder she questioned him about it.[24]

71. Then did Hara say, O Beloved! as thy nature is incomprehensible, so is the meaning of the Gitā difficult to understand, being for ever new.[25]

72. For it was given forth by the Supreme Being himself, from whose voice, in sleep, emanated the ocean of the text of the Vedas.

73. How, therefore, can I, who am dull of intellect, hope [to understand such a work]? This work is unfathomable and even the Vedas were bewildered by it.

74. Who can grasp the infinite, or illuminate the great light? How could an insect hold the firmament in its grasp?

75. But in this matter there is one source of strength, through which I may speak with confidence; that is, my gracious preceptor. So says Jnānadeva.

76. But for this I would be a fool. Though I have been thoughtless, the light of the grace of the saints enlightens me.

77. It is the property of the philosopher's stone to turn iron into gold; so also the dead regain life through the power of nectar.

78. If Sarasvati herself were to appear to him a dumb man would obtain the gift of speech. Is this any cause for wonder? This is but the nature of such power.

79. Can anything be unobtainable for one whose mother is Kāmadhenu? For this reason I have set out to expound this work.[26]

80. I beseech you, therefore, to add whatever may be found deficient, and to reject what may be superfluous.

81. Now, I beg of you, pay heed to me; what you inspire in me I will speak, as the puppet dances when moved by a cord.

82. Blessed by your grace I am obedient to the saints; make of me therefore whatever you please.

83. Whereupon the Teacher says, Enough of this, there is no need to say all this; now give your mind to this work.

84. The disciple of Nivritti, rejoicing at these words said, Listen attentively [to my exposition].

Dhṛtarāṣṭra said:

> 1. *In the field of righteousness, the field of the Kurus, when my people and the sons of Pāṇḍu had gathered together, eager for battle, what did they do, O Saṃjaya?*

85. Dhritarashtra, moved by affection for his sons, said, O Sanjaya, tell me [what occurred on] the battle-field of the Kurus.[27]

86. On the field which is said to be the abode of righteousness my sons and the Pāndavas have arrayed themselves, intent on fighting.

87. Tell me now what they have been doing there so long, thus facing each other.

    II. *Then, Duryodhana the prince, having seen the army of the Pāṇḍavas drawn up in battle order, approached his teacher and spoke this word:*

    III. *Behold, O Teacher, this mighty army of the sons of Pāṇḍu organized by thy wise pupil, the son of Drupada.*

88. Then said Sanjaya, The army of the Pāndavas rose up like the spread jaws of death at the time of the universal dissolution,[28]

89. as the gathering of a dense mass of clouds. It was like the Kālakuta poison seething everywhere; who could control it?[29]

90. [It seemed like] the sea fire which, fanned by the wind of the universal destruction, rises up in flames to the very heavens, having dried up the waters of the ocean.

91. So this invincible army, arranged in various positions, was at that time a terrifying sight.

92. But Duryodhana regarded it with contempt, as a lion would despise a herd of elephants.

93. Then he approached Drona and spoke to him thus, Seest thou this huge army of the Pāndavas,

94. skilfully arrayed like a moving hill fortress in order of battle by the highly intelligent son of Drupada?

95. See how [that son of Drupada], to whom as thy pupil thou didst teach the art of war, making him expert in it, has spread out his army like the sea!

    IV. *Here are heroes, great bowmen equal in battle to Bhīma and Arjuna—Yuyudhāna, Virāṭa and Drupada, a mighty warrior.*

96. There also are matchless warriors, skilful in the use of weapons and missiles, well versed in the art of war.

97. By their strength and valour they are equal to Bhima and Arjuna. I will tell you their names in turn.

98. Here is that great warrior Yuyudhāna, the King Virāta, and Drupada that great chariot-fighter.

    V. *Dhṛṣṭaketu, Cekitāna and the valiant King of Kāshi, also Purojit, Kuntibhoja and Śaibya the foremost of men.*

99. See here Cekitāna, Dhrishtaketu, and the valiant king of Kāshi, Uttamauju the best of kings, Shaibya.

100. Here is Kuntibhoja, Yudhāmanyu has come and all other kings including Purujit.

> VI. *Yudhāmanyu, the strong and Uttamauja, the brave; and also the son of Subhadrā and sons of Draupadi, all of them great warriors.*

101. Here is the joy of Subhadrā's heart, the youthful Arjuna named also Abhimanyu. Duryodhana said, See, O Drona.
102. Many more there are, like the sons of Draupadi, and all of them great chariot warriors, far too numerous to mention, all gathered together.

> VII. *Know also, O Best of the twiceborn, the leaders of my army, those who are most distinguished among us. I will name them now for thine information.*

103. Now listen, I will tell you the names of the famous warriors on our side, the leaders of our armies.
104. To give you some idea, I will mention but a few; in the first place, yourself as chief.

> VIII. *Thyself and Bhīṣma and Karṇa and Kṛpa ever victorious in battle; Asvatthāmā, Vikarna, and also the son of Somadatta.*

105. Here is Bhishma, son of Gangā adorned with valour and resplendent as the sun; Karna, the lion among these elephants in the form of his enemies,
106. who even in thought would be able to destroy the whole universe single-handed. Is not Kripācārya enough even by himself?
107. Here is Vikarna the brave, and a little further thou canst see Ashvatthāmā who is feared even by the god of death.
108. There are Samitinjaya, Saumadatta and many more, whose valour even the creator cannot measure;

> IX. *And many other heroes who have risked their lives for my sake. They are armed with many kinds of weapons and are all well skilled in war.*

109. These are expert in the use of weapons, as the incarnate power of the mantras, from whom has been learnt the use of all kinds of missiles.

110. All are matchless warriors in this world, full of perfect valour. They have nevertheless followed me with all their heart and soul.

111. As in her heart a chaste wife consorts only with her husband, I am all in all to these warriors.

112. In the interest of my cause, they consider their lives as of no value, so pure and selfless are they in their loyalty to their lord.

113. They are conversant with all the art of war, they are victors even over fame; in short, they are the very pattern of warrior-ship.

114. Our army is thus composed of soldiers of every branch, and it would not be possible to count them.

> x. *Unlimited is this army of ours which is guarded by Bhīṣma while that army of theirs which is guarded by Bhīma is limited.*

115. Moreover to Bhishma, the best of warriors and the most valiant fighter in battle, is given the command of our army.

116. Under his power this army is arranged like a fortress, and even the three worlds are insignificant.

117. The ocean itself is impassable, but what if added to this there were the great sea-fire?

118. As the fire of destruction and the great wind combine [to bring about the end of the universe], so is our army with our general, the son of Gaṅgā.

119. Who then will fight with him? This army of the Pāndavas certainly appears to be of no account compared with ours.

120. Besides, the mighty Bhimasena is its general. Whereupon he ceased speaking.

> xi. *Therefore do ye all support Bhīṣma, standing firm on all the fronts, in your respective ranks.*

121. Then Duryodhana said again to all the troops, Arrange yourselves in your respective detachments.

122. The command should be given to those great chariot fighters who command the various sections on the battle-field.

123. They should each command their own troops, obeying Bhishma. To Drona he said, You watch over everything.

124. Especially protect Bhishma; you must regard him as my very self, for our whole army depends entirely on him.

> XII. *In order to cheer him up, the aged Kuru, his valiant grandsire, roared aloud like a lion and blew his conch.*

125. Hearing these words of the king, the commander rejoiced, and sent forth a roar like a lion.
126. The marvellous sound of it was heard throughout the three worlds and resounded on all sides.
127. In harmony with the reverberating echoes, the god-like Bhishma blew his divine conch with all his strength.
128. The two sounds, in combination, seemed to deafen the three worlds, as if the skies were crashing down.
129. The heavens were [shattered] by the thunder, the ocean heaved and the whole of creation trembled.
130. The hollows of the hills were filled with the great noise and then all the warriors beat on their war drums.

> XIII. *Then conches and kettledrums, tabors and drums and horns suddenly blared forth and the noise was tumultuous.*

131. Then could be heard the terrific roaring of innumerable battle instruments so that it was thought that the doom of the universe had come.
132. What then was the state of the faint-hearted, for the timid [were blown away like] dried leaves? Even the god of death was frightened beyond measure.
133. There were kettledrums, tabors and drums, also horns, conches and bugles, with the terrible war cries of the warriors.
134. Some beat their arms with violence, shouting with fury, so that the elephants could not be restrained.
135. Some even died where they stood, the teeth of brave men chattered, and matchless fighters also shook with fear.
136. The terrible and deafening sound of all those martial instruments reverberated so that even the creator was afraid, and the gods exclaimed, The day of universal destruction will surely come!

> XIV. *When stationed in their great chariot, yoked to white horses, Kṛṣṇa and Arjuna blew their celestial conches.*

137. While even in the abode of the gods this commotion
prevailed, listen to what occurred in the army of the
Pāndavas.

138. Behold, [the chariot which was] the very essence of victory,
and the treasure-house of light, and to which were yoked
four horses as swift as Garuda,[30]

139. resplendent as a winged Meru, the brilliance of it shining
in all the four quarters of the earth,[31]

140. with the lord of Vaikuntha himself as the charioteer! Who
could describe its quality?[32]

141. On the banner pole of the chariot sat the monkey god,
the very incarnation of Shri Shankara; and the Holder of
the Shānga bow was the charioteer, with Arjuna.[33]

142. Behold this wondrous act of the Lord, His great love for
His disciple, that he serves Pārtha as charioteer![34]

143. Seated in front and with His disciple behind Him, He
joyfully blew His conch called Pāncajanya.

144. While the deep sound was vibrating, just as all the stars
fade out when the sun rises,

145. all the martial sounds in the Kuru army were silenced
and it was not possible to tell at what moment they faded
away.

146. Similarly, Arjuna, the Wielder of the bow, blew loudly on
his conch, named Devadatta, with a deep and resounding
note.

147. These two terrible sounds combined into one and thereupon the whole universe appeared to be shattered to
pieces.

148. At that moment Bhimasena grew furious, as if the god of
destruction were enraged, and he blew on his great conch
called Paundra.

149. The noise of the blowing was as the thunder clouds at
the time of the day of destruction. Yudhishthira also
sounded his Anantavijaya.

11

150. Then Nakula blew on his conch Sughosa, and Sahadeva on Manipushpaka; hearing these sounds, even the god of death trembled with fear.[35]

> XVII. *And the king of Kāśi, the Chief of archers Śikhaṇḍin, the great warrior, Dhṛṣṭadyumna and Virāṭa and the invincible Sātyaki.*

151. On the field there were many kings, such as Draupada and the sons of Drupadi, the King of Kāshi, of the long arm,

> XVIII. *Drupada and the sons of Draupadī, O Lord of earth, and the strong armed son of Subhadrā, on all sides blew their respective conches.*

152. and Sātyaki, the unconquerable, the son of Arjuna, Dhrishtadyumna, the best of kings, and Shikhandi,[36]
153. and others like Virāta, all leading warriors. They blew their conches continuously.

> XIX. *The tumultuous uproar resounding through earth and sky rent the hearts of Dhṛtarāṣṭra's sons.*

154. Terrified by the vibrations of these sounds Shesha and Kurma were confused and tried to throw off the burden of the earth.[37]
155. Thereby the foundations of the three worlds were shaken; Meru and Mandāra began to rock, and the ocean heaved itself up to the skies.[38]
156. The earth was about to turn upside down, the sky became terrified and the stars ready to fall.
157. A cry arose in the highest heaven that the universe had perished and the gods were rendered helpless.
158. The sun did not shine by day, and in all the three worlds arose cries of lamentation, as if the great light of the final destruction had vanished.
159. Even the Supreme Being was astonished and exclaimed, Is this the end of all things? Then suddenly this unusual turmoil ceased.
160. Thus was the universe saved, when Shri Krishna and the others blew on their great conches, for otherwise the end of the cycle might have occurred.
161. Although the deep sounds had ceased, their echoes continued to vibrate, so that the army of the Kauravas was destroyed.

162. As a lion may easily destroy a herd of elephants, so the
sound struck terror into the hearts of the Kauravas.

163. As they heard the thunder of them, they lost all heart and
cried out to each other, Beware! Beware!

> xx. *Then Arjuna, whose banner bore the crest of Hanumān,
> looked at the sons of Dhṛtarāṣṭra drawn up in battle
> order; and as the flight of missiles [almost] started, he
> took up his bow.*

164. Then those great undaunted chariot fighters, full of valour
began to gather the army together.

165. Thereupon the latter rushed forward with redoubled
vigour, so that the three worlds trembled at that army.

166. Those brave bowmen sent forth a stream of arrows, like
the unrestrained showers from the clouds on the day of
universal destruction.

167. At the sight of it Arjuna rejoiced in his heart and hastily
turned his glance in the direction of the two armies.

168. When he saw [the soldiers of] the Kauravas well arranged
in order of battle, the son of Pāndu gracefully took up
his bow.

> xxi. *And, O Lord of earth, he spoke this word to Hṛṣikeśa
> [Krṣṇa], Draw up my chariot, O Acyuta [Krṣṇa],
> between the two armies.*

169. Thereupon Arjuna addressed these words to the Lord,
Now, quickly place my car between the two armies,

> xxii. *So that I may observe these men standing, eager
> for battle, with whom I have to contend in this strife of
> war.*

170. while I look for one moment at all these warriors gathered
here for battle;

171. for though they have all come together in this place, I
wish to see on the field those with whom I will have to
fight.

> xxiii. *I wish to look at those who are assembled here,
> ready to fight and eager to achieve in battle what is dear
> to the evil-minded son of Dhṛtarāṣṭra.*

172. These evil-minded and impatient Kauravas pretend that
they love fighting, though they have not the spirit for it.

173. They make believe that they are eager to fight, but they have no valour in battle. Having narrated all this to the King, Sanjaya said—

> XXIV. *Thus addressed by Gudākeśa [Arjuna], Hṛṣikeśa [Kṛṣṇa] drew up that best of chariots, O Bhārata [Dhṛtarāṣṭra], between the two armies.*

174. When Arjuna spake thus, Shri Krishna drove his chariot and placed it between the two armies.

> XXV. *In front of Bhīṣma, Droṇa and all the chiefs he said, Behold, O Pārtha [Arjuna], these Kurus assembled [here].*

175. There before him were to be seen Bhishma, Drona and other relatives and many kings.

176. His chariot having been driven in front of them, Arjuna glanced round eagerly at them all.

177. Then he said, See, O Lord! All these are our kith and kin, our elders and teachers. Shri Krishna was for a time astonished [at this remark].

178. He said to Himself, What is the meaning of this? What has he in mind?

179. Then He looked into the future and at once knew what was in Arjuna's mind, but nevertheless He remained silent.

> XXVI. *There saw Arjuna standing fathers and grand-fathers, teachers, uncles, brothers, sons and grandsons and also companions.*

180. There on the field of battle Arjuna could see all his elders, grandparents and teachers, kinsmen and maternal uncles;

181. he saw his friends and sons and brothers-in-law among them.

> XXVII. *And fathers-in-law and friends in both the armies. When the son of Kuntī [Arjuna] saw all these kinsmen thus standing arrayed,*

182. His dear ones, fathers-in-law and the rest of his relations, his young grandsons, all these the Wielder of the Bow saw there.

183. All of them old and young, those who were under an obligation to him and those whom he had protected in distress.

184. Thus could Arjuna see in both armies all his relatives, at that moment standing ready to fight.

> XXVIII. *He was overcome with great compassion and said in sadness, When I see my own people arrayed and eager for fight, O Kṛṣṇa,*

185. At this his heart was perplexed and naturally he felt pity; and his valour, [unable to bear such] humiliation, deserted him.
186. As highborn women, virtuous and beautiful, cannot tolerate another woman superior in these qualities;
187. as a voluptuous man enraptured by another woman, forgets his own wife, and recklessly follows his passion,
188. or as a man, by practising penance, obtains spiritual powers and becomes mentally confused and forgets the fulfilment of his goal,
189. so it was with Arjuna, and being overcome by compassion, his manliness left him.
190. Lo! as a reciter of mantras, when he himself becomes mad, is as though possessed by an evil spirit, so was the Holder of the Bow, overpowered by infatuation.
191. Therefore when his heart melted with compassion his manliness deserted him, just as a moonstone melts on being touched by the rays of the moon.
192. In this way Pārtha was overcome by pity and being full of sadness, he thus addressed Shri Acyuta,
193. Listen to me, O Lord! when I behold this assemblage [of warriors], everywhere I see my kindred.
194. All these warriors stand here ready [to fight], but how can this be right for me?
195. The very thought of it perplexes and unnerves me, my mind has almost lost its balance.

> XXIX. *My limbs quail, my mouth goes dry, my body shakes and my hair stands on end.*

> XXX. *[The bow] Gāndiva slips from my hand and my skin too is burning all over. I am not able to stand steady. My mind is reeling.*

196. See how my body trembles, my mouth is parched, and weakness overtakes my limbs.
197. My hair stands on end, [my body] is feverish and because of this distress I cannot hold my Gāndiva bow.[39]

198. I cannot hold it; without my knowledge it slips from my hand, and my heart is weighed down with foolishness.

199. Though my heart is harder than adamant, bold and valiant, this madness is stronger still.

200. Arjuna, who conquered Shankara in fight and overcame the god of death, was in an instant overpowered by this confusion,

201. as a bee can pierce with ease the hardest wood but may be caught in a tender bud.

202. There it may lose its life, but it knows not how to tear apart the petals. Thus is pity, so soft and yet so hard.

203. Sanjaya said, O King, listen! [This affection] is the illusion of the Supreme Being and not even the Creator himself can control it; hence the confused state of Arjuna.

204. Hear, O King! Arjuna, seeing all his relatives and friends, forgot all the honour of battle.

205. I do not understand how this compassion has arisen in Arjuna's heart. Then he said, O Krishna! It is not right for me to remain here.

206. My mind is completely bewildered, my speech is confused at the thought of killing all these [relations of mine].

> XXXI. *And I see evil omens, O Keśava [Kṛṣṇa], nor do I foresee any good by slaying my own people in this fight.*

207. If the Kauravas are to be killed, then why not kill Yudhishthira and those others? For all of them are equally my relations;

208. Therefore fie on this war! I do not like it at all. What is the use of this evil?

209. O Lord! from every point of view this fighting is evil and therefore, if it can be avoided, it would surely be an excellent thing.

> XXXII. *I do not long for victory, O Kṛṣṇa, nor kingdom nor pleasures. Of what use is kingdom to us, O Kṛṣṇa, or enjoyment or even life?*

210. The desire to gain a victory is nothing to me; what would even the acquirement of kingship avail me?

> XXXIII. *Those for whose sake we desire kingdom, enjoyments and pleasures, they stand here in battle, renouncing their lives and riches.*

211. Away with these pleasures, which can only be enjoyed after slaying all these! So said Pārtha.

212. I can bear anything else but such enjoyment. I am prepared even to die to gain them.

213. But that we should kill those men and then enjoy the pleasures of kingship, my mind cannot entertain such a thought, even in a dream.

214. Of what use would our birth be to us? For whom should we wish to live, if in our minds we were to think evil of our elders?

215. Every family desires a son; is this to be the fruit of it, that we should destroy our families?

216. How can we hold such a thought in mind, or speak with words as hard as adamant? We should always seek their good.

217. All these should enjoy whatever we acquire in this world; even our lives should be spent in their interest.

218. We should overcome all the kings in the world that our families should be satisfied,

219. and here they stand [before us]. What curious turn of fate is this? They are arrayed here ready to fight with us.

220. Having left behind them their wives and children and all their treasures, submitting their lives to weapons of destruction,

221. how can I kill these, with what weapons attack them, how can I strike at my own heart?

> XXXIV. *Teachers, fathers, sons and also grandfathers; uncles and fathers-in-law, grandsons and brothers-in-law and [other] kinsmen,*

222. Dost Thou not know who they are? Over there are Bhishma and Drona, who have been our great benefactors,

223. our brothers-in-law, fathers-in-law, uncles, and those other kinsmen, sons and grandsons, so dear to us.

224. Listen! These are all our close relatives, so that it is a sin even to speak of [killing] them.

> XXXV. *These I would not consent to kill, though killed myself, O Madhusūdana [Kṛṣṇa], even for the kingdom of the three worlds; how much less for the sake of the earth?*

225. Rather let them perform any unworthy action and now
kill us, than that I should think of killing them.

226. Even could I attain to the undisputed sovereignty of the
three worlds, I could never commit such an evil action.

> XXXVI. *What pleasure can be ours, O Kṛṣṇa, after we
> have slain the sons of Dhṛtarāṣṭra? Only sin will accrue
> to us if we kill these criminals.*

227. Were I to act thus today, who would hold me in respect,
and how could I look Thee in the face, O Krishna?

228. If I were to kill my kinsmen, I would become the abode
of all sin. I should lose Thee who hast become so dear to
me.

229. If I became burdened with the sins of family destruction,
then how could I look up to Thee?

230. As the cuckoo when it sees a fierce fire spreading in a
garden, does not remain there;

231. or the chakora bird, seeing a lake full of mud, abandons it
and departs,

232. so, O Lord, if the store of righteousness in me were
destroyed Thy love for me would vanish, and Thou
wouldst desert me.

> XXXVII. *So it is not right that we slay our kinsmen, the
> sons of Dhṛtarāṣṭra. Indeed, how can we be happy, O
> Mādhava [Kṛṣṇa], if we kill our own people?*

233. I will not do this therefore, nor take a weapon in my hand
in this struggle, for it seems in every way contemptible.

234. Were we to lose Thee, what would become of us? Without
Thee my heart would be broken with grief.

235. Therefore, said Arjuna, it would be impossible for us to
enjoy the reward if we were to destroy these Kauravas.

> XXXVIII. *Even if these whose minds are overpowered by
> greed, see no wrong in the destruction of the family and
> no crime in treachery to friends;*

> XXXIX. *Why should we not have the wisdom to turn
> away from this sin, O Janārdana [Kṛṣṇa], we who see
> the wrong in the destruction of the family?*

236. Even if, deluded by the force of pride, these men have
come to fight, it behoves us to recognize our own good.

237. If a lion appeared suddenly in our path, we would save our lives by avoiding it.

238. How can we do this and at the same time kill our kinsmen? Would we knowingly swallow virulent poison?

239. What gain is there, O Lord, if, forsaking the light which we have, we choose a pit of darkness?

240. Were we to find ourselves near a fire and make no effort to avoid it, we could be burnt to death in an instant.

241. So knowing that we are approaching the very incarnation of sin, should we knowingly go forward into it?

> XL. *In the ruin of a family, its ancient laws are destroyed: and when the laws perish, the whole family yields to lawlessness.*

242. As when two pieces of wood are rubbed against each other fire is produced, and all the wood in the world would be burnt up by it,

243. so if the members of a family kill each other through spite, from that sin the whole family will perish.

244. So through this sin, all the inherited duty of the family is brought to nought, and then unrighteousness enters the family.

> XLI. *And when lawlessness prevails, O Vārṣṇeya [Kṛṣṇa], the women of the family become corrupted and when women are corrupted, confusion of castes arises.*

245. Thereupon, all considerations of right and wrong, the correct performance of duties, all the precepts of conduct and prohibition are ignored.

246. As a man is in danger of falling when his lamp is extinguished and he walks in the darkness, even though he may walk straight,

247. so if a family is destroyed, its immemorial traditions will be lost and nothing will remain.

248. When self-control fails the senses run amok and the women of the family commit adultery.

> XLII. *And this confusion brings the family itself to hell as well as those who have destroyed it. For the spirits of their ancestors fall, deprived of their offerings of rice and water.*

249. The noblest consort with the meanest, castes are mingled and all the family traditions destroyed.

250. As if an oblation of rice were thrown out on the public road, crows will fall on it from every side, great sin enters into such a family.

251. Then the whole family and those who have thus wrecked it have to descend into hell.

252. In this way that family will be degraded and its forefathers in heaven will be drawn down into hell.

253. So then the daily and the periodical duties cease to be properly performed; then who will be left to carry out the rites of the dead?

254. How then would it be possible for the ancestors to live in the heaven-world? They too [would have to enter hell] along with the family.

255. As when the tip of a man's finger is bitten by a serpent, his whole body soon becomes affected [by the poison], so such a sin would overwhelm the whole family even from [its very origin in] Brahma.

> XLIII. *By the misdeeds of those who destroy a family and create confusion of the varṇas, the immemorial laws of the race and the family are destroyed.*
>
> XLIV. *And we have heard it said, O Janārdana [Kṛṣṇa], that the men of the families whose laws are destroyed needs must live in hell.*
>
> XLV. *Alas, what a great sin have we resolved to commit in striving to slay our own people through our greed for the pleasures of the kingdom!*

256. O Lord, listen to me further. This great sin would by its contagion corrupt all men.

257. If a fire should break out in one's house, with its inner apartments, others would soon be enveloped in flames, and everything in it be burnt.

258. So all others who come in contact with this family are themselves beset with troubles.

259. Then owing to manifold sins the family will experience the deepest horrors of hell, said Arjuna.

260. Once fallen into hell there is no escape from it, even at the end of the great age, so abysmal would be the ruin of the family, said Arjuna.

261. O Lord, so it is heard in various ways. Should not this,

even now, trouble us? Please listen! Why are our hearts
so hard?

262. Should we not avoid this sin, realizing that the enjoyment
of kingship which we desire is really momentary.

263. Tell me, is it then so small a sin to have looked on these
our elders with the idea of killing them?

> XLVI. *Far better would it be for me if the sons of
> Dhṛtarāṣṭra, with weapons in hand, should slay me in
> the battle, while I remain unresisting and unarmed.*

264. Far better that I, laying aside my weapon, should be
struck by their arrows, than live in this way.

265. Death itself would be more welcome, but I cannot commit
such a sin.

Sanjaya said:

> XLVII. *Having spoken thus on the [field of] battle, Arjuna
> sank down on the seat of his chariot, casting away his
> bow and arrow, his spirit overwhelmed by sorrow.*

266. Thus spoke Arjuna at that time on the field of battle,
Sanjaya said to Dhritarāshtra, Listen!

267. He [Arjuna] was greatly dejected; he became choked with
uncontrollable grief and leapt down from his chariot.

268. As a prince deprived of his throne is distressed or as the
sun when eclipsed by Rāhu is bereft of his splendour,[40]

269. or as an ascetic, overcome by the fascination of psychic
powers, becomes dominated by desire and helpless

270. so the Wielder of the bow seemed unnerved by grief when
he abandoned his chariot.

271. Flinging away his bow and arrows, he wept in spite of
himself. Thus, O King, did it happen, said Sanjaya.

272. Now the Lord of Vaikuntha, on seeing Pārtha so dejected
expounded to him the great truth.

273. Jnānadeva, disciple of Nivritti, will tell in detail this
most interesting story'.

*In the Upanishad of the Bhagavadgītā, the science of the Absolute,
the scripture of Yoga and the dialogue between Shri Krishna and
Arjuna, this is the first chapter called the Depression of Arjuna.*

1. *Shri Ganesha.* The name of a Hindu god whose special feature is the elephant head. Ganesha, also called Ganpati, is especially popular in Mahārāshtra. The image of this god is used in the opening section of this chapter for a wealth of figurative expression. The particle 'Shri' prefixed to names is honorific and occurs with the majority of names of gods as a sign of reverence; e.g. Shri Krishna.
   Om, the 'sacred syllable'. The written form of the syllable is given below in Note 10. This syllable is uttered at the beginning of sacred reading, recitation or prayer.
   Vedas. Sacred scriptures of the Hindu religion. These are the Shrutis, i.e. 'that which is heard', 'revealed'.
2. *Smritis.* These are writings which are based on 'that which is remembered', a body of literature produced by human authors, not 'revealed'.
3. *Purānas.* The 'ancient stories' and legendary history.
4. *Vyāsa.* The sage to whom the authorship of the Mahābhārata is attributed.
5. *Six systems of philosophy.* The six systems of Hindu philosophy and their concepts are represented here by the objects and weapons held in the hands of the traditional form of the image of Ganesha.
6. *Vedānta.* One of the six systems of philosophy.
7. *The two hands.* The images and statues of the Buddha often show the hands in two positions: the left hand is raised to an upright position as the hand of reassurance, 'Be not afraid', and the right hand is extended as the hand of blessing and the giving of boons.
8. *Two systems.* The two systems propounded in this work are that of 'Karma' (action) and 'Jnāna' (knowledge, discrimination). They are treated respectively in Chapters II and III of the text.
9. *Upanishads.* Mystical writings expounding the meaning of the Vedas.
10. *A-U-M.* These are three phonetic elements of the sacred syllable, here related to parts of the body in the image of Ganesha. In the Sanskrit system the vowel 'o' is considered as being a compound of the vowels 'a' and 'u'. The relation of this syllable to the body of Ganesha can be understood by referring to the shape of the written form: ॐ o; ⌣ m; ॐ om.
11. *Shārada.* The goddess of learning, an alternative name for Sarasvati, goddess of speech and learning.
12. *The Stone of Desire.* A magical gem which is said to fulfil every desire of the one who possesses it.
13. *The three worlds.* This refers to the whole universe: earth, heaven and the underworld.
14. *The nine sentiments.* These are the nine emotional tones in poetry. They are often referred to as eight, with the edition of tranquillity as the ninth. They are: love or passion, humour, pity, wrath, heroism, horror, disgust, wonder, tranquillity.

15. *Bhārati.* The goddess of speech. See note 11 above.
16. *Janmejaya.* The last king of the Pāndu dynasty, to whom the Mahābhārata is said to have been related. See following note.
17. *Mahābhārata.* The legendary history of the descendants of Bharata. See Introduction.
18. *Gitā.* This is the shortened form of the name of the poem at the heart of the Mahābhārata, the Bhagavadgitā, 'The Song of the Lord', relating to conversation between Krishna and Arjuna. See Introduction.
19. *The Churning Rod.* The process of churning usually refers to the churning by the gods of the Ocean of Milk in Hindu mythology, using the mountain Mandāra as the churning rod.
20. *Ghi.* Butter clarified by heating, much used in Hindu rites and sacrifices.
21. *Bhishmaparva.* The section of the Mahābhārata in which the story of the warrior Bhishma is recounted.
22. *Shiva.* One of the highest gods of the Hindus, the 'destroyer'.
Sanaka. One of the great Hindu sages.
23. *Chakora bird.* A bird similar to a partridge, said to subsist on moonbeams.
Shārdā. One of the six seasons of the Hindu year, approximately from mid-September to mid-November.
24. *Shambhu.* Another name of Shiva.
Bhavāni. The consort of Shiva.
25. *Hara.* One of the names of Shiva.
26. *The desire-fulfilling Cow.* The 'kāmadhenu' is the mythical cow which fulfils all desires.
27. *Dhritarāshtra.* The blind king of the Kurus to whom his charioteer Sanjaya is describing the battlefield where the Kurus and the Pāndavas are about to fight. See Introduction. *Note:* The names of the chief warriors in the two armies, and their relationships, occurring in the verses from here to 120, are given below in a special note.
28. *Universal dissolution.* At the end of a world age there is said to take place a general dissolution of the world through fire, flood and destruction.
29. *Kālakuta poison.* This deadly poison which was churned out of the Ocean of Milk and was drunk by Shiva.
30. *Garuda.* The mythical bird which is the vehicle of the god Vishnu.
31. *Meru.* The name of a mountain said to be made of gold.
32. *Vuikvntha.* Vaikuntha is the heavenly abode of Vishnu, one of whose epithets is 'Lord of Vaikuntha'. This epithet is here transferred to Krishna, identified with Vishnu of whom he is an incarnation.
33. *The Monkey.* The head-piece of the chariot is the effigy of a monkey, the symbol of the Monkey god who is said to have delivered the island of Ceylon (Lankā) from the possession of Rāvana, the great demon.
Shankara. An incarnation of Shiva.

Shārnga.   The name of Krishna's bow; hence the epithet 'Holder of the Shāranga bow'.
34. *Pārtha.*   Another name of Arjuna.
35. *Nakula.*   One of the brothers of Arjuna.
   Sahadeva.   One of the brothers of Arjuna.
36. *Sātyaki.*   Dhristhadyumna, Skanda, Virāta. See note 27 above.
37. *Shesha.*   The mythical serpent which supports the world.
   Kurma.   A tortoise; the second incarnation of Vishnu.
38. *Mandāra.*   See above, note 19.
39. *Gāndiva.*   The name of Arjuna's bow.
40. *Rāhu.*   The name of a planet, which periodically 'swallows' the sun or moon in an eclipse.

Names and relationships of the chief persons taking part in the battle on the great plain of Kuruksetra:

Kuru.   A country in northern India; the name of the king of this country.

Kauravas.   Descendants of the king Kuru.

Pāndu.   The brother of Kuru; Kunti, his wife, mother of Arjuna.

Pāndavas.   The descendants of Pāndu.

Arjuna.   One of the sons of Pāndu; also called Pārtha.

Nakula and Sahadeva.   Sons of Arjuna by his wife Mādri; Karna, a half-brother.

Bhima.   The commander of the Pāndavas.

Dhritarāshtra.   The blind king of the Kauravas.

Duryodhana.   The eldest son of Dhritarāshtra who has seized the kingdom destined by his father's wish to pass to Yudhishthira, son of Pāndu.

Bhisma.   The old sage who taught and trained Pāndu and Dhritarāshtra in the art of warriorship. See note on Bhishmaparva in the Introduction.

Kripācārya.   The teacher of the Kauravas.

Drona.   The preceptor of the sons of Pāndu and Dhritarāshtra.

Yādavas.   The descendants of the king Yadu; Krishna is referred to as the Lord of the Yādavas.

Drupada.   The king of Kāshi (Benares).

Sātyaki.   Krishna's charioteer.

Sanjsayas.   The charioteer of Dhritarāshtra.

CHAPTER II

Sanjaya said:

> 1. *To Him [who was] thus overcome by pity, whose eyes were filled with tears and troubled and [who was] much depressed in mind, Madhusūdana [Kṛṣṇa] spoke this word.*

1. Then Sanjaya said to the King, Listen, O King! Arjuna, being overcome with grief, began to weep.
2. Seeing all his kinsmen before him, deep affection was aroused within him and his heart was melted with pity. To what can it be likened?
3. Like salt dissolving in water, or clouds driven by the wind, his heart though valiant became tender.
4. Overcome by compassion he seemed to wither, as a swan caught in the mud.
5. Seeing Arjuna overcome with deep emotion, Shri Shārngadhara spoke thus:

The Blessed Lord said:

> 11. *Whence has come to thee this stain [this dejection] of spirit in this hour of crisis? It is unknown to men of noble mind [not cherished by the Aryans]; it does not lead to heaven; [on earth] it causes disgrace, O Arjuna.*

6. He said, O Arjuna, first consider if thy behaviour is proper in this place. Who art thou? What art thou doing?
7. What is the matter with thee? What prevents thee from action? Why this grief?
8. Do not allow unworthy thoughts to enter thy mind. Do not lose courage, for at the mention of thy name defeat would flee to the four quarters.
9. Thou art the incarnation of heroism, a prince among Kshatriyas, the fame of thy might echoes throughout the three worlds.[1]

10. Didst thou not overcome Hara in battle? Were not the demons Nivātakavaca slain by thee? Hast thou not made the heavenly bards sing of thy brave deeds?[2]
11. When compared with thee the three worlds are insignificant, O Pārtha, so great is thy valour.
12. In spite of this today thou weepest, thy head droops, abandoning all thy courage.
13. Consider, O Arjuna. You are weakened by compassion. Tell me, is the sun ever swallowed up by darkness?
14. Does the wind stand in terror of a cloud? Can nectar ever die? Is fire ever consumed by fuel?
15. Will salt ever dissolve water? or will the Kālakuta poison die from the touch? Say, will a small frog ever swallow the great serpent?
16. Has such a wonder ever happened, that a jackal should fight against a lion? But thy actions seem to prove that these things might really happen.
17. Therefore, even now, O Arjuna, pay no heed to these unworthy thoughts, wake up and take courage.
18. Rid thyself of this folly; arise and take up thy bow. Of what use is pity on the field of battle?
19. So! Arjuna thou hast wisdom, why then dost thou not now reflect? Say, is pity appropriate at the time of battle?
20. Shri Krishna, the Abode of the Worlds, said, This will mar thy present fame and prevent thee from entering heaven, O Arjuna.

> III. *Yield not to this unmanliness, O Pārtha [Arjuna], for it does not become thee. Cast off this petty faint-heartedness and arise, O Oppressor of the foes [Arjuna].*

21. Therefore, do not grieve, O Son of Pāndu; be full of courage and shake off this dejection.
22. This ill befits thee, by this all that thou hast acquired will be lost; even now consider this.
23. At the hour of fighting pity is of no value; have these men only now become thy kith and kin?
24. Hast thou not already known them as such? Hast thou not recognized them as kinsmen? This excess [of feeling] is out of place.
25. Is today's fighting a new thing thy life? In thy race these is always some occasion for strife?
26. Then what has come over thee today, and why has pity

thus come to you? I know not, O Arjuna; but thou hast acted wrongly.

27. If thou holdest on to this illusion, the reputation thou hast will vanish, and then for thee both heaven and earth will be lost.

28. Faint-heartedness is never a sign of goodness; to a Kshatriya moreover it is equivalent to defeat in battle.

29. Thus, in various ways, did the Most Merciful One teach him. Hearing this the son of Pāndu spoke.

Arjuna said:

 IV. *How shall I strike Bhīṣma and Droṇa who are worthy of reverence, O Madhusūdana [Kṛṣṇa], with arrows in battle, O Slayer of foes [Kṛṣṇa]?*

30. Arjuna said, O Lord! There is no need to say any more. Listen! Do Thou Thyself first consider this fight.

31. It is wrong to think of this as war; it seems rather that a great crime is committed; it has fallen to us to have to destroy our elders.

32. See! reverence is due to parents and our actions should give every satisfaction to them. So how can we slay them with our own hands?

33. O Lord! our salutations are due to saints and sages; we should, when possible, worship them; how can we, in spite of this, abuse them with our own speech?

34. Likewise, too, we should show proper reverence to our family preceptors. I am greatly indebted to Bhishma and Drona.

35. How then, O Lord, can we slay them now, when even in our dreams we have never harboured any spite against them?

36. Fie upon this life! What fate has befallen all these? Should we display our [warrior's] training in the killing of them?

37. I, Pārtha, was taught by Drona. He it was who instructed me in the science of archery. Shall I then repay this by taking his life?

38. Arjuna said, Am I Bhasmāsura, to betray one from whom I have received such kindness?[3]

39. We are told that the sea is calm, and on the surface it seems to be so. But Drona's heart seems never to be disturbed.

40. The sky appears to be limitless, yet can it be measured?
Drona's heart is deep and unfathomable.

41. Nectar perchance might be spoilt, or the force of time
might break the thunderbolt, but nothing could ever shake
his purpose.

42. No greater love is there than a mother's, but Drona is
kindness incarnate.

43. Arjuna said, Drona is the source of all compassion, the
storehouse of all virtue, the boundless ocean of learning.

44. Therefore [we regard him as] a great saint and for us he is
full of compassion. How then can we consider his
destruction?

> v. *It is better to live in this world by begging than to slay
> these honoured teachers. Though they are mindful of their
> gains, they are my teachers and by slaying them I would
> enjoy in this world delights that are smeared with blood.*

45. I cannot find it in my heart to slay such men in battle
and then to enjoy a kingdom.

46. Rather than enjoy even more unattainable things than
this it would be far better to go begging for alms.

47. It may be better to leave one's country or to retire into
solitude in the mountains; but I will not take up a weapon
against them.

48. Shall we drown in blood by shooting sharp arrows into
their hearts to win the pleasure [of kingship]?

49. Having won it, what should we do then? How could we
enjoy such tainted pleasures? I cannot accept this
proposition.

> vi. *Nor do we know which for us is better, whether we
> conquer them or they conquer us. The sons of Dhṛtarāṣṭra,
> whom if we slew we should not care to live, are standing
> before us in battle array.*

50. So then spoke Arjuna, Listen O Krishna! But hearing
Arjuna's words, Murāri was not pleased.[4]

51. Realising this, Arjuna was afraid and again he said, Why
O Lord, dost thou not give heed to my words?

52. I have expressed thoughtfully what is in my mind, but
Thou knowest best what is right.

53. Those [in conflict with whom] we should be ready to die,
are arrayed here for the purpose of battle.

54. Should we slay them or abandon at once the field of battle? We know not which is the better of these two courses.

> VII. *My very being is stricken with the weakness of pity. With my mind bewildered about my duty, I ask Thee. Tell me, for certain, which is better. I am Thy pupil; teach me, who am seeking refuge in Thee.*

55. I feel confused when I think of what is proper for us; for my mind is distracted with this confusion.

56. When darkness pervades all space, the sight of the eyes is dimmed, and then even things which are near are invisible.

57. O Lord! I am in this predicament—for the mind being overcome by confusion cannot understand wherein lies its own good.

58. Therefore, O Krishna, Thou knowest all and shouldst tell us what is right, for Thou art everything to us, our friend.

59. Thou art indeed our teacher, brother, father. Thou art our chosen deity. Thou alone art our protector in time of difficulty.

60. The guru never forsakes his disciples; the sea never refuses the waters of a river;

61. how could a child live, being abandoned by its mother? O Krishna, listen!

62. So also, O Lord, Thou art all in all to us, we have none but Thee. If what I have already said is displeasing to Thee,

> VIII. *I do not see what will drive away this sorrow which dries up my senses even if I should obtain a rich and unrivalled kingdom on earth or even the sovereignty of the gods.*

63. tell us quickly, O Purushottama, what is befitting for us, and how we may not deviate from our duty.[5]

64. The grief that has arisen in my heart at the sight of these my kinsmen cannot be removed except by Thy words.

65. Even should I obtain the whole earth and gain the sovereignty of Indra, the doubt in my mind could not be resolved.

66. As seeds once fried can never germinate, even though sown in the richest soil, and plentifully watered;

67. or as when a man's days are numbered, no medicine can
have any effect, for only the purest nectar would be of
any avail,

68. so even all the enjoyments of a kingdom can in no way
encourage me. In this, O Storehouse of mercy, Thy
compassion alone is my support.

69. Thus spoke Arjuna, and for a time his confusion disappeared; but then a fresh wave [of distraction] overwhelmed him.

70. To me it seemed that there was in reality no wave; it was
something else; he was swallowed up by the great serpent
of infatuation,

71. which, at the most intense moment of his pity, attacked
his innermost heart and thus the waves of grief would
not subside.

72. Realizing the force of this, Shri Hari, who even with his
sight can destroy poison, hastened towards him like a
snake-charmer.[6]

73. Shri Krishna was near Arjuna when he was thus afflicted.
By the power of his grace he will be able to protect him.

74. Therefore, bearing this in mind, I have said that Arjuna
was attacked by the serpent of infatuation.

75. So here was Phālguna overcome by infatuation, just as
the sun is sometimes overshadowed by a mass of clouds.[7]

76. Like a mountain consumed by fire in summer, Arjuna,
the Wielder of the Bow, was afflicted with grief.

77. Then Shri Gopāla turned towards him, like a cloud, deep
blue in colour and moist with the nectar of kindness, and
spoke to him.[8]

78. The brilliance of his glance was as the flashing lightning,
the deep speech as the roar of the thunder.

79. Now that generous cloud will send down such a shower of
rain that the mountain that is Arjuna will cool and the
green shoots of knowledge begin to break forth.

80. Jnānadeva, disciple of Nivritti, says, Listen with full
attention to that story.

Sanjaya said:

IX. *Having thus addressed Hṛṣikeśa [Kṛṣṇa], the mighty
Guḍākeśa [Arjuna] said to Govinda [Kṛṣṇa] 'I will not
fight' and became silent.*

81. While narrating this, Sanjaya said, O King, what did Pārtha, again overcome with grief, say?

82. Hear now. Sorrowfully he said to Shri Krishna, Assuredly will I not fight; do not try to persuade me.

83. With these words he suddenly ceased speaking. Shri Krishna was astonished to see him in such a condition.

> X. *To him thus depressed in the midst of the two armies, O Bhārata [Dhṛtarāṣṭra], Hṛṣikeśa [Kṛṣṇa], smiling as it were, spoke this word.*

84. And He said to Himself, What is he thinking of? Arjuna is quite ignorant, what can be done?

85. How can he be brought to his senses? How can he be made to take heart? Just as an exorcizer considers [how to cast out] an evil spirit,

86. or as a physician, finding someone suffering from a dangerous illness, at the approach of the crisis, instantly prescribes some magic remedy such as nectar,

87. so, between the two armies, Ananta reflected upon how Arjuna could cast off his infatuation.[9]

88. Having decided what to do, He began to speak in an angry tone, as in a mother's anger is often concealed her affection,

89. or as in the bitter taste of medicine the full power of nectar is hidden, which, though not outwardly apparent, is shown in its efficacy.

90. So Hrishikesha addressed Arjuna in words which, though seemingly casual, in reality were very sweet.[10]

The Blessed Lord said:

> XI. *Thou grievest for those for whom thou shouldst not grieve, and yet thou speakest words about wisdom. Wise men do not grieve for the dead or for the living.*

91. Then He said to Arjuna, I am astonished at what thou sayest in the midst of all this.

92. Thou pretendest to be wise, and yet thou dost not abandon ignorance. Thou desirest to be taught, yet thou talkest over much.

93. Thy wisdom is as that of a man who, being born blind, afterwards loses his reason and wanders about at random.

94. Thou art altogether ignorant of thyself, and yet art ready to grieve for these Kauravas. This constantly surprises me.

95. O Arjuna, tell me if thou believest that the three worlds owe their existence to thee? Is it untrue that the structure of the universe is without beginning?

96. Is it falsely said in the world that there is but one Supreme Being from whom all creatures emanate?

97. After all, does it come to this, that thou hast created this life, and is it true that all who are to die are destroyed by thee?

98. Through the blindness of egoism dost thou say that those are immortal because thou hast not thought of killing them?

99. Thou art allowing confusion to enter thy mind [in thinking] that thou art the only destroyer, and that all these are those who perish.

100. All this has existed from beginningless time; it is born and it dies according to its own nature; tell me then why thou shouldst grieve.

101. It is ignorance which causes thee to believe thus, and thou shouldst not think these false thoughts; yet thou speakest to Me of morality!

102. The wise grieve for neither [the living nor the dead], whether these exist or pass away.

> XII. *Never was there a time when I was not, nor thou, nor these lords of men, nor will there ever be a time here-after when we shall cease to be.*

103. Arjuna, listen to what I tell thee. Lo! here art thou and I and these kings and all others.

104. Such ideas, that we should remain for ever, or that we should certainly perish, do not exist, when seen without confusion.

105. The idea that things can be born or die is but an illusion; in reality matter is indestructible.

106. The surface of water is agitated by the wind and waves appear on it; yet who can say what it is that is born and whence?

107. Similarly when the wind ceases to blow and the surface of the water once more becomes calm, consider, what is it that has died.

XIII. *As the soul passes in this body through childhood, youth and age, even so is its taking on of another body. The sage is not perplexed by this.*

108. Moreover, there is only one body, but there are different stages of life. Surely this is self-evident.
109. Thou mayest see boyhood, and yet in youth that vanishes; still the body does not perish with each stage.
110. Likewise, in the realm of spirit, bodies eventually die. He who knows this is not perturbed by any grief arising from confusion of mind.

XIV. *Contact with their objects, O Son of Kuntī [Arjuna], give rise to cold and heat, pleasure and pain. They come and go and do not last for ever, these learn to endure, O Bhārata [Arjuna].*

111. It is due to the domination of the senses that this is not understood. For the heart is in their power and so they are confused.
112. Objects are enjoyed through the senses and from these arise joy and grief; from such contacts the inner self is plunged into confusion.
113. The effect of the object of sense is not uniform, sometimes pain is the result, sometimes pleasure.
114. Behold! both censure and praise are associated with the realm of words; when these are heard they give rise to hate or love.
115. Softness and hardness are both qualities experienced by touch; when through contact they are felt by the body, they cause pleasure or pain.
116. Forms may be ugly or beautiful and yet through the eye they produce dislike or delight.
117. Fragrance and stench are different odours, but again through the sense of smell they arouse disgust or satisfaction.
118. Likewise taste is twofold, likes and dislikes arising from it; the contact with sense objects is, therefore, the cause of corruption.
119. If one yields to sense desire, one feels heat and cold and is caught up in pleasure and pain.
120. It is in the nature of the senses that they should find nothing more attractive than objects of sense.

121. But what is the real nature of these objects? They are as the water of a mirage, and like an elephant seen in a dream.

122. Like these, they are ephemeral. Do thou, therefore, reject them, O Wielder of the Bow. Do not let thyself be affected by contact with them.

> XV. *The man who is not troubled by these, O Chief of men [Arjuna], who remains the same in pain and pleasure, who is wise, makes himself fit for eternal life.*

123. He whom these objects do not bind is not affected by pleasure or pain, and for him there is no need for rebirth.

124. O Arjuna! thou shouldst understand that he is indeed immortal who does not fall into their power.

> XVI. *Of the non-existent there is no coming to be; of the existent there is no ceasing to be. The conclusion about these two has been perceived by the seers of truth.*

125. Now, Arjuna, I will tell thee something more; listen. Wise men realize this.

126. Within this bodily life dwells that same consciousness which pervades all things. Philosophers accept this.

127. As milk when mingled with water becomes one with it, still it can be separated by the royal swans.

128. As by means of fire the alloy mixed with gold is burnt out, and those who have the knowledge can extract the pure gold;

129. or as when curdled milk is churned by those who have the skill, butter at last appears;

130. or as when grain and chaff are winnowed together, the husks are blown away, while the heavy grain is left,

131. so when this matter is properly understood, the external visible world vanishes, and then for the wise only the first principle, Brahma, remains.

132. They do not concede real existence to impermanent things, for they have realized the true nature of both.

> XVII. *Know thou that that by which all this is pervaded is indestructible. Of this immutable being, no one can bring about the destruction.*

133. Considering the real and the unreal, thou wilt see that

the unreal is illusory, while the real in its very nature is
eternal.

134. That of which the three worlds are a manifestation has
neither name, colour, form nor sign.

135. It is eternal, all-pervasive, and beyond the reach of birth
and death. None can ever destroy it however much he
may try to do so.

> XVIII. *It is said that these bodies of the eternal embodied
> [soul] which is indestructible and incomprehensible come
> to an end. Therefore fight, O Bhārata [Arjuna].*

136. All bodies are by their very nature destructible. Therefore
do thou fight, O son of Pāndu.

> XIX. *He who thinks that this slays and he who thinks
> that this is slain; both of them fail to perceive the truth;
> this one neither slays nor is slain.*

137. With pride in its form, having thought only of thy body,
thou sayest, I am the killer, and these are those who die.

138. But, O Arjuna, thou dost not understand. If thou dost
think in terms of reality, thou art not the slayer, nor can
these be killed.

> XX. *He is never born, nor does he die at any time, nor
> having [once] come to be does he again cease to be. He
> is unborn, eternal, permanent and primeval. He is not
> slain when the body is slain.*

139. As whatever is seen in a dream appears at the time to be
real, but recollected on waking it has no reality,

140. so know this to be an illusion, and thy confusion therefore
is vain. As a shadow cut with a weapon is not cut in
itself;

141. or as when a pot full of water is turned upside down, the
surface can no longer reflect the sun; but nevertheless the
sun is not destroyed with the reflection.

142. As also the air in a house seems to have the shape of the
house, but if the latter is broken up, [the air again has its
natural] form.

> XXI. *He who knows that it is indestructible and eternal,
> uncreate and unchanging, how can such a person slay
> anyone, O Pārtha [Arjuna], or cause anyone to slay?*

143. In the same way though the body may die, the Self does
not. Therefore, O Beloved, do not cling to this delusion.

> XXII. *Just as a person casts off worn-out garments and
> puts on others that are new, even so does the embodied
> soul cast off out-worn bodies and take on others that are
> new.*

144. As an old garment is cast aside, and then a new one is
put on, so does the Self take to itself a new body.

> XXIII. *Weapons do not cleave this self, fire does not burn
> him; waters do not make him wet; nor does the wind
> make him dry.*

> XXIV. *He is uncleavable, he cannot be burnt. He can be
> neither wetted nor dried. He is eternal, all-pervading,
> unchanging and immovable. He is the same for ever.*

145. It is without beginning, eternal, without limitation and
pure. It cannot, therefore, be cleft by any weapon.
146. It cannot be submerged by the final flood of waters,
flames of fire can never consume it. Even the strongest
winds cannot wither it up.
147. This, O Kiriti, is not visible to the eye of reason; but
meditation eagerly reaches out for it.[11]

> XXV. *He is said to be unmanifest, unthinkable and
> unchanging. Therefore, knowing him as such, thou
> shouldst not grieve.*

148. It is ever inaccessible to the mind; it is not attainable by
any special practices. O Arjuna, this Supreme Being is
immeasurable.
149. O Arjuna, this is everlasting, immovable, all pervading
and eternally perfect.
150. It transcends the three qualities, beyond form, without
source or change, all pervading.[12]
151. O Arjuna, know it to be such, see it to be the Self in all.
Then will all thy grief pass away.

> XXVI. *Even if thou thinkest that the self is perpetually
> born and perpetually dies, even then, O Mighty-armed
> [Arjuna], thou shouldst not grieve.*

152. Or if thou dost not believe this, and thinkest of it as
subject to death, still thou shouldst not grieve, O son of
Pāndu.

153. For birth, life and dissolution follow each other in eternal progression, like the ceaseless flow of the waters of the river Ganges.

154. At its source it never fails, it always flows into the ocean, while in its middle course it is seen to be flowing onwards.

155. So too, at these three stages it passes on in succession and no creature can ever arrest its flow.

156. Thou shouldst not, therefore, grieve for these warriors, for these three conditions have been the same from all time;

157. or if thou agreest not, O Arjuna, seeing that men are subject to birth and death,

158. even then there is no cause for thee to grieve, for truly birth and death are unavoidable.

> XXVII. *For to the one that is born death is certain and certain is birth for the one that has died. Therefore for what is unavoidable, thou shouldst not grieve.*

159. What is born, dies; what dies, is born again. Like the wheels of a water-clock this cycle continues.

160. Or as sunrise and sunset follow each other, so in this world birth and death are inevitable.

161. At the time of the great dissolution even the three worlds perish. Therefore birth and death are inevitable.

162. If thou believest this, then why dost thou grieve, O Wielder of the bow? Knowing this already, why shouldst thou profess ignorance?

> XXVIII. *Beings are unmanifest in their beginnings, manifest in their middles, and unmanifest again in their ends, O Bhārata [Arjuna]. What is there in this for lamentation?*

163. Moreover, Arjuna, from no point of view is there any reason for grief.

164. All these beings are formless before birth; being born they take on individual form.

165. In that state to which they depart after the dissolution of their bodies, they do not certainly exist separately, but revert to their primal state.

166. Now, what is manifest in the life between is as a dream to one who sleeps. Likewise form appearing in the Self is due to the power of cosmic illusion.[13]

167. As water, when agitated by the wind, appears in the form of ripples, or as gold is fashioned by a man's desire into the shape of ornaments,

168. so all that has form is the result of illusion as the clouds which appear in the sky. Thou shouldst realize this.

169. Why then dost thou grieve for that which is not subject to birth? Consider rather that spirit which never fades away,

> XXIX. *One looks upon him as a marvel, another likewise speaks of him as a marvel; another hears of him as a marvel; and even after hearing, no one whosoever has known him.*

170. that spirit for which, when the longing for it is experienced, the saints renounce all desire, become dispassionate and retire into the wilderness,

171. and seeing which great sages have observed vows of celibacy and practised austerities.

172. Some while singing the praises of it, with detached minds, have become altogether absorbed in it.

173. Some, steadfast in heart, even at the sight of this, forget all the activities of this world.

174. Others, again, even hearing of it, have become subdued and lost all consciousness of their bodies. Others attain to union with it through experience.

175. As all the currents of rivers reach the ocean and never flow back again,

176. so the minds of the masters of yoga, once turned towards it, are merged in the Self and through the power of thought they do not experience rebirth.

> XXX. *The dweller in the body of everyone, O Bhārata [Arjuna], is eternal and can never be slain. Therefore thou shouldst not grieve for any creature.*

177. Behold! that which is everywhere and in everyone, which, though threatened, cannot be killed, is the one life infusing the whole universe.

178. It is owing to the nature of this that everything is born and dies; say then what can cause thee to grieve?

179. O Pārtha, I cannot understand why thou canst not accept this; moreover, lamentation is unbecoming in every way.

180. Why dost thou not now consider? What is it that thou art thinking? Thou hast forgotten thine own duty by which alone thou canst obtain salvation.

181. Should any calamity befall the Kauravas, should any mishap overtake thee, or were the great age to come to an end now,

182. even then one's own sacred duty must never be abandoned; canst thou then save thyself by compassion?

183. O Arjuna! though thy heart has melted with pity, it is out of place on the battlefield.

184. Though there may be cow's milk, it must not be given as a diet during fever, where if given it will act as a poison;

185. so, if action is not suitable for the occasion, one's welfare suffers. Arouse thyself, therefore.

186. Why grievest thou without reason? Attend to thy duty; if thou wilt follow it, no evil will at any time befall thee.

187. If one keeps to the road one encounters no mishap; if one carries a lamp one does not stumble.

188. So, O Pārtha, by the observance of one's duty all desires are easily fulfilled.

189. Thou shouldst know, therefore, that nothing is more worthy of a Kshatriya than fighting.

190. Free thy mind of deception, and fight blow for blow; but what need is there to speak to thee of what is obvious?

191. O Arjuna, consider this war, it is indeed fortunate for thee; perhaps it reveals the whole of thy life's calling.

192. Should it be called a battle, or is it that in this form heaven has become manifest, revealed by thy valour?

193. Or that Fame herself, attracted by thy qualities, eager with passion, has come to choose thee for her lord?

194. A Kshatriya who has acquired great merit, having such an opportunity of battle, would be as one who has found a stone of desire in his path,

195. or like a man into whose mouth, opened to yawn, nectar unexpectedly drops, so has this battle fallen to thy lot.

196. If thou dost shun this war and grievest unnecessarily, thou canst only harm thyself.
197. If thou castest away thy weapon in this battle today, assuredly wilt thou lose all that thy forefathers have gained.
198. Then will thy present fame be lost, the world will curse thee, and great sins will find thee out.
199. Just as a woman who has no husband is scorned on every side, so is the state of one who has abandoned his duty;
200. or as a corpse thrown out on waste land is attacked on all sides by vultures, so will the man who fails to perform his duty be beset by great sin.
201. If thou, therefore, dost abandon thy duty, thou wilt incur guilt, and thou wilt be dishonoured to the end of the age.

202. So long as he is not stained by dishonour a wise man should wish to live. How then canst thou flee from here?
203. Being free from malice and full of compassion, thou mayest perhaps turn back, but others will not approve of thy action.
204. They will attack thee on every side and will discharge arrows against thee; thou wilt not escape because of thy compassion.
205. If, however, thou art able to escape such dangers to thy life, even then existence would be to thee worse than death.

206. There is one other matter which thou dost not consider. Thou hast come here eager to fight, and if through compassion thou shouldst return,
207. tell me, is it likely that thy wicked enemies will understand this?
208. They will say, Arjuna has gone! He is afraid of us! Would such a slander be pleasing to thee?

209. Men make great efforts and even sacrifice their lives, O Wielder of the bow, but they increase their good name.
210. Thy fame has been easily won, unbroken, incomparable as the heavens,
211. so is thy fame without limit or equal; thy merit is the finest in all the three worlds.
212. The princes of all countries are the bards who chant thy praises, at which the hearts of the god of death and all others tremble with fear.
213. So great is thy renown, clear as the waters of the Ganges; the sight of it has astonished the foremost warriors of the earth.
214. Hearing of thy marvellous valour, they have come here, in despair of their lives.
215. As the roar of a lion seems as terrible as death to a raging elephant, so art thou a terror to the Kauravas.
216. As mountains regard the thunderbolt, as serpents dread the eagle, so do all these regard thee, O Arjuna.
217. If without fighting thou shouldst now turn back, all this greatness will be lost and worthlessness will come to thee.

> XXXVI. *Many unseemly words will be uttered by thy enemies, slandering thy strength. Could anything be sadder than that?*

218. Fleeing, they will prevent thee; they will hold and surround thee, despising thee, they will utter abuse in thine own hearing.
219. Then will thy heart break. Why shouldst thou not fight bravely now? If thou conquerest thine opponents thou wilt enjoy the whole earth.

> XXXVII. *Either slain thou shalt go to heaven; or victorious thou shalt enjoy the earth. Therefore arise, O Son of Kunti [Arjuna], resolved on battle.*

220. Or if, fighting in the battle, thou shouldst lose thy life, thou wilt enjoy heavenly bliss to the full.
221. Therefore, Arjuna pay no attention to these thoughts; stand up and grasp thy bow, ready to fight.
222. Behold! by fulfilling one's duty, present sin is destroyed; what is this confusion in thy mind about sin?
223. Do we drown in a boat, or stumble on the high road? Calamity may befall one who knows not how to walk.

224. One can even die from taking nectar, if poison is taken
with it; so sin can arise from duty performed, if the motive
is [wrong].
225. Therefore, O Pārtha, there is no sin against thy duty as a
warrior in fighting without [selfish] purpose.

> XXXVIII. *Treating alike pleasure and pain, gain and
> loss, victory and defeat, then get ready for battle. Thus
> thou shalt not incur sin.*

226. Rejoice not in happiness, be not downcast through pain;
do not consider gain or loss.
227. To consider whether victory will be won, or one's life be
lost, such thoughts of the future should not be considered
beforehand.
228. Performing one's own proper duty, come what may, one
should endure it with a steady mind.
229. When the mind is in this state, naturally no sin is incurred;
fight, therefore, with confidence.

> XXXIX. *This is the wisdom of the Sāṃkhya, given to thee,
> O Pārtha [Arjuna]. Listen now to the Yoga. If thine
> intelligence accepts it, thou shalt cast away the bondage
> of works.*

230. This path of wisdom has here been briefly expounded to
thee; now listen to the explanation of the path of union
through reason.[14]
231. O Pārtha, he who is altogether detached in performing
actions, cannot be troubled by the bonds of action,

> XL. *In this path, no effort is ever lost and no obstacle
> prevails; even a little of this righteousness [dharma] saves
> from great fear.*

232. as when clad in armour of adamant it is possible to
endure the attack of any weapon and remain unharmed
and victorious.
233. Life in this world is not lost and liberation is still won,
when this path has been faithfully followed.
234. Continue all prescribed action, but do not desire the fruit
thereof. As an exorcist cannot be harmed by an evil spirit,
235. so when a man has attained full enlightenment, then the
limitations of matter cannot bind him.
236. That wisdom which is subtle and steady, where sin has

no place and which the contacts of the three qualities cannot contaminate—

237. O Arjuna, should thy heart, through merit, be illumnated even a little by such wisdom, then every fear of life in this world would be removed.

> XLI. *In this, O joy of the Kurus [Arjuna], the resolute understanding is single; but the thoughts of the irresolute are many-branched and endless.*

238. As the flame of a lamp, however small, sheds a great light, so this wisdom should not be despised.

239. O Pārtha, this wisdom, the true desire for which is rare in this world, is sought after by many learned men.

240. As the touchstone is rarely found, in comparison with other objects; as it is only by good fortune that one finds even a drop of nectar,

241. so is wisdom difficult of attainment, the goal of which is the highest Self, as the ocean is for ever the goal of the Ganges.

242. So, O Arjuna, see! There is but one wisdom in the world, of which the sole abode is none other than the Supreme.

243. All other forms of enlightenment than this are evil. They are for the most part full of passion, and it is only the thoughtless who indulge in them.

244. So, O Pārtha, they experience heaven, existence and hell. The bliss of self-realization they never find.

> XLII. *The undiscerning who rejoice in the letter of the Veda, who contend that there is nothing else, whose nature is desire and who are intent on heaven,*

245. They speak with the authority of the Vedas, teaching action only, and that, with desire for the fruit of action.

246. They say, We must be born into this world, and perform sacrificial rites in order to enjoy heavenly pleasures

247. O Arjuna, such men of erring reason say, Beyond desire there is no happiness in the universe.

> XLIII. *Proclaim these flowery words that result in rebirth as the fruit of actions and [lay down] various specialized rites for the attainment of enjoyment and power.*

> XLIV. *The intelligence, which is to be trained, of those who are devoted to enjoyment and power, and whose*

248. Lo! such men, overcome by desire, perform action, setting their hearts only on the enjoyment of pleasure.
249. They perform many ceremonies, omitting no rites and so carry out their religious duties with great care.
250. In one thing only are they at fault; they set their hearts on the desire for heaven, and so lose sight of the Lord of Sacrifices, the real enjoyer.
251. It is as if a heap of camphor were made and set on fire, or rich dishes were mixed with poison;
252. or as if a vessel full of nectar, found by good luck, were overturned by the foot; so do these men destroy any merit they may gain by their desire [for the fruit of action].
253. Merit should be striven for with great effort; why then should they long for earthly existence? But if they do not know this, what can help those who have not attained wisdom?
254. As a cook might prepare choice dishes and then sell them for money, so the unenlightened throw away merit for the sake of enjoyment.
255. Know therefore, O Pārtha, evil inclinations beset the minds of those who indulge in controversies about the Vedas.

> XLV. *The action of the three-fold modes is the subject matter of the Veda; but do thou become free, O Arjuna, from this threefold nature; be free from the dualities [the pairs of opposites], be firmly fixed in purity, not caring for acquisition and preservation, and be possessed of the Self.*

256. Know certainly that the Vedas are pervaded by the three qualities; for this reason all the Upanishads are pure spirit,
257. while all else in which performance of action is described and which teaches that heaven is the only goal, is enveloped in passion and ignorance.
258. Therefore know this, that these lead only to pleasure and pain; do not set thy heart on them.
259. Reject all thought of the three qualities; speak not of

'me' and 'mine'; let only the bliss of the Self rest in your heart.

> XLVI. *As is the use of a pond in a place flooded with water everywhere, so is that of all the Vedas for the Brāhman who understands.*

260. Though in the Vedas much is said, and various distinctions are suggested, still we should only accept that which is for our good.
261. As when the sun is risen, all paths become visible, yet, tell me, is it possible to travel by all of them?
262. Even if the earth's surface is flooded with water, yet we take only enough to quench our thirst.
263. So do wise men examine the meaning of the Vedas and accept only what they desire and what has to do with the eternal.

> XLVII. *To action alone hast thou a right and never at all to its fruits; let not the fruits of action be thy motive neither let there be in thee any attachment to inaction.*

264. Listen therefore, O Pārtha, understood in this way, it is best for thee to perform thine own duty.
265. When we have considered all things, we realize that we should not abandon our appointed duty.
266. But do not desire the fruit of action, avoid action which is prohibited. Perform right action with no thought for the result.

> XLVIII. *Standing firm in yoga, do thy work, O Winner of wealth [Arjuna], abandoning attachment, with an even mind in success and failure, for evenness of mind is called yoga.*

267. Steadfast in yoga, renouncing attachment to the fruit of action, perform all actions with an attentive mind, O Arjuna.
268. If by good fortune the action undertaken is successfully accomplished, do not, on the other hand, rejoice unduly;
269. or if, for any reason, an action is prevented from fulfilment, thou shouldst not be disturbed by disappointment.
270. If, during its performance, it meets with success, well and

good; if it is prevented from completion, even so regard it as good.

271. If thou dost make an offering to the Supreme of every action thou mayest undertake, know that it will surely be accomplished.

272. Such mental equilibrium, in right action as in wrong, is the state of yoga, which is highly esteemed by the best of men.

> XLIX. *Far inferior indeed is mere action to the discipline of intelligence [buddhiyoga], O Winner of wealth [Arjuna]; seek refuge in intelligence. Pitiful are those who seek for the fruits [of their action].*
>
> L. *One who has yoked his intelligence [with the Divine] [or is established in his intelligence] casts away even here both good and evil. Therefore strive for yoga; yoga is skill in action.*

273. O Arjuna, the evenly balanced mind is the essence of yoga; wherein the mind and pure intelligence are united.

274. When we consider this yoga of pure intelligence, the yoga of action with attachment appears in many ways to be inferior, O Pārtha.

275. But this yoga of pure intelligence only becomes attainable when the yoga of action is practised; for action that remains after desire for its fruit is renounced naturally leads to evenness of mind.

276. The yoga of pure intelligence, therefore, is steady, O Arjuna. Concentrate on it and relinquish any desire for the fruit of action.

277. Those who have practised this yoga have reached the other shore and have freed themselves from the bondage of sin and merit.[15]

> LI. *The wise who have united their intelligence [with the Divine] renouncing the fruits which their action yields, and freed from the bonds of birth reach the sorrowless state.*

278. They perform action, but they are not caught in the bondage of it and thus, O Arjuna, they are freed from the cycle of births and deaths.

279. Then, O Wielder of the bow, those who are united with pure intelligence [the Supreme] arrive at the unshakable state of perfection.

LII. *When thine intelligence shall cross the world of delusion, then shalt thou become indifferent to what has been heard and what is yet to be heard.*

280. When thou hast thrown off this delusion, thou shalt become like them, and non-attachment will pervade thy mind.
281. Then having acquired deep and faultless knowledge of the Self, thy mind will easily become detached.
282. Then, O Arjuna, all need of knowing anything else or of recalling any past knowledge will disappear.

LIII. *When thine intelligence, which is bewildered by the Vedic texts, shall stand unshaken and stable in spirit [samādhi], then shalt thou attain to insight [yoga].*

283. Thy mind hitherto distracted owing to the activity of the senses, will stand as before firmly established in the life of the Self.
284. When the mind has become steady in the joy of contemplation, then thou shalt attain to the state of complete union.

Arjuna said:

LIV. *What is the description of the man who has this firmly founded wisdom, whose being is steadfast in spirit, O Keśava [Kṛṣṇa]? How does the man of settled intelligence speak, how does he sit, how does he walk?*

285. Arjuna said, O Lord! who art the ocean of mercy, now I will ask Thee to explain to me the meaning of all this.
286. Acyuta said readily, O Kiriti, Ask me with an open heart whatever seems good to thee.[16]
287. At this Pārtha said to Shri Krishna, Tell me who is the man with stable mind and how he is to be recognized.
288. Who is so called? What are the characteristics of one of stable mind who enjoys the bliss of contemplation?
289. In what state does he live, what does he look like, O Lord of Lakshmi? Tell me all this.[17]

The Blessed Lord said:

LVI. *When a man puts away all the desires of his mind, O Pārtha [Arjuna], and when his spirit is content in itself, then is he called stable in intelligence.*

290. Then what did Shri Nārāyana, the incarnation of the Highest Self and the abode of the six qualities, say?[18]
291. Shri Krishna said, Hear, O Arjuna! all the strong desires of the heart are a hindrance to the experience of the highest bliss.
292. He whose heart is always satisfied in the Self but who, as regards the contact by which a man is drawn into the enjoyment of sensual pleasures,
293. has renounced all desire and whose mind rests in the joy of the Self, know such a man to be one who is stable-minded.

> LVI. *He whose mind is untroubled in the midst of sorrows and is free from eager desire amid pleasures, he from whom passion, fear and rage have passed away, is called a sage of settled intelligence.*

294. He whose mind is not disturbed though he may suffer pain and who is not troubled by the desire for pleasures,
295. he into whose mind, O Arjuna, desire and anger do not enter, who knows no fear, is perfect.
296. The sage who is beyond limitation and without earthly bondage or sense of difference should be known as even-minded.

> LVII. *He who is without affection on any side, who does not rejoice or loathe as he obtains good or evil, his intelligence is firmly set [in wisdom].*

297. He is everywhere and always the same, as the moon in shedding her light does not say, This is good, or that is bad,
298. so is his unbroken even-mindedness, his compassion towards all creatures, and his mind is at no time subject to change.
299. He who is not overjoyed when he receives something good and is not distressed when evil befalls him,
300. know him to be stable-minded, free from joy or sorrow and filled with the enlightenment of the Self, O Wielder of the bow.

> LVIII. *He who draws away the senses from the objects of sense on every side as a tortoise draws in his limbs [into the shell], his intelligence is firmly set [in wisdom].*

301. Now, Arjuna, there is one more thing I will tell thee,

listen. There are some seekers who resolutely abandon the pleasures of sense.

302. As a tortoise, when at ease may extend its limbs or draw them in at will,

> LIX. *The objects of sense turn away from the embodied soul who abstained from feeding on them, but the taste for them remains. Even the taste disappears when the Supreme is seen.*

303. so is the understanding of the well-balanced man whose senses are under his control and act according to his bidding.

304. Those who his bidding subdue their hearing and other senses but do not control their taste, are consequently bound by them in a thousand ways.

305. If the upper leaves of a tree are plucked off and yet the tree is watered at the roots, how can it be destroyed?

306. In the same way that such a tree branches out luxuriantly owing to the power of the water, so attachment to objects of sense is nourished in the mind through the sense of taste.

307. The other senses can be separated from their objects but taste cannot be easily controlled, for no living thing can exist without it.

308. So, O Arjuna, when a man experiences the state of union with the Supreme, he is easily able to control these desires also.

309. When a man realizes that he and the Supreme are one, awareness of bodily feelings ceases, and the objects of sense are forgotten by the senses.

> LX. *Even though a man may ever strive [for perfection] and be ever so discerning, O Son of Kunti [Arjuna], his impetuous senses will carry off his mind by force.*

310. Moreover, O Arjuna, even they who ceaselessly strive to curb their senses are not always successful.

311. Those who dwell in the house of the practice of yoga, who build walls of mind-control around themselves and keep their minds in a firm grip,

312. even they also are tormented, so great is the power of the senses that even a knower of incantations may be deceived by an evil spirit.

313. Of such a nature are the objects of sense, which appear in
     the disguise of psychic powers, and in contact with the
     senses ensnare [the mind].
314. At such a time the mind goes astray and practice of
     control is crippled. Such is the strength of the senses.

> LXI. *Having brought all [the senses] under control, he
> should remain firm in yoga intent on Me; for he, whose
> senses are under control, his intelligence is firmly set.*

315. Hear, therefore, O Arjuna! Whoever, abandoning attach-
     ment to all pleasures of sense, destroys their power, is
     known
316. to be steadfast in yoga; whose mind is not deluded by the
     pleasures of the senses,
317. and who is always full of the knowledge of the Self, and
     who never forgets Me in his heart.
318. On the other hand, earthly existence never ceases for the
     man who outwardly gives up objects of sense and yet
     dwells upon them in his heart.
319. As when a drop of poison is taken its effect increases and
     inevitably destroys the life,
320. so even if a doubt about objects of sense remains in the
     mind it may destroy all understanding.

> LXII. *When a man dwells in his mind on the objects of
> the senses, attachment to them is produced. From attach-
> ment springs desire and from desire comes anger.*
>
> LXIII. *From anger arises bewilderment, from bewilderment
> loss of memory; and from loss of memory, the destruction
> of intelligence and from the destruction of intelligence he
> perishes.*

321. Should a man dwell on objects of sense in his mind then
     attachment will arise within detachment; in attachment
     is the very image of desire.
322. Where there is desire anger has first been present, and
     in anger there has been delusion.
323. When delusion appears, memory will be lost, as a flame
     is extinguished by a gust of wind.
324. Then, blinded through ignorance, everything is lost, so
     that the pure reason in his mind is confused.
325. As at sunset the night envelops the light of the sun, so is
     that man's condition when memory breaks down.

326. As a man born blind, when he has to run, rushes piteously hither and thither, in the same way pure wisdom becomes bewildered, O Wielder of the bow.

327. Memory being thus confused, reason is entirely defeated, and all knowledge is destroyed.

328. As the body is reduced to a sorry plight when consciousness fails, so is the state of the man who loses his reason.

329. Hear, therefore, O Arjuna! As a spark applied to fuel, which bursts into flame and could set fire to the three worlds,

330. so reflection on objects of sense, even unwittingly, leads to great loss.

> LXIV. *But a man of disciplined mind, who moves among the objects of sense with the senses under control and free from attachment and aversion, he attains purity of spirit.*

331. If all sense objects are entirely driven from the mind, attraction and aversion will perish of themselves.

332. O Pārtha, there is one thing more. If attraction and aversion die out, no harm can ensue when the senses are interested in objects of sense.

333. As the sun in the sky is not contaminated by the earth which it touches with its rays,

334. so is one who is indifferent to the pleasures of the senses, free from desire and anger and filled with the bliss of the Self.

335. Then when he sees none other than himself in the universe how can sense pleasures disturb him?

336. If water could be drowned in water, or fire burn fire, then it would be possible for the perfect man to be affected by contact with sense objects.

337. In such a manner he becomes steadily one with everything and so his understanding is well balanced. Believe this to be so.

> LXV. *And in that purity of spirit, there is produced for him an end of all sorrow; the intelligence of such a man of pure spirit is soon established [in the peace of the self].*

338. When the heart is always at peace, the miseries of his worldly existence cannot enter it.

339. As he in whose body there is a fountain of nectar is not troubled by hunger or thirst,

340. so, if the heart is peaceful, where can any place be found for pain? The mind thus naturally dwells in the highest Self.
341. As a light in a place where there is no wind will not flicker, so that man who is even-minded remains united in mind with the Self.

342. He who does not reflect upon this union in his heart is bound by objects of sense and their qualities.
343. For him, O Pārtha, steady understanding is quite impossible, and even a longing for it is never aroused in him.
344. If there is no sense of stability in the mind, O Arjuna, how can it be at peace?
345. Where there is no centre of peace, bliss can never enter in even unawares, for salvation is not for the sinner.
346. If seeds could germinate after being cast in the fire, then might happiness come to a man without peace.
347. Therefore the unharmonized state of the heart is the cause of all pain, and so it is essential for the senses to be controlled.

LXVII. *When the mind runs after the roving senses, it carries away the understanding even as a wind carries away a ship on the waters.*

348. They whose actions follow the bidding of the senses, do not cross over the ocean of earthly life, though they may seem to do so.
349. As when a boat has arrived at the shore a tempest may arise, and the boat will be overtaken by the disaster from which it had recently escaped,
350. so, even if a man who has attained to this state indulges his senses for pleasure, he is overcome by the pain of worldly life.

LXVIII. *Therefore, O Mighty-armed [Arjuna], he whose senses are all withdrawn from their objects his intelligence is firmly set.*

351. Therefore, O Conqueror of wealth, if the senses are kept
under control, what greater goal is there than this?[9]
352. So the understanding of the man whose senses are obedient
to his command has reached a state of wisdom.
353. Now, O Arjuna, there is still one more subtle characteristic
of the perfect man, which I will tell thee, Listen!

> LXIX. *What is night for all beings is the time of waking
> for the disciplined soul; and what is the time of waking
> for all beings is night for the sage who sees [or the sage
> of wisdom].*

354. One who remains conscious when all other beings are
asleep, or apparently asleep when others are awake,
355. he alone is beyond limitation, well balanced and a lord
among sages.

> LXX. *He into whom all desires enter as waters into the
> sea, which, though ever being filled is ever motionless,
> attains to peace and not he who hugs his desires.*

356. O Arjuna, by one further characteristic may he be known;
now listen to it. As the ocean is continuously calm,
357. even though the streams of all the rivers flow into it,
filling it to the full, it does not increase nor does it pass
beyond its boundaries;
358. or in the summer, O Arjuna, if all the rivers were to dry
up, even then it would not decrease;
359. so, even if that perfect one should acquire psychic powers,
his reason would not be disturbed by them, nor would he
be discouraged if he did not gain them.
360. Tell me, is any light needed in the house of the sun, or
would it be enclosed in darkness, if no lamp were placed
there?
361. Similarly, whether psychic powers are gained or not, he is
unaware of them, for he is absorbed in the highest bliss.
362. How can one who, in his own cleverness, considers
Indra's heaven as mean, like living in the hut of the
forester?
363. One who finds fault with nectar will not drink gruel. In
the same way he who has experienced the bliss of the
Self has no interest in psychic powers.
364. How surprising this is, O Pārtha! When even the bliss of

heaven is considered as of little value, are psychic powers of any significance?

> LXXI. *He who abandons all desires and performs actions from longing, without any sense of mineness or egotism, attains to peace.*

365. Thou mayest know him to be well balanced in understanding who takes delight in the bliss of the Self, and feeds on the highest joy.
366. Overcoming all egoism, abandoning all desires, he moves through the universe, for he has himself become that universe.

> LXXII. *This is the divine state [brahmasthiti] O Pārtha [Arjuna], having attained thereto, one is [not again] bewildered; settled in that state at the end [at the hour of death] one can attain to the bliss of God [brahmanirvāna].*

367. This is the boundless divine state enjoyed by those whose desires are dead; they easily reach union with the highest Self.
368. The pains of death have no power to disturb the mind of such an enlightened man when he reaches the state of union with the divine wisdom.
369. This is that state of which Krishna spoke with his own lips to Arjuna. So said Sanjaya.
370. Hearing these words of Krishna, Arjuna thought to himself, This teaching which I have heard is good.
371. The Lord has forbidden all action and therefore it is forbidden to me to fight.
372. With these words of Shri Acyuta the Wielder of the bow was inwardly delighted. Being still in doubt, he will now ask further questions.
373. Such an occasion is highly to be esteemed, for it is the store of all duty, the limitless ocean of the nectar of pure wisdom.
374. Shri Ananta, Lord of the enlightened, will himself propound all this. Jnānadeva, disciple of Nivritti, will comment upon it.

In the Upanishad of the Bhagavadgitā, the science of the Absolute, the Scripture of Yoga and the dialogue between Shri Krishna and Arjuna, this is the second chapter called the Yoga of Knowledge.

NOTES

1. *Kshatriya.* The 'warrior' caste, second among the four Hindu castes.
2. *Nivātakavaca.* The name of a pair of demons.
3. *Bhasmāsura.* The name of a demon who, having been given special powers of destruction, then used these against his benefactor.
4. *Murāri.* One of the names of Krishna, the 'enemy of Mura' (a demon).
5. *Purushottama.* The highest spirit, the 'best of persons', here referring to Krishna.
   Dharma. The sacred duty of a man in accordance with his caste; religious practice; religion in general.
6. *Hari.* One of the names of the god Vishnu, of whom Krishna was an incarnation. Here the name is given to Krishna.
7. *Phālguna.* One of the names of Arjuna. Also the name of one of the months of the Hindu calendar.
8. *Shri Gopāla.* One of the names of Krishna, the 'cowherd'. This name derives from a period in Krishna's life when he lived in the role of a cowherd.
   deep blue colour. Krishna is usually pictured as having a blue complexion; the word krishna is an adjective with the meaning 'dark', 'blue', etc.
9. *Ananta.* A name of Krishna, meaning 'without end', 'infinite'.
10. *Hrishikesha.* Another epithet of Krishna, 'the one with the bristling hair'.
11. *Kiriti.* Another name for Arjuna.
12. *the three qualities.* The three basic properties of nature governing human life are referred to as the 'qualities' (guna); ignorance, passion and spirit, or truth. See also later under note 18.
13. *Cosmic Illusion.* Illusion, māyā, is the condition in which all creatures live in this world, a condition which disturbs true perception of reality.
14. *the path of wisdom.* This is the philosophy of the Sānkhya system, the jnānayoga.
    the path of union through reason. A yogic discipline leading to union with the Absolute through intellectual training.
15. *the other shore.* Life in this world is thought of as a river to be crossed and the goal is to reach salvation as 'the other shore'.
16. *Acyuta.* A name of Vishnu, here used in reference to Krishna, 'permanent', 'not fallen'.
17. *Lord of Lakshmi.* Lakshmi is the name of the consort of Vishnu, the epithet referring here to Krishna.
18. *Nārāyana.* One of the names of Vishnu and referring here to Krishna.
    the six qualities. The six qualities, or virtues, in a man's life are glory, heroism, victory, prosperity, wisdom and renunciation.
19. *Conqueror of wealth.* One of the epithets of Arjuna.

CHAPTER III

Arjuna said:

> *1. If thou deemest that [the path of] understanding is more excellent than that of action, O Janārdana [Kṛṣṇa], why then dost thou urge me to do this savage deed, O Keśava [Kṛṣṇa]?*

1. Then said Arjuna, O Lord! I have listened to Thy words attentively, O Consort of Kamalā.[1]
2. O Ananta, it would appear from them that action and agent no longer exist. If this be Thy definite opinion,
3. then why, O Hari, dost Thou call on me to fight; art Thou not ashamed to incite me to this terrible action?
4. Thou condemnest all action, and then dost Thou urge me to cause this destruction?
5. Shri Hrishikesha, consider this, Thou approvest of cessation of action and yet, at the same time, Thou dost command me to kill.

> *II. With an apparently confused utterance thou seemest to bewilder my intelligence. Tell me then decisively the one thing by which I can attain to the highest good.*

6. O Lord! if even Thou shouldst advise us thus, what shall we ignorant people do? Is it that this would be the end of all discrimination?
7. If this is indeed Thy teaching, what can false teaching be like? Now indeed all our eagerness for knowledge of the divine is finished.
8. If a physician were to prescribe a healing diet and then himself administer poison, tell me, how could the patient live?
9. This [seemingly] good advice that thou has given to us is like setting a blind man on the wrong road, or giving an intoxicating potion to a monkey.

10. In the first place I am ignorant, and then I am overcome
    with this confusion; that is why, O Krishna, I have asked
    for Thy guidance.
11. How strange are Thy ways! There is confusion in Thy
    teaching. Shouldst Thou behave in this way towards a
    disciple?
12. With body, mind and soul I ought to place confidence in
    Thy words, and if Thou behavest thus, then all is finished.
13. If this is truly Thy teaching, then it is well for us. Arjuna
    said, How is there any hope of gaining knowledge?
14. Not only is there nothing fresh to learn, but still further
    harm has been done. My mind which was steady has
    become disturbed.
15. Moreover, Shri Krishna, I cannot understand Thy ways.
    Dost Thou wish to test my mind under this pretext?
16. Art Thou deceiving me or has Thy teaching a hidden
    implication? Considering it, indeed I cannot understand.
17. Therefore listen, O Lord, do not speak of such deep
    meaning. Tell me those things in Marāthi.[2]
18. Indeed I am very dull of understanding. But I will listen
    well, O Krishna. Speak with certainty.
19. If a disease is to be cured, medicine must be given, but it
    ought to be sweet and palatable.
20. These truths so full of meaning should be suitably told,
    but in a way that will enlighten my mind.
21. O Lord! Thou art my own Teacher! Why then shouldst
    Thou not fulfil my desire? Why should I stand in awe of
    anyone? Thou art our mother!
22. If anyone were to obtain through good fortune the milk
    of the cow who satisfies all desire, why should he refrain
    from asking what he wants?
23. If the wishing-stone were to fall into one's hand, why
    should one hesitate to express his wishes? Why should he
    not ask for what pleases him?
24. If a man should reach the ocean of nectar and then suffer
    from thirst, of what use would be the trouble he has
    taken to reach it?
25. Similarly, O Lord of Lakshmi, if having worshipped Thee for
    many lives it is now my good fortune to have found Thee,
26. then, O Highest Lord, why should I not ask Thee for
    what pleases me? O Lord, what a rich harvest there is
    now for my mind!

27. Today my desires have been fulfilled, my merit has borne
fruit, and all my longings have been crowned with success.

28. Thou who art the abode of all auspiciousness, the Lord
of all the gods, hast now become mine.

29. As there is no time when a child may not suck at the
breast of its mother,

30. so, O Lord, the storehouse of mercy, I will ask Thee
whatever I wish, if it pleases you.

31. Pārtha said, Tell me clearly what I should do, and what
will be beneficial to me hereafter

The Blessed Lord said:

> III. *O blameless One, in this world a two-fold way of life
> has been taught of old by Me, the path of knowledge for
> men of contemplation and that of works for men of action.*

32. Surprised by these words, Shri Acyuta said, O Arjuna,
listen to the deeper meaning [of what I have said].

33. While explaining the yoga of discrimination, I have at
the same time expounded the system of the Sānkhya
philosophy.[3]

34. Thou hast not understood my purpose, hence thou hast
been needlessly perplexed. Thou shouldst realize that I
have spoken of both these.

35. Listen! O Best of warriors, these two paths have been
revealed by Me in this world and they have existed
eternally.

36. One is called the path of knowledge, followed by the sages,
and they who travel along it attain to the realization of
the Self.

37. The other is known as the path of action, whereby seekers
who become proficient in it in course of time reach
Nirvāna.[4]

38. Though these paths are two, ultimately they become one,
as food whether prepared or unprepared give the same
satisfaction;

39. or as rivers flowing east and west seem separate, but
eventually both merge into the same ocean,

40. so both these teachings have in view the one goal, but the
practice of them depends on one's ability.

41. Behold! how a bird can seize a fruit even when it is in
flight; but can a man do so with such swiftness?

42. Gradually, springing from bough to bough, eventually in this manner he will reach [the fruit].

43. By the same method as that of the bird, wise men who follow the path of knowledge may quickly attain to liberation,

44. but resorting to the path of action, performing their duties, yogis also attain perfection in due time.

> IV. *Not by abstention from work does a man attain freedom from action; nor by mere renunciation does he attain his perfection.*

45. Besides, a man cannot, by omitting to perform his prescribed duties, become free from the obligation of action as is the perfected sage.

46. For, O Arjuna, it is useless and foolish to say that a man can be free from his allotted action by merely abstaining from it.

47. When it is necessary to cross a river, can it be done by abandoning one's boat?

48. Or if hunger is to be satisfied surely one must cook food oneself, or accept what is already prepared.

49. As long as there is no freedom from desire, so long action must be performed; when contentment is gained, then activity naturally ceases.

50. Hear then, O Arjuna, proper action is unavoidable for him whose heart is set on liberation.

51. Moreover, is action something that can be performed or abandoned at will?

52. To say so would be idle talk; this must be carefully thought out. Bear in mind, beyond all doubt, that action is not renounced merely by avoiding it.

> V. *For no one can remain even for a moment without doing work; everyone is made to act helplessly by the impulses born of nature.*

53. As long as a man is born of nature, it is ignorance to say that action may be performed or avoided. Action is under the sway of the qualities inherent in matter.

54. Even if every obligatory action were abandoned, would the tendencies of the sense organs cease?

55. Would the ears cease to hear? Would the light of the eyes

fail? Would the nostrils be closed and incapable of smelling?

56. Would the rhythm of breathing cease or the mind be unable to function, or would the desires of hunger and thirst come to an end?

57. Would waking and sleeping stop, or the feet forget how to walk? Would birth and death cease?

58. If these do not cease, then has anything been abandoned? Therefore it is not possible for those who are in the body to avoid action.

59. Action is born of, and is dependent on, the qualities of nature; thus is it useless to say that one can choose whether to act or not.

60. If one enters a carriage and remains motionless in it, still one moves as one travels, dependent on the carriage.

61. As a dried leaf, lifted by the force of the wind, circles in the sky although it does not move of itself,

62. so by the force of nature, and through the tendencies of the organs of action, even one who is detached from action is always active.

63. Therefore, so long as there is any connection with matter, abandonment of action is impossible. Those who say, in spite of all this, that they can cease from action are merely obstinate.

> VI. *He who restrains his organs of action but continues in his mind to brood over objects of sense, whose nature is deluded is said to be a hypocrite.*

64. They who abandon proper action and seek to become freed from action only by controlling the tendencies of the sense organs,

65. have not really abandoned action, for the thought of the action still remains in the mind. Such outward show is to be despised.

66. O Pārtha, there is no doubt whatever that such men can be truly known as wholly attached to the objects of sense.

67. Now, O Wielder of the bow, listen to me, and I will explain to thee in order the characteristics of those who are detached from sense.

> VII. *But whoever controls the senses by the mind, O Arjuna, and without attachment engages the organs of action in the path of work, is superior.*

68. He whose mind is firm, absorbed in the Self, yet outwardly active as other people,

69. who does not act under the impulse of his senses, who does not fear contact with objects of sense, who does not avoid any proper action,

70. who, although he does not curb his senses when performing action with them, is not carried away by the waves of their influence,

71. such a man is not bound by mere desire, nor contaminated by the darkness of delusion, as a lotus leaf remains untainted by the water in which it floats,

72. so in this earthly life such a man appears as others, in the same way that the reflection of the sun in water seems to be part of it.

73. Similarly such a man seems to be quite ordinary, but, observed more closely, one does not know his true disposition.

74. Recognizing him by these signs thou wilt know him to be liberated and free from the bonds of desire.

75. He is a yogi, O Arjuna, highly esteemed in this world. I tell thee, seek to be like him.

76. Control thy mind, be steady of heart, and then thy senses may engage freely in activity.

> VIII. *Do thou thy alloted work, for action is better than inaction; even the maintenance of thy physical life cannot be effected without action.*

77. Thou sayest thou wouldst be free from action, but that is not possible in this world; consider then how one can transgress the law.

78. Therefore, perform whatever action is right and proper, according to the occasion without selfish purpose.

79. O Pārtha, there is one thing more which thou knowest not, how a man may easily obtain freedom from action.

80. He who performs the duties proper to his station in life, most certainly attains liberation by that very practice.

> IX. *Except for work done as and for a sacrifice, this world is in bondage to work. Therefore, O Son of Kuntī [Arjuna], do thy work as a sacrifice, becoming free from all attachment.*

81. O Beloved! know that a man's duty is his daily sacrifice, and acting therein he can incur no sin.

82. When such individual duty is relinquished and there arises a liking for wrongful action, then bondage to earthly life follows.

83. Therefore the performance of one's own duty is ceaseless sacrifice. He who performs it creates no bonds for himself.

84. This world is bound by action; he who is under the sway of the senses is deprived [of the efficacy] of daily sacrifice.

85. O Pārtha, now I will relate to thee a story concerning this. When Brahma created the whole structure of nature,

> x. *In ancient days the Lord of creatures created men along with sacrifice and said, 'By this shall ye bring forth and this shall be unto you that which will yield the milk of your desires'.*

86. he created all beings with perpetual sacrifice; but as the meaning of the sacrifice was very subtle they did not understand it.

87. His creatures prayed to Brahma saying, O God, what refuge is there for us here? Then Brahma, born of the lotus, said to them,[5]

88. According to your castes your duties have been prescribed for you; follow them and your desires will be naturally fulfilled.

89. You need to practise no vow or rule, nor need you mortify your bodies; there is no necessity to visit any distant place of pilgrimage.

90. Do not undertake yogic practices, devotions with special intent, charms or incantations.

91. Worship no other deity, and doing none of these things, perform without striving the sacrifices that are ordained for you.

92. Perform them with disinterested mind, as a chaste woman [is devoted] to her husband.

93. The ordained sacrifice is the only one which you need to perform, so said the Lord of the highest heaven.[6]

94. So if you will practise your own duty, it will be to you as the cow who satisfies all desires. O my people, it will never forsake you.

> xi. *By this foster the gods and let the gods foster you;*

thus fostering each other you shall attain to the supreme good.

95. By this all the gods will be propitiated and will fulfil all your desires.
96. If you worship the hierarchy of the gods through the performance of your duty, they will assure your welfare and security.
97. If you will worship the gods, they will be pleased with you; thus an attachment will spring up between you;
98. thereby whatever you wish to do will be easily accomplished, and all the desires of your heart will be fulfilled.
99. All that you may say will prove to be true, you will be able to command others and psychic powers will do your bidding,
100. as the wealth of the forest is always in attendance at the door of spring, the lord of the seasons, gracefully bearing abundance of fruit.

> XII. *Fostered by sacrifice the gods will give you the enjoyments you desire. He who enjoys these gifts without giving to them in return is verily a thief.*

101. In this way fortune incarnate will seek you out with all delights.
102. O Beloved, if you will only act thus, devoted solely to your duty, you will be rich in all happiness and free from all desire.
103. If having acquired all wealth a man should be carried away by the excitement of the senses, and long for objects of sense,
104. or if he does not worship the highest god, according to the requirements of his caste, with the wealth given to him by the gods who are pleased with his sacrifice,
105. if he were not to offer oblations of fire, worship the gods, or on suitable occasions give food to brāhmans,
106. if he were to turn away from devotion to his guru, or if he were not to offer hospitality to guests, or give satisfaction to his caste fellows,
107. if, failing in those things that pertain to his duty, and being vain in his prosperity, he were to be solely engrossed in the enjoyment of sensual pleasures,
108. great harm will befall him, all that he possesses will be

lost, and he will not even be able to enjoy his present pleasures.

109. As consciousness departs from the body of a dead man, or as the goddess of wealth leaves the house of a man of ill-fortune,

110. so, if a man loses sight of his duty, then happiness will be cut off from its source. As when a lamp is extinguished, the light also disappears,

111. so if one departs from his own nature, then freedom no longer exists. So Virinci said clearly, This is true; listen, O my people![7]

112. Death will punish him who abandons his duty and, calling him a thief, will take everything from him.

113. Then as ghosts surround a graveyard at night so will all kinds of sins encompass him.

114. All the afflictions of the three worlds and every kind of sin and misery will be with him.

115. O my creatures! when such a man, having gone mad, is reduced to such a state weeping will not set him free even at the end of the world.

116. Do not, therefore, abandon your own duty, or let your senses go astray. So the four-faced one teaches all men.[8]

117. As water animals will soon perish if they leave the water, so should you not forget your duties.

118. Therefore do I tell you all again and again that you should be zealous in the performance of your proper duty.

> XIII. *Good people who eat what is left from the sacrifice are released from all sins, but those wicked people who prepare food for their own sake verily eat their sin.*

119. Behold! he who uses what wealth he possesses for carrying out his duty with no desire for the fruit,

120. who worships his preceptors, his kinsmen and the fire, who pays due reverence to brāhmans and on proper occasions gives offerings for the sake of his forefathers,

121. throwing into the fire during the performance of these sacrifices whatever remains from the offerings,

122. and who eats all this happily in his own house, with his family, his sins are thereby destroyed.

123. Because he enjoys the remains of the sacrifice, he is freed from all his sins, as a leprous man is healed by nectar.

124. He whose mind is firmly fixed on the real cannot be

deceived by illusion, so he who eats of the remains of the sacrifice is free from sin.

125. Therefore whatsoever a man gains in the performance of his duty should be used for the discharge of that duty, and what remains, he should enjoy in contentment.

126. O Arjuna, thus only shouldst thou act. Thus did Shri Murāri recount to him the ancient story.

127. Those who regard the body as the Self, who consider that sense pleasures are to be enjoyed, see nothing except this;

128. ignorant of any act of sacrifice, they seek only the selfish enjoyment of pleasure;

129. they prepare dishes to satisfy their senses, these are sinful men nourishing themselves on evil.

130. Thou shouldst regard all worldly riches as material for offerings and dutifully pour it out as an oblation to the Supreme.

131. See how the foolish, instead of acting thus, prepare all kinds of food for their own satisfaction!

132. The food with which a sacrifice is performed and which is pleasing to the Highest, is no common food.

133. Do not consider it as ordinary food, but as a form of Brahma, for it is the means of life for the whole of creation.

> XIV. *From food creatures come into being; from rain is the birth of food; from sacrifice rain comes into being and sacrifice is born of work.*
>
> XV. *Know the origin of karma [of the nature of sacrifices] to be in Brahma [the Veda] and the Brahma springs from the Imperishable. Therefore the Brahma, which comprehends all, ever centres round the sacrifice.*

134. All creatures grow from the food they eat; and everywhere the rain produces this food.

135. The birth of the rain is in the sacrifice, and the cycle of action gives rise to sacrifice; Brahma in the form of the Veda is the source of all action.

136. The Imperishable, Higher than the highest, sends forth the Vedas; therefore all this movable and immovable creation is bound up in Brahma.

137. But hear, O Subhadrāpati, the Vedas have their permanent abode in the sacrifice, which is the embodiment of action.[9]

XVI. He who does not, in this world, turn the wheel thus set in motion, is evil in his nature, sensual in his delight, and he, O Pārtha [Arjuna], lives in vain.

138. Thus, O Arjuna, I have briefly recounted to thee the origin and tradition of the sacrifice.
139. Therefore is sacrifice in the form of your own duty proper from the beginning. He who is full of vanity never performs it in this world.
140. Know him to be a store of sin and a burden to the earth who by doing evil serves his senses only.
141. O Arjuna, his life and actions are as fruitless as a mass of untimely clouds,
142. and the existence of one who fails to perform his proper duty is as useless as the false teat hanging from the neck of a goat.
143. Therefore listen, O Arjuna, let no one abandon his duty, but follow it with his whole heart.
144. Moreover, where there is an embodied life, duty as a matter of course accompanies it. Why should one abandon what is right?

XVII. But the man whose delight is in the Self alone, who is content with the Self, who is satisfied with the Self, for him there exists no work that needs to be done.

XVIII. Similarly, in this world he has no interest whatever to gain by the actions that he has done and none to be gained by the actions that he has not done. He does not depend on any being, for any purpose of his.

145. He alone who, while the functions of the body continue, rejoices always in the Self, is unaffected by action.
146. For he is content in the illumination of the Self, and as his work is accomplished, he is naturally free from the contact of action.
147. As when any of the senses are gratified the means of gratification passes away there is satisfaction in the Self, there is no need for action.
148. O Arjuna, so long as the mind does not reach illumination, one must resort to some means of reaching it.

XIX. Therefore, without attachment, perform always the work that has to be done, for man attains to the highest by doing work without attachment.

149. Therefore, perform thy own appointed duty, with restraint and without attachment.

150. For, O Pārtha, those who attain to that state of non-attachment to the fruit of action by performing their duty, do indeed reach the highest bliss even in this world.

151. Janaka and others, without abandoning any action, attained to the bliss of liberation.

152. Therefore, O Pārtha, let duty be carefully observed. There is also one other good which results from it.

153. For if we ourselves perform action others will follow [our example], and so in time they will avoid calamity.

154. They who have realized their desires and have reached non-attachment, yet for them also action has to be performed for the sake of the people.

155. As on the road a man with sight will walk in front of a blind man, so should those who know point out the path to those who do not.

156. Were we not to do so, how could the ignorant understand? How could they know this path?

XXI. *Whatever a great man does, the same is done by others as well. Whatever standard he sets, the world follows.*

157. In this world, whatever the elders do, other people regard as a duty and usually seek to follow it.

158. So, naturally, action should never be abandoned; especially should good men perform action.

XXII. *There is not for me, O Pārtha [Arjuna], any work in the three worlds which has to be done nor anything to be obtained which has not been obtained; yet I am engaged in work.*

XXIII. *For, if I ever did not engage in work unwearied, O Pārtha [Arjuna], men would in every way follow my path.*

XXIV. *If I should cease to work, these worlds would fall in ruin and I should be the creator of disordered life and destroy these people.*

159. Now, O Kiriti, why need I speak to thee of others? Behold, I act myself in the same way.

160. Wert thou to say that I perform duty because I am in some difficulty, or I am in need of something,

161. thou knowest that I posses powers in the fullness of which no one in the world can equal me.

162. How then do I perform My duty? I do it as if I desired the fruit of it. In this I have only one motive.

163. All creatures are dependent on Me and they must not be led astray.

164. If with all desires satisfied I were to remain content in the Self how could men obtain salvation?

165. Were they to see My ways they would follow My ways and the stability of all worlds would be overthrown.

> XXV. *As the unlearned act from attachment to their work, so should the learned also act, O Bhārata [Arjuna], but without any attachment, with the desire to maintain the world-order.*

166. Therefore, especially he who is powerful and has all knowledge should never cease from action.

167. The disinterested man should act wholeheartedly, in the same way that a foolish man works who hopes for the fruit of his actions.

168. O Arjuna, the stability of the worlds must be steadily maintained,

169. and we should, therefore, follow the path of duty and show the way to the people, and we should not consider ourselves as different from them.

> XXVI. *Let him [jnānin] not unsettle the minds of the ignorant who are attached to action. The enlightened man, doing all works in a spirit of yoga, should set others also to act.*

170. How can a child only just able to suck the breast eat seasoned food? Therefore, O Wielder of the bow, such food should not be given to it.

171. So non-attachment [to the fruit of action] should especially not be indiscriminately taught to such as are unworthy.

172. They should be encouraged to perform proper action; such action alone must be extolled and the disinterested should show it by their conduct.

173. When, in such a manner, action is performed for the welfare of the world, it can have no power to bind.

> XXVII. *While all kinds of work are done by the qualities of nature, he whose soul is bewildered by the self-sense thinks 'I am the doer'.*

174. Moreover, O Wielder of the bow, if we take the burden of another on our head, will it not weigh us down?
175. Similarly good and evil actions are wrought by the qualities of nature, but a deluded fool imagines that he is the doer.
176. It is not right, therefore, to reveal this highest truth to an ignorant man deluded by egoism.

> XXVIII. *But he who knows the true character of the distinction [of the soul] from the qualities of nature and their works, O Mighty-armed [Arjuna], understanding that it is the qualities which are acting on the qualities [themselves], does not become attached.*

177. Know that this feeling of egoism, from which all actions proceed, is not found in those who are knowers of the truth.
178. Free from the egoism of the body, controlling its qualities and functions, they live in it, as it were, as spectators.
179. Therefore, although living in the body, they are not bound by the fetters of action any more than the sun is affected by the actions of the creatures [upon which it shines].

> XXIX. *Those who are misled by the qualities of nature become attached to the works produced by them. But let no one who knows the whole unsettle the minds of the ignorant who know only a part.*

180. Action affects only one who is deluded by the qualities and is living under the power of nature.
181. The senses carry on their activities prompted by the qualities; one who takes upon himself [the responsibility for] those activities is bound by action.
182. O Arjuna, now listen attentively while I tell thee what is for thy good.

> XXX. *Resigning all thy works to Me, with thy consciousness fixed in the Self, being free from desire and egoism, fight, delivered from thy fever.*

183. When performing all appointed actions, surrender them to Me, but concentrate all the thoughts of thy heart in the Self.

184. 'This is action', 'I am the doer', 'I will perform it', allow no such pride to enter thy mind.

185. Do not be attached to the body, give up all desire, and then thou mayest enjoy all pleasures at the appropriate time.

186. Now, taking thy bow in thy hand, mount this chariot, and with an easy mind embrace the duties of warriorship.

187. Let thy fame increase throughout the world, enhance the dignity of performing one's duty, and release the earth from this burden.

188. Now, O Pārtha, leaving aside all doubt, do naught else but turn thy mind to fighting.

> XXXI. *Those men, too, who, full of faith and free from cavil, constantly follow this teaching of Mine are released from* [*the bondage of works*].

189. O Wielder of the bow, this is my firm opinion; those who accept it eagerly and practise it with faith,

190. are freed from the bondage of works even while engaging in them. Action, therefore, should certainly be performed.

> XXXII. *But know those who decry My teaching and do not follow it to be blind to all wisdom, lost and senseless.*

191. On the other hand, those who, attached to nature and indulging their senses, disregard My teaching,

192. think it to be of small account, despise it or speak of it in extravagant chatter,

193. know these to be intoxicated with the wine of infatuation, overcome by the poison of sense pleasures and plunged in the mire of ignorance.

194. As a jewel placed in the hand of a corpse would be useless to it, or as dawn has no meaning for a blind man,

195. or as the rise of the moon is of no use to the crow, so is discrimination not valued by the fool.

196. For not only do they disregard our words, but they even scorn them. Can a moth bear the light?

197. So, Arjuna, enter into no discussion with those who turn away from this highest teaching.

198. Therefore in the first place a wise man should not pander to his senses for the sake of pleasure.

199. Should one play with a serpent? Or would it be good to associate with a tiger? If virulent poison were swallowed, could it be digested?

200. Even if fire is kindled in play, it rises in flames and cannot be controlled; so it is not good to encourage the activity of the senses.

XXXIV. *For sense attachment and aversion are fixed [in regard] to the objects of each sense. Let no one come under their sway for they are his two enemies.*

201. Moreover, O Arjuna, why should a man give pleasure to his body, which is subject [to nature]?

202. Why should we pamper our bodies day and night regardless of the cost in wealth secured by great efforts?

203. This body is composed of the five elements and at death is resolved into them again; where then shall we seek for the labour [undertaken for its benefit]?

204. Therefore the mere indulgence of the body is obviously disastrous. Do not set thy heart on it.

205. In another sense it is true that the enjoyment of sensual objects gives gratification of the mind.

206. It is like the accomplice of a thief who, posing as an honest man for a time remains quiet, till he has passed beyond the boundaries of the town.

207. O Beloved, the pleasures of sense are sweet; do not let longing for them arise in the mind. Do not partake of them without considering the consequences.

208. So also desire, which resides in the senses, arouses a harmful yearning after pleasures, just as the bait attached to a hook allures the fish.

209. As the hook within, which can deprive it of its life, is not seen because it is concealed,

210. so is he cast into the fire of wrath who, allured by passion, seeks pleasure from sensual objects.

211. As a hunter tempts [his prey] to the very place of its death in order to accomplish his purpose,

212. so also it is [with sense desires]. Therefore avoid contact with them; know also, O Pārtha, that both desire and wrath are destructive.

213. Do not resort to them, nor let thy mind even remember them; let nothing destroy thy devotion to the Self.

> XXXV. *Better is one's own law though imperfectly carried out than the law of another carried out perfectly. Better is death in [the fulfilment of] one's own law, for to follow another's law is perilous.*

214. O Beloved! it is best to perform our own duty, however difficult it may be.

215. The duty of another may seem more attractive to us, but, nevertheless, we should carry out our own.

216. How could a brāhman, however poor, eat food in a shudra's house though it may be delicious?[10]

217. Why should anyone perform an improper action, or wish for what is undesirable? Or consider, does one get what one desires?

218. Is it wise to destroy one's own straw hut because one sees the attractive mansions of others?

219. As one's own wife, however uncomely, is well appreciated when one lives with her,

220. so will our own duty, however arduous and difficult in practice, lead us to the happiness of heaven.

221. Sugar and milk are both well known for their sweetness, but as they are injurious to a man suffering from worms, should he take them?

222. O Arjuna, if he does take them, they may give him temporary satisfaction, but in the end he will not be able to digest them.

223. We should not therefore practise what is proper for another and not for ourselves, if we seek our own welfare.

224. Even if we spend our life in the performance of our own duty, it will be well with us both here and hereafter.

Arjuna said:

> XXXVI. *But by what is a man impelled to commit sin, as if by force, even against his own will, O Vārṣṇeya [Kṛṣṇa]?*

225. When Shārngapāni, crowning jewel among the gods, had

thus spoken, Arjuna said, O Lord, I have a request to
make.[11]

226. Indeed I have listened to all that Thou hast told me, but
I will now ask Thee what I wish to know.

227. O Lord, how is it that we see the equanimity of even wise
men disturbed, and that, leaving the right path, they go
astray?

228. They who are very wise know which methods to use and
which to avoid; under what influence do they undertake
the duties of others?

229. A blind man cannot discriminate between seed and husk;
how is it that sometimes a man with good sight commits
the same fault?

230. The very men who have abandoned their [original]
attachments are now not satisfied with [new] attachments.
Even those who resort to the life of the hermit [return to]
the habitations of man.

231. They go into seclusion and escape from evil, but are
dragged into it by force.

232. The fiend which seizes this life grips hold of them and
when they try to escape it seeks them out.

233. This is a kind of tyranny; what is the nature of this
dominating power? Tell me this, O Hrishikesha, said
Pārtha.

The Blessed Lord said:

XXXVII. *This is craving, this is wrath, born of the quality
of passion, all devouring and most sinful. Know this to
be the enemy here.*

234. Then that highest of all beings, the resting-place of the
lotus-like heart and the desire of yogis, said, I will tell
thee, listen.

235. Know then these are desire and wrath, which are both
devoid of compassion and regarded as [the equal of] death
itself.

236. They are serpents in the storehouse of knowledge, tigers
in the desert land of sense-objects, mean men of violence
on the path of devotion.

237. They are rocks [endangering] the fortress of the body, as
a wall surrounding the village of the senses; as mental

confusion and other states they cause disturbance throughout the whole world.

238. These are the influence of passion in the mind, born of daemonaical forces, fostered by ignorance.

239. They are indeed passionate, but favoured by the quality of darkness, which also invests them with its power of error.

240. In the house of death are they regarded as friends, for they are the enemies of life.

241. When hungry even the whole universe would not be enough as a morsel to satisfy them; they extend their greed towards the manifold activities of men.

242. Delusion is the younger sister of hope, for whom the fourteen worlds are but a small trifle for her to hold in her grasp.[12]

243. Through the power of her service lust thrives, for whom the three worlds are but a mouthful eaten with delight.

244. They are esteemed by illusion and selfishness, which makes the world dance for its delight, trades with them.

245. Dost thou not know that it is through these that hypocrisy has spread throughout the world, by which truth has been robbed of its possessions and filled with the straw of improper action.

246. The chaste figure of peace has been ravished by them and having adorned lowborn delusion with ornaments, through her they have polluted numberless sages.

247. They have devastated the place of discrimination, dispassion has been stripped bare and the neck of tranquility twisted.

248. They have destroyed the forest of contentment, demolished the fortress of courage and rooted up the plant of joy.

249. They have plucked the tender shoots of understanding, wiped out the name of happiness and kindled the fire of threefold afflictions in the heart.[13]

250. They were formed with the body and are attached to life, but when sought for cannot be found either by Brahma or any other.

251. They are the neighbours of consciousness and are seated alongside of wisdom; they are ever ready to fight and cannot be driven off.

252. They can drown without water, burn without fire and silently they hold fast all creatures.

253. They kill without weapons, bind without ropes and strike
down a wise man for a wager.

254. They bury a man without earth, ensnare without a noose
and are unequalled in strength.

> XXXVIII. *As fire is covered by smoke, as a mirror by dust,*
> *as an embryo is enveloped by the womb, so is this covered*
> *by that [passion].*

255. As serpents encircle the roots of a sandalwood tree; as the
membrane of the womb surrounds the embryo,

256. as there can be no sun without light, no smoke without
fire, no mirror without dust,

257. so we have never known knowledge to exist without these.
As seed grows enveloped by the husk,

> XXXIX. *Enveloped is wisdom, O Son of Kuntī [Arjuna],*
> *by this insatiable fire of desire, which is the constant foe*
> *of the wise.*

258. so wisdom, however pure, is surrounded by these and it is
thus made difficult to reach.

259. First overcome these and then obtain wisdom; till then
attraction and aversion cannot be overcome.

260. All the strength that is exercised to control them is as
fuel which feeds a fire.

> XL. *The senses, the mind and the intelligence are said to*
> *be its seat. Veiling wisdom by these, it deludes the embodied*
> *[soul].*

> XLI. *Therefore, O Best of Bhāratas [Arjuna], control thy*
> *senses from the beginning and slay this sinful destroyer*
> *of wisdom and discrimination.*

> XLII. *The senses, they say, are great; greater than the*
> *senses is the mind; greater than the mind is the intelligence*
> *but greater than the intelligence is he.*

261. So then whatsoever means may be used to overcome them
does but assist them, and for this reason those who
practise hathayoga have been overcome by them in the
world.[14]

262. In such a difficulty there is only one effective method,
which I will explain to thee if thou wilt accept it.

263. The senses are their principal seat; nature gives birth to activity. First destroy them utterly.

264. Then the activity of the mind will be checked, the reason will be set free, and so the home of these sinful actions will be demolished.

> XLIII. *Thus knowing him who is beyond the intelligence, steadying the [lower] self by the Self, smite, O Mighty-armed [Arjuna], the enemy in the form of desire, so hard to encounter.*

265. If these are driven from the heart, they will undoubtedly be destroyed as a mirage fades away without the sun.

266. Similarly if attraction and aversion disappear, the dominion of Brahman will be established; then each may enjoy his own bliss.

267. This is the true relationship of guru and disciple, as that of body and soul. Standing firmly in it never depart from it.

268. In this way spoke the Master of all perfected beings, the consort of Lakshmi, the lord of the gods.

269. Now Ananta will return to the matter about which the son of Pāndu will question him.

270. With what words can we tell it? Who can describe the sweetness of it? The listeners will be contented with the happiness of hearing this.

271. Jnānadeva, disciple of Nivritti, says, My friends, let your understanding be awakened, and so enjoy the dialogue between Shri Hari and Pārtha.

In the Upanishad of the Bhagavadgitā, the science of the Absolute, the scripture of Yoga and the dialogue between Shri Krishna and Arjuna, this is the third chapter called the Yoga of Action.

NOTES

1. *Kamalāpati.* Kamalā is another name for the wife of Krishna, Lakshmi. The epithet 'husband of Kamalā' refers therefore to Krishna.

2. *Marāthi.* The name of the language, the author's mother-tongue, is used here in the text to indicate what is 'easily understood'.

3. *Sānkhya.* One of the six systems of Hindu philosophy; the doctrine of the final emancipation of the soul.

4. *Nirvāna.* Final emancipation from worldly life.
5. *Lotus-born.* Brahma is thought to have been born of a lotus which grew from the navel of Vishnu.
6. *highest heaven.* Of the seven heavens in Hindu belief the highest is that of 'truth'.
7. *Virinci.* One of the names of Brahma, Vishnu, and here referring to Krishna.
8. *the four-faced god.* An epithet of Brahma, used here in reference to Krishna.
9. *Subhadrā.* The name of Krishna's sister, Arjuna's wife.
10. *Shudra.* The lowest of the four castes, the 'servers', menial workers.
11. *Shārngapāni.* 'One who has the Shārnga bow in his hand', Krishna.
12. *fourteen worlds.* In Hindu mythology there were said to be fourteen worlds, seven terrestrial and seven celestial.
13. *threefold afflictions.* These are afflictions, or limiting conditions, related to all beings in this world: ādhibhautika (material), ādhidaivika (spiritual), and ādhyātmika (individual, i.e. selfhood).
14. *hathayoga.* A form of yoga which is practised through severe bodily discipline with meditation.

CHAPTER IV

1. Lo! the day of good fortune for the ear has come, for it has seen the treasure of the Gitā, as though its dream had come true.
2. Firstly, the subject of this chapter is discrimination; besides this it is being propounded by Shri Krishna, the lord of the world; Kiriti, best of devotees, is listening.
3. It is as if the fifth note were mingled with sweet fragrance, or fragrance with fine taste, so great is the beauty of this story.[1]
4. What excellent good fortune! For here we find the Ganges of nectar. Or it may be that the austerities of the hearers have borne fruit.
5. Now let all the other senses enter the dwelling of the ear and the happiness of hearing of this dialogue, called the Gitā.
6. Enough of this digression; let me now turn to the discourse between Krishna and Arjuna.
7. At that time Sanjaya said to the king, Arjuna was visited by good fortune, for Shri Nārāyana spoke to him with great affection.
8. Even the divine Lakshmi, so near to him, had not experienced the joy of this love; the ripening of Krishna's affection for Arjuna has brought this to him.
9. The hopes of Sanaka and others were greatly increased, but these were not fulfilled in this way.
10. The affection of the Lord of the world for Arjuna seems incomparable. What is that high merit he has earned?
11. I am much moved by the intimate affection between Krishna and Arjuna, for love of whom the immortal Krishna took on human form,
12. whereas he cannot be reached by yogis; he is incomprehensible to the Vedas and to the eyes of meditation He remains invisible.

13. What impulse can have moved Him to such compassion,
    He who is one with the Self, who is immutable and
    eternal?
14. See how He who is beyond form, the folds of the garment
    of the three worlds, has been overcome by His affection
    [for Arjuna]!

The Blessed Lord said:

> 1. *I proclaimed this imperishable yoga to Vivasvān;
>   Vivasvān told it to Manu and Manu spoke it to Īkṣvāku.*

15. Then said Krishna to the son of Pāndu, This very yoga
    we declared to Vivasvat but many ages have passed since
    then.[2]
16. Then Vivasvat taught the whole knowledge of yoga to
    Manu.[3]
17. Manu practised it himself and taught it to his son,
    Ikshvāku; in this way it has been handed down from age
    to age.

> 11. *Thus handed down from one to another the royal sages
>   knew it till that yoga was lost to the world through long
>   lapse of time, O Oppressor of the foe [Arjuna].*

18. Thereafter many royal sages knew this yoga; but since
    then it has remained unknown.
19. For creatures are addicted to sensual enjoyments and are
    attached to their bodies; therefore they have forgotten
    the knowledge of the Self.
20. Eagerness for Self-knowledge has wandered away from
    them, sensual pleasures are the object of their lives; and
    so existence and the limitations of the body have become
    dear to them.
21. What would be the use of costly garments in a village of
    naked ascetics? Of what use is the sun to a man born
    blind?
22. Who, in an assembly of the deaf, could appreciate singing?
    How can jackals enjoy the light of the moon?
23. How can crows, whose eyes are then blind, recognize the
    moon as it rises?
24. Similarly, how can these foolish people reach God who
    have not even come to the borders of dispassion and who

are unacquainted with even the language of discrimination?

25. No one knows how this infatuation has developed, for owing to it the time has passed away and so yoga has disappeared from the world.

> III. *This same ancient yoga has been today declared to thee by Me; for thou art My devotee and My friend; and this is the supreme secret.*

26. That same yoga have I taught thee today, O Son of Kunti, in truth; be in no doubt about it.[4]
27. It is My deep secret, but how can I hide it from thee, who art so dear to Me?
28. Thou art the embodiment of love, the heart of devotion, the very art of friendship, O Wielder of the bow.
29. Thou art the home of intimacy, so how can I deceive thee now? Though we are ready to fight,
30. still for a time we must be patient and not be confused, for first of all thy ignorance must be cleared away.

Arjuna said:

> IV. *Later was Thy birth and earlier was the birth of Vivasvat. How then am I to understand that thou didst declare it to him in the beginning?*

31. Thereupon Arjuna said, O Shri Hari, Thou store of all mercy, listen to Me; what wonder is it that a mother loves her child?
32. Thou art a shelter to all those afflicted by worldly life, a mother to the helpless; verily it is Thy kindness that has given us birth.
33. O Lord, if a child is born lame, all its life this burden has to be borne. Why should I speak of this before Thee?
34. Pay heed to what I ask Thee. Be not angry with me for questioning Thee.
35. O Ananta, thou hast spoken to me of former things, but for a moment I do not understand.
36. For even our forefathers did not know who Vivasvat was; how then didst Thou teach them about him?
37. We are told that he belonged to the remote past; Thou, O Krishna, art of the present time and hence there is inconsistency in this matter.

38. Moreover of Thy life we know nothing, how then should we ever say that Thou speakest a falsehood?

39. Tell me, therefore, the whole story of how Thou didst teach this yoga to the sun, that I may clearly understand it.

40. Then said Shri Krishna, O Son of Pāndu, should there be any thought in thy mind that I was not in existence when Vivasvat lived,

41. knowest thou not that thou and I have had many births? Yet of thine own thou hast no memory.

42. I remember every occasion when my incarnations have been taken place, O Wielder of the bow.

The Blessed Lord said:

> v. *Many are My lives that are past, and thine also, O Arjuna; I know all time, but thou knowest not, O Scourge of the foe [Arjuna].*

> vi. *Though [I am] unborn, and My Self [is] imperishable though [I am] the lord of all creatures, yet establishing Myself in My own nature, I come into existence through My power [māyā].*

43. Therefore I remember everything in the past. I am ever unborn, and yet I become incarnate through the power of illusion.

44. Even then, this in no way affects my eternal nature. The birth and death which apparently I undergo, are expressions of the power of illusion working in Me.

45. Thereby My freedom does not suffer, though I still seem to be bound by action. Such, in reality, is only delusion caused by distorted reason.

46. By means of a mirror one object may seem to be two; but in point of fact, are there really two?

47. So, verily, I am formless, O Kiriti, but when I resort to the world of nature for a special purpose I behave as though I were incarnate.

> vii. *Whenever there is a decline of righteousness, O Bhārata [Arjuna], then I send forth [create incarnate] Myself.*

48. That I should watch over the strict performance of all

duties and rites from age to age is but the natural course
[of the world] from the beginning.

49. When, therefore, unrighteousness overpowers righteousness, then I lay aside My birthlessness and, disregarding
My formlessness, [I become incarnate].

50. Then for the sake of my devotees, I take on form and,
becoming incarnate, drive out the darkness of ignorance.

> VIII. *For the protection of the good, for the destruction of
> the wicked and for the establishment of righteousness, I
> come into being from age to age.*

51. Then I break the bonds of unrighteousness, tear up all the
records of sin, and through righteous men raise the banner
of happiness.

52. I destroy the families of demons, increase the honour of
saints and sages and unite morality with religion.

53. Having removed the soot of indiscrimination, I light the
lamp of discrimination, and then yogis enjoy a perpetual
feast of light.[5]

54. The universe becomes filled with the joy of the Self,
righteousness dwells on the earth and My devotees feast
on virtue.

55. When I manifest Myself in the flesh, the mountain of sin
is shattered and the day of righteousness dawns, O son
of Pāndu.

56. For this purpose I am born from age to age. He who
knows this is truly wise in this world.

> IX. *He who knows in its true nature My divine birth and
> works, is not born again; when he leaves his body he
> comes to Me, O Arjuna.*

57. One who knows My birth although I am unborn; who
knows My action, though I am above all action; and who
knows Me to be immutable, may be called liberated.

58. In the company of those who move he remains still; being
in the body, he is not bound by it; and at death he attains
to My true nature.

> X. *Delivered from passion, fear and anger, absorbed in
> Me, taking refuge in Me, many, purified by the austerity
> of wisdom, have attained to My state of being.*

59. Moreover, those who grieve neither for themselves nor for

others, who are freed from desire, who never walk on the path of anger,

60. who dwell always in Me, who live only to serve Me who are content in the realization of the Self, free from all attachment,

61. who, filled with the fire of penance, the sole resort of wisdom and add holiness to the holy places of pilgrimage,

62. easily attain to My nature and become one with Me, for between them and Me there exists no separation.

63. If the alloy of brass were entirely removed from gold would it be necessary to add anything in its place?

64. Similarly those who are purified by restraint of the senses and purified by penance and wisdom, are merged into My being; what doubt is there of this?

> XI. *As men approach me so do I accept them; men on all sides follow My path, O Pārtha [Arjuna].*

65. Know this also, that in whatever way men are devoted to Me, so do I serve them.

66. Behold all mankind are by nature solely devoted to Me and live only in Me.

> XII. *Those who desire the fruition of their works on earth offer sacrifices to the gods [the various forms of the one Godhead], for the fruition of works in this world of men is very quick.*

67. Lacking wisdom they have gone astray and come to believe in duality; as a result of this they have imputed diversity [to Me who am] one.

68. Therefore they see diversity where there is oneness, give names to the nameless, and speak of the one who is inexpressible as a god or a goddess.

69. Deluded by their intelligence, they divide that which is ever unchangeable into 'higher' and 'lower'.

70. Then with diverse purposes and with appropriate ceremonies they worship those whom they believe to be their deities.

71. Thus they obtain in full whatever they desire, but thou shouldst recognize that this is undoubtedly the fruit of action.

72. Know that, except for action, there is nothing that gives

or takes; properly speaking, it is certain that action alone is the bearer of fruit in the world of men.

73. Only that which is sown in a field can grow there, only what is reflected in a mirror can be seen there.

74. As when we stand at the foot of a hill what we hear, O Kiriti, is by a natural law the sound of our own words, which returns to us as an echo,

75. so, O Arjuna, I am the witness at all forms of worship, and the fruit [which each obtains] is in accordance with his faith.

> XIII. *The fourfold order was created by Me according to the divisions of quality and work. Though I am its creator, know Me to be incapable of action or change.*

76. In the same manner I have created the four castes by the different distribution of qualities and actions.[6]

> XIV. *Works do not defile Me; nor do I yearn for their fruit. He who knows Me thus is not bound by works.*

77. This system has come about through Me, but I did not establish it. He who realizes this is liberated.

> XV. *Knowing this, work was done also by the men of old who sought liberation. Therefore do thou also work as the ancients did in former times.*

78. For according to the mixture of qualities derived from nature their functions have been allotted to each.

79. [Actually] all are one, O Wielder of the bow; the four castes, however, were built up by the distribution of qualities and action.

80. Therefore, O Arjuna, from this point of view, I am not, in reality, the author of this system of caste differences.

81. Knowing Me to be thus, they who sought for liberation in earlier times performed all action, O Wielder of the bow.

82. As seeds which have been fried can never germinate although sown in the ground, so the very actions of these people proved to be the cause of liberation for them.

83. One thing more, O Arjuna, the wise should never seek to determine what is action and what is inaction by their own judgement.

> XVI. *What is action? What is inaction? As to this, even*

*the wise are bewildered. I will declare to thee what action
is, knowing which thou shalt be delivered from evil.*

84. What is action, and what characterizes inaction? Even
wise men when they consider this problem are perplexed.
85. As a counterfeit coin, when looked at, makes us doubt
what our eye sees by its semblance to one that is genuine,
86. so, in the delusion of non-attachment to action, even such
souls as are able by thought power to create another
world become involved in actions.
87. Then what of the foolish? In this matter the wise, with
subtle vision, are perplexed. Therefore listen to Me, and
I will explain this to thee.

> XVII. *One has to understand what action is, and likewise
> one has to understand inaction. Hard to understand is
> the way of work.*

88. Action is that natural action through which the manifestation of the universe becomes possible. First understand
this thoroughly.
89. Then that particular action which is prescribed, proper
for the various castes and the stages of life, with their
practice, should be thoroughly understood.[7]
90. Know also the nature of that action which is prohibited as
unlawful, so that you may not be entangled in it.
91. Generally speaking, however, the world is dependent on
action, so great is its universality. Now listen to the
characteristics of those souls who have attained their
goal.

> XVIII. *He who in action sees inaction and action, is wise
> among men; he is a yogī and he has accomplished all his
> work.*

92. He who, while carrying out his duties, knows non-
attachment and has no desire for the fruit of action,
93. and to whom nothing in the world matters more than his
duty, has truly understood freedom from action.
94. Yet he is seen to perform well all religious ceremonies.
By these signs he is known to be wise.
95. As a man standing near water perceives his own reflection
in it, and yet knows well that he is different [from the
reflection],

96. or as a man who enters a boat sees trees on the bank passing rapidly by him, yet knows when he looks that they are all actually stationary,

97. so he, while in the midst of action, knows clearly that it is illusory and that he himself is detached from it.

98. As, also, owing to the rising and setting of the sun, it seems to move though in reality it is stationary, so realize that freedom from action lies in action.

99. Such a man seems to be as other men, but he is not affected by human nature, like the sun which can never be drowned in water.

100. He has seen the universe without seeing it, he does all without doing it and he enjoys all pleasures without involvement in them.

101. Though seated in one place, he travels everywhere, for even while in the body he has become the universe.

> XIX. *He whose undertakings are all free from the will of desire, whose works are burned up in the fire of wisdom, is called by the wise a man of learning.*

102. One who is not weary of action, and yet in whom the desire for the fruit of it is not present,

103. whose mind is not tainted by any such thought as 'I will perform this action', or 'I will carry out what I have undertaken',

104. who has burned up all action in the flames of the fire of wisdom, know such a man to be Brahma in human form.

> XX. *Having abandoned attachment to the fruit of works, ever content, without any kind of dependence, he does nothing, though he is ever engaged in work.*

> XXI. *Having no desires, with his heart and self under control, giving up all possessions, performing action by the body alone, he commits no wrong.*

> XXII. *He who is satisfied with whatever comes by chance, who has passed beyond the dualities [of pleasure and pain], who is free from jealousy, who remains the same in success and failure, even when he acts, is not bound.*

105. So also is one who is indifferent towards his body, without desire for the enjoyment of the fruit of action, is full of joy,

106. who, O Wielder of the bow, is the sanctuary of content-

ment and who while feasting on the food of self-illumination, is never satiated.

107. Having rejected all desire and selfishness, he enjoys in
increasing measure the delights of heavenly bliss.

108. One who, therefore, is content with whatsoever he obtains
from time to time, for whom there is no thought of either
'mine' or 'not mine',

109. becomes whatever he sees with his eyes, or hears with
his ears.

110. The way of his feet, the words of his mouth, in fact all
his activities are the Supreme [moving through him].

111. More than this, to him the whole universe is seen as not
different from himself. How and in what way then can
action affect him?

112. Nothing is left in him of the duality from which envy
springs, so he is without envy. Is there any need to say
more?

113. Therefore he is in every way free and even though acting
he is free from action; though possessing attributes he is
beyond all attributes. This is beyond all doubt.

> XXIII. *The work of a man whose attachments are sundered,
> who is liberated, whose mind is firmly founded in wisdom,
> who does work as a sacrifice, is dissolved entirely.*

114. Though dwelling in a body he appears as the Self; tested
by the touchstone of Brahma he is utterly pure.

115. Being so, should he perform any actions such as sacrifice
even for interest, they are absorbed completely into
himself.

116. As untimely clouds appearing in the sky without giving
rain are suddenly lost again and become as they were,

117. so though such a man performs all actions in accordance
with prescribed rites, by his state of harmony he attains
to union with all.

> XXIV. *For him the act of offering is God, the oblation is
> God. By God is it offered into the fire of God. God is
> that which is to be attained by him who realizes God in
> his works.*

118. 'This is an oblation', 'I am the sacrificer', 'This is the
partaker in this sacrifice', such differences do not exist
for his mind.

119. Therefore the sage, performing the sacrifice, regards the ritual such as the offerings and the incantations as the Eternal Self.

120. One who understands that all action is Brahma, O Wielder of the bow, is free from the bonds of action even though he performs actions.

    xxv. *Some yogins offer sacrifices to the gods while others offer sacrifice by the sacrifice itself into the fire of the Supreme.*

121. Now those who, having left behind the youth of indiscrimination, have committed themselves to nonattachment and who perform the worship of the fire of yoga,[8]

122. who perform sacrifices night and day, who burn up the ignorance of their minds in the fire of the words of their spiritual teachers,

123. make offerings in the fire of yoga, which is called the 'divine sacrifice'. By this means, O Son of Pāndu, strive after the joy of the Self.

124. Listen, I will tell you more. There are those who maintain the sacrificial fire in the form of Brahma and offer as an oblation in that fire the sacrifice itself.

    xxvi. *Some offer hearing and the other senses into the fires of restraint; others offer sound and the other objects of sense in the fibres of sense.*

125. Some perform the sacrifice in the form of restraint; they make the pure offering of the senses as the oblation, with prayers proceeding from the three lower centres.[9]

126. Others, when the sun of dispassion breaks forth, then prepare the sacrificial hearth of restraint and uncover the fire of the senses.

127. Then when the flames of dispassion arise, the fuel of the passions is burnt up and the smoke of desire disappears from the five-fold vessel [of the senses].

128. Then in the cauldron of the fire of the senses they offer up constant oblations of the objects of sense, following with great care the injunctions of the Vedas.

    xxvii. *Some again offer all the works of their senses and the works of the vital force into the fire of the yoga of self-control, kindled by knowledge.*

129. O Pārtha, others again wash entirely away all evil tendencies; still others churn the power of discrimination
using the heart as the churning rod,

130. hold it firmly with tranquility, pressing it down with the
power of fortitude, and churn it vigorously with the
words of the guru.

131. When they churn thus, with concentrated minds, the
action quickly bears fruit and the fire of wisdom is
kindled.

132. When the smoke of the allurement of psychic powers
disperses then a subtle flash appears,

133. and the passions of the mind which have been rendered
powerless by means of acts of restraint are thrown into it.

134. The fire flares up with these [passions] as fuel and they
are burnt up with the oil of all the desires of the heart.

135. Such sacrificers, chanting 'I am He' throw into the
kindled fire of wisdom offerings of the activities of the
senses.

136. Having completed the offering, using the breathing
processes as a ladle, they perform naturally the ablutions
in the [waters of] union with Brahma.

137. Then the bliss of self-realization, which is all that remains
from the offerings poured into the fire of restraint, is the
rice-cake of which they partake.

138. Some by this kind of sacrifice have freed themselves from
the limitations of the three worlds. There are many such
sacrifices, but there is only one goal of attainment.

> XXVIII. *Some likewise offer as sacrifice their material
> possessions, or their austerities or their spiritual exercises,
> while others of subdued mind and severe vows offer their
> learning and knowledge.*

139. Of these, which have been described, one is called the
sacrifice of wealth, others arise from the practice of
austerity, others again are called sacrifices of yoga.

140. In some, words are poured out in sacrifice, called the
sacrifice of speech. That by which knowledge is imparted
is called the sacrifice of wisdom.

141. All such sacrifices are difficult to perform, O Arjuna, but
to the man who is self-controlled they are possible through
his merit.

142. The sacrificers are most proficient and they possess a

wealth of yoga. Therefore they sacrifice their personal selves on the altar of the Self.

> XXIX. *Others again who are devoted to breath control, having restrained the paths of prāna [the outgoing breath] and apāna [the incoming breath], pour out as sacrifice prāna into apana and apāna into prāna.*

143. Some pour out as sacrifice their vital breath by regular practice, the oblation of the incoming breath in the fire of the outgoing breath.
144. Some pour out as sacrifice the incoming in the outgoing breath; others again control both. These are called pranāyāmi, O Son of Pāndu.

> XXX. *While others, restricting their food, pour as sacrifice their life breaths into life breaths. All these are knowers of sacrifice and by sacrifice their sins are destroyed.*

145. There are still others who regulate all kinds of food by using the yogic posture of vajrāsana and earnestly sacrifice their vital breath [by pouring it out into life].
146. These are all seekers after liberation who by means of such sacrifices wash away all impurities of the mind.

> XXXI. *Those who eat the sacred food that remains after sacrifice attain to the eternal Absolute; this world is not for him who offers no sacrifice, how then any other world, O Best of the Kurus [Arjuna]?*

147. There are those in whom ignorance has been removed and there remains only the essence of the self in which there is no longer any sense of difference between the fire and the sacrificer.
148. The desire of the sacrificer being attained, the performance of the sacrifice ends and no further action remains to be done.
149. This is the state into which thought does not enter, desire has no place and which is not contaminated by any contact with the evil of duality.
150. That pure and eternally perfect knowledge which is the result of the sacrifice is enjoyed by those who are established in the Self, as they chant 'I am Brahma'.
151. As they are satisfied with the nectar which remains from

the sacrifice, or as they attain to the state of immortality, they are easily united with Brahma.

152. For those who, being in the body, allow no place in themselves for dispassion, who do not worship the fire of restraint, who never perform the sacrifice of yoga,

153. their worldly welfare comes to nought; so why consider their heavenly state? Think about this, O Son of Pāndu.

> XXXII. *Thus many forms of sacrifice are spread out in the face of Brahman [set forth as the means of reaching the Absolute]. Know thou that all these are born of work, and so knowing thou shalt be freed.*

154. All these many and various sacrifices I have described are fully explained in the Vedas.

155. But what need is there of this description? Know that they result from action, and knowing this the bonds of action will not easily be formed.

> XXXIII. *Knowledge as a sacrifice is greater than any material sacrifice, O scourge of the foe [Arjuna], for all works without any exception culminate in wisdom.*

156. All such grosser actions, O Arjuna, of which the Veda is the source, and of which the highest reward is happiness in heaven,

157. are sacrifices of objects, but altogether inferior to the sacrifice of wisdom, as the light of the stars fades with [the rising] of the sun.

158. See here the treasure of supreme joy, to attain to which yogis do not hesitate to apply to their eyes the pigment of understanding,

159. which is the goal of all action for all seekers, the mine of understanding for those [who have reached] detachment, the means of satisfaction for the hungry.

160. [Having obtained this], mental activity is impaired, the power of reason loses its insight, and the senses forget the contact with the objects of sense.

161. The mind can no longer function, words lose their power of expression and, when a man reaches this state, he finds that which he desires to know.

162. In this, the longings of dispassion are fulfilled, the quest for discrimination is satisfied and without further striving self-realization is attained.

163. Such knowledge is the best, O Arjuna; if one desires to
find it he should serve these sages with all thy heart.

> XXXIV. *Learn this by humble reverence, by inquiry and
> service. The men of wisdom who have seen the truth will
> instruct thee in knowledge.*

164. They are the home of all knowledge and service to them
is the threshold for entry; lay hold of it, O Best of warriors,
165. Therefore prostrate thyself at their feet, with body, mind
and soul and serve them in all humility.
166. Then whatever thou askest they will explain to thee, thy
heart will then be enlightened and all desire will vanish.

> XXXV. *When thou hast known it, thou shalt not fall
> again into this confusion, O Pāṇḍava [Arjuna], for by
> this thou shalt see all existences without exception in the
> Self, then in Me.*

167. With the illumination of their teaching thy mind will lose
its fear and thou wilt become as free from doubt as
Brahma himself.
168. Then wilt thou see thyself, with all other beings, as being
for ever [absorbed] in My eternal Form.
169. O Pārtha, thus the morning of wisdom will dawn, the
darkness of confusion be dispelled, through the mercy of
one's teacher.

> XXXVI. *Even if thou shouldst be the most sinful of all
> sinners, thou shalt cross over all evil by the boat of wisdom
> alone.*

> XXXVII. *As the fire which is kindled turns its fuel to
> ashes, O Arjuna, even so does the fire of wisdom turn to
> ashes all work.*

170. Though thou shouldst be a mine of sins, an ocean of
confusion, a mountain of infatuation,
171. yet all this will be insignificant before the pure power of
wisdom, so great is it.
172. See! This illusory universe, which is the shadow of the
Formless, cannot equal the light of it.
173. What are impurities of the mind before it? Even to speak
of them would be insulting. In this world nothing can be
compared with its magnitude.

174. Could the clouds withstand the whirlwind at the t me of
the great dissolution, which disperses into space the ashes
of the three worlds?

175. Could grass suppress the fire of this destruction, which
with the fury of the wind can be kindled even by water?

> XXXVIII. *There is nothing on earth equal in purity to
> wisdom. He who becomes perfected by yoga finds this of
> himself, in his self in course of time.*

176. This can never be; even to consider it would be improper.
Nothing is so sacred as wisdom.

177. Wisdom is the highest thing, for what can equal it? As
spirit is one without a second, so also is wisdom.

178. Compared with the sun is there any reflection as brilliant?
Could the sky be held in anyone's grasp?

179. If one could find a match for the earth, then might
wisdom find its equal, O Son of Pāndu.

180. Therefore from whatever point of view and however often
it is considered, the sacredness of wisdom will be found
only in wisdom itself.

181. As the taste of nectar can only be described as like nectar,
so can wisdom be compared only with itself.

182. To say more than this would be waste of time Then
Arjuna said, What thou sayest is indeed true.

183. But when Arjuna was about to ask how this wisdom
might be known, the Lord was aware of his thought.

184. He said, O Kiriti, listen well to what I say, I will tell thee
a way in which you may acquire this wisdom.

> XXXIX. *He who has faith, who is absorbed in it [that is
> wisdom] and who has subdued his senses gains wisdom,
> and having gained wisdom, attains quickly the supreme
> peace.*

185. He who, for the sake of the bliss of the Self, feels aversion
for all objects of sense, in whom there is no thought for
the senses,

186. to whose mind desires make no appeal, who has no interest
in the material world and who takes pleasure in the
enjoyment of faith,

187. is surely sought out by wisdom, in which perfect peace is
found.

188. When that wisdom is established in the heart and the

tender shoots of peace break through, then at once the light of the Self shines forth.

189. Then wherever he looks, he will see only peace of which no limit is conceivable.

190. In short it would be impossible to describe how the seeds of wisdom are spread far and wide. But enough of this.

XL. *But the man who is ignorant, who has no faith, who is of a doubting nature, perishes. For the doubting soul, there is neither this world nor the world beyond nor any happiness.*

191. Listen! how can I describe the existence of a man who has no desire for this wisdom? Death would be preferable to such a life.

192. Like an empty house, or a body without consciousness, existence without wisdom would be a mere illusion.

193. But if a man does not possess wisdom and yet has a strong desire to obtain it, there is some hope of his gaining it.

194. Failing such a desire, it is out of the question. Know him to have fallen into the fire of doubt, in whose mind there does not exist this eagerness.

195. When distaste becomes so strong that even nectar is not relished, one realizes clearly that death is near.

196. So, he who delights in sensual pleasures and has no regard for wisdom is obviously entangled in doubt.

197. Then, should he thus fall into doubt, he is most certainly destroyed and loses all hope of happiness in this world and the next.

198. Just as a man suffering from continuous fever is unable to sense heat and cold and regards fire and moonlight as the same,

199. so the doubting man cannot distinguish between truth and untruth, right and wrong, or the beneficial and the harmful.

200. As a man born blind does not recognize night and day, so also there is no understanding of truth by one who doubts.

201. There is no sin greater or more terrible than doubt; it is a dangerous snare to all creatures.

202. Therefore cast away this doubt and overcome first that state which arises from lack of wisdom.

203. When the mind is overclouded by the darkness of ignorance, this increases in strength and the path of faith
becomes completely blocked.

204. Not only can it not be contained within the heart, but it
envelops the reason also and even the three worlds are
pervaded by doubt.

> XLI. *Works do not bind him who has renounced all works
> by yoga; who has destroyed all doubt by wisdom and who
> ever possesses his soul, O Winner of wealth [Arjuna].*

> XLII. *Therefore, having cut asunder with the sword of
> wisdom this doubt in thy heart that is born of ignorance,
> resort to yoga and arise, O Bhārata [Arjuna].*

205. Though [this ignorance] may increase in strength, there
is one way of overcoming it, if the sword of wisdom is
held in the hand.

206. It is completely destroyed by this sharp weapon of wisdom
and then all impurity vanishes from the mind.

207. Therefore, O Pārtha, rise up at once and smite this doubt
which resides in thy heart.

208. Hear, O King [said Sanjaya] how Krishna, the father of
omniscience, the light of wisdom, spoke with compassion;

209. how, pondering on this whole discourse, the Son of Pāndu
will ask questions from time to time.

210. The excellence of this narration should be saluted by the
eight sentiments. It is the resting place in this world for
the minds of all good men.

211. So tranquility will be renewed; listen, therefore, to this
Marāthi speech, full of meaning and deeper than the
ocean.

212. As the disc of the sun appears to be no larger than the
palm of the hand, yet for its light even the three worlds
are too small, so is the content of these words. This should
now be experienced.

213. As all desires are satisfied by the wish-fulfilling tree, so
are these words most significant. Give attention to them.

214. Be it so. What more need be said? Though the wise know
this already, still it is my request that they give full
attention to it.

215. This poem displays poetic power and tranquility, as a

young woman with beauty and virtue should be devoted to her husband.

216. It is natural to like sugar, and if to it is added medicine, why should it not be tasted cheerfully from time to time?

217. The breeze from the mountains of Malaya is gentle and fragrant; if by good fortune it bears the taste of nectar and is mingled with the sound of music,

218. then will its touch calm the body, its flavour delight the tongue, and the ears will hail it with joy.

219. The hearing of this story is the same; it will be a feast for the ear and with little difficulty will remove all the pains of life.

220. If an enemy can be killed by a charm, what need is there to take up a weapon? If a disease can be cured by milk and rice, why drink the juice of neem leaves?

221. So in this way liberation may be gained by means of the ear without doing harm to the mind or mortifying the senses.

222. Therefore, for the solace of all minds the words of the Gitā are excellent. Jnānadeva, the disciple of Nivritti, says, Listen!

In the Upanishad of the Bhagavadgitā, the science of the Absolute, the scripture of Yoga and the dialogue between Shri Krishna and Arjuna, this is the fourth chapter called the Yoga of Divine Knowledge.

NOTES

1. *the fifth note.* The sound of the fifth note of the musical scale is considered to be particularly sweet.

2. *Vivasvat.* The sun, personified as one of the gods.

3. *Manu.* The father of the human race; alternatively, the name of the first of fourteen progenitors of the race, and the law-giver.

4. *Kunti.* The mother of Arjuna.

5. *Divāli.* The traditional Festival of Lights, taking place in the month of October. Here it indicates a time of great enjoyment.

6. *four castes.* These are: brāhmans, kshatriyas, vaishyas (merchants) and shudras.

7. *the stages of life.* The four stages of the life of a brāhman are that of boyhood and celibacy (the period of study and training), the life of a householder with a family, retirement as a forest-dweller for further religious observance, and the last stage as the homeless life

of one who is emancipated from involvement in wordly life, complete
renunciation.

8. *the fire of yoga.*   The passage from v. 121 to v. 138 gives a description
of the discipline of the sacrifice of the individual self in the figurative
terms of the actual ritual of the sacrifice in the fire.

9. *three lower centres.*   The three lower centres of the psychic energy
in the body.

CHAPTER V

Arjuna said:

> 1. *Thou praisest, O Kṛṣṇa, the renunciation of works and again their selfless performance. Tell me for certain which is the better of these two.*

1. Then said Pārtha to Shri Krishna, Oh! what art Thou saying? If Thy words were consistent the mind might consider them.
2. Previously Thou hast well expounded renunciation of actions, so how canst Thou now encourage the yoga of action?
3. It seems that Thou speakest with a double meaning; our ignorant minds are unable to understand it as Thou wouldst wish us to, O Shri Ananta.
4. Listen. If Thou teachest but one truth, tell us plainly of it; is there any need for others to tell Thee this?
5. For this very reason did I request Thee, who art as a mother, not to explain this truth in an ambiguous manner.
6. Let the past be forgotten, O Lord; tell us definitely now which of these two paths is the better.
7. The path Thou showest must have a sure end, bearing certain fruit, and be straight and easy to follow,
8. just as it is easy to make a journey in a comfortable vehicle which travels fast and in which one's sleep is not disturbed.
9. With these words of Arjuna the Lord was pleased and said gladly, It shall be so, therefore listen!
10. He who is fortunate enough to have the Cow of Plenty for his mother, could get even the moon to play with.
11. Think of the compassion of Shri Shambhu, did he not give the ocean of milk to satisfy Upamanyu's desire for rice and milk?[1]

12. So, Shri Krishna, the storehouse of generosity, giving
     Himself to the great warrior, why should he [Arjuna] not
     become the home of bliss?
13. What wonder is this? With the consort of Lakshmi as his
     master should he not ask for all that he desired?
14. Therefore what Arjuna asked for, the Lord gladly gave; I
     will now tell you what Krishna said.

The Blessed Lord said:

> II. *The renunciation of works and their selfless performance,
> both lead to the soul's salvation. But of the two, the selfless
> performance of works is better than their renunciation.*

15. He said, O Son of Kunti, of a truth, renunciation and
     yoga, properly understood, are both means of attaining
     liberation.
16. Yet to all, the wise as well as the ignorant, this yoga of
     action is indeed easy to practise, just as it is safer for
     women and children to cross over water in a boat.
17. So, in comparison, [the yoga of action] by which the
     fruit of renunciation is acquired without effort is the easier.

> III. *He who neither loathes nor desires should be known
> as one who has ever the spirit of renunciation; for, free
> from dualities, he is easily released from bondage, O
> Mighty-armed [Arjuna].*

18. I will therefore describe to thee the characteristics of the
     sannyāsi. Then thou wilt realize that [these two paths]
     are not different.[2]
19. One who does not grieve for what he may lose, nor care
     if he obtains nothing, and who is as steady in mind as
     Mount Meru,
20. whose heart has forgotten the sense of 'I' and 'mine', such
     a man is the eternal ascetic, O Pārtha.
21. He who attains to such a condition of mind is freed from
     the bondage of desire and finds eternal joy in the heart of
     all bliss.
22. Now there is no need to give up home or anything else,
     for [the mind] which is subject to desire has become free
     [from its influence].
23. As when a fire has been extinguished, it is possible to
     place cotton on the ashes which remain,

24. so, in the midst of worldly conditions, an ascetic whose mind is free from attachment is not aware of the bonds of action.
25. Therefore when desire has been given up renunciation is attained. Then renunciation and yoga are found to be linked together.

> IV. *It is the ignorant who speak of renunciation [sāṃkhya] and practice of works [yoga] as different, not the wise. He who applies himself well to one, obtains the fruit of both.*

26. Besides, O Pārtha, how can the completely ignorant understand the systems of sānkhya and yoga?
27. Naturally the ignorant regard these two as different; but is the light different in every lamp?
28. But those who from their own experience have perceived the truth look on both as one.

> V. *The status which is obtained by men of renunciation is reached by men of action also. He who sees that the ways of renunciation and of action are one, sees [truly].*

29. Whatever is gained by sānkhya, is likewise reached by means of yoga. Therefore they are one by nature.
30. As the sky and the heavenly spaces are not different, so for one who recognizes that sānkhya and yoga are one,
31. day has dawned in the world; he alone has seen the Self who has realized that sānkhya and yoga are without difference.

> VI. *But renunciation, O Mighty-armed [Arjuna], is difficult to attain without yoga; the sage who is trained in yoga [the way of works] attains soon to the Absolute.*

32. O Pārtha, he who climbs up the mountain of liberation by the pathway of yoga, swiftly reaches the summit of the highest bliss.
33. The eagerness of another who abandons this yoga is in vain; he will not attain to renunciation.

> VII. *He who is trained in the way of works, and is pure in soul, who is master of his self and who has conquered the senses, whose soul becomes the Self of all beings, is not tainted by works, though he works.*

34. If a man has freed his mind from doubt, has purified it
by the words of the guru, and then has become absorbed
in the Self—

35. as salt, before it is put into the sea, is in separate and
small grains, but when thrown into it rapidly becomes
one with it—

36. he, whose mind is free from desire, becomes one with the
Self and, though apparently limited by space, pervades
the three worlds.

37. Then such ideas as 'agent', 'act' or 'ought' cease to exist
for him, and even should he perform actions, he is not
the agent of them.

> VIII. *The man who is united with the Divine and knows
> the truth thinks 'I do nothing at all', for in seeing, hearing,
> touching, smelling, tasting, walking, sleeping, breathing,*
>
> IX. *in speaking, emitting, grasping, opening and closing
> the eyes, he believes that only the senses are occupied with
> the objects of sense.*

38. For in his personality, O Pārtha, there remains no thought
of egoism. How then can any thought remain in his mind
that he is the agent of his actions?

39. Thus though he has not relinquished the body, every
characteristic of a disembodied person may be seen in
such a yogi,

40. yet like other men he has a body, and outwardly it seems
as if he participates fully in men's activities.

41. Observe this wonder! He also sees with his eyes, hears
with his ears, though he himself is not concerned in these
actions.

42. He experiences touch, with his nose he enjoys fragrance,
he also speaks when it is appropriate.

43. He takes food, gives up that which should be thrown out
and at the proper time he is ready to sleep.

44. He goes wherever he desires, and thus he performs all
actions.

> X. *The yogins [men of action] perform works merely
> with the body, mind, and understanding or merely with
> the senses, abandoning attachment, for the purification of
> their souls.*

45. What need is there to mention every action? Breathing in and out, opening and closing the eyes and the rest, all these things he does.

46. O Pārtha, all actions seem to be performed by him, but owing to the power of Self-realization, he is not the doer.

47. So long as he lay asleep on the bed of delusion, he was deluded by the pleasure of his dreams, then he awakened in the dawn of wisdom; this is the reason.

> XI. *He who works, having given up attachment, resigning his actions to God, is not touched by sin, even as a lotus-leaf [is untouched] by water.*

48. Now the tendencies of the senses are attracted towards the appropriate objects of sense, activated by the energy of spirit.

49. Just as all domestic activities may be carried on by the light of a lamp, so are all actions performed by the body of a yogi.

50. Though he performs all actions, he is not bound by them, as a lotus leaf in the water is not touched by it.

51. That is called action of the body in which reason takes no part and which does not originate as an idea springing up in the mind.

52. To speak simply, yogis perform actions with their bodies, like the movements of children.

53. Thus, when the body, born of the five elements, is asleep, the mind alone functions as in a dream.

54. Hear this wonder, O Wielder of the bow, this strange working of desire; it does not allow the body to waken and yet causes it to experience pleasure and pain!

55. The actions which occur without the awareness of the ten senses are said to be solely of the mind.

56. Yogis perform these also, but they are considered as beyond action, having abandoned egoism.

57. Now when the mind has fallen a victim to confusion and resembles the mind of a ghost, these activities become disorderly.

58. Such a man sees form, hears when called, speaks with his mouth, but he has no understanding.

59. In short, any action which is performed without purpose is purely action of the senses.

60. But be sure that whatever is universally known is the pure work of reason. So said Shri Hari to Arjuna.

61. With reason as their guide, they perform actions attentively but they seem to be free from the bondage of action.

62. From the reason through to the body itself they have no trace of egoism, and thus though performing action they remain pure.

63. O Beloved! An action which is performed with no thought for the fruit is alone truly selfless. Yogis, learning it from their gurus, know well this principle.

64. Now, such words as surpass all speech and in which the spirit of tranquillity is overflowing its bounds have been uttered by thee.[3]

65. Only those are worthy to listen who have completely freed themselves from the crippling senses.

66. Let us end this digression, lest the thread of the narrative be lost and the connected sequence of the verses should be broken.

67. Fortunately that which is too difficult for the mind to grasp, or which is unattainable by any effort of reason, thou hast been able to explain with ease.

68. If what is by nature beyond verbal expression has nevertheless been put into words, why indulge in any digression? Let us proceed with the story.

69. Knowing the eagerness of his listeners, the disciple of Nivritti said, Now listen further to the conversation of these two.

70. Then Shri Krishna said to Pārtha, I will now explain to thee clearly and fully the characteristics of one who is perfect.

> XII. *The soul in union with the divine attains to peace well-founded, by abandoning attachment to the fruits of works; but he whose soul is not in union with the divine is impelled by desire, and is attached to the fruit [of action] and is [therefore] bound.*

> XIII. *The embodied [soul], who has controlled his nature having renounced all actions by the mind [inwardly], dwells at ease in the city of nine gates, neither working nor causing work to be done.*

71. The Eternal Peace takes home to herself in this world

him who has through yoga attained to union with the Self, and who has become detached from the fruit of action.

72. O Kiriti, others are fastened to the stake of the enjoyment of fruit with the knot of desire, because of the bondage of action.

73. He performs all actions, as would a man desirous of the fruit of it, and then renounces the same as though he had not performed them,

74. In whatever direction he looks he will see a world of joy, and wherever he says [it shall be] he finds the great illumination.

75. He seems to dwell in the nine-gated body [of the sense organs], and yet he is not there. Renouncing all fruit, he engages in action, yet he does not act.[4]

> XIV. *The Sovereign Self does not create agency for the people, nor does He act; nor does He connect work with their fruits. It is nature that works out [these].*

76. As the Lord of all is considered to be free from all action, it is he who orders the whole expanse of the three worlds.

77. Even if it is said that he is the agent, still he is unaffected by any action; no part of his indifference is tainted by it.

78. The great sleep of Brahma is not disturbed nor is he distressed by the absence of agency; nevertheless the whole array of the five elements are generated by him.[5]

79. He pervades the life of the world, but he himself belongs to none and he is quite unaware of the creation or dissolution of this world.

> XV. *The All-pervading Spirit does not take on the sin or the merit of any. Wisdom is enveloped by ignorance; thereby creatures are bewildered.*

80. Though all merit and sin are very close to him, yet he does not see them, nor does he even stand as a witness to these. Why say any more?

81. Assuming bodily form he sports with mortals but the formlessness of this master is not corrupted by this.

82. Creatures say that he creates, sustains and destroys, but listen, O Son of Pāndu, this is ignorance.

> XVI. *But for those in whom ignorance is destroyed by wisdom, wisdom lights up the Supreme Self like the sun.*

83. When ignorance is destroyed utterly, and the darkness of ignorance is dispelled, it can be realized that the Lord does not perform actions.

84. Thus when a man understands that the Lord is not an agent and that from the beginning he is one with the Supreme in his nature,

85. when through discrimination this idea arises in his mind, how can any sense of duality remain in him in all the three worlds? From his own experience he recognizes that the whole world is in a state of liberation,

86. in the same way as when the sun rises radiant in its mansion in the eastern quarter, darkness vanishes at the same time from all four quarters of the earth.

87. How can I fully describe that feeling of equilibrium in the hearts of those who are filled with this all-embracing wisdom?

> XVII. *Thinking of THAT, directing one's whole conscious being to THAT, making THAT their whole aim, with THAT as the sole object of their devotion, they reach a state from which there is no return, their sins washed away by wisdom.*[6]

88. Is it strange to say that they regard not only themselves, but the whole universe as Brahma?

89. As good fortune never even out of interest looks on misery, as true discrimination does not know delusion,

90. or as the sun sees no trace of darkness even in a dream; as nectar hears no tale of death—

91. But let this be!—as the moon has no memory of heat, so such wise men can perceive no difference between creatures.

> XVIII. *Sages see with an equal eye, a learned and humble Brāhman, a cow, an elephant or even a dog or an outcaste.*

92. How can any thought remain such as to imagine that this creature is a fly, that an elephant, this man an outcaste, that one a brāhman or that this is my son and that another's?

93. Still further, that this is a cow, that a dog, this a noble man and this a base one—how can any conscious man entertain such a dream?

94. How can such differences exist? If any egoism remains,

when that has been utterly destroyed, what is left that can produce any sense of separateness?

95. Then mayest thou know that Brahma is everywhere, eternal and unvarying, and that thou thyself art that unequalled Brahma. Know fully that this is the secret of an evenly balanced mind.

> XIX. *Even here [on earth] the created [world] is overcome by those whose mind is established in equality. God is flawless and the same in all. Therefore are these established in God.*

96. Such a man may not have abstained from contact with sense objects, nor mortified his senses, yet being free from desire he experiences non-attachment.

97. Like others he follows worldly pursuits, yet at the same time he has freed himself from the unawareness of ordinary people.

98. Though in the body, he is not recognized by other men, just as a ghost which is in the world and yet never visible to men;

99. and as water plays upon water when agitated by the wind and people think the wave is different from the water.

100. Such is the name and form of one whose mind has reached equilibrium in all things; he is indeed Brahma himself.

> XX. *One should not rejoice on obtaining what is pleasant nor grieve on obtaining what is unpleasant. He who is [thus] firm of understanding and unbewildered, a knower of God, is established in God.*

101. O Arjuna, he who has reached this state of even balance is, verily, distinguished by one other characteristic, of which I will tell thee briefly, said Acyuta.

102. As a high mountain cannot be washed away by a flood which is a mirage, so he who is not affected by weal or woe,

103. is indeed firmly established in equilibrium. Hari says, He indeed is Brahma, O Son of Pāndu.

> XXI. *When the soul is no longer attached to external contacts one finds the happiness that is in the Self. Such a one who is in union with God enjoys undying bliss.*

104. Is it any wonder that one who does not wish to forgo
the bliss of the Self in order to return to the domination
of the senses takes no pleasure in objects of sense?

105. Enjoying to the full the bliss of the Self, once his heart is
established in it he will never leave it.

106. Will the chakora bird lick the sand, when among the
beds of lotus flowers it has once fed on the clear beams
of the moon?

107. Need it be said that, similarly, he who has attained to the
bliss of the Self and has thereby gained self-realization,
naturally abandons all contact with sense objects?

> XXII *Whatever pleasures are born of contacts [with
> objects] are only sources of pain, they have a beginning
> and an end, O Son of Kuntī [Arjuna]; no wise man
> delights in them.*

108. Now, thy curiosity will certainly prompt thee to think,
Who then are deluded by the pleasures of the senses?

109. They, indeed, who do not know themselves indulge in
the pleasures of sense as a hungry man will even eat
husks;

110. or as a deer afflicted with thirst and in its distraction
forgetting to look for water, will rush to a mirage in the
desert,

111. so those who have not seen the Self, who are always
lacking the bliss of the Self, regard objects of sense as
desirable and relish them.

112. Otherwise it is absurd to say that there is happiness in
sensual objects. Why is it not possible to make use of
lightning for lighting the world?

113. Tell me, if the mere shade of clouds could afford protection
against wind, rain, and heat, why should three-storeyed
houses be built?

114. Therefore it is as idle to talk ignorantly of sensual pleasures
as if a poisonous root might be called sweet!

115. Just as Mars might be called 'auspicious' or as a mirage
be called 'water', so there is no sense in talking of the
'pleasures' derived from sense objects.

116. Enough of all this talking. Would the shade of a serpent's
hood be cool enough for a mouse?

117. O Son of Pāndu, as the piece of bait attached to a hook

is good so long as it is not eaten by the fish; so it is with all contact with sense objects. Understand this clearly.

118. Seen with a dispassionate eye, they would appeal, O Kiriti, as much as the fatness of a jaundiced body.

119. Therefore know that the happiness obtained from the enjoyment of sense is entirely painful. But what can fools do? They cannot live without it.

120. These poor people have no understanding of inner happiness, and therefore they are obliged to indulge the senses. Do maggots born of sores ever feel disgusted by them?

121. To such unfortunate beings pain itself appears to be the heart of pleasure, they are like frogs immersed in the mire of objects of sense. How can fish abandon water?

122. If all creatures became indifferent to sense pleasures, the births which are the source of suffering would serve no purpose.

123. Who, otherwise, would suffer without relief the pangs of ante-natal life, or the pains of life and death?

124. Were those who are addicted to sensual enjoyment to give it up, what place would there be for great sins, and would not the word 'earthly existence' then lose its meaning?

125. So those who have come to believe that the pain of sense experience is pleasure prove to themselves that the falsities of ignorance are true.

126. For this reason, O noble warrior, rightly viewed, objects of sense are evil; beware lest, in forgetfulness, thou shouldst walk in that path.

127. Men of dispassion, however, renounce them as if they were poison. To the dispassionate the pleasure shown [by the senses in the form of] pain makes no appeal.

XXIII. *He who is able to resist the rush of desire and anger, even here before he gives up the body, is a yogin, is the happy man.*

128. Indeed in the hearts of the wise there is no trace of this, seeing that they have learnt to control physical tendencies in their bodies.

129. They are entirely unaware of outward affairs; in their hearts there is only the experience of bliss.

130. Even so they enjoy it in a different manner, and not as a

bird pecking at a fruit, for they are unaware of the separateness [of the enjoyer from the object enjoyed].

131. [The enjoyer] becomes one with the object of enjoyment, the mountain of egoism is removed and then they cling firmly to their inner joy.

132. In that embrace they are united, as when water is mixed with water there is no sign of any separation.

133. As when the wind [falls and] is lost in the sky their separateness vanishes, so in such a union there remains only the bliss in the Self.

134. When all trace of duality is lost, could one say that one alone remains? For who would there be to bear witness of it?

135. Let us leave all this now; should we try to express the inexpressible? Those who enjoy inner happiness know the secret.

136. Those who enjoy to the full this bliss, who are absorbed in the Self, I know to be indeed moulded in the bliss of the Self.

137. They are the very image of bliss, the green shoots of [the tree of] joy, a palace built by the great wisdom.

138. They are the dwelling place of discrimination, the very nature of Brahma, or the ornamented limbs of the knowledge of the Self.

139. They are the essence of truth and forms of the spirit. Is this not enough of praise for all these?

140. When thou delightest in the praises of the saints thou forgettest the subject of thy talk, though thou speakest excellently of other matters.

141. But control thy overflowing enthusiasm, light the lamp of the meaning of the Gītā and bring the auspicious dawn into the temple of the hearts of the righteous.

142. These quiet words of the guru were heard by Nivritti's disciple and he said, Listen to what Krishna says.

> XXIV. *The yogin who finds his happiness within, his joy within and likewise his light only within, becomes divine and attains to the beatitude of God [brahmanirvāṇa].*

> XXV. *The holy men whose sins are destroyed, whose doubts [dualities] are destroyed, whose minds are disciplined and who rejoice in [doing] good to all creatures, attain to the beatitude of God.*

143. O Arjuna, those who plunge into the depths of the infinite bliss, establish themselves in it and become one with THAT.

144. One who, through the clear illumination of the Self, sees his unity with the universe can be regarded as the highest Self while still in the body.

145. This Self is truly the supreme, immutable and infinite, and the dispassionate are worthy to attain to it.

146. It flourishes in the great sages, and is shared by those who are freed from desire; they who are free from doubt enjoy the rich harvest.

XXVI. *The beatitude of God lies near to those austere souls [yatis] who are delivered from desire and anger and who have subdued their minds and have knowledge of the Self.*

147. Those who have become liberated from the pleasures of objects of sense, and have control over the mind, sleep in this Self and do not again waken.

148. That is the peace of the Eternal, the goal of all who have attained enlightenment; O Son of Pāndu, these are that Self.

149. If thou seekest to know how they become so, how they attain to the state of the Eternal while still in the body, I will briefly explain.

XXVII. *Shutting out all external objects, fixing the vision between the eyebrows,*

XXVIII. *making even the inward and the outward breaths move within the nostrils, the sage who has controlled the senses, mind and understanding, who is intent on liberation, who has cast away desire, fear and anger, is ever freed.*

XXIX. *And having known Me as the Enjoyer of sacrifices and austerities, the Great Lord of all the worlds, the Friend of all beings, he [the sage] attains peace.*

150. When they have, by means of dispassion, cast out all sense desires, they concentrate the mind within the body.

151. With the gaze turned inwards and fixed on the space between the eyebrows where the three meet,[7]

152. stopping the breath through the right and left nostrils

and making the outgoing and ingoing breaths equal, they cause the mind to remain steadfast in the crown centre. [8]

153. As when the Ganges reaches the ocean, carrying with it the waters from the streets, the different streams cannot be distinguished,

154. so, O Arjuna, all distinction between various desires ceases when by means of restraint of the breath the mind becomes stilled within the inner cavity.

155. Then, behold, the canvas of the mind on which is painted the picture of worldly existence is torn apart, just as reflections disappear when a lake dries up.

156. When the mind has ceased to function, where is there any place for egoism or other passions? Therefore a man [who has realized the Self] becomes Brahma even when still in the body.

157. I have spoken earlier of those who, while in the body, have attained to the Self; they have reached this by following this path.

158. Ascending the mountains of restraint and crossing the ocean of constant practice, they have attained their goal.

159. Having purified themselves and carried out their earthly tasks, they have become one with the essential truth.

160. When Hrishikesha expounded the purposes of yoga in this manner, the intelligent Arjuna was filled with wonder.

161. Krishna, realizing this, smiled and said to Pārtha, Have these words brought peace to thy mind?

162. Then Arjuna replied, O Lord, Thou art the master in understanding the minds of others and hast well understood the inclination of my mind.

163. Thou hast already understood what I wish to ask Thee for further explanation. Show me again clearly, therefore, what Thou hast already told me.

164. Listen, however, to me. The path Thou hast pointed out is as a ford [by which a river] may be more easily crossed than by swimming.

165. Similarly, [the path of yoga] is easier than the path of knowledge for people as weak as we are; but still it takes time to learn it, though we will be patient.

166. Wilt Thou therefore now test our understanding? Let Thy explanation be complete, even if it is extensive.

167. Then Krishna said, If thou findest this path to be good, what can I lose by explaining it to thee again? I will gladly speak of it.

168. O Arjuna, if thou wilt listen, and having heard wilt practise it, will it be a waste of time to explain it?

169. Already [Krishna's] heart was compassionate, added to which there was his special affection for Arjuna. Who then can understand the wonder of his love?

170. It was like the shower of the waters of compassion, or the creation of a new love. It would be difficult to describe that compassionate look of Hari.

171. It was as though moulded out of nectar, an intoxication of affection; so it was caught in the fascination of Arjuna and could not be withdrawn.

172. The more we digress in this matter the lengthier will be our account; but the nature of His love defies all description.

173. Is there any cause for wonder in this? Who could possibly fathom that Lord who is unconscious even of Himself?

174. However, from those last words of His, it would seem that He was bewitched, so that he said forcefully to Arjuna, Listen, O Beloved!

175. O Arjuna, I will joyfully explain all this in such a manner that thou wilt understand.

176. What that yoga represents, what its usefulness is, who is qualified to practise it,

177. all that has been said about these things I will now explain.

178. Listen attentively to Me. With these words Krishna will begin to speak of the subject of the next chapter.

In the Upanishad of the Bhagavadgitā, the science of the Absolute, the scripture of Yoga and the dialogue between Shri Krishna and Arjuna, this is the fifth chapter called the Yoga of Renunciation of Action.

NOTES

1. *Upamanyu.* The son of a celebrated sage. The verse refers to a legendary story of the giving of the ocean of milk to him by Shiva.
2. *Sannyāsi.* One who practices sannyāsa, renunciation of sense pleasures and of involvement in worldly life; the last of the four stages of a brāhman's life.
3. Here there is a change of speaker, Jnāneshvara himself addressing his audience.
4. *the nine-gated body.* The body is referred to in this way on account of the nine orifices of the physical body.
5. *the sleep of Brahma.* It was believed that Vishnu would enter into prolonged sleep at the end of a world age.
6. *THAT.* The absolute, without attributes and beyond time and space, is referred to as 'THAT', in opposition to the 'This', the world of man and nature. Bhag. XVII.
7. *the three.* The three main arteries of the body, one on the right, one on the left and one in the centre. These form the basis of the system of psychic centres, meeting in the 'brow' centre, in the forehead. They are named *ida, pingala* and *sushumna.* Further information about these centres may be found in *The Serpent Power*, Avalon, Arthur.
8. *the crown centre.* The 'crown' of the psychic system is on the top of the head, corresponding to the position of the fontanelle This is the highest centre of all to be reached in yoga.

E*

113

CHAPTER VI

1. Then Sanjaya said to the king, O great king! listen to the teaching of yoga which Shri Krishna will now expound to Arjuna.
2. It was as if a great feast of the essence of Brahma had been prepared for Arjuna by Nārāyana, and we as guests have arrived at the right time.
3. I cannot express how great our good fortune is. It is as though a thirsty man, on tasting water, were to find that it is nectar,
4. so it has been with you and me, for without effort on our part we have this truth. Then Dhritarāshtra said, I do not ask this of thee.
5. From these words of the king, Sanjaya understood what was in the king's heart, possessed by his affection for his sons.
6. Perceiving this, he smiled to himself, saying, The old king has been blinded by his love for his children; otherwise my words were relevant at this time.
7. But how can he regard them as such? How can a blind man see the light of day? But Sanjaya feared to say this lest the king should be offended.
8. However, inwardly he was delighted that he had an opportunity of hearing the discussion between Shri Krishna and Arjuna.
9. In the fullness of joy and with steady purpose, he will begin to speak respectfully to the king.
10. This is the sixth discourse of the Gitā, of Sanjaya's narration. As nectar was born from the milky ocean,
11. so is laid before us here the essence of the meaning of the Gitā, the other shore of the ocean of discrimination, the treasure of the riches of yoga,
12. the resting place of primordial matter, which cannot be expressed by the Vedas, and from which springs the root of the creeper of the Gitā.

13. Such is this sixth discourse, which will be explained with literary beauty. Listen to it attentively, therefore.

14. My language is Marāthi, but it easily surpasses nectar, with such beauty of words and expression will I compose it.

15. Even the melody of the seven notes will fall short of its sweet delicacy, and the power of fragrance will be subdued by its charm.

16. Moreover, overcome by its sweetness, tongues will spring up in the ears and hearing it the various sense organs will begin to quarrel among themselves.

17. Listening to speech is the function of the ears, but the sense of taste will say, This joy is mine. My words will be the fragrance enjoyed by the sense of smell.

18. Marvelling at the flowing style the eyes, filled with satisfaction, will exclaim, O wonder! Here is opened for us the mine of beauty!

19. When the sentences have been arranged the mind will rush forward with outstretched arms to embrace the words.

20. In this way the senses will vie with each other, but each in its own way will understand the meaning, as the sun illuminates the whole world.

21. The wide range of meaning of the words is rarely to be found, and he who understand their sense will find therein all the qualities of the stone of desire.

22. I am offering respectfully, to those who are dispassionate, full dishes of food in the form of these words, served with the essence of eternal bliss.

23. Now only those who have lighted the lamps of the ever new radiance of the Self can partake of this food without the awareness of the senses.

24. In doing so the listeners must disregard the craving of the ears, for the mind alone should enjoy it.

25. With the personality merged in Brahman, and the veil withdrawn from the inner meaning of the words, the experience of the supreme bliss of the Self should be freely enjoyed.

26. If such pleasure is the result this exposition will serve a good purpose; otherwise the whole would be but a story told to the deaf and dumb.

27. But enough of all this! There is no need to arouse the listeners further. The dispassionate naturally have the right to hear it.

28. Only those who out of their love for realization of the Self have given up all thought of heaven and earth can appreciate its sweetness.

29. As crows cannot recognize the moon, so ordinary people will never be able to understand this work. As the chakora bird feeds on moonbeams,

30. so this writing is meant only for wise men; as the ignorant can make nothing out of it, there is no need to enlarge further on the subject.

31. All this have I spoken of in my disgression and the good men must forgive it; so now will I speak of Shriranga's teaching.[1]

32. It is difficult for the mind to grasp; scarcely, therefore, can it be expressed in words, but with the light of the grace of Nivritti I will be able to understand it.

33. That which cannot be seen with the eyes, may be perceived without their aid if the subtle power of wisdom has been acquired.

34. The gold which the alchemist cannot make can be found in iron if by good fortune he can discover the touchstone.

35. So what can we not do if we have the favour of the Guru? Jnānadeva says, This I have in abundance.

36. In the strength of it I will speak; in words I will give form to the formless and cause the senses to experience what is beyond their power to know.

37. He in whom dwell the six qualities—success, wealth, benevolence, knowledge, dispassion and sovereignty,

38. who, therefore, is called 'Blessed', that Lord, the friend of the selfless, said to Pārtha, Now pay attention to Me.

The Blessed Lord said:

> *1. He who does the work which he ought to do, without seeking its fruit, is the sannyāsin, he is the yogin, not the man who merely does not light the sacred fire, and performs no rites.*

39. Listen! Among men the yogi and the sannyāsi cannot be regarded as different; rightly viewed the two are indeed but one.

40. Apart from the apparent difference of name, even yoga itself is sannyāsa; seen in the light of the Self there is no difference between these.

116

41. As different names may be given to the same man, as two roads may lead to the same place,

42. as different vessels may be filled with the same kind of water, so should we regard this apparent difference between yoga and sannyāsa.

43. Listen, O Arjuna, he is considered by all to be a true yogi who, while performing actions, yet is not desirous of their fruit.

44. Just as the earth naturally produces vegetation, without any awareness of itself, and does not look forward to the grain that grows,

45. similarly, the yogi performs actions whenever occasion demands, according to his circumstances and appropriate to his caste duties and the stage of his life.

46. He does what is right, but he has no egoism in his nature nor does he set his heart on the fruit of action.

47. Such a man is a true yogi. Listen, O Pārtha! He is most surely a master of yoga.

48. Moreover, if there is some duty to be performed he says 'I will abandon this work, for it incurs bondage', but he immediately sets his hand to another task.

49. He labours in vain, like an obstinate servant who, washing off a liniment already applied, persists in binding on another.

50. According to his destiny he has already on his shoulders the burden of a householder's duties; the practice of sannyāsa only adds to it.

51. So, one should not abstain from worshipping the fire or fail to carry out one's appointed duties. The bliss of yoga is within one's Self.

> II. *What is called renunciation, know to be the same as disciplined activity, O Pāṇḍava [Arjuna], for no one becomes a yogin who has not renounced his selfish purpose.*

52. Know that a sannyāsi is the same as a yogi; this truth has been universally proclaimed by many in various scriptures.

53. When the will, being renounced, is finally given up, then the essence of yoga is discovered through the poise gained from experience.

> III. *Work is said to be the means of the sage who wishes*

*to attain to yoga; when he has attained to yoga, serenity
is said to be the means.*

54. Now, O Pārtha, if thou wishest to ascend to the summit
of the mountain of yoga, do not fail to do so by the pathway of action.

55. From the lower levels of the restraint of the senses by the
footpath of the postures of yoga, thou mayest mount
upwards by the steep ascent of the restraint of breathing.[2]

56. Then canst thou reach the cliff of pratyāhāra, which is
slippery even for the feet of reason and whence hathayogis,
in spite of their boasts, are hurled down.[3]

57. While on pratyāhāra they are helpless but with the
strength derived from discipline they cling with the claws
of dispassion.

58. In this way, helped by the power of the wind, he comes
to the broad road of mental concentration and may proceed onward till the peak of meditation has been passed.

59. Then the end of the path will be reached, all desire for
further advance satisfied, and in the joy of the Self the
seeker after the goal will be united with it.

60. Where no further path remains, where memories of the
past fade out, there, in that highest level, comes samādhi.[4]

61. Now I will tell of the distinctive characteristics of him
who, enthroned in yoga by these means, reaches the
limitless perfection.

> IV. *When one does not become attached to objects of sense
> or to works, and has renounced all purposes, then he is
> said to have attained to yoga.*

62. For him who sleeps in the chamber of the consciousness
of the Self, sense objects do not pay frequent visits to the
house of the senses,

63. His mind is not disturbed when pleasure or pain touches
his body, and when sense objects come within his purview
he is not concerned about what they are.

64. His senses are engaged in their appropriate functions, yet
his heart entertains no desire for any fruit.

65. While fully awake in the body, he is yet like one who has
fallen asleep. Know such a man to be perfectly established
in yoga.

66. Here Arjuna said, O Ananta! all this fills me with wonder;
tell me who has endowed him with such merit.

v. *Let a man lift himself by himself; let him not degrade himself; for the Self alone is the friend of the self and the Self alone is the enemy of the self.*

67. Then Shri Krishna smiled and said, Is not thy question a strange one? In this state of union who will give what, and to whom?

68. When in a state of deep ignorance, a man falls asleep on the bed of delusion, then he experiences the painful dream of life and death.

69. Afterwards when he suddenly awakens he realizes that all this was an illusion, and the realization of his own being also arises from within himself.

70. Therefore, O Conqueror of wealth, such a man brings about his own ruin by indulging in self-conceit.

vi. *For him who has conquered his [lower] self by the [higher] Self, His Self is a friend; but for him who has not possessed his [higher] Self, his very Self will act in enmity.*

71. From this point of view, egoism should be given up and then the man will become what he really is; then will he have secured the welfare of his own self.

72. Otherwise, like a chrysalis in its cocoon, the self will be its own enemy, when it imposes on the fair body the concept of self-hood.

73. How strange it would be if some unfortunate person should wish to be blind at the very moment when he discovers a treasure, or that he should close his eyes;

74. or that a man out of sheer madness should entertain some false idea in his heart, such as 'I am not I, I am lost.'

75. Nevertheless he is the same person. Yet what can be done if he does not think so? Can death follow from a wound received in a dream?

76. [The unenlightened man is] like a parrot who, perplexed by the fact that the rod revolves in the opposite direction because of the weight of its body, is unable to fly away when it should do so.[5]

77. In vain it twists its neck and contracts its chest in order to clasp the pipe more and more firmly with its claws.

78. It fancies that it is really bound, caught up in this illusion it grasps the rod even more firmly, although its feet are free.

79. Can it be said that it is caught by another, when in reality it is not held at all? Even if it were dragged away by force it would not loosen its hold.
80. Therefore the man who is filled with conceit is his own enemy. The man who is enlightened does not hold on to such illusions, said Shri Krishna.

> VII. *When one who has conquered one's [lower] self and has attained to the calm of self-mastery, his supreme Self abides ever concentrated, he is at peace in cold and heat, in pleasure and pain, in honour and dishonour.*

81. The higher Self is not far distant from him who has conquered his inner sense and whose every desire has been subdued.
82. As when all the impurities have been separated from it pure gold remains, so the individual self becomes Brahma when the will has ceased to function.
83. When the shape of a pot no longer exists, the space therein becomes merged in the outer air; it does not have to move to another place,
84. so he whose false individuality is destroyed becomes the original highest Self.
85. Then currents of cold and heat, the turmoil of pleasure and pain, the concepts of honour and dishonour no longer exist for him.
86. Wherever the sun goes on its path, the universe becomes light; so whatever such a man acquires becomes indeed himself.
87. As showers of rain falling from the clouds do not pierce the ocean, so good or evil are not different for the master yogi.

> VIII. *The ascetic [yogī] whose soul is satisfied with wisdom and knowledge, who is unchanging and master of his senses, to whom a clod, a stone and a piece of gold are the same, is said to be controlled [in yoga].*

88. When he considers worldly knowledge, he perceives it to be false, and when he sees aright he knows that he himself is wisdom.
89. As no sense of duality remains in him, naturally there is no further need to consider such ideas as 'partial' or 'all-pervasive'.

90. In this way, he who has conquered his senses, though still in the body, is naturally equal in bliss to the highest Self.

91. Being self-subdued and harmonized, for him there is neither 'small' nor 'great' at any time.

92. Behold! he regards a heap of gold as great as Mount Meru and a clod of earth as the same.

93. He values even a jewel, so precious that in comparison the whole earth is of little worth, as no more than a stone.

> IX. *That man excels who is equal-minded among friends, companions and foes, among those who are neutral and impartial, among those who are hateful and related, among saints and sinners.*

94. How can he imagine such strange differences as a friend or a foe, one who is indifferent or one who wishes one well.

95. Who is a relative or who is a hater to him who has realized his unity with the whole universe?

96. Further, O Kiriti, in his sight there can be neither 'high' nor 'low'. Tested by the touchstone, are differences of value made [in measuring gold]?

97. As by its means only the purest possible gold is procured, so is it evident that the reason of such a man regards with complete impartiality all living and non-living beings.

98. All created things, varying though they may be in form, are nevertheless made out of the same gold—the eternal Parabrahman.[6]

99. This supreme wisdom he has gained in its fullness, so he is not deceived by the outward appearance of this array of forms.

100. When we look at a piece of cloth, we find thread throughout the whole texture; in fact there is nothing but the thread.

101. He who has gained this perception in experience has formed evenness of mind which does not vary.

102. He is worthy to be called the holiest of the holy, the mere sight of him commands respect and in his company even a deluded person experiences absorption in Brahma.

103. Religion lives through his words, the sight of him produces the highest psychic powers, and in heavenly bliss he takes constant pleasure.

104. If by any chance the memory of him comes to our mind

his greatness is imparted to us. Let it be so; even to praise him will be of great profit to us.

> x. *Let the yogin try constantly to concentrate his mind [on the Supreme Self] remaining in solitude and alone, self-controlled, free from desires and any longing for possessions.*

105. He for whom there dawns the day of non-duality, which knows no setting, remains in the unceasing bliss of the Eternal.
106. O Pārtha, the man who possesses discrimination in such a manner is unique, for in all the three worlds he is the only one who has no household possessions.
107. These are the exceptional characteristics of the perfected man, said Krishna out of the fullness of his knowledge,
108. He is the parent of all wise men, light to the eyes of those who see and the one whose masterly thought created the universe,
109. to encompass whose glory the rich garment of the Vedas, fashioned in the workshop of the sacred syllable, is inadequate.
110. From the lustre of his body the sun and moon derive their greatness and give forth their light. Is it possible for the world to exist without that lustre?
111. How canst thou comprehend his qualities, whose name alone the whole of space would be insufficient to contain?
112. Enough, therefore, of this praise; under this pretext I cannot tell whose qualities He has actually described and why.
113. Moreover were I to reveal the whole secret of the Eternal which casts out all thought of duality, then the joy of my affection for Arjuna would be destroyed.
114. Therefore he [Krishna] did not tell Arjuna everything but drew a thin veil over it. He allowed the sense of his mind being separate [to remain with Arjuna] in order that Arjuna should be able to enjoy the experience.
115. [For this enjoyment] oneness with Brahma is an obstacle; those who seek after it are poor and the sight of them may affect his love for Me.
116. If, perchance his egoism vanishes and he becomes one with Me, what can I do alone [without his love]?
117. Who then could soothe Me with the sight of him, speak

to Me when My heart is full, or embrace Me in the warm clasp of love?

118. If this state of union with Me were reached, with whom could I speak of the precious secret that cannot be contained in the heart?

119. With this compassionate thought Janārdana reached out with his mind to draw to Himself the mind of Arjuna in conversation, under the pretext of this exposition.[7]

120. If, hearing this, it seems difficult to understand, remember that Pārtha is but an image moulded out of the bliss of Shri Krishna.

121. As a childless woman, bearing a child in her old age, dances in deep ecstasy,

122. so it was with Shri Ananta; I would not have said this if I had not seen this great love for Arjuna.

123. See how strange this is! On the one hand this teaching, and on the other the battle! Krishna danced with the delight of Arjuna's love.

124. How could love feel shame, or passion become weary, and how can there be madness without delusion?

125. The meaning of all this is that Arjuna was the refuge of Krishna's affection, or that he was as a mirror reflecting the heart of Krishna overjoyed with love;

126. or being so pure and holy, his heart was the most fertile field in the world in which to plant the seed of devotion; therefore he is most worthy of the grace of Shri Krishna.

127. It is as though Pārtha were the chief deity presiding over worship in the form of 'fellowship', which is the pedestal of the attainment of 'the oblation of the self'.

128. Arjuna is so dear to Hari that, though the master is near, He is not praised, while His servant's virtues are recited.

129. Consider how a wife is lovingly devoted to her husband, and he holds her in high esteem; is not such a virtuous woman more worthy of praise than her husband?

130. In the same way it has delighted me to praise Arjuna more than Shri Hari, who has become the abode of the good fortune of the three worlds?

131. Being possessed by love of him the Formless One has taken form, and in spite of His perfection has felt a longing for him.

132. Then exclaimed the listeners, O what good fortune! What beauty of language! Does not its excellence surpass even the Vedas!

133. There is nothing strange in this for, speaking in my mother-tongue, Marāthi, literary excellence will appear in it like the different colours in the sky.

134. How clearly shines the moonlight of divine knowledge, with the cool rays of the meaning and so the sense of the verses, like lotus flowers, naturally comes into bloom!

135. [See now], desire has been awakened in the desireless [listeners]. Such desire arises also in the great, and they sway with it, being enlightened in their hearts.

136. Realizing this the disciple of Nivritti said, Pay heed and learn that in the coming of Shri Krishna a great day has dawned for the Pāndava race.

137. Born of Devaki, reared with great care by Yashodā, now He has come to the help of the Pāndavas.[8]

138. Therefore there has been no need for the fortunate Arjuna to serve Him for long years, or to await opportunities to seek His favour.

139. Enough of this digression! Continue the story without delay. Then Arjuna said in a friendly manner, O Lord, these signs of saintliness are not to be found in me.

140. Moreover, judged by such a standard, undoubtedly I should fall far short of it, but by hearing Thy teaching I should become great.

141. If Thou willest it I shall become Brahma; and shall I not practise what Thou teachest?

142. I do not understand what it is that Thou sayest; but hearing it I extol it in my heart. What high qualities are needed to attain to this?

143. May they be also in me! Wilt Thou with Thy great saintliness make me Thine? Thereupon Shri Krishna smiled and said, Why should I not? I will do this.

144. Behold! so long as contentment has not been gained, there are many difficulties concerning happiness; when however it has been acquired, what can a man lack?

145. So that a devotee of the Supreme may become Brahma without difficulty. See how Krishna bends under the weight of the harvest of Arjuna's good fortune!

146. He who has been so difficult of attainment even for Indra and all the other gods, who have spent thousands of lives

striving for it, has become the servant of Arjuna. This cannot be described in words.[9]

147. Now listen to me. When Arjuna asked the Lord to make him one with Brahma, the Lord heard him attentively.

148. Thus He realized the great longing in Arjuna's heart and knew that [the seed of] dispassion had entered the womb of reason.

149. But the days of fulfilment were not completed, and yet, with the fullness of the spring of dispassion the flower of union with Brahma is ready to break forth.

150. Now it will not be long before the fruit of union with Brahma will be realized, for he has developed dispassion. Shri Ananta was sure of this.

151. He knew that whatever practices Arjuna might follow they would bear fruit even from the beginning, that if he were taught the method of yoga it would not be without result.

152. With such thoughts in his mind Shri Hari then said to Arjuna, Listen, while I tell three of this royal path.

153. [Already] there can be seen the abundant fruit of liberation lying at the foot of the tree of earthly existence. Even Shankar is still a pilgrim on this path.

154. Multitudes of yogis have set out by various by-ways to find Brahma, and the foot-prints of their experience have made an easy path.

155. By the straight path of Self-realization they have travelled steadily, avoiding the side roads of ignorance.

156. All the sages have come by this path; seekers have attained to perfection in this way; exalted positions have been reached by those who know the Self.

157. When once this path is perceived, hunger and thirst are forgotten, and travelling on it there is no awareness of night and day.

158. Wherever the pilgrim sets his foot, there will the mine of eternal bliss be open to him, and even should he go astray in the end he attains to heavenly bliss.

159. This path [like the sun] proceeds from the east towards the west and one has to walk along it steadily, O Wielder of the bow.

160. He who travels on this road becomes identified with the place to which he is going. Why should I say this? Thou wilt easily understand.

161. Thereupon Arjuna exclaimed, O Lord, when will this be? Why dost Thou not rescue me from the ocean of expectant desire in which I am plunged?

162. Then Shri Krishna said, Why this impatient talk? I am explaining it all to thee; besides, thou has asked Me to do so.

XI. *He should set in a clean place his firm seat, neither too high nor too low, covered with sacred grass, a deerskin and a cloth, one over the other.*

163. Now it will be described in detail. But it can only be profitable through experience. First a suitable place must be found.

164. It should be a place where one can sit comfortably and not desire to rise; and such that when one sees it, one's intention towards dispassion will increase.

165. The place should be one frequented by saints, which would induce a feeling of contentment and fill the mind with courage.

166. Such a place should be very beautiful so that one would wish to practise yoga there and the heart would experience Self-realization.

167. Should a heretic enter the place unawares, even he would feel a strong inclination to practise penance.

168. If some pleasure loving man chanced to come that way and unexpectedly found it, he would not think of returning [to the life of worldly desire].

169. One who is reluctant to stay there would be forced to remain, the deluded would be persuaded to sit there; and dispassion would be awakened with a tap on the shoulder.

170. A sensuous person beholding it, would experience such delight that he would be willing to sacrifice even a kingdom for the sake of resting there.

171. It must be as clean as it is beautiful, where the highest bliss is revealed.

172. There is one more condition: it should be frequented by seekers of yoga and not disturbed by the footsteps of passers by.

173. It should be surrounded by a grove of shady trees which have roots as sweet as nectar and which are always bearing fruit.

174. Here and there should be streams, clear even in the rainy season, with springs nearby.

175. The air should not be hot but cool, and gentle breezes should blow softly over it.

176. Quiet should reign there, it should not be a resort of animals, nor should there be parrots or bees near it.

177. Swans, however, may be floating on the water, a few cranes nearby, and cuckoos now and then.

178. There would be no harm in the occasional presence of peacocks, but not all the time.

179. O Pāndava, it would be better if there were a secluded hermitage near the spot, or a temple of Shiva,

180. either of these, according to one's preference. The yogi should for the most part sit in solitude.

181. One should seek out such a place, and if it is felt to be suitable; the seat for meditation should be set up there.

182. On carefully laid young blades of kusha grass should be placed a pure deer skin and, on that, a clean folded cloth.[10]

183. The tender grass should be placed with care so that it remains well bound together.

184. If the seat were too high, the body might sway; if too low, it would be affected by contact with the earth.

185. It should be neither too high nor too low. So should this seat be evenly poised. Enough has been said.

> XII. *There taking his place on the seat, making his mind one-pointed and controlling his thought and sense, let him practise yoga for the purification of the soul.*

186. Then, with concentration of mind, the aspirant should recall the presence of his guru.

187. Remaining thus, until the respectful calling to mind of his guru causes a sense of purity to pervade the heart, the hardness of egoism is melted away.

188. The sense of objects is forgotten, the restlessness of the senses stopped and the mind becomes quietened within the heart.

189. This should be continued until a sense of union is reached and the yogi should remain seated with this awareness.

190. Now the body will maintain its poise, the breathing will keep its own rhythm, and perception will be heightened.

191. The outgoing activities of the mind are withdrawn and a

sense of repose will be felt within; at the moment of adopting this posture, the exercise begins.

XIII. *Holding the body, head and neck erect and still, looking fixedly at the tip of the nose without looking around [without allowing the eyes to wander],*

192. Now listen, I will tell you how the yogic posture should be taken up. Lifting the calves of the legs up on to the thighs [seated on the ground],

193. the soles of the feet should be placed firmly against the perineum so that they will remain in position.

194. Let the right foot press against the base so that the left foot rests on it easily.

195. Between the anus and the penis there are exactly four inches; leaving a space of one and a half inches on each side,

196. in the remaining one inch span the back part of the right heel should be forced and the body balanced on it.

197. The ankles should be held in such a way that the lower part of the body is raised so slightly that one is not aware of it.

198. O Pārtha, the form of the whole body will come to be resting on the top of one heel.

199. O Arjuna, know that this is what is called the mulabandha posture, otherwise known as vajrāsana.

200. In this way the proper position is established and the lower passages [of the body] are closed, and the breath is restrained within the body.

201. The cupped palms of both hands will rest upon the left foot and the shoulders will appear to be raised.

202. Between the upper arms the lotus-like head is held firm and the eyelids will begin to close.

203. The upper eyelids will drop and the lower ones extend; thus the eyes remain half open.

204. The vision remains within and does not wander outside; it continues to be focused on the tip of the nose.

205. In this way the sight remains firmly inside and does not move outside again; its focus remains steadily downwards.

206. Then any interest in looking in all directions or noticing [external] forms ceases completely.

207. The neck and throat are compressed, the chin pressed
into the cavity between the collar-bones and forced down
on to the breast,

208. and the larynx is hidden [in this position]. O son of Pāndu,
this posture is called jālāndhara.[11]

209. The navel rises upwards and the stomach is compressed
and the heart cavity is expanded;

210. O Kiriti, the yogic posture formed by drawing the navel
and the penis towards each other is called odhiyāna.[12]

XIV. *Serene and fearless, firm in the vow of celibacy,
subdued in mind, let him sit, harmonized, his mind
turned to Me and intent on Me alone.*

211. Then the signs of the yogic experience appear outwardly
on the body and inwardly the working of the mind ceases.

212. The activity of thought subsides, mental energy dies
down, and body and mind find rest.

213. Hunger is forgotten, sleep disappears; even the memory
of them is lost, no trace is to be found.

214. The downward life-breath being confined in the vase of
the body, turns back and, becoming compressed, begins
to expand.

215. More and more it is agitated and in the freer space above
it rumbles and struggles against the solar plexus.

216. The struggle ceases and the whole body trembles to its
very centre; thus the impurities of childhood are driven
out.

217. It does not then turn downwards but moves in the interior
of the body. It expels the bodily secretions.

218. It looses the ocean of the humours of the body, reduces
the fat, and even draws out the marrow from the bones.

219. It clears the arteries, loosens the limbs; but the seeker
should not allow himself to be frightened by any of these.

220. It reveals and removes diseases; it stirs up the soil and
the water.

221. On the other hand, O Wielder of the bow, the heat
induced by the practice of this posture awakens the force
called Kundalini.[13]

222. As the brood of a she-serpent bathed in turmeric lie
curled up in sleep,

223. so lies this Kundalini, very small and curled in three and

a half circles, like a female serpent with her head turned downwards.

224. It is like a ring of lightning, or folds of flaming fire, or a bar of pure gold.

225. Thus bound fast by threads it is confined between two folds, but being compressed by the vajra posture, it is awakened.

226. Then, as a star shooting through space, as the sun falling from its place in the sky, or as a point of light bursting forth as a sprouting seed,

227. it breaks its bonds, grips the body, and appears mounted upon the navel.

228. For long years it has hungered for this awakening, and, the pretext having occurred, it extends its mouth upwards with great eagerness.

229. Then, O Kiriti, it holds firmly in its clasp the air which fills the cavity below the heart.

230. The fire arising from it spreads upwards and downwards and begins to consume the flesh.

231. Not only does it do this, however, but it consumes the fleshy tissue of the heart also.

232. It attacks the palms of the hands and the soles of the feet, penetrates the upper parts and passing through them it searches out the joints of the limbs.

233. It does not leave its place in the lower body but draws the vitality from the nails, and cleansing the skin causes it to cleave to the bones.

234. It cleanses the hollow of the bones, scours the inner recesses of the heart and withers the hair of the body.

235. It drains the ocean of the seven bodily humours, parches the whole of the body and brings about a state of intense heat.

236. The air which passes twelve inches out of the two nostrils is perforce again inhaled.

237. Then the exhaled breath is drawn upward and the inhaled breath downward, their meeting being prevented by the petals of the psychic centres.[14]

238. Otherwise the two would intermingle, but Kundalini would be displeased at this and would say, 'Go back! What are you doing here?'

239. Arjuna, listen! All the earthly matter is entirely consumed and the watery element dried up.

240. When these two elements have been consumed, Kundalini is fully satisfied and being pacified remains close to the sushumna.

241. The poison which in its satisfaction it sends forth from its mouth is the nectar by which vitality is sustained.

242. This fire rises from within, but when it begins to cool down both internally and externally the limbs regain the strength which they had lost.

243. The arteries are blocked, the nine types of vital air disappear and the functions of the body cease.

244. The ida and pingala arteries merge into one, the three knots are loosened, and the six petals of the psychic centre [at the spleen] open out.

245. Then the two breaths, thought of as the sun and the moon, cannot even cause the flame of a lamp to flicker.

246. The energy of mental activity dies down and the sense of smell which remains in the nose enters the sushumna and joins the Kundalini.

247. Slowly from above the reservoir of the moon-nectar pours itself into the mouth of the Kundalini, turning downwards on one side.

248. This nectar fills the passages and circulates throughout the whole body and together with the life-force is absorbed in it.

249. As in a heated mould the melted wax pours out [when molten metal is poured in], and only the metal shape remains, having taken on the form of the mould.

250. so is beauty incarnated in the shape of the body, covered over by a veil of skin.

251. As the sun remains concealed under a veil of clouds, but when they pass its light is beyond bounds,

252. so the dried surface of the skin flakes off as the husks are shed from grain.

253. The beauty of the limbs seems like natural marble or the sprouting of seed-jewels,

254. as if the lovely hues of the evening sky were transferred to the body, or an image were fashioned from an inner radiance of the spirit,

255. which, when it is seen, is like the richness of turmeric moulded from the essence of nectar; it seems to me to be the very incarnation of peace;

256. as if it were made of the colours in a picture of joy, the

very form of heavenly bliss or growing saplings of the tree of desire.

257. [It may be likened to] a bud of the golden champak tree, or an image of nectar, or a ripe plantation of tenderness;

258. the disc of the moon saturated with the moisture of the sharada season or splendour itself incarnate seated in this yogic posture.

259. So appears the body [of the yogi] when Kundalini has drunk of the nectar, and even the god of death is afraid to look at it.

260. Old age vanishes, the knot of youth is loosened, and the lost bloom of childhood reappears.

261. Whatever his age, the word 'youth' should be interpreted as 'strength', such is his incomparable fortitude.[15]

262. Just as the ever new jewel-buds open on the boughs of a tree of gold, fine new finger-nails grow;

263. new teeth appear, very small, set like rows of diamonds on each side.

264. Over the whole body tiny new hairs spring forth like small splinters of rubies.

265. The palms of hands and feet are as red lotus flowers and in the eyes there shines an indescribable lustre.

266. As the shell of an oyster no longer holds the pearl when it is fully developed and it bursts open at the joint with the force of its growth,

267. so the sight, which strives to pass outwards when it cannot be held within the eye lids, embraces the whole heavens, even with half-open eyes.

268. Listen, though the body has the appearance of gold, yet it has the lightness of air, for no earthly or watery particles remain in it.

269. The yogi can then see beyond all oceans, hear the thoughts of the heavens and read the mind of the ant.

270. He rides on the horses of the winds, walks on the surface of the water, though his feet do not touch it, and in such ways he acquires many super-human powers.

271. Hear this. Grasping prana by the hand, ascending the stairway of the ether, Kundalini enters the heart by the steps of the middle artery.

272. She is the Mother of the worlds, the glory of the empire of the soul, who gives shelter to tender sprouts of the seed of the universe,

273. the phallic symbol of the formless Brahma, the containing vessel of Shiva, the supreme soul, and the true source of the life breath.

274. When the young Kundalini enters the heart, the force-centre there is awakened and sounds are heard.

275. They are faintly heard by the consciousness of pure reason, which is attached to the power of Kundalini.

276. In the volume of that sound lie pictured in the form of the sacred syllable the four divisions of speech.[16]

277. This has to be experienced to be understood, but how can it be imagined? Therefore we cannot know what are the sources of this sound.

278. O Arjuna, one thing I have forgotten to tell thee; so long as the air exists the sound arises in the etheric space and so vibrates.

279. That etheric space reverberates with the thunder of this sound, and the windows of the crown centre burst suddenly open.

280. Listen; here exists still another great space in the form of a lotus bud, where consciousness seems to be appearing.

281. In the innermost cavity of the heart the divine Kundalini lays out before consciousness the feast of her own lustre.

282. She offers a morsel of food, dressed with the green vegetable of reason, in which no trace of duality is visible.

283. Her brilliance then vanishes and is transformed into the life-force. How can I describe its appearance?

284. It is like an image formed out of air and the golden cloth in which it was wrapped has been withdrawn.

285. Like a flame which, coming into contact with the air, flickers out, or like a streak of lightning which flashes across the sky and instantly disappears.

286. It appears as a necklet of gold as far as the lotus-like heart centre, or a fountain of brilliant light.

287. On entering the hollow of the heart, it loses its separateness and is merged into the power dwelling within it.

288. Then though it is called power, yet it should be known as the life-force and nāda, bindu and kalā and jyoti became imperceptible.[16]

289. Control of the mind, restraint of the breath and inclinations towards meditation are of little consequence.

290. To think this thought or reject it, such an idea is now irrelevant. The subtle elements are clearly destroyed.

291. 'One body devours another.' This is the secret of the teaching of Nātha, but it has now been revealed by Shri Vishnu.[17]

292. Imagining my hearers to be customers, I have untied the bundle of that secret and opened out before them the folded sheet of the inner meaning of these wares.

XV. *The yogin of subdued mind, ever keeping himself thus harmonized, attains to peace, the supreme nirvāṇa, which abides in Me.*

293. Listen! When the Kundalini loses its lustre, the gross form of the body disappears and its is no longer visible to physical sight.

294. In reality it is the same body, and is seen to possess the same limbs, yet it looks as if it were moulded out of air.

295. Like the inner stalk of a plantain tree standing erect divested of its sheath or as limbs fashioned from the ether.

296. When such is the condition of the body the yogi seems to be a spirit; when this happens it seems like a miracle to those still in the body.

297. See! As the adept walks he leaves psychic powers in the train of his footsteps.

298. But we are not concerned with these; O Arjuna, bear in mind that the three grosser elements of the body have disappeared with the body itself.

299. The water dissolves the soil, the light absorbs the water, and in the heart centre the vital air consumes the light.

300. It alone is left, but it continues in the form of the body and after a time it even is merged into etheric space.

301. Then the word Kundalini loses its significance, and the appropriate name is Māruti, but the force remains until it is absorbed into Shiva.[18]

302. Now it leaves the heart centre, breaks through the end of the sushumna artery and enters the space in the roof of the mouth.

303. Forthwith, climbing upon the back of the sacred syllable, it passes beyond the form of speech called pashyanti.[19]

304. Thereupon, as rivers flow into the ocean, [the subtle elements] enter into the space of the brow centre symbolized by the ardhamātrā of the sacred syllable.[20]

305. After settling in the Brahma centre, it reaches out with the arms of its consciousness of unity with the Self and embraces the image of the Supreme.

306. At that moment the veil of the five elements is rent asunder and the individual self and the supreme Self are united; then all, including etheric space, is absorbed in that union.

307. As water from the ocean is drawn up into the clouds and pours down again into itself as rain,

308. So the Self, having lived in bodily form, enters into the supreme Self. Such, O Pāndava, is this union.

309. There even remains no such thought as to whether it is separate or whether it is indeed one with the supreme Self.

310. As it happens that space merges into space, so is this state of union realized by experience and the yogi remains in it.

311. It would be impossible for words to describe this state nor can even discuss it in conversation.

312. O Arjuna, this being so, anyone who is ambitious enough to express an opinion on this, even vaikhari, is far from this state.[21]

313. The 'm' of the sacred syllable cannot enter the space behind the brow, for the life-force moving alone fails to reach that etheric space.

314. As soon as it appears there the power of speech vanishes, whilst the etheric space is destroyed.

315. How can speech plumb the depths of the great void of the Supreme, where there is no place even for the ether?

316. Therefore it is a threefold truth that this could neither be expressed in words nor be heard by the ear.

317. If by good fortune self-realization can be attained through experience, then one should strive to remain in it.

318. Beyond this there is no more to know. So then, O Arjuna, let this be enough; there would be no purpose in saying more.

319. In this state language withdraws, imagination dies away and not even the wind of thought can enter.

320. This is the highest principle, without beginning and beyond measure, the beauty of the supra-mental state and the dawning of the experience of the soul's oneness with Brahma,

321. the end of all form, the goal of the search for liberation, that in which beginning and end merge into one.

322. It is the root of the universe, the fruit of the tree of yoga, the very essence of bliss.

323. It is the seed of the subtle elements, the light from which emanates the sun; O Pārtha, it is My own nature.

324. This four-armed one has manifested itself in its splendour, seeing that the godless have persecuted the multitudes of My devotees.

325. Those who persevere unswervingly towards the goal enjoy the indescribable bliss of being one with the Self.

326. They who follow the method prescribed by Me, even with their bodies, having purified themselves, reach a state comparable to Mine.

327. It seems as though the liquid of the supreme Self had been poured into the mould of their bodies.

328. If this realization were to shine from the inner Self, the whole universe would be overshadowed by it. Whereupon Arjuna said, Verily it is so.

329. For, O Lord, the method described by Thee, being the way to attainment, leads surely to the goal,

330. and they who steadfastly tread this path unfailingly attain to union with Brahma. This I have understood from Thy teaching.

331. O Lord, even to hear this teaching brings enlightenment to the mind; how then could the realization of it not lead to union with the Self?

332. There is no fault in this; but listen for a moment, I pray Thee, O Krishna, to what I say.

333. O Krishna, I appreciate the yoga Thou hast taught; but for lack of worthiness I am unable to practise it.

334. If with my whole heart I gladly follow this path successfully, I will willingly practise this way.

335. Otherwise, if I am unable to do as the Lord commands me, I would ask Thee what can be done without such worthiness.

336. Impelled by such a desire I must question Thee further. Therefore, O Lord, be pleased to listen attentively to my words.

337. I have listened patiently to the method described by Thee. If a man who wishes practises this can he succeed in it?

338. Or is there nothing that can be gained without worthiness? Thereupon Shri Krishna said, O Arjuna, what is this thou askest?

339. This question relates to the ultimate; but even in the case of ordinary tasks is it possible to succeed without adequate ability?

340. Whether a man has this fitness or not can only be known by his success; but what is done by a man who is worthy bears fruit from the beginning.

341. Here nothing can be obtained without effort; besides, is there any great store [from which worthiness can be easily drawn]?

342. Would not a man who is inclined to dispassion and restrains his bodily needs be regarded as worthy for this purpose?

343. By this means thou also mayest become worthy. In such a way did the Lord remove the difficulty in Arjuna's mind at this time.

344. Again, he said, O Pārtha the gist of this teaching is that an undisciplined man is entirely unfit for this work.

345. He is not fit for the practice of yoga who is in bondage to his palate or spends his life in sleep.

346. or if he too rigidly restricts his hunger and thirst and rejects all food;

347. or refuses to sleep, and plays the role of obstinacy incarnate; his body will not be his own, so how can he possibly practise yoga?

348. Therefore both excessive enjoyment of sensual pleasures and the complete abstention from them, are to be avoided.

> XVI. *Verily, yoga is not for him who eats too much or abstains too much from eating. It is not for him, O Arjuna, who sleeps too much or keeps awake too much.*
>
> XVII. *For the man who is temperate in food and recreation, who is restrained in his actions, whose sleep and waking are regulated there ensues discipline which destroys all sorrow.*

349. Sufficient food should be taken, but with proper restraint, and all actions performed in the same way.

350. Speech should be moderated, walking should be steady, the need for regular sleep respected.

351. When waking occurs it should be quiet; thereby the humours of the body will be balanced and tranquil.

352. When the sense organs are satisfied in this way with moderation and regularity, happiness of mind increases.

> XVIII. *When the disciplined mind is established in the Self alone, liberated from all desires, then is a man said to be harmonized.*

353. The more the outward discipline is established, the greater the inner happiness and then without much effort yoga may be practised.

354. As when a man's good fortune is in the ascendant, diligence is incidental, all manner of prosperity will come to him unsought,

355. so the disciplined man may easily turn to yogic practice; his experience will ripen into Self-realization.

356. Therefore, O Arjuna, that fortunate one who has discipline, bears the royal adornment of the final beatitude.

357. One in whom there is this holy confluence in the union of moderation and yogic practice, and whose mind is resolved ever to remain in this holy place,[22]

> XIX. *As a lamp in a windless place does not flicker, to such is likened the yogi of subdued thought who practises union with the Self [or discipline of himself].*

358. may be said to be harmonized in yoga; moreover, one characteristic of such a man is that his mind is like a lamp set in a windless place.

359. Knowing thy desire, I will now tell thee something more. Listen carefully.

360. For thou art eager to know yoga and yet thou carest not to practise it. Does thou fear the difficulty of it?

361. Do not let your mind be troubled thus, O Pārtha. The wicked senses try in vain to frighten men.

362. Does not the tongue regard medicine as an enemy, when, in reality, it steadies the life which is coming to an end?

> XX. *That in which thought is at rest, restrained by the practice of concentration, that in which he beholds the Self through the self and rejoices in the Self;*

> XXI. *That in which he finds this supreme delight, perceived by the intelligence and beyond the reach of the senses,*

wherein established, he no longer falls away from the truth;

363. Similarly that wich is really conducive to our welfare is painful. Apart from this is there anything as easy as yoga?
364. Therefore the senses may be curbed by the resolute practice of yogic posture of which I have spoken to thee.
365. Moreover, when in this manner the senses have been restrained, the mind reaches out to meet the Self.
366. It turns away [from sense objects] and begins to look within its own self; at once it recognises its own true nature [saying], 'I am the Self'.
367. When this recognition takes place, it seats itself on the imperial throne of supreme bliss, and the mind becomes absorbed in this union.

XXII. *That which, on obtaining, a man thinks that there is no greater gain beyond it, established wherein he is not shaken even by the heaviest sorrow,*

368. Then if mountains of bodily trouble greater even than Mount Meru should oppress such a man, his mind would in no way be crushed by their weight.
369. Or if he should be struck by weapons, or burnt by fire, his mind, absorbed in the bliss of the Self, is in no way disturbed.
370. Having entered into the Self, he is unaware of the body, in the fullness of joy he even forgets it.

XXIII. *Let that be known by the name of yoga, this separation from union with pain. This yoga should be practised with determination, with heart undismayed.*

371. Because of the sweetness of this joy, the mind which is held in the grip of worldly life, gives up all desire.
372. This beauty of yoga, this kingdom of contentment for which wisdom is essential,
373. must be clearly seen by the mind through the practice of yoga, and seeing it the seer becomes transformed into it.

XXIV. *Abandoning without exception all desires born of [selfish] will, restraining with the mind all the senses on every side;*

374. So, Beloved, in one sense this yoga is easy to practise. If desire experiences sorrow at the death of her children

375. when she learns that the power of sense objects has been destroyed, and perceives that the senses have been subdued, she dies of a broken heart.

376. Strive for such dispassion, and then the pilgrimage of desire is finished and pure reason dwells in happiness in the mansion of courage.

> XXV. *Let him gain little by little tranquillity by means of reason controlled by steadiness and having fixed the mind on the Self, let him not think of anything [else].*

> XXVI. *Whatsoever makes the wavering and unsteady mind wander away let him restrain and bring it back to the control of the Self alone.*

377. If reason, supported by steadfastness, slowly leads the mind by the pathway of Self-realization to the temple of the Self, and installs it there,

378. this is one way of attaining to the Self; consider this, but should it be found impracticable, there is still another easy method; listen.

379. A vow should be taken to adhere to a resolute determination and not to depart from it.

380. If by this means the mind can be steadied, then the work will be easy. If not, it may be allowed to move freely.

381. Then, wherever it goes, the resolution will bring it back, and the steadiness will be restored.

> XXVII. *For supreme happiness comes to the yogin whose mind is peaceful, whose passions are at rest, who is stainless and has become one with God.*

382. Thus in course of time it will acquire steadiness and will easily approach the Eternal.

383. On beholding THAT it will become one with it, duality will be lost in non-duality, and the universe will become illuminated by the splendour of unity.

384. Just as the sky alone fills the universe when the clouds which seemed separate from it have melted away,

385. so also when the mind has become absorbed [in the divine consciousness] that alone is the all-pervasive essence. This result is easily obtainable in such a way.

386. Being utterly indifferent to the riches of imagination
many have experienced this simply acquired yogic
condition.

    XXVIII. *Thus making the self ever harmonized, the yogin,
who has put away sin, experiences easily the infinite bliss
of contact with the Eternal.*

387. With joy they have easily entered into the Eternal. As
salt cannot separate itself from water,

388. so they attain to union and then in the palace of oneness
with the Eternal and the illuminated festival of Supreme
Bliss is seen by the world.

389. This is [as difficult] as if one had to walk with one's legs
upon one's back. If this is not attainable, however, O
Arjuna, listen to another way.

    XXIX. *He whose self is harmonized by yoga sees the Self
abiding in all beings and all beings in the Self; everywhere
he sees the same.*

390. There it no doubt that I exist in all forms, and that
everything abides in Me.

391. Thus has everything been created, and the two [spirit
and matter] are intermingled. Thy reason should come to
understand this.

    XXX. *He who sees Me everywhere and sees all in Me;
I am not lost to him nor is he lost to Me.*

392. O Arjuna. Whoever through his conscious realization of
unity worships Me as one existing in all beings,

393. and who knows that notwithstanding the multiplicity of
beings there is no duality in their hearts and that My
essence pervades everything everywhere,

394. it is irrelevant to say that he and I are one. Do not speak
thus, O Arjuna, for I am indeed he.

395. As there is oneness between a lamp and its light, so is he
in Me and I in him.

396. As wetness is essentially one with water, space and ether
are coterminous, so a man has a body because it is infused
with My form.

    XXXI. *The yogin who established in oneness, worships
Me abiding in all beings, lives in Me, howsoever he may
be active.*

397. As the woven thread is one with the cloth, so, O Kiriti, he sees Me everywhere, one and the same.

398. Ornaments are fashioned in many shapes, yet there are not different kinds of gold; so it is with him who has attained to the rock-like stability of union.

399. He for whom the night [of delusion] has been followed by the daybreak of unity, is like a tree, whose leaves are many yet not all of these were planted as saplings.

400. What power can bind him, though he may be imprisoned in a body composed of the five elements who by his experience of Self-realization is equal to Me?

401. On account of this experience he is embraced by My all-pervasiveness, although he should not be called all-pervasive.

402. Now, though he has a body, he is not of the body. Can one express what is beyond the power of speech?

> XXXII. *He, O Arjuna, one who sees with equality everything in the image of his own self, whether in pleasure or in pain, is considered a perfect yogi.*

403. Let us leave this now. He who regards the whole of creation as similar to himself,

404. whose mind is no more aware of feelings of pleasure and pain, than of good and evil deeds,

405. sees all kinds of distinctions and all strange things as only the limbs of his own body.

406. But what need is there to specify? A man who has realized that he is one with everything in the universe,

407. although he has a body, and the world may consider him as being happy or unhappy, yet am I sure that he is indeed the Eternal.

408. Therefore, O Pāndava, strive to realize this oneness, to see the universe in thyself and thyself in the universe.

409. For this reason I tell thee repeatedly that there is no realization higher than the consciousness of unity.

Arjuna said:

> XXXIII. *This yoga declared by you to be the nature of equality [evenness of mind], O Madhusūdana [Kṛṣṇa], I see no stable foundation on account of restlessness.*

410. Thereupon Arjuna said, True, O Lord, prompted by Thy

kindness towards me, Thou hast explained this; but it is not sufficient for the nature of man's mind.

411. One cannot know the nature and extent of the mind; the three worlds are too small for its activities.

> xxxiv. *For the mind is very fickle, O Kṛṣṇa, it is impetuous, strong and obstinate. I think that it is as difficult to control as the wind.*

412. Could it ever happen that a monkey should practise meditation, or will the strong wind stop in its course when told to do so?

413. Will the mind which harasses the reason, shakes the resolution, and plays games with courage,

414. which deludes discrimination, disturbs contentment, and compels us, though we want to be still, to wander in every direction,

415. which becomes excited when it is curbed, and is even encouraged by control of the senses, [can such a mind] give up its own nature?

416. It can never happen that such a mind will ever remain stable and allow the Self to acquire equanimity.

The Blessed Lord said:

> xxxv. *Without doubt, O Mighty-armed [Arjuna], the mind is difficult to curb and restless but it can be controlled, O Son of Kuntī [Arjuna], by constant practice and by non-attachment.*

417. Then Shri Krishna said, Thou speakest truly; the mind is indeed of a fickle nature;

418. but if by the aid of dispassion it can be led into constant practice, in due course it will become stable.

419. For in this one respect it is good, that it frequents places familiar to it; therefore the delight of experience of the Self should be shown to it often.

> xxxvi. *Yoga is hard to attain, I agree, by one who is not self-controlled; but by the self-controlled it is attainable by striving through proper means.*

420. On the other hand it must be admitted that for those who are not dispassionate and who do not engage in

discipline the mind is hard to control. Do we not agree
on this?

421. But those who never practise self-restraint, in whose minds
there is no thought of dispassion and who are submerged in
the waters of sense-objects,

423. who during their lives have never been supported by the
practice of yoga, tell me, can the minds of such men ever
become stable?

424. Therefore begin the restraint of the mind by this method,
then how can that resolution fail to be achieved.

425. Is all the practice of yoga useless? Rather confess that
thou art unable to practise it.

426. If thou possess the strength of yoga, how can the mind
be restless? Cannot even all the primordial elements be
under our control?

Arjuna said:

> XXXVII. *One who cannot control himself though he has
> faith, with the mind wandering away from yoga, failing
> to attain perfection in yoga, which way does he go, O
> Kṛṣṇa?*
>
> XXXVIII. *Does he not perish like a rent cloud, O Mighty-
> armed [Kṛṣṇa], fallen from both and without any hold
> and bewildered in the path that leads to the Eternal?*
>
> XXXIX. *Thou shouldst dispel completely this my doubt,
> O Kṛṣṇa, for there is none else but Thyself who can
> destroy this doubt.*

427. At this Arjuna said, True, what Thou sayest, O Lord, is
right; the strength of the mind verily cannot be compared
with the power of yoga.

428. But what is that yoga? How can I know it? Even still
I have no idea of it; therefore, O Lord, I said that the
mind is uncontrollable.

429. For the first time in my life, O Purushottama, I have
heard of this yoga through Thy grace.

429. I have one other doubt, O Lord, and none but Thee is
able to resolve it.

430. So tell me, O Govinda, a man may strive to attain to
Self-realization through faith, but without any yogic
method;[23]

431. he leaves the village of the senses, and starts out on the road of earnestness, intending to reach the city of attainment to the Self.

432. But he does not reach Self-realization, neither can he retrace his steps, and at such a point the sun of his life sets.

433. As untimely clouds, thin as a veil, neither remain [in the sky] nor turn to rain,

434. so both ways are lost to such a man; his goal is far off, but also on account of his faith he loses his [former] state of not seeking for it.

435. If a man, though full of faith, [loses his goal] through delaying, is he entirely lost? What is his fate?

The Blessed Lord said:

XL. *O Pārtha [Arjuna], neither in this life nor hereafter is there destruction for him; for no one who does good, dear friend, ever treads the path of woe.*

436. Then Shri Krishna said, O Pārtha, is there any other goal than liberation possible for a man who is striving for deliverance?

437. One thing may happen, that for a time he may have to rest [from his efforts], but during that delay he may still enjoy happiness unattainable even by the gods.

438. Had he, however, made greater progress in the practice of yoga he would certainly have reached the consciousness of his unity with the Eternal before the end of his life.

439. As he did not make a sufficiently rapid advance, naturally he had to wait. There is no doubt that he will achieve deliverance eventually.

XLI. *Having attained to the world of the righteous and dwelt there for very many years, the man who has fallen away from yoga is again born in the house of such as are pure and prosperous.*

440. Hear how wonderful this is! Such a man easily finds the blessedness which is difficult [even for Indra] to attain to with a hundred sacrifices.

441. There he enjoys the wonderful but unprofitable pleasures [of that world] but his mind becomes satiated with them.

442. Consequently he is reborn into the world of mortals, but
in a family which is the mother of all righteousness and
[as it were], will grow as a shoot in a prosperous field.

443. In a family which follows the path of rectitude, speaks
pure truth, and considers whatever is to be done in the
light of the scriptures,

444. in which the Veda is the living god, whose only concern
is the performance of its own proper duty, and for whom
the discrimination between good and evil is the only
counsellor,

445. in a family where the consort of Vishnu takes thought
for its welfare, and prosperity is the presiding goddess.

446. A man fallen from yoga is reborn into a family possessing
such merit and the harvest of all happiness.

> XLII. *Or he may be born in the family of yogins who are
> endowed with wisdom. For such a birth as this is more
> difficult to obtain in the world.*

> XLIII. *There he regains the [mental] impressions [of union
> with the Divine] which he had developed in his previous
> life and with this [as the starting point] he strives again
> for perfection, O Joy of the Kurus [Arjuna].*

447. Or into [a family] which burns the sacrificial fire of
wisdom, is versed in the knowledge of the Eternal and
is heir to the land of the highest bliss;

448. who, seated on the throne of the highest truths, rules over
three worlds, and who are as birds singing in the garden
of contentment;

449. who sit in the chief place of the city of discrimination
[enjoying] the fruit [in the form of Brahma]. In the
family of such yogis he may be born.

450. In outer form he may appear small, but as the light
precedes the rising of the sun, so in him there appears
the dawning of Self-knowledge.

451. Without waiting to attain this state, or reaching mature
age, already in youth he became possessed of all knowledge.

452. With the acquirement of such a perfected intellect, his
mind freely gives forth learning, and from his lips are
revealed all branches of knowledge.

453. He enters into such a birth as the gods in heaven crave
for, constantly performing sacrifices, repeating prayers,

454. and for which the immortal ones become bards and sing
the praises of this mortal world. So, O Pārtha, is such a
one reborn.

> XLIV. *By his former practice, he is carried on irresistibly.
> Even the seeker after the knowledge of yoga goes beyond
> the Vedic rule.*

455. The pure reason which was his when he left his former
life, he obtains anew in full measure in this life.
456. As a fortunate man who is born feet first could easily see,
with an application of magic ointment, treasures of the
lower world,
457. so the intellect of such a man grasps without effort the
most abstruse problems, knowledge which ordinarily may
only be gained by the aid of the guru.
458. The powerful senses are under the control of his mind,
the mind becomes one with the vital air, while that begins
to mingle with the etheric space.
459. We do not know how this comes about that owing to past
practice, meditation itself seeks out the house of his mind.
460. Know that [such a man] is the presiding deity of yoga, the
glory of the beginning of yoga practice, the incarnation
of the experience of perfection in yoga.
461. [He is] that by which worldly happiness is measured, the
lamp which reveals the whole sum of eight-fold yoga. As
if fragrance were to take on the form of a sandal wood
tree,
462. so he appears to be the embodiment of contentment, or
one drawn out from the great store of those who have
reached perfection. To such a condition the seeker after
yoga seems to have risen.

> XLV. *But the yogi who strives with assiduity, cleansed of
> all sins, perfecting himself through many lives, then attains
> to the highest goal.*

463. After millions of years and thousands of births, he arrives
at the shore of Self-realization.
464. Thus all means to the end come naturally to him, and
he sits on the very throne of discrimination.
465. Then with the speed of thought itself even discrimination
is left behind, and he becomes one with that which is
beyond thought.

466. The cloud in the form of the mind vanishes, the air loses its very nature, and is absorbed into itself.

467. He enjoys indescribable bliss, such that the sacred syllable lowers its head, and language retreats before him.

478. Thus he becomes the embodiment of the state of Brahma, that which promotes all activity, and is indeed the very form of the Formless.

469. During many past lives he has swept away the mass of confusion, and the moment of his birth is the final moment of his marriage [with Brahma],

470. and entering into non-duality he becomes wedded with the Eternal, as the clouds merge into the sky.

471. So while still in the body, he becomes one with the Eternal, from which the universe proceeds and into which it will again be absorbed.

> XLVI. *The yogin is greater than the ascetic; he is considered to be greater than the man of knowledge, greater than the man of ritual works, therefore do thou become a yogin, O Arjuna.*

472. Men of devotion, supported by the arm of fortitude, plunge into the sixfold course of action in the hope of attaining to this union,

473. for which very purpose the wise, clad in the armour of knowledge, fight with worldly existence in the battle-field of life,

474. or, longing earnestly for which ascetics cling fast, un-supported, to the steep precipice of the fortress of penance,

475. which is the object of worship for all worshippers, the sacrificial objects of those who sacrifice in short, that which is ever to be venerated by all,

476. which is the final goal, that highest truth which is to be attained to by all seekers, the Eternal, which he himself becomes.

477. Therefore he is respected by all men of action, worthy to be known by the wise, the highest lord among ascetics.

478. He whose whole mental activity is directed towards the union of the self with the Self [as of the confluence of two rivers], rises to greatness even while still in the body.

479. Therefore, O Son of Pāndu, I always say to thee, Be thou a yogi with all thy heart.

XLVII. *And of all yogins, he who full of faith worships Me, with his inner Self abiding in Me, him I hold to be the most attuned [to Me in Yoga].*

480. O Beloved, know that the man who is called a yogi is the god of the gods, My greatest joy, My very life.

481. To such a man, worshipper, worship and the object of worship, [these three] are always, through experience of union, Myself.

482. Then it is certain, O Consort of Subhadrā, that the love existing between him and Me cannot be described in words.

483. Sanjaya said, Thus spoke [Krishna] who is [to his devotees] as the moon to the chakora bird, the only lord of the three worlds, the ocean of all virtues.

484. Then the Lord of the Yadus realized that Pārtha's eagerness to hear more of this matter had become twice as strong as before.[24]

485. So He was happier in His mind for His words had found a mirror [of response]; therefore He will now joyfully expound everything.

486. This subject will be treated in the following chapter, in which the sentiment of tranquillity will be explained and in which the seeds of this knowledge will be loosened for the shoots to come forth.

487. With showers of the quality of purity the soil of the spiritual sowing ground in the minds of the wise has been prepared.

489. It has been made ready for sowing by the attentiveness [of the hearers] precious as gold, and now the disciple of Nivritti is eager to sow the seed.

489. Jnānadeva says, Truly a wish has been fulfilled by my guru, for he has laid his hand on my head and the seeds of knowledge have been sown.

490. So whatever is spoken by my lips will be acceptable to the hearts of the good. But let that be; I must now tell of what has been taught by Shriranga.

491. It must be heard with the ear of the mind, the words must be seen with the eye of the intellect, and thus mutual profit will be derived.

492. These words must be embraced in the heart with the arms of attention and then they will delight the minds of the good.

493. These words will being peace of mind, revive the sense of
purpose and bring immeasurable joy into the soul.

494. Now Mukunda will joyfully converse with Arjuna. That
I will now recount in the Ovi metre.[25]

*In the Upanishad of the Bhagavadgitā, the science of the Absolute,
the scripture of Yoga and the dialogue between Shri Krishna and
Arjuna, this is the sixth chapter called the Yoga of Meditation.*

NOTES

1. *Shri Ranga.* One of the names of Krishna.

2. *yogic postures.* Formal postures are assumed in meditation in the
practise of yogic disciplines. There follow here various particulars of
such postures, or 'āsanas', used figuratively to describe the religious
path of the yogi. See *The Serpent Power*, Avalon, for these, and
for the psychic centres.

3. *pratyāhāra.* The name given to a particular exercise in restraining
the breath and various organs of the body.

4. *samādhi.* The eighth and highest stage of development in yogic
practice, leading to union with the Supreme Spirit; the final stage
in renunciation.

5. *the parrot and the pipe.* It was a practice in entrapping parrots to
use the method of a revolving pipe. The parrot feels that it is
bound to the pipe and clings more firmly to it, making it easier for
it to be caught.

6. *Parabrahma.* The highest Brahma, the Absolute.

7. *Janārdana.* One of the names of Krishna.

8. *Devaki* The mother of Krishna.
Yashodā. The nurse of Krishna in childhood.

9. *Indra.* The Lord of all the gods.

10. *Kusha grass.* A species of grass regarded as sacred.

11. *jālāndhara.* The name of a particular yogic posture.

12. *odhiyāna.* Another yogic posture.

13. *Kundalini.* The coiled female serpent seated at the base of the
spine and channel of psychic energy which, when activated through
yogic practices, passes upwards through the psychic centres. See
The Serpent Power, Avalon.

14. *petals of the psychic centres.* In the psychic system each centre is
represented by a lotus of a certain number of petals of which the
highest centre has one thousand. See Avalon, *The Serpent Power*.

15. *'youth' and 'strength'.* Here there is a pun in the original Marāthi
text; the word 'bāla' means 'youth' or 'child', while 'bala' means
strength'.

16. *four divisions of speech.* These divisions are as follows:

parā vāc	The highest reality, all-embracing Logos in which no individual sound or concept is manifest,
pashyanti vāc	A first step towards manifestation,
madhyamā vāc	Phonological and semantic concepts,
vaikhari vāc	Articulate speech.

17. *Nātha.* A sect of the Hindus in Mahārāshtra. See Introduction. *Vishnu.* The Hindu god who is the 'preserver'. Contrast Shiva, the destroyer. See note Ch. I. 32. Vaikuntha.

18. *Māruti.* The 'vital air'; the wind. A special name given to Kundalini in certain contexts.

19. *pashyanti.* See note 16, above.

20. *ardhamātra* The 'half-syllable', that is, the last element in the word Om, which is not a full consonant in the Sanskrit script but a nasal sound in speech which is written as a 'half consonant' and can be written in roman as -m. This is uttered by holding the nasal resonance of 'm' without releasing the consonant by opening the lips.

21. *vaikhari.* See note 16 above.

22. *Prayāga.* A holy place; specifically, Allahabad, at the confluence of the rivers Ganges and Jamna.

23. *Govinda.* One of the names of Krishna.

24. *Yadunātha.* Lord of the race of Yadu, an ancient king: an epithet of Krishna.

25. *Mukunda.* Another of the names of Krishna. *Ovi.* The metre in which the *Jnāneshvari* is written. See Introduction.

CHAPTER VII

The Blessed Lord said:

I. Hear then, O Pārtha [Arjuna], how practising yoga, with the mind clinging to Me, with Me as thy refuge, thou shalt know Me in full, without any doubt.

II. I will declare to thee in full this wisdom, together with knowledge by knowing which there shall remain nothing more to be known.

1. Hear now! Then Shri Ananta said to Arjuna, Indeed thou hast now become perfected in yoga.
2. Now I will declare to thee the wisdom together with practical knowledge, by means of which thou shalt know Me fully, as a jewel that is lying in the palm of the hand.
3. Shouldst thou sincerely ask what may be the use here of worldly knowledge, I would answer that it must first of all be acquired.
4. Then, when true wisdom is gained, consciousness closes its eyes, just as a boat moored to the shore does not move.
5. So, where the personal consciousness cannot enter, thought withdraws and the skill of logical reasoning is ineffective.
6. There is wisdom, O Arjuna; on the other hand knowledge of worldly affairs is practical knowledge, and the apparent sense of reality in it is in truth ignorance; distinguish these three.
7. Now, how ignorance can be entirely dispelled, worldly knowledge burnt up, and wisdom, in its real nature, made manifest,
8. that deep secret will now be revealed, by which, being understood even a little, many longings of the mind will be satisfied.
9. As a result of this the voice of the speaker ceases, the

longing of the hearer vanishes, and there remain no distinctions such as great and small.

> III. *Among thousands of men scarcely one strives for perfection, and of those who strive and succeed, scarcely one knows Me in truth.*

10. Among thousands, O Beloved, rarely is there one who has an earnest desire for it, and among these, hardly one attains to a knowledge of it.
11. As in the world full of men an army of thousands is formed of chosen warriors, O Arjuna,
12. and as from amongst them all, when the weapons strike them down in battle one warrior alone is seated on the throne of victory,
13. so also thousands enter the great waters of the eager search but scarcely one is able to reach the further shore of attainment.
14. Therefore, O Beloved, this is no ordinary matter, but is of great import. It will be explained in due course. Now let us return to the present subject.

> IV. *Earth, water, fire, air, ether, mind, understanding and self-sense, this is the eightfold division of My nature.*

15. O Conqueror of wealth, listen! As reflections are shadows of our own bodies, so are divine intelligence and other primary elements shadows of Myself.
16. It is called My nature, and is eightfold in its parts, and the three worlds are emanations from it.
17. If thou desirest to know what these eight divisions are, listen to this explanation:
18. Water, fire, air, earth, ether, mind, reason and individuality, these are the eight parts.

> V. *This is My lower nature: know My other and higher nature which is the soul, by which this world is upheld, O Mighty-armed [Arjuna].*

19. The equilibrium of this eightfold Matter is My higher nature, O Pārtha, and is called the life-element.
20. It is this which quickens dead matter, awakens consciousness, and is that which causes the mind to feel sorrow and delusion.

21. By association with awareness reason acquires discrimination and by the skill of its principle of individuality the world is upheld.

> VI. *Know that all beings have their birth in this. I am the origin of all this world and of its dissolution as well.*

22. When the higher nature by its own innate tendency intermingles with the lower, the creation of beings takes place.
23. The fourfold imprint of form begins spontaneously; the value is the same, but the classes are various.[1]
24. Millions of species are formed with innumerable subdivisions, and the store-house of space can hardly contain them; the womb of the original void is filled with these types, as coins in a treasure-house.
25. From the five elements many coins of the same kind are minted and the divine nature alone can keep the tally of their number.
26. The coins which she produces are multiplied and then melted down. [In the time of their circulation] they are occupied with the commerce of good and evil deeds.
27. Let us leave that metaphor; I will explain to thee clearly. It is nature who creates the multitude of name and form,
28. and this divine nature is reflected in Me, none other. I am therefore the beginning and end of the universe.

> VII. *There is nothing whatever that is higher than I, O Winner of wealth [Arjuna]. All that is here is strung on Me as rows of gems on a string.*

29. The universe is like a mirage of which on closer observation, the cause is found to be the sun and not its rays;
30. similarly, O Kiriti, when the created world, emanating from this higher nature vanishes, it will be found that I am the only reality.
31. So whatsoever is born, exists and disappears, rests wholly in Me. The universe is held by Me as gems are threaded on a string.

> VIII. *I am taste in the waters, O Son of Kuntī [Arjuna], I am the light in the moon and the sun. I am the syllable Aum in all the Vedas; I am the sound in ether and manhood in men.*

32. Know therefore that, I am the moisture in water, the touch of the wind and the radiance in the sun and moon.
33. I am also that natural pure fragrance of the earth, the sound in the heavens and the sacred word in the Vedas.
34. I must be thought of as the humanity in man, the principle of individuality, and the essence of human activity. This truth I declare to thee.
35. The word "fire" is the outward covering of the inward light; when this is removed, the light is Myself.
36. All creatures born in their varied species in the three worlds are sustained by the food necessary for each.
37. Some live on air, others on green herbs, others on other food or on water.
38. These various forms of nourishment, differing according to the nature of each creature, are all permeated with My undivided life.
39. The principle which at the beginning of time diffuses itself through the germinating activity of space and at the end engulfs the letters of the sacred syllable,

40. which, so long as creation continues, seems to exist in the form of the universe, but which in the dissolution of it becomes formless,
41. is indeed Myself, eternally existent, the seed of the universe. This is now revealed to thee,
42. and when it is made clear to thee and through discrimination thou makest it thy own, thou wilt understand its highest purpose.
43. But to leave this digression, briefly, this nature of Mine is the austerity in the ascetic,
44. I am the enduring strength of the strong, the intellect of those endowed with intelligence;

45. I am desire in all creatures, said Krishna, that desire through which religion becomes the highest aspiration.

46. This desire, through the channel of feeling, generally follows the path of the senses but is not allowed to work against religion.

47. Leaving then the wrong road of prohibited actions it goes onward by the path of prescribed duties, and travels with the help of the torch of discipline.

48. When desire follows the true direction, duty is fulfilled, and a man participates in worldly life with the freedom obtained at the holy place of liberation.

49. Desire causes the creeper of the whole created nature to spread on the arbour of the greatness of the Vedas until it sends forth new foliage, with the fruits of action, and reaches the Absolute.

50. Such restrained desire, the source of all created objects am I, says the Father of yogis.

51. It is not possible to describe this in detail, thou shouldst know that all created objects are evolved from Me.

> XII. *And whatever states of being there may be, be they harmonious [sāttvika], passionate [rajasa], slothful [tamasa]—know thou that they are all from Me alone. I am not in them, they are in Me.*

52. Every condition of the mind, whether pure, active or slothful, is born of My nature; thou shouldst realize this.

53. Though evolved from My nature, I am not in them any more than the waking consciousness is lost while one is in deep sleep.

54. Although a seed may be solid with compressed sap yet through its shoots it will become wood;

55. but canst thou say that there is actually any seed quality in the wood? So I am not in these varying states, though I may appear to be subject to modification.

56. Indeed, clouds form in the sky, but the sky is not in the clouds; or [we can say that] there is water in the clouds and yet the clouds are not in the water.

57. Lightning, born of the agitation of water, flashes brilliantly, but is there any water in that flash of lightning?

58. Smoke emerges from the fire, but there is no fire in the smoke; so all creatures have emanated from Me, yet I am not in them.

XIII. *Deluded by these threefold modes of natures [guṇas]
this whole world does not recognize Me who am above
them and imperishable.*

59. Water is covered by the weeds growing in it, or the sky
becomes veiled in masses of useless clouds;

60. we may say that a dream is false, but during sleep it
appears to be a reality; during that time are we aware
of it as a dream?

61. Is it not so that the eye is deprived of its sight when it is
veiled by a cataract?

62. So also all this is a reflection of Me, the shadow of the three
qualities has spread itself over Me as if with a screen.

63. Therefore My creatures do not know Me. Though they are
Mine, they are not one with Me, as pearls born of the water
do not melt in it.

64. If a pot is made out of earth, and is broken up again
immediately it becomes one with the earth; if however
it be baked in the fire it remains separated from it.

65. So indeed all creatures are parts of Me, but on account of
the great illusion, they have acquired the state of individuality.

XIV. *This divine māyā of Mine, consisting of the qualities,
is hard to overcome. But those who take refuge in Me alone
cross beyond it.*

66. O Conqueror of wealth, how is it possible to enter into
union with Me, having passed over the great river of
illusion?

67. First there gushes out from the rocky side of the mountain
of Brahma a stream in the form of desire, and from that
the great elements emerge in small bubbles.

68. Then in the manifestation of the created world it flows on,
and gathering speed with time, it overflows the high
banks of activity and cessation from activity.

69. With showers of rain from the clouds in the form of the
basic qualities, the great flood of delusion swells the stream
and it sweeps away the cities of restraint and self-control.

70. Upon its surface swirl the whirlpools of hate, and the cross
currents of envy, and in it flash the great fish of error and
many sins.

71. In its course too are eddies of worldly affairs, and the

rapids of action and wrong action on which the weeds of pleasure and pain are swept along.

72. On the island of sexual love dash the billows of sexual desire and masses of foam in the form of selves are cast up on it.

73. In the stream of egoism spouts of the threefold infatuation are thrown out and waves of sense-objects leap forth.[2]

74. The rise and fall of the flood of day and night causes the great depths of birth and death in which the bubbles of the five elements come and go [in the form of bodies].

75. The fishes of infatuation and delusion swallow the bait of courage and swirling eddies of ignorance are formed.

76. In the turbid water of perplexity, they are sunk in the mire of the expectation of happiness and heaven resounds with the gurgling of passion.

77. The streams of the quality of darkness are powerful, the stillness of the waters of purity is deep. In short, this river of illusion is difficult to cross over.

78. With the constant gushing out of the waves of birth and death even the bastions of the highest heaven collapse and the rocks of the universe crash down under the blows.

79. This terrible deluge of illusion has not yet subsided; who is there who can cross over it?

80. Those who have plunged into this river, in order to swim across with the arm of his own intellect, have been lost; some have been sucked down into the deep pool of knowledge by their own pride.

81. Others who embarked on the raft of the Vedas, with stones of egoism fastened to them, were swallowed up by the fish of infatuation.

82. Some again girded up their loins with the vigour of youth, and seeking the support of the god of love, have been eaten by the crocodile of sensual pleasure.

83. Then caught in the net of confusion, on the waves of old age, and bound fast on every side,

84. they were dashed against the rocks of grief, and being whirled round in the eddies of anger, wherever they rose to the surface they were attacked by the vultures of misfortune.

85. Sunk in the mud of sorrow, they were drawn into the sands of death. Thus their reliance on the help of desire was in vain.

86. Some, fastening to their waist a bundle of sacrificial rites, were trapped in the cave of heavenly bliss.

87. Others placing their faith in external action, in the hope of reaching the other bank through liberation, became entangled in the whirlpool of prescribed and prohibited duties.

88. It is wellnigh impossible to cross [this river] where the boat of dispassion cannot land and the rope of discrimination cannot reach to the other side.

89. If we say that someone could cross over this river of illusion by his own efforts, I will tell thee what such language is like.

90. If disease will not attack a man addicted to immoderate eating, if the evil thoughts of the wicked can be understood by a good man, or if a sensuous man will refuse to accept prosperity;

91. if thieves could come together in an assembly; if a fish could safely swallow the hook of the angler, or a coward chase away a ghost,

92. if a young deer could gnaw away a net, or an ant be able to climb to the top of Mount Meru, then perhaps a living creature might see the other bank of the river of illusion.

93. So, O Son of Pāndu, as a lascivious man cannot resist a woman, so is it impossible for an individual self to cross over this river of illusion.

94. Only those who have served Me with devotion have succeed in crossing it; to them even while on this side the waters of illusion have vanished;

95. and, casting off the burden of egoism, avoiding the winds of desire, searching the water of earthly love [to find] a shallow inlet,

96. if he has found the food of pure reason, at the descent of union, he leaps forward to the further bank of emancipation,

97. If a man finds the boat of self-examination, places his whole trust in Self-experience, with a good preceptor as his ferryman,

98. then strikes through the water with the arms of disinterest and, supported by the strength of oneness with the Self, he reaches without hindrance the shore of the cessation of all activity.

99. Those who have served Me in these ways, have crossed

over My [river of] illusion, but devotees such as these are
very few.

> xv. *The evil doers who are foolish, low in the human
> scale, whose minds are carried away by illusion and
> partake of the nature of demons, do not seek refuge in Me.*

> xvi. *The virtuous ones who worship Me are of four kinds,
> the man in distress, the seeker for knowledge, the seeker
> for wealth and the man of wisdom, O Lord of the Bhāratas
> [Arjuna].*

100. Besides these there are many others who have forgotten
     their true self-hood, having become possessed by the evil
     spirit of egoism.
101. They have forgotten the garment of a well-disciplined life,
     have lost all sense of shame about their future state of
     degeneration, and they perform actions prohibited by the
     Vedas.
102. Behold, O Son of Pāndu, they abandon the very purpose
     for which they have entered into the life of the body.
103. On the main streets they gather an assembly of varied
     emotions in order to satisfy their craving for the vain
     prattling of egoism.
104. It is needless to say that having been swallowed up by
     illusion they are unable to remember the wounds of sorrow
     and affliction.
105. Therefore they fail to find Me. Hear now the four ways in
     which these worship Me, and seek to increase their own
     spiritual welfare.
106. The first should be called those who suffer, the second are
     said to be the seekers after knowledge, the third are known
     as those who crave for wealth and the fourth are the wise.
107. Of all these, the sorrowful ones worship Me on account of
     their sorrow, the seekers after knowledge for the sake of
     knowledge and the third desiring to gain wealth.
108. The fourth, however, are not impelled by such motives;
     know the wise, therefore, to be true worshippers of Me.

> xvii. *Of these the wise one, who is ever in constant union
> with the divine, whose devotion is single-minded, is the
> best. For I am supremely dear to him and he is dear to Me.*

109. For by the light of his wisdom the darkness of separateness

is removed and then he becomes fully united with Me. Nevertheless he remains still My devotee.

110. But the strange thing is that, as to the eyes of many, a crystal may for a moment appear to be water, so the wise man seems to them [separate from Me].

111. Just as when the wind ceases to blow, it no longer appears to be separate from the sky, so is that devotee certainly united with Me, though his individuality as a devotee remains the same.

112. When the wind moves it appears distinct from the sky, and yet the sky remains as it was.

113. So also, while acting in the body he appears to be worshipping Me, but having attained to Self-realization, he is one with Me.

114. Through the dawning of wisdom he knows Me to be his Self. I, too, joyfully regard him as My Self.

115. Having reached the state that is beyond the individual self, is one who performs actions in the world different from Me, owing to the separateness of the body?

> XVIII. *Noble indeed are all these but the sage, I hold, is verily Myself. For being perfectly harmonized, he resorts to Me alone as the highest goal.*

116. All devotees cling to Me, some having self-interest as their motive, but the wise alone I love.

117. With the hope of milking a cow one ties it with a rope, but so strong is her affection for her calf [that she gives milk to it] without being tied.

118. For the calf, in the whole of its being, knows none [but its mother]; seeing her it says 'This is my mother.'

119. In this way the calf is solely dependent on its mother and the cow is devoted to its calf for this reason. The Lord of Lakshmi has spoken truly.

120. Again the Lord said, These devotees whom I have already described are very dear to Me.

121. For when they learn to know Me, they never look back, as a river flowing towards the ocean never turns back from it.

122. Similarly one in whom Self-realization like a river flows from the deep place of the heart and unites with Me, indeed become Myself.

123. The wise man, however, is the soul of My soul; this should not have been spoken, but how could I not do so?

XIX. At the end of many lives, the man of wisdom resorts to Me, knowing that Vāsudeva [the Supreme] is all that is. Such a great soul is very difficult to find.

124. For he, avoiding the dangers of desire and anger, in the midst of the dense forest of sense-objects, reaches the ascent of good desire.

125. Then, O Chief of warriors, in the company of the righteous, he follows the straight road of right action, avoiding the by-way of unrighteousness.

126. Not making use of the sandals of attachment, he proceeds on his journey through countless births; can he care about the fruit of desire?

127. Thus travelling onwards alone, through the night of union with the body, he sees the end of action and the dawn appears.

128. Then the morning rays of the favour of the guru and the sunshine of wisdom fall on him and the glory of equanimity is revealed to his sight.

129. Thereupon, wherever he turns his gaze I am there before him; even when he is alone, I am present there.

130. In short, there is none but Me everywhere, as a pot immersed in deep water has water both inside and outside.

131. So he is in Me and I am within him and without. This [experience] cannot be spoken of in words.

132. In this way he sees the storehouse of wisdom, and because of this he lives knowing he and the universe are one.

133. He is the best among devotees and he alone is wise, for he has realized the consciousness that everything is pervaded by Shri Vāsudeva.[3]

134. That great soul, O Arjuna, is rare indeed, in the treasure-house of whose Self-realization the whole of creation is contained.

XX. But those whose minds are distorted by desires resort to other gods, observing various rites, constrained by their own natures.

135. Beside him, O Kiriti, many worship Me, but their worship is offered for their own satisfaction, for they are blinded by the darkness of desire.

136. Desire has entered their hearts, through greed for the fruit of action, and from constant contact with it the lamp of their wisdom is extinguished.

137. Thus they sink into the inner and outer darkness and, losing sight of Me who am so near, earnestly worship other gods.
138. Being already slaves of material life they are impoverished by their enjoyment of some pleasures. See how eagerly they worship [these gods]!
139. They take certain vows, perform many and various rites, and offer all manner of oblations.

> XXI. *Whatever form any devotee with faith wishes to worship, I make that faith of his steady.*

140. Whatever desires a man may seek in the worship of other deities verily it is I who fulfil them.
141. Thus they worship those deities in whom they have placed their trust, practising the proper rites until they obtain the fruit of their devotion.

> XXII. *Endowed with that faith, he seeks the worship of such a one and from him he obtains his desires, the benefits being decreed by Me alone.*

142. Serving the gods in such a way a man reaps the fruit of it; but nevertheless it proceeds from Me.

> XXIII. *But temporary is the fruit gained by these men of small minds. The worshippers of the gods go to the gods but My devotees come to Me.*

143. These worshippers do not know Me, for they can never rise above desire, so that they acquire passing and imaginary satisfaction.
144. Truly speaking, such worship only serves worshippers in this worldly life, for the enjoyment of its fruit is as momentary as a dream.
145. But let us leave this matter here. Whatever deity may be the chosen one, he who worships other gods acquires their nature.
146. They who follow the path of devotion to Me, with body, mind and soul attain to Me at the end of life.

> XXIV. *Men of no understanding think of Me, the un-manifest, as having manifestation, not knowing My higher nature, changeless and supreme.*

147. But men do not do this, they rather destroy their own good; they try, as it were, to swim in water held in the palm of the hand.

148. Why should a man keep his mouth fast closed while, immersed in an ocean of nectar, he meditates on a pool of water?

149. Why should he die when he is bathing in nectar? Being in it why should he not become one with it?

150. Similarly, O Wielder of the bow, why should not a man escape from the snare of the fruit of action, soar high on the wings of Self-realization towards the sky to become its master?

151. Then, rising upwards with courage he reaches those higher regions and can wander there at his pleasure.

152. Why seek to measure the immeasurable? Why consider Me the unmanifest as manifest? When I am present here, why do they weary themselves [with efforts to reach Me]?

153. If all this is really considered, O Arjuna, even so, it appears that creatures cannot comprehend Me.

> XXV. *Veiled by My creative power [yogamāyā] I am not revealed to all. This bewildered world knows Me not, the unborn, the unchanging.*

154. For these have become blinded by the veil of illusion, so that they fail to perceive Me even in the full light of day.

155. Can it be said that anything exists in which I am not found? Can there be water without the quality of wetness?

156. What is there that is not touched by the wind? Is there anything which is not contained in space? I, indeed, am the One alone who pervades the whole universe.

> XXVI. *I know the beings that are past, that are present, O Arjuna, and that are to come, but Me no one knows.*

157. All creatures who have existed have become Me, and those who exist in the present, I am in them also.

158. Neither will they be apart from Me who may be born in the future. These are mere words, for nothing is ever born, nor can anything ever die.

159. Thus, O Son of Pāndu, I am eternally present and the whole of creation has come about in another way.

XXVII. *All beings are born deluded, O Bhārata [Arjuna],
overcome by the dualities which arise from wish and hate,
O Conqueror of the foe [Arjuna].*

160. Listen, while I explain all this briefly to thee. When
Egoism and Body were attracted towards each other,
161. a daughter called Desire was born to them. When she
reached maturity in love she was married to Hate.
162. To them was born a son called Duality-veil; the child was
brought up by his grandfather Egoism.
163. He was always opposed to resolution and refused all
discipline; and grew fat on the juice of yearning.
164. Intoxicated with the wine of dissatisfaction, he disported
himself with passion in the precincts of objects of sense,
O Wielder of the bow.
165. He scattered thorns of doubt on the pathway of devotion,
and opened up the byways of wrong action,
166. whereby creatures are deluded, and being involved in the
complexity of this worldly life, are beaten about with the
cudgels of great sorrows.

XXVIII. *But those men of virtuous deeds in whom sin has
come to an end, freed from the delusion of dualities,
worship Me, steadfast in their vows.*

167. Those who, however, seeing the sharp thorns of illusion
do not allow themselves to be distracted by them,
168. trample under foot these sharp thorns, in the pathway of
steadfast devotion, and cross over the forest of great sins.
169. Moreover they run towards Me on the swift course of
righteousness and are saved from the attack of wayside
robbers.

XXIX. *Those who take refuge in Me and strive for
deliverance from old age and death, know the Brahman
[or Absolute] entire, [they know] the Self and all about
action.*

170. On the other hand, O Pārtha, for those who are earnest in
their efforts to achieve liberation from birth and death,
171. their struggles one day will blossom into the fruit of the
supreme consciousness, and this on ripening yields in
abundance the juice of perfection.

172. At such a time the supreme goal of life is reached, the glory of Self-knowledge is fully experienced; the life of action is fulfilled and mental activity ceases.

173. Such is the reward of Self-knowledge reaped by the man whose wealth is invested in Me.

174. Then indeed he draws the interest of an evenly balanced mind, his commerce in union prospers and he knows no longer the calamity of separateness.

> xxx. *Those who know Me as the one that governs the material and the divine aspects, with their minds harmonised, have knowledge of Me even at the time of their departure [from here].*

175. They who, having understood Me in my earthly form, with the help of experience, have reached the highest deity,

176. who with the power of Self-knowledge see Me in the sacrifice, do not grieve at the separation from the body.

177. Otherwise, when the thread of life is cut, spirits are plunged into confusion. What wonder then that one who is alive feels as though the day of final destruction is upon him?

178. But who knows how to tell this? They who are attached to Me do not fall away from Me at this time.

179. Know that such perfected yogis are whole-heartedly attached to Me.

180. Arjuna had not caught in the cupped hands of his attention the draught of words which Shri Krishna had poured out to him, for he had fallen behind for a moment.

181. At that moment, the fruit in the form of the words of Brahma, succulent with the juice of much meaning, and fragrant with the perfume of devotion,

182. fell suddenly into the hollow of Arjuna's ears from the tree in the form of Shri Krishna, shaken by the wind of His great compassion.

183. This fruit was created from the great truths dipped in the water [of the essence of Brahman], and covered with the sweetness of the highest bliss.

184. Owing to its purity and excellence Arjuna began to feel a longing [for this higher wisdom] and to drink draughts of the nectar of wonder.

185. He mocked at heaven and its pleasures, and in his heart of hearts were vibrations [of ecstasy].

186. Fascinated by the beauty of that fruit, his delight increased and he felt an ardent desire to taste it.

187. At once he took this fruit in the form of the spoken word, in the hand of inference and placed it in the mouth of self-experience,

188. but the tongue of thought could not soften it, and the teeth of reasoning could not bite it. Realizing this the Lord of Subhadrā did not even suck it.

189. He became perplexed and, Are not these like stars [reflected] in water? How I have been deceived by the simplicity of the words!

190. They indeed are not litters but folds in the garment of the heavens, the meaning of which our intellects are utterly unable to fathom.

191. Then wondering in his heart how the things can be explained, he looked again towards the Lord of the Yādavas.[4]

192. Then the great warrior besought Him, saying O Lord, it is strange that I have not [previously] heard of these seven words associated together.[5]

193. Ordinarily it is possible to explain quickly, with attentive listeners, the meaning of various principles.

194. But here it is not so, O Lord; for one sees the assemblage of words and even wonder itself experiences wonder.

195. As soon as the rays of Thy words entered the openings of my ears, wonder arrested my attention.

196. O Lord, I am eager to learn their meaning, so please explain it, for I am not able to bear the delay caused by the effort to express this desire.

197. So, reflecting on what had already been said, and concentrating on what was yet to come, he was able to restrain his eagerness.

198. Notice how cleverly Arjuna has asked for this wisdom; he has touched the heart of Shri Krishna without transgressing the bounds of reverence and is ready to embrace the heart of the Lord.

199. Whatever we need to learn from our teachers we should ask them in this way; Savyasāci knew this well.[6]

200. See with what delight Sanjaya tells of Arjuna's questions and the manner in which the omniscient Hari replied!

201. Pray listen to the narrative, which will be recounted in clear Marāthi, for as the eye will perceive the meaning before the ears hear it,

202. so will the senses be revived by the beauty of the words,
even before the inner meaning has been tasted by the
tongue of reason.

203. The fragrance of Mālati buds is enjoyed by the nose but
does not their outward beauty also please the eye?[7]

204. So will the senses, after enjoying the beauty of the Marāthi
language, be made ready to approach the deeper truths.

205. Jnānadeva, disciple of Nivritti, says, Listen, for I am
going to utter such words as will surpass in culture all other
speech.

*In the Upanishad of the Bhagavadgitā, the science of the Absolute,
the scripture of Yoga and the dialogue between Shri Krishna and
Arjuna, this is the seventh chapter called the Highest Order of
Ascetism.*

NOTES

1. *The fourfold imprint of form.* The four classes of beings here referred,
to are: those born of eggs; those born of warm vapour (sweat), i.e
insects; those born of earth (mineral and vegetables); those born in
the womb.

2. *threefold infatuation.* The temptations of learning, wealth and power.

3. *Vāsudeva.* Any descendant of Vasudeva, the father of Krishna;
here the epithet is one of the names of Krishna.

4. *Lord of the Yādavas.* Krishna is here referred to as the lord of the
descendants of the race of Yadu, an ancient king.

5. *the Seven words.* These are the concepts of Brahma, the Absolute;
the Self, karma (action, duty, fate, etc.), material nature, the soul,
the supreme sacrifice and death.

6. *Savyasāci.* The 'left-handed one', an epithet of Arjuna.

7. *Mālati.* A tree of which the buds are specially fragrant.

CHAPTER VIII

Arjuna said:

> 1. *What is Brahman [or the Absolute]? What is the Self
> and what is action, O Best of persons? What is said to
> be the basis of the elements? What is called the basis of
> the gods?*

1. Thereupon Arjuna said, O Lord, hast thou heard? Please
   reply to what I have asked.
2. Wilt Thou tell me what Brahma is; what is action and
   who is the Supreme Spirit? I am listening, tell me clearly.
3. What are the highest being and the highest deity?

> 11. *What is the basis of sacrifice in this body and how,
> O Madhusūdana [Kṛṣṇa]? How again art Thou to be
> known at the time of departure by the self-controlled?*

4. O Lord, what is present in all sacrifice, and how can it be
   recognized in this body? It cannot be understood by
   mere logical reasoning.
5. Also, O Shārngadhara, show me in what way Thou art
   known by one who is disciplined at the time of his death.
6. If a fortunate man were asleep in a house constructed
   out of the stone of desire, his words, even though uttered
   in a dream would not be meaningless.
7. So, no sooner did Shri Krishna hear what Arjuna said
   than he replied Listen, O Arjuna, while I answer thy
   question.
8. Arjuna was like the young calf of the wish fulfilling cow,
   as though resting in a grove of trees which grant desires.
   Small wonder then that his longing was to be satisfied.
9. Even one whom Shri Krishna kills in anger attains to the
   realization of the Eternal; why then should not another
   so attain whom out of kindness He teaches?

10. As Arjuna alone bore such boundless love for Him, his desires were always gratified.

11. So, aware that Arjuna was about to ask Him a question, He prepared to serve him with the answer as with a dish of food.

12. A mother's love for her infant is so great that even when it has left the breast she knows when the child is hungry; she does not only suckle the child when it tells her.

13. It is not surprising, therefore, that the guru is filled with affection for his disciple. Listen to what the Lord said.

The Blessed Lord said:

> III. *Brahman [or the Absolute] is the indestructible, the Supreme [higher than all else]; essential nature is called the Self. Karma is the name given to the creative force that brings beings into existence.*

14. Then said the Lord of All, That which pervades this perishable body never seeps out of it.

15. In its subtlety it is as the void but in its nature it is not so; though it is as subtle as though it had been strained through a cloth of ether.

16. Yet it is so subtle that it would pass even through a bag of worldly knowledge; even with shaking it does not pass out [of this bodily life]. That is the Eternal.

17. It brings forms to birth, yet does not experience birth; when they pass away, it does not know death.

18. This is the very essence of the everlasting existence of Brahma, the Supreme. This is what is called adhyātmā, O Lord of Subhadrā.[1]

19. Then as in a clear sky a bank of clouds of different colours suddenly appears, no one knows how,

20. so in that pure formless Eternal arise the various subtle elements, appearing in the form of world systems.

21. From the fallow soil of the changeless Eternal shoot forth the primal thought and all the differentiated forms of the original Brahma are produced.

22. If we examine each of these closely we will find that they are infused with the life-force of Brahma, and countless lives appear and disappear in them.

23. Then the individual lives that make up these systems

give rise to innumerable primal desires, and in such manifold ways the universe expands.

24. Brahma, alone and without a second, pervades the whole, and pours forth a flood of varieties.

25. It is not possible to know how this unity and diversity arose; all movable and immovable beings come into existence for apparently no purpose; but countless numbers of species appear to be generated.

26. The number of these lives is as limitless as the leaves of a tree. When it is considered how all this comes to birth, the source is found to be the Zero.[2]

27. So then, in short, there is no visible creator, nor any origin, nor, in the end, any cause; only the spontaneous process of generation.

28. In this manner the process whereby forms become manifest in the unmanifested, without a creator, is called activity.

> IV. *The basis of all created things is the mutable nature; the basis of the divine elements is the cosmic spirit. And the basis of all sacrifices, here in the body is Myself, O Best of embodied beings [Arjuna].*

29. Now I will explain briefly to thee what is called adhibhuta.[3] In the same way that a cloud appears and then vanishes,

30. so this has no real existence in itself and will inevitably disappear, which obtains its form from the five elements,

31. which is manifested by the combination of these elements and has these for its basis, and the name and form of which melt into nothingness when they are dissolved.

32. That is what is meant by adhibhuta. Now we must consider adhidaiva, who partakes of what is created by matter.[4]

33. It is the eye of consciousness, the ruler of the province of the senses, the tree on which the bird of desire rests at the time of the death of the body.

34. He is a reflection of the supreme soul, but is wrapped in the slumber of egoism, and is alternately pleased and displeased with the dreamlike concerns of the world.

35. By his nature he is called the individual soul, dwelling in the house of the body.

36. O Son of Pāndu, he who while still in the body subdues

the power of sensation in the body, is adhiyajna—that is, Myself.[5]

37. In fact, I am, in every way, both adhidaiva and adhiyajna. When gold is mixed with alloy does it not become impure gold?

38. but still the quality of the actual gold is not spoiled nor does it really become one with the alloy; but so long as it is thus mixed it is considered to be alloyed gold.

39. In the same way, so long as adhibhuta and the others are concealed by the garment of ignorance they are thought to be different.

40. When this covering is withdrawn, the boundaries of separateness removed can it be said that having been separate they have become one? But were they ever two?

41. If some hairs were placed under a piece of crystal the stone would appear to the eye to be split into pieces.

42. Then if the hair is removed, can one say where the division was? Were the pieces cemented together? Was [the split] in the stone?

43. It is a whole, as it always was, but the presence of the hairs made it appear to be divided; these being removed, the stone appears again as before.

44. Similarly when egoism disappears, the original unity can be seen. In the same way I am that adhiyajna through which this unity is always present.

45. It is that sacrifice which I had in mind when I said before that all sacrifice is but action.

46. It is the refuge of all creatures, the storehouse of disinterested happiness, O Pāndava; I am now revealing it to thee.

47. First, in the blazing fire of the senses, burning with the fuel of dispassion, oblations of the material of sense-objects having been offered,

48. with the vajrāsana posture as the ground and gestures proper to the ādhāra position an altar should be built on the lap of the body.

49. Then plentiful oblations of the senses should be poured into the caldron of the fire of restraint, while many hymns in the form of yoga should be recited.

50. The mind, breathing and self control, an abundant supply of offerings; these feed the smokeless fire of wisdom.

51. All these are offered in the sacrifice of wisdom; then

wisdom loses itself in the object of wisdom, till there remains only the pure object of wisdom.

52. This, O Beloved, is called adhiyajna. When Krishna, the all-wise one spoke thus the intelligent Arjuna understood.

53. Knowing this Shri Krishna said, Well hast thou heard, O Pārtha. Arjuna was very happy at Krishna's pleasure.

54. Behold, only a mother can be pleased at the satisfaction of her child; only a good teacher is able to rejoice in the attainment of his disciple.

55. Therefore Krishna's heart could not contain his pure joy before Arjuna could be affected by it, but he restrained it with his mind.

56. He spoke gentle and kind words, like the fragrance of ripened joy or billows of cool nectar, and said,

> v. *And whoever, at the time of death, gives up his body and departs, thinking of Me alone, he comes to My status [of being]; of that there is no doubt.*

57. Hear, O Arjuna, best of listeners! When illusion is burnt out, then, [that wisdom which consumed it] is burnt up also.

58. That of which I have just told thee, which is called adhiyajna, means that those who know that to be Me in the beginning, know it also at the time of death.

59. They regard the body as but a sack and, attaining to their true nature, the Self, as the space enclosed in a house is still space,

60. they sleep in the chamber of determination, in the dwelling place of Self-realization and there remains no memory of the external world.

61. Achieving the sense of complete union they become Me, and the external sheaths of the five elements fall off from them without their knowing it.

62. When a man has no awareness of the existence of the body, although it may be still alive, how can he be distressed when it falls away from him? Therefore [at the end of his life] there can be no suffering for his Self-realizing consciousness.

63. That consciousness is moulded out of unity, or poured into the heart of eternity, and, as though washed in the ocean of union with the Supreme, it is never corrupted.

64. If a pot be submerged in water, it is filled with water as well as immersed in it; then, should the pot be accidentally broken would the water itself also be broken?

65. If a serpent sheds its skin, or on account of the heat a garment is thrown off, is there any change in the limbs [of the body]?

66. Likewise this outward form perishes but the Self which exists without it continues. When the reason grasps this knowledge, how can it be disturbed?

67. Therefore those who know Me at the hour of death give up their bodies and become one with Me.

> VI. *Of whatever state [of being] he is thinking when at the end he gives up his body, that he attains to, O Son of Kuntī [Arjuna], being ever absorbed in the thought thereof.*

68. Usually when death strikes in the breast, a man becomes that which his heart remembers at the final moment.

69. If some unfortunate man, running at full speed, inadvertently falls into a well with both feet,

70. now, as before his fall, there is no one to help him to avoid it, he simply has to fall in.

71. So whatever comes before his mind at the moment of death, he cannot avoid becoming one with it.

72. In the same way whatever desires a man forms while he is awake he sees [in his dreams] as soon as his eyes are closed.

73. The longings that a man feels when alive, which remain fixed in his heart, come to his mind at the moment of death,

> VII. *Therefore at all times remember Me and fight. When thy mind and understanding are set on Me, to Me alone shalt thou come without doubt.*

74. and whatever he remembers at the time of death he will attain that state. Therefore remember Me at all times.

75. Whatever is seen with the eye, heard with the ear, thought of in the mind, or spoken,

76. both the inner and the outer, thou shouldst know that it is all Me, so that at all times I am present in everything.

77. If this union happens, O Arjuna, a man does not die even

though his body may die; then in this fighting can there
be any fear for thee?

78. If thou wilt surrender thy mind and reason wholeheartedly
into My being, then I give my word that thou shalt come
to Me.

> VIII. *Whoever meditates on the Supreme Person with his
> thought attuned by constant practice and not wandering
> after anything else, Pārtha [Arjuna], reaches the Person,
> Supreme and Divine.*

79. If any doubt arises in thy mind of how this may be,
practise it, and if it does not happen [as I tell thee],
then be angry [with me].
80. With such practise harmonize thy mind, O Beloved, for
even a lame man can climb a mountain by dint of effort.
81. Similarly with practice keep constantly before thy mind
the Highest Being, then let the body live or die!
82. When the mind, having wandered after manifold objects,
chooses the Self, who then will remember whether the
body is or is not?
83. Behold, when the currents of rivers rush to meet the sea,
do they turn back to see what is happening behind them?
84. No, they remain merged in the ocean; and so also, the
mind becoming united with the spirit, birth and death
cease, for this is the supreme bliss.

> IX. *He who meditates on the Seer, the ancient, the ruler,
> subtler than the subtle, the supporter of all, whose form is
> beyond conception, who is sun-coloured beyond the darkness,*

85. He is older than the heavens, smaller than the smallest
particle, by whose power the universe is activated,
86. [This Seer] has being without form, in him there is neither
birth nor death, and he sees the totality of all that is.
87. From him the whole creation was born and through him
everything lives, reason dreads him, and he is beyond
the power of imagination to conceive.
88. Behold, a moth cannot consume fire nor can darkness
enter the light; so, he, in full daylight, appears as darkness
to the human eye.
89. But to the enlightened he is perpetual dawn, brilliant as
the solar rays, wherein there is no trace of setting

90. If a man, knowing that unblemished Supreme Spirit when the hour of death has struck, remembers it with a steady mind,

> x. *He who does so, at the time of his departure, with a steady mind, devotion and strength of yoga and setting well his life force in the centre of the eyebrows, attains to this Supreme Divine Person.*

91. outwardly assuming the lotus posture, facing towards the north and holding in his heart the joy of the yoga of action,
92. with the functions of his mind concentrated within, possessed by love for Self-realization, and eagerly reaching out to attain it,
93. with the practice of yoga completed his life sets forth from the lower centre by the middle pathway of the central artery, towards the crown centre.
94. Though outwardly it appears that the vital air has become one with the mind, in fact it then enters the space in the head and, thus prepared,
95. it enters the space between the eyebrows, destroying both active and lifeless matter just as the sound of a bell dies away inside a bell.
96. Or the dying man may leave his body, O Pāndava, like a lamp covered over with a vessel so that no one can tell when and how it was extinguished.
97. Such a man is the pure Highest Self, he is called the Highest, he reaches My eternal abode.

> xi. *I shall briefly describe to thee that state which the knowers of the Veda call the Imperishable, which ascetics freed from passion enter, and desiring which they lead a life of self-control.*

98. This is called 'the indestructible' by the intelligence of those wise men who are the mine of that wisdom which is the aim of all knowledge.
99. The true ethereal space is that which a whirlwind could not break up; without it how could clouds remain in existence?
100. Similarly what can be grasped by knowledge is bounded by its limits; what is beyond those limits is called the indestructible.

101. Therefore what the knowers of the Vedas describe as indestructible is higher than matter; it is the essence of the Highest Spirit.
102. Overcoming the evil of objects of sense, mortifying their senses and seated at the foot of the tree of the body,
103. such dispassionate ones wait for this without ceasing, which is always deeply loved by those who are detached,
104. yearning after it seekers consider of no account the difficulties of celibacy, and mercilessly subdue their senses.
105. That place which is inaccessible and unfathomable, on the edge of which even the Vedas sink exhausted,
106. those go to who relinquish their bodies in this manner. Once again I will speak to thee of this state, O Arjuna.
107. Thereupon Arjuna said, O Lord, I was about to speak to thee of this very thing. But thou Thyself hast shown me this favour. Do Thou tell me,
108. but I pray Thee explain it simply. [He who is] the light of the three worlds replied, Do I not know thee? I will be brief.

> XII. *One should have all the gates of the body restrained, the mind confined within the heart, one's life force fixed in the head, established in concentration by yoga.*

109. See to it that thy mind will remain fixed in the innermost place of thy heart, curbing the tendency to run after external objects.
110. But this is only possible when the gateways of the senses are firmly closed by the doors of restraint.
111. Then the mind, being easily confined, remains silent in the heart, just as a man with his arms and legs broken cannot leave his house.
112. The attention thus remaining fixed, O Pāndava, the life-breath should be transmuted into the sacred syllable and brought up by the central path to the brow-centre.
113. As soon as it arrives at this centre it should be held there with firm resolution, until the three elements of the sacred syllable are merged together in the crown centre.

> XIII. *He who utters the single syllable Aum [which is] Brahman, remembering Me as he departs giving up his body, he attains to the highest goal.*

114. Till then the life-breath should be held quiescent in the

space of the brow-centre and after its union with the sacred syllable it begins to rejoice in the half-syllable.

115. Then all memory of the Aum ceases and with it the life breath is lost, beyond that only the Eternal remains.

116. Therefore he who, remembering the one name, the sacred Brahma syllable which is My highest form,

117. gives up his body in this way, most certainly comes to Me, than whom there is no higher goal.

> XIV. *He who constantly meditates on Me, thinking of none else, who is a yogin ever disciplined [or united with the Supreme], by him I am easily reached.*

118. Perhaps O Arjuna, thy mind is still doubtful how a man may remember Me at the moment of death,

119. At this time, when the senses have lost their power and the joys of life have departed, and all the inner and outer signs of death present themselves,

120. who is then able to sit up, restrain activity and in his heart remember the sacred syllable?

121. Thou mayest perchance have such doubts in thy mind, but him who has served Me [in life], I serve at the hour of his death.

122. Those who have given up all sense-objects, with their desires controlled, having installed Me in their heart, enjoy [eternal bliss].

123. But if, experiencing Me, they feel dissatisfied, hunger and thirst do not affect them, what then can their sight and other senses do?

124. They who have thus realized union with Me, have clung to Me in their hearts, worship Me, becoming one with Me.

125. If it were necessary for such men to remember Me at the moment of death, and for Me to come to them, what would be the value of their devotion to Me?

126. Should a poor man in his distress call to Me pitifully to come to his aid, should I not hasten to relieve him in his plight?

127. If My devotees were in this position, who then would feel any longing for devotion? So this doubt need not be entertained at all.

128. O Pāndava, I could not bear the burden [of thought] that I should have to remember to go to them whenever they turn towards Me.

129. and knowing My debt to them, I repay it by being the servant of my devotees at their death.

130. Lest My beloved devotees may feel the wind of the weakening of the body, I enclose them in a case of Self-realization.

131. Moreover, I cover this case with the cool shadow of remembrance of Me, and in this way I bring to them steadfastness of mind.

132. Therefore the distress of death never affects my own people and I bring them joyfully to Myself.

133. When he relinquishes the sheath of this body, and shakes off the surface dust of egoism, by arousing in My devotee a pure feeling for Me, I make him one with Me.

134. My devotees feel no attachment to their bodies, therefore at the moment of leaving it they do not feel it as separation.

135. Nor do they expect Me to come to them at death and take them to Myself, for naturally they have already become one with Me.

136. The bodily form has existence only as a shadow reflected in water; after all, moonlight is in the moon itself.

137. To those who are thus always devoted to Me I am easy of attainment; therefore, they are surely united with Me at death.

> xv. *Having come to Me, these great souls do not return to rebirth, the place of sorrow, impermanent, for they have reached the highest perfection.*

138. A plantation of trees of distress, the hearth of the fire of threefold calamity, an oblation to the crow of death,

139. the nourisher of poverty, which increases the great fear and is the store of all the pains of life,

140. the root of evil tendencies, the fruit of evil conduct, the very being of delusion,

141. the basis of worldly existence, the garden of passions, a meal offered to all the diseases,

142. the remains of the mixed dish of death, the body of desire, the high road of life and death,

143. a fund of deception, the outpouring of doubt, a cellar full of scorpions,

144. a den of tigers, the friend of harlots, a favourite device for the knowledge of objects of desire,

145. the solicitude of a witch, the cool draught of poison, the trust placed in cunning thieves disguised as honest men,
146. the embrace of a leper, the softness of the serpent of death, the very song of the hunter,
147. the hospitality of enemies, the respect of evil-doers, the very ocean of calamity,
148. the vision seen in a dream, a forest watered by a mirage, or a sky filled with smoke—
149. such a body is not obtained in a later birth by those men who have become one with My limitless form.

> XVI. *From the realm of Brahma downwards, all worlds are subject to return to rebirth, but on reaching Me, O Son of Kuntī [Arjuna], there is no return to birth.*

150. Even one who has acquired the greatness of oneness with Brahma cannot escape from the round of births and deaths; but as a dead man cannot suffer from stomach pains,
151. or as a man on awakening is not drowned in a flood seen in a dream, so they who have come to Me are not even touched by worldly existence.

> XVII. *Those who know that the day of Brahma is of the duration of a thousand ages, and that the night [of Brahma] is a thousand ages long, they are the knowers of day and night.*

152. Truly speaking, it is that which is the head of the whole universe of form, the chief of all permanent things, the loftiest peak of the mountain of the three worlds, the world of Brahma,
153. that place in which a portion of an hour lasts longer than even the life of Indra, and of which a day is longer than the lives of fourteen Indras.
154. When a cycle of the four aeons passes away a thousand times, that is a day of Brahma; similarly when another thousand have passed, that is a night of Brahma.
155. Those fortunate ones who do not die within the duration of such a day and night are the deathless ones of heaven.
156. And [compared with these] what can be said of the multitude of the gods? Consider the state of the great Indra—fourteen days of Indra in one day of Brahma!

157. They who are witnesses of the passage of the eight divisions of a day and night of Brahma should be called knowers of day and night.

158. When the day breaks in the world of Brahma, countless numbers of worlds come into existence out of the unmanifested.

159. Again at the end the four divisions of the day of Brahma pass away, the ocean of manifested creation dries up, and again at dawn the waters begin to rise.

160. As at the advent of the season of sharat clouds disappear from the sky, and at the end of the hot season they again gather in the sky,[6]

161. so, at the beginning of a day of Brahma, multitudes of created beings come forth until a thousand of these periods of four yugas have passed.

162. After that the time of the night begins and the universe remains absorbed in the unmanifested during a period of a thousand years of Brahma, of four yugas each; when the dawn comes and the process of creation begin again.

163. Why should all this be said, that in one day and night of Brahma the universe is destroyed and recreated?

164. Behold what glory there is in this! He is the reservoir of the seeds of the universe, and yet He is as the peak of the full measure of the cycle of birth and death.

165. This universe, O Wielder of the bow, is an extension of the world of Brahma, which is spread out as soon as the day dawns.

166. Then the nightfall comes, when all by its own nature returns whence it came, to a state of equilibrium.

167. As the nature of a tree is inherent in a seed or a cloud becomes one with the sky, the state in which diversity becomes merged in unity is called equilibrium.

168. Then there is neither likeness nor unlikeness, and no

trace of created beings remains, in the same way that milk which has become curds loses its name and form.

169. So, as soon as it loses form the world loses its own nature, but that [the unmanifest] from which it arose remains.

170. Then it is called the 'unmanifest'; when again it assumes form it is called 'manifest'. These two concepts seem to be mutually dependent, but this is not so.

171. When [a metal] is melted it is called a bar of metal, but the metal loses its solid form on being made into ornaments.

172. These two events happen also in the case of gold; so does the idea of 'manifest' and 'unmanifest' inhere in Brahma.

173. In itself it is neither manifest nor unmanifest, permanent or destructible, it is beyond both and eternally self-existent.

174. It is perceived in the form of the universe, but with the destruction of the universe it is not itself destroyed, as one may erase writing but the meaning [remains].

175. Behold! waves rise and fall again, but the water in them always remains; so that which is in the perishable elements is itself imperishable,

176. or as when ornaments are melted down, the gold is not destroyed, so is the immortal within the mortal body.

> xx. *But beyond this unmanifested, there is yet another Unmanifested Eternal Being who does not perish even when all existences perish.*

> xxi. *This Unmanifested is called the Imperishable. Him they speak of as the Supreme Status. Those who attain to Him do not return. That is My supreme abode.*

177. It may easily be called the 'unmanifest', but this would not be a worthy name for it; for it is beyond the reach of mind or reason.

178. It is also that which, though manifested in form, does not lose its formlessness, and whose permanency is not affected by the loss of form.

179. It is therefore called the 'unchangeable', which conception is [more easily] understood. There is no space to be seen beyond it. It is called the final beatitude.

> xxii. *This is the Supreme Person, O Pārtha [Arjuna], in*

whom all existences abide and by whom all this is pervaded;
[who] can, however, be reached by unswerving devotion.

180. Pervading this body, it is dormant, for it does not work,
nor does it cause another to work.

181. Meanwhile, O great warrior, none of the physical functions
ceases, the activities of the ten sense organs continue.

182. The market of the sense-objects is opened and the mind
becomes the centre of trade, in the midst of which transactions of pleasure and pain are carried on.

183. But as the trade of his kingdom does not cease while the
king rests peacefully, for his subjects carry it on as they
please,

184. so it is with the activity of the reason, the transactions of
the mind, the functioning of the sense organs, and the
movements of the vital airs.

185. All bodily functions continue to function without being
activated by the Self, just as men carry on their work
without being impelled by the sun.

186. Being in the same way asleep in the body, O Arjuna,
he is called Purusha.

187. Or it may be also that being faithful to his devoted wife
Prakriti, he is called Purusha.[7]

188. Even the greatness of the Vedas cannot see his courtyard;
see how he covers the whole ethereal space.

189. Knowing him to be so, the greatest yogis describe him as
the highest of the high, who enters the house of those
who have no other resort.

190. He is the fruitful soil in which ripens the devotion of
those who with body, speech or mind attend to no other
matter.

191. He is the refuge, O Pāndava, of those believers whose
firm conviction it is that the whole universe is the highest
Purussa.

192. He is the glory of the humble, the realization of those who
are beyond the attributes, the highest happiness for the
dispassionate.

193. He is as choice food set before the contented, as the heart
of a mother for those helpless ones who have no worldly
longings, and a straight road for devotion to seek his
abode.

194. O Arjuna, it is unnecessary to describe this in detail. It

is that with which, when a man reaches it, he becomes
united.

195. As hot water becomes cold in a cool breeze, as darkness
becomes light on the approach of the sun,

196. so, O Pāndava, arriving at that place even worldly
existence is transformed into liberation.

197. As fuel thrown on the fire becomes fire and cannot in
any way again be distinguished as wood;

198. as sugar cannot by any skill be made again to become
sugarcane, O son of Pāndu;

199. as iron may be changed into gold only by the philosopher's
stone, and no other substance can make it into iron again;

200. as clarified butter cannot again become milk, so there is
no return from the attainment of union with the Supreme.

201. That is indeed My highest abode. I have now revealed
to thee this hidden secret.

> XXIII. *Now I shall declare to thee, O Best of Bhāratas [Arjuna], the time in which yogis, departing, never return; and also that wherein, departing, they return.*

202. In another way it is easy to understand this place,
whither yogis go when they abandon their bodies.

203. It may happen that if the body is given up at an inauspicious moment they must return again to bodily life.

204. If they relinquish their bodies at an auspicious time, they
at once become one with Brahma. On the other hand,
should they die at an inauspicious time, they must return
to earthly existence.

205. Hence union and return to birth are dependent on time.
That time I will describe to thee now, in due order.

> XXIV. *Fire, light, day, the bright [half of the month], the six months of the northern path [of the Sun], going forth at these times men who know the Absolute go to the Absolute.*

206. So, O great warrior, listen to Me. At the crisis of death,
the five elements leave the body last,

207. If at the moment of dying reason is not overcome by
confusion, memory does not become blind, and the mind
does not become deadened,

208. then the organs of perception retain their vigour, and

union with the Eternal which has been experienced becomes a protective sheath.

209. In such a way the senses remain conscious and this condition lasts till death supervenes. This is only possible so long as the heat of the body is maintained.

210. Look, when owing to the action of wind or water a lamp is extinguished, is the sight of the eyes of any use, though we still have it?

211. Similarly at death, owing to the action of wind the body becomes full of mucus and the spark of the inner fire is put out.

212. When the vitality of life is lost, what can reason so? Consciousness, therefore, cannot remain active in the body without heat.

213. O Beloved, when the fire in the body ceases, then the body is no longer a body, but merely a lump of damp clay, and the life-span struggles in vain to find its end in the darkness.

214. At this time one should preserve all memories of the past and, leaving the body, attain to union with Brahma.

215. The perception of consciousness is drowned in the phlegm of the body and all awareness of past and future ceases.

216. Therefore the benefit accruing from the previous practice of yoga is lost even before death occurs, as though the lamp held in the hand were extinguished before one has found what was lost.

217. Know then that the [gastric] fire is the basis of consciousness. This fire is the source of all strength at the moment of death.

218. Within, [there should be] the light of the gastric fire; without, the time should be the bright half of the month, during daylight, and during one of the six months of the northern path of the sun.

219. He who gives up his body under the conjunction of such auspicious conditions becomes one with the Eternal, for he is a knower of Brahma.

220. Listen now, O Wielder of the bow, such is the power of this conjunction and hence this is the straight path by which it is possible to reach Me.

221. Here the gastric fire is the first step, the light of the fire the second, the daytime the third, and the bright half of the month the fourth.

222. [The requirement of] one of the six months of the northern path is the highest step of this ascent, by which the yogi arrives at the place of perfection in union with Brahma.

223. This is known to be the best time and it is called the 'arcira' path. Now listen and I will now describe to thee the inauspicious time.[8]

> xxv. *Smoke, night, so also the dark [half of the month], the six months of the southern path [of the sun], going forth at such a time, the yogi obtains the lunar light and returns.*

224. At the moment of dying the heart is compressed in darkness, owing to the pressure of air and phlegm.

225. Sense organs are blocked, memory is lost in confusion, the mind becomes bewildered, and the life force is constricted.

226. The fire of the gastric juices becomes extinguished and smoke pervades the whole, owing to which consciousness in the body is confined within,

227. just as when heavy watery clouds hide the moon, there is neither brilliance not darkness but only a dim light.

228. So a man does not die, nor does he remain conscious; he becomes motionless, his earthly life awaits the moment of death.

229. When a mist has spread over the sense organs, the mind and intellect, all the gains of the life are lost.

230. When a man loses what he has possessed, what value is there in gaining anything more? Such is a man's state at the moment of death.

231. This is the condition in the body; in the external conditions the time is night, in the dark half of the month, these together with one of the six months of the southern path.

232. If all these, which bring about rebirth in the cycle of birth and death come together at a man's dying moment, how can he attain to union with Brahma?

233. A man, being a yogi, dying at such a juncture, reaches the moon-world, and then he descends again into earthly existence.

234. Know that I have spoken here of the inauspicious time, O Son of Pāndu; this is the dark path leading to the recurrence of birth.

235. The other, called the path of light, the busy high road, straight and easy, leading to Self-realization.

> xxvi. *Light and darkness, these paths are thought to be the world's everlasting [paths]. By the one he goes not to return, by the other he returns again.*

236. O Arjuna, these are the two everlasting paths, the one, straight, the other crooked, I have purposely pointed them out to thee,

237. in order that for thy welfare thou shouldst see the right path and the wrong, recognize the true and the false, and know what is good and what is harmful.

238. Is a man likely to plunge into deep water when he sees a good boat near him? Will a man go by a side path when he knows the right road?

239. Will a man who can distinguish between nectar and poison be able to give up the nectar? Likewise he who sees a straight road will not take a side path.

240. So one should discriminate clearly between good and evil, and then one will avoid the inauspicious moment.

241. However, at the time of dying there is a great danger inherent in the dark path, in that all the practice of a lifetime will be in vain.

242. Should the path of light be missed, and the yogi enter by chance upon the path of darkness, he will be bound to the revolving cycle of life and death.

243. Seeing this great danger, I have clearly explained both yogic paths to thee, so that thou mayest know once and for all how it may be avoided.

244. By the one the yogi reaches the Eternal, by the other he comes back to the cycle of rebirths; but [he will go by] the path by which he is destined to travel at the time of death.

> xxvii. *The yogin who knows these paths, O Pārtha [Arjuna], is never deluded. Therefore, at all times, O Arjuna, be thou firm in yoga.*

245. At that time this cannot be known; it is useless to ask what may happen. [It is not known] by which path one may attain to Brahma at the time of death.

246. Yogis know that they are indeed the Eternal whether they are in the body or out of it, just as the appearance

of being a snake is illusory from the point of view of a rope.

247. Is water aware of whether it has waves or not? The water itself remains the same at all times.

248. The water is not born of the waves, nor does it disappear when they subside. Those who become Brahma while still in the body are the 'disembodied' ones.

249. For them there remains no memory even of the body. Consider then, when do they die?

250. Why then should the path be sought for? Is there anything to lose at any time once a man has become one with time, place and the rest?

251. When an earthen pot is broken, the space within it goes on its way; its way leads it at once to merge in all space. Otherwise it would get lost.

252. Consider also this. Only the form is lost but the space was in space even before the pot took on the form of a pot.

253. In accordance with this concept, yogis who have realized their oneness with Brahma are not concerned with the rightness or wrongness of the path.

254. For this reason, O Son of Pāndu, thou shouldst become absorbed in yoga, and thus thou wilt have perpetual evenness of mind.

255. Then whether the body is retained or cast off at any time or in any place, there can be no change in separation from that unlimited and perpetual union with the Eternal.

256. Such a man is not born at the beginning of a great world age, nor does he die at the end of an age; nor is he deluded by the temptations of heaven or earthly life.

257. One who has becomes a yogi through this teaching knows the rightness of it; having weighed up the experience of it he comes to self-realization.

258. For he has rejected as worthless, O Son of Pāndu, even the royal glory which Indra and all the other gods extol.

> XXVIII. *The yogin having known all this, goes beyond the fruits of meritorious deeds assigned to the study of the Vedas, sacrifices, austerities and gifts and attains to the supreme and primal status.*

259. Even if a man has made a study of the Vedas, or if for him the field of sacrifice has borne fruit, or if he has gathered riches from austerities and almsgiving,

260. and if the plantation of all this merit were to yield abundant fruit, it cannot be compared with [the realization of] the purest Brahma.

261. This would not fall short if measured against the final beatitude, to attain which the Vedas and sacrifices are the means.

262. It neither spoils nor fades away, it satisfies the desire of those who experience it and becomes as a loved brother to the Eternal bliss;

263. it would give delight to the divine eye, it is founded on unseen merit, and it is unobtainable even by a thousand sacrifices.

264. When yogis take the measure of this heavenly happiness, with the divine eye, they find it to be of very little worth.

265. Then, O Kiriti, using it as a stepping stone, they ascend to the Eternal bliss.

266. He who is the glory of the whole animate and inanimate creation, worthy to be worshipped by Brahmā and Shiva, and who is the only wealth to be enjoyed by yogis,[9]

267. who is the art of all arts and the image of the highest bliss, the life and soul of the whole universe,

268. who is the essence of omniscience, and the shining light of the family of the Yādavas, that is Krishna, spoke thus with Arjuna.

269. This account of [what happened] on the field of Kurukshetra Sanjaya related to the King. Listen further to this story, says Jnānadeva.

In the Upanishad of the Bhagavadgitā, the science of the Absolute, the scripture of Yoga and the dialogue between Shri Krishna and Arjuna, this is the eighth chapter called the Yoga of the Highest Brahma.

NOTES

1. *adhyātma.* See above, VII, note 5. The Self.
2. *Zero.* The nought, the great void of non-being, the symbol of Brahma.
3. *adhibhuta.* See above, VII, note 5. The elemental and material.
4. *adhidaiva.* See above, VII, note 5. The divine.
5. *adhiyajna.* See above, VII, note 5. The supreme sacrifice.
6. *cycle of seasons.* The seasons in the region of Mahārāshtra (Bombay Province) can be broadly described as three: the cool season, mid-November to end of February, the hot season, March to beginning of June, and the rainy season (monsoon), June till September with an intermediate period between mid-September and the end of October. In the traditional Hindu year there are six seasons, each of two months; the 'hot' season is the period from mid-May to mid-July and the rainy season is the period from mid-July to mid-September. It is not possible to equate either months or seasons to English names or periods. The season of sharat (sharadā) lies between the end of the rains and beginning of the cold season.
7. *Purusha and Prakriti.* Purusha, the Supreme Spirit, the creative force as the passive spectator of the activity of Prakriti, nature, regarded as the wife of Purusha.
8. *arcira.* The path of light leading to Brahma.
9. *Brahmā.* The god, not the Supreme Spirit; he is highest god of the triad of Brahma, Vishnu and Shiva.

190

CHAPTER IX

1. I promise you that if you give me your attention, you will be worthy to enjoy all happiness,

2. But in an assembly of wise people like yourselves, I do not speak with arrogance; my affectionate request is that you will pay heed to what I say.

3. For if I have such wealthy ones as yourselves as my home, all desires are satisfied and all wishes fulfilled.

4. Seeing the cool shade of the garden of your favour, enriched by graciousness, I whom am weary rest in it.

5. Sirs, you are the deep waters of the nectar of happiness, so that we long for its coolness. If I fear to approach you here in friendliness, where indeed should I refresh myself?

6. As a child uses its own childish words and its steps are stumbling and unsure, still its mother wonders and is delighted,

7. So let the love of you saintly ones be given to me in some way. This is my great desire, approaching you affectionately.

8. Besides, am I worthy to speak before such wise listeners as you are? Does a son of the goddess of learning have to be taught how to study?

9. Listen! However large a glow-worm may be, could it ever equal the sun in brightness? How could this be? Who can prepare food worthy of being served in a dish of nectar?

10. Is there any need to fan the moon, with its cool rays? Who would sing before the mystic sound? Can ornaments be further ornamented? How could this be done?

11. Is there anything that perfume itself can smell, or where could the ocean bathe itself? What space is there that could contain the whole firmament?

12. What man possesses that power of oratory which could satisfy your interest and entertain you well enough to call forth your applause?

13. But is it wrong to worship the sun which lightens the universe with a simple oil lamp? Should we not pay homage to the ocean by offering a handful of water?

14. Sirs, you are the incarnation of the great Shiva, while I am a simple man serving you with devotion. Therefore though I offer only the leaves of the nirgudi shrub, be pleased to accept them as though they were those of the bela tree.[1]

15. If a child approaches his father's plate and offers him food out of it, the father delighted opens his mouth eagerly [to receive it].

16. Similarly though I, like a child, am boring you with my talk, because of your affection I feel sure you will be pleased.

17. You saintly ones are moved by the power of your love for me so you should not be offended by my familiarity [in speaking thus to you].

18. Behold how a cow's milk flows more freely when her calf strikes her; so anger against some beloved one increases affection for him.

19. I have spoken to you thus, believing that your hidden compassion has been aroused by my child-like words.

20. Can the moon be ripened like a layer of mangoes? Can anyone impart motion to the wind? Can the heavens be restrained by a cage?

21. One does not have to make water liquid, nor to churn butter with a churning-staff; so my diffidence prevents me from speaking before you.

22. But am I worthy to expound in Marāthi that Gitā which is the bed upon which lie resting the words of the Vedas, wearied [in their attempt to describe the eternal truth]?

23. Nevertheless I am eager to do this, and besides I have the hope that through my boldness I may win your affection.

24. So, with your attention, which is more cooling than the moon and more life-giving than nectar, satisfy, I pray you, my desire.

25. For if you shower upon me your kindly looks, the seeds of exposition will germinate in my mind; otherwise, if you remain indifferent, the tender shoots of knowledge will wither.

26. So listen to me, for when my power of speech is fed by

attention, a wealth of propositions will come forth in my words,

27. The sense waits on the words, meaning brings forth further meaning, and there is a full blossoming of feeling in the mind.

28. When, therefore, the favourable wind of dialogue begins to blow, clouds of learning gather in the sky of the heart; but if listeners are inattentive the essence of the exposition will melt away.

29. Now, the moonstone melts; but this is due to the action of the moon itself. So the speaker cannot be a speaker without hearers.

30. Do grains of rice have to ask eaters to sweeten them? Do puppets have to ask the showman to move them?

31. Does he make them dance for their own sake? Is it not to display his own skill? So, what need have I to behave in a similar way?

32. Thereupon the Guru exclaimed, What is all this about? We have understood your request. Now tell us what the Lord Krishna taught to Arjuna.

The Blessed Lord said:

> 1. *To Thee, who doth not cavil, I shall declare this profound secret of wisdom combined with knowledge, by knowing which thou shalt be released from evil.*

33. Now Arjuna, I will proceed to tell thee the inner meaning of the cherished secret of My heart.

34. Thus the disciple of Nivritti, delighted, joyfully agreed saying, Listen to the words of the Lord!

35. If, naturally, thou shouldst wonder why I should reveal to thee in this way My innermost secret,

36. then listen, O thou wise one; thou art the very symbol of earnestness, and never dost thou disregard what I teach thee.

37. If the secrecy is to be broken, let it be so; let that be spoken which should be spoken, but allow this secret of My heart to enter thine.

38. There is milk concealed in the udders, but they do not know of its sweetness. So [a cow] lets it be drawn, provided it satisfies the one who desires it and can get it from no other source.

39. If seed is taken from the storing jar and sown in prepared soil, can it be said that the seed is wasted by being scattered about?

40. Therefore, to such as are of goodwill, pure mind, and respectful, who take their sole refuge in Me, I will gladly impart to them My most secret wisdom.

41. So as there is none other like thee endowed with these virtues, it is not right for Me to keep this wisdom hidden from thee although it is secret.

42. If I keep on repeating 'this is secret', thou wilt think it strange; so I will explain to thee wisdom combined with worldly knowledge,

43. with this sole purpose that thou mayest be able to discriminate carefully between true and false wisdom, intermingled as they seem to be.

44. As a royal swan is able to separate milk from water with the grip of its beak, I will explain to thee separately wisdom and knowledge,

45. As in a current of wind the sifted chaff is blown away whilst the grains of corn fall together in a heap,

46. so, knowing this wisdom, the things of this world are joined with the life of this world, and the knower is placed on the throne of Self-liberation.

47. Among all branches of knowledge, this is worthy of the highest position in the realm of teaching, the foremost of all secrets, the sovereign of all pure things,

48. the abode of righteousness, best among the best, which, having once been gained, there is no question of any rebirth.

49. However small a part of it may be revealed by the mouth of the preceptor, that self-existent one residing in the heart is spontaneously experienced.

50. Moreover it is that which a man may ascend to by easy steps, and, having reached it, all other experience falls away.

51. Not only so, but even while standing only on the border of the enjoyment of that wisdom the mind rejoices in it; it is so easily attained, and yet it is also the highest Brahma.

II. *This is sovereign knowledge, sovereign secret, supreme sanctity, known by direct experience, in accord with the law, very easy to practise and imperishable.*

52. It has still another characteristic; when once it has been gained, it does not perish; when experienced, it is never lost, nor does one weary of it.

53. At this point thou mayest wonder, O thou questioning one, how it is that such a treasure should have escaped the hands of men.

54. It is holy and delightful, simple to attain to, a natural joy, yet righteous, and experienced within oneself.

55. When therefore, it is in every way desirable, how is it that men have let it escape them? Such a doubt is reasonable, but thou shouldst not entertain it.

> III. *Men who have no faith in this way, not attaining to Me, O Oppressor of the foe [Arjuna], return to the path of mortal living [saṃsāra].*

56. Sweet and pure is the milk of the cow, and only just beneath skin; yet do not lice leave the milk and suck the impure [blood]?

57. Lotus roots and frogs live together in the same pond, but bees feed on the pollen of the lotus, while the mud is left [for the frogs].

58. Again there may be thousands of gold coins buried in the house of a man of ill-luck, yet he will starve himself, living in poverty.

59. So although I may in My heart be the garden of all joys, still a deluded man will seek for sensual pleasures.

60. Similarly a man, seeing a mirage, might spit out a mouthful of nectar as he was swallowing it; or another might cut off the philosopher's stone hanging round his neck for the sake of an oyster-shell.

61. So preoccupied are they with self that these wretched ones fail to reach Me, and so are tossed back and forth between the banks of life and death.

62. What am I like, in reality? I am not as the sun which at times is visible and at others hidden from sight. I do not fail in this way.

> IV. *By Me all this universe is pervaded through My unmanifested form. All beings abide in Me but I do not abide in them.*

63. Is not this whole universe but the manifestation of My

own Self? Just as milk when curdled is naturally called
'curds',

64. or as a tree grows out of a seed, or as gold is made into
ornaments, so this universe is but a manifestation of Me.

65. My nature is confined when unmanifested; it becomes
diffused [when manifested] in the form of this universe.
Know thou that I, the Form of the Formless, am manifested in the three words.

66. All forms from the most subtle of the elements to physical
matter are reflected in Me like foam on water.

67. But, O Son of Pāndu, as when this foam is seen from within
no water is found, or as on awakening what is seen in a
dream ceases to have a separate existence,

68. so are all these beings reflected in Me, but I am not in them.
I have already taught all this to Thee,

69. so there is no need to enlarge upon it now. Let the eye of
thy mind remain fixed on My inner nature.

v. *And [yet] beings do not dwell in Me: behold My divine
mystery. My spirit which is the source of all beings sustains
the beings but does not abide in them.*

70. If thou wilt endeavour to see without misconception, My
real nature underlying all matter, thou wilt then understand that it is untrue to say that beings are in Me, for
I am everything.

71. But when the twilight of mental bewilderment fails, the
eyes of the intelligence are for a time darkened, My
eternal form is dimly perceived and beings appear to be
distinct from each other.

72. Again when this bewilderment passes, as soon as doubt is
destroyed, My indivisible form is seen. In the same way
the error of mistaking a wreath for a snake is removed
[by clearer perception].

73. Do pitchers and jars spring up of themselves like shoots
from the earth? No, they are the offspring of the mind of
the potter.

74. Are there waves stored up in the water of the ocean? Is
not this change in the water brought about by the wind?

75. Are there bundles of cotton within the cotton-plant? In
the eye of the weaver it has been made into cloth.

76. When gold is formed into ornaments it does not lose its

nature as gold, but seen by him who wears it, it appears
on the surface to be the ornament.

77. Tell me, are not the answering echo, and forms seen in a
mirror, in reality our own creations, or do they appear
from elsewhere?

78. Whoever attributes the existence of beings to My nature,
in his thought sees only their appearance in the world.

79. When matter, which produces these appearances, passes
away, the illusion of created beings is removed, and only
My pure and unchanging nature remains.

80. When one spins one's body round rapidly everything
appears to be revolving round one; so to the imagination
separate beings appear to exist in My indivisible form.

81. Relinquish these notions; there are no grounds for thinking
that beings are in Me, and I in them, even in a dream.

82. Such words as 'I alone am the supporter of beings' or
'I am in them' are merely the delirious utterances of the
imagination.

83. Listen therefore, O beloved! I am the Self which pervades
the universe, and also the resort of all the creatures of the
illusory world of nature.

84. As owing to the rays of the sun an unreal mirage seems to
exist, so is the false concept that all beings are in Me, and
this unreality is imposed on Me.

85. I am the ground of the illusion of the existence of this
world, and yet I am in no way different from it, as the sun
and its radiance are one.

86. Now thou hast seen My supreme nature. Tell Me now,
what is the relation of difference between Me and these
beings?

87. It is clear, therefore, that beings are not different from Me;
and do not imagine Me to be different from them.

> VI. *As the mighty air moving everywhere ever, abides in
> the etheric space [ākāśa], know thou that in the same
> manner all existences abide in Me.*

88. The extent of the sky is the same as that of the wind in it;
when the one moves it appears to be different from the
other; yet in reality they are the same.

89. Similarly when it is thought that all beings are in Me,
something seems to exist; in the absence of thought,
nothing remains but Myself, who am all.

90. So their existence or non-existence depends on such thought; with its disappearance they vanish, and with it again they appear.

91. When that original thought is destroyed, where can existence or non-existence be found? Consider again, therefore, My supreme nature.

92. Become as a wave in the ocean of the realization of this wisdom, and then, seeing all this animate and inanimate creation, thou wilt see thyself.

93. Then the Lord said, Has this wisdom now been awakened in thee? Has not the delusion of duality been realized as false?

94. If again, perchance, thy understanding were overcome by the slumber of such thoughts, that realization of unity in thee would vanish, and thou wouldst fall into the dream of separateness.

95. I am now about to reveal to thee a secret, [knowing which] this sleep will never occur, and through the awakening of pure wisdom thou wilt realize thyself as one with all.

96. Therefore, O fearless archer, Dhananjaya, listen attentively to My words. It is illusion which creates all beings and again destroys them.

> VII. *All beings, O Son of Kuntī [Arjuna], pass into nature which is My own at the end of the cycle; and at the beginning of the [next] cycle, I send them forth.*

97. It is called primordial matter and it is of two kinds, as I have told thee; one is eightfold in form, the other is the life-element.

98. Thou hast already heard all about this matter, O Son of Pāndu, so there is no need to repeat it; *this* is primordial matter.

99. Now, at the end of a great world-age, all beings are reabsorbed into My unmanifested nature.

100. As owing to the extreme heat of summer all grass seed is reabsorbed into the earth,

101. or as when the vehemence of the rainy season is over, the Sharadā season sets in, and masses of clouds then disappear from the sky,

102. or as the wind abates and vanishes from the dome of the sky, or the restlessness of waves subsides in the water,

103. or as a dream, on awakening, sinks back into the mind, so

at the end of a world-age everything formed out of matter is reabsorbed into the primal matter.

104. Then, it is said, at the beginning of another world age I again create everything. Listen while I explain this to thee clearly.

> VIII. *Taking hold of nature which is My own, I send forth again and again all this multitude of beings which are helpless, being under the control of nature [prakṛti].*

105. O Kiriti, I pervade this very matter, which is My own, just as the texture of warp and woof can be seen in a piece of woven cloth.

106. During the process of weaving, small squares [of crossing threads] take on the form of cloth; so does matter show itself in the forms consisting of the five elements.

107. Owing to the presence of that which thickens it, milk is transformed into curds, and nature is formed out of matter in the same way.

108. The seed in contact with water germinates and large and small branches grow from it; so is the creation of all beings due to Me.

109. It would be true to say that a town has been made by a certain king; but in reality, did the hands of the king take part in the making of it?

110. If thou askest Me how I pervade this matter, it may be compared to a man awakening from sleep.

111. Do the legs, O Son of Pāndu, feel pain when one wakes from sleep? Do they actually travel in a dream?

112. If you ask what the import of all this is, it is that in the evolution of this created world I am not required to do anything at all.

113. As the subjects of a king follow their individual occupations, so am I related to matter; all the actual work is performed by it.

114. Behold! at the sight of the full moon, the ocean rises in full tide; but, O Kiriti, does this involve any effort for the moon?

115. Does not the lifeless iron move when brought near a magnet? But is the magnet disturbed by the proximity of the iron?

116. In short, in a similar way, when I assume My natural form the creation of beings then begins to proceed of itself.

117. All these innumerable creatures are dependent on matter, O Son of Pāndu. As the earth is capable of producing plants and leaves from seeds,

118. as childhood and the other ages of man [evolve] under the direction of the body, as the rainy season is the cause of the clouds in the sky,

119. or as sleep is the cause of dreams, so, O Best of men, does this matter direct the production of all created things.

120. Matter is the root of the whole creation, animate and inanimate, gross and subtle.

121. Therefore, that beings are created, and, once created, are maintained, this whole process has no relation to Me.

122. The moonlight spreads over the water like a creeper, but that does not cause the moon to increase. Similarly, all actions, though resting in Me, are apart from Me.

ix. Nor do these works bind Me, O Winner of wealth [Arjuna], for I am seated as if indifferent, unattached in those actions.

123. As it would be impossible for a handful of salt to stem the onward rush of the waters of the ocean, similarly, can actions which end in Me bind Me?

124. Can a cage made of smoke restrain the force of the wind; or darkness enter the disc of the sun?

125. Are [minerals] in the heart of a mountain damaged by showers of rain? So all actions performed by matter do not affect Me.

126. However, understand that I am the sole cause underlying all the effects of matter, but, like one dejected, I do nothing, nor do I cause anything to be done.

127. As a lamp placed in a house neither directs nor restrains anyone, nor does it know who is engaged in what work;

128. as it is a mere witness without interest in household activities, so though unattached to all works of creatures, I am nevertheless in these creatures.

129. What need is there to repeat this argument in different ways? Thou shouldst bear it always in mind, O lord of Subhadrā.

x. Under My guidance, nature [prakṛti] gives birth to all things, moving and unmoving and by this means, O Son of Kuntī [Arjuna], the world revolves.

130. O lord of Subhadrā, as the sun is but the mere instrument of all the activities of beings, so I am the cause in the production of this universe.

131. Since matter, established by Me, is the producer of all moving and immovable things, it follows that I am the root cause of all this.

132. In the light of this thou mayest clearly understand this principle, that beings are in Me, but I am not in them.

133. That beings are not in Me, not I in them; do not let these points ever be forgotten.

134. This is My deep secret, to thee only have I disclosed it. Closing fast [the doors of] the senses, experience it in thy heart.

135. So long as this secret is not fully grasped, My real nature will not be understood, O Pārtha, as grains [cannot be found] in husks.

136. A man may think that he can learn it from inference; but does the soil become damp with the moisture of a mirage?

137. When a net is thrown into the water the reflection of the moon seems to be caught in it; but when the net is pulled into the shore and shaken, where is the moon?

138. Likewise men covet in vain the eyes of experience with words and speech, but when it is a matter of real experience, behold, there is nothing.

XI. *The deluded despise Me clad in human body, not knowing My higher nature as Lord of all existence.*

139. What more can be said? If thou fearest this earthly life, and hast a true longing for Me, remember carefully this secret.

140. A man suffering from jaundice will say that the moonlight is yellow; so there are some who see blemishes in My pure form.

141. The mouth loses its power of taste because of fever, and finds milk like poison; so there are those who regard as human Me who am without human form.

142. So I say again, O Dhananjaya, beware lest thou forget this truth; if thou regardest it with thy grosser understanding, it is worthless.

143. However, some see Me with their grosser vision, but know thou that their seeing is as blindness, as nectar found in a dream has no power to make a man immortal.

144. The foolish think that they know Me completely by means of their earthly vision, but in fact such knowledge becomes a hindrance to the attainment [of true knowledge],

145. as a swan would perish, entering the water for the sake of the reflections of stars, [in the hope of finding jewels].

146. Is any gain lost by passing by a mirage [which can give no water]? Can any wish be fulfilled by resorting to the thorny bābul, thinking it to be the tree of the gods?[2]

147. A man might put out his hand to grasp a poisonous snake, imagining it to be a two stranded necklace of sapphires, or gather pebbles thinking them to be jewels,

148. or one might pick up a live ember of wood in his garment thinking he has found a treasure; or a lion might leap down a well, not realizing that in it is his own shadow.

149. So those who have jumped to the conclusion that I dwell here in earthly existence are like men who take the moonlight shining on water to be the moon itself.

150. Their belief is as useless as that of a man who drinks gruel, expecting that it will have the effect of nectar.

151. How can I manifest Myself to those who believe that they see Me, the imperishable, in a form destructible and material?

152. O Beloved, can a man reach the western shore of the ocean by setting out in an easterly direction? O good warrior, can grains of rice be obtained by thrashing the husks?

153. Similarly, can My true nature be known by knowing this gross body form? If a man takes foam in his mouth, has he drunk water?

154. Thus with deluded minds, they erroneously identify Me with this body and attribute to Me birth and action.

155. As a result of this they impute names to Me, who an nameless, action to Me the actionless, and bodily attributes to Me who am bodiless.

156. They think that I have form, who am formless, they worship Me who am without attributes, and they believe that I perform rites and duties, who am beyond the precepts laid down in scripture.

157. They impute to Me caste, who am without caste, attributes, who am beyond these, feet and hands, when I have none.

158. They measure Me who am infinite, restrict Me within the

limit of place, who am all-pervading. As a man who though asleep in his bed may see a forest,

159. so they imagine Me to have eyes and ears who have none; they think I have family descent who am without it, and that I have form who am formless.

160. They suppose that I am manifested who am unmanifest, they impute desire to Me who am passionless, they believe I experience satisfaction though I am self-sufficient.

161. They give Me clothing who cannot be clothed, ornaments, who cannot be adorned, they imagine I am the result of some cause, whereas I am the cause of all.

162. Though I am uncreated they [think they] create Me; though I am self-existent they set up [images of] Me; though I am timeless they call Me into existence and dismiss Me.

163. Though always complete within Myself, they attribute to Me boyhood, youth, old age, and they impute these various states to Me who am unvarying in form.

164. They infer that I am dual who am beyond duality, that I who am actionless perform actions, and state that I experience enjoyment, who am indifferent to it.

165. They describe My ancestry who have none, grieve at My death though I am everlasting, and assume that I have friends and enemies who am within all.

166. Though absorbed in the bliss of My own nature, still they regard Me as desirous of pleasure and though all-pervasive they believe that I belong to one place.

167. I am the one Self, in all creatures, imminent in all, and yet they declare that I favour this one, and being angry with some other, kill him.

168. In short, they attribute to Me all manner of human qualities, so perverted is their knowledge.

169. When they perceive before them an image they worship it as a god; when it is broken they throw it away believing that it is not.

170. They regard Me as human in all these various ways and thus their beliefs obscure their understanding.

> XII. *Partaking of the deceptive nature of friends and demons, their aspirations are vain, their actions vain and their knowledge vain and they are devoid of judgement.*

171. Therefore they are born in vain, like the clouds out of the

rainy season or as the waves of a mirage seen from a distance.

172. They are thus no better than riders made out of earth, ornaments produced by juggling, or walls of a celestial city seen in the clouds. All are mere appearances.

173. They are like a silk-cotton tree which has grown very high, but is hollow inside and bears no fruit, or like the [false] teat on the neck of a she-goat.

174. So is the life of such fools, like the fruit of a silk-cotton tree that can neither be given nor taken. Fie upon their works!

175. Whatever they have learned is like a coconut plucked by a monkey or a pearl fallen into the hands of a blind man.

176. Their scriptural knowledge is of as little use as a weapon in the hands of a girl, or as secret mantras taught to the unclean.

177. O Arjuna, the knowledge and actions of such men is useless for they are stupid.

178. The she-demon of the quality of darkness consumes their clear intelligence and, like an ogress, destroys the whole mind.

179. Overcome by this demon they are constantly troubled by anxiety and so fall into the jaws of the quality of darkness.

180. [In her mouth] the saliva of hope flows, the tongue of slaughter rolls, and endlessly she chews up morsels of the meat of content.

181. She licks her lips, thrusting out her tongue to reach the ears of her victims, filling the valley of the mountain of error with her intoxication.

182. Her jaws of hatred grind down wisdom, and to foolish men of dull intellect it is like the covering of Agastya.[3]

183. All who fall into the jaws of this fiend of darkness become immersed in the pitcher of confusion.

184. Those who thus fall into the pit of ignorance cannot be reached by the hand of discrimination; moreover, there is no trace of where they have gone.

185. Enough of these unnecessary words; for what use is there in describing a fool? To continue with their story can only weary the voice.

186. Shri Krishna having thus spoken, Arjuna replied, Yes, O Lord; and then Krishna said again, Listen to the description of the good, which will rest the voice.

> XIII. *The great-souled, O Pārtha [Arjuna], who abide in
> the divine nature, knowing [Me as] the imperishable
> source of all beings, worship Me with an undistracted
> mind.*

187. These are they in whose pure hearts I dwell permanently,
     as in a sacred place, and on whom non-attachment attends
     even during sleep,
188. over whose ardent desire and good faith religious duty
     reigns supreme, whose minds are the very essence of
     wisdom,
189. who have bathed in the river of wisdom and in whom,
     satisfied with the food of perfection, new foliage sprouts
     on [the tree of] peace.
190. They are the tendrils of Self-realization, the pillars of the
     hall of fortitude, and pitchers filled to the brim with the
     ocean of joy.
191. In them the spirit of devotion is so fervent that they even
     dismiss liberation [as worthless], and in whose every
     activity is visible the life of morality.
192. Their senses are adorned with the ornaments of restraint
     and their minds are a shelter for Me, the all-pervading.
193. These men of deep experience, the glory of the God-like
     nature, knowing everything to be a manifestation of Me,
194. the high-souled ones, worship Me with ever increasing love
     and their attitude is such that the sense of separation is
     never even touched by them.
195. Becoming one with Me, O Pāndava, they serve Me alone.
     The wonder of this must be told, so listen!

> XIV. *Always glorifying Me, strenuous and steadfast in
> vows, bowing down to Me with devotion, they worship Me,
> ever disciplined.*

196. With religious recital, drama and dance they have des-
     troyed [the necessity] for all acts of repentance, and not
     even the name of sin exists any longer.
197. They have made restraint of the senses and control of the
     mind of no importance, removed places of pilgrimage
     from their high rank, and the committal [of sinners] to
     hell ceases.
198. Restraint says, What is there for me to curb? Control asks,
     What is there to subdue? Pilgrimages to holy places say,

What is there for us to consume? For there are no sins for which our remedies are needed.

199. Thus by extolling my name they remove all the pains of the world, and fill the whole universe with the joy of the Highest Bliss.

200. They enable others to see even without the dawn, give creatures life without nectar, and enable them to see liberation with their own eyes without the practice of yoga.

201. They honour equally both king and peasant, make no distinction between high and low; therefore they are always a source of bliss to all the world.

202. Rarely does anyone reach heaven, but these saints have made the whole earth into heaven, and have purified everything with the power of singing My praise.

203. They are as radiant as the light of the sun but the sun is defective in that its sets. The moon also is only full at times; but these are eternally perfect.

204. Clouds give generously, but they disappear; so such a comparison is inadequate. They are veritable lions of compassion.

205. My name, to utter which only once a thousand births must be lived through, dances with delight before their speech.

206. I do not dwell in heaven, nor am I seen in the orb of the sun; more than that, I transcend even the minds of yogis;

207. yet, O Pāndava, though I am lost [to others] I must be sought in those who unceasingly extol My name.

208. How content they are in [singing of] My qualities! They forget even time and place and in the joy of their song they experience the inner bliss.

209. Joyfully they recite My names, Krishna, Vishnu, Hari, Govinda, interspersed with many enlightened discussions on the Self.[4]

210. Enough has been said. Hear, O Son of Pāndu, Thus praising Me they move about among all creatures.

211. O Arjuna, there are others who, with great efforts restraining the vital airs, and taking the mind as a guide,

212. erecting a hedge of control and restraint, they build within it an enclosing wall of the vajra posture, and on them they mount the cannons of breath-control.

213. With the light of Kundalini and the aid of the mind and the life-force, they capture the water-tank of the realization of ultimate reality.[5]

214. Self-restraint performs mighty deeds which silence passion, and the organs of sense are bound and imprisoned within the heart.

215. The steeds of self-control are massed together, all the elements are united, and the fourfold army of thought is destroyed.

216. Then with victorious battle-cries the drums of contemplation are sounded, and absorption in the Absolute shines forth in supremacy.

217. Finally, in the joy of the kingdom of Self-realization, the glory of perfect Union is enthroned and anointed with the experience of oneness with the Supreme.

218. O Arjuna, devotion to Me is so mysterious that I will now describe some other ways in which it is practised.

219. As there is but one thread running through a woven garment from one end to the other, so they recognize no one except Me in the whole universe.

220. From Brahma at the beginning to an insect at the end, they regard everything in the universe as manifestations of Myself.

221. They see no difference between great and small, animate or inanimate, gathering all together they know it to be Me.

222. Unaware of their own greatness, they do not distinguish between the worthy and the unworthy, classing all together, they like to bow down before all.

223. As water pouring from a height flows downwards without effort, so is it their nature to pay respect to every creature that they see.

224. As the branches of fruit-laden trees bend towards the earth, so they humble themselves before all creatures.

225. They are always free from conceit; humility is their wealth which they offer to Me with words of homage.

226. Being thus always humble, honour and dishonour do not exist for them, and they easily become united with Me; always absorbed in Me, they worship Me.

227. O Arjuna, I have described to thee the highest form of devotion. Now listen while I tell thee of those devotees who worship Me with sacrifice in the form of wisdom.

228. O Kiriti, already thou knowest the method of their worship, for I have described it earlier.

229. Arjuna replied, That is so, O Lord, it was Thy act of grace.

Can anyone, however, become satiated when feeding on nectar?

230. Hearing this, Shri Ananta knew that Arjuna was eager to listen to him. So he swayed with a joyful heart,

231. and said, It is well, O Pārtha, This would not be the occasion [to repeat it], but this eagerness makes Me speak.

232. Whereupon Arjuna said, Why is this? Does the moon shine only for the chakora bird? Is it not the nature of the moon to cool the whole world?

233. The chakora raises its beak towards the moon for its own satisfaction; so we make but a small request, O Lord who art the ocean of mercy.

234. The clouds, out of their generosity, relieve the thirst of the earth, but how small is the thirst of the chātaka bird, compared with the showers of rain that fall?

235. To obtain even a mouthful of water a man has to go to a river, so whether our desire be small or great, we must express it, O Lord.

236. The Lord replied, Say no more. After the pleasure I have experienced, it would not be possible to bear any more praise.

237. Thou dost listen so attentively that thou dost encourage my eloquence. Thus did the Lord speak appreciatively of what Arjuna had said.

> xv. *Others again sacrifice with the sacrifice of wisdom and worship Me as the one, the distinct and the manifold, facing in all directions.*

238. This is the nature of the sacrifice of wisdom. The primal thought is the sacrificial post, the five elements are the canopy, and the sense of separateness is the sacrificial beast.

239. The special qualities of the five elements, the senses and the vital airs are the materials used in the sacrifice and ignorance is as the clarified butter poured over them.

240. Mind and reason are as the vessel in which the fire of wisdom burns, and the even-balanced mind is to be understood as the altar of sacrifice, O My friend.

241. Keenness of intellect combined with discrimination are the proper incantations; the spoon [for pouring oil] is restraint, the individual self is the sacrificer.

242. That sacrificer, with the vessel of Self-realization, by means of the powerful mantra of discrimination, and wisdom as guardian of the fire, destroys the sense of separateness.

243. At that moment ignorance is removed and when the sacrificer has performed the purifying ablutions of the water of union with the Self, even the sacrificer and the sacrifice cease to exist.

244. No longer does he think of the five elements or the senses or sense objects as separate, for, through Self-realization, he knows all to be one.

245. O Arjuna, as a man suddenly awakening might exclaim, 'Was it not I who, while sleeping, was that army in my dream?

246. Now the army is no army and I alone am everything!' So does he realize his unity with the universe.

247. Then the concept of the individual self is lost, and he is filled with the realization of the unity of all created things, beginning with Brahma himself. So do they, realizing unity, worship Me with the sacrifice of wisdom.

248. From the beginning of time this diversity exists, by which all things are different; for even the names and forms of all things are unique.

249. Therefore, though there is difference in the world, yet there is no duality in their wisdom, as the limbs may seem to be separate, but they belong to the same body.

250. There are great and small branches, yet they are of one tree; as the rays of the sun are many but there is only one sun.

251. So, likewise, beings may be of many kinds, having many different names, and possessing various qualities; but I am known as indivisible among all these separate creatures.

252. These perform the sacrifice of wisdom, O Pāndava, conscious of this multiplicity; for, having attained Self-knowledge, they do not become separated.

253. So whatever objects they may perceive, at any time anywhere, they are conscious that there is nothing in them except Me.

254. A bubble [on the surface of water], wherever it may be floating, has only water round it; whether it floats or bursts, it is still in the water.

255. When the wind raises particles of dust, these cannot lose

their earthly nature, and when they fall down again it is on to the same earth.

256. So wherever and of whatever nature a thing may be, whether it exists or not, all things are in Me.

257. O Beloved, the extent of their experience [of oneness] is as wide as My omnipresence, so they become many and are active in many forms.

258. O Arjuna, as the sun is apparent to everyone, so are they seen ever before the world.

259. Their wisdom is not two-sided, as wind blows in all quarters of the sky.

260. As is the extent of My infinity, so is the measure of their faith, O Pāndava, and even if such men do not actually worship Me, still their worship is accomplished.

261. In fact, I am all that is. Who, therefore, is there who does not worship Me? But without real knowledge this worship cannot take place.

262. Now have I explained to thee those who worship Me with the sacrifice of Right Knowledge.

263. Whatever actions may be performed, all are offered to Me alone; but the foolish, unaware of this, cannot attain to Me.

> XVI. *I am the ritual action, I am the sacrifice, I am the ancestral oblation, I am the [medicinal] herb, I am the [sacred] hymn, I am also the melted butter, I am the fire and I am the offering.*

264. When such awareness is awakened, then will it be found that I am the basic scriptures, the practices arising from them.

265. Then, O Pāndava, I am the sacrifice to be performed strictly according to the precepts.

266. I am also the oblation and the food offered to the ancestors. I am the soma and the other the herbs; I am the butter, the fuel, the oblation and the incantations.[6]

267. I am the priest maintaining the fire which is a form of Myself and I am even the offerings themselves.

> XVII. *I am the father of this world, the mother, the supporter and the grandsire, I am the object of knowledge, the purifier. I am the syllable Aum and I am the rk, the sāma and the yajus as well.*

268. I am that father through whose union with the eightfold primordial matter the worlds are brought to birth.

269. As in the play of Shiva the man acts the part of the woman also, so I am also the mother of all animate and inanimate beings.[7]

270. In Me alone is the universe born, in Me it is maintained, and certainly in Me it evolves and in no other.

271. In the three worlds I am the grandsire of the universe from whose primal unconditioned mind was born pure Spirit and primordial matter.

272. I am the meeting point to which the various paths of knowledge lead; O Best of warriors, I am He who is called 'the one who should be known' in the central place of the Vedas.

273. I am the holy place where all the diverse theories are unified, wherein the different philosophies become reconciled, and in which devious forms of knowledge converge.

274. The seed of Brahma sends forth the shoot of the fourfold speech. I am the sacred syllable, the abode of this speech.

275. In the womb of this syllable are conceived the letter 'a' and the others. These as they are born give rise to the three Vedas.

276. I am these three, the Rik, Yajur and Sāma, say I Rāma, and I am also all that proceeds from these three.[8]

> XVIII. *[I am] the goal, the upholder, the lord, the witness, the abode, the refuge and the friend. [I am] the origin and the dissolution, the ground, the resting place and the imperishable seed.*

277. I am that highest goal in which primordial matter, wherein lies latent the whole movable and immovable universe and which, becoming exhausted, finds rest.

278. In Me this matter lives, and receiving support from Me, it gives birth to the universe. Moreover through it the universe experiences the three qualities.

279. I am the consort of Laksmi, the riches of the universe, O Son of Pāndu, and the lord of all the three worlds.

280. That ether should pervade the whole universe, that the wind should not for a moment cease to blow, that fire should burn and waters flow,

281. that the mountains should not leave their foundations,

that the ocean should not go beyond its bounds, and the earth should bear the burden of all creatures, all this is at My command.

282. It is I who cause the Vedas to speak, the sun to move in its course, moved by Me that vital air stirs which keeps the world in motion.

283. O Son of Pāndu, in accordance with laws prescribed by Me, at whose command all actions are performed, all creatures are overtaken by death.

284. I am He who am the all powerful lord of this universe; I am also the witness, like the ether of space.

285. I am that which pervades all names and forms, O Pāndava; I am also the refuge of them all.

286. As waves are of water, and the water is also in the waves, I establish all and I am the abode of all.

287. I am one, yet many, with all the diversity of the attributes of matter; I am the life-force active in all beings of the living world.

288. As the sun sheds his rays on all, not distinguishing between the ocean and the smallest pool, so I am the friend of all from Brahma to all creatures.

289. O Son of Pāndu, I am the life-essence of all the three worlds, and am the root-cause of the birth and death of all creation.

290. A seed sends forth branches and thus the quality of becoming a tree lies in the seed. Therefore, everything is the product of thought and ultimately is reabsorbed into thought.

291. I am He into whom, at the end of a world-age, is reabsorbed that unmanifested thought in the form of desire, which is the cause of the whole creation.

292. At that time all that has name or form passes away, both classes and individuals vanish, differences of kind cease to exist; and when space is no more,

293. I am that dwelling-place of the immortal gods whose function is to recreate form through thought and desire.

> XIX. *I give heat; I withhold and send forth the rain. I am immortality and also death, I am being as well as non-being, O Arjuna.*

294. As the sun, I send out heat and dry up [the earth]; again, as Indra, I send down rain and refresh the world.

295. All that is encompassed by death is a manifestation of Me, and I am the imperishable in all that does not die.

296. More need not be said, take it all in once and for all; understand that I alone am all that is and is not.

297. Hence, O Arjuna, is there any place where I am not? What is the fate of living beings, however, that they do not perceive Me?

298. Everything is filled with Me, both inwardly and outwardly; verily the whole universe is moulded in My form; but because they are involved in the process of action, they say that I do not exist.

299. Waves dry up when there is no water, a ray of light cannot be seen without a wick. How strange! I am they, [but they think that] they are not in Me.

300. But if one were to fall into a well of nectar, would one climb out on to the bank? What can be done for a man who does not attain to Me?

301. As a blind man, O Kiriti, running in search of a morsel of food, stumbles and kicks aside a desire-stone in his blindness,

302. so when true knowledge forsakes a man, he is in a similar state. All action, therefore, performed without wisdom is worthless.

303. Of what use would the wings of Garuda be to a blind man? So without wisdom every right action is wasted.

xx. The knowers of the three Vedas who drink the soma juice and are cleansed of sin, worshipping Me with sacrifices, pray for the way to heaven. They reach the holy world of Indra [the lord of heaven] and enjoy in heaven the pleasures of the gods.

304. O Kiriti, in accordance with the duties prescribed for each stage of life, they become the model for the performance of rites.

305. When they perform the sacrifice with natural ease, the three Vedas bow their heads and ritual itself stands before them offering them the fruit of it.

306. Such consecrated men, drinkers of the soma juice, become the incarnation of sacrifice, but realize that by the merit which they acquire, they incur sin;

307. for, knowing the Vedas and performing even a hundred

sacrifices, and they lose sight of Me, who am the object of sacrifice, and prefer heaven.

308. O Arjuna, it is just as if a poor beggar who, seated at the foot of the tree of desire, were to tie up the corners of his begging-cloth and set out to beg in poverty.

309. So, worshipping Me with a hundred sacrifices, they seek for heavenly pleasures. Is it not really sin they accumulate, rather than merit?

310. Therefore, the attainment of heaven without Me is but the path of merit resulting from ignorance. Wise men regard it as the path of calamity and destruction.

311. Compared with the pains of hell, heaven may be a place of joy, but the pure bliss of the Eternal is My true form.

312. In coming to Me, O great warrior, heaven and hell are the two false paths, the ways of robbers.

313. Men ascend to heaven by means of sin, which is thought of as merit; they descend to hell as a result of actual sin. But I can only be reached by pure merit.

314. O Arjuna, since all things are in Me, is it not a lie to say that that which alienates Me from them is merit?

315. But enough for the moment; now listen! Consecrated men who thus perform sacrifices in worship of Me are but seeking the pleasures of heaven

316. But by means of that merit which is sin and by which they cannot reach Me, they go to heaven,

317. where immortality is their throne, their steed is like Airāvata and Amarāvati is their royal palace.[8]

318. There they enjoy treasures of the highest psychic powers, jars full of nectar, and possess herds of desire-fulfilling cows.

319. There the gods themselves are their servants, there are fields of desire-stones, and gardens of wishing-trees for their delight.

320. There are songs of the heavenly bards, dances of the celestial dancers like Rambhā. Urvashi is chief of the maidens who minister to their pleasure.[10]

321. The god of love serves them in their bedchamber where the moon sprinkles water; heralds as swift as the wind [do their bidding].

322. The heavenly priest Brihaspati himself is chief among the company of brāhmans who chant blessings and they enjoy all things in company with the gods.[11]

323. Mounted troops of the princely guardians of the quarters of the earth accompany them, and Uccaishravā is the leader of the horses on which they ride.[12]

324. Enough of this now. Thus they experience pleasures such as those of Indra, so long as their store of merit lasts.

> XXI. *Having enjoyed the spacious world of heaven, they enter [return to] the world of mortals, when their merit is exhausted; thus conforming to the doctrine enjoined in the three Vedas and desirous of enjoyments, they obtain the changeable [what is subject to birth and death].*

325. But when they lose the rank attained by their merit, they fall down again from that exalted Indra-like state, and return to the mortal world.

326. The state of these sacrificers is as shameless as that of a man who, having spent all his wealth [on visiting harlots] dare not even knock at their doors. How can it be told?

327. Thus they miss Me, who am always with them, they who desired to enjoy heaven through their acquired merit; their immortality has become worthless and they return to earthly existence.

328. O Beloved, as treasure may be found in a dream but vanishes when a man awakens, so is the heavenly happiness of these knowers of the Vedas.

329. O Arjuna, though a man may know the Vedas, without knowing Me it is like husks of corn winnowed without the grain.

330. Therefore without Me the three rites [described in the Vedas] are meaningless. So knowing Me, if none else, thou wilt obtain happiness.

> XXII. *But those who worship Me, meditating on Me alone, to them who ever persevere, I bring attainment of what they have not and security in what they have.*

331. Those who have offered their whole heart and mind to Me, as the child in the womb knows nothing of striving,

332. those to whom I alone am dear, and those who have devoted their lives to Me,

333. who meditate on Me with undivided minds, and who worship Me only, these I Myself serve.

334. As soon as they have become one with Me, they follow My path, and all thought for their welfare falls on Me.

335. The performance of all that they have to do devolves on
Me, as a mother bird lives only to sustain the life of her
fledgelings.

336. A mother has to do all that is good for her child before
it knows hunger and thirst; so for creatures who follow
Me I do not hesitate to do everything.

337. Should they desire union with Me, I satisfy their longing;
to those who seek to serve Me, I give My love.

338. Whatever wish they have in their hearts, that I grant them
first of all; and the support which is given to them is given
by Me.

339. Their whole welfare is in My hands O Pāndava, for I am
their sole refuge.

XXIII. *Even those who are devotees of other gods, worship
them with faith, they also sacrifice to Me alone, O Son of
Kuntī [Arjuna], though not according to the true law.*

340. There are other traditional paths, but in them men do not
know Me as all-pervading; they worship Me as Fire,
Indra, the Sun or the Moon.

341. Such worship does indeed reach Me, for I am all these;
but the way of their worship is not the straight path but
crooked.

342. Are not the branches and leaves of a tree born of the same
seed? and it is the roots which absorb the water, so it is
the roots which must be watered.

343. Or, though the ten sense organs belong to the same body,
the sense-objects experienced through them are enjoyed
by only one person.

344. Should one put well-prepared food in the ear? Should one
bring flowers and attach them to the eyes?

345. Food must be tasted by the tongue, fragrance must be
smelt by the nose; so, I must be worshipped in My true
nature, as Myself.

346. Worship performed without knowing Me is worthless and
irrelevant; so knowledge, which is as the eyes of these acts,
must be free from blemish.

XXIV. *For I am the enjoyer and lord of all sacrifices. But
these men do not know Me in My true nature and so they
fall.*

347. Moreover, behold, O Son of Pāndu, of all the offerings in sacrifice, is there any other enjoyer but Myself?

348. I am the source of all sacrifice, I am also the end of them; still men of perverted minds forget Me and worship other gods.

349. As the water of the Ganges is poured out into the Ganges itself in the name of the gods and ancestors, so these men offer Me what is Myself, but in various forms of faith.

350. Therefore, O Pārtha, they fail to reach Me, and attain to that state which in their minds they have desired.

> xxv. *Worshippers of the gods go to the gods, worshippers of the manes go to the manes, sacrificers of the spirits go to the spirits and those who sacrifice to Me come to Me.*

351. Those whose devotion is offered to the gods, with their whole mind and speech and senses, become gods as soon as they relinquish the body.

352. Again they who faithfully observe the rites due to ancestors, attain to the state of those ancestors when they die.

353. Still more, those whose chief deities are the lower divinities and elemental spirits whom they worship with magic practices,

354. they themselves become elementals when the veil of the body is removed; so in accordance with their thoughts they receive the fruit of their actions.

355. On the other hand, [there are] those who have seen only Me with their eyes, heard of only Me with their ears, who have no thought except for Me, who extol Me with their voices;

356. who everywhere prostrate themselves [before Me] with their bodies, they who offer alms and carry out other practices for My sake;

357. who have studied [My wisdom], who inwardly and outwardly are satisfied by Me and who have come to birth solely for My sake;

358. who proudly boast that they exist for the glory of Hari, and whose only greed is their greed for Me;

359. who are filled with passion, desiring Me, filled with love, loving Me, fascinated by their attraction to Me they forget the world;

360. who know only Me as their sacred books and who recite

hyms only in order to reach Me, who worship Me thus in every activity.

361. These men certainly have become united with Me even before death; so at death how could they pass on to any other state?

362. Therefore those who have become worshippers of Me and have made offering of themselves to Me attain to union with Me.

363. O Arjuna, without giving himself to Me, none can please Me; I cannot be reached by any [other] offering.

364. He who claims knowledge [of Me] does not know Me; he who boasts of his self-realization is imperfect; he who declares that he has reached his goal has attained nothing.

365. O Kiriti, sacrifices, charity, austerities or any such efforts of which a man is proud are worthless; they are as ineffective here as a blade of grass.

366. Consider, is there anything superior in knowledge to the Vedas? Is there any other who is a greater talker than Shesha?

367. Even Shesha hides beneath My bed; the Vedas themselves withdraw saying 'Not thus, not thus', while Sanaka and other great sages are perplexed [as to My nature].

368. Among those who practise severe penance, who is worthy to be placed beside Shankara? Yet he humbly bears on his head the waters which flow from My feet.

369. Is there anyone to equal in greatness Lakshmi who is waited upon in her house by serving maids like success?

370. If in play they were to build toy houses and call them Amarapura, would not Indra and other gods be their dolls?[13]

372. When tired of them, she breaks up these toys and Indra would then become destitute. Whatever trees they see are changed into wishing trees.

371. Even [Lakshmi] the chief mistress, in whose presence the servants of the house possess such power, is not worthy to be mentioned here.

373. For serving Me with her whole heart, and humbling herself before Me, O Pāndava, she has become worthy of the honour of washing My feet.

374. So then, all greatness should be left aside, all learning forgotten, for when a man has become lowly in terms of the world, he is near to Me.

375. O Kiriti, if the moon fades before the light of the sun with its thousand rays, how can a glow-worm boast of its light?

376. How then can an ordinary wretched human being come to Me, when the glory of Lakshmi is of no avail and even the penance of Shiva does not suffice?

377. Therefore relinquish the body, cast away every virtue, abandon all pride in riches.

> XXVI. *Whoever offers to Me with devotion a leaf, a flower, a fruit, or water, that offering of love, of the pure of heart, I accept.*

378. Thus if any devotee, with the joy of boundless devotion [brings] as an offering to me a fruit from whatever tree he may choose,

379. he shows it to Me, however small it is, I hold out both hands to receive it, and without even removing the stalk, I taste it respectfully.

380. Also if a flower is given to Me in the name of devotion, I place it in My mouth, though truly speaking I should smell it.

381. But why a flower, when even any leaf would be accepted, it matters not whether it is fresh or dry or in any other condition.

382. If it is offered to Me with the utmost love, even though it may be a mere leaf I take it with the same delight as a hungry man would rejoice at a draught of nectar.

383. A leaf would do, but it may happen that one cannot be found; then there is no difficulty in finding water.

384. Water is found anywhere, without price, and one finds it even without searching for it. He who offers Me even that in the spirit of the purest devotion,

385. builds for Me a temple more spacious than Vaikuntha, offers Me jewels more perfect than the Kaustubh diamond [in My crown].

386. He makes for Me many bedrooms of milk as delightful as the milky ocean.

387. He gives Me delights of sweetly scented substances such as camphor, sandalwood and aloe-wood, and lays on Me with his own hand a garland of lights like the sun.

388. He offers Me vehicles like Garuda, gardens filled with wishing trees, and herds of heavenly cattle.

389. Tasty dishes served to Me are sweeter than nectar, the smallest drop of water delights Me.

390. But why need I say any more, O Kiriti? Thou has seen with thy own eyes how, with My own hands, I unloosed the knot in Sudāma's cloth to take out a few grains of rice.[14]

391. True devotion is the only thing I recognise; I make no distinction of great and small. I am ready to be welcomed by the devotion of any man.

392. Indeed, a leaf, a flower, a fruit, is to Me but a means of devotion; in short, what I desire is complete devotion.

393. Listen to Me, therefore, O Arjuna, gain ready control over thy mind and then wilt thou never forget Me, who dwell in the temple [of thy heart].

> XXVII. *Whatever thou doest, whatever thou eatest, whatever thou givest away, whatever austerities thou dost practice, do that, O Son of Kuntī [Arjuna], as an offering to Me.*

394. However thou mayest act, whatever pleasures thou mayest enjoy, whatever sacrifices of many kinds thou mayest perform,

395. whatever gifts thou mayest grant to deserving suppliants, whatever wages thou mayest pay thy servants, whatever austerities and vows thou mayest observe,

396. all such actions, according to they own nature, which thou mayest do with steadfast devotion, should be offered to Me.

397. But in thy mind let there remain no memory of having performed these actions; thus purified, offer every action to me.

> XXVIII. *Thus shalt thou be freed from the good and evil results which are the bonds of action. With thy mind firmly set on the way of renunciation, thou shalt become free and attain to Me.*

398. As seeds thrown into a fire lose their power to germinate, so also deeds either good or bad do not bear any fruit when offered to Me.

399. O Beloved, when actions remain [without such offering], they bear the fruit of either pleasure or pain, and a man must be born again to experience these.

400. When, however, actions are offered up to Me then death

and birth cease, and all trouble arising from birth also disappears.

401. Therefore, O Arjuna, there is no need to spend time thinking this over for I have told thee the easy way of renunciation.

402. Do not fall into the bondage of the body nor become engulfed in the ocean of pleasure and pain. Experience of eternal bliss in Me will come to thee.

> XXIX. *I am alike to all beings. None is hateful nor dear to Me. But those who worship Me with devotion they are in Me and I also in them.*

403. If thou askest what My nature is, I would say that I am the same in all beings; with Me there is no distinction of 'I' and 'the other.'

404. They who know Me as such and destroy the seat of egoism, worship Me with their whole soul and in every action,

405. these, though seemingly acting in the body, are not really in their bodies, but are in Me, and I dwell wholly in their hearts.

406. As the complete nature of a banyan tree lies hidden in each of its seeds, and the seeds live within the tree,

407. so are we mutually related, I and they, though externally we differ in name. Still, the inner truth of this is that I and they are one.

408. As borrowed ornaments are only worn on the outside of the body, so these are indifferent concerning life in the body.

409. As when its fragrance is carried away by the wind, a flower remains abandoned on its stem, so the body of such men is only retained for the span of their earthly life.

410. Verily, O Pāndava, one whose egoism is absorbed in devotion to Me enters into union with Me.

> XXX. *Even if a man of the most vile conduct worships Me with undistracted devotion, he must be reckoned as righteous for he has rightly resolved.*

411. Thus they who worship Me with devoted affection are not reborn into a body of whatever caste they are.

412. O good warrior, considering their conduct, for the most

part it has been bad, but they passed [the rest of] their days at the meetingplace of the four ways of devotion.

413. O Beloved, whatever is the last thought at the moment of death, so will certainly be a man's state in after life; if therefore, in the end, he spends his life in devotion,

414. though his earlier conduct may have been sinful, he is the best of men; he is like a man who has fallen into a great flood, but emerges alive.

415. When he reaches the other bank alive, as the possibility of drowning has passed, so too, as a result of a man's devotion in his last years, none of his past sin remains.

416. Even had he been very wicked, he would be bathed in the holy waters of repentance, and thus cleansed he comes to Me by his earnest devotion.

417. His family also is made holy, pure and noble; such a man certainly fulfils the purpose of his life.

418. He has acquired knowledge, practised austerities, and studied the eightfold yoga.

419. In short, O Arjuna, he who is wholeheartedly devoted to Me has become free from the bonds of the fruit of action.

420. O Kiriti he has gathered up all the activities of heart and mind in his single-minded devotion and has offered it to Me.

> XXXI. *Swiftly does he become a soul of righteousness and obtain lasting peace. O Son of Kuntī [Arjuna], know thou for certain that My devotee never perishes.*

421. Thou wilt suppose that in the course of time will be united with Me; but how is it possible for anyone to die who lives on nectar?

422. So long as the sun does not rise it is called night; so is not any action performed without love for Me a great sin?

423. So, O Son of Pāndu, whenever the mind of a man reaches Me, he has indeed become one with Me.

424. When one lamp is lighted from another, it is difficult to say which was the first; so he who worships Me with his whole heart, becomes one with Me.

425. Then he remains in My eternal peace which is his glory; in fact, he lives by My life.

426. O Pārtha, shall I tell thee of this again and again? He who longs for Me must never cease from practising devotion.

427. Purity of family is not needed, nobility of birth is not to

be praised; and why should he bear the burden of useless learning?

428. Being fascinated by beauty or youth, or boasting of wordly wealth, are but empty show without devotion to Me.

429. Of what use are empty ears of corn, without the grain, however plentiful? Of what value is a forsaken city, however beautiful?

430. [What is the good of] a lake that is dry? If two distressed men meet in a forest, [what can they do?] [What is the use of] a tree whose flowers are sterile?

431. Equally vain are riches, and the pride of race and caste; no better, in fact, than a body with all its limbs but no head.

432. So, too, is a life accursed without devotion to Me. After all, are there not stones on the earth?

433. As a good man will avoid the deep shade of a harmful tree, so a man who does not worship Me is deserted by merit.

434. A neem tree may be breaking with its own seeds, but only the crows benefit by it; so a man without devotion has lived only for sin.

435. Should well flavoured food be put into an earthen dish and left at night at the cross roads, it would only be food for dogs.

436. The life of a man without devotion would be similar. Not even in his dreams can he realize what are good actions. He is but offering hospitality to all the sorrows of worldly life.

437. So the family [into which a man is born] need not be noble; a man might be born as an outcaste, or even the body of an animal would be acceptable.

438. Behold when the elephant was seized by the crocodile he piteously remembered Me; in spite of his animal nature he was able to reach Me.[15]

> XXXII. *For those who take refuge in Me, O Pārtha [Arjuna], though they are lowly born, women, Vaiśyas, as well as Śudras, they also attain to the highest goal.*

439. O Kiriti, those who are born in the lowest of all castes, the utterance of whose name is a pollution, the wombs of sin,

440. even such ignorant ones, as stupid as a stone, if devoted to Me with all their heart and soul,

441. chanting My praises with their voices, their sight contemplating only My form, and thinking only of Me with their minds,

442. whose ears listen to nothing but My glory, the only ornament of whose body is service of Me,

443. whose consciousness is aware of no sense object, but knows only Me, and who regard the attainment of such a state as life and all else as death,

444. who, O Pāndava, by their complete devotion have made Me the sole essence of their lives,

445. such may be born in the most degraded caste, they may be entirely unlearned, still when measured against Me they are not inferior.

446. Behold! the demons through the fullness of their devotion excelled the gods and on account of their greatness I had to become incarnate as the Lion-man.[16]

447. O Kiriti, many have always taken Prahlāda in place of Me and he has received what should have been given to Me.[17]

448. It is true that he came from a family of demons but even Indra could not surpass him [in devotion]. Therefore caste is of no consequence, devotion is the essential thing.

449. When the royal cipher is impressed on a piece of leather, [if a man has these pieces] everything may be obtained with it.

450. Again, even gold and silver are of no value as money; it is the royal decree that can give them value. Even a piece of leather stamped with it can purchase anything.

451. Similarly, greatness and the highest knowledge are of value only when the mind and the reason are filled with love of Me.

452. Therefore, race, caste and colour are all meaningless. It is only by union with Me that the goal of life can be reached, O Arjuna.

453. In whatever way devotion is practised, the mind should be directed towards Me; that being accomplished, all those things are useless.

454. As smaller streams exist as streams until they merge in the river Ganges; once they have joined the river they become one with it.

455. The distinction between sandalwood and acacia exists only until they are cast into the fire and become one.

456. The divisions of Kshatriya, Vaishya, women, Shudra and outcastes remain different only until they worship Me.[18]

457. Like grains of salt thrown into the ocean, such distinctions as caste and person pass away when through devotion men become united with Me.

458. Different rivers are called by various names and are said to flow eastwards or westwards until they reach the ocean.

459. So it is when, by whatever means, a man's mind has entered into Me; then it follows naturally that he becomes one with Me.

460. If a piece of iron, even if lifted only for cleaving, comes into contact with the magic stone, at that very moment it will become gold.

461. Were not the women of Vraja united with Me when, through their love, they came to meet Me?[19]

462. Did not Kansa come to Me through fear and Chaidya and others through their great hostility to Me?[20]

463. O Pāndava, the Yādavas were united with Me through kinship, and Vasudeva and others through affection.[21]

464. As Nārada, Dhruva, Akrura, Shuka and Sanatkumāra were able to reach Me through their devotion, O Wielder of the bow,[22]

465. so the Gopis came to Me through love, Kansa through the confusion of fear, Shishupāla and others through their wicked intent.[23]

466. O Beloved, I am the final haven for all, though coming by various ways, whether devotion, desire, dread, dispassion or enmity.

467. See! There is no lack of means whereby to enter into Me.

468. Let a man be born in any caste, let him serve Me or oppose Me, whether he is a devotee or an enemy, he must become Mine.

469. Under whatever pretext a man enters into Me, he is certain to attain to union with Me.

470. Therefore, O Arjuna, even outcastes, a Vaishya, a Shudra or a woman, when they worship Me, enter My abode.

XXXIII. *How much more then, holy Brāhmans and devoted saints; having entered this impermanent sorrowful world, do thou worship Me.*

471. Then [come] the brāhmans, the highest of all castes, for
whom heaven is a royal right, who are the home of the
knowledge of incantations,

472. who are gods upon earth, austerities incarnate, through
whom the good fortune arises in all places of pilgrimage.

473. In them all sacrifices everlastingly dwell, they are the
armour of the Vedas and in the lap of their sight all
auspiciousness grows.

474. Virtue flourishes by the essence of their ardour and truth
lives through their thoughts.

475. Fire was given life at their bidding, and for love of them
the ocean gave them its waters.

476. [To approach them] I pushed Lakshmi on one side, took
My divine necklace in My hand and laid bare the cavity
of My breast to receive the dust of their feet.[24]

477. I still bear the impress of that foot in My heart, O Auspicious One, to preserve My divine wealth, vast as the ocean.[25]

478. O good warrior, their wrath is the dwelling place of Rudra,
the bringer of the final conflagration, and through their
grace supernatural powers are obtained.[26]

479. Is it necessary to prove that such brāhmans, worthy to be
revered for their great merit and filled with devotion for
Me, obtain union with Me?

480. The leaves of a nearby neem tree, touched by the wind
passing by a sandalwood tree [absorb its fragrance and],
though lacking awareness, are placed on the forehead of
the god.

481. How could it be thought, therefore, that the sandalwood
tree itself cannot attain to such a state? Would this only
be true if it were proved that it had happened?

482. Hari himself wore on his head the half-moon in the hope
that it might cool his brow.

483. So why should not the sandalwood tree, which is whole
and which has power to cool, and by its fragrance is
superior to that of the moon, be freely applied to the
whole body?

484. If water from drains reaches the sea easily with the help
of the river into which it flows, can the river do otherwise
[than carry it to the sea]?

485. So, therefore, for princely sages and brāhmans, for whom
I am the sole refuge of both action and thought, and I am
most surely their ultimate state, their very being.

486. How can a man be carefree when he sets out in a boat full of holes? How can one expose oneself to a shower of weapons?

487. When stones are thrown at one's body surely a shield must be held [in front of it]? Or if attacked by disease should one be reluctant to take medicine?

488. O Pāndava, surely one should escape when surrounded on all sides by a forest fire? So then why should not a man worship Me, when born into affliction?

489. Has any man such strength that he can reject the worship of Me? Is he able to rest carefree in his home or in his pleasures?

490. Can anybody trust happily in knowledge or youth and yet not worship Me?

491. O Beloved, all the pleasures of the world do but gratify the body, and that, after all, eventually falls into the jaws of death.

492. Man has arrived at the market-place [of the end of the world], where the merchandise of sorrow has been brought in for sale and is being meted out by the measuring hand of death.

493. O Son of Pāndu, can the commodity of happy living be bought there? Can a lamp be lit by blowing a heap of ashes?

494. Or can the juice pressed out of poisonous roots, though it may be called nectar, make a man immortal?

495. Objects in the mortal world are of as much use as if the head were cut off and bound on to a wound in the leg.

496. Who could ever hear the report of any true happiness in this mortal world? How would it be possible to sleep at ease on a bed of live embers?

497. The moon of this world is forever waning, where the sun must rise only to set, and where sorrow, in the guise of happiness, harasses all men,

498. where the tender shoot of well-being is at once blighted by evil, and where death seeks out even a child still in the womb.

499. Men become anxious about the unobtainable, and even if they get it, it is carried off by demigods and no trace of it is left.

500. O Kiriti, though a man may search in every path, there is no trace of anyone who has returned and the only stories are those of the numberless dead.

501. Listen! Even if one were to describe the extent of the impermanency of that world for as long as Brahma, the creator of it, exists, the tale would never be finished.

502. It seems strange that those who are born in a world in which this kind of life is lived can be without care.

503. A man will not give a trifle of his wealth for spiritual gain in the visible or invisible world, yet he will still spend a fortune for something which can only bring ruin.

504. A man who in this life is absorbed in worldly pleasures is at present called happy, and one who bends under a burden of greed is called wise.

505. A man who has but little left of his span of life and whose strength and mental powers are deteriorating, is saluted humbly by others as an elder.

506. As a child grows in strength [its parents] dance with joy; and yet there is no regret that its life is becoming shorter.

507. Since the day of its birth, every day brings it nearer to death, and yet they celebrate its increasing years by raising flags.

508. Beloved, they cannot bear to hear the word 'May you die!' and they weep for the dead; but because of their ignorance they do not value life while it is there.

509. Behold, a frog, about to be swallowed by a serpent, will still wave its tongue to catch flies; so do creatures increase their desire with greed of some kind or other.

510. Shame on such evil! Everything in this world is distorted; as thou hast chanced to be born in this world, O Arjuna,

511. leave it at once and follow the path of devotion by which thou shalt reach My perfect abode.

> XXXIV. *On Me fix thy mind; to Me be devoted; worship Me; revere Me; thus having disciplined thyself, with Me as thy goal, to Me shalt thou come.*

512. Let thy mind be united with Me, devote thy love to worship of Me, and everywhere pay thy homage only unto Me.

513. When, under My direction, a man's personal will is burnt out, then he is called a true worshipper of Me.

514. When in this manner thou hast become one with Me, then

wilt thou enter into My form. I am telling thee this secret of My heart.

515. Entering into possession of these riches that I have kept concealed from all others, thou shalt be forever happy.

516. Sanjaya said, So spoke Krishna, the Great Soul, the tree that satisfies the desires of His devotees, the dark-hued [incarnation of] the Highest.

517. Listen! The old king quietly listened to this, silently, as a buffalo will lie still in the flooding waters.

518. Then Sanjaya nodded his head and said [to himself], O what showers of nectar have fallen on us, and yet the king seems as it were to have withdrawn to some neighbouring place.

519. As he is my patron, however, it would be improper for me to tell him this. It is his nature, and it cannot be helped.

520. I am indeed blessed in that the divine sage Vyāsa has preserved me in order that I should be able to tell this story.

521. As he was speaking thus, with great effort and mental stress, he was overcome by uncontrollable emotion.

522. His mind was stupefied and he became speechless, while his body vibrated from head to foot.

523. Tears of joy flowed from his half-closed eyes and waves of inner joy caused him to tremble all over.

524. Beads of perspiration formed on the pores of his skin like pure wheat grains so that he seemed to be covered with a net of pearls.

525. His life seemed to be passing out in the ecstasy of his joy but his life was preserved by the task of narration laid upon him by Vyāsa.

526. Then he suddenly began to hear again the conversation between Krishna and Arjuna and this brought him back to full consciousness.

527. Brushing away the tears from his eyes and wiping the perspiration from his body, he said to Dhritarāshtra, Listen to me, O King.

528. Now the listeners will gather a rich harvest of great truths, the words of Krishna being the choice seeds sown in the fertile soil of Sanjaya's mind.

529. O listeners, you should give some attention so that you may ascend the heights of joy; the good fortune of your ears have brought you blessing.

530. So the Lord of all perfected souls will show to Arjuna
the place of His glory. Listen to this, said Jnānadeva,
disciple of Nivritti.

*In the Upanishad of the Bhagavadgitā, the science of the Absolute,
the scripture of Yoga and the dialogue between Shri Krishna and
Arjuna, this is the ninth chapter called the Description of Sovereign
Knowledge.*

NOTES

1. *the bela tree.* This tree was sacred to Shiva. The nirguda was an inferior thorny shrub.
2. *the tree of the gods.* This is the 'wishing-tree' which grants the desires of those who approach it.
3. *Agastya.* A sage who was said to have been born in a pitcher.
4. *recitation of names.* The recitation of all the various names of Krishna is a special form of worship.
5. *the 'seventeenth'.* The seventeenth is the highest level of experience, realization of the ultimate. The 'seventeen' consist of the five senses, five actions, five vital airs, mind and realization.
6. *Soma.* The juice of the soma plant was used in sacrificial offering; also nectar, the beverage of the gods.
7. *ardhanārinateshvar.* This compound word used in the Marāthi text refers to the hermaphroditic form of Shiva and the drama based on this form is known by the same compound ending in -i; hence the reference to Shiva playing the role of both man and woman.
8. *Rik, Yajur, Sāma.* These are the names of the first three of the four Vedas; the fourth is the Atharvaveda.
   Rāma. This, as a name of Krishna is probably a shortened form of Ātmārāma, 'rejoicing in the Spirit'.
9. *Airāvata.* The name of the elephant on which Vishnu rode.
   Amarāvati. The palace of Indra, lord of the gods.
10. *Rambhā* and *Urvashi.* The names of two mythological nymphs.
11. *Brihaspati.* The priest of the gods.
12. *Uccaishravā.* The name of Indra's horse, said to have been produced out of the churning of the ocean.
13. *Amarapura.* The city of the immortals.
14. *Sudāmā.* A boyhood friend of Krishna who was so poor in later life that when he went to visit Krishna to ask for help all he could bring as a gift was a few grains of rice.
15. *the elephant and the crocodile.* The two doorkeepers of Vishnu were transformed by a certain sage into an elephant and a crocodile, but they were eventually released from this curse.
16. *Narsinha.* One of the incarnations of Krishna, the Lion-man.

17. *Prahlāda.* The son of a demon king who opposed Krishna. Prahlāda was persecuted because he persisted in serving Krishna.
18. *Women and outcastes.* The brāhman caste was the privileged caste in every way; they alone were educated for the religious life. The remaining castes—warriors, merchants, servers—with women and outcastes, were prohibited from religious practice according to tradition. It was at the time of Jnāneshvar and the 'bhakti' movement that all came to be included in the practice of loving devotion to Krishna.
19. *Vraja women.* These were women of a certain region, cowherdesses, who came to meet Krishna to welcome him when he visited the region. Through their devotion they attained to union with him.
20. *Kansa.* The maternal uncle of Krishna, ruler of the Vraja district. *Chaidya.* This king of the Chedis was also called Shishupāla. Both he and Kansa were hostile to Krishna but nevertheless won his blessing.
21. *Yādavas.* Descendants of the king Yadu.
Vasudeva. The father of Krishna.
22. *Nārada.* and others. The names of others who attained to union with Krishna through their devotion to him. Nārada was the messenger between gods and men.
23. *the Gopis.* These were women in charge of cows who were devoted to Krishna, who in his youth sported with him.
24. *The dust of the feet.* The deepest form of obeisance was made by touching the feet of the object of worship and then touching one's forehead with hands folded together.
25. *Bhrigu.* This was a sage who, to test whether Vishnu was worthy of worship, kicked him in the breast. Vishnu treated him with generosity. Here the reference is to Krishna, the incarnation of Vishnu.
26. *Rudra.* Rudra is the horrific form of Shiva.

CHAPTER X

1. Salutation to thee, [O Preceptor], skilful in clarity of exposition, causing the lotus of knowledge to bloom, delighting in the beauty of the first stage of speech as in a lovely maiden![1]
2. Salutation to thee who art the sun in the darkness of worldly life, possessed of the highest powers; who art endowed with youthfulness and dost delight to foster [in Thy disciples] attainment to the highest stage of knowledge of truth.
3. Salutation to thee! who art the protector of the whole world, the storehouse jewels of auspiciousness, the sandal-wood tree in the forest of righteous men, object most worthy to be worshipped.
4. Salutation to thee! who in the minds of the wise art as the moon to the chakora bird, king in the realm of Self-realization, ocean of the essence of the Vedas, the cupid who inspires the god of love.
5. Salutation to thee! who art worthy to be worshipped by all the faithful, who hast destroyed the temples of the elephant of this worldly existence, the source from which the whole universe has evolved, O prince among teachers!
6. Thy grace is [personified by] Ganesha, and favoured by him even a child may enter into every branch of learning.
7. When the word of reassurance has been spoken by the beneficent voice of the Preceptor, the island of the nine sentiments will be reached.
8. Even a dumb man can rival Brihaspati, lord of eloquence, in the art of composition when he is favoured by thy love, which is as the goddess Sarasvati.
9. Moreover, he on whom thy gracious sight shines or on whose head thy lotus-like hand is placed, though he be an individual soul, becomes equal with the great god Shiva.

10. With what further words can I extol his greatness? Is there any need to make the sun shine more brightly?

11. or to cause the desire-tree to bear flowers? What feast can be offered to the ocean of milk, or who would wish to add fragrance to camphor?

12. What ointment can be applied to sandalwood? What need is there to cook nectar? Is it possible to place anything above the sky?

13. Such is the greatness of the spiritual teacher, and therefore by what means is one to understand him? Realizing all this, I silently salute him!

14. Were I to say that I could describe my revered teacher by the power of intelligence, it would be like adding gloss to pearls.

15. But let these words be. [To say more would be like applying] a touchstone to the finest gold. It is better to fall silently at his feet.

16. Then I said, O Master, because thou has shown me such affection I have become as a banyan tree in the holy city of this meeting place of Krishna and Arjuna.

17. Once when Upamanyu asked for a cup of milk, the god Shiva offered him the whole milky ocean in a bowl.

18. The Lord of Vaikuntha presented the discontented Dhruva with the gift of the place of the polar star.[2]

19. In the same way I have been able to sing, in the Ovi metre, of the Bhagavadgitā which is the crown of the Brahma philosophy and the seat of all the sciences.

20. When I was wandering in the forest of language I could not hear what was said by the words, as it were the fruit borne by the trees; but thou hast made of that speech a wish-fulfilling creeper of understanding.

21. My consciousness has now been made into a treasure-house of spiritual joy, and my heart has become a couch of rest in the ocean of the meaning of the Gitā.

22. Now by thy grace I have been able without difficulty to explain the first part of the Gitā in the Ovi metre.

23. In the first chapter was described the despondency of Arjuna, in the second the yoga [of action] was made clear, in which also the difference between the yoga of wisdom [and that of action was explained].

24. In the third chapter the yoga of action was propounded; in the fourth the same was shown in relation to the

philosophy of wisdom. In the fifth chapter the secret [of the eight branches of yoga] was presented.

25. This same yoga was explained in detail in the sixth chapter, beginning with a description of yogic posture, the yoga by which the individual soul attains to union with the Highest Spirit.

26. In the same chapter was taught the complete theory of the realization of union and the fate of those who fall away from this path.

27. After this, in the seventh chapter, at first the abandonment of matter was explained and then the nature of the four classes of worshippers of the Highest was described.

28. Then in the eighth chapter, after answering [Arjuna's] seven questions, the Lord explains in the rest of the chapter all matters concerning the condition in which men find themselves at the time of death.

29. Whatever teaching there is in the whole of the Vedas is to be found in the hundred thousand verses of the Mahābhārata.

30. Now [the teaching comprised] in the whole of the Mahābhārata is found in the seven hundred verses of the discourse of Krishna and Arjuna and the essence of all these is contained in the ninth chapter.

31. I would not dare to set my seal on the ninth chapter, claiming that its meaning had been fully expounded. Why should I speak with such boldness?

32. Sugar and molasses are made from the same sugarcane juice, but they are very different in the sweetness of their taste.

33. Some chapters describe Brahma, realizing Him to be all-pervading; others help us to realize His immanence; when we try to understand others, we ourselves, with all our powers of perception, become absorbed in Him.

34. Such are the chapters of the Gitā, but the ninth surpasses all description; that I have been able to expound it is [the work of] thy grace, O Lord.

35. There was [Vasishtha] whose cloth shone as the sun [Vishvamitra] who was able to create another world; and [Nala] who brought stones [and made a ford by which the monkey armies] crossed the sea.[3]

36. [Māruti] caught the sun in the heavens, and [Agasti]

drained the ocean in one gulp. So hast thou enabled me, ignorant as I am, to relate that indescribable chapter.[4]

37. If a description of the fight between Rāma and Rāvana were asked for, their meeting on the field of battle should be narrated exactly as it happened.[5]

38. So I say that Krishna's teaching in the ninth chapter is as it is given in the ninth chapter. Those learned ones who understand the meaning of the Gitā will realize this.

39. I have expounded the first nine chapters in accordance with my views. Now begins the second part of this book, to which please listen.

40. In this chapter Shri Krishna will explain to Arjuna in a skilful and interesting way his special and his general powers.

41. With the eloquence of our Marāthi language, the sentiment of tranquillity will be found to surpass that of love, and even the Ovi metre will be an ornament to poetic composition.

42. If my Marāthi version of the original Sanskrit [Gitā] is read carefully, with a clear understanding of its meaning, no one could say which is the original.

43. Owing to the beauty of the body, it becomes an ornament to the very ornaments that it wears, and one cannot say which of the two beautifies the other.

44. So do the Sanskrit and Marāthi languages display their beauty in the place of honour in the meaning of the Gitā; listen carefully.

45. If one has to express the feelings aroused [by the Gitā] one needs showers of the nine sentiments, whereby one's literary powers are enriched.

46. So, taking the beauty of the Marāthi tongue and adding to it the youth of the sentiments, the precious truths of the Gitā are set forth.

47. Hear now what is said by the Lord of the Yādavas, who is the greatest teacher in the whole world and who causes the minds of men of intelligence to marvel.

48. Jnānadeva, disciple of Nivritti says, Hear what the Lord Krishna said, O Arjuna, thy mind is well able to understand all these things.

The Blessed Lord said:

1. *Again, O Mighty-armed [Arjuna], hearken to My*

supreme word. From a desire to do thee good, I will declare it to thee, now that thou art taking delight [in My words].

49. [I wished to see whether] thou hast paid attention to the exposition of the truth previously given, and [I find that] thou hast done very well.

50. As by pouring a little water into a pot one can see whether it leaks and then more can be added, so I have tested thee to see whether I can teach thee more.

51. If one wishes to leave a stranger in charge of one's possessions one makes him treasurer only if he is honest; so now I can place confidence in thee, O Kiriti.

52. Thus the Lord of all addressed Arjuna with respect, as clouds, on perceiving a mountain, gather around it.

53. That Prince of all compassionate ones said, O Mighty-armed, listen. I will explain again the truths which I have imparted to thee.

54. When a field is sown every year and yields a drop, it will yield more and more if the farmer does not weary of cultivating it.

55. Gold which is heated again and again in a crucible should not be said to deteriorate [for its quality increases].

56. So here, O Pārtha, I am not speaking for your sake but for My own purposes.

57. When a child is covered with ornaments it does not really appreciate them; it is the mother who is delighted at the sight of them.

58. So one should say that as it benefits thee more and more, so My love for thee is doubled.

59. O Arjuna, enough of this elaboration, clearly I love thee and there is no end to my satisfaction in talking with thee.

60. For this reason I repeat these things; listen to Me with full attention.

61. Arjuna, hear this secret, My sublime teaching; it is the highest Brahma, taking on the form of words, which comes to embrace thee.

   11. *Neither the hosts of gods nor the great sages know any origin of Me for I am the source of the gods and the great sages in every way.*

62. But, O Kiriti, dost thou not truly know Me? It is I who am here; the universe is but a dream.

63. Here the Vedas are silent, the mind and the vital air become powerless, and the sun and the moon set in darkness, though it is not night.

64. As the child in the womb does not know its mother's age so am I unknown to all the gods.

65. As fish cannot measure the ocean, as a gnat cannot traverse the whole sky, so the great sages even with their wisdom cannot know Me.

66. Aeons have passed in trying to know clearly who I am, how great, whence I come and when.

67. O Pāndava, though I am the primal source from which all the gods, the great rishis and the whole of creation have sprung, it is very difficult for them to know Me.

68. If water having flowed downwards could flow up again to a mountain or a grown tree return to its own roots, then could I be known by the world which has emanated from Me;

69. or if it were possible for a banyan tree to be contained in one of its shoots, if the sea could be contained in a single wave, or the whole earth be stored in a single atom,

70. then there would be a possibility of My being known by the souls of men, the great rishis and the gods who have been created by Me.

> III. *He who knows Me, the unborn, without beginning, also the mighty lord of the worlds, he, among mortals is undeluded and freed from all sins.*

71. Though I am thus, one who by chance withdraws from further worldly life, and turns away from all activities of the senses,

72. even though he is drawn back into these he can quickly recover and, abandoning the life of the body, can rise above the power of the elements.

73. His mind being firmly established thus, by the light of his own Self-illumination, he realizes clearly that by nature I am unborn.

74. He is as the touchstone compared with other stones, as nectar in comparison with all fluids, or as a part of Me in human form.

75. He is the living image of wisdom and the limbs of his body are as the offshoots of bliss. His human form is an illusion for ordinary men.

76. If by chance a diamond were found in a lump of camphor
and water fall upon it, would it not emerge with its
form preserved?

77. So though this man may seem in the human world to be
an ordinary man, the weaknesses of nature are unknown
in him.

78. Sins avoid him, for fear of their lives, and as a serpent
will leave a burning sandalwood tree, so desires will pass
by the man who knows Me.

79. Now if thou desirest to learn how I may be known, hear
what I am and what are My states of being.

80. These are spread throughout the whole world, expressing
themselves in many and various creatures according to
their individual nature.

> IV. *Understanding, knowledge, freedom from bewilder-
> ment, patience, truth, self-control and calmness; pleasure
> and pain, existence and non-existence, fear and fearless-
> ness.*

> V. *Non-violence, equal-mindedness, contentment, austerity,
> charity, fame and ill-fame [are] the different states of
> beings proceed from Me alone.*

81. Of these the first is intellect, then follows limitless wisdom,
freedom from confusion, forbearance, forgiveness and
truth,

82. then tranquillity and restraint, joy and grief found among
men, birth and destruction, these all exist in my nature.

83. Fear and fearlessness, harmlessness and equanimity,
contentment, austerity and charity, O Son of Pāndu,

84. fame and disgrace, success and failure, all these moods
which are found in every place, emanate from Me, in all
creatures.

85. Just as all men are different, so regard also these moods.
Some proceed from My wisdom, some know nothing of me.

86. As light and darkness are caused by the sun; when it
rises light appears and darkness comes with its setting.

87. Similarly knowledge and ignorance of Me are due to the
destiny of creatures; for this reason they are of different
kinds.

88. Thou shouldst know, O Son of Pāndu, that the whole
world of sentient beings is involved in My nature.

89. Now will I speak of eleven other manifestations of Myself, those which protect the created world and under whose power the worlds live.

90. [There are] those illustrious seven seers, Kashyapa and others, most advanced [in all virtues], and wisest among the sages;[6]

91. fourteen Manus will be mentioned, of whom there are four principal ones and of these Svayambhu is the chief.[7]

92. These eleven were conceived in My mind, O Wielder of the bow, for the conduct of the affairs of the created world.

93. Before the order of men had been evolved or individuality developed, the group of the primary elements was still undivided.

94. These being created they then established [the guardians of] the world; these created the peoples.

95. So these eleven are as kings and the evolved worlds are their subjects, therefore know that all this world-manifestation is Mine.

96. [As an example] first there is only a seed, from that there grows a stem, and out of that branches shoot out;

97. from the main branches others shoot out and from all these appears the foliage,

98. then the flowers and fruit; so the whole tree grows; and, if we consider rightly, the seed is all this.

99. So, in the beginning I alone was; then awareness of mind was born. Out of that arose the seven great rishis and the four Manus.

100. They created the guardians [of different worlds], and these brought into being the various worlds. From the worlds were created the whole of mankind.

101. In this way, the whole universe has developed from Me. Only through faith is this realized.

VII. *He who knows in truth this glory and power of Mine is united [with Me] by unfaltering yoga; of this there is no doubt.*

VIII. *I am the origin of all; from Me all [the whole creation] proceeds. Knowing this the wise worship Me, endowed with meditation.*

102. Therefore, O Consort of Subhadrā, these are the aspects of My powers and the whole universe is pervaded by them.

103. In this manner, [from Brahma the Creator down] to the ant, there is nothing else but me.

104. One who knows this to be true has indeed attained the awakened state of wisdom and is not aware of the illusion of distinctions between superior and inferior.

105. Thou shouldst know, through experience of oneness, that I Myself, those manifestations of Me, and all separate things comprised in them, all these are one.

106. So, therefore, he who by means of the yoga of certainty is united with Me through his mind, has attained his goal; concerning this there is no doubt.

IX. *Their thoughts [are fixed] on Me, their lives [are wholly] given up to Me, enlightening each other and ever conversing of Me, they are contented and rejoicing in Me.*

107. As though the sun were to encircle the sun with light, or the moon embrace the moon, or two brooks of like size meet,

108. so the streams of union with the Supreme meet, the quality of purity floating as plant leaves on the surface of the waters, and [these devotees] become as the image of Ganesha, seated in a group of four for discussion together.

109. In their great delight they leave the village of their bodies and begin to proclaim aloud their joy in Me.

110. The great truth of Brahma which the teacher conveys to his disciples, withdrawing to a quiet place, these men proclaim like the clouds in heaven till it resounds throughout the three worlds.

111. Just as the lotus bud, on opening, knows not how to keep its fragrance to itself, but offers it as a feast of fragrance alike to king and beggar,

112. so do these enlightened ones tell of Me throughout the universe. In the joy of the telling they forget their tale; in this forgetfulness they lose all awareness of body and soul.

113. In the fullness of their love they know neither day nor night; they have made themselves one with the perfect bliss of union with Me.

114. Then they win for themselves the priceless gift, O Arjuna, which I Myself should grant them,

115. and, O good warrior, compared with the path by which they set out, both heaven and final emancipation are as a by-path.

116. So, that love which they have for Me is the gift I have to bestow, but they have made it their own before even I could grant it.

117. All therefore that remains to be done is [to ensure that] such love increases and that the evil eye of death does not fall on them. This is what I have always to do.

118. O Kiriti, as a mother follows after her beloved child and watches over it lovingly while it plays,

119. and she turns into gold whatever game it wants to play; so do I foster in them every kind of worship.

120. I take special delight in encouraging them along the path which brings them joyfully to Me.

121. I love all creatures who are devoted to Me, and they are devoted to Me as their only resort; for there are few such lovers in My abode.

122. The two paths leading to heaven and to liberation have been made for them to travel, I Myself and My consort Lakshmi spend ourselves [in their service].

123. But the supreme and selfless joy is reserved for those devotees who are united with Me through their loving devotion.

124. O Kiriti, to such a degree [am I attached to them] that I take these loving ones to Myself. These things are such that they are not to be spoken of.

xi. *Out of compassion for those same ones, remaining within My own true state, I destroy the darkness born of ignorance by the shining lamp of wisdom.*

125. They who have made of Me, who am the true Self, the only centre of their lives, thinking of nought else but Me,

126. for those pure enlightened ones, O great warrior, I Myself am the torch bearer, going before them with the camphor torch.

127. I dispel the thick cloud of the night of ignorance, and I create for them the dawn.

128. When He who is best of all, beloved of the hearts of His steadfast devotees, had spoken thus, Arjuna said, My mind is at rest.

Arjuna said:

> XII. *Thou art the Supreme Brahman, the Supreme Abode and the Supreme Purifier, the Eternal Divine Person, the First of the gods, the Unborn, the All-pervading.*

129. Hear, O Lord, well hast Thou swept away the dust of worldly life and I am set free from the pains of human birth and rebirth.

130. Today have I seen my [spiritual] birth and found my own true life. I am content.

131. Wisdom has been born, the day of my good fortune has dawned, in that I have received the grace of Thy words from Thy divine lips.

132. With the light of Thy teaching the inner and outer darkness has been dispelled and I see Thy nature in its full reality.

133. Thou art the Supreme Brahma, the resting place of the great elements, the most holy abode, O Lord of all the worlds.

134. The highest among the three gods art Thou, the spirit of the twentyfifth principle, the divine one beyond all forms of matter.[8]

135. Thou art without origin, O Lord, free from the grasp of the birth and action. Thee I have realized this day.

136. Thou dost control this wheel of time, Thou dost govern all life, Thou dost rule over the cauldron of the universe. Now I understand this clearly.

> XIII. *All the sages say this of Thee, as well as the divine seer Nārada, so also Asita, Devala, Vyāsa and Thou Thyself declare it to me.*

137. In another way I see the greatness of this experience; the great sages of old have spoken of Thee thus,

138. but through Thy grace my heart understands the truth of all they taught.

139. Though Nārada always came to us and sang of Thee, yet, in spite of not understanding the meaning of his words, I merely enjoyed his singing.

140. If the sun shines on a habitation of blind men, they would feel its warmth, but how could they know its light?

141. In the same way when the great sage sang of the Supreme, I enjoyed the sweetness of the melody, but did not understand anything else with my mind.

142. I heard also from Asita and Devala that 'Thou art thus'; but then my mind was overpowered by the poison of sense desires.

143. Why mention the names of others? Even when the great Vyāsa came to us he always spoke of Thy nature.

144. His teachings were like the desire-stone found in the dark, which remains unnoticed; but when daylight comes it appears and we say it is here.

145. Thus the teachings of Vyāsa and other sages were a mine of precious truth for me; but they were as though wasted without Thee, O Krishna,

> XIV. *I hold as true all this that Thou sayest to Me, O Keśava [Kṛṣṇa]; neither the gods nor the demons, O Lord, know Thy manifestation.*

146. Now the rays of the sun [of Thy teaching] have shone forth and my ignorance of all the paths spoken of by the sages has been dispelled.

147. Their teaching, the seeds of life, have fallen deep into the soil [of my heart] and, watered by Thy grace, they have borne fruit in this conversation.

148. The discourse of Krishna has brought juice into the flowers and these have given me delight.

149. The sayings of Nārada and the other saints are as rivers in the form of devotion and I, O Ananta, am the ocean of the joy of this dialogue [into which they flow].

150. O Lord, what all the merit which I have accumulated in past lives could not achieve, Thou, O Teacher, [hast given to me].

151. Often I have heard the elders speak of Thee, but until Thy grace was bestowed on me, I could understand nothing.

152. When a man's fortune is favourable, whatever he under-

takes prospers. Similarly, all that is heard or studied
bears fruit through the favour of the teacher.

153. My Lord, a gardener spends his life toiling and tending
his trees, but the fruit will be seen only when the spring
comes.

154. When fever abates, what is sweet [again] tastes sweet and
even medicine is thought sweet when health returns.

155. Moreover, as the senses, speech and breath serve their
purpose only when consciousness is active in the body,

156. so all enquiry into the scriptures, all exercises practised
in yoga, can only become our own under the direction of
the teacher.

157. With the realization of this experience, Arjuna, dancing
with the joy of conviction, said, O Lord, I know Thy
words are true.

158. O Lord of blessedness, I have indeed had the clearest
realization that Thy nature is beyond even the understanding of the gods and demons.

159. Now I realize that unless Thy teaching is revealed to us,
we can never understand it with only our own intelligence.

> xv. *Verily Thou Thyself knowest Thyself by Thyself, O
> Supreme Person; the Source of beings, the Lord of
> Creatures; the God of gods, the Lord of the world.*

160. As the sky is aware of its own vastness, and the earth
knows its own weight.

161. so also Thou knowest Thyself through Thy omnipotence,
O Lord of Lakshmi! The Vedas even boast in vain of
their knowledge of Thee.

162. How may [the speed of] the mind be outrun, or the wind
be measured in a fathom? How can the original void be
crossed [by swimming] with human arms?

163. So it is with the knowledge of Thee; there are none who
can grasp it. Thou alone art able to impart knowledge
of Thyself.

164. Thou alone knowest Thyself and art able to reveal Thyself
[to others]; so wipe from thy brow once and for all, the
sweat of my desire to know.

165. Hast Thou heard me, O Creator of all beings, who art as a
lion to [the elephant of] worldly existence, and revered
by all gods and deities, O Lord of the universe?[10]

166. If we see Thy greatness [we know that] we are not worthy

to stand before Thee; on account of this unworthiness we fear to approach Thee, yet we have no other way.

167. Everywhere seas and rivers are full, but to the chātaka bird they seem dry, for only when rain falls from the clouds does it drink.

168. Similarly are there many teachers, O Krishna, but Thou alone art our refuge. Describe to me, then, Thy divine manifestations.

> XVI. *Thou shouldst tell me of Thy divine manifestations, without exception, whereby, pervading these worlds, Thou dost abide [in them and beyond].*

169. Show to me those of Thy manifestations which are most permeated with Thy divinity.

170. O Ananta, reveal to me those principal and best known manifestations which pervade all worlds.

> XVII. *How may I know Thee, O Yogin, by constant meditation? In what various aspects art Thou, O Blessed Lord, to be thought of by me?*

171. How may I know Thee? What must I know in order to meditate constantly on Thee? Were I to say that Thou art all, meditation on Thee would be impossible.

172. So do Thou once more describe to me in detail those manifestations to which Thou has earlier referred.

173. Speak to me clearly of them all, that I may find no difficulty in meditating on Thee in them.

> XVIII. *Tell me again in detail, O Janārdana [Kṛṣṇa] of Thy power and manifestation; for I am not satiated with Thy nectar-like speech.*

174. O Lord of Creation, I pray Thee to tell me of all those manifestations of Thine about which I have asked Thee. If Thou askest why I repeat this request,

175. [I would reply], Do not misunderstand this, O Janārdana; when one is drinking nectar one can never have enough.

176. After all, [the nectar which was drawn] from the same source as the Kālakuṭa poison, was drunk by the gods through fear of dying, and yet in one day of Brahma fourteen lives of Indra passed away;

177. but even so, anyone for whom the taste of this liquid of the Milky Ocean has the semblance of being nectar has such faith in it that he cannot refuse it.

178. It is self-existent and eternal, and easily obtained without turning the mountain Mandāra or churning the Milky Ocean.

179. It is neither liquid nor solid, has no distinction of taste and is obtainable by anyone who merely remembers it.

180. No sooner has its sweetness been tasted than earthly existence becomes meaningless and he who has acquired it becomes immortal.

181. No further mention is there of birth and death and the highest bliss increases in the whole man.

182. When by good fortune it is tasted it leads at once to Self-realization. Now when Thou Thyself givest this to me, I cannot refuse it.

183. Thy name is a great delight to me, acquaintance has become friendship, and besides this Thou art pleased to talk with me.

184. With what can I compare this joy? I cannot speak for delight. But this much I know, that [I would like Thee] to repeat what Thou hast said.

185. Does the sun ever grow stale? Does the moon ever shrink? Do the constantly flowing waters of the Ganges ever become unclean?

186. What Thou hast spoken with Thy lips [is to us as though] we have seen the form of Brahma. Today we enjoy the fragrance of the flowers of sandalwood.

187. Krishna swayed with pleasure at Arjuna's words and thought to Himself, His heart is a receptacle for the wisdom of devotion.

188. In the joy of His loved one affection for Arjuna welled up in His heart but, controlling it, what did Ananta say?

The Blessed Lord said:

> xix. *Yes, I will declare to thee of My divine forms but only of those which are prominent, O Best of the Kurus ; [Arjuna], for there is no end to My extent.*

189. Knowing this, thou wilt know all, O Kiriti, as a man who holds a seed in his hand holds the whole tree.

190. When a man obtains possession of a garden, he may easily get flowers; so if all these manifestations are seen the whole universe can be perceived.

191. Knowing well that He was the Father of the Father of all
and yet at the time forgetting it, Krishna said, O son of
Pāndu, My father, thou hast done well.
192. There is no cause for surprise that He called Arjuna
'Father', for was he not actually the son of Nanda?[11]
193. But let this be, such things are due to great affection.
Then He said, O Wielder of the bow, listen to what I am
about to say.
194. O Lord of Subhadrā, those My manifestations about which
thou hast asked Me are so countless, that though they are
Mine, yet I Myself cannot keep them in mind.
195. Even I Myself do not know clearly My own nature, or
how great I am. Therefore listen [while I tell thee of] My
principal and best known manifestations.
196. Truly, O Wielder of the bow, there is no limit to all that
emanates from Me. Even so wide an expanse as the
heavens can be contained in Me.

> XX. *I, O Gudākeśa [Arjuna], am the self seated in the
> hearts of all creatures. I am the beginning, the middle
> and the very end of beings.*

197. Listen, O thou of the curling hair, who art as Shiva in
the art of archery, in each and every created being I am
the Self.
198. I am enshrined within their hearts and I am also as a
sheath around them; I am the beginning, middle and end
of all.
199. As the sky surrounds the clouds above, below and on
every side, and they are both of the sky and in it,
200. as when they disappear they merge with it, so I am the
origin, the existence and the end of all creatures.
201. In such a way thou mayest know My manifold and all-
pervading being through My manifestations. Listen with
thy heart, with full attention.

> XXI. *Of the Ādityas I am Visnu; of the lights I am the
> radiant Sun; I am Marīci of the Maruts; of the stars I
> am the moon.*[12]

202. With these words the Compassionate One continued,
Among the heavenly deities I am Vishnu; among the
radiant worlds of light I am the Sun,

203. Among the companies of winds I am Marici, said Shārngi,
and of all the stars of heaven I am the moon.

> XXII. *Of the Rudras I am Śankara [Śiva]; of the Yakṣas
> and the Rakṣasas [I am] Kubera; of the Vasus I am
> Agni [Fire] and of the mountain peaks I am Meru.*

204. Among all the Rudras I am Shankar, the enemy of the
god of love; have no doubt about this.[13]
205. I am the wealthy Kubera, [friend] of Shambhu among
the Yakshas and Rakshasas. So say I, Ananta.[14]
206. Know Me to be Fire, among the eight Vasus, and Meru
among the high peaked mountains.[15]

> XXIII. *Of the Vedas I am the Sāmaveda; of the gods I am
> Indra; of the senses I am mind and of beings I am
> consciousness.*

207. Of the Vedas I, Govinda, am the Sāmaveda and among
the gods I am known as the great Indra.
208. Of the senses I am the eleventh, the mind, and of every
creature I am naturally the living spirit.

> XXIV. *Of the household priests, O Pārtha [Arjuna], know
> Me to be the chief, Bṛhaspati; of the [war] generals I am
> Skanda; of the lakes I am the ocean.*

> XXV. *Of the great sages I am Bhṛgu; of utterances I am
> the single syllable Aum; of offerings I am the offering of
> silent meditation and of immovable things [I am] the
> Himālayas.*

209. I am Brihaspati, the prince among all priests, ministering
to the heavenly throne, the primal storehouse of all
knowledge.
210. O wise one, of all generals in the three worlds I am
Skanda who was born of the union of Fire with the
semen of Shiva in Krittikā.[16]
211. Of all waters I am that great store of water, the ocean; of
the great sages I am Bhrigu, the treasure-house of austerity.
212. In the whole of speech I am that sacred syllable in which
is contained the highest truth. So say I, the beloved one
of Vaikuntha.
213. Among all the forms of worship in this world I am the
repetition of the names [of the Highest], I who, having

abandoned action, give rise to action and other [forms of religious activities].

214. Of all immovable mountains I am the most holy Himālaya, said the Lord of Lakshmi.

> XXVI. *Of all trees [I am] the Aśvattha and of divine seers [I am] Nārada; among the gandharvas [I am] Citraratha and of the perfected ones [I am] the monarch.*

> XXVII. *Of horses, know Me to be Uccaiśravas, born of nectar; of lordly elephants [I am] Airāvata and of men [I am] the monarch.*

215. Among all such trees as the Kalpa, Pārijāta and the sandalwood trees, well known for its qualities, I am Ashvattha.[17]

216. Among all the heavenly sages, O Son of Pāndu, know Me to be Nārada; of all the celestial songsters I am Citraratha.[18]

217. O Wise one! Chief of all the enlightened ones I am the venerable Kapila; among all horses I am Uccaishrava.[19]

218. Of elephants who are the ornaments of kings, O Arjuna, I am Airāvata, churned out of the ocean by the gods.[20]

219. Among men my special manifestation is the king, whom all men serve as his subjects.

> XXVIII. *Of weapons I am the thunderbolt; of the cows I am the cow of plenty; of the progenitors I am the god of love; of the serpents I am Vāsuki.*

> XXIX. *Of the nāgas I am Ananta; of the dwellers in water I am Varuṇa; of the [departed] ancestors I am Aryamā; of those who maintain law and order, I am Yama.*

220. Of all great weapons, I am the thunderbolt, O Wielder of the bow, the weapon of Indra, performer of a hundred sacrifices.

221. Of cows I am the Cow of Plenty, of unlimited powers; of progenitors know Me to be Madana.[21]

222. Of the genus of serpents I am the foremost Vāsuki, O Son of Kuntī; I am Ananta of the Nāgas.[22]

223. Among those that inhabit the waters I am Varuna, the consort of the western quarter, say I, Ananta.[23]

224. Of ancestors I am Aryamā, the divine forefather, I tell you this truly, O Arjuna.[24]

225. Of those who record the virtues and vices of men, who
search their hearts, and grant them liberation according
to their deeds,

226. of those who exercise control over men, I am Yama, the
witness of the deeds of men; this I, Ātmarāma, say to
thee, Arjuna.[25]

> XXX. *Of the demons I am Prahlāda; of calculators I am
> Time; of beasts I am the King of beasts [lions] and of
> birds [I am] the son of Vinatā [Garuḍa].*

227. Look on me as Prahlāda, of the race of demons; for this
reason he was never tainted by hatred or other vices of
the demonic nature.

228. Of all those who persecute I, Gopāla, say that I am Death
and among all beasts the lion is the manifestation of Me.

229. Of birds know Me to be Garuda; that is why he is able
to carry Me safely on his back.

> XXXI. *Of purifiers I am the wind; of warriors I am
> Rāma; of fishes I am the alligator and of rivers I am
> the Ganges.*

230. Of those that can traverse the world in a moment of time,
O Wielder of the bow, I am that which can circle the
earth in one leap.

231. Of all such swiftly moving things I am the wind, O Son
of Pāndu. Among all who wield weapons, I am Rāma,

232. who, when righteousness was in peril, transformed himself
into a bow in its defence, and in the Tretā age made the
glory of success his goal.[26]

233. Then, standing on the summit of Mount Suvela, he boldly
presented Rāvana's ten heads as an offering to those in
heaven who were praying for his victory?[27]

234. That Rāma restored to the gods their rightful dignity,
re-established righteousness, rising as the sun of the great
Solar Race.[28]

235. I am that Rāma, the consort of Jānaki, among all the
great wielders of weapons. Among all creatures dwelling
in the waters, I am the tailed crocodile.

236. Of all streams I am the Ganges brought down from
heaven by Bhāgirathi, who was swallowed [by Janhu]
and was given forth again from his thigh, ripped open.[29]

237. Among all rivers know Me to be the Ganges, the only
river of the three worlds, O Son of Pāndu.

> XXXII. *Of creations I am the beginning, the end and also
> the middle, O Arjuna; of the sciences [I am] the science
> of the self; of those who debate I am the dialectic.*

238. Were I to attempt to name all the various manifestations
of Myself in the universe, a thousand births would not be
enough to mention even half.

> XXXIII. *Of letters I am [the letter] A and of compounds
> [I am] the dual; I also am imperishable time and I the
> creator whose face is turned on all sides.*

239. If one desired to gather together all the stars, he would
need to enclose the whole heavens in a cloth.

240. If one wished to count all the atoms of which the earth is
composed, one would have to hold it under the arm. So
anyone who wishes to see the whole extent [of My
manifestations] must first know Me.

241. If a man wanted to grasp all the branches, flowers and
fruit of a tree at the same moment, it would be necessary
for him to pull up the root;

242. so if My different manifestations are to be known entirely,
My faultless nature must first be known.

243. Otherwise, of all these varied forms how many canst thou
listen to? Therefore know once and for all, O wise one,
that everything is indeed Me.

244. I am the beginning, the middle and the end of all creation,
O Kiriti, as the thread is woven throughout the warp
and woof of cloth.

245. When a man understands Me as pervading all, what need
is there to know My separate manifestations? Thou art
not yet worthy [to realize this].

246. So, O Lord of Subhadrā, as thou hast asked me, listen
while I tell thee more of those manifestations. Now of all
branches of knowledge, I am the knowledge of the Self.

247. Among speakers I am the discourse of which there is no
end, in spite of the principles laid down in the traditional
teachings.

248. It grows as the discussion develops, it adds strength to
the power of imagination in all who listen, and adds value
to the words of the speaker.

249. So I, Mukundu, say. I am the argument in all controversy.
Of all letters I am the pure A.

250. Of compounds know Me to be the dvandva and I the one
who, as death, seizes all, from the smallest gnat to the
Creator Himself.[30]

251. O Kiriti, I am he who, grasping the light of the universal
dissolution, swallows up the winds and into whose belly
the whole of space is absorbed.

252. I who sport with Lakshmi am death, the infinite; and
again I recreate everything.

> XXXIV. *I am death, the all-devouring and [am] the origin
> of things that are yet to be; and of feminine beings, [I am]
> fame, prosperity, speech, memory, intelligence, firmness
> and patience.*

253. I sustain all created things; I am their very life, and at
the end, when I destroy them all, I am death; hear this.

254. Now among feminine characteristics, My manifestations
are seven. Listen with care and I will tell thee of them.

255. Fame, which is ever new, O Arjuna, is the embodiment
of Me, and generosity with wealth is also Myself.

256. In all men I am intelligence accompanied by steadiness;
I am also universal fortitude and forbearance.

257. In the feminine qualities I am these seven powers. [So
said Krishna] who is as the lion to the elephant of earthly
experience.

> XXXV. *Likewise of hymns [I am] Bṛhatsāman, of metres
> [I am] gāyatrī; of months [I am] mārgaśīrṣa and of
> seasons [I am] the flower-bearer [spring].*

258. O Beloved, of the wealth of hymns in the Vedas I am the
much-loved Brihatsāma; so say I, the Lord of Lakshmi.[31]

259. That which is called the Gāyatri is of all metres My own
form. Know this for sure.[32]

260. Of months I am mārgashirsha, and of seasons I am the
flower-laden spring. It is I, the Wielder of the Shārnga
Bow, who say this.[33]

> XXXVI. *Of the deceitful I am the gambling; of the splendid
> I am the splendour; I am victory, I am effort and I am
> the goodness of the good.*

261. O wise Arjuna, among all tricks in games I am the dice. For this reason, no one should be turned away if there is theft in the market-place.

262. Of all brilliant things I am the light, believe this; and in all undertakings I am success.

263. My nature is at the heart of all manner of dealing where justice prevails, said the Lord of all the gods.

264. I am the goodness in all good things, and it is I who am the glory of all the Yādavas, I Ananta, say this.

265. I am he who was born to satisfy the wish of Devaki and Vāsudeva, who went to Gokula to please the Gopi maidens and who [sucking at her breast] drew out the life-breath of Putanā [with her milk],[34]

266. who even in his boyhood rid the earth of demons, and holding up the mountain [Govardhana] in His hand, humbled the greatness of Indra;[35]

267. who destroyed the serpent piercing the heart of Kālindi, saved Gokula from being burnt, and for the sake of the cattle drove Brahmā mad;[36]

268. who in early youth destroyed with ease such huge monsters as Kansa.

269. What more shall I say of all this? Thou thyself hast seen and heard it all. But still, thou shouldst know that I am manifested among the Yādavas;

270. and of all the Pāndavas of the Lunar race, I am thou, Arjuna; it is for this reason that our friendship endures.

271. Among the sages I am Vyāsa, said the lord of the Yādavas, and of the great seers I am Ushanā, who is the abode of all fortitude.

272. Of all the restraining powers I am the rod of chastisement by which all are held in restraint, from the smallest insect to the Creator himself.

273. Of all the sciences of those who decide between good and

evil and who uphold righteousness, I am the science of
ethics.

274. O, My friend, in every secret thing I am silence. Even the
Creator remains ignorant in the presence of those who
do not speak.

275. Know Me to be the knowledge of those that know. But
let this be enough; there is no end [to these manifestations].

> XXXIX. *And further, whatsoever is the seed of all existences
> that am I, O Arjuna; nor is there anything moving or
> unmoving that can exist without Me.*

276. Canst thou count the streams of rain, O Wielder of the
bow, or number the blades of grass on the earth?

277. As no one can tell how many are the billows of the ocean,
so My forms are countless.

> XL. *There is no end to My divine manifestations, O
> Conqueror of the foe [Arjuna]. What has been declared
> by Me is only illustrative of My infinite glory.*

278. I have now told thee of seventyfive of My chief manifestations; yet, O Arjuna, it seems very little.

279. It is impossible to keep count of the great extent of My
Manifestations; couldst thou hear them all, or could I
tell them?

280. For this reason I will now reveal to thee My great secret:
I am the seed from which all created beings arise and
grow.

281. Therefore thou shouldst regard Me as everything that is,
without considering such concepts as great or small, high
and low.

282. Listen now to one more simple sign by which thou mayest
recognize a manifestation of Me.

> XLI. *Whatever being there is, endowed with glory and
> grace and vigour, know that to have sprung from a
> fragment of My splendour.*

283. Wherever both wealth and compassion are found together,
these thou shouldst know, O Conqueror of wealth, are
part of Myself.

284. As there is but one sun in the heavens, yet its light
shines throughout all worlds, so is My law alone obeyed
by all men.

285. Do not say that He is alone nor call Him poor. Does the Cow of Plenty have to carry anything with her [with which to satisfy desires]?
286. She begins at once to bring forth whatever a man may ask at any time, and in this way all powers are granted to Me.
287. By this sign mayest thou know those men whose commands are obeyed by all to be manifestations of Me, O wise one.

> XLII. *But what need is there, O Arjuna, for such detailed knowledge by you? I support this entire universe pervading it with a single fraction of Myself.*

288. It is wrong to consider that one is common, another good, for I am the one who pervades the whole universe.
289. Why should we imagine distinctions such as 'ordinary' and 'good'? Why let our minds be unnecessarily contaminated by the thought of difference?
290. Or what need is there to churn butter? Why reduce nectar by pressing it? Is there any left [or right] in a shower of rain?
291. We could ruin our sight by looking for the front or back of the disc of the sun; so in My form there is no such thing as general and particular.
292. My manifestations are infinitely various. How wilt thou measure My limitless form? Already thou knowest enough, O Consort of Subhadrā.
293. With one fragment of Myself this whole universe is permeated; so, setting aside all distinctions, worship Me with single-mindedness.
294. So spoke the glorious Lord Krishna who is as the spring in the garden of the wise, the beloved of the dispassionate.
295. Then Arjuna said, O Lord, Thou hast spoken inconsistently when Thou didst say that we who must abandon difference are separate from that very difference.
296. Does the sun tell the earth to drive away darkness? But to call Thee thoughtless, O Lord, would be presumption.
297. O Lord, when Thy name is uttered or heard even once, all idea of separateness vanishes from the mind.
298. Can heat be felt by one who has entered the very centre of the moon? Thou hast spoken impetuously, O Wielder of the Shārnga bow.

299. Then the Lord, being naturally pleased, closely embraced him and said, Beloved, do not be angered by what I say.

300. I have told thee about My manifestations in terms of diversity [in order to see] whether thou hast understood in thy heart this absence of separation.

301. For the sake of knowing this I spoke for a moment after the manner of outward appearances; then thou didst understand well My manifestation.

302. Thereupon Arjuna said, O Lord, Thou indeed knowest. I see that the whole universe has been brought into being by Thee.

303. While Sanjaya told Dhritarāshtra that Arjuna had thus experienced Self-realization, the king remained unmoved.

304. Sanjaya, with a sad heart, said to himself, Is it not strange that he should throw away such good fortune? I believed that he had good understanding but now I find him to be blind inwardly [as well as outwardly].

305. But let us leave [what Sanjaya said]. Arjuna's respect for non-duality had so increased that his eagerness to hear more was intensified.

306. Following this desire to see with his own eyes an outward form of what he had experienced in his heart, this thought arose in his mind,

307. that he should grasp with his eyes the Cosmic Form [of Krishna]. It was his great good fortune which brought him this longing.

308. Arjuna is like a bough of the desire-tree which bears no sterile flowers. Whatever he may ask for, [Krishna] will surely grant him.

309. Arjuna has been given as his teacher Krishna, who became poison for the sake of Prahlāda.

310. In the next chapter, therefore, I will describe the manner in which Arjuna will express his request to see the Cosmic form of Krishna. So says Jnānadeva, the disciple of Nivritti.

In the Upanishad of the Bhagavadgitā, the science of the Absolute, the scripture of Yoga and the dialogue between Shri Krishna and Arjuna, this is the tenth chapter called the Yoga of Manifestation.

NOTES

1. *the first stage of speech.* For the stages of speech, see Ch. VI, note 16. Here the first stage is used figuratively to express appreciation of the talents of his guru.
2. *Dhruva.* The polar star; the name of the son of Uttānapāda, an ancient king. See IX, v. 464.
3. *Purānic literature.* In this and the following few verses there are references to traditional stories from the Purānas. See Introduction. *Vasishtha, Vishvamitra.* Two of the great sages of mythological stories. The names given in brackets would be familiar to all the listeners.
4. *Māruti, Agasti.* The Monkey god. See Ch. I, note 32 and Ch. IX, note 3.
5. *Rāma, Rāvana.* Rāma is the hero of the other great Sanskrit epic, the Rāmāyana, the central story of which is the capture of his wife Sitā by the demon Rāvana and her rescue by Rāma.
6. *Kashyapa.* A celebrated sage.
7. *Manu.* See Ch. IV, note 3. *Svayambhu.* The 'self-existent one', Brahma. Also Vishnu.
8. *the twentyfifth principle.* The 24 'forms of matter' evolve as a result of the connection between Soul (the 25th principle) and Matter (the first). The principles enumerated are Matter, Consciousness, Individuality, Thought, the five senses, five basic 'activities', five objects of sense-perception (form, etc.) and five elements (ether, air, fire, water and earth). The 'three gods' are Brahma, Vishnu and Shiva.
9. *Asita, Devala.* The names of two sages.
10. *The lion and the elephant.* The lion is traditionally the destroyer of the elephant.
11. *Nanda.* The foster father of Krishna when his life was threatened by Kansa.
12. *Ādityas.* One of the twelve Suns; *Marici*, one of the Maruts, or winds; Vedic gods. (Bhaga. XXI).
13. *Rudras.* A group of eleven gods, said to be inferior manifestations of Shiva.
14. *Kubera.* The god of wealth and riches. *Yakshas.* A class of demi-gods. *Rakshasas.* Demons.
15. *Vasus.* A class of eight gods.
16. *Skanda.* A son of Shiva.
17. *Kalpa.* The heavenly tree which grants all wishes. *Pārijāta.* The 'coral' tree, *Erythrina Indica*. *Ashvattha.* The fig tree; the Tree of Life.
18. *Chitraratna.* The king of the gandharvas, the heavenly bards.
19. *Uccaishrava.* The horse of Indra, said to have been churned out of the Ocean of Milk. *Kapila.* A great sage.
20. *Airāvata.* The elephant of Indra.

257

21. *Madana.* The god of love.
22. *Vāsuki.* The king of the serpents.
    Nāgas. The serpent-demons.
23. *Varuna.* The regent of the ocean and of the western quarter; the deity of rain.
24. *Aryamā.* Another name of the sun.
25. *Yama.* The god of death. *Rāma.* See Ch. IX, note 8.
26. *Tretā.* The third of the four yugas, or ages of the world.
27. *Rāvana.* This god was said to have had ten heads. See above, note 5.
28. *The Solar race.* A dynasty of kings who ruled over the district which is now the province of Oundh.
29. *Bhāgirathi.* The name of one of the three great branches of the Ganges. This name is also used for the Ganges itself.
    Janhu. An ancient king who was angry with the Ganges for flowing over his territory.
30. *dvandva.* A pair, double; in grammar, one of the classes of compound words.
31. *Brihatsāma.* Hymns composed in a particular metre.
32. *Gāyatri.* A Vedic metre; a sacred verse recited daily by brāhmans.
33. *Mārgashirsha.* The ninth month of the Hindu year, from mid-November to mid-December.
    Vasanta. One of the six seasons in the Hindu year, approximately from mid-March to mid-May.
    Vrishnis. The ancestors of Krishna. (Bhag. XXXVIII).
34. *Gokula.* The village where Krishna was brought up.
    Putanā. A female demon who tried to kill Krishna.
35. *Govardhana.* A mountain near Gokula.
36. *Kālindi.* The river Jamnā in the heart of which there dwelt a serpent.

CHAPTER XI

---

1. Now in the eleventh chapter the story in which Pārtha will encounter the Cosmic Form [of Krishna] is permeated by two of the sentiments.[1]
2. In it the sentiment of wonder has come as a guest to the house of tranquillity, and the remaining sentiments have received the honour of being invited [to the feast].
3. As at the wedding of a bride and bridegroom, their relatives put on fine garments and ornaments, so in the palanquin of the Marāthi language all the sentiments are carried in the procession.
4. But here tranquillity and wonder, which will be appreciated easily by the eye, are predominant, like Hari and Hara affectionately embracing each other.
5. Or, as on the day of the new moon, when the orbs of the sun and moon meet, so these two sentiments are here united.
6. The two sentiments flow together, like the confluence of the two streams of the Ganges and the Jamnā, so that the whole world may bathe there and be purified.
7. The Gitā is the hidden stream of Sarasvati and the two sentiments are as the two visible rivers. So, O fathers, this great triple confluence is formed.[2]
8. It is easy to enter this holy place by the medium of the ear. Jnānadeva says, This has been brought about by the grace of my patron.
9. Overcoming [the difficult ascent of] the steep banks of Sanskrit, Nivrittideva, the treasure house of all righteousness, has made a ladder of Marāthi words.
10. So that any man can bathe here and behold the Cosmic Form of Krishna, as Mādhava can be seen at Prayāga; thereby he can be freed from worldly existence.[3]

11. Enough has been said. The sentiments are fully developed here and to the world is given the highest delight of hearing.

12. It is not enough to say that the sentiments of tranquillity and wonder are clearly to be seen here, for all the others acquire added beauty. Here is the highest bliss.

13. This eleventh chapter is the resting place of the Lord and Arjuna is prince among the fortunate in that he has arrived here.

14. But why should I say that Arjuna alone is so fortunate? For this opportunity is today available for every man, the Gitā being here explained in Marāthi.

15. Therefore, listen now to my request that all you good men should give your careful attention.

16. It is indeed improper for me to be so familiar in your presence, but as your own [child] you should treat me with affection.

17. After all, if we teach a parrot and it learns well, we nod in approval. Is not a mother delighted when her child does as she tells it?

18. O masters, whatever I can say is only what you yourselves have taught me; so surely you should listen to it.

19. You yourselves have planted this sweet tree of knowledge and you should therefore nourish it with the nectar of your attention.

20. Then it will produce the flowers of the sentiments, bear the fruit of meaning, and thus through your devotion the whole world will benefit.

21. The good men were pleased at hearing these words and exclaimed, We are delighted; you have done well. Now tell us what Arjuna said.

22. Then the disciple of Nivritti said, How can an ordinary man like me tell of the dialogue between Krishna and Arjuna? But you must help me to tell it.

23. The defeat of Rāvana was brought about by the monkeys, eaters of the forest leaves; could not Arjuna alone defeat the eleven armies of the Kauravas?

24. Can it be said that whatever can be done by a competent man cannot be achieved by all other beings? So you who are saints can enable me to expound the Gitā.

25. Now please listen to this clear explanation of the Gitā which comes from the mouth of the Lord of Vaikuntha.

26. [Blessed is] the book of the Gitā, for Krishna who is the subject of exposition in the Vedas is also the author of it.

27. How can I describe the greatness of that which even the great mind of Shambhu failed to grasp? That should now be saluted with reverent heart.

28. Now listen to the way in which Arjuna, fixing his gaze upon the Cosmic Form of the Supreme Being, began to speak of the matter.

29. All things are a manifestation of the Almighty; this experience which Arjuna had had of his beloved Lord he now wished to see with his eye of the senses.

30. Being so diffident about expressing his wish to the Lord, how can he suddenly ask for the mystery of the Cosmic Form to be shown to him?

31. [Arjuna said], How could I mention that which not even a beloved one had ever before asked for?

32. Though I am his dear friend, am I closer to Him than His mother? Yet even she feared to speak to him of this.

33. However deep has been my devotion to Him, can it be compared with that of Garuda? But he, too, did not dare to speak of this.

34. Am I closer to him than Sanaka and the other sages? Yet they did not [dare to ask for this]. Am I dearer to Him than the women of Gokula?

35. [Some failed to recognize Him], misled by His youthful form. Another underwent the experience of birth, yet the vision was withheld. To no one has it been revealed.

36. So profound is the mystery of His Being, hidden deep in His heart; how can I demand this impatiently?

37. Nevertheless if I do not ask for it, there is no joy in my heart, perhaps not even the possibility of living.

38. So I will approach the matter tentatively and will do as the Lord may wish. So Pārtha, with some fear, began to speak,

39. but in such a way that the Lord, after replying to him once or twice, will reveal to Him without reserve His Divine Form.

40. A cow, moved by affection on seeing her calf, stands up; then as soon as its mouth touches her udders will her milk not flow?

41. So, will the Lord, who at the sound of the name of the

Pāndavas ran to help them in the forest, disappoint Arjuna when he asks Him about this?

42. The Lord is the very incarnation of love, and this love has been aroused [by Arjuna]. When these come together, how can any sense of difference remain?

43. Therefore as soon as Arjuna speaks the Lord will at once manifest His Cosmic Form. I pray you, listen to the first episode.

Arjuna said:

> 1. *The supreme mystery, the discourse concerning the Self which thou hast given out of grace for me—by this my bewilderment is gone from me.*

44. Then Arjuna said to the Lord, O Compassionate One, for my sake hast Thou spoken to me of that which is inexpressible.

45. When the great elements had been reabsorbed [into the Absolute] and individual souls and other manifestations of matter no longer existed, then God alone remained, that is the final cessation.

46. It was this knowledge which Thou hast kept hidden within the recesses of Thy heart, like a miser, and which was withheld even from the Vedas.

47. This heart Thou hast laid open before me today, the secret to gain which Shankara laid aside his glory.

48. O Lord, thou hast conferred this on me in a moment; yet were I to say this, how [can it be said that] I am one with Thee?

49. Perceiving that I was submerged in the flood of the great illusion, Thou, Hari, didst indeed plunge into it and rescue me.

50. There is none other beside Thee in the whole world; but see our fate, that we imagined ourselves existing [apart from Thee].

51. Filled with pride in my personality I thought that I was Arjuna in this world and said that the Kauravas were my relatives.

52. In addition to that, I had the evil dream that I would kill them and then what should I do? But the Lord wakened me from my sleep.

53. It was as though I had abandoned a celestial home; and

was seeking to drink water from a mirage, O Lord of Lakshmi;

54. or as though, if one were to touch a snake made of cloth, one would actually feel waves of its poison. Thine, O Ananta, is the credit of saving the soul of one who was about to die in a similar delusion.

55. A lion, not recognizing his own shadow may jump into a well, thinking it sees another lion; thou has saved me, O Ananta, from a similar plight.

56. Until now I had resolved [not to fight against my kinsmen], even should all the seven seas be merged in one,

57. the whole world be submerged and the skies crash down; still I would not fight with my kinsmen.

58. In this way, in an excess of egotism, I had leapt into the waters of self-will. It is well that Thou wert near, otherwise who would have saved me?

59. I, being no one, thought I was a person and called those my relatives who in reality did not exist. Thou hast saved me from this great madness.

60. Already Thou has rescued me from burning in a fire of wax, but then it was only the body [which was in danger]. Now it is a fire of another kind and my soul as well [is threatened].

61. [The earth of] my reason was carried away under his arm by the Hiranyāksha of wrong determination and into a cavity in the ocean of infatuation.[4]

62. Through Thy power my reason has been restored to me. For this thou didst have to make another incarnation, as the boar.[5]

63. Thus Thy deeds on my behalf have been endless; how can I describe them all, with but one voice? Thou gavest Thy very life for my sake.

64. Nothing, however, of all this has been in vain for, O Lord, thou hast overcome all, in that my illusion has been completely dispelled.

65. How could one, for whom Thy eyes, which are as lotuses in a lake of joy, have become the temples of Thy favour,

66. have anything to do with illusion? How meaningless a thing is this? How could a flood of mirages quell the great sea-fire?

67. And yet even I, O bountiful Lord, [am permitted to]

enter the inmost chamber of Thy grace and eat the food
of Brahma.

68. Is it then any cause for wonder that my infatuation has
been dispelled? I vow at Thy feet that Thou hast saved
me.

> 11. *The birth and passing away of things have been heard
> by me in detail from Thee, O Lotus-eyed [Kṛṣṇa], as also
> Thy imperishable majesty.*

69. O Lord of the lotus-eyes, brilliant as a myriad suns,
today, O Great God, I have heard from thee

70. how all things came to be and how they passed away.
The Lord has explained to me the whole process of
creation.

71. Not only hast Thou described nature to me, but Thou
hast also shown me the place of the Spirit, whose greatness
forms the garment adorning the Vedas.

72. The Vedas live and increase and the jewel of religion has
come to birth; all this is due to the power of worshipping
at Thy feet.

73. Thy might is unfathomable, the goal of attainment for all
paths, and the supreme delight of the experience of Self-
realization. This Thou hast shown to me.

74. In the same manner as when the sky is clear of clouds the
orb of the sun can be seen; when weeds are cleared from
its surface water can be seen,

75. when the coils of a serpent are removed from a sandalwood tree it can be touched, or when an evil spirit has
left it a hidden treasure can be secured,

76. so, when the Lord had dispelled the illusion clouding my
mind, He brought the great truth within reach of my mind.

77. In regard to this, O Lord, my heart is convinced; and yet
another desire had arisen in my mind.

78. Though I might remain silent from a feeling of awe, yet
whom else can I ask? Is there any other refuge but Thee?

79. Do not aquatic creatures depend upon water? If a child
draws back from its mother's breast is there any other
means by which it can live, O Hari?

80. So, setting aside fear I will tell thee all that I wish to say.
Thereupon the Lord said, Enough, ask me whatever thou
wishest.

III. *As Thou hast declared Thyself to be, O Supreme
Lord, even so it is. [But] I desire to see Thy divine form,
O Supreme Person.*

81. Then said Kiriti, My intuitive perception has been
satisfied by what Thou hast told me.
82. Now, that by whose thought all these worlds have been
created and destroyed, and that of which Thou sayest, 'I
am all this',
83. is Thy original Form from which, in order to carry out
the purposes of the gods, Thou hast become from time
to time incarnate in two-armed and in four-armed figures.
84. When Thou hadst finished Thy manifestations in the
guise of Vishnu sleeping upon the ocean, and in the form
of the Fish and the Tortoise, Thou didst gather up [Thy
properties] as a juggler [at the end of his performance].[6]
85. This is that of which the Upanishads sing, which yogis
perceive in their hearts, and which has been embraced
by Sanaka and other sages.
86. O Lord, my mind is eager to see that unfathomable
Cosmic Form of which I have heard with my ears.
87. Having dispelled my fear, if in Thy affection for me Thou
askest what I wish, then [I would say that] this is my
greatest desire,
88. that Thy Cosmic Form should be shown to me. This is the
deepest longing of my heart.

IV. *If Thou, O Lord, thinkest that by me, It can be seen,
then reveal to me Thy imperishable Self, O Lord of yoga
[Kṛṣṇa].*

89. One doubt have I here, O Holder of the Shārnga Bow;
am I worthy to behold that Form?
90. I do not know this myself; and shouldst Thou ask me
why, I would answer, Does a sick man know the cause of
his illness?
91. As a man impelled by some strong desire forgets his own
worth, or a thirsty man thinks that the whole ocean
would not satisfy him,
92. so, in the confusion of my powerful longing I have not
been able to keep a proper sense of my worth. Therefore,
as a mother knows the true nature of her child,
93. Thou, O Janārdana, shouldst consider my worthiness and
then begin to show me the vision of Thy Cosmic Form.

94. If I am worthy, bestow on me this favour; otherwise tell me that it cannot be. How can one give pleasure through music to a deaf man?

95. The cloud gives rain not only to satisfy the chātaka bird, but for the whole world; yet the shower is wasted if it falls on rocky ground.

96. The chakora bird draws nectar from the light of the moon; are others therefore prevented from doing the same? Yet, because they are blind, the moonlight is wasted.

97. I trust that Thou wilt show me Thy Cosmic Form. For art Thou not ever [revealed] anew to the intelligent as to the unintelligent?

98. Thy generosity is not conditioned [by him who asks], Thou dost not distinguish between the worthy and the unworthy, and even such a sacred thing as salvation Thou hast granted to Thine enemies.

99. Liberation is indeed difficult to attain, and yet it too serves at Thy feet, and like a servant goes wherever it is sent.

100. To Putanā, who angrily [came to kill Thee] with poison in her breast, Thou didst give a place in union with Thyself worthy of the sage Sanaka.

101. How wert Thou dishonoured and abused with many evil words in the presence of the three worlds assembled together at the time of the Rājasuya sacrifice![7]

102. Yet, O Gopāla, Thou didst give a place to that wicked Shishupāla. Did the young son of Uttānapāda desire to be raised to the place of the polar star?[8]

103. In order that he might seat himself on his father's lap, he withdrew to the forest; nevertheless Thou didst honour him like the sun and moon.

104. Thou art he who is especially merciful towards those who are overcome with distress; Thou didst offer union with Thyself to Ajamila who uttered Thy name on seeing his son [of the same name].[9]

105. O Thou generous one, Thou dost still bear on Thy breast the imprint of the kick [of Bhrigu] and Thou dost not even yet abandon the body of Thy enemy.

106. Thus Thou hast given help to Thy malefactors and been generous even to the unworthy. Thou didst beg a gift from Bali, for which Thou didst become his doorkeeper.[10]

107. Thou didst bestow [the joy of] Vaikuntha on that courtesan

who did not even know how to worship Thee, but [who merely uttered Thy name] when calling her parrot.

108. Considering these trivial pretexts on which Thou hast granted the gift of Thy presence, wilt Thou then turn me away?

109. Can the calves of that celestial Cow, who with her plentiful milk satisfies the needs of the world, be left hungry?

110. Surely the Lord will not refuse to show me what I have requested, but He will make me worthy to see it.

111. If Thou thinkest that my eyes can contemplate Thy Cosmic Form, then, O Lord, satisfy my desire to see it.

112. When Arjuna had finished expressing his entreaty in these various ways, the Ruler of the six qualities was not able to restrain Himself.[11]

113. He was like a cloud full of the nectar of compassion, while Arjuna was as the approaching rainy season; or, Krishna was like the kokila bird for whom Arjuna was the spring.

114. As the tides of the sea begin to rise at the sight of the full moon, so the Lord was joyful in his increasing affection for Arjuna.

115. Swaying with his feeling of delight, the Lord, full of compassion, said, O, Pārtha, behold all My infinite Forms!

116. Pāndava had desired only to see His Cosmic Form; but the Lord showed him the whole universe [as a manifestation of Himself].

117. How abundant is the grace of the Lord! He always grants of Himself a thousandfold to one who seeks him.

118. The innermost secret which was kept from Shesha, which was hidden from the Vedas, and which was not even shown to Lakshmi, His dearest one,

119. will now be revealed in many forms to Arjuna. How great is the good fortune of Arjuna!

120. As when a waking man falls asleep he seems to become all that he experiences in a dream, so the Lord appeared in the form of the infinite bowl of the universe.

121. He laid aside His mortal form and removed the veil of [Arjuna's] human sight; in short, He displayed the glory of His yogic power.

122. Giving no thought to whether Arjuna would be able to bear the sight or not, He exclaimed in the ecstasy of love, Behold!

The Blessed Lord said:

> v. *Behold, O Pārtha [Arjuna], My forms, a hundredfold, a thousandfold, various in kind, divine, of various colours and shapes.*

123. O Arjuna, thou hast asked Me to show thee one form, but that would be hardly worth giving; behold now all that is contained in My Cosmic Form.

124. Some are lean, some fat, some short, others great; some massive, others slender; some are boundless.

125. Some are wild, others calm; some active, others motionless; some indifferent, some affectionate and some fierce.

126. Some are senseless, some alert; some are simple, others profound. Some are liberal, others miserly, and some are very wrathful.

127. Some are tranquil, some riotous; some are quiet and others joyful. Some are loud, others silent and others are mild.

128. There are those who are full of desire, while others are passionless. Some are awake, some asleep; some are contented, others anxious, others serene.

129. Some carry weapons, others are unarmed; some submissive, others daring; some threatening and some friendly; some are absorbed [in contemplation].

130. Some revel in the sport of creation, others protect by their love; some destroy with their ardour, some are merely spectators.

131. Thus these shapes are infinite in form and variety, brilliant with light and no two are of the same colour.

132. Some are as heated gold, some tawny, some red as the tinted clouds [at sunset].

133. Some scintillate with natural beauty as though the universe were ornamented with rubies. Some, like the dawn, are of the colour of red turmeric.

134. There are some as clear as pure crystal, some tinted with the sapphire blue of Indra, others black as collyrium. Some are of the colour of Krishna.

135. Some are yellow as shining gold, others black as a new storm cloud. Some pale as the flowers of the champak tree, others green.

136. Some are red as heated copper, others clear as the whiteness of the moon. Behold My Forms of many and varied hues.

137. As the colours are of every variety so are the shapes, some so beautiful that even the god of love would be put to shame.

138. Some are revealed with shapes of matchless beauty, others with most beautiful bodies, as though the treasure-house of the goddess of wealth were opened.

139. Some with fleshy heavy-limbed bodies, others emaciated and ugly, some as clear as light, others massive.

140. Thus, O Consort of Subhadrā, My forms are of infinite shapes, there is no end to them; thou mayest see a world in each part of the body of this Form.

> VI. *Behold, the Ādityas, the Vasus, the Rudras, the two Aśvins and also the Maruts. Behold, O Bhārata [Arjuna], many wonders never seen before.*

141. Whenever I open My eyes there appear whole worlds of suns and when I close them, these all vanish.

142. From the breath of My mouth everything is filled with flames and from these fire and multitudes of Vasus emerge.

143. When in anger the points of My eyebrows draw together, groups of the Rudras come forth.

144. In the mildness of My benign aspect countless Ashvin gods appear and from My ears many winds rush out.[12]

145. In such a manner from the simplest action of Mine races of gods and adepts are brought forth; behold all these great and infinite forms.

146. The Vedas speak of them with halting tongue and even the whole span of time would not suffice to see them all; the Creator himself is unable to comprehend them.

147. Behold now those infinite [manifestations of Myself] which are not known to the divine Triad and so experience joyfully the glory of this marvel.[13]

> VII. *Here today, behold the whole universe, moving and unmoving and whatever else thou desirest to see, O Gudakeśa [Arjuna], all unified in My body.*

148. O Kiriṭi, as the tender shoots of grass sprout round the trunk of the tree of desire, behold the created worlds springing from the roots of the hair of this Form.

149. As we see atoms floating in space because of currents of air, so universes hover around each joint of My limbs.

150. In each part of My body, behold a universe spread out, and if thou desirest to see what lies beyond this universe,

151. there will be no difficulty in this, for thou canst behold whatever thou wishest to see in this body.

152. When Krishna in His Cosmic Form spoke thus, full of compassion, Arjuna remained silent, without saying whether he was seeing [this Form] or not.

153. Krishna looked at him, wondering why he did not speak, [and realized] that Arjuna was still absorbed in his desire [for the vision].

> VIII. *But thou canst not behold Me with this [human] eye of thine; I will bestow on thee the supernatural eye. Behold My divine power.*

154. Then He said, His eagerness has not abated; but he has not yet found the way to happiness. It has been shown to him clearly, yet he cannot comprehend it.

155. Saying this, the Lord smiled and said [to Arjuna], who was still gazing at Him, I have shown thee My Cosmic Form, yet thou art unable to perceive it.

156. At this the wise Arjuna replied, Who is at fault in this? Thou art feeding a crane with moon beams!

157. Thou art, as it were, holding a mirror before a blind man, O Hrishikesha, or singing a song to a deaf man.

158. Thou art deliberately offering a meal of honey to a frog! Why then shouldst Thou be angry, O Holder of the Shārnga bow?

159. Thou dost place before my human sight that which is known to be beyond the reach of the senses and is open only to the eye of wisdom. How could I see this?

160. But I should not speak of Thy fault; it would be better for me to bear with it. Thereupon the Lord said, O Beloved, I agree with that.

161. If I wanted to show thee the vision of My Cosmic Form I should first have given thee the power to see it; but speaking with thee affectionately, I was thoughtless.

162. What would be the use of sowing seed in a field without first ploughing it? It would be waste of time. But now I will give thee the vision by which thou mayest perceive My Cosmic Form.

163. With that sight thou canst behold the majesty of My

divine power, O Pāndava, and know it from inner experience.

164. Thus spoke the Lord, the object of all knowledge in the Upanishads, the precursor of all worlds and the adored of all the earth.

Sanjaya said:

   IX. *Having spoken thus, O King, Hari, the great lord of yoga, then revealed to Pārtha [Arjuna] His supreme and divine Form.*

165. Sanjaya continued, O Emperor of the Kurus, I have often wondered if there is anyone more fortunate than Lakshmi in all the three worlds.

166. Show me anything that can vie with the Shrutis in the statement of eternal truths. Or is there any more devoted servant than Shesha?

167. Among yogis who weary themselves by their ceaseless endurance [in devotion], who is to be compared with Garuda?

168. All this, however, is changed since the birth of the Pāndavas, in whom is centred the joy of the Lord.

169. But among the five [Pāndavas], it is to Arjuna that Krishna yields willingly, as a lover is brought under the sway of a woman.

170. A well trained bird would not talk [so easily] nor a tame animal behave [so well]. Who knows how such good fortune has come to Arjuna?

171. Today his sight is so blessed as to experience the highest Brahma. See how the Lord treats Arjuna's words indulgently!

172. When he is angry the Lord quietly bears with it; when he is displeased, He coaxes him. He is strangely infatuated by Arjuna.

173. Great masters like Shuka, who even before birth had conquered desire, became His bards and sang about His adventures in love.

174. O King, It astonishes me that He who is the wealth of concentration in yogis should be so captivated by Arjuna.

175. Then Sanjaya continued, O Lord of the Kurus, is there any cause for wonder in this, for great good fortune comes to him who is accepted by Krishna.

176. Then the Lord of all the gods said to Arjuna, I will give thee that sight whereby thou mayest see My Cosmic Form.

177. No sooner were these words uttered by Krishna than the darkness of ignorance passed away.

178. Then Arjuna was endowed with supernatural sight, the eye of wisdom shone forth and the Lord displayed His glory to Arjuna.

179. All these incarnations [of Krishna] are as waves on the ocean; the whole universe is like a mirage arising out of His radiance.

180. Krishna displayed His Form against the eternal background on which the picture of all created things is imprinted.

181. Once in His childhood Krishna had eaten some earth, and His mother Yashodā caught Him up in anger,

182. but in fear He opened His mouth and, under the pretext of showing her [what He had eaten], He showed her all the fourteen worlds [revealed] within it.

183. Again, when in the Madhu forest [Krishna] touched Dhruva on the cheek with His conch, he began to utter His praises in such a manner that even the Vedas were silenced.

184. O King, Krishna showed such favour to Arjuna that he wondered where his perplexity had gone.

185. Suddenly the light of His glory dawned on all sides, as though a miraculous deluge had poured forth, so that Arjuna's mind seemed to be submerged in a sea of wonder.

186. As Mārkandeya alone swam in the full waters even up to the heaven of the Creator, so did Arjuna, marvelling, float in the ocean of [Krishna's] Cosmic Form.

187. He exclaimed, Here was the wide firmament; who has carried it away? What has become of all created things, and the great elements?

188. The four quarters have disappeared, and above and below are no longer discernible. All the worlds [have vanished] as a dream passes on waking.

189. As in the bright light of the sun the moon and the stars become invisible, so by this Cosmic Form the whole structure of the world is engulfed.

190. Then Arjuna's mind ceased to function, his reason could

not be restrained, and the activity of his senses was withdrawn into his heart.

191. He remained in deep silence and paralysed by astonishment, as though his thought had been struck by a stupefying weapon.

192. While, overcome with amazement, he was gazing [at the vision], the four-armed figure of Krishna assumed many forms and spread out in all directions.

193. As during the rainy season clouds [spread over the whole sky], as on the day of the final dissolution the light of the sun [envelopes everything] so here nothing remained [but that Form].

> x. *Of many mouths and eyes, of many visions of marvel, of many divine ornaments, of many divine uplifted weapons.*

194. Then he saw many faces [resplendent] as the royal mansions of Krishna, or like the open treasury of [Lakshmi's] beauty.

195. So beautiful were the faces of Krishna which he saw that they were as gardens of joy in full bloom, or as beauty itself endowed with royalty.

196. Others came forth infinitely terrible as the legions [of death] on the night of universal destruction.

197. These were perhaps the very faces of death, or fortresses built of fear, or cauldrons filled with the fire of the final holocaust.

198. Thus the warrior beheld many faces, wonderful, terrible or gentle; some ordinary, some beautiful.

199. With his divine eye he gazed at these faces but there was no end to them; then he began in wonder to look at the eyes.

200. Then Arjuna saw eyes like gardens of blooming lotuses of many colours and shining like clusters of suns.

201. And under the eyebrows he saw, among masses of dark clouds, yellow fire like flashes of lightning on the day of final destruction.

202. While Arjuna was watching these marvels with astonishment, the great variety of phenomena in this one Form unfolded before him.

203. Wondering then where the strong arms, the legs, and the crowns upon the head were to be seen, Arjuna's longing for the vision grew more intense.

204. Is it possible that the desire of Arjuna, who is the very storehouse of good fortune, will not be fulfilled? Could there be any useless arrow in the quiver of the wielder of the Pināka bow?[14]

205. Can a faulty word be uttered by the four-faced Brahma?[15] Therefore Arjuna saw the whole extent of this limitless universe.

206. With his own two eyes Arjuna in one moment enjoyed a vision of every limb of that one whose path even the Vedas do not know.

207. He saw the glory of the full stature of that Cosmic Form shining with jewelled ornaments.

208. How shall I describe these various ornaments which the great Brahma fashioned out of Himself for the adornment of His body?

209. A radiance of light which could illuminate even the sun and moon, as the innermost centre of that sun which lights the whole world—

210. with such brilliance of adornment as would be beyond the conception of any mind did the Lord invest Himself; thus Arjuna saw Him.

211. Then, when Arjuna looked with his supernatural sight at the extended hands, he saw shining in them such weapons as would strike down the flames of the holocaust at the end of the world.

212. The stars were parched by the fierceness of this radiance and even fire [scorched] by its brilliance, longed to cast itself into the ocean.

213. He saw innumerable hands with raised weapons, as though engulfed in waves of Kālakuta poison or like great forests of ignorance.

> XI. *Wearing divine garments and raiments, with divine perfumes and ointments, made up of all wonders, resplendent, boundless, with faces turned in all directions.*

214. When Kiriti turned his gaze aside in fear, and looked at the neck and crown, he saw that they were as the stems of divine trees.

215. [Set in the crown] he saw lotuses as pure and fragrant as those on which the tired Lakshmi rested, where the great supernatural powers have their origin.

216. On the crown of the head were bunches of flowers arranged as though for worship, and round the neck hung superb garlands.
217. Round the loins was a yellow silken garment, as though the heavens had clothed themselves in the light of the sun, or the mountain Meru were covered with gold.
218. [His body was as that of] Shankar anointed with camphor, or the mountain Kailās covered with quicksilver, or as the milky ocean covered with milk.[16]
219. He saw the whole body covered with sandalwood paste as though a garment of moonlight were unfolded and wrapped as a cloak round the heavens,
220. that fragrance by which lustre is added to light itself, by which the intensity of the joy of union with Brahma is assuaged and which gives life to the earth;
221. who can describe that pure unguent used by Brahma and smeared on his body [by the god of love]?
222. Perceiving the beauty of each adornment Arjuna was agitated and could not understand whether the Lord was seated, standing, or lying fown.
223. Opening then his physical eyes he saw that the whole of space was pervaded by this Form; then reluctant to look at this he remained silent; but he saw the same thing with his inner sight.
224. He saw before him countless shapes; in fear he turned his back on them, but there too he saw the same faces, hands and feet of this Form.
225. Is there any wonder that he could see the vision with open eyes? But it is marvellous that he could see it even when his eyes were closed.
226. See the gracious work [of the Lord]! Arjuna perceived that He pervaded all things not only when he looked but also when not looking.
227. Scarcely had he regained the shore after being immersed in the waters of one marvel than he plunged into the sea of another.
228. Thus the Lord encompassed Arjuna with the miraculous feat of the vision of His manifold forms.
229. This Form faced in all directions and it was this that Arjuna had asked to be revealed to him. Now He was seen as all that is.
230. The Lord gave to Arjuna a power of sight which would

endure whether the light of a lamp or of the sun shone forth or were dimmed.

231. Thus Arjuna was able to see both in the light and in the dark. Sanjaya related all this to Kings Dhritarāshtra in Hastināpur.

232. He said, O King, thou hast heard how Pārtha saw that wonderful omnipresent Form adorned with many ornaments.

> XII. *If the light of a thousand suns were to blaze forth at once in the sky, that might resemble the spendour of that exalted Being.*

233. O King! how can I describe the splendour of the Lord's Form? [It is said that] on the day of final destruction twelve suns will rise together in the sky;

234. but were thousands of such resplendent suns to appear at the same moment could they be compared with the splendour of that vision?

235. If all lightning were brought together in one flash and fuel for the final holocaust be gathered, and still the ten great luminaries be added to them,

236. even then such accumulated brilliance would be insignificant beside the splendour of the Lord's appearance; never could it be so radiant.

237. Thus was displayed the radiance of the Cosmic Form of the great-souled Hari. I was able to see it by the grace of the sage Vyāsa.

> XII. *There the Pāṇḍava [Arjuna] beheld the whole universe, with its manifold divisions gathered together in one, in the body of the god of gods.*

238. There in that Cosmic Form was seen in one place the whole world in its abundance, as bubbles appear separately on the surface of the great ocean,

239. or imaginary cities in the heavens, or ants building their nests in the earth, or again, as small atoms lying on Mount Meru.

240. In such a way Arjuna saw at that time the whole universe in the body of the Lord of lords.

> XIV. *Then he, the winner of wealth [Arjuna], struck with amazement, his hair standing on end, bowed down his head to the Lord, with hands folded in salutation, said,—*

241. What faint sense of dualism remained between the universe and himself faded away and his heart was absorbed in the vision.

242. He was filled with ecstasy, while outwardly his limbs lost their strength and from head to foot his whole body vibrated.

243. His hair stood on end, as when the first monsoon rains pour down a mountain side the tender blades of grass shoot forth.

244. His body was covered with beads of perspiration as when water begins to ooze from the moonstone when the rays of the moon touch it.

245. When a cluster of bees is caught in a [lotus] bud, it begins to sway on the water; so did Arjuna tremble with the power of the waves of inner joy.

246. From his eyes teardrops began to fall, as camphor drips out of a camphor tree when its folds open with the fullness of the sap.

247. In such a manner all the eight elements of the state of purity vied with each other [in their eagerness to possess him] and the supreme joy of the bliss of Brahma arose in his heart.

248. Waves of joy swelled [in his heart], as the ocean rises into full tide with the rising moon,

249. so, after this experience of joy the human sight which perceives duality was restored to Kiriti and, giving a deep sigh, he waited.

250. Then, turning to where Krishna was seated he bowed his head to the god and with joined hands he spoke.

Arjuna said:

> xv. *In Thy body, O God, I see all the gods and the varied hosts of beings as well, Brahma, the lord seated on the lotus throne and all the sages and heavenly nāgas.*

251. O Lord, glory to Thee! Through Thy wonderful grace I, an ordinary man, have beheld Thy Cosmic Form.

252. It is well, O Lord, and great is my satisfaction in seeing that in Thee the whole universe is contained.

253. Within Thy body I perceive many worlds, as on the mountain Mandār forests full of beasts are to be seen everywhere.

254. In the heavenly spaces are numberless groups of stars,
on some huge tree may be found nests of birds;

255. so too, O Hari, in Thy Cosmic Form I see heaven and all
the gods.

256. Therein also I see many groups of the five primal elements
and numberless creatures of many worlds come forth.

257. In Thy body I see the Satya heaven; and is not this
Brahma Himself? On another side Kailās is also to be seen.

258. Mahādeva with his consort Bhavāni is in one part of
Thy body, and there also Thou Thyself art seen, O
Krishna,[17]

259. In this Form I see too the long line of all the sages, with
Kashyapa, and there too is the nether world with all the
serpents.

260. In short, O Lord of beatitude, pictured on the walls of
each of Thy limbs are the fourteen worlds, as though
supported by them.

261. And when I look at the people of those worlds as Thou
hadst depicted them in Thy Form, I see Thy incomparable depth.

> XVI. *I behold Thee, infinite in form on all sides, with
> numberless arms, bellies, faces and eyes, but I see not
> Thy end or Thy middle or Thy beginning, O Lord of
> the universe, O Form Universal.*

262. When I glance around with that divine eye I see space
stretching forth in Thy strong arms.

263. Then I see all things accomplished eternally and simul-
taneously by Thy hands alone.

264. In Thy body I perceive countless bellies, as though the
whole extent of the divine bliss had opened up the
treasury of the created world.

265. As though myriads of images of the thousand-headed one
appeared in one moment, or the great Brahma [as a tree]
were weighed down with fruit in the form of faces,

266. I see Thy Form as having such countless mouths and
similarly numberless rows of eyes.

267. All is pervaded by Thy Form; whether it be heaven or
hell, earth, distant direction or firmament, one can no
longer tell.

268. The universe is so filled with Thee that I search in vain
for one atom in any place that is not pervaded by Thee.

269. I see all the primal elements gathered together, with all
created beings to be permeated by Thee, O Ananta.

270. Whence comest Thou? Art Thou seated or standing? In
what womb wert Thou born? Of what stature art Thou?

271. Of what nature are Thy form and limbs, what is beyond
Thee and on what dost Thou rest? When I began to
ponder these things,

272. then I understood that Thou art all; Thou art born of
none, Thou art without beginning and self-existent.

273. Thou art neither standing nor seated, neither of great
nor of small stature, extending far above and below
Thyself;

274. in form Thy very own, Thyself in age, O Lord, before
and behind Thou art Thy very Self, O great Lord.

275. That is to say, I have now seen, over and over again, O
Ananta, that Thou Thyself art all.

276. If there is anything that Thou lackest, it is that in Thy
Form there is neither beginning, middle nor end.

277. I have searched everywhere, but I have indeed found no
trace of any of these three.

278. So have I truly seen Thy Form without beginning, middle
or end, O Thou infinite Lord of the universe.

279. Within the body of this great Form are depicted many
individual forms and Thou seemest to have clothed
Thyself in garments of various kinds.

280. Thou art like an immense ocean heaving with the waves
of infinite shapes or a huge tree bearing them as its fruit.

281. As the surface of the earth is covered with trees and the
heavens are studded with stars, so Thy Form is filled
with these created forms.

282. In each of these shapes the threefold universe arises and
disappears; they are but the hair upon Thy body.

283. When I considered the extent of this universe [within
Thee] and asked who Thou art, I realized that it is Thou
who art my charioteer.

284. O Mukunda, when I see all these things I think that
Thou art eternally all-pervading, but through compassion
for Thy devotees, Thou dost assume bodily form.

285. What is Thy azure-tinted, four-armed body which, when
we see it, both mind and sight are satisfied and which,
if we reach out towards it, can be grasped in our arms?

286. O Lord of the Cosmic Form, Thou hast appeared in this

beautiful body. But our mortal sight is blurred so that
we see it only imperfectly.

287. But now our sight is purified and Thou hast endowed me
with the supernatural vision and I have beheld Thy
greatness as it truly is.

288. Now have I seen clearly that it is Thou who hast assumed
Thy Cosmic Form, Thou who art the charioteer seated
behind the head-piece on the yoke of my chariot.

> XVII. *I behold Thee with Thy crown, mace and discus,
> glowing everywhere as a mass of light, hard to discern,
> [dazzling] on all sides with a radiance of the flaming fire
> and sun, incomparable.*

289. O Hari! is not that Thy diadem placed upon Thy head?
But now the lustre and glory of it are wondrously enhanced.

290. O Lord of the Cosmic Form, there in Thy raised hand is
the discus, held ready [for throwing]; the sign of it is
unmistakable.

291. Is not that Thy mace, O Govinda, in the other hand?
Are not thy lower hands, free of weapons, used for
holding the horse's reins?

292. I know well, O Lord of the Universe, that in Thy eagerness
Thou didst at once assume Thy Cosmic Form to satisfy
my desire.

293. What wonder is this! My astonishment knows no bounds,
and my imagination is bewildered by the marvel of it.

294. Trying to perceive whether Thy form is here or not
leaves one breathless; the lustre of that body pervades
the whole of spcce.

295. In the light of it one's very sight is scorched; even the
sun is lost in it like a firefly, so fierce is its light.

296. It is as though the whole created world had become
submerged in the ocean of the great light, or that the
heavens were enveloped in the lightning flashes of the
last day,

297. or one might say that the flames of the final holocaust had
broken loose and had built for themselves a stage in the
firmament. Even possessed as I am with the eye of
wisdom I am unable to look at it.

298. It grows brighter and brighter, burning with fierce flames,

so that the supernatural sight of my eyes cannot bear to gaze on it.

299. It may be described as the consuming fire of the day of destruction, or as the bursting forth of the hidden third eye of the god Rudra, the destroyer.[18]

300. With the spreading of this light a whirlpool of the flames of the fivefold fire forms and the universe is seen to be reduced to cinders.

301. Never in my life have I seen Thee as this wonderful blaze of light. One cannot realize how limitless is Thy extent.

> XVIII. *Thou art the Imperishable, the Supreme to be realized. Thou art the ultimate resting-place of the universe; Thou art the undying guardian of the eternal law. Thou art the Primal Person, I think.*

302. O Lord, Thou art changeless and beyond [the mystery of] the sacred syllable.[19] The Vedas search for Thee,

303. who art the origin of all form, the one treasure-house of the whole universe, unmanifest, unfathomable, imperishable.

304. Thou art the essence of all religion, uncreated and ever new; I know Thee to be the supreme Spirit beyond the thirty-six principles.[20]

> XIX. *I behold Thee as one without beginning, middle or end, of infinite power, of numberless arms, with the moon and the sun as Thine eyes, with Thy face as a flaming fire whose radiance burns up this universe.*

305. Without beginning, middle [or end], Thy power is infinite; Thou art the hands and feet, without limit, of the whole universe.

306. The sun and moon are Thine eyes, through which Thou showest anger and compassion; O Gopāla, Thou dost show displeasure to one, Thou dost protect another.

307. This is indeed Thyself that I behold. Thy mouth appears as though the fire of the final destruction were flaming in it.

308. Thy tongue rolling in Thy mouth is licking the teeth as the rising flames of a conflagration envelope a mountain.

309. With the heat proceeding from Thy mouth and the radiant glory of Thy whole body, the scorching universe is writhing in distress.

xx. *This space between heaven and earth is pervaded by Thee alone, also all the quarters. O Exalted One, when this wondrous, terrible form of Thine is seen, the three worlds tremble.*

310. The created world, the nether regions, the earth and the firmament, with the horizon surrounding the ten quarters,

311. I see with wonder that all is filled with Thee. It is as though with all the heavens everything were engulfed by some horror.

312. Or [one might say] that the fourteen worlds were surrounded by great waves of the miraculous. How can I comprehend such a marvel?

313. Thy vast extent cannot be encompassed and the fierceness of its brilliance is intolerable; all my joy is gone and only with great difficulty can the world continue to exist.

xxi. *Yonder hosts of gods enter Thee and some, in fear, extol Thee, with folded hands. And bands of great seers and perfected ones cry 'Hail' and adore Thee with hymns of abounding praise.*

314. O God, I do not know whence this tide of fear comes at the sight of Thee, or why the threefold world should be engulfed by waves of grief.

315. On the contrary, should the sight of Thee, the great souled one, inspire fear and distress? but I realize why I feel [no joy] from this vision.

316. So long as men have not seen Thy Form they take delight in things of this world; but now that I have seen Thee I am troubled by a loss of all interest in pleasure.

317. Am I able immediately to embrace Thee whom I have seen? If I should not do so then how can I remain in this plight?

318. If I turn back, the life of birth and death confronts me; yet Thou art in front of me, unrestrainable, and I cannot grasp Thee.

319. It seems clear to me now that the three worlds are tormented, as parched grain, between these dangers.

320. As a man burnt by fire rushes to the sea to alleviate his pain, and then fears even more the force of the waves,

321. so is the state of uneasiness into which the world is thrown at the sight of Thee. Behold! yonder are groups of wise men;

322. these wise ones are absorbed into Thy being through devotion, the seeds of action having been burnt up in them by the radiance of Thy body.

323. Others, naturally fearful, pray to Thee with folded hands, keeping the vision of Thee ever before them.

324. O Lord, we are drowned in the ocean of ignorance and entangled in the snare of worldly pleasure; we are trapped between heaven and earthly existence.

325. Who but Thou canst release us? With all our heart and soul we turn to Thee.

326. Sages and adepts, the hosts of demigods, all bless and praise Thee.

XXII. *The Rudras, the Ādityas, the Vasus, the Sādhyas; the Viśvas, the two Aśvins, the Maruts and the spirits of the ancestors and the hosts of Gandharvas, Yakṣas, Asuras and Siddhas, all gaze at Thee and are amazed.*

327. The hosts of Rudras and Ādityas, Vasus and all the Sādhyas, the Ashvins, the devas and the wind,[21]

328. the fire and the Gandharvas, all the hosts of demons, Indra with his gods, and the Siddhas,[22]

329. all these eagerly behold this divine vision of Thee, each from his own world.

330. Every moment, as they look upon Thee with hearts amazed, they worship Thee, O Lord, circling their crowns around Thee.

331. The heavens resound with their cries of 'Victory to Thee!', and [they bow before Thee] with folded hands raised to their foreheads.

332. In the form of the quality of purity the season of spring has come to the forest full of trees of humility, and Thou art the fruit growing in the tender leafage of their hands joined in salutation.

333. The day of good fortune has dawned for the eyes of those who have seen Thy unfathomable Cosmic Form, and abundance of joy to their minds.

334. Even the gods were filled with awe at the vision of that Form, which pervades the whole world and which presents itself to the sight from every direction.

XXIII. *Seeing Thy great form, of many mouths and eyes, O Mighty-armed, of many arms, thighs and feet, of many*

335. Though it is but one, it has strange and terrible mouths,
innumerable eyes, and countless arms holding weapons.

336. It has many legs, many bellies of various colours; and see
how all the mouths are full of fury!

337. It is as though at the end of a world age these mouths
had been scattered abroad with flames of fire lit in them.

338. These flames are like the missiles of Shiva, destroyer of
Tripura, or the assemblage of Bhairavas on the day of
dissolution; or like the wielders of the powers of destruction with which, at the end of an age, all creatures
are struck down.[23]

339. In every direction Thy terrible mouths are to be seen,
and Thy fierce teeth cannot be restrained within them,
like lions [roaming] in a valley.

340. In the dark night at the end of time devouring spirits
come out into the open and in Thy mouths [we see], as
in theirs, jaws smeared with the blood of the final day
of destruction.

341. Thy faces are as terrible to look on as the god of death
challenging to battle or the widespread slaughter on the
last day.

342. If one glances round this pitiful universe [it seems to
have] become as a tree growing on the banks of the
Jamnā river full of [the waters of] distress.

343. The ship of the life of the three worlds is being tossed on
the waves of the storm of anguish in the ocean of death
which is Thyself.

344. O Lord, if Thou wert to ask me suddenly, in anger, what
I think about this world, saying that I should experience
the joy of realization,

345. [I would reply], What can I say? I myself am full of
dread; the distress of this world is but a thin veil of
pretext [concealing my own fear].

346. Even I, who was dreaded by Rudra and for fear of whom
the god of death hid himself, have been filled by Thee
with terror.

347. This is the great calamity; it is strange that it should be
called Thy Cosmic Form! For it has the power to defeat
even fear itself.

xxiv. *When I see Thee touching the sky, blazing with many hues, with the mouth opened wide, and large glowing eyes, my inmost soul trembles in fear and I find neither steadiness nor peace, O Viṣṇu!*

348. Some of Thy mouths are so fierce that they challenge even the god of death; their vast extent dwarfs the whole of space.

349. The wide expanse of heaven cannot contain them, the winds of the three worlds cannot encircle them; see how even fire itself is consumed by the vapour issuing from them!

350. No two of them are alike and they are of many different colours; and their flames assist the work of universal destruction.

351. So fierce is the glow from them that it reduces the three worlds to ashes, and in all those mouths too are more large and small teeth.

352. Gale seems to be added to wind, deluge to the ocean; or the fire which lies beneath the ocean has come forward to meet the fire of poison.

353. See, the glow in Thy mouth is as fierce [as if] it had drunk the Halāhala poison and death had set fire to death.[24]

354. Who can tell their extent? It is as though space had broken open, or the sky cleft asunder;

355. or it is like the cavern of the nether world opened by Shiva when the demon Hiranyāksha escaped into a cave with the world under his arm.

356. So wide are these mouths, and the tongues within them so ravenous that the whole world would be too small a mouthful to satisfy them.

357. In the hollows of the mouths the tongues are spread out, like those poisonous flames emitted by the hissing of the serpents of the nether regions which rise up to the heavens.

358. The tips of those teeth protruding beyond the lips are as the flashing lightning on the day of destruction illuminating the bastions of the sky.

359. How those great eyes in their sockets below the forehead fill even fear with terror, as though they were waves of the great death lying in wait.

360. I know not why Thou hast assumed this terrifying Form, but I am filled suddenly with the fear of death.

361. I have longed to see this Form of Thine, and my desire has been fulfilled. I have beheld it with my eyes and they are satisfied.

362. This earthly body will die, and who cares about this? But now [I begin to wonder] whether my spirit will survive.

363. My limbs tremble with fear, and if this should increase my mind would be affected; my intelligence is failing and I have lost all self-respect.

364. Even more than this, that still inner soul, the very essence of all bliss, is overcome by fear.

365. O Beloved, I truly yearned [for the vision of Thy Form]; but now my understanding has left me, and our relationship of teacher and disciple can scarcely endure.

366. O Lord, I have striven courageously to overcome the weakness which has come into my heart after seeing this vision.

367. Already I had lost courage and now I have had this vision of Thy Form. Let that be; Thy teaching has filled me with perplexity.

368. My weary spirit has fled in every direction hoping to find rest, but there is none to be found anywhere.

369. So through this terrifying vision the whole universe has been afflicted. How could I refrain from speaking to Thee of this, O Krishna?

> xxv. *When I see Thy mouths terrible with their tusks, like Time's devouring flames, I lose sense of the directions and find no peace. Be gracious, O Lord of gods, Refuge of the worlds!*

370. In front of the huge eyes Thy vast mouths spread out as though they were the shattered vessels of the great fear.

371. The teeth are so thickly set that in each mouth the two lips cannot cover them, and they seem like dense rows of the weapons of the final destruction.

372. It is as though the great serpent Takshaka were filled with poison, as when spirits wander abroad on the darkest night, or fiery shafts of lightning are brandished in the sky.

373. Not only are Thy mouths so huge, but the fury within pours out so that the waves of death engulf us.

374. What can fail to be consumed when the storm wind of the day of doom and the fire of the final holocaust come together?

375. My courage fails when I behold these devouring mouths;
I am bewildered and have lost all sense of direction; I
no longer even know who I am.

376. Even after a short glance at Thy Form all my joy has
left me. Withdraw, I entreat Thee, this huge limitless
Form of Thine.

377. If I had realized Thy intention, would I have [asked Thee
to show this to me]? I beseech Thee to save me now from
this vision!

378. If, O Ananta, Thou art my master, shield my life from
this danger; draw back into Thyself this display of deadly
destruction.

379. Hear, O Thou ruler of the gods, Thy energy sustains the
whole universe, but Thou hast forgotten this and hast
begun to destroy it.

380. Be gracious, therefore, O Lord; withdraw swiftly Thy
mystic power and save me from this terror.

381. I have experienced such dread of this Form that again
and again I have implored Thee mercifully to remove it.

382. When Amarāvati was attacked was it not I alone who
saved it? I am not afraid to meet death face to face.

383. But this is quite different, O Lord, for Thou, rivalling
death itself, art about to engulf us with Thy universal
Form.

384. How can it be that though this is not the time of the
universal dissolution, yet even now Thou art amongst us
as death and the life of this wretched world is nearing its
end.

385. O perversity of fate! Calamity has arisen even while we
were seeking for peace. Alas! the universe is passing away
as Thou hast begun to consume it.

386. Do I not see that with Thy wide open mouths Thou art
swallowing up our armies in all directions?

XXVI. *All yonder sons of Dhṛtarāṣṭra together with the hosts
of kinsmen and Bhiṣma, Droṇa and Karṇa along with
the chief warriors on our side,—*

387. Are not the youths of the Kaurava race the sons of the
blind Dhritarāshtra, with all their friends and followers
being drawn into these mouths?

388. And all those kings of different countries who have come

together to support them are being swept away so that
none will be left to tell the tale.

389. Thou dost seize herds of raging elephants and swallow
up the whole array of the battlefield.

390. Troops firing with cannon and foot soldiers armed with
clubs are lost in Thy mouth.

391. All these numberless weapons as destructive as death,
even one of which could swallow up the universe, are
being seized up.

392. O great god, what pleasure does it give Thee to swallow
whole these fourfold armies, their followers and their horse
drawn chariots?

393. Who can compare with Bhishma in bravery and truth-
fulness? Alas! Even he and Drona, the brāhman, are
being devoured.

394. Now the brave Karna, son of the sun, has disappeared! I
see too that all of us are brought to nothing as dead leaves.

395. Alas! How strange is the favour of the Lord Creator!
For my request has brought its fate to this poor world.

396. The Lord explained formerly to me in various ways some
of His divine manifestations, but not satisfied with that
I pressed Him to show me His Cosmic Form.

397. We cannot avoid our destiny and our mind brings about
that which is to be; I am fated to bring about the destruction of this world, so how can it be avoided?

398. In earlier times the gods obtained nectar [by churning
the ocean], but they did not stop there and eventually
they stirred up the Kālakuta poison.

399. But in one way little harm was done, however, for [a
remedy was found] and Shiva overcame the calamity.

400. But now, how can this tempest of fire be controlled? Who
can swallow the heavens filled with poison? Who can
wrestle with death?

401. In this way Arjuna was distressed and lamented in his
heart; but he could not understand the Lord's motive
in this.

402. He was overwhelmed by the belief that he was the slayer
and that the Kauravas had died by his hand; but it was
in order to remove this illusion that Ananta had given
him the vision of Himself.

403. The Lord had revealed through that vision that no man
is killed by another, for He Himself is the only destroyer;

404. but, unable to understand this intention, Arjuna grieved in vain and his groundless fear increased.

> XXVII. —*are rushing into Thy fearful mouths set with terrible tusks. Some caught between the teeth are seen with their heads crushed to powder.*

405. Again Arjuna said, Look! Both armies at once, complete, are engulfed in Thy mouth, as clouds are merged in the sky.
406. As at the end of a great age the god of death, angered against the world, seizes in his grasp hell and the twenty-one heavens,
407. or as when a miserly man's luck has turned his hoarded treasure is immediately lost,
408. all the armies gathered here are at once drawn into Thy jaws, not one being able to escape. See the work of destiny!
409. As all these men enter Thy mouth they are as nothing, like the shoots of an Ashoka tree when stripped off by a camel.
410. See how their crowned heads have fallen into the grip of Thy jaws and are being ground to powder!
411. The jewels of their crowns stick in the crevices of the teeth and the powder of them adheres to the tongue; the edges of some of the teeth are smeared with it.
412. And yet, though Thy Form, as death, has laid hold of their bodies, the heads of the individual bodies are preserved.
413. The heads, the spiritual part of their bodies, have been left intact though they are in the mouths of the great death.
414. Then Arjuna said, He who is born can have no other fate, and for that reason the whole world is moving forward into the cavities of these mouths.
415. All the created worlds are pouring into these mouths, and silently Thou dost swallow them as they come.
416. Brahma and all the highest spiritual beings are rushing into the higher mouths, ordinary men into the nearer ones.
417. Other creatures are seized at the moment of their birth. Truly nothing is able to escape the clutch of those jaws.

> XXVIII. *As the many rushing torrents of rivers race towards the ocean, these heroes of the world of men rush into Thy flaming mouths.*

418. From all directions this world enters Thy mouth, as great rivers flow swiftly into the ocean.

419. Hastening through the span of their earthly life on the ladders of day and night, all creatures move onwards to meet these mouths.

> XXIX. *As moths rush swiftly into a blazing fire to perish there, these men rush into Thy mouths with great speed to their own destruction.*

420. All these fall into Thy mouths as moths fly into the recesses of a blazing mountain.

421. Whatever enters Thy mouth is swept away leaving no trace behind it, as water vanishes when falling on [heated] iron.

> XXX. *Devouring all the words on every side with Thy flaming mouths, thou lickest them up. The fiery rays fill this whole universe and scorch it with their fierce radiance, O Viṣṇu.*

422. Having consumed as a meal the whole world, why art Thou still hungry? What is this extraordinary power of consumption?

423. As a sick man recovering from a fever [is overcome with hunger] or a beggar in time of famine, so, licking Thy lips, the strange movements of the tongues are seen in Thy mouths.

424. How wonderful is that insatiable hunger! Nothing that is eatable escapes from Thy mouths.

425. Dost Thou wish to swallow the ocean in one gulp, to consume a mountain as one mouthful, or to set Thy teeth into the whole universe?

426. Such is Thy voracity that Thou dost swallow up all the quarters of the globe and with one lick of the tongue wipe away the stars.

427. As desire increases with enjoyment, as with fuel a fire grows fiercer, so Thy mouths as they eat seek for more.

428. Even one of these mouths is so vast that the three worlds could hang on the tip of its tongue, as though an apple were thrown into the great fire beneath the sea.

429. Thy mouths are so numerous that there are not enough worlds to fill them all. There is no purpose in multiplying them when there is no food for them.

430. Alas for this poor world, caught in the flames of Thy
mouth as animals encircled by a forest fire.

431. The universe is in such plight that Thou art not its god;
an evil fate has come upon it as though it were a fish
floundering in the net of death.

432. How can any creature escape from the meshes of the
radiance of Thy body? These are not mouths; they are,
for the world, as wax houses.²⁵

433. Fire does not know its own power of burning because it
cannot be burnt; yet those whom it touches cannot
escape from it.

434. Does a weapon know how it may destroy with its sharp-
ness, or poison know its own power to kill?

435. So, too, Thou art unaware of Thy fierceness; yet on this
side Thy mouth has devoured the whole world.

436. Thou, O Lord, art the one all-pervading spirit; why hast
Thou become for us the god of death?

437. I have relinquished all desire for life; be Thou not afraid
but tell me, without reserve, what is in Thy mind

438. How much more wilt Thou extend Thy terrifying Form?
Remember Thy divine nature, or at least have mercy on
me!

> XXXI. *Tell me who Thou art with form so terrible.
> Salutation to Thee, O Thou great Godhead, have mercy.
> I wish to know Thee [who art] the Primal One, for I
> know not Thy working.*

439. O Lord, known to us in the Vedas, existing before all
worlds, worshipped by the whole universe, listen to my
entreaty.

440. With these words the warrior bowed low at the feet of the
Lord and said, Listen, O Lord of lords.

441. I have asked Thee to show me Thy Cosmic Form, that I
might be satisfied; but at once Thou didst begin to swallow
up the universe.

442. Who art Thou and what is Thy motive for assembling all
these terrible faces? Wherefore dost Thou wield those
weapons in every hand?

443. Why dost Thou in wrath grow even greater than the sky?
Why dost Thou terrify us by producing these terrifying
eyes?

444. Wherefore dost Thou enter into rivalry with the god of death? Wilt Thou explain all this to me?

445. To this Ananta replied, Thou askest Me who I am, why I have so extended [My Form] and what this violence is.

The Blessed Lord said:

> XXXII. *Time am I, world-destroying, grown mature, engaged here in subduing the world. Even without thee [thy action], all warriors standing arrayed in the opposing armies shall cease to be.*

446. I am clearly the god of death and [My Form] is thus extended for the destruction of the world. For this purpose are these mouths spread out and I will devour all that is.

447. Arjuna replied, alas, I was sorely tried by earlier perplexities; and so I besought Thee, whereupon all these misfortunes arose.

448. Feeling that such harsh words would cause Arjuna to be dejected, Krishna said at once, But there is another thing.

449. Thou, Pāndava, art set apart from this great calamity [Thou wilt not perish]. At this point Arjuna, about to give up, gradually recovered his spirit.

450. As the fear of this great destruction passed, Arjuna came to himself and began to give his attention to the words of the Lord.

451. The Lord continued, O Arjuna, It is only you who are Mine; I am about to destroy all others.

452. Thou hast seen the whole world drawn into My mouths, [and consumed] as a protective offering cast into the submarine fire.

453. Certainly nothing will remain of all this, but see how these armies vainly boast!

454. These armies mustered here arrogantly claim, with all the power of their warrior-like qualities, that their elephant troops are superior even to the god of death.

455. They say that they can create worlds upon worlds, and claim that they could even slay death itself and swallow the whole universe in one gulp.

456. They boast that they will eat up the whole earth, burn up the whole of space and nail down the wind with their arrows.

457. By means of the wealth of weapons of this fourfold array and elated by their achievements, they emulate the great death.

458. Their words seem to be sharper than their weapons and fiercer than fire and compared with their power to destroy the Kālakuta poison is sweet.

459. But all these warriors seem to be hollow masses of plaster or fruit [painted in] a picture.

460. These figures parading in grand attire are as the flood waters of a mirage; not armies, but resembling a snake made of cloth.

> XXXIII. *Therefore arise and win glory. Conquering thy foes, enjoy a prosperous kingdom. By Me alone are they already slain. Be thou merely the occasion, O Savyasācin [Arjuna].*

461. I have already consumed all the power which activates them; they are as lifeless as ghostly figures in a potter's shop.

462. They are like puppets at the end of a stick which tumble down in all directions as soon as the cord which moves them is broken.

463. Such are these armies which it would take me but a moment to overcome. So arise! Come to thy senses!

464. When the cattle [of Virāta] were stolen [by the Kauravas] thou didst render them unconscious with thy magic weapon, so that even the timid Uttara laid hold of them and stripped off their clothes.[26]

465. These armies are even more worthless than those enemies; now that they have come to this battlefield, slay them and win for thyself the glory of having vanquished them single-handed.

466. This is no empty glory, O Arjuna; the whole kingdom will be thine, so do thou act as a weapon in My hand.

> XXXIV. *Slay Drona, Bhīṣma, Jayadratha, Karṇa and other great warriors as well, who are already doomed by Me. Be not afraid. Fight, and thou shalt conquer the enemies in battle.*

467. Have no care for Drona, no fear for Bhishma; why shouldst thou hesistate to take up arms against Karna?

468. Do not be concerned about killing Jayadratha and all these other renowned warriors.[27]
469. Consider them as merely painted lions, to be wiped out with the hand.
470. So, O Pāndava, what is this great battle array? It is but an outward show; for I already hold it in My grasp.
471. At the moment when thou didst see them caught in My mouth, their lives were ended; now they are like empty husks.
472. Therefore arise at once, slay those whose lives I have already taken and do not give way to senseless grief.
473. Realize that thou art a mere instrument; shoot them down like a man who, as a game, piles up wooden blocks and knocks them down again.
474. Beloved, those who have arisen to oppose thee, were already dead [at the moment of birth]; so enjoy renown with the conquest of this kingdom.
475. Arjuna, in his bravery, destroyed utterly his kinsmen who were filled with pride and drunken with their power in the world.
476. O Kiriti, write these words on the tablet of the world's records and be thou victorious.

Sanjaya said:

> xxxv. *Having heard this utterance of Keśava [Krṣṇa], Kirīṭin [Arjuna], trembling, saluted again with folded hands and prostrating himself in great fear, spoke in a faltering voice to Krṣṇa.*

477. Sanjaya narrated the whole of this story to the lord of the Kurus, who listened to it eager to hear more. So says Jnānadeva.
478. Then Krishna spoke with a full-toned voice like the rushing sound of the Ganges pouring down from the highest heaven,
479. as the roaring of heavy clouds sending down their torrents of rain, or as the milky ocean reverberated when churned with the mountain Mandāra.
480. So Krishna, the root of the universe, unknowable and of infinite form, spoke to Arjuna in deep resounding tones.
481. Arjuna had scarcely heard it when his whole body began

to tremble, whether with excess of joy or grief it would
be hard to know.

482. Bending very low and joining his hands in salutation,
again and again he touched the Lord's feet with his
forehead,

483. and when he tried again to speak, his throat was choked
with emotion. Imagine whether this was through joy or
fear.

484. This was Arjuna's condition brought about by the words
of the Lord. This is how I interpret the verses of the story.

485. Being full of fear, again he bowed his head at the feet of
the Lord and said, O Lord, this is how Thou didst speak—

Arjuna said:

xxxvi. *O Hṛṣikeśa [Kṛṣṇa], rightly does the world
rejoice and delight in Thy magnificence. The Rākṣasas are
fleeing in terror in all directions and all the hosts of
perfected ones are bowing down before Thee [in adoration].*

486. O Arjuna, I am death, and it is my game that I devour
all.—This saying I accept as unalterable;

487. but I cannot understand why Thou who shouldst preserve
art today destroying all.

488. How can youth be removed from the body and untimely
age be brought in? Therefore what Thou claimest to do is
impossible.

489. Can the sun ever set at midday, O Ananta, before the
day has reached it close?

490. For Thee, who art endless time, there are three states,
each one all powerful in its own period.

491. When existence begins, continuation and dissolution cease
to be; during the continuation of existence, creation and
dissolution have no place.

492. Moreover at the moment of dissolution, creation and
existence cease. This system is eternal and immutable.

493. For this reason I cannot understand how Thou dost
devour the world while it is living in the enjoyment of
the state of existence.

494. Then the Lord signed to Arjuna, as though to say, I have
shown thee how these two armies are doomed and the
destruction of others will happen in due time.

495. Ananta had hardly spoken when Arjuna saw that the worlds were restored to their previous state.

496. Arjuna said, O Lord, Thou dost hold the strings controlling the puppet show of the universe. [See], the world has returned to its former state.

497. I remember how it is said of Thee that Thou savest those who have fallen into the ocean of sorrow.

498. Whenever I remember this I experience the highest bliss and seem to float on the waves of the nectar of joy.

499. O Lord, this world is filled with love for Thee on account of its very existence; but the wicked, on the other hand, suffer increasing destruction.

500. O Hrishikesha, Thou art a source of terror to the demons of the world, who flee from Thee beyond its confines.

501. While gods, men of perfection and the kinnaras, in short, the whole of animate and inanimate creation, salute Thee in great joy.[28]

> XXXVII. *And why should they not do Thee homage, O Exalted One, who art greater than Brahma, the original creator? O Infinite Being, Lord of the gods, Refuge of the universe, Thou art the Imperishable, the being and the non-being and what is beyond that.*

502. O Nārāyana! why should the demons flee at sight of Thee, instead of finding refuge in Thee?

503. Why should I ask Thee this? This much we know. How can darkness remain after the rising of the sun?

504. As Thou who art the storehouse of the light of the soul, hast made Thyself visible to us today, it is but natural [that the demons] should take to flight.

505. This for long was hidden from me, O Rāma, but now I have beheld Thy profound greatness.[20]

506. Thy divine desire has brought forth the Supreme Spirit from which proceed whole series of worlds and all manner of created beings.

507. Thou, Lord, art that which is eternally limitless, the one who is not confined by the qualities, the same for all time; Thou art indeed the whole process of speech in its four stages.[30]

508. Thou art the essence sustaining all the worlds; O Sadāshiva Thou art indestructible, being and yet non-being, and all that is beyond this.[31]

XXXVIII. *Thou art the First of the gods, the Primal Person, the Supreme Resting-place of the world. Thou art the knower and that which is to be known and the supreme goal. And by Thee is this universe pervaded, O Thou of infinite form.*

509. Thou art the source of both spirit and matter, the whole extent of the great first principle, without beginning, self-existent, the ancient one.

510. Thou art the life of all the universe, the storehouse of the life of the world, the knowledge of past and future is in Thy hands.

511. Through the eyes of the Vedas we see the joy of union with Thee, O Thou who art one with the universe; Thou art the highest resort of the three worlds.

512. Therefore Thou art called the ultimate refuge, for at the end of the world even the supreme spirit merges into Thee.

513. In short the whole universe is pervaded by Thee. Who can describe Thy infinite Form?

XXXIX. *Thou art Vāyu [the wind], Yama [the destroyer], Agni [the fire], Varuna [the sea-god] and Śaśānka [the moon], and Prajāpati, the grandsire [of all]. Hail, hail to Thee, a thousand times. Hail, Hail, to Thee again and yet again.*

XL. *Hail to Thee in front, hail to Thee behind and hail to Thee on every side, O All; boundless in power and immeasurable in might, Thou dost penetrate all and therefore Thou art all.*

514. Art Thou not the One? Is there any place where Thou art not? Hail to Thee, all that Thou art.

515. O Ananta, Thou art the God of the wind and of death who is the punisher of all; Thou art the fire residing in all beings.

516. Thou art the god of the waters and of the moon; Brahma the creator of all, and also the progenitor of the great ancestor of all.

517. Salutation to Thee, O Lord of the world, we hail Thee as all that Thou art, be Thou with or without form.

518. So, with a devoted mind, the Son of Pāndu praised the Lord and again and again saluted Him.

519. Once more looking at the Form of the Lord from head to foot, he cried, Hail, all hail to Thee, O Lord.

520. Having observed all the animate and inanimate forms that were to be seen in His body, he exclaimed again, O Lord, salutation to Thee.

521. At the sight of many still stranger forms and marvels appearing he was filled with amazement and exclaimed again and again, All hail to Thee!

522. He could think of no other words of praise, nor could he remain silent; he began to shout aloud in the fervour of his love.

523. Thus he saluted the Lord a thousand times and exclaimed again, I bow down to Thee, Hari, who art here before me!

524. Of what consequence is it to us whether Thou hast front or back; from behind I salute Thee.

525. There is no end to Thy different limbs and forms. Therefore hail to Thee who dost pervade all.

526. I salute Thee in whom are contained all mighty power and immeasurable prowess; Thou art ever the same one [manifested] in all lands.

527. Thou art all in all, and fillest all, as in the sky the whole space is sky.

528. All this art Thou, as in the milky ocean every wave is of milk.

529. In no way art Thou different from all this; now I realize that Thou Thyself art all.

XLI. *For whatsoever I have spoken in rashness to Thee, thinking that Thou art my companion and unaware of this [fact of] Thy greatness, [saying] 'O Kṛṣṇa, O Yādava, O Comrade'; out of my negligence or maybe through fondness,*

530. I have never realized that Thou art thus, O Lord, and so I have behaved towards Thee in the manner of a close relationship.

531. How great was my impropriety! [It was as if I had used] nectar to cleanse the ground, or given away the boon-giving cow in exchange for a bull;

532. as if, having found a touchstone, I had broken it up unwittingly for use in building, or cut down the tree of desire to make a hedge for a field:

533. or, having found a mine of desire-jewels, had used them to drive away unruly [cattle], not recognizing them. So even while Thou wert so near we have rejected Thee as a friend.

534. Considering the present situation, this war after all is not important; yet have I used Thee, the Highest Brahma, as my charioteer!

535. O Thou generous one, we sent Thee as a mediator to the Kauravas, using Thee, the living Lord, as a common go-between.

536. Fool that I am, how could I not recognize Thee, the bliss of the highest attainment of yogis? And yet before Thy very face I have treated Thee with discourtesy.

> XLII. *And for whatsoever disrespect was shown to Thee in jest, while at play or on the bed or seated at meals, either alone or in the presence of others, I pray, O Unshaken One, forgiveness from Thee, the Immeasurable.*

537. Thou art the eternal origin of the universe, and yet we jested with Thee on familiar terms as friends gathered together.

538. When at times we visited Thy home we were received by Thee with respect yet, disregarding this, we would take offence.

539. O Holder of the Shārnga Bow, to appease us Thou didst have to touch our feet, and so in many ways [we slighted Thee].

540. As though Thou wert one of us we turned out backs on Thee. O Vaikuntha, in all these things we behaved so wrongly.

541. We crossed swords with Thee, wrestled with Thee constantly, playing chess we treated Thee with scorn, and quarrelled with Thee fiercely.

542. We demanded the best of everything, offered advice even to Thee and at times treated Thee as of no account.

543. Our fault is so great that the threefold world cannot contain it; but touching Thy feet [we assure Thee that] we did not understand.

544. The Lord would lovingly remember me at meals, but shamelessly I would remain silent.

545. Thoughtlessly I played in the Lord's inner chamber and rested beside Him on the couch.

546. I would call out to Thee, Krishna! and look on Thee as a
Yādava, and fling an oath at Thee when Thou didst go
away.

547. We would sit together and I would disregard Thy words;
many such things happened through our familiarity. What
more can I relate?

548. O Ananta, how much more shall I recount? I am nothing
but a great mass of offences.

549. Whatever faults I have committed either in Thy presence
or behind Thy back, take them all upon Thyself, O Lord,
as a mother would.

550. Whenever rivers flow with their turbid waters into the
ocean, must it not receive them or can it reject them?

551. So, O Mukunda, Thou shouldst forgive me for all that I
have spoken against Thee, whether out of love or thought-
lessness.

552. It is through Thy forgiving nature that the earth has
been able to bear on its surface all these creatures.
Therefore, O Highest Being, is there any need to entreat
Thee?

553. O Thou who art immeasurable, grant pardon for all my
faults to me who have sought refuge in Thee.

> XLIIII. *Thou art the father of the world of the moving and
> the unmoving. Thou art the object of its worship and its
> venerable teacher. None is equal to Thee, how then could
> there be one greater than Thee in the three worlds, O Thou
> of incomparable greatness?*

554. Now, O Lord, have I realized Thy true greatness, who
art the origin of the whole creation.

555. Thou art the highest deity of all the gods of Hari, Hara
and every other. Thou art the First Teacher, teaching
even the Vedas.

556. Thou art profound, O Rāma, sole abode of all creatures,
the image of all virtues, one without a second.

557. What need is there to state that none is equal to Thee?
Is not the whole world contained in that space created
by Thee?

558. One should hesitate to declare that there is any one to
match Thee. How then could one say that any other is
greater than Thee?

559. Thou art the One in the universe, and there is none equal

to or greater than Thee. Thy incomparable greatness
cannot be told.

XLIV. *Therefore bowing down and prostrating my body
before Thee, adorable Lord, I seek Thy grace. Thou, O
God, shouldst bear with me as a father with his son, as a
friend with his friend, as a lover with his beloved.*

560. Thus spoke Arjuna and prostrated himself before the
Lord, being filled with pure reverence.
561. Then he exclaimed in choking voice, I entreat Thee, have
mercy, save me from the ocean of my faults.
562. Thinking of Thee, who art the friend of the whole world,
as a personal relation, I did not treat Thee with proper
respect, but behaved arrogantly towards Thee who art
the Lord of all the gods.
563. Thou Thyself who art worthy to be extolled, but through
Thy affection for me Thou hast praised me before others
and in my excitement I boasted more and more.
564. There is no limit to such mistakes, O Mukunda; so save
me, save me from my faults.
565. How can I be worthy to ask this of Thee? But I speak
familiarly, as a child to his father.
566. When a man meets a close friend, he does not hesitate
to tell him freely of the troubles that have befallen him
in the world.
567. A faithful wife having surrendered herself wholeheartedly
to her husband cannot conceal from him, when he meets
her, what is in her heart.
568. So too, O Lord, I have implored Thy pardon. There is
one more thing I wish to say to Thee.

XLV. *I have seen what was never seen before and I rejoice,
but my heart is shaken with fear. Show me that other
[previous] form of Thine, O God and be gracious, O
Lord of the gods and Refuge of the universe!*

569. I took the liberty of urging the Lord to reveal to me His
universal Form, and Thou, my father and my mother,
didst lovingly fulfil my desire.
570. I desired to have wish-granting trees planted in my
courtyard and wanted Thee to give me a calf of the
boon-giving cow to play with.

571. I wished to play dice with the stars and to have the moon for a ball. All these desires Thou hast fulfilled, O my mother!

572. Thou hast showered down on me, like the four months of the rainy season, nectar, a small particle of which can be obtained only with difficulty. Preparing the soil Thou hast sown desire-stones in every furrow.

573. In this way Thou hast fulfilled the longing of my life, Thou hast treated me indulgently and hast shown me [Thy Form] of which even Hara and Brahma have never heard.

574. Still less have they seen it. Thou hast unravelled for me the knot of that secret which even the Upanishads failed to discover.

575. Even in all the lives through which I have passed from the beginning of the age until now,

576. searching through them all I cannot perceive that this has even been seen or heard.

577. The knowledge of the intellect has been unable to penetrate even its outer court, nor can it be imagined by the heart.

578. How then can it be said that the eyes have ever seen it? Never before has it been seen or heard.

579. This is that Cosmic Form which Thou didst reveal to me and it has gladdened my heart.

580. But now I long to talk with Thee, to enjoy Thy company, to embrace Thee.

581. How is this possible with that Cosmic Form of Thine? To which of Thy faces shall I address myself? Whom shall I embrace, as there is no end to Thy Form?

582. How can one run with the wind, embrace the sky or play and sport in the ocean?

583. Great dread of the Form had arisen in my heart; so grant me this indulgence, let this vision be withdrawn.

584. As a man, having seen with pleasure the whole created world, then remains happily at home, so Thy four-armed form is our resting place.

585. If we practise yoga, that leads to the experience of Thy finite form; we may study all the scriptures but we attain to the same end.

586. Whatever activities we undertake, they are rewarded with this same fruit; this is the goal of all pilgrimages to the holy places.

587. The charity we perform, the merit we acquire, all bring
the reward of the vision of Thy four-armed form.

588. It is for that that my heart longs, but it is difficult to
see it. Do Thou hasten to remove my distress.

589. O Thou who knowest our hearts, who dost establish the
whole universe, who art to be worshipped, God of gods,
have mercy on me.

> XLVI. *I wish to see Thee even as before with Thy crown,
> mace and disc in Thy hand. Assume Thy four-armed
> shape, O Thou of a thousand arms and of universal form.*

590. See how that Form tints the flowers of the blue lotus,
adds colour to the azure sky, and gives lustre to the
sapphire.

591. It is as though the emerald were endowed with fragrance,
as though arms were to grow on [the body of] joy and
all these lend beauty to Cupid himself.

592. On Thy head is a crown, but Thy head has become as a
crown to the crown. Thy body itself is the ornament of
the ornaments which adorn it.

593. O Wielder of the Shārnga bow, Thy necklace Vaijayanti
is given added radiance by Thee, as clouds in the sky
set in the span of the rainbow.[32]

594. How noble is Thy mace, which gives the bliss of heaven
to the demons with [the force of] its blow and, O Govinda,
Thy discus glows with gentle radiance.

595. O Lord, I pray Thee to assume at once that familiar
form that I am so eager to see.

596. Having experienced the joy of Thy Cosmic Form, my
eyes are satisfied and long now to see Thee again as
Krishna.

597. I desire to see no other than Thy finite form; if [my
eyes] may not see that, they can no longer appreciate
that other Form.

598. For us this simple form is our only source of joy and
means of liberation. Therefore gather in Thy Cosmic
Form and become again the embodied Krishna.

The Blessed Lord said:

> XLVII. *By My grace, through My divine power, O Arjuna
> was shown to thee this supreme form, luminous, universal,
> infinite and primal which none but thee has seen before.*

599. The Lord of the Cosmic Form, wondering at Arjuna's words, said, I have never seen anyone so foolish.

600. What a wonderful thing thou hast obtained! Yet thou hast no joy in it, but like an obstinate man thou knowest not, in thy fear, what thou sayest.

601. At times, when I have been pleased, I have been willing even to give My body [for my devotees]. But to whom does one offer one's whole heart?

602. For thee today I have given My all to prepare for thee this vision of My Form.

603. My love for thee is so great that I have displayed the banner of the supreme secret before the world.

604. This is My matchless, highest Form, out of which [proceed] the incarnation such as that of Krishna.

605. It is infused with the purest light of wisdom, pervading all worlds, eternal, immovable, the source of all.

606. Except for thee, O Arjuna, never before has this happened, nor is it obtainable by any means or practices.

> XLVIII. *Neither by the Vedas, nor by sacrifices, nor by study, nor by gifts, nor by ceremonial rites, nor by severe austerities, can I be seen with this form in the world of men by any one else but thee, O Hero of the Kurus [Arjuna].*

607. When the Vedas set out to find it, they were silent; sacrifices turned back from heaven [in despair].

608. Seekers encountering many difficulties abandoned the practice of yoga; study of the sacred writings is of no effect in this matter.

609. The highest works of merit pursued it eagerly but in spite of all their efforts, most of them reached only as far as the seventh heaven.

610. They saw heaven and immediately abandoned their severe austerities; the means of penance also failed them; the goal was beyond their reach.

611. Without any such effort thou hast seen this Cosmic Form which none else in the world of men has been able to see.

612. Thou alone hast been [found worthy] of this the goal of meditation; even the Creator himself has not been so blessed.

> XLIX. *May you not be afraid, may you not be bewildered, seeing this terrible form of Mine. Free from fear and glad at heart, behold again this other form of Mine.*

613. Rejoice in having seen this Form; have no fear of it, and do not regard anything as good except this.

614. If a man were to come suddenly upon an ocean filled with nectar, would he abandon it for fear of drowning in it?

615. Should a man find a mountain of gold, would he pass it by, deeming it too heavy to be moved?

616. If by good fortune one were to wear a desire-stone would he reject it as a burden? Would a man drive away the boon-giving cow because he was unable to feed her?

617. If the moon were to appear in one's house, would one say, Depart, do not bring heat? Would a man say to the sun, Begone, thou dost cast shadows!

618. Today thou hast been given the glorious vision of the great light; why shouldst thou be so perturbed?

619. Thou ignorant one, thou dost not understand, O Arjuna; but should I be angry with thee? Thou dost abandon the true body and cling to the shadow.

620. Is not this Form truly Myself? In thy timidity thou givest thy love to the semblance of Me in My four-armed form.

621. O Pārtha, relinquish thy former conceptions and do not remain attached to that form.

622. Though that Cosmic Form is fierce, terrifying and vast, let that be the only goal of thy desire.

623. A miser's whole heart is bound up in his treasure and he lives [outwardly] only as a body.

624. A mother bird leaves her heart in the nest with her unfledged young ones when she flies away into the sky.

625. A cow roams on the mountain though her love remains with her calf; so, O Pārtha, set thy affection on My Form alone.

626. So enjoy My four-armed form, for the sake of external pleasure,

627. but, O Pāndava, again and again [I urge thee] never to forget My words, that thou shouldst not withdraw thy devotion from My Cosmic Form.

628. Never having seen this [vision] before, thou art afraid; give up this fear and let thy love be given wholly [to this Form].

629. Then Krishna said, I will do as thou sayest; I will gladly give thee again [the vision of] My [four-armed] form.

L. *Having thus spoken to Arjuna, Vasudeva [Kṛṣṇa] revealed to him again his own form. The Exalted One, having assumed again the form of grace, comforted the terrified Arjuna.*

630. As soon as He had spoken these words, the Lord resumed His human shape. See how wonderful is His love [for Arjuna].

631. Shri Krishna is the highest bliss and in the vision of His Cosmic Form He gave His all; yet Arjuna was not content with it.

632. He was like a man who accepts something and throws it away; like one who finds fault with a jewel, or who having seen a maiden rejects her.

633. See how Shri Krishna by displaying His Cosmic Form, showed His great love! In this He gave to Arjuna the essence of all His teaching.

634. As a piece of gold made into ornaments according to one's wish is again melted down if the ornaments do not please,

635. so Krishna, who out of love for His disciple had transformed Himself into His Cosmic Form, assumed again His personal form when Arjuna was not pleased.

636. Seeing this [we may ask] where there could be any teacher so patient with the demands of his disciple. Sanjaya said, I do not understand such love.

637. Then that Cosmic Form embracing all things around it, the divine radiance which had been revealed, was drawn back into the personal form of Krishna.

638. As the concept of 'thou' is embraced by the [wider] concept of 'THAT', as the seed is contained in the tree,

639. as the fantasy of a dream is destroyed by the return to consciousness, so did Shri Krishna withdraw His Cosmic Form.

640. The light of the sun is held within the disc of the sun, as clouds form part of the sky, and the fullness of the tide lies in the bed of the ocean, O King.

641. So, to please Arjuna, the Lord spread out as the folds of a new garment that Cosmic Form which had been concealed within His personal form;

642. and when Arjuna, as though he were a customer, had examined its measure and its colour, it did not please him and was again folded away.

643. So it was that the Cosmic Form, which overpowers the world by the vastness of its extent, changed again into the gentle and beautiful finite form.

644. Or perhaps Ananta returned to His lesser form in order to reassure the frightened Arjuna.

645. Then Arjuna was filled with amazement as a man waking suddenly from a dream in which he has been in heaven;

646. or [one might say that] Arjuna looked at Krishna in the same way as a man whose interest in worldly affairs had been withdrawn through the grace of his guru might suddenly realize the eternal truth.

647. It seemed good to him that the Cosmic Form, which had been as a veil [between them], had been withdrawn.

648. Then, as a man who had overcome death, or had escaped from a terrible storm, or had crossed the seven seas by the strength of his own arms,

649. Arjuna rejoiced that after the Cosmic Form was removed he could see Krishna as before.

650. Then as after sunset the stars appear again in the sky, Arjuna began to see the two armies on the earth.

651. He looked round and saw the battlefield of the Kauravas and his relatives ranged on the two sides, as before, the warriors hurling masses of weapons against each other.

652. His chariot was still standing there, as though under a canopy of the enemies' arrows with Krishna seated at the front of his chariot, himself on the ground.

Arjuna said:

> LI. *Beholding again Thy gracious human form, O Janārdana [Kṛṣṇa], I have now become composed in mind and am restored to my normal nature.*

653. When everything was thus restored to its previous state, Arjuna, the joy of heroes, said, my mind is restored!

654. Knowledge, abandoning intelligence, had strayed in fear into the wilderness, and my mind in company with egotism was wandering from place to place.

655. My senses became inactive and speech ceased to exist; such was the state of disorder within my body.

656. These are now restored to their proper activity and revitalized [by the sight of] Thy finite form.

657. Feeling such inward joy Arjuna said to Krishna, Again I see this Thy human form.

658. O Lord, by showing it to me Thou hast treated me as a mother would coax an erring child and suckle it.

659. I who was immersed in the ocean of Thy Cosmic Form, struggling through the waves one by one with my hands, have arrived at the shore of this personal form.

660. O Thou who art the friend of the city of Dvārkā, this is no mere gift, but is as though Thou didst shower down rain upon me, a withering tree.[33]

661. I who was overcome with thirst have come upon an ocean of nectar, and now confidence in my understanding is restored.

662. Thou hast planted in the garden of my heart the creeper of happiness, and my experience of joy is renewed.

The Blessed Lord said:

> LII. *This form of Mine which is indeed very hard to see, thou hast seen. Even the gods are ever eager to see this form.*

663. After Arjuna had spoken thus, Shri Krishna said, Fix thy affections on My universal aspect,

664. and then thou mayest turn to this finite form with outward worship only. O husband of Subhadrā, hast thou forgotten all My teaching?

665. O Arjuna! Once a man possesses even Mount Meru, he will think it of little value. Such false dreams do we have!

666. Even with all his penances Shiva was not able to attain to the vision of that Cosmic Form which I have shown to thee.

667. Arjuna, yogis become weary through the practice of yogic discipline, but do not obtain that vision.

668. The gods themselves spend the whole of their lives in the hope that one day they may catch a glimpse of it.

669. As the chātaka bird looks up to the clouds with longing, holding out, as it were, the cup of hope,

670. so do gods and men, with eager desire, repeat day and night their prayer for that vision.

671. Yet thou hast seen so easily, face to face, this Cosmic
Form which no one had seen even in a dream.

> LIII. *In the form in which Thou hast seen Me now, I
> cannot be seen either by the Vedas or by austerities or by
> gifts or by sacrifices.*

672. Behold, O Arjuna! This vision cannot be reached by any
road, and the Vedas have turned back [in their search
for it].
673. O Wielder of the bow, My Cosmic Form cannot be reached
through the practice of manifold penances,
674. nor can that vision, which thou hast seen with so little
effort, be won by gifts, by ascetic practices or by sacrifices.
675. Thou shouldst know that there is but one path by which
I can be reached; the heart must be filled with devotion.

> LIV. *But by unswerving devotion to Me, O Arjuna, I can
> be thus known, truly seen and entered into, O Oppressor
> of the foe [Arjuna].*

676. This devotion must be like showers of rain which has
no other place to go to apart from the earth;
677. or like the river Ganges, which with its abundant waters
again and again seeks out the ocean which is its only
refuge.
678. In such a way [a devotee] lives his life in Me with whole-
hearted and unswerving love, becoming one with Me.
679. As I Myself am like the milky ocean, which from shore
to shore consists only of milk,
680. Have no doubt that from Myself down to the ant, in fact,
in the whole creation, there is none other to be worshipped.
681. As soon as thou believest this thou wilt know My true
nature; and when this is known, it follows that thou wilt
see me.
682. Then, in the same way when fire is lit from fuel the fuel
is lost to sight, having become fire itself,
683. or as the sky remains dark so long as the sun has not
risen, but when it appears, the light shines forth,
684. so through direct experience of Me, egotism vanishes and
with the disappearance of egotism, duality passes away.
685. Thus I am all that is; I am by nature the only one who
exists; what more can I say? A man [who knows this]
is absorbed into union with Me.

686. A devotee who performs every action for My sake and for whom there is no one in the world so dear as I am,

687. for whom among all things visible and invisible I am the only goal, and whoever has chosen me as the final purpose of his existence.

688. one who has forgotten the language of created beings, and who reveres all things because, seeing Me in all things, he is free from enmity,

689. becomes united with Me, O Pāndava, when he leaves his mortal body.

690. Sanjaya said, O King! the Lord who contains within Himself the whole universe spoke thus with words full of compassion.

691. Then Arjuna, endowed with the riches of supreme joy, and the one in all the world most fitted to serve at the feet of Krishna,

692. did indeed see with his mind both the manifestations of the Lord; but he preferred Krishna in His human form to the vision of the Cosmic Form.

693. Krishna, however, did not approve of Arjuna's opinion; for the finite is not superior to the infinite.

694. In support of this the Lord gave him several explanations.

695. Hearing these, Arjuna said to himself, Now I will ask which is the better of these two.

696. With this thought in mind, Arjuna found appropriate ways of asking Krishna about it; listen now to the continuation of the story.

697. Jnānadeva says, This story will now be told in an interesting way in the simple Ovi metre, by the grace of Nivritti.

698. At the feet of the Cosmic Form of the Lord I now offer the open flowers of my Ovi verses, held in the hands of my pure devotion.

In the Upanishad of the Bhagavadgitā, the science of the Absolute, the scripture of Yoga and the dialogue between Shri Krishna and Arjuna, this is the eleventh chapter called the Vision of the Cosmic Form.

1. *rasas.* See Ch. I, v. 13. Here and in the next verse the implication is that the sentiment of tranquility predominates, that of wonder is subordinate, and the remaining sentiments are present from time to time.
2. *triple confluence.* The third river is the Sarasvati which formerly flowed into the confluence of the Ganges and the Jamnā but was hidden. This triple junction made Prayāga especially sacred.
3. *Mādhava.* One of the names of Krishna, the vision of whom can be seen at Prayāga, or Allahabad, at the confluence of the Ganges and the Jamnā.
4. *Hiranyāksha.* The name of a demon who took the earth under his arm and threw it into the ocean.
5. *the boar.* The third incarnation of Krishna.
6. *the fish and the tortoise.* Two of the ten incarnations of Vishnu.
7. *Rājasuya sacrifice.* A great sacrifice performed by a universal monarch.
8. *Uttānapāda.* The father of Dhruva, the polar star. Dhruva was rejected by his father and was told by his mother that the attainment of high places was only to be reached by great efforts. After practising great austerities Vishnu raised him to the position of the polar star.
   Shishupāla. An ancient king who continuously opposed Krishna.
9. *Ajamila.* The name of a brāhman who attained to union with Krishna.
10. *Bali.* The name of a demon.
11. *Ruler of the six qualities.* An epithet of Krishna. See Ch. II, note 8 for the six qualities.
12. *Ashvin gods.* A group of gods who were physicians.
13. *the divine Triad.* Brahma, the creator, Vishnu, the preserver and Shiva, the destroyer.
14. *Pināka bow.* The name of Shiva's weapon.
15. *Four-faced.* One of the epithets of Brahma. He is said to have had five heads, of which one was destroyed.
16. *Kailās.* A peak in the Himālayan mountains said to be the dwelling of Shiva.
17. *Mahādeva.* One of the names of Shiva.
18. *the third eye of Rudra.* Rudra, the god of destruction, was said to have a third eye, in his forehead.
19. *the sacred syllable.* In the Marathi text this is referred to here as the 'three and a half mātras' (three and a half sound-units). See Ch. VI, note 20.
20. *thirty-six principles.* These extend the list of the 'twenty-four' given above; see Ch. X, note 8. One enumeration gives the following: Shiva, Shakti, Vishnu; twenty elements, sense-objects, activities and senses; five vital airs; thought, individuality, consciousness, matter, soul; three 'qualities'. The 'thirty-seventh principle' is the Supreme Spirit.

21. *Rudras.* A class of gods who are inferior manifestations of Rudra (Shiva). *Sādhyas.* A class of celestial beings. *Devas.* An inclusive word for gods.
22. *Gandharvas.* Celestial singers. *Siddhas.* Those who are perfected in religious development.
23. *Tripura.* The name of a demon presiding over three cities.
Bhairava. Bhairava is another name of Shiva; Bhairavas are a group of gods associated with Shiva.
24. *halāhala.* A deadly poison. Cf. kālakuta, Ch. I, note 38.
25. *wax houses.* These were huts made of flammable material to be set alight as a defence in battle.
26. *Uttara.* The son of the king Virāta, whose cattle were stolen by the Kauravas in battle. Uttara overcame them and stripped them of their clothes.
27. *Jayadratha.* The name of a king fighting on the side of the Kauravas.
28. *Kinnaras.* Mythical beings with human bodies and horse heads.
29. *Rāma.* See Ch. IX, note 8.
30. *four stages of speech.* See Ch. VI, note 16.
31. *Sadāshiva.* Another name of Shiva.
32. *Vaijayanti.* The necklace of Indra, here attributed to Krishna.
33. *Dvārkā.* The capital of Krishna in northern India.

CHAPTER XII

Salutation to Ganesha!

1. Hail to thee, O Grace of the Preceptor,—who art pure, famous for thy generosity, ever pouring out showers of joy!
2. When a man is overcome by the grasp of the serpent of sense pleasures, it is rendered harmless by one glance from thy grace.
3. If thou dost flow over us with the waves of thy favour, whom can the heat [of passion] burn or the fire of grief consume?
4. O blessed grace, thou dost reveal to thy disciples the bliss of yoga, and their yearning after Self-realization is satisfied by thee.
5. Thou dost rear them lovingly in the lap of the power seated in the ādhāra centre and rock them to sleep in the cradle of the heart centre.[1]
6. Thou dost encircle them with the light of discrimination; thou dost give them mind control and the vital airs as toys for their play; and dost wrap them in the garments of the bliss of the Self.
7. Thou dost suckle them with the supreme spirit and sing them songs of the mystic anāhata sound as lullabies, and lull them to sleep by telling them of the final absorption in the spirit.[2]
8. Thus art thou the mother of spiritual seekers, all knowledge matures at thy feet; therefore I will not leave the shadow of thy protection.
9. O Grace of the Guru, one who is supported by thy favour becomes as the creator of the whole world of knowledge.
10. Therefore, O wealthiest of mothers, the tree of desire to thy devotees, do thou bid me expound this work.
11. O Mother, let the ocean of the nine sentiments fill my speech, create mines of the finest figures of speech, and raise mountains of the interpretation of the meaning.

313

12. I pray thee, open up in the soil of this Marāthi language a mine of the gold of literary composition and cultivate in it creepers of discernment.

13. [Jnāneshvar] says, Plant in it dense gardens ever full of abundant fruit of discussion and philosophical problems.

14. Break up the ravines of heresy, destroy the by-paths of controversy and slay the evil beasts of false reasoning.

15. Make me always remain seated at the feet of Shri Krishna and set the listeners on the throne of hearing.

16. Let the blessed day of the knowledge of Brahma come to the city of the Marāthi language and let the world trade only in the bliss of union.

17. Wrap me in the garment of thy blessed favour and soon I will accomplish all this.

18. Hearing this prayer of the disciple, the grace of the Preceptor looked at him, and he was told to say no more but to begin at once the exposition of the Gitā.

19. Jnāneshvara filled with joy exclaimed, Lord, Lord, I will do so! Then he said [to his hearers], I will now begin to expound the work. Listen!

Arjuna said:

> *1. Of those devotees who, ever harmonized, worship Thee, and those again [who worship] the Imperishable and the Unmanifested, which have the greater knowledge of yoga?*

20. Then the greatest of all warriors, the victorious leader of the Lunar race, the son of Pāndu began to speak.[3]

21. He said to Krishna, Hast Thou heard? Thou didst show me Thy Cosmic Form, and I was terrified by this marvellous vision.

22. Being familiar with Thee as Krishna in human form, my desire at once turned to that, but Thou didst forbid me to entertain such a wish.

23. O Lord, Thou art indeed both the manifest and the unmanifest. The manifest is reached through devotion; the unmanifest is attained by yoga.

24. These are the two paths by which Thou mayest be reached, O Lord of Vaikuntha, and the manifest and the unmanifest are the two thresholds [by which they are approached].

25. See, when a bar of gold of a hundred grains [is tested with] a touchstone the effect is the same as it would be with a

piece of one grain; in the same way there is the same value
in both the limited and the limitless.

26. The power that lies in an ocean of nectar is found equally
    in a handful taken from a wave of it.

27. Verily I believe this in experience, but there is one question
    which I desire to ask Thee, O Lord of Yoga.

28. Wilt Thou tell me, O Lord, whether that Cosmic Form
    which for a time Thou didst assume is real, or merely a
    display of Thy power?

29. Those devotees whose actions are consecrated to Thee, for
    whom Thou art the highest goal, and whose hearts are
    wholly given to devotion,

30. and who in many other ways worship Thee, O Hari, with
    all their heart and soul,

31. and [on the other hand] those wise ones who worship Thee,
    the Unmanifest, who art beyond even the sacred syllable
    and inexpressible in speech, unfettered by any bondage,

32. the imperishable one, unmanifest, beyond space or defini-
    tion,

33. of these two, the devotees and the wise—who, O Eternal
    One, are more truly the knowers of yoga?

34. The Friend of the World was pleased with these words of
    Kiriti and said, It is well, Thy question is a good one.

The Blessed Lord said:

> II. *Those who fixing their minds on Me worship Me, ever
> harmonized and possessed of supreme faith, I consider
> perfect in yoga.*

35. As the rays of the sun follow the orb as it reaches the
    border of the western mountain,

36. so is [the devotion] of those who, with their senses merged
    in Me, serve Me without awareness of day or night.

37. Similarly their love abounds as the waters of the Ganges
    seem to increase even after they have poured into the ocean.

38. As the waters of a river rise in the rainy season, O Son of
    Pāndu, their devotion seems to increase more and more.

39. Such devotees, who devote themselves entirely to Me, I
    deem to be the ones who are the most perfected in yoga.

> III. *But those who worship the Imperishable, the Undefin-
> able, the Unmanifested, the Omnipresent, the Unthinkable,
> the Unchanging and the Immobile, the Constant.*

40. Also, O Pāndava, those whose minds, filled with the thought
    of oneness with the Absolute, reach out for that which is
    formless and imperishable and indivisible,

41. that one whom the mind is unable to grasp, who cannot be
    perceived by the intellect nor apprehended by the senses,

42. who, not being confined by space nor limited by form, is
    even beyond the reach of meditation,

43. who exists in every place, every form and at all times, and
    in the contemplation of whom the mind is utterly confused,

44. who comes into being and yet does not become, exists yet is
    non-existent, and to reach whom all means are unavailing,

45. who neither moves nor sways, is neither diminished nor
    sullied, and whom [these devotees], by their [spiritual]
    power, have made their own.

> IV. *By restraining all the senses, being even-minded in all
> conditions, rejoicing in the welfare of all creatures, they
> too, indeed, come to Me.*

46. Burning up the whole army of sense pleasures in the great
    fire of dispassion, they have brought their scorched
    passions under control.

47. Driving them back in the noose of self-restraint, they
    confine them within the inner recesses of the heart.

48. Constraining the down-going breath with the help of the
    [proper] yogic posture they build up the fortress of
    mulābandha.[4]

49. They break the bonds of desire, remove the rocks of timi-
    dity, and dispel the darkness of sleep.

50. They burn the humours of the body in the flames of the
    thunderbolt, make an offering of all diseases at the altar of
    the six centres of the body.

51. They set the torch of Kundalini at the ādhāra cakra and
    with this light they find the way to the crown centre.

52. Closing fast the nine doors of the body with the strong bar
    of self-control they open the window of the sushumna
    artery.

53. With the help of the goddess of the vital airs they kill the
    'sheep' of ideas and sacrifice it and the 'buffalo's head' of
    the mind.

54. Bringing together the two passages ida and pingala and
    thus calling forth the sound called anāhata, they rise
    swiftly to the source of the vital principle.[5]

55. Through the central cavern of the sushumna they ascend the stairway and reach the peak of Brahmārandhra.

56. Again ascending the steps of Makāra and having passed beyond the abysss, they support themselves by the heavens and become absorbed in the Absolute.[6]

57. In this way those who have an evenly balanced mind capture the boundless fortresses of yoga in order to attain to union with the Absolute.

58. Thus, O Kiriti, in exchange [for their self-renunciation], they at once attain to the Unmanifest and are united with Me.

59. Not that they acquire anything more by these practices of yoga; rather, for them much more effort is required.

> v. *The difficulty of those whose thoughts are set on the Unmanifest is greater, for the goal of the Unmanifest is hard to reach by the embodied beings.*

60. For those who, abandoning the path of devotion, have set their minds on the Unmanifest, the self-existent One, [source of] the welfare of all beings,

61. aspirations to highest heavenly rank are as highway robbers and they are laid low by the combined assault of prosperity and psychic powers.

62. Many disturbances arise from desire and anger, and the body has to wrestle with the Spirit.

63. Their thirst they must quench with thirst, when hungry they must feed on hunger; day and night they strive to measure the wind with the span of their arms.

64. Wakefulness is their rest, for pleasure they have but restraint, and their only fellowship is with trees.

65. They wear cold as a garment, and clothe themselves with heat, and they dwell in the rain as in a house.

66. In short, O Pāndava, such practices are as the constant self-immolation of a widowed woman.

67. Herein the purpose of the husband is not served, nor is there fulfilment of family duty; it is merely an ever recurring struggle with death.

68. Is it possible to drink boiling poison more stinging than death itself? Would not the mouth that swallows a mountain be torn to pieces?

69. Therefore, O good warrior, many difficulties will be in the path of those who set out on the way of yoga.

70. If a toothless man were to chew pieces of iron, would they satisfy his hunger, or would it not be certain death?
71. Can a man swim across the ocean by the strength of his arms or can he walk on the air?
72. Can a man going into battle expect to reach heaven without a single wound?
73. O Pāndava, it is as difficult for an embodied man to reach the Unmanifest as it would be for a lame man to compete with the wind.
74. All the same, if they summon all their courage and ardently seek the Unmanifest, only distress will befall them.
75. So, O Pārtha, the lot of those who resort to the path of devotion.

> VI. *But those who, laying all their actions before Me, intent on Me, worship with unswerving devotion, meditating on Me.*

76. They who, according to the characteristics of their caste fulfil peacefully their duties through the organs of action,
77. carry out prescribed actions, omitting those that are forbidden, and burning up the fruits of actions offer them to Me.
78. See further, O Arjuna, when they yield them all up to Me, they annul [the fruits of] these actions.
79. Further, all actions performed by body or mind have no other goal but Me.
80. Those who serve only Me, and ever worshipping and contemplating Me have thereby become My abode,
81. who, setting on one side as of no account all pleasure and enjoyment, even the hope of liberation, ever commune with Me in love.
82. For those who have, as it were, sold to Me wholly their bodies and soul, how can I tell what I do?

> VII. *These whose thoughts are set on Me, I straightway deliver from the ocean of death-bound existence, O Pārtha [Arjuna]*

83. To be brief, O wielder of the bow, thou knowest how close is the relationship between a mother and the child born in her womb.
84. So it is with My devotees and Me, O Winner of wealth; in whatever state they may be I have pledged Myself to overcome death for them.

85. Besides this, my devotees have no need to be anxious on account of their worldly affairs. Does the wife of a rich man have to beg for food?

86. Know them to be as members of My own family; I do not feel ashamed in anything that I do for them.

87. Seeing this world of nature struggling in the surging waves of life and death, I felt thus in My heart—

88. What man would not feel afraid in an ocean? No wonder then that My devotees should be overcome with fear.

89. This, O Pāndava, is why I have become incarnate and come in haste to them.

90. Those who were unattached I induced to meditate on Me; to those with families I recommended the recital of My names.

91. With my many names as boats [in the ocean of worldly life], I have become the ferryman.

92. With My love bound to them as a safety raft I have led them to the other shore of liberation.

93. In this way, all My devotees, from animals to mankind, I have made them worthy of the throne of My Heaven.

94. Thus, My devotees suffer no anxiety, for I am he who ever lifts them up.

95. When they devote their hearts to Me, they bind Me to themselves.

96. Therefore, Dhananjaya, if thou art resolved to follow this path,

> VIII. *On Me alone fix thy mind, let thy understanding dwell in Me. In Me alone shalt thou live hereafter. Of this there is no doubt.*

97. concentrate thy mind and will earnestly on My nature,

98. and when in this manner thy mind and will have entered into Me through thy loving devotion, thou wilt attain union with Me.

99. When mind and will both abide in Me, how can there remain any distinction of 'I' and 'thou'?

100. When a lamp is extinguished, its light fades out; when the sun sets, daylight vanishes;

101. when the vital airs leave the body the senses also depart with them; in the same way consciousness of self follows wherever the mind and will go.

102. Therefore fix thy mind and will firmly on Me, and assuredly thou wilt be one with Me, the All-pervading One.

103. I assure thee with a solemn pledge that there is no other teaching than this.

IX. *If, however, thou art not able to fix thy thought steadily on Me, then seek to reach Me by the practice of concentration, O Winner of wealth [Arjuna].*

104. But if with all thy will and mind thou art not able to fix thy attention wholly on Me,

105. devote [to this concentration] at least a brief space during the twenty-four hours of the day.

106. Then so long as the mind contemplates My joy, sense pleasures will have no attraction for it.

107. As at the end of the rains the rivers begin to subside, thy mind will withdraw itself from worldly activities.

108. As the moon begins to wane from the day of the full moon and is lost to sight by the day of the new moon,

109. so, withdrawing itself from the pleasures of sense and entering into Me thy mind will gradually be united with Me, O son of Pāndu.

110. O Beloved, this is what is known as the yoga of constant practice; there is nothing that is not obtainable by this method.

111. Some are able to pass through the air through the power of this yoga; some have been able to tame the tiger and the serpent.

112. Some can consume poison with impunity, some may walk upon the waters; others again, through this yoga, have found it a simple matter to study even the Vedas.

113. There is nothing, in fact, too difficult to achieve by means of this practice; so strive to reach Me by this path.

X. *If thou art unable even to seek by practice, then be as one whose supreme aim is My service; even performing actions for My sake, thou shalt attain perfection.*

114. If thou art unable to follow this path of practice, then continue in thy present way of life.

115. Do not restrain thy sense organs, nor abstain from the enjoyment of pleasure nor relinquish thy pride of caste.

116. Carry out thy family duties, perform prescribed actions

and avoid those that are prohibited; thus wilt thou be free to act as thou wishest.

117. But do not say of thy thoughts, words and bodily actions that thou thyself art the doer.

118. Realize that the Supreme Spirit by whom the whole universe is promoted alone knows what is to be done and what not done.

119. Do not concern thyself with deficiency and sufficiency but carry on the life appropriate to thy caste.

120. Thy life should be conducted as the water which flows quietly in the channel made for it by the gardener.

121. O good warrior, is a chariot concerned whether the road be straight or crooked?

122. Do not take on thyself the burden of outgoing life activities or the cessation of them; let thy mind be solely directed towards me.

123. So, whatever action thou performest, surrender it wholeheartedly to Me and do not consider whether it is great or small.

124. Thus fixing thy heart on Me in renunciation of the body, thou wilt certainly attain to the abode of perfect union with Me.

> XI. *If thou art not able to do even this, then taking refuge in My disciplined activity, renounce the fruit of all action, with the self subdued.*

125. O Son of Pāndu, if thou canst not offer up all thy actions to Me, then worship Me thus.

126. O Kiriti, if it is hard for thee to fix thy heart on Me before ordering the intention to act, or before or after the action,

127. let this be; leave aside remembrance of Me and direct thy mind towards the control of the senses,

128. As trees and plants throw off the fruit that is ripe, so do not consider the result of any action when it is completed.

129. Let no such idea concern thee that thou fix thy mind on Me, or that actions should be done for My sake. Cast away this thought.

130. As rain falling on a rock or seed thrown into the fire come to naught, so regard thy actions as though they were a dream.

131. As a father's love for his daughter is free from passion, so do thou remain unaffected by the fruit of any action.

132. As flames of fire vanish they rise in the air, so let thy actions end in nothing.

133. To relinquish the fruit of action may thus appear easy; still this yoga is superior to all others.

134. By relinquishing all attachment to their fruit actions cease to bear fruit, as the bamboo tree which bears seed but once.

135. In this manner there can be no rebirth of this body, and even the cycle of birth and death comes to an end.

136. O Kiriti, through climbing the ladder of practice understanding is obtained, and through understanding one can reach the stage of meditation.

137. When all levels of feeling are merged in meditation, all activity is laid aside.

138. When action ceases, abandonment of its fruits takes place, and through abandonment of fruit peace is attained.

139. Therefore, O consort of Subhadrā, these are the stages in the attainment of the peace [of Brahma]. For this reason thou shouldst begin with [the yoga of practice].

> XII. *Better indeed is knowledge than the practice [of concentration]; better than knowledge is meditation; better than meditation is the renunciation of the fruit of action; on renunciation [follows] immediately peace.*

140. Deeper than practice is knowledge, O Pārtha, and meditation transcends knowledge.

141. Selfless action is higher than meditation and enjoyment of peace is better than selfless action.

142. Such are the stages on the road by which peace is reached, O Great Warrior.

> XIII. *He who has no ill will towards any being, who is friendly and compassionate, free from egoism and self-sense, even-minded in pain and pleasure and patient—*

143. Such a man entertains no feeling of hatred for any creature, as the spirit of life has no sense of 'myself' and 'another',

144. as the earth does not say, 'I will welcome the best man and reject the worst',

145. as life, ever kind, does not say, 'I will treat well the body of a king and thrust aside that of a beggar',

146. and water makes no distinction, nor says, 'I will quench the thirst of a cow, and kill the tiger by turning it into poison',

147. or as a lamp does not give light to a household and leave others in darkness.
148. This man gives his friendship equally to every creature and is the very source of compassion.
149. In his mind the idea of 'I' and 'he' has no place, who calls nothing his own, is indifferent to either pleasure or pain,
150. his power of forgiveness is as that of the earth and he holds contentment in his lap.

XIV. —*who is ever content, self-controlled, unshakeable in determination, with mind and understanding given up to Me, My devotee, is dear to Me.*

151. Even without the rainy season the sea is full of water, so is such a man full of contentment, though he may not strive for it.
152. He has pledged himself to retain control over his heart and carries out every resolve;
153. In the palace of his heart the individual self and the Supreme are seated together in splendour.
154. Being thus perfected in yoga, he merges his mind and will entirely in Me.
155. He is purified both inwardly and outwardly in yoga and is wholly devoted to Me.
156. Such a man, O Arjuna, is a real devotee, a perfect yogi and has found liberation; his love towards Me is as that of a wife to her husband.
157. Nay, he is dearer to Me than life itself; but even this is but a poor comparison.
158. Indeed, the story of the beloved is enchanting and though it cannot be told, my love of thee forces Me to speak of it.
159. For this reason such a simile came to My mind; otherwise what comparison can be found?
160. This is enough, O Kiriti; love is intensified by speaking of the beloved.
161. If the teller has a loving [listener], can the delight ever pall?
162. O Son of Pāndu, thou art both the beloved and the listener, and the time has come to speak of this love.
163. So I will speak. It is good that we have come to this happy occasion. Speaking thus, Krishna began to sway with joy.
164. Then again He said, Listen now to the qualities possessed by those devotees whom I hold in My heart.

xv. *He from whom the world does not shrink and who does not shrink from the world, and who is free from joy and anger, fear and agitation, he too is dear to Me.*

165. As creatures living in the water are not afraid of the sea, nor the sea of them,

166. so such a man is not distressed by the pleasure-loving world, and the world does not weary of him.

167. As the body never tires of its own limbs, so is he never tired of any creature, looking on it as his own self.

168. In fact, it is as though the world is his own body, so that he is free from all likes or dislikes, as from joy and anger.

169. Who thus is free from the pairs of opposites, from fear and dejection, remains always devoted to Me.

170. Such a man is very dear to Me. How can I describe him? He lives in My life.

171. He is content with inner bliss and in him the highest Brahman dwells; he is Lord of fulfilment.

xvi. *He who has no expectation, is pure, skilful in action, unconcerned and untroubled, who has given up all initiative [in action], he, My devotee, is dear to Me.*

172. Such a one, O Arjuna, is free from ambition and his very existence causes joy to increase.

173. The Ganges is pure and all sin and passion are purified in its waters; but it is necessary to sink in them.

174. It is well known that Benares generously bestows liberation, but those who go there have to sacrifice the life of the body.

175. All impurities disappear [when one goes to] the Himālayas, but it involves risking one's life. There is no such danger to the purity of a good man.

176. The depths of devotion are not known but a man does not drown in them; liberation is attained immediately even without death.

177. The impurities of the Ganges are removed by the touch of saintly men; then how great must be the purity derived from the company of such devotees?

178. Let that be! A good man imparts his purity even to holy places, and dissipates entirely all impurities of mind.

179. Both inwardly and outwardly he is as pure as the light of the sun, and as a man born lucky [has second sight], he is endowed with the vision of the highest truth.[6]

180. As the sky is limitless yet indifferent, so such a man's mind reaches everywhere, [yet nothing can sully it].
181. A bird escaped from a snare no longer has any fear, so is he free from worldly distress and regards everything with indifference.
182. Likewise he who is always contented is free from anxiety as a dead man feels no shame.
183. When he undertakes anything there is no awareness of self, a fire without fuel will die out.
184. He who is at peace within himself, is already on the threshold of self-liberation.
185. O Arjuna, he who, full of the sense of his oneness with Brahma, is about to reach the further bank of [the ocean of] dualism,
186. then, in order to enjoy the bliss of devotion, he divides himself as it were into two parts, taking to himself the role of devotee.
187. The other part he calls Me and thus points out the path of devotion to those yogis who do not serve Me.
188. Such a man is very dear to Me; he is My dwelling-place and I am not happy till I reach him.
189. For his sake I must become incarnate and for him I must live in this world; I feel that I should embrace him with my very life.

XVII. *He who neither rejoices nor hates, neither grieves nor desires, has renounced good and evil, and is thus devoted, is dear to Me.*

190. He considers knowledge of the Self as the highest attainment and therefore is not carried away by the enjoyment of worldly pleasure.
191. Being at one with the whole world he is free from any sense of separateness, and consequently feels no hatred.
192. Recognizing that that which is really his own can never be lost, even at the end of a world age, he does not grieve for what he may lose [in this world].
193. He realizes that he has within himself that which is more precious than all else and he has no further desire.
194. He makes no distinction between the evil and the good, in the same way as the sun does not consider light and darkness.

195. A man who has thus reached the highest self-realization,
and as well as this still lives in devotion to Me,

196. is more beloved of Me than the dearest relative; I assure
thee that this is true.

XVIII. *He who [behaves] alike to friend and foe, also to men
of good and evil repute, does not in cold and heat, pleasure
and pain and who is free from attachment;*

197. O Pārtha, he has no sense of inequality and to whom friend
and foe are alike to him.

198. A tree gives the same shade to the man who planted it as to
another who strikes at its roots to fell it.

199. Sugarcane is sweet to the man who cultivates it and equally
[sweet] to him who extracts its juice.

200. The man who has the same attitude towards friend and foe,
or fame and shame are alike to him.

201. He does not vary in heat or cold, as the sky remains the
same throughout all seasons.

202. O son of Pāndu, as Mount Meru bears the north and the
south winds equally, so such a man remains steady whether
joy or sorrow come to him.

203. He preserves the same attitude towards all creatures as
moonlight shines with sweetness alike on king or beggar.

204. Water is acceptable to everyone on this earth; so is he
desired by all three worlds.

205. Laying aside all contact of inner and outer objects, he lives
apart, his soul absorbed in Brahma.

XIX. *He who holds as equal blame and praise, who is
silent [restrained in speech], content with all that comes,
who has no fixed abode and is firm in mind,—such a devotee is dear to Me.*

206. The sky suffers no pollution, such a man is neither offended by scorn nor elated by praise.

207. Therefore, regarding praise and blame with equal indifference, he moves among men or in seclusion, [freely] as the
air.

208. Indifferent as to whether truth or untruth is spoken, he
remains silent; for he is absorbed in his state of freedom
from illusion.

209. He takes no delight in the satisfaction of desires, nor is he disappointed by any loss, as the sea does not dry up when there is no rain.

210. As the wind has no fixed abode, he seeks no refuge.

211. He believes that everywhere is his home; indeed, he regards himself as one with all movable and immovable things.

212. Furthermore, if as well, O Pārtha, he is devoted to worship of Me, I place him as a crown upon My head.

213. Is it strange that men should bow their heads before such a great one? Even the three worlds reverence the water touched by his feet.

214. Only if Shankar himself were to be one's teacher could one know how to appreciate such great devotion.

215. But enough of Shankar! In praising him I would be giving praise to Myself.

216. The consort of Rāma said, This is not an adequate illustration, for I bear him upon My head.

217. Bearing in the palms of their hands the fourth human attainment, Self-realization, such men tread the path of devotion, bestowing their gift on the world.

218. Having in himself the authority to give to other the Highest Bliss, he takes, like water, the lowest place.

219. Let us salute him and place him as the crown upon our heads and his feet upon our breasts.

220. Let us beautify our speech with the jewels of his praise and adorn our ears with his fame.

221. Desiring to see such a one, I whom am sightless have taken human eyes and I worship him with My lotus in hand.

222. I have assumed My four-armed body that I may embrace him.

223. To delight in his company, I, the formless one, have become incarnate; indeed, My love for him is incomparable.

224. Is it to be wondered at that he is so dear to Me? Those who listen to the story of his life,

225. those who praise the lives of the saints, are dearer to Me than My very soul.

226. O Arjuna, what I have so far expounded to thee is the whole yoga of union through devotion.

227. It is a state so high that they who attain to it are very dear to Me; I meditate upon them and hold them in the highest esteem.

228. Those who listen to this teaching, full of beauty, sweet as a stream of nectar, leading to righteousness, and understand it in experience,

229. who realize within themselves the proper state of mind already described as seed in well-tilled soil,

230. who with a perfect faith in its truth allow it to grow within them and practise it with all their heart,

231. such, O Pārtha, are My beloved devotees; they alone are true yogis in this world, and for them I feel the deepest love.

232. They are the true holy streams and sacred places; they alone in the world are pure, those men who give themselves up to devotion.

233. He is the succourer of the gods, delighting in the care of the world, whose pleasure it is to protect those who resort to him.

234. He is ever beneficient to his devotees and is open-hearted to those who love him; the supporter of truth, the storehouse of all arts.

235. Let us contemplate them as the deity whom we worship; nothing is more acceptable to Me than such men.

236. They are My delight, My store of treasure and the source of My contentment.

237. O son of Pāndu, those also who tell of this devotion I regard as my highest deity.

238. So said Mukunda, the giver of joy to all his people, the source of all created things.

239. O King, he who is the pure, perfect and merciful protector of all those who take refuge in him,

240. who shines with the lustre of His glory and righteousness and famed for His unbounded charity, who by His incomparable strength bound the powerful Bali,

241. Krishna, the supreme sovereign of Vaikunta, spoke thus and Arjuna listened to what he said.

242. Sanjaya said to Dritarāshtra, Listen now to what is described after this.

243. This story, full of interest, will be set forth in the Marathi language; listen to it earnestly.

244. Jnānadeva says, My guru, Nivrittidās has taught me how
I should supplicate you saintly men.

*In the Upanishad of the Bhagavadgitā, the science of the Absolute,
the scripture of yoga and the dialogue between Shri Krishna and
Arjuna, this is the twelfth chapter entitled the Yoga of Devotion.*

NOTES

1. *The ādhāra and heart centres.* Notes on the psychic centres of the
body are given in Vol. I, Chapters V and VI.
2. *anāhata.* A mystic sound proceeding from the psychic centre of the
heart.
3. *Somavansha.* The Lunar race. See Vol. I, Ch. X, vv. 234, Solar race
and 270.
4. *mulabandha.* One of the yogic postures. See Ch. VI, notes on postures.
5. *ida and pingala arteries.* See Ch. VI, notes.
6. *Makāra.* The 'half' syllable, m, at the end of the sacred syllable,
Aum. This refers here to the highest form of spiritual experience to
which the yogi can ascend.

---

CHAPTER XIII

1. I salute the holy feet of my Guru, the remembrance of which leads to the acquisition of all branches of knowledge,
2. by thinking of which one can command the power of literary composition and all learning comes readily to the tongue.
3. Eloquence surpasses even nectar in its sweetness and the nine sentiments wait upon the words.
4. The symbols bring about the revelation of deep meaning and particular truths are discerned and understood.
5. When the feet of the Guru are held in remembrance in the heart, good fortune is added to wisdom.

Arjuna said:

> 1. *Praktṛi and puruṣa, the field and the knower of the field, knowledge and the object of knowledge, these I should like to know, O Keśava [Kṛṣṇa].*

6. Then Arjuna said, I wish to know certainly from Thee about nature and spirit, and about the field and the knower of the field.
7. Jnāneshvari says, I will bow to them. [Krishna], Father of the Creator, husband of Lakshmi, spoke thus:

The Blessed Lord said:

> II. *This body, O Son of Kunti [Arjuna], is called the field, and he knows this is called the knower of the field by those who know thereof.*

8. Hear, O Pārtha, that the body is called the field, and he who knows it is called the knower of the field.

> III. *Know Me as the Knower of the field in all fields, O*

Bhārata [Arjuna]. The knowledge of the field and its knower, I regard as true knowledge.

9. Here I am He who is known as the knower of the field, and the supporter of all fields.
10. To understand clearly what this field is and who it is that knows it, is to My mind true knowledge.

> iv. *Hear briefly from Me what the Field is, of what nature, what its modifications are, whence it is, what he [the knower of the field] is, and what his powers are.*

11. Now I will explain fully to thee why this body is referred to as the field.
12. I will tell thee why it is called the field, how and where it is born, and by what changing processes it grows.
13. Does it measure three and a half spans of the hand? What is its size? Is it barren or fertile? To whom does it belong?
14. Listen then; I will tell thee of all the properties of this field.
15. The Vedas frequently speak of its place and speculation with regard to it has been constant.
16. The Darshanas have exhausted themselves discussing it and their conflicting views have come to no agreement.[1]
17. All the sciences have failed to agree concerning it and discussions have spread over the world on this very subject.
18. No one man agrees with another and opinions contradict each other; argument and vain talk have flourished.
19. Nothing is known as to who inhabits it, but so great is the eagerness in the dispute that in every direction people come to blows.
20. In order to refute the agnostics the Vedas have risen in rebellion, and seeing this, the heretics have raised their voices.[2]
21. They say, You have no foundation [in truth], your wordy arguments are false. If you deny this, we challenge you.
22. Naked ascetics, tearing out their hair, laid before the heretics fallacious arguments, but they too fell to the ground.
23. Dreading that death would overtake them with the problem still unsolved, yogis came forward to join the quest.
24. They feared death and so they withdrew to the forest practising severe restraints to the very end.

25. Out of his deep respect for this field, Shiva abandoned his
heavenly kingdom, regarding it as a hindrance, and re-
sorted to the burning ground [as a penance].
26. With firm resolve [to pursue this quest] he stripped himself of everything, and burnt to ashes the god of love who
had tempted him.[3]
27. The Lord of Satyaloka had the advantage of four faces, but
even he also failed to understand [the nature of this field].

> v. *This has been sung by sages in many ways and
> distinctly, in various hymns and also in well-reasoned and
> conclusive expressions of the aphorisms of the Absolute
> [brahmasutra].*

28. There are those who say that this field is basically the
home of the living spirit and the vital air is the tenant.
29. In the house of this vital air work four brothers as labour-
ers and mind directs the work.[4]
30. This life has under its command a team of ten oxen in the
form of the ten senses who labour unceasingly in the field
of sense objects, ignoring observances of the new moon
day or dawn.
31. Man avoids the practice of prescribed duties, sows the
seed of unrighteousness and cultivates the soil with evil
actions.
32. Then, according to the nature of the seed there results a
plenteous harvest of sins, from which he suffers misery
through countless lives.
33. On the other hand, he may sow good seed in the prepared
soil of prescribed duties and enjoy happiness through
hundreds of lives.
34. Others again say that this is not so, the individual soul is
not [master of the field]. It is we who should be consulted
about the field.
35. The soul is a stranger here, a sojourner on a long journey,
and the vital air is the watchful supervisor of the field.
36. The eternal root matter, which the Sānkhyas describe, is
said to be the hereditary owner of this field.
37. She owns all the equipment and directs its cultivation.
38. The three who are the primal cultivators of the land, the
three qualities, are born of her.
39. Rajas sows the seed, sattva preserves it, and tamas alone
gathers in the harvest.

40. Making of Mahātattva a threshing floor, with the help of the ox called Kāluga, she threshes out the corn from which arises the great heap of unmanifest nature.[5]

41. Other philosophers, despising this explanation, state that the theory is meaningless and of recent origin.

42. They say, What is Matter, compared with Brahma, who is All in All? Listen quietly to our explanation of the field.

43. Once all powerful thought slept on the softest cushions in the bedchamber of the primal void.

44. Suddenly he awoke, but being always fortunate in his affairs he obtained his treasure according to his desire.[6]

45. Through him, the garden of Parabrahma, vast as the three worlds, came into being.

46. Placing all the five elements together and confining the fallow land, he separated it into four parts in the fourfold division of creatures.

47. Then, binding together the five elements, he made from them the human body with its five functions.

48. On both sides he built a wall of Action and Inaction, and made a barren region of the unproductive creatures.

49. For passing back and forth between these regions the primal thought made the beautiful path of life and death.

50. Combining with individuality he formed the intellect [to guide] the whole created world.

51. Thus in the great void there grew the branches of the tree of Thought, which is the origin of all this worldly existence.

52. Others examined these [theories as] pearls of wisdom and they say, You are very wise, are you not?

53. If you assume that thought exists in the Absolute, why should you not also accept that Matter is also included in it?

54. You need not trouble yourselves any further, however, for everything will now be explained to you.

55. Who is it that stores the water in the rain clouds? Who holds up the stars in the heavens?

56. Who has stretched out the wide canopy of the sky? Who is it that causes every wind to blow?

57. Who makes the hair grow on the body? Who fills up the ocean and sends down the showers of rain?

58. This field [of the body] is a natural phenomenon and belongs to no one. He who tills it receives its fruits, others gain nothing.

59. Then other philosophers came forward and said angrily,
    You say well; but how is it then that time dominates the
    whole field?

60. We believe that death is like an angry lion in a cave, so
    why do you argue in this useless manner?

61. The hand of death will surely strike, but still they all
    assert their own opinions.

62. This [lion of death] throws his grasp suddenly beyond the
    cycle of time and attacks even the elephant in the form of
    the highest of all worlds.

63. Entering into the heavenly forest, he destroys ever more
    guardian deities and companies of the elephants of the
    four quarters.

64. Through the wind of their passing bodies, beasts in the
    form of human souls perish and are left wandering in the
    pit of the cycle of life and death.

65. See how widespread is the grasp of time in which he holds
    this elephant which represents the universe of form.

66. It is true therefore to say that everything in this universe
    is ruled by time. O son of Pāndu, these are the various opi-
    nions held about this field [of the body].

67. Frequent discussions were held by the seers in the Nai-
    misha forest, to which the Purānas bear testimony.

68. The poetic discourses in various forms of verse are still
    quoted arrogantly in support of these opinions.

69. The verses of the great Sāmaveda, the most holy from the
    point of view of insight, did not understand what this
    field is.

70. Many great and wise sages have devoted their minds to
    this question.

71. But no one has been able to expound clearly what it is,
    how great it is, or to whom it belongs.

72. I will now explain this field to thee as fully as possible.

> VI. *The great [five gross] elements, self-sense, under-
> standing, as also the unmanifested, the ten senses and
> mind and the five objects of the senses.*
>
> VII. *Desire and hatred, pleasure and pain, the aggregate
> [the organism], intelligence and steadfastness described,
> this in brief is the field along with its modifications.*

73. The five great cosmic elements, self-sense, understanding,
    unmanifested matter, and the ten senses,

74. also the mind, the activities of the ten organs of sense; pleasure, pain and aversion; the whole range of desire;

75. consciousness and resolution—all these, I have told thee, constitute the Field.

76. Now will I tell thee separately which are the five great elements, the sensory activities and their organs.

77. Earth, water, fire, air and ether are the five great elements; these I have told thee.

78. As during the waking state the dream condition recedes or as the moon is hidden on the day of the new moon;

79. youth lies latent in early childhood, fragrance is hidden in the bud until it expands into the full-blown flower,

80. and fire lies dormant within fuel, so, O Kiriti, does [consciousness] lie latent in the womb of primal matter.

81. A fever lying within a bodily humour awaits the pretext of an unsuitable diet; then what was already within pervades the body without.

82. So when the five elements unite and assume the form of a body, that which causes it to function is self-consciousness.

83. Now what is called understanding is known by these signs; listen and I will tell you, said the Lord of the Yādavas.

84. Impelled by the god of passion, the activity of the senses overcomes the objects of sense.

85. At the time when the individual soul has to render an account of its experiences of pleasure or pain, the understanding enables it to determine which is the better.

86. By exercising the understanding it is able to discriminate between pleasure and pain, good and evil action, purity and impurity.

87. It makes possible the distinction between base and noble, high and low, and the scrutiny of objects of sense.

88. It causes the development of the sensory organs, stores up the quality of harmony and establishes the union between the spirit and the individual soul.

89. Know, O Arjuna, that by these things one can recognize consciousness. Now listen to the ways of recognizing the Unmanifest.

90. O wise one, that which the Sānkhya philosophers term primordial matter, is also called the unmanifest.

91. Already I have explained to thee the nature of this pri-

mordial matter as it is expounded by the Sānkhyayoga philosophy.

92. O warrior, the condition of the individual soul, called the Lord of Heroes, is also known as the unmanifest.

93. At dawn the light of the stars disappears from the sky; at sunset the activities of all creatures cease.

94. O Kiriti, with the casting off of the physical body all its activities and conditions are hidden in the karma of the individual.

95. The entire tree lies hidden in its seed, and the existence of woven cloth in the threads [of which it is to be made].

96. So do the great elements, and the beings which have proceeded from them, become subtle and fade away when they leave their material forms.

97. This, O Arjuna, is known as the unmanifest. Now listen to the description of the sense organs.

98. The ear, the eye, the skin, the nose and the tongue are the five organs of perception.

99. By means of this system the intelligence can express through the five organs its experience of pleasure and pain.

100. Speech, hands, feet and the excretory and sexual organs are the five organs of action.

101. The Lord of Beatitude says that these are to be known as the organs of action.

102. That power of activity which is, as it were, the wife of the life-principle enters and leaves the body by these five ways.

103. The Lord said, In this manner I have described to thee the ten organs of sense; now listen and I will tell thee clearly what mind is.

104. It is that which forms a link between the organs and the intelligence and hovers on the shoulders of passion.

105. The mind is as the blueness in the sky or the illusory waves of a mirage.

106. When the male semen meets the blood of the female, the combination of the ten elements is produced.

107. Through the power inherent in the bodily function these ten settle into their appointed parts.

108. Therein there is only one power of activity which is the basis of passion.

109. This power is outside the control of the will but dominates the realm of self-consciousness.

110. This activity is wrongly called mind but is in fact thought, through the medium of which the Universal Spirit assumes the condition of individuality.
111. This is the source of all tendencies, the ground of all passion and activates self-consciousness.
112. It increases desire, encourages hope, and fosters fear.
113. It awakens the sense of duality, fortifies ignorance, and plunges the senses into contact with sense objects.
114. It first intends to create, then purposes destruction; it raises a pile of fantasies and then shatters them.
115. It is like a cave of delusion, the heart of the element of air, and it conceals all the channels of the intellect.
116. O Kiriti, this is undoubtedly what is known as mind. Now listen to the [names of the] various pleasures of the senses.
117. Touch, sound, form, taste, and smell are the faculties of the five organs of perception.
118. Through the doors of these five organs perception reaches out of the body as cattle stray towards green pastures.
119. The utterance of vowels, consonants and aspiration, the acceptance or rejection of objects, walking, the action of the sexual and excretory organs,
120. these are the functions of the five organs of action, and from the creation built of these, all action is carried on.
121. These are the ten functions of the body; now it is necessary to explain desire.
122. Its activity is awakened by remembering past experience, or by hearing the sayings of others.
123. Supported by passion it is aroused as soon as the senses come into contact with sense objects.
124. When it is awakened the mind rushes hither and thither, and the senses are thrust towards undesirable objects.
125. Through its love of activity, the mind is disturbed by its delight in sense objects. This is desire.
126. But if it so happens that the senses do not find the desired satisfaction, [the disappointment they experience] leads to aversion.
127. Now [let us consider] what pleasure is like, by experiencing which one becomes oblivious to all things.
128. When bodily actions, speech and thought cease and all consciousness of the body is lost,

129. after which the vital breath becomes subdued and the state of harmony increases twofold,

130. the whole activity of the senses is withdrawn to the solitude within the heart and peaceful sleep is induced.

131. In short, pleasure is a state in which it is possible for the soul to realize union with the Spirit.

132. O Arjuna, the condition in which this state is not experienced is properly called pain.

133. These states are not brought about by any intention; they arise naturally, for they are the bases of pleasure and pain.

134. Now the power of the Spirit in the body, the detached witness of all that happens, is called consciousness, O Arjuna.

135. From the toe-nails of the feet to the hair of the head it is alert in the body and remains unchanged throughout the three stages of life.

136. It gives freshness to the mind, will and other functions, like the eternal sweetness of spring in the forest of the world of matter.

137. It is this consciousness which is the moving force in both organic and inorganic matter. I am not deceiving thee.

138. A king does not know every one of his subjects, and yet at his order, they overthrow the invading enemy; at the full moon the waters of the ocean rise to high tide.

139. The contact of a magnet sets in motion fragments of iron; the rising of the sun arouses all men to work.

140. The tortoise feeds her young one when she sees it, not waiting for the contact with its mouth.

141. So too, O Pārtha, inorganic matter is infused with life through the presence of the spirit in the body.

142. This, then, is called consciousness, O Arjuna. Listen now to the explanation of firmness.

143. The elements by their very nature are at enmity with each other. Does not water destroy the earth?

144. Heat dries up water, wind fights with fire and the firmament devours the wind.

145. Ether does not mingle with any element, and, though it penetrates all, yet it is entirely separate from all.

146. In such a way all these five elements contend with each other. Yet when they come together in one body,

147. they lay aside their differences, live in unity and even nourish one another with their own particular qualities.

148. The strength which holds these elements together in spite
of their natural antipathy is called firmness.
149. O Pāndava, together with the individual soul, this conjunction of the thirty-six parts constitutes the field.
150. Thus have I explained to thee clearly all the thirty-six
components which go to form the body.
151. O Pāndava, the parts of a chariot when assembled together are called a chariot; so also the combined upper
and lower parts of the body are referred to as the body.
152. Again, an assembly of horses and elephants constitutes
what is called an army; groups of syllables are called sentences.
153. Masses of clouds are referred to as the sky; the various
peoples on the earth make up the world.
154. Oil, wick and fire, held together, are known among men as
a lamp.
155. In a similar way these thirty-six elements united together
in groups are called the field.
156. Through the cultivation of the body the crops of merit and
demerit are produced and we therefore call it figuratively
'the field'.
157. According to some it is called the body, but let this be;
its names are without number.
158. Gods, men and serpents are all born in accordance with
their kind and so find themselves caught within the system of particular qualities and set duties.
159. From the supreme spirit down to inanimate matter, whatever exists and then dies, all these are part of the field.
160. Arjuna, the consideration of these qualities will be spoken
of later; here I will explain the nature of knowledge.
161. I have already described to thee in detail the characteristics of the field and its modifications; now listen to what I
have to say about knowledge,
162. in order to obtain which yogis overcome all obstacles to
reach heaven, and swallow up the ether [in the sacred
centre].⁷
163. They do not care for spiritual attainment nor have any
regard for worldly prosperity, and despise such austerities as yogic practice.
164. They surmount the fortresses of penance, set aside [the
advantage accruing from] the performance of hundreds of
sacrifices.

165. Some adopt various forms of worship, others roam about naked, while some enter the deep places of the Sushumna.

166. To acquire it great Sages in their ardent search wander from page to page in the leaves of the great tree of the Vedas.

167. O Arjuna, they vow to pass their lives in the service of their spiritual teachers.

168. The acquisition of this knowledge dispels ignorance and brings about the union of the individual self with the Supreme Self.

169. It closes the doors of the sense organs, takes away the power from the outgoing activities and removes the poverty of the mind.

170. When this knowledge is obtained, the famine of duality passes away and the abundant life of non-duality ensues.

171. It leaves no trace of pride, overcomes all illusion, and no place is left for the thought of self and others.

172. It uproots worldly existence, washes away the mire of thought, and makes it possible to grasp the unattainable goal of the highest knowledge.

173. By its light the eyes of intelligence are opened, and the soul is able to enjoy the highest bliss.

174. Such is knowledge, the only treasure house of all holiness, and through it even the unclean mind is made pure.

175. Contact with it at once heals a soul suffering from the disease of pride in the self.

176. It is impossible to describe it, though it will be described; when heard it is discernible only by reason; nor is it visible to the eye.

177. When this knowledge appears in the body, it can be perceived by the eyes, expressing itself through the activities of the sense organs.

178. Its presence may be realized in the same way that the advent of spring is recognized by the freshness of the trees.

179. When water is poured on the roots of a tree, its effect is shown in the sprouting of leaves on the branches.

180. The softness of the earth is proved by the tenderness of the shoots of plants; noble behaviour in a man is evidence of good breeding.

181. A man's friendly nature is expressed in his acts of hospitality and when the very sight of a man brings comfort, we know him to be good.

182. The existence of camphor in a tree is known by its fragrance and the light of a lamp enclosed in glass is seen outside it.

183. Now listen carefully while I tell you how in the same way the signs are visible in the body through the dwelling of this knowledge in the heart.

> VIII. *Humility [absence of pride], integrity [absence of deceit], non-violence, patience, uprightness, service of the teacher, purity [of body and mind], steadfastness and self-control.*

184. Such a man does not want to strive after success in any worldly matter and feels any honour to be a burden.

185. Should his qualities be praised, high respect be shown to him, or his greatness be recognized,

186. he feels embarrassed like a deer trapped by a hunter, or a swimmer caught in a whirlpool.

187. O Pārtha, in the same way he is disturbed by expressions of respect and will not accept any suggestion of greatness.

188. He does not wish to see any sign of his worthiness nor to hear any word of fame and prefers not even to be remembered by others as having any special qualities.

189. Such a man has no wish to receive respect or honour; he prefers death to receiving a salutation.

190. He, like Brihaspati, possesses all knowledge, yet for fear of greatness he hides among madmen.

191. He conceals his knowledge, makes no use of his high attainments and prefers to be considered mad.

192. Worldly renown distresses him, he is averse to learned discussion, and likes to live in silence.

193. He much prefers to be ignored and desires that his own relatives should take no notice of him; this is the way he likes to live.

194. He behaves in such a way that he will be known as lowly and baseness will be as a jewel to him.

195. He tries to live in such a way that people will be unaware of whether he is alive or dead.

196. He desires that men should not ever know whether he walks by himself or is propelled by the wind.

197. He prefers that his very existence should be hidden and even his name unknown, so that no creature will fear him.

198. A man who has taken such vows, lives always in seclusion and delights in the very idea of solitude.

199. He is content with the company of the wind, takes pleasure in conversing with the sky and loves trees as his own life.

200. He in whom such characteristics are found is the intimate companion of this knowledge.

201. A man's humility is known by these characteristics. Now I will tell you how to recognize the quality of candour.

202. This quality is like the mind of a miser who though his life is threatened will nevertheless refuse to reveal his hidden treasure.

203. So also, O Kiriti, a man [of candour] will never reveal, even at the risk of his life, by word or gesture, any good action that he may perform.

204. O Arjuna, a vicious cow drives its calf away, a whore endeavours to conceal her advancing age;

205. a rich man overtaken in a forest conceals his wealth, a girl of noble birth conceals her limbs;

206. a cultivator covers the seed sown in the ground; so does such a man remain silent about his charitable deeds.

207. He does not adorn his body [to impress others], he abstains from flattery, and does not boast of his own righteousness.

208. He does not speak of good done to others nor display his knowledge, nor will he sell it for the sake of celebrity.

209. He is miserly concerning the pleasures of the body, yet he does not count the cost in the matter of charity.

210. There is always scarcity in his household and his body is very lean, but when there is need for charity he can rival the tree of desire.

211. In fact, he is noble in the performance of duty, is generous when occasion demands; he is skilful in discussion of the self, yet at other times appears to be mad.

212. The trunk of the plantain tree seems to be light and hollow, yet the fruit when formed is firm and sweet.

213. Clouds may look light in weight as though easily driven before the wind, yet they can send down torrents of rain.

214. If one studies such a man closely he seems to be fully satisfied, but outwardly he seems to lack everything.

215. Enough has been said. Understand that he in whom these

indications are present to the fullest extent is one who has acquired wisdom.

216. All this is called candour. Now listen to the signs of harmlessness.

217. Hear how different schools of thought have described this quality according to their various opinions.

218. As if one should break off the branches of a tree to form a fence round the trunk,

219. cut off his arm and sell it in order to satisfy his hunger, or demolish a temple, and then use the stones to build a wall round the god,

220. so the ritualists held that harmlessness could be cultivated by slaughtering animals [for sacrifice].

221. They offer various sacrifices in order to obtain rain, at times when the world is suffering from lack of water.

222. Clearly the basis of these sacrifices is the slaughter of animals, and how can harmlessness be practised in this way?

223. If the taking of life is the only seed that is sown, how can harmlessness spring from it? Arjuna, how great was the presumption of those ritualists!

224. O Son of Pāndu, the whole science of Vedic medicine is equally strange in this respect, for to save one life it prescribes the taking of another.

225. When men suffer from disease and groan under the pain of it this science prescribes medicine to remove it;

226. to prepare this treatment plants are dug up or entirely uprooted.

227. Sometimes trees are cut through to the centre, or the bark may be removed. In some the growing centre is boiled in a crucible.

228. O Warrior, some, knowing nothing of enmity, were struck in such a way that they withered and died.

229. Sometimes bile is taken from the bodies of animals and used for treating other suffering creatures.

230. All this is like pulling down good houses to build temples and shrines or despoiling traders to set up free houses for the distribution of food.

231. It is as though a man were to wrap his head in a garment leaving the rest of his body naked, or as if a house were to be demolished to build a large shed.

232. It is like a man who sets his clothes on fire in order to warm himself, or the bathing of an elephant.

233. It is like selling cattle to build a cattle pen, setting a parrot free and then making a cage to keep it in. Are such things done seriously or in jest? Should we laugh at them?

234. Some strain the water they drink as a religious practice and many lives are lost in the process.

235. There are some who refrain from cooking grain for fear of doing harm. In this they torment the body, and that again is harmful.

236. O wise Arjuna, even harmlessness and destruction both amount to the same in the code of the ritualists; thou shouldst realize this.

237. When I began to explain true harmlessness I intended to describe the true characteristics of it.

238. Then I thought I must not avoid mention of these different views regarding it, so that thou shouldst know them also.

239. This is all inherent in the subject. Otherwise thou wilt be led astray.

240. Moreover, O holder of the bow, in order fully to establish one's point of view, one must also understand the opinions of others.

241. This is the method of explanation. Now listen carefully, for this is the most important point.

242. I will now express My own views so that thou mayest understand the inner meaning of harmlessness.

243. [Whether a man] has fully understood the [nature of harmlessness may be judged] from his daily life, as a touch stone reveals any inferior quality in gold.

244. As soon as mind and knowledge come together, the mind receives the impress of harmlessness.

245. Avoiding any disturbance of the waves, without breaking the ripples with its legs nor agitating the calm of the surface,

246. a crane passes through the water swiftly but cautiously watching its prey,

247. a bee alights gently on a lotus flower, fearing lest the pollen might be disturbed.

248. In the same way [he who is full of harmlessness], believing that the smallest atom is full of minute lives, walks over the ground softly and with compassion.

249. He bestows kindness as he goes and spreads goodwill in all directions, protecting other creatures with his own life.

250. O Arjuna, one who walks with such care is beyond praise and no words suffice to describe him.

251. A mother cat lovingly carries her young in her mouth and her sharp teeth touch them [but they are not hurt].

252. When an affectionate mother waits for her child her eyes fill with tenderness;

253. when a man gently fans himself with a lotus leaf his eyes are refreshed with the cool wind.

254. even so a man who practises harmlessness step gently upon the gound, and joy comes to all men.

255. O son of Pāndu, when such a man, walking so quietly, notices a worm or an insect in his path, he turns back.

256. He feels that if he should tread heavily he might disturb someone's sleep and his peace would be disturbed.

257. In his compassion he would turn back and would not harm anyone.

258. He does not walk over a blade of grass, as there is life within it; how then could he unwittingly cause harm to any creature?

259. As it would be impossible for an ant to cross over Mount Meru or a gnat to swim across the ocean, so he could not step over any creature he might meet.

260. His behaviour is like the very fruit of kindness; see, his speech is full of compassion.

261. His breathing is tranquil, his face is like the source of all affection, even his teeth seem to send forth sweetness.

262. Even before beginning to speak love springs from him and compassion expresses itself before any word is uttered.

263. He prefers not to speak, for fear that he may hurt someone's feelings.

264. He avoids unnecessary speech, so that no one should be distressed or be caused to suffer doubt,

265. so that his words may not divert anyone from his project, cause anyone to fear or, hearing him, to scorn him.

266. He maintains silence so that he may not hurt the feelings of others nor cause them to frown; this is his attitude.

267. If at any time he is requested to speak, he would speak with affection and those who listen would feel that he was a parent.

268. His words would be to his hearers like the reverberating voice of Brahma, or the waters of the Ganges or [as chaste as] a virtuous wife who has grown old.

269. In such a manner are his words tender and true, moderate and sincere, like waves of nectar.

270. His speech is free from sarcasm, hurting no one, never provoking ridicule or wounding deeply.

271. In his speech there is no agitation or haste, no guile or false hope, doubt or deceit; he eschews all such faults.

272. O Kiriti, his look is steady, O Arjuna, and his brow unruffled,

273. for he holds that the universal spirit is in all beings and so usually he avoids looking at them lest this spirit be harmed.

274. Should his inward kindliness impel him to look at another,

275. [his glance brings comfort] even as the moonrays, though invisible, bring immediate satisfaction to the chakora bird.

276. The effect of his look on all creatures is such that even the tortoise does not know the depth of its tenderness.

277. Thou wilt see that the hands of one who looks on another in this way are just [as harmless].

278. His hands are as still as those of one who has attained his goal and has no further desire.

279. As what cannot endure is abandoned, as a fire without fuel ceases to burn, or as a dumb man must remain silent,

280. so have this man's hands apparently nothing to do and therefore remain at rest.

281. He does not move his hands lest the wind should receive a shock, or the sky be pierced by his nails.

282. Then how could he brush away a fly settling on his body, or gnats buzzing round his eyes, or frighten birds or beasts with his glance?

283. O Kiriti, how then could he take up a weapon when he is unwilling to grasp even a stick in his hand?

284. He avoids playing with a lotus, or tossing a garland of flowers, as this would seem to him like playing with a sling.

285. He will not pass his hand over his body lest he cause the hair on it to tremble, and allows his nails to grow till they wrap round his fingers.

286. Normally his hands are inactive, but if an occasion arises for using them he folds them.

287. He raises them to reassure the fearful, to raise the fallen or to lay a hand on the distressed.

288. Even though he does this with reluctance, he helps those
in distress or fear. Even moonbeams cannot know the
tenderness of his touch.

289. Compared with the gentleness with which he touches
animals, even the [breezes from the] Malaya mountains
would seem harsh.

290. His hands are always empty and free, like the sandalwood tree, which though bearing no fruit cannot be called
barren.

291. But enough has been said. The hands of a good man are
gentle, like his character.

292. If now I were to tell thee truly about such a man's mind,
[I would say] Of whose activity have I spoken?

293. Are not the branches one with the tree? Can there be the
ocean without water? Is there any difference between
light and the sun?

294. Are the limbs of a body in any way separate from it? Are
water and wetness different from each other?

295. So, too, all these outward expressions which I have
described are only the manifestations of mind.

296. As it is the seed sown in the ground which becomes the
tree so it is the inner mind which manifests itself through
the senses.

297. If harmlessness has no place in the mind, how can it find
outward expression?

298. O Kiriti whatever inclination [may arise] it is first of all
awakened in the mind; then it is passed either to the
speech, the eye or the hand.

299. Indeed, how can anything that is not first in the mind
expressed itself through the body? Can a sprout grow in
the ground without a seed?

300. How can a stream flow if its source dries up? How can a
lifeless body be active?

301. In the same way, as soon as the mind ceases to function,
the senses become inactive, as in the absence of [the
showman holding] the threads puppets are motionless.

302. The mind, O Pāndava, is the mainspring of all sensory activities and it works through the channel of the
senses.

303. Whenever there is any impulse in the mind, it is expressed
through the activity of the senses.

304. When harmlessness is well established in the mind, [it

spreads out as] the fragrance pouring out from the centre of a flower.

305. So the senses carry out the activity of harmlessness, spending freely its abundant riches.

306. As the water of the ocean at high tide flows into every inlet, so the mind pours out its wealth through the senses.

307. Enough! As a teacher holds the hand of a child and writes the line of words easily,

308. so the mind transmits its kindliness to the hands and feet and through them brings about harmlessness.

309. Know, therefore, O Kiriti, that by describing the activity of the senses, the activity of mind itself has been described.

310. When thou seest that a man has entirely renounced the doing of harm in speech, in thought or in outward action,

311. know him to be an abundant storehouse of wisdom, indeed, he is the very incarnation of wisdom.

312. If thou dost desire to understand this harmlessness, which is heard, spoken and written of in books, we have only to look at such a man.

313. [Jnānadeva says], I ought to have told you in a few words what the Lord said; forgive me for explaining this at such length.

314. You may say that cattle put to graze in a green pasture constantly move onwards, leaving [what lies behind]; birds, too, flying with the wind, are lost in the sky.

315. Inspired by the theme and tempted by poetic sentiment, my mind was carried away.

316. But listen, I would rather say that there is better reason for this expansion; otherwise the word itself consists of but three syllables!

317. Harmlessness seems but a small thing but it can only be explained clearly when all the many views regarding it are considered.

318. Were I to explain harmlessness without referring to all the opinions held about it, my explanation would not be accepted by you.

319. If a stone were taken to an expert in jewels, it would be thrown away and praising it would be futile.

320. Consider, [in a market where] the scent of camphor is finely judged, could anyone sell flour [as a substitute]?

321. Sirs, in such an assembly as this, no response would be
called forth by a flow of eloquent words.

322. You would listen to me only if I speak of both the general
and particular theories about this subject.

323. Moreover should I mingle the purity of the exposition
with the turbid waters of doubt, your attention would be
diverted from it.

324. Do swans seek out water covered with weeds?

325. The chakora bird will not open its beak to feed on the
moonbeams if the moon shines through a cloudy sky.

326. Likewise if my exposition were not indisputable, not only
would you reject it but it would provoke your anger.

327. If this discourse does not help you to understand or dispel
doubts it would not be acceptable to you.

328. All this writing has been undertaken for the purpose of
pleasing you saintly men

329. and knowing how deeply interested you are in understanding the Gitā, I have held it faithfully in my heart.

330. You are ready, I feel sure, to give all you have and abandon all to gain a knowledge of the teachings of the Gitā;
my work, for this reason, is a pledge of your kindness.

331. On the other hand, if you consider only your own interest
and disregard [the search for] salvation, then listen, the
Gitā and myself will bear the same fate.

332. In short, I desire to win your favour and I have written
this book to that end.

333. I decided to speak of the various opinions [about this
doctrine] so that I should find a discourse which would
appeal to you appreciative listeners,

334. so I have made this digression and left aside the meaning
of the verses; forgive me for this, for I am your child.

335. It takes time to remove grains of sand from rice, but
there is no fault in that, for such particles must be removed.

336. If a child takes time to come home in order to avoid
meeting a thief, should his mother be angry with him or
perform the ceremony of preserving his life.

337. But my discourse has not been like this, and it is good that
you have been tolerant with me. Now listen to what the
Lord said.

338. O Arjuna, who hast the vision of wisdom, attend to Me;
I will explain to thee how to recognize wisdom.

339. Thou mayest know wisdom in the man who has patience without intolerance.

340. He is like lotuses on the surface of a deep lake, or wealth in the house of a fortunate man,

341. O Pārtha, I will tell you clearly the characteristics of one who possesses forbearance.

342. He is a man who patiently bears all things, as one wears on the body his favourite ornaments.

343. Even should the three great calamities befall him at the same time, he is not overwhelmed by them.[8]

344. His attitude is one of glad acceptance whether he obtains what he desires or what he does not desire.

345. He bears with equanimity both honour and shame, is the same in happiness or in sorrow, and he is not affected differently by censure or by praise.

346. He does not feel scorched by heat, nor does he shiver with cold; he is daunted by nothing.

347. As Mount Meru does not feel the weight of its own peaks nor the boar feel the burden of the earth,[9]

348. or as the whole creation does not weigh down the earth, he does not sweat under the pressure of the pairs of opposites.

349. As the ocean swells to receive the water of all the rivers flowing into it,

350. so there is nothing that such a man cannot bear with equanimity, and he has no memory even of what he has suffered.

351. Whatever befalls his body he accepts as his own and takes no credit to himself for what he suffers.

352. He who practises such quiet endurance, O best beloved, adds greatness to wisdom.

353. O Pāndava, that man is the essence of wisdom. Now listen as I tell you about uprightness.

354. It is like the generosity of the vital air, in which there is the same attitude of benevolence towards all.

355. The sun sheds its light without discrimination; the sky, too, gives its space to all,

356. in the same way that man's attitude does not vary with different men and his behaviour is the same.

357. The whole world seems familiar to him as if all men were to him close friends; he has no thought of 'self' and 'others'.

358. He meets with everybody, as water mixes with anything; his mind turns against no one in any matter.

359. Like the swiftly moving wind, his mind is straight forward and doubt and hope do not exist for it.

360. A child does not hesitate to come to its mother, so he freely expresses his thoughts to others.

361. O wielder of the bow, he does not pass his life in concealment but [lives as] a full blown lotus which spreads its fragrance freely.

362. Like the purity of a jewel whose lustre shines from its surface his pure mind is always in advance of his actions.

363. He does not need to think ahead, he is satisfied in the experience of union, and his heart is free and candid.

364. His glance is frank and open, his speech is sincere, and he bears malice towards no one.

365. All his senses are pure and the five vital airs are unrestricted throughout the twenty-four hours.

366. His heart is honest as a stream of nectar; indeed he is the very source of this quality.

367. O good warrior, such a man is the embodiment of uprightness and wisdom has made its abode in him.

368. Now, O best of wise men, I will explain to thee the nature of devotion to the Teacher.

369. How devotion is the soul from which springs prosperity, and the way in which it enables the distressed soul to reach Brahma,

370. I will now explain to thee; pay attention steadily.

371. The Ganges enters the ocean with all the wealth of its waters. The Shrutis all culminate in the place of Brahma

372. As a wife surrenders herself to her husband with her whole being, with all her virtues and faults,

373. so, too, a man who is devoted to his spiritual teacher offers to him all that he has and makes of himself a temple of devotion.

374. As a woman parted from her husband constantly thinks of him so does [the man of devotion] always remember the place where his teacher lives.

375. He hastens to meet the breeze which blows from his teacher's house and meeting it on the way begs it to enter his house.

376. Carried away by love he delights in turning his speech in

that direction and established himself as resident in his teacher's house.

377. He remains in his own dwelling only to obey his command, like a calf tied to a rope.

378. He is always wondering when the tether will break, so that he may meet his teacher and the time of waiting seems to be longer than a world age.

379. Should someone come to him from his teacher or bring a message from him, he feels like a dead man brought back to life.

380. Like streams of nectar falling on parched shoots or as if a fish from a pool were to find itself in the ocean;

381. or like a poor man seeing a store of treasure, a blind man recovering his sight, or a beggar who is raised up to the throne of Indra,

382. so the mention of his teacher's house fills him with joy and [he longs to be tall enough] to embrace the whole sky.

383. When thou seest a man who has this attachment for his teacher's house, thou wilt realize that wisdom itself is his servant,

384. and with the force of love in his heart he worships and meditates on the form of his teacher.

385. In his pure heart he makes a temple for his teacher, sets him in the place of honour and with heart and soul becomes all that is needed for worship.

386. In the courtyard of his consciousness, within the temple of his joy, he sprinkles on the image of his revered teacher the nectar of meditation.

387. When the sun of enlightenment dawns, he makes to Shankar [in the form of his teacher] the many-flowered offering, filling the basket of his intelligence with the pure sentiments.

388. At the three appointed times for worship and he burns the incense of his inner self waving around it the lamp of wisdom.

389. He offers constantly to his teacher the food of union with the Self and becomes the worshipper, regarding the teacher as the object of worship.

390. It is as though his inner heart were the bed on which the teacher, as a husband, enjoys union with him and his intelligence delights in that love.

352

391. When at times his heart overflows with love, it could be called the Ocean of Milk.

392. The bliss of meditation [on his teacher] is to him as the pure couch of Shesha on which his teacher seems to be sleeping.[10]

393. He thinks she is Lakshmi, bathing the feet of her lord, or he may even [imagine] he is Garuda standing in his presence.[11]

394. In his affection for his teacher he feels he is Brahma, being born from the navel [of Vishnu] and through this desire he experiences the bliss of meditation.

395. Sometimes in the intensity of his love he fancies that his teacher is his mother and he is lying in her lap being suckled;

396. or else, O Kiriti, he will think of his teacher as a cow at the foot of the tree of consciousness and himself as her calf;

397. or at times he imagines himself as a fish swimming in the waters of his teacher's love;

398. or he may feel as though he is a plant receiving from his teacher a shower of nectar. Such fantasies arise in his mind.

399. He may think of himself as a fledgeling with his teacher as the mother bird, so boundless is his love.

400. Again, he imagines his teacher as the mother bird feeding him with her beak, or as a boat to which he is clinging in the water.

401. As wave after wave arises on the sea, so through the depth of his love one meditation follows on another.

402. Briefly, in such ways he enjoys in his heart the contemplation of the image of his teacher. Now I will tell thee of his outward service.

403. Reflecting in his heart he says, I will serve my teacher well so that, pleased with me, he will say, Ask for some boon.

404. When my teacher, satisfied with my sincere devotion, [wishes me to make some request to him], I will entreat him like this.

405. I will say, O Lord, I desire to be myself the whole body of your servants;

406. I wish to become to you all the things that you need for conducting worship.

407. This is the boon that I would ask of him, and if he consented, I would be the minister to his every need.
408. If I were myself to be all the means required by him for worship, he would appreciate my devotion to him.
409. The teacher is as the mother to many disciples; but only I will serve him in all things; in this way I could even make a vow on his kindness.
410. I will so strongly draw his love that he will be like a husband devoted to only one wife, and his desire will be directed to me alone, as a devotee dwelling in one sacred place.
411. As the wind can never pass beyond the limits of the four quarters, I will be the cage that traps the entire benevolence of my teacher.
412. All the ornaments of my virtues will I offer to his service as to a queen, and I will be the only vessel of devotion to him.
413. I will be as the deep earth on which the love of the teacher falls like showers of rain.
414. I will be the home of the teacher and becoming his servant, I will carry out every form of service to him.
415. He says, I will willingly be the threshold of the door over which he passes when entering or leaving his dwelling; I will be both the door and the doorkeeper.
416. I will be the shoes he wears, myself putting them on his feet, and both his umbrella and the holder of it.
417. I will be his herald and the holder of his fly-wisk; I will be his forerunner.
418. I will prepare his betel nut and serve his personal needs; I will make the preparations for his bath.
419. I will be the seat he rests on, his garments and ornaments, his sandalwood paste and other articles for his use.
420. I will be his cook, serve his food and myself be the lamp which is waved around him.
421. When the teacher takes his meals, I will be his companion and come forward to offer him his betelnut roll.
422. I will remove the dishes, make his bed and massage his feet,
423. I will be his seat of honour; thus I will serve him in every way.
424. I will even perform the miracle of being the subject on which he meditates.

425. I will be those legions of words that may fall on his ear, and the sensation aroused by whatever may touch his body.

426. I will be all those objects that the loving glance of the teacher rests on.

427. I will be all the savoury things he may taste, and will provide the fragrances that delight his sense of smell.

428. In such a way, becoming everything in the world, I will surround my teacher with every external service.

429. As long as my body lasts I will serve him thus, and after death I will still long to do so.

430. I will mix the soil of my body with that earth on which the revered feet of my teacher will tread.

431. I will take the watery element to a good place mixed with the water touched by my master's hand.

432. The fiery part of me I will merge into the lights that are circled around him and the lamps that give light in his dwelling.

433. I will cause my vital air to be one with the air wafted towards him by the whisk or fan, and so serve his body.

434. The etheric force in me will be absorbed into the ether of the space wherever the teacher may be with his followers.

435. Living or dead I will never give up serving him, nor leave anyone else to serve him even for a moment, and so will I attend on him for many lives.

436. [The devotee is one] in whose mind is the eagerness described above and he is incomparable [in this service].

437. He does not consider day or night, more or less, and the more arduous the service the happier he is.

438. He feels as great as the sky when called on to work, and delights to serve alone at every time.

439. His body runs ahead of his mind, and there is constant rivalry between the two in the performing of any service.

440. At any time he is ready to sacrifice his life for the slightest whim of his Master.

441. His body may be emaciated by this service of his teacher, but he is nourished by the love of his teacher and is the dwelling place of the teacher's command.

442. He is of noble birth by virtue of his teacher's noble family, kindly through the kindness of his teacher's relatives and diligent because of his preoccupation with the teacher's service.

443. He sees as his daily duties those which belong to the religious tradition of his teacher and he occupies himself solely in his service.

444. His guru is to him a holy place, his deity, his father and mother, and he knows no other path than service to him.

445. It is the joy of his life to live in his guru's house, and loves others who serve him as his own brothers.

446. His lips speak no other prayer than the repetition of the guru's name, and he has no other scripture but his words.

447. The water may be impure that touches his guru's feet, but for him it is as a holy pilgrimage embracing all the sacred places of the three worlds.

448. Should he by chance obtain some of the leavings of his guru's meal, [they would be a feast compared with which even] the bliss of samādhi would disgust him.

449. O Kiriti, he would take a speck of dust raised by his guru's feet [as the price with which] to obtain eternal joy.

450. How can I say more? His devotion is boundless. It is from overpowering inspiration [that I describe it thus].

451. A man who has such devotion, whose sole delight is in this and who values nothing but such service,

452. is a treasure house of wisdom; wisdom is even honoured by his existence; he is a god and wisdom is his devotee.

453. Indeed, wisdom entering through open doors dwells in him; this is sufficient to satisfy the whole world.

454. My whole soul delights in the service of the guru and therefore I have wandered in my discourse.

455. [If I am not occupied in his service], having hands I am helpless, [having eyes] I am blind to worship, I am less able to process round the temple than a lame man.

456. Having a voice I am dumb in praising the guru, an idler to be fed by others; yet in my heart is the sincere desire to serve him.

457. Jnānadeva says, This is what has compelled me to enter into this long explanation.

458. But I beg you to forgive me and allow me to serve you. Now I will continue the exposition in a better way.

459. Listen, O Pārtha, to what was said by Shri Krishna, the incarnation of Vishnu, and the bearer of the burden of the world.

460. Now I will speak of purity. The pure man is pure as camphor in both mind and body.

461. as a jewel is of one clear quality all through, or as the sun which is altogether pure light.

462. Good actions serve to cleanse his body, within he is enlightened by wisdom, and by these two means he is full of purity.

463. According to the rules of the Vedas water and earth together cleanse a man outwardly.

464. Wherever there is dust on the mirror of the mind it is cleansed by the intelligence, as stains are removed from cloth in the washerman's cauldron.

465. Similarly that man is pure who is clean outwardly and has the light of wisdom within his heart.

466. Otherwise, O son of Pāndu, if there is no inner purity, all outward effort is indeed a mockery.

467. It would be like decorating a corpse with ornaments, bathing a donkey in holy water or smearing a bitter pumpkin with sugar,

468. or like hanging flags on a deserted house, pasting food on the body of a hungry man, or like a widow wearing the auspicious mark on her brow.

469. A gilded pinnacle is but a hollow ball and its glitter is worthless. What is the use of an imitation fruit if it is only cowdung within?

470. So it is with an impure man and his outward deeds; inferior goods cannot be sold for a high price. A pitcher of wine is not made holy by being immersed in the Ganges.

471. Therefore when wisdom enters the heart, outward cleanliness naturally follows. How can wisdom arise out of external works?

472. Thus the outward part, the body, is purified by means of religious observances while inner impurities are cleansed by wisdom.

473. Then the distinction of inner and outer disappears and purity takes their place; in fact, purity alone remains,

474. so that the good qualities of the inner self shine through the outer life like a light set in a crystal lamp.

475. Whatever gives rise to evil thoughts, arouses undesirable feelings, or sows the seeds of evil tendencies,

476. whether actually seen or heard or encountered, makes no impression on such a man's mind, as the sky is not sullied by the tint of the clouds.

477. Yet, though his senses may enjoy sense objects, he himself is not contaminated by passion.

478. He knows how to remain untouched by these things, as a
high caste and a low caste woman meet on the road without coming into contact with each other.

479. As a young woman embraces both her husband and her
son, and yet the latter arouses no passion in her,

480. so a man who is pure in spirit takes no account of good
and evil desires; he knows clearly which actions are right
and which are wrong.

481. As a diamond cannot be permeated by moisture, or sand
cooked in boiling water, so his heart is not contaminated
by any kind of evil thought.

482. All this is known as purity in its fullest sense and thou
shouldst realise that in this dwells wisdom.

483. The man in whom steadfastness is found is the very life of
wisdom.

484. His body may behave in many ways but the equanimity
of his mind is never disturbed.

485. A cow does not withdraw her affection for her calf even if
she is wandering in the forest; the ornaments worn by a
woman [who burns herself in company with her dead
husband] do not give her any pleasure.

486. The [heart of a miser] remains with his treasure however
far he may be from it; so too such a man's mind is
unperturbed even while his body is moving from place to
place.

487. The sky does not move with the fleeting clouds as the
pole star remains fixed while the stars revolve round it.

488. O wielder of the bow, travellers come and go, but the road
does not move nor do the trees leave their places.

489. So [the pure minded man] even while in the body activated
by the five elements is undisturbed by the waves of
natural feelings.

490. The swirl of calamitous events leaves him unperturbed,
as the earth is not shaken by the force of a whirlwind.

491. He is not distressed by the misery of poverty, is never
overwhelmed by fear or sorrow, nor does he fear the death
of the body.

492. Swayed by anxiety or hope, threatened by old age or
sickness, his mind remains steady and never turns back.

493. Contempt or dishonour may beat upon him or he may be

overcome by passion or desire, but not even a hair of his head is disturbed.

494. The sky may fall on him, or the earth crumble, but still would his mind remain unshaken.

495. He does not feel wounded by abuse as an elephant could not be driven off by throwing flowers.

496. As the waves of the Milky Ocean do not move Mount Mandāra, and the sky is consumed by a forest fire,

497. so the passing waves of passion do not disturb his mind; he remains courageous and patient even at the end of a world age.

498. O Arjuna who hast inner vision, such is the condition of steadfastness of which I have spoken to thee in detail so far.

499. He in whose heart and mind is this unswerving steadfastness is an open storehouse of wisdom.

500. A greedy man thinks only of his home, a warrior is always mindful of his weapon, a miser clings to his hoard of wealth;

501. a mother has no thought but for her only son; the bee is always greedy for honey;

502. so, O Arjuna, does such a man place a guard over his mind and does not allow it to stand [expectant] at the door of the senses.

503. He fears that some creature of passion may hear or some fiend of desire see, and lay hold on his heart.

504. As the outraged husband of an unruly wife confines her to the house, so this man keeps watch over the moods of his mind.

505. He exercises rigid control over his senses, He mortifies his body and subdues all actions.

506. At the great doorway of the mind, with withdrawal of senses from external contacts, he imposes restraint on all activity.

507. Placing the three lower centres of psychic energy under the watchful guard of the three bodily postures, he focuses his mind at the junction of the ida and pingala arteries.

508. On the couch of highest contemplation he concentrates on meditation and becomes absorbed in the union of mind and spirit.

509. This is what is termed the control of the heart and when this comes about wisdom rises supreme.

510. The man whose heart obeys his every command, is wisdom incarnate.

> IX. *Indifference to the objects of sense, self-effacement and the perception of the evil of birth, death, old age, sickness and pain.*

511. Complete indifference to sense objects fully occupies his mind.
512. The tongue has no liking for food that has been vomited, there is no pleasure embracing a corpse;
513. no one wants to take poison, to enter a burning house, or to dwell in a tiger's cave.
514. One would not leap into molten iron or use a serpent as a pillow.
515. In the same way, O Arjuna, such a man eschews all contact with sense objects and does not allow his thoughts to go out towards them.
516. His mind is altogether indifferent [to sense enjoyment] and his body is emaciated, yet he still has a great desire for the practice of self-control.
517. O Pāndava, he practises all manner of penance, and finds the company of others as intolerable as the end of an age.
518. He is strongly attracted towards yoga, desires to live in seclusion and cannot bear even the mention of the society of others.
519. To him the enjoyment of worldly pleasures is like lying on a bed of arrows or rolling in mire.
520. Even hearing such an idea as heaven seems to him like the decaying flesh of a dog.
521. This is dispassion and is the great good fortune of Self-realization, and through it the soul becomes worthy of the joy of union with Brahma.
522. Wisdom will be found in the man in whom there is this strong antipathy for the pleasures of this world or of heaven.
523. Like a man who has not renounced passion, he performs his religious duties, but cherishes no sense of merit.
524. He carries out all his caste and family obligations and regular religious rites, but without personal involvement in them.
525. His mind is not disturbed by any feeling that it is he who

has performed them or that they have been accomplished
by him.

526. The wind blows in any direction at any moment, the sun
shines with no sense of its own importance;

527. the Vedas speak spontaneously and the Ganges flows
without a sense of purpose. So is this man's behaviour
without pride.

528. He engages in action as trees bear their fruit in due season,
not knowing what they do.

529. The illusion of egotism is as little present in his heart,
his deeds and his speech as would be like a necklace from
which the string had been removed.

530. Clouds float in the sky without being attached to it;
so are the bodily actions of such a man.

531. He is like the garment worn by a drunkard, the weapon
held in the hand of a clay image, or as books tied on the
back of a bull.

532. Similarly he has no awareness of being in bodily life, and
this is what is termed selflessness.

533. When all these signs are found in a man, wisdom dwells
in him. There can be no gainsaying this.

534. He is capable of understanding birth, death, sorrow,
disease, old age and sin, even before they approach him.

535. A man with special powers protects himself against evil
spirits, yogis take precautions against obstacles and a
mason makes use of a plumbline;

536. a serpent retains its enmity even from a former birth, so
this man is always mindful of the sins of past lives.

537. A grain of sand does not melt into the eye, a weapon in-
serted into a wound is not absorbed into it; so he never
forgets the pain of a former life.

538. He exclaims, Alas! I have fallen into a pool of mire, I came
to birth through the lowliest passage, I tasted sweat as I
fed at the breast.

539. In such ways he is disgusted by the remembrance of
birth, and declares that he will never allow it to happen
again.

540. A gambler plays another game to make up for his losses, a
son will avenge a wrong done to his father,

541. and a younger brother will seek revenge for [the murder
of an elder brother]; with the same impulse such a man
will strive to avoid rebirth.

542. The shame of his birth never leaves him, as a noble-minded man is unable to tolerate dishonour.

543. Though death is for him still in the future, he is as vigilant about its approach as if it might occur that very day.

544. O son of Pāndu, when a swimmer is told that the river is deep in the middle, he adjusts his garment in readiness while still on the bank.

545. A warrior, about to go into battle makes careful preparation and with his shield wards off blows before they strike him.

546. A traveller anticipates the danger of finding robbers at his next halting place; medicine is sent for before a man's life can pass out.

547. What would be the use of digging a well only when one is caught in a burning house?

548. When a man has fallen like a stone into deep water and is drowning, who will respond to his cries for help?

549. A man at enmity with another powerful man would keep himself always armed with weapons;

550. or as a betrothed girl [must be ready to leave her father's house] or a man renouncing the world [must abandon all ties]; so will such a man always meditate on the idea of death even before it comes to him.

551. Thus he wards off rebirth even in this life, overcomes future death by dying [to the life of the body] and lives only in his true nature.

552. There is no lack of wisdom in such a man, in whose heart the thorns of anxiety about life and death no longer exist.

553. In this way, before his body is borne down with old age, he gives thought [to death] while still in the heyday of youth.

554. He says to himself, At present my body is well nourished, yet eventually it will become as lean as a piece of dried fruit.

555. My limbs will become useless, like a bankrupt business or a kingdom which has lost its power for lack of a minister [to guide it].

556. The nose which now delights in the fragrance of flowers will be as insensitive as the knee of a camel.

557. My head will become like the sore hooves of a restless cow stamping in the cowpen.

558. The eyes that now rival lotus flowers, will then be as lustreless as a dry snake-gourd.

559. The eyelids will hang down like the dry bark of a tree, and the chest will waste away under the constant falling of tears.

560. Like the trunk of the Bābul tree, sticky with the licking of a chameleon, the face will be smeared with saliva.

561. Mucus will collect round his nose like the droppings of dirty water that fall at the foot of a cooking stove.

562. The mouth, now red with betel nut juice, the teeth that are shown as I laugh and which I now use for elegant speech,

563. will then be clogged with phlegm and all the teeth will have fallen out of their sockets.

564. The tongue will not be able to move, like a farmer caught in the meshes of debt, or cattle sunk in the mud after a rain storm.

565. The hair on the face will fall off like dry straws blown away by the wind on fallow land.

566. The spittle will run down from the mouth as rain water pours down a mountain creek at the first burst of rain in the monsoon.

567. Speech will fail, the ears lose their power of hearing, and the condition of the body be like that of an old monkey.

568. As a scarecrow made of grass shakes in the wind so will the whole body tremble.

569. The legs will totter, the arms are weighed down and the beauty of the body will become a travesty of its former state.

570. Control of the organs of the body will weaken and my death will be the object of vows made by others.

571. Should death be delayed, people seeing me will spit upon me and relatives will be tired of my existence.

572. Women will call me a ghost, children will faint at the sight of me and so I will become an object of loathing.

573. When a fit of coughing troubles me my sleeping neighbours will say, That old man exhausts everybody.

574. So, therefore, while still young he worries about old age, and the thought of it fills him with revulsion.

575. He says to himself, Youth will pass away and old age will overtake me, what then will be left of good for me?

576. I will therefore spend my time listening to what is worthy before I lose my hearing; before I become lame I will go and visit holy places.

577 I will see all that is to be seen before sight fails and I will say all the good that should be said before I lose the power of speech.

578. I know my hands will become weak, so now will I use them for charity and good works.

579. When this state comes upon me my mental powers will deteriorate so I will occupy myself now in thinking of the Spirit.

580. As men should conceal their wealth lest thieves may one day seize it, or hide everything at nightfall before the lights go out,

581. so it is wise to accomplish all that should be done now so that it may not be left undone when old age approaches.

582. If a traveller enters a place [surrounded by] forts, [at night fall] when birds are returning to their nests, and abandons his journey from exhaustion, he is likely to be robbed.

583. So, if old age comes to a man and his coming to birth has been fruitless, can one say that he has yet a long life to live?

584. Seed-pods of sesamum that have been threshed do not yield more seeds if threshed again; can a fire burn once it has become ashes?

585. A man is wise, who, bearing in mind the thought of old age, tries to rob it [of its grimness].

586. He takes every precaution to prevent disease attacking his body.

587. A sensible man will reject anything that has fallen from the mouth of a serpent.

588. Such a man will abandon the attachment which fosters separation, pain, disaster, and distress and becomes indifferent.

589. He blocks up with the stones of self-restraint the doors of the senses through which sin might thrust itself in.

590. In short, the man who in this way uses all possible means is a master of the wealth of wisdom.

591. I will now speak of an unusual characteristic of such a man; listen, O Dhananjaya.

x. *Non-attachment, absence of clinging to son, wife, home and the like and a constant equal-mindes to all desirable and undesirable happenings.*

592. He is as indifferent to his body as a man living in a lodging house.

593. A traveller finding the shade of a tree does not regard it with the same interest as he feels for his own house.

594. He is as desireless towards his wife as a man is unaware of the shadow that is always with him.

595. As for any children he may have, [he cares no more for them than] a stranger come to his house or than a tree may care for the cattle lying under it.

596. In the midst of his possessions, O son of Pāndu, he is as indifferent as a mere observer passing by.

597. He is fearful of the authority of the Vedas as a parrot restricted in a cage.

598. The man who has no affection for wife, children or home is the source of all wisdom.

599. Good and evil mean as little to him as the hot or rainy seasons to the ocean.

600. His mind is as unaffected by the desired and the undesired as the sun does not vary with the morning, noon or evening.

601. Where, as in the sky, there is complete equanimity, there you may see true wisdom.

xi. *Unswerving devotion to Me, with whole-hearted discipline, resort to solitary places, dislike for a crowd of people.*

602. He is firmly convinced in body, speech and mind that there is nothing more desirable than Me.

603. In these three ways he has drunk to the full the store of conviction that I am the sole refuge, there is no other.

604. Indeed, his mind has become so merged in Me that he and I dwell together.

605. As a woman with her husband feels no restraint in heart or in body, he is altogether one with Me.

606. As the river Ganges, when it reaches the ocean, merges with it, so, united with Me he worships Me with his all.

607. The light of the sun, rising with it and setting with it, is one with it and enhances its brilliance.

608. Water sparkles playfully on the surface and then men call it waves, but in reality it is only water.

609. So the man who is devoted to Me and has become one with Me, is wisdom incarnate.

610. He is drawn to holy places, the banks of sacred rivers, purified groves where penance is practised, and caves where he can retire.

611. He likes to dwell in mountain caverns, on the shores of lakes, and prefers to avoid cities.

612. He loves solitude and grows weary in the company of people; he is indeed wisdom in human form.

613. O wise Arjuna I will explain to thee also other features of wisdom, for the sake of definition.

> XII. *Constancy in the knowledge of the spirit, insight into the end of the knowledge of Truth—this is declared to be [true] knowledge and all that is different from it is non-knowledge.*

614. He realizes that the highest Self is the one reality, and

615. he is convinced that the knowledge by which heaven and earthly life are known is but ignorance.

616. Therefore, he gives up the goal of reaching heaven, rejects worldly life and in full faith plunges himself into the knowledge of the Self.

617. As [a traveller], arriving at a point where the road divides, seeks [to avoid] a by-path and continues along the high-way,

618. so the wise man lays aside all kinds of ignorance and directs his mind and intelligence towards the knowledge of the supreme Spirit.

619. He says that this is the only truth and all else is delusion; and his conviction of this is as firm as Mount Meru.

620. In this certitude regarding the knowledge of the Self, he is as fixed as the pole star in the sky.

621. Knowledge dwells in him. If thou deniest this [I would say that] one whose mind is devoted to knowledge is one with it.

622. Now the act of sitting does not take place merely by saying the word. So is it also in the matter of knowledge.

623. There is one result to be gained from pure knowledge of the Self; that is the object of knowledge, towards which he steadily looks.

624. Otherwise if through awakened knowledge the object of it is not seen, knowledge will be of no value even though he may acquire it.

625. Of what use is a lamp in the hands of a blind man? So all knowledge is futile [which does not result in Self-realization].

626. If with the light of knowledge the mind cannot reach the supreme Spirit, the urge towards it is as though blind.

627. Therefore the insight must be purified so that whatever knowledge reveals [is known to be] Brahma.

628. So, the object revealed by pure knowledge is apprehended by such insight.

629. His reason develops along with the development of this knowledge, and he does not need to state in words that he himself is knowledge.

630. So then, he whose mind grasps reality with the illumination of knowledge, easily reaches the highest truth.

631. O son of Pāndu, is it strange that such a man should be described as the incarnation of knowledge? Does one need to say that the sun is the sun?

632. Then those who were listening said, You have said enough; do not digress too far, you are diverting our interest in the discourse.

633. Already have you generously entertained us with eloquence expounding fully what knowledge is;

634. there should not be too much sentiment, you are using too many [poetic] devices and you will only arouse opposition in us.

635. Of what value would the hospitality of a hostess be if she removed all the dishes as soon as her guest sat down to eat?

636. Who would feed a cow who, though good in all other respects, only kicks and will not let anyone sit near her at milking time?

637. You have not behaved like those writers who idly prattle without developing their minds with knowledge; but you have done well.

638. That knowledge of which to gain even a little man will practise many austerities, is good, and so has been your exposition of it.

639. [Would anyone complain if] a shower of nectar fell on him continuously for seven days? Who, moreover, would

trouble to count the days if his happiness lasted for thousands of years?

640. Would the chakora bird [ever tire of] looking [at the moon] even if there were a whole age of full moon nights?

641. So, listening to a discourse on knowledge, full of poetic sentiment, who would say, It is enough!

642. If a fortunate guest should be served by a beautiful woman, there is great reluctance to bring the meal to an end.

643. So it is with us, for we desire knowledge and you also have a great love for it.

644. For this reason your explanation has a fourfold inspiration. No one could deny that you have deep insight into knowledge.

645. Therefore you should bring to this the inspiration of wisdom and expound the meaning of the verses.

646. In response to these words of his saintly listeners, Jnānadeva, disciple of Nivritti, said, This was my intention.

647. Now that you have commanded me, I will waste no further words.

648. So listen to the eighteen characteristics of knowledge, of which the Lord spoke to Arjuna.

649. Then Krishna said, True knowledge is what has been explained by Me and many other wise men.

650. In short I have made knowledge as clear to thee as though it were a fruit being turned round in the palm of the hand.

651. O high-souled Arjuna, I will now tell thee plainly what is called ignorance, with its manifest characteristics.

652. Having now a clear understanding of knowledge, O winner of wealth, it is easy to see that what is not knowledge is of course ignorance.

653. When the day is over, night takes its place; beyond these two there is no third possibility;

654. so where there is no knowledge, there is ignorance. But I will tell you some of its features.

655. He who lives for greatness, seeks esteem, and is pleased when honoured by others;

656. one whose pride is as a mountain peak and who will not climb down from his greatness, is full of ignorance.

657. He displays his righteousness in his speech like a rope bound to a pimpal tree and sets it up like a broom on a temple roof.

658. He proclaims his learning and makes great show of his good deeds and does everything to bring him fame.

659. He smears his body [with ash] and deceives others, but he is a veritable mine of ignorance.

660. His conduct is a pain to all and is like a fire passing through a forest consuming all nature in its path.

661. His casually spoken words are more hurtful than an iron bar, his purposes are more deadly than poison.

662. He is full of ignorance, indeed a very storehouse of ignorance, and his life is a dwelling place of destruction.

663. As an inflated bellows is first distended and collapses when deflated, so is such a man now elated by good fortune, now depressed by misfortune.

664. When people praise him he leaps with joy like dust blown into the air by a whirlwind.

665. At the slightest rebuff he is at once cast down, as a little earth is damped by a few drops of rain but is dried again by the wind.

666. A man who is so hypersensitive to praise and blame is full of ignorance.

667. He keeps his thoughts to himself while seeming to behave with frankness, mixes with everybody but in his heart deceives them.

668. Such a man behaves outwardly in a friendly way but sets everybody against him as a hunter may spread food [for birds in order to catch them].

669. Like a stone covered with moss, or a ripe neem fruit, his deeds seem on the surface to be good.

670. Believe me, ignorance is stored up in such a man. This is indeed the truth.

671. He is ashamed of his guru's house, cares nothing for serving him, treating with disrespect the one from whom he has gained his knowledge.

672. To speak of him is as like eating the food of an inferior caste, but it cannot be avoided when describing such a man.

673. I will now speak of devotion to one's guru, which will expiate the sin of speech; the mention of one who serves his guru is like the light of the sun.

674. To speak of such a man saves one from sin and wards off even the worst of evil deeds;

675. it destroys even the fear [of sin]. Listen now to other signs of the ignorant man.

676. One who neglects the performance of good deeds and whose mind is full of doubts is like a disused well in a forest.

677. The opening of such a well is overgrown with thorns and it is full of bones; a man who is entirely evil is like such a well.

678. He sees no difference between his own wealth and that of another, like a dog which, to satisfy its hunger, makes no distinction between food that is exposed and that which is covered.

679. As a pig will come together with its mate regardless of the place, such a man is careless in his dealings with women.

680. He does not trouble if he misses the hour for performance of his duties and religious observances are omitted.

681. Shameless in committing sin, indifferent in the doing of good deeds, his mind is full of evil thoughts.

682. His eyes are always fixed on the acquisition of wealth. Such a man is the very image of ignorance.

683. For even the smallest gain will he swerve from the path of firmness, like a blade of grass swayed by an ant.

684. He is disturbed by any hint of fear as water in a pond becomes muddy if touched by the foot.

685. He is distracted by sorrow in the same way that mist is scattered in every direction by the wind.

686. His mind is carried away by the current of his desires, like a gourd that falls into flood waters.

687. Like a gale of wind, he cannot rest in any one holy place of pilgrimage by a holy river or in a town.

688. Like an excited chameleon running up and down a tree, he wanders aimlessly about.

689. As an earthen pot can only stand where it is placed firmly on the ground, he stays wherever he happens to be, otherwise he roves from place to place.

690. Such a man is full of ignorance, and as to fickleness, he is own brother to the monkey.

691. O wielder of the bow, his mind is entirely without restraint.

692. He is no more concerned about committing prohibited actions than a stream in flood would be hindered by a sandbank.

693. He disregards the fulfilment of vows, transgresses against religious duty; and his deeds break the bounds of prescribed rules.

694. He is never tired of sin, he rejects right action and uproots all the boundaries of shame.

695. He turns his back on family duties, avoids all the injunctions of the Vedas, and cannot discriminate between a righteous and an unrighteous action.

696. Like an unrestrained bull or the wind blowing freely, like an overflowing stream in a forest,

697. like a blind elephant running wild or like a fire spreading on a hill, his mind wanders among the pleasures of sense.

698. What is there that may not be thrown on a rubbish heap? Who is there who may not encounter an animal let loose? Or can one know who will pass over a village boundary?

699. As any man may eat the food [offered to brahmans], as authority may fall into the hands of indifferent men or all and sundry may enter the shop of a merchant [who is giving away his goods],

700. so is that man's heart; in him ignorance thrives abundantly.

701. He will not relinquish his desire for sense pleasures in life or death, and he seeks the enjoyment of them even in heaven.

702. He strives constantly after such pleasures, is addicted to action with selfish motives; yet if he sees a man who has renounced these he bathes to purify his body and his clothes.

703. Sensual pleasures fade away, but he neither wearies of them nor guards against them; he is like a leper eating with leprous hands.

704. A female donkey does not allow itself to be approached by the male but kicks him on the muzzle, yet he does not withdraw.

705. Such a man will jump into a burning fire to experience pleasure, and boasts of his addiction as though it were an adornment.

706. A deer will exhaust itself following a mirage with increasing desire, yet not realize that it is an illusion.

707. So will such a man after pleasure of sense all his life, but instead of becoming weary, his passion increases.

708. During childhood he is devoted to his father and mother, but when he grows up he indulges in sensual pleasures with women;

709. then, still resorting to this pleasure, old age approaches and he transfers this love to his children.

710. As a woman who has borne a blind child always remembers it, he never ceases to long for sense pleasures in life or death.

711. Know that in him there is unbounded ignorance. Now I will tell you other characteristics of such a man.

712. He begins to act holding fast to the idea that his body is his self.

713. Whatever he does, whether completed or not, he strives to display it before everyone.

714. As an exorcist is proud of the burden [of responsibility] laid on him, so this man is bowed down by his age and his learning.

715. He claims that he alone exists, that in his house is the greatest wealth and that his conduct is superior to all.

716. He considers that no one is so great as he, that he is supremely learned; he is thus full of arrogance.

717. As sense pleasures should not be displayed before a sick man, so he is unable to tolerate the good of others.

718. In a lamp the wick is burnt as well as the oil; it leaves soot wherever it is placed;

719. if it is sprinkled with water it will splutter; if it is fanned it will be blown out and if it is placed near a straw it will burn it up.

720. It gives but little light and warmth only in proportion; that learned man is like such a lamp.

721. Milk given as medicine to a patient with a nine days' fever only increases the fever; if it is given to a serpent it turns into poison.

722. So does that man envy virtuous men; he is vain about his erudition, and puffed up with pride about his wisdom and his austerities.

723. He is as inflated as a low caste man would be if seated in glory, or as a great snake who has swallowed a pillar.

724. He is as unbending as a beam, as unyielding as a rock, and [as cunning as] a reptile which eludes the control of the snake-charmer.

725. I tell thee truly that in such a man ignorance continues to increase.

726. Moreover, O winner of wealth, [being engrossed in] his

house, his family, his possessions, he gives no thought to his former births.

727. He forgets them as an ungrateful man forgets obligations, as a thief forgets money given to him or a shameless man disregards praise.

728. A dog who has had its ear and tail cut off and been driven out on account of harm that it has done will return to the house to do more.

729. A frog already in the mouth of a snake is interested only in catching flies, unaware [of its fate].

730. Though all his limbs and sense-organs may have lost their vitality and his body is decaying with disease, he is not troubled by the thought of how this has come about.

731. While he lay warmly for nine months in the womb among the layers of the soil of his mother's body,

732. he remembers nothing about the pains suffered during birth.

733. He is not troubled or disgusted at the sight of a child delivered from the womb.

734. Has not the last birth passed away? and will not another come? He does not consider such questions as these.

735. Seeing the whole panorama of life unfold, he gives no thought to death.

736. He is so confident in the reality of life that he does not recognize the fact of death which it implies.

737. A fish which lives in shallow water, assuming that the water will not dry up, does not seek a deeper part of the river.

738. A deer lured on by the hunter's song does not notice the hunter himself; a fish will swallow the bait unaware of the hook it conceals.

739. Similarly a moth does not know that the glittering flame of a lamp can burn it.

740. As a foolish man enjoying sleep, does not see that his house is on fire, and he might easily cook food with poison.

741. So such a man absorbed in the pleasures of passion, does not realize that death comes in the guise of living.

742. He considers as real the growing strength of his body, the sequence of day and night, and the intensity of sensual pleasures;

743. But the wretched man does not realize that all this is like

surrendering himself to a whore and will lose him all his wealth.

744. Association with a gentil robber may mean loss of life; or a painting [on a wall] is easily destroyed [by washing].

745. As a body may swell because of jaundice, it seems well nourished, but it means the end of life; in the same way a deluded man does not know that a life of food and sleep [leads to death].

746. For a man running towards a stake, death draws nearer with every step.

747. In the same way, as such a man's body ages, as his days increase, and as he continues to enjoy the pleasures of the senses,

748. so death gradually gains dominion over life; as salt is gradually washed away by water,

749. so as life passes by death approaches; he fails to recognize this continuous process.

750. In brief, O son of Pāndu, deluded by pleasure, he does not see that the death of the body is gradually approaching.

751. O mighty Arjuna, he is the king of the land of ignorance. There is no more to be said about this.

752. Engrossed in the pleasures of life he does not notice death; youthful enjoyment does not concern itself with age.

753. He does not see that old age is in front of him, any more than a wagon falling over a cliff or a rock slipping from a mountain top is aware of its end.

754. Like a low lying stream in flood, or as two buffaloes fighting with each other become wild, he is carried away by the passions of youth.

755. His body shrinks, beauty fades, his head begins to tremble;

756. the beard grows grey, he shakes his head in refusal, but still seeks after what he desires.

757. A blind man does not know what is in front of him until he runs into it; an indolent man is pleased when the feeling of drowsiness comes to his eyes.

758. So even in the full enjoyment of youth, such a man does not see that old age is approaching; he is indeed ignorant.

759. Whenever he sees a man decrepit and bowed down, he begins to mock at him, not considering that that will be his own condition later.

760. The illusion of youth is not dispelled even when old age, the mark of death, is already impressed upon him.

761. Believe me that such a man is the home of ignorance. Now listen to more of these chief characteristics.

762. A bull, which has grazed in a forest full of tigers, and is fortunate enough to come back safely, will return confidently to the same place.

763. A man who finds by chance a hidden treasure in a serpent's hole concludes that there is no serpent there,

764. and after several visits to the treasure becomes convinced that there is none.

765. A man who, when his enemies are sleeping thinks that all his enmities are at an end, will lose his life with all his family..

766. In the same way the ignorant man will have no anxiety about disease so long as he has food and sleep and good health.

767. He acquires more wealth, enjoys more the company of his wife, children and relations, and through this pleasure he loses his insight.

768. He does not foresee the tragedy that he may suddenly lose his wife and children or be deprived of his wealth.

769. O Pāndava, he is ignorant; know him to be so, as he encourages his senses in every way.

770. In the heat of youth and with the aid of his wealth he enjoys impulsively all sorts of pleasures.

771. He does what he should not do, dwells on improper ideas and allows his mind to entertain undesirable thoughts.

772. He enters where he should not, asks for what he should not have, and in mind and in body touches those things that are forbidden.

773. He goes where he has no right to go, sees things he should not look at, eats what he should not and even enjoys it.

774. He keeps undesirable company; maintains relations with those he should avoid, following a wrong path of action.

775. He listens to what he ought not to hear, speaks what should be left unsaid, but while behaving in this way he is unaware that he is doing wrong.

776. Swayed by his inclinations he disregards good and evil and acts at random, without considering what should or should not be done.

777. He does not consider whether he is sinful or whether he will have to suffer later the pains of hell.

778. Through contact with him ignorance increases in the world so that even wise men may be affected by it.

779. That is enough; there are still other signs that mark such men, and by them thou mayest know clearly [what ignorance is].

780. He is attached to his house and family like a bee attracted to the pollen of a newly opened flower.

781. As a fly is unable to leave a heap of sugar, this man's mind is always occupied with thoughts of women.

782. He is like a frog caught in a pond or a fly stuck on a slimy surface, or a beast sunk deep in mud;

783. he does not stir from his house in life or death, as a [dead] snake remains on the earth.

784. He holds fast to his body as a wife clings to her husband.

785. He watches over his house diligently, like a bee in search of honey.

786. As a treasured child born to parents in their old age means everything to them,

787. so, O Pārtha, is he devoted to his house, and nothing is more valued by him than his wife.

788. When a saintly man has reached the stage of union with Brahma worldly activities cease,

789. so this man lives only for women and does not realize who he is or what he ought to do.

790. So the man whose desires are centred on women cares nothing for loss, shame or censure.

791. He strives to please his wife and dances attendance on her, behaving like a monkey dancing round its master.

792. As an avaricious man exhausts himself and alienates his friends while he amasses wealth,

793. he curtails his charity, deceives his relatives, and satisfies every wish of his wife, depriving her of nothing.

794. He is negligent about worshipping the family gods, deceives his guru and pretends poverty to his parents.

795. On the other hand in the matter of his wife's pleasure he has no lack of money and buys for her any good thing that he sees.

796. In fact he serves his wife as devotedly as one who worships the family gods.

797. He considers that the whole world would collapse if anyone looks at or opposes his wife.
798. He gives her the most precious things while for others he
does not even provide for their maintenance.
799. As one would be very careful to keep a vow made to the
god Nāga for fear of catching ringworm, so he satisfies
her desires.
800. In short, O conqueror of wealth, his wife is all in all to
him, and he loves those who are born to her.
801. All her possessions are more dear to him than his life.
802. Such a man is the root of all ignorance and ignorance becomes stronger through him; indeed, he is ignorance incarnate.
803. As boats on a stormy sea are tossed about by the waves,
804. he is overcome by joy when he obtains what he desires
and in the depths of depression if any misfortune happens
to him.
805. O high-souled Arjuna, a man who is thus disturbed by joy
or misery is indeed ignorant.
806. As for his devotion to Me, it is prompted only by his desire for its fruit and such a man will make a show of
detachment in order to gain money.
807. He is like an unfaithful wife who behaves lovingly to her
husband in order to go on associating with her lover.
808. O Kiriti, he begins to worship Me, but his mind is set on
pleasure,
809. and should he fail to gain his object through worship, he
abandons it, declaring it to be an illusion.
810. He sets up one deity after another, as a peasant cultivates
one field and then another.
811. He follows the guru whom he considers eminent, learning
some incantation from him while ignoring everything else.
812. He is unkind to all living creatures, and expresses devotion to an image, but even in this he shows no steady purpose.
813. He makes an image of Me, sets it up in a corner of his
house and then proceeds on pilgrimages to worship other
gods and goddesses.
814. He worships Me daily, while on various occasions he
worships his family deity, and again at special times he
offers his devotions to other gods.
815. In his house is My shrine, but he pays his vows to other

gods, and on the day of memorial ceremonies for his father he worships his ancestors.

816. He feels as much devotion for Me on the eleventh day of the month as he does for the serpent god on the day of Nāga Panchami.[12]

817. At dawn on the fourth day he will worship the god Ganesha, and on the fourteenth he will declare his devotion to Durga.

818. On the day of the worship of Chāndi, he relinquishes his daily observances and offers his devotion to that goddess, and on Sundays he offers food at the feet of Bhairava.[13]

819. Again on Mondays he goes to the temple of Shiva and there offers leaves of the Bel tree; in such ways he shows devotion to all manner of gods.

820. In this way he worships continuously, with never a moment of silence, as a whore sits at the city gates.

821. He who thus seeks to follow any and every deity is the incarnation of ignorance.

822. So he too [is ignorant who] dislikes holy places of seclusion, groves in which penance is performed, places of pilgrimage, or the banks of lakes.

823. Also a man who, though learned, scorns the knowledge by which the realization of the Spirit is reached, [is ignorant].

824. He will not turn to the Upanishads, has no interest in the study of yoga, and pays no attention to knowledge of the supreme Spirit.

825. He is unwilling to acknowledge with his intellect the importance of metaphysical discussion and his mind is without discipline.

826. He is well versed in ritualistic teaching, knows the Purānas by heart and is an expert in astrology.

827. He is expert in the art of sculpture, skilled in the art of cookery and knows all the rituals in the Atharva Veda.

828. He is well versed in treatises in love, has read the whole Bhārata, and has mastered all the scriptures.

829. He understands the sciences of morality and medicine and has no rival in his knowledge of poetry and the drama.

830. He is versed in the Smritis, knows the secrets of the juggler and has at his command the whole glossary of Vedic roots.

831. He is a master of grammar, highly proficient in logic:

but nevertheless he is as one born blind in the understanding of the supreme Spirit.

832. Even should he be like the earth which is creator of all basic principles, in every science except that of the Spirit he is like a child born under Mula on whom no one will look.[14]

833. He is as useless as the numberless 'eyes' in the tail feathers of a peacock, which are sightless.

834. If even the smallest portion of life restoring root is found, what is the use of cartloads of other herbs?

835. So all sciences are invalid without the one supreme science of the Spirit.

836. Therefore, O Arjuna, know that a man unversed in the scriptures, who does not study this science with resolution,

837. bears a body in which the seed of ignorance is growing, and his learning is as the vines that spring from it.

838. All that he says is but the flower of ignorance and any meritorious deeds he may perform are its fruit.

839. It is needless to say that a man who does not believe in this science can never realize the highest truth.

840. How can anyone learn about the opposite bank of a river who runs away even from this side before he reaches it?

841. Or can a man know what is inside a house if his feet are bound together on the very threshold?

842. In the same way, how can a man realize the supreme truth who knows nothing of the science of the Spirit?

843. It is quite needless to tell thee therefore that such a man cannot possibly understand the one reality.

844. When a woman with child is fed, her unborn infant is nourished at the same time; so if the characteristics of knowledge are described above, those of ignorance will be implied in that description.

845. When a blind man is invited to dine, someone else must go with him; in the same way the signs of ignorance do not need to be described separately [from those of knowledge].

846. The characteristics of knowledge which are contrary to those of ignorance, such as humility and others, have already been explained in previous verses.

847. When those eighteen signs of knowledge are inverted the nature of ignorance will become apparent.

848. Shri Mukunda has already said in earlier verses that ignorance is the opposite of what has been said about knowledge.

849. For this reason I have been careful to dilate on this subject; otherwise it would have been like adding water to increase the quantity of milk.

850. So without any idle talk and keeping within the limits of the texts, I have been prompted to expand the original.

851. The listeners thereupon exclaimed, Wait! Why all this explanation? Why dost thou fear, O thou supporter of poets?

852. The Lord Murāri has told thee to reveal those difficult matters He Himself has kept concealed.

853. Thou art actually expounding to us the hidden thoughts of the Lord. Even the very thought of this might inhibit thy mind.

854. So then we will say no more. We have been granted the joy of hearing of the boat of knowledge [in which to cross the ocean of this life].

855. Tell us now without further delay what Shri Hari said.

856. At these words of his saintly hearers the disciple of Nivritti answered, Now listen to what the Lord said.

857. O Pāndava, all these characteristics of which thou hast heard represent the section on ignorance.

858. Turn away from all these things and set thy heart firmly on the attainment of knowledge,

859. then thou wilt be able to penetrate with a clear mind that which is the object of all knowledge. Arjuna expressed his desire to know this.

860. The Prince of wise men, aware of his desire, said to him, Listen while I tell thee of that which is to be known.

> XIII. *I will describe that which is to be known and by knowing which life eternal is gained. It is the Supreme Brahman who is beginningless and who is said to be neither existent nor non-existent.*

861. Brahma is the object of all knowledge, and knowledge is the only means by which that may be comprehended.

862. When He is known, nothing more remains to be known and that knowledge alone brings [the knower] into union with It.

863. When He is known all worldly activities cease for the knower, who becomes absorbed in the eternal bliss.

864. That One, the object of knowledge, is without beginning and is called the Highest Brahma.

865. If it is said that He does not exist, it will be seen that He is one with the universe; and again if it is said that He Himself is the universe this is illusion.

866. He has no form, no colour, nor manifest form; nor is His condition such that he can be seen by anyone. How can anyone say that He exists?

867. If it said that He is not, then how did all the elements come into existence, in whom had they their being, and is there indeed anything other than He?

868. Therefore the declaration that He is or is not is meaningless and access to Him through thought is impossible.

869. As earth is visible in the form of clay pots and vessels, jars of every kind, so Brahma is everything and is in everything.

XIV. *With his hands and feet everywhere, with eyes, heads and faces on all sides, with ears on all sides, He dwells in the world, enveloping all.*

870. In all times and places he remains unchanged by time and space; His hand alone promotes the activity of both gross and subtle elements.

871. For this reason He is called the Universal-armed One, for in all actions, in all times, it is He who acts.

872. And because He is everywhere at one and the same moment; O winner of wealth, He is called the Omnipresent One, having feet everywhere.

873. As the sun has no distinct body or eyes, [yet illuminates all] so He, being in all, sees all.

874. Thus the Vedas were wise in calling the sightless Brahma the Universal-eyed One.

875. As the body of the sacrificial fire is one with the mouth which consumes the oblations, so the supreme Being partakes of all through its presence in all beings.

876. He is therefore called, in the words of the Vedas, O Pārtha, the Universal-mouthed One.

877. As the ether pervades everything, so His ear hears every spoken word,

878. and thus we call Him the All-hearing One, for he pervades all.

879. O high-souled Arjuna, the Shritis describe Him as Universal-eyed in order to indicate His all-pervading nature.

880. Otherwise any reference to His hands, ears or feet is meaningless, it is of His very nature that He is without attributes.

881. Similarly as one wave appears to swallow up another, yet is the one separate from the other?

882. So when there is in reality only one Being, can it be said that one pervades and another is pervaded? Yet in speaking of these things one must make such a distinction.

883. When it is necessary to indicate zero one must use the sign for nought; similarly one has to use the language of duality for describing non-duality.

884. Otherwise, O Pārtha, the relationship between guru and disciple would be impossible and speech be silenced.

885. The Shrutis, therefore, have adopted the language of duality in order to express non-duality.

886. Now listen to the way in which Brahma, by means of sight and other sensory functions, pervades all.

> xv. *He appears to have the qualities of all the senses and yet is without senses, unattached and yet supporting all, free from the guṇas [dispositions of prakṛti] and yet enjoying them.*

887. O Kiriti, He is as the ether pervading all Space, and like the threads of the warp and woof of a piece of cloth,

888. as the quality of moistness becoming water is found in water, and the quality of light in a lamp,

889. as the quality of camphor is in camphor and as bodily activity manifests itself in a body,

890. and, O Pāndava, as gold exists in every piece of gold, so Brahma both is all and is in all.

891. Gold in the lump seems to have all the properties of gold; yet though it is in a lump it is still only gold.

892. When a stream follows a winding course [the water in it seems to bend and yet], O Friend, the water flows without bending; when iron is heated by fire, the fire does not become iron.

893. Ether appears to be round when enclosed in a pot, but square when it is in a house;

894. but as ether does not cease to exist when the enclosing
spaces are destroyed, so Brahma, though existing in forms
subject to change, does not undergo change.

895. O winner of wealth, He appears to have mind and sense
organs, also the three qualities;

896. but as sweetness in a lump of sugar is not in its form, so
these sense organs and qualities are clearly not Brahma.

897. O Arjuna of the monkey banner, ghi is in the form of milk
when it is milk, but [after it has been made into ghi] it is
no longer milk.

898. Similarly, thou shouldst understand that in spite of all
these modifications Brahma himself undergoes no modification. An ornament is a form of gold, but it is still gold.

899. Therefore I say in plain language [Marathi], O winner of
wealth, there is a complete difference [between Brahma
and] the qualities and the sense organs.

900. Such modifications as name, form, relationship, kind, activity and separation belong entirely to the outward form.

901. Brahma is not the qualities, nor connected with them,
though they appear to belong to Him.

902. Owing to this, O Kiriti, the deluded man imagines that
they are attributes of Brahma.

903. To think that they are so would be like believing that the
sky is one with the clouds, that a mirror is one with the
form reflected in it,

904. or that the sun is one with its own image in water or a
mirage the same as the rays of the sun [which cause it].

905. It is entirely a false idea, therefore, that Brahma is one
with the attributes which appear to be imposed on Him,
as He is without connections.

906. To impute attributes to Brahma is [as foolish as saying
that] a poor man really enjoys the kingship [he experien-
ces] in a dream.

907. It is altogether incorrect, therefore, to say that Brahma is
related to the attributes or that He enjoys them.

> XVI. *He is without and within all beings.*
> *He is unmoving and also moving.*
> *He is too subtle to be known.*
> *He is far away and yet He is near.*

908. O son of Pāndu, Brahma is in everything both movable
and immovable, as heat is the same in all forms of fire.

909. Know thou that that Being which is the object of knowledge is in all things, subtle and indestructible.

910. It is within and without, near and yet far off. It is one without a second.

> XVI. *He is undivided [indivisible] and yet he seems to be divided among beings. He is to be known as supporting creatures, destroying them and creating them afresh.*

911. As the sweetness of the ocean of milk is not greater at the centre and less near the banks, so is this Being the same everywhere.

912. In the whole creation of beings of every class it is without exception immanent in all.

913. O thou Best of listeners, it is like the reflection of the moon which is the same in every vessel containing water,

914. or the taste of salt in every grain of a heap of salt, or the sweetness in every one of a thousand sugar canes.

915. It is that alone which pervades the whole of creation and, O wise one, it is the sole cause the universe.

916. Brahma is the supporter of all forms which proceed from Him as the sea supports the waves in it.

917. As the body passing through the three ages of childhood, boyhood or manhood is still a body, so He is unchanging through the beginning, the middle and end [of creation].

918. As there is no change in the sky during the three periods of each day, [He is unchanging].

919. O dearest one, at the moment of manifestation He is called Brahma [the Creator]; during the period of existence He is called Vishnu, the Sustainer,

920. and when all forms are dissolved He is called Rudra the Destroyer. Again when the three qualities cease to be active in Him, He is the great Void.

> XVIII. *He is the Light of Lights, said to be beyond darkness. Knowledge, the object of knowledge and the goal of knowledge—He is seated in the hearts of all.*

921. From this Being comes the flame of fire, the life of the moon and through it the sun is endowed with vision.

922. It is the origin of all origins, the growth in all that grows, the intelligence in all minds and the life in all that lives.

923. Through it the stars throw down their light and the sun sends out its brilliance.

924. It is the activity in all minds, all eyes see through it, the nose detects scents and through it speech is uttered.

925. It is the breath in breathing, it is the feet in all motion, and that through which all activity takes place.

926. It gives form to everything, is the means by which everything expands and promotes all destruction.

927. It forms the substance of earth and of water, and everything that has lustre derives its brilliance from it.

928. It is the breathing of the wind, it is the space of the firmament; in short, it is that through which all manifestation appears.

929. In short, O Pāndava, it is all in all and therefore there remains no place for duality.

930. When insight is awakened, it is both vision and seer, bringing about his union with Brahma.

931. It is at the same time knowledge, the knower and that which is to be known, and it is that by which the goal is reached.

932. As one figure is arrived at when a calculation is complete, so both the goal and the means of reaching it become one.

933. In it there remains no trace of duality; in short, O Arjuna, it is found in every heart.

XIX. Thus the field, also knowledge and the object of knowledge, have been briefly described. My devotee who understands this becomes worthy of My state.

934. Thus, O good friend, I have clearly explained to thee the Field of knowing.

935. After that, O Kiriti, I have told thee of the nature of knowledge, in a way that thou canst understand.

936. I have also clearly expounded the nature of ignorance, till thy longing has been satisfied.

937. Further, I have described, clearly and with plenty of sound argument, the object of all knowing.

938. O Arjuna, meditating over these problems with their intellect, [My devotees] with full faith, become united with Me.

939. Passing beyond the necessity of controlling body and mind, they have found in Me their true heritage.

940. Knowing in the end that I am all this, O Kiriti, they become one with Me.

941. Listen now to the principal way in which I may be reached. I have made an easy path for this,

942. as steps are cut on the slope of a hill, a wooden frame for reaching upwards to the sky, or a boat for crossing deep water.

943. Otherwise, O best of warriors, were I to tell thee that all this is Spirit, thy mind would be unable to grasp it.

944. I have, therefore, divided the subject into four parts, realizing the difficulty of understanding.

945. As a child is fed only a little at a time, so that One has been described to thee in four sections.

946. First there is the field of knowledge, then knowledge itself, then that which is to be known, and ignorance, knowing [the extent of] thy comprehension, I have made these four sections.

947. O Pārtha, should this method of explanation still be unintelligible to thee I will present the subject to thee once more.

948. I will speak neither under four forms nor as one only, but as the Self and the Not-Self.

949. But for this thou shouldst give to Me what I ask of thee; that is, listen with complete concentration.

950. Hearing these words of Krishna, Arjuna trembled with joy, and the Lord said, That is good, but do not let thyself be overwhelmed by this.

951. Thus restraining Arjuna's emotion, He said, Listen now to the two divisions of Spirit and Matter.

952. The path of knowledge in the world known to the yogis as Sānkhya, for proclaiming which I incarnated as Kapila,[15]

953. [I will now describe to thee.] Listen carefully to the exposition of spirit and matter, said the Supreme Being to Arjuna.

> XX. *Know thou that prakṛti [nature] and puruṣa [soul] are both without beginning and know also that the forms and modes are born of prakṛti [nature].*

954. The spirit is eternal and so too is matter, the two are united as day and night.

955. The body is not a phantom, but its shadow is attached to it; O winner of wealth, the grain and husk of a seed grow closely together.

956. So are Matter and Spirit inseparable, two in one, both existing eternally.

957. What has been previously described as the field is to be understood as this same matter,

958. and what has been referred to as the 'Knower of the Field' is the spirit; this cannot be denied.

959. Though different names are given to these two, the description of them is the same. As the discussion proceeds this should not be forgotten.

960. O son of Pāndu, spirit is pure existence, and matter is the name given to all activity.

961. Intelligence, the sense organs, and the heart, with all their modifications as well as the three qualities of sattva, rajas and tamas,

962. the combination of all these arises from matter, and matter is the promoter of all action.

> XXI. *Nature is said to be the cause of effect, instrument and agent, and the soul is said to be the cause, in regard to the experience of pleasure and pain.*

963. [Matter] first brings forth desire and intelligence along with egoism, after which they arouse the longing for satisfaction.

964. O winner of wealth, that which activates the means of satisfaction is called the effect.

965. The force of desire awakens the mind and the mind impels the senses to act; this is called action.

966. Know that matter is the origin of that sequence of cause, effect and action. So spoke Krishna, the prince of adepts.

967. Thus with the union of these three, matter takes the form of action, carried out in accordance with the dominant quality.

968. Actions promoted by the quality of goodness are called virtuous deeds, those springing from passion may be termed medium,

969. and those that arise solely from darkness are to be considered as unrighteous and evil.

970. It will be seen therefore that good and evil actions proceed from matter and result in happiness and misery.

971. Evil actions breed sorrow, good actions produce joy, while that which experiences both is called the spirit.

972. In describing this interaction of spirit and matter there is

an inconsistency, for here it is the wife who labours but the husband who enjoys [the fruits].

973. So long as happiness and misery arise, activity belongs to matter and experience to spirit.

974. Here the husband and wife are not united and yet the wife gives birth to the world. Listen now to this strange thing.

XXII. *The soul in nature enjoys the modes of nature. Attachment to the modes is the cause of its births in good and evil wombs.*

975. This Spirit, in itself, is formless, crippled, destitute, alone, hoary with age, the most ancient of all things ancient.

976. He is called Spirit and yet is neither female or neuter; in fact, it cannot be said who he is.

977. He is without eyes, ears, hands or feet; he has neither form, colour or name.

978. Though having neither possession nor attributes, yet he is the husband of matter and experiences happiness and misery.

979. He is inactive, indifferent and without capacity for experience; but his wife renders him capable of experience.

980. With the least movement of her form and attributes, she can bring about any and every activity.

981. For this reason she is called the one who possesses attributes; indeed, she is the very embodiment of the qualities.

982. She is renewed at every moment, is all form and qualities, and her force activates even lifeless substance.

983. Names are known through her, love is love through her, and the sense organs derive their activity from her.

984. Is not mind neuter? Yet she causes it to be active throughout the three worlds, so wonderful is her power.

985. She is the great island of delusion, the essence of the power to pervade all, and the creator of an infinite variety of moods.

986. She is like an arbour made of [the creeper of] desire, spring in the forest of infatuation; she is known as the Divine Illusion.

987. She inspires literature, she is the giver of form to the formless and the indestructible impetus behind all worldly existence.

988. All art springs from her, all learning comes from her, and
she gives birth to desire, knowledge and action.

989. She is the chamber in which all sound is produced, the
treasure-house of all marvels; in fact, all things arise from
the play of her power.

990. Evolution and dissolution are her morning and evening;
enough has been said, she is the great enchantress.

991. She is the counterpart of the One, the companion of the
detached spirit, and dwells with him in the great void.

992. So great is the power of her good fortune, that she is able
to control the one who is uncontrollable.

993. He has indeed no attributes or moods, but she herself
becomes all these things in him.

994. She makes birth possible for the self-existent one; she is
the manifestation of the unmanifest and the condition and
locality of him [who is without these limitations].

995. She is desire in the one who is devoid of desire, satisfaction
in him who is complete, caste and lineage in him [who is
beyond these definitions].

996. She is the visible sign of that which is indescribable;
imparts measure to the immeasurable, and mind and intelligence to the mindless one.

997. She is the form of the formless, the activity of the inactive
and the individuality [of him who has not this attribute.]

998. She is the name of the nameless one, birth in the unborn
one and deed and action in him [who is incapable of
action].

999. She is the attributes of the one who is beyond all attributes, the feet of the footless one, the ears of the earless
one, and gives eyes to him who is eyeless.

1000. She endows the passionless one with feeling, the limbless
one with limbs; in fact, she is all things in him.

1001. Thus with her power to encompass all things, the function
of all attributes in him who is without attributes is performed by matter.

1002. The male element which is in Brahma is there by virtue
of matter, as the light of the moon [is not lost though it] is
dimmed at the time of the new moon.

1003. If even a grain of alloy be mixed with pure gold, it will
lessen its value.

1004. As an evil spirit possessing a good man will lead him into
sin, as [clouds] in the sky will spoil a fair day,

1005. as milk hidden within a cow's udder, and fire latent in a piece of wood, or as the lustre of a diamond hidden in a cloth,

1006. as a king overcome by his enemy, a lion infected by some weakening disease, so the spirit when in contact with matter loses its inherent splendour.

1007. A man fallen suddenly into deep sleep becomes a victim to the experiences in his dreams,

1008. so the spirit in contact with matter becomes affected by the qualities, as a dispassionate man can be disturbed by contact with a woman.

1009. Thus the unborn spirit becomes subject to experiences of birth and death as long as there is contact with the qualities.

1010. But, O son of Pāndu, this would be the same as if it were said that fire suffers the blows when heated iron is struck with a hammer,

1011. or that there are many moons because there are many reflections of it on the rippling surface of water.

1012. A face seems to be double when near to a mirror; red powder gives to crystal the appearance of redness.

1013. Similarly, the unborn spirit appears to have come to birth through contact with the qualities; yet it is never born.

1014. He is thought to take birth in a high-born or a low-caste family, as an ascetic might dream that he had been born an outcaste;

1015. so in pure spirit there is neither birth nor experience; it is contact with the qualities which is the cause of all this.

XXIII. *The Supreme Spirit in the body is said to be the Witness, the Permitter, the Supporter, the Experiencer, the Great Lord and the Supreme Self.*

1016. Spirit is always present in matter; they are like a creeper and its supporting post. Spirit and matter are [to each other] as earth to sky.

1017. O Kiriti, spirit is like Mount Meru on the bank of the river of matter; it is reflected in the water but cannot be carried away by the current.

1018. Matter forms and dissolves, but spirit exists eternally; therefore spirit is the ruler of creation from Brahma downwards.

1019. Matter lives through spirit and through its power brings the world to birth; hence spirit is the husband of matter.

1020. O Kiriti, the universe, existing in matter for untold ages, is dissolved into spirit at the end of a great world age.

1021. Spirit is the great lord of matter, directing the course of the universe, and the visible world is measured by his infinite being.

1022. When it is said that the Great Spirit inhabits the human body, thou shouldst understand it in this way.

1023. O son of Pāndu, the belief that there is a being beyond matter refers, in fact, to this spirit.

> XXIV. *He who thus knows soul [puruṣa] and nature [prakṛti] together with the modes, though he takes part in action in every way, is not born again.*

1024. If a man knows this spirit truly and knows that the activity of the qualities is derived from matter,

1025. in the same way, O winner of wealth, that one must discriminate between an object and its shadow, the distant water and a mirage,

1026. and similarly he has arrived at a clear distinction between spirit and matter, O Arjuna,

1027. he may perform, while in the body, any act whatever; he is no more contaminated by action than is the sun by smoke.

1028. He who during bodily life does not let himself to be deluded by its activities is not reborn after death.

1029. Such is the unique advantage that he receives from that discriminative knowledge of spirit and matter.

1030. Listen now to the many methods by which this discrimination may be awakened so that it may shine in the heart like the sun.

> XXV. *By meditation some perceive the Self in the Self by the Self; others by the path of knowledge and still others by the path of works.*

1031. O good warrior, there are some who burn up in the fire of discrimination the impure mixture of the non-self and the purity of the Self,

1032. and break completely through the thirty-six principles, extracting from them the pure essence of the Self.[16]

1033. O Kiriti, these, through the insight of meditation, see
their own selves within the Supreme Self.
1034. Others, according to their destiny, concentrate on the
Self through the medium of Sānkhya yoga, and yet others
seek Him by relying on the path of Karmayoga.

> XXVI. *Yet others, ignorant of this [these paths of yoga]
> hearing from others worship; and they too cross beyond
> death by their devotion to what they have heard.*

1035. In such various ways they do indeed pass beyond the
confusing fear of worldly existence.
1036. There are others again who, overcoming all pride, trust
in the teachings [of a guru],
1037. one who, knowing what is good and what is harmful,
compassionately removes all loss, dispels weariness and
brings them joy.
1038. Listening with respect to whatever falls from the guru's
lips and follow him devotedly.
1039. In order to listen to him, they aside all other activity and
reverence his words with all their heart.
1040. O thou bearer of the monkey banner these men at last
pass easily over the ocean of death.
1041. Thou mayest see that there are many such ways of attaining the realization of Brahma.
1042. But enough has been said; let me give thee the distilled
essence of all these teachings.
1043. O son of Pāndu, thou mayest come in this way to experience true self-knowledge and find no difficulty in what
lies beyond.
1044. So let us consider this well, refute all these divergent
views and clarify the inner meaning.

> XXVII. *Whatever being is born, moving or unmoving,
> know thou, O Best of the Bhāratas [Arjuna], that it is
> [sprung] through the union of the field and the knower of
> the field.*

1045. I have revealed Myself to thee as the knower of the field
and described the Field fully.
1046. From the union between these two springs all creatures
evolve just as waves rise on the surface of water through
the force of the wind,

1047. As the rays of the sun shining on a desert creates illusion
of a flood in a mirage, O warrior,

1048. or as many showers of rain falling on the earth cause a
great variety of plants to spring up,

1049. so also, know thou that all movable and immovable creatures, in fact, all that lives, is evolved from the union of
these two,

1050. and, therefore, O Arjuna, all such beings are in no way
separated from the all important knower of the field.

> XXVIII. *He who sees the Supreme Lord abiding equally in
> all beings, never perishing when they perish, he, verily, sees.*

1051. As the woven state of cloth is not the same as the threads
yet it is dependent on them, so is this union; consider this
deeply.

1052. All manifested creatures are evolved from the one and are
one; but they appear in experience to be several.

1053. Their names are different and they behave in different
ways; their outward forms vary.

1054. But if, O Kiriti, seeing this, thou shouldst entertain the
idea that they are inherently different, thou couldst not
escape from the clutches of rebirth.

1055. As a gourd plant will bear fruit that, owing to various
influences, is long, curved or round,

1056. and does not the jujube tree have both crooked and
straight branches? Yet these branches belong to the same
plant; so there may be variety of forms, but the spirit
within them is one.

1057. The same Lord pervades all beings, as there is the same
heat in every particle of fire.

1058. He exists in all created forms, as the rain pouring down
from the sky consists only of water.

1059. Creatures may be varied, but the essence within them is
the same, just as it is the same ether which fills both a pot
and a house.

1060. All these creatures, moreover, are subject to dissolution,
but the Self in them is imperishable, in the same way that
the value of the gold in bracelets and other ornaments [is
not destroyed with them].

1061. Thus he who sees that the One who is without attributes
is not separated from all creatures is the most perceptive
among seers.

1062. O great warrior, among all those who have the inner sight
of wisdom, his is the clearest vision. This is not empty
praise; such a man is truly fortunate.

> xxix. *For, as he sees the Lord present, equally every-
> where, he does not injure his true Self by the self and then
> he attains to the supreme goal.*

1063. This body is like a bag containing the dualities and the
senses, the threefold blend of the humours, and the evil
and terrible collection of the five elements.
1064. It is indeed like a scorpion with five tails, stinging in five
places, or a lion in the form of the soul which has come
upon the lair of a deer.
1065. Though it is all this, there is no one who thrusts the knife
of the knowledge of the Eternal into the vitals of the
Consciousness of the Non-Eternal.
1066. But, O son of Pāndu, no man should become his own
destroyer while he is in the body; then ultimately he will
reach Brahma.
1067. Yogis, relying on their knowledge and yogic practice,
having passed through thousands of lives, plunge into
union with Brahma knowing that they will never return.
1068. That is the further shore of the river of the form, the home
of highest contemplation, the last boundary of sound;
it is the supreme Brahma.
1069. All conditions, including final liberation, there come to
rest, as rivers like the Ganges find their refuge in the ocean.
1070. Such supreme bliss is experienced even while still in the
body by those men who, while recognizing the diversity
of all creatures preserve the sense of unity in their minds.
1071. So the same Lord is present in all as there is only one light
that shines in a thousand lamps.
1072. O son of Pāndu, he who lives with the perception of the
unity underlying all things is not caught in the grip of
life and death.
1073. For this reason I have described again and again the fortunate man who rests on [the belief in] unity.

> xxx. *He who sees that all actions are done by nature
> [prakṛti] and likewise that the self is not the doer, verily
> sees.*

1074. An enlightened man knows that all actions proceeding
from the five organs of sense, the mind and the intelligence, and the five organs of action, are prompted by
nature.

1075. In the same way that the people living in a house are all
active though the house itself remains inactive, and
clouds pass across the sky yet the sky remains undisturbed,

1076. so nature, activated by the light of the spirit, disports herself in various ways according to the qualities while the
spirit remains as motionless as a pillar.

1077. He who through accepting this concept has seen this light
in himself, has truly realized that the spirit is without
action.

> XXXI. *When he sees that the manifold states of beings
> are centred in the One and from just that it spreads out,
> then he attains Brahman.*

1078. O Arjuna, a man is blessed with the knowledge of Brahma
when he understands all these diverse forms to be within
one unity.

1079. As waves in water, atoms and grains in the earth, rays in
the sun,

1080. as the limbs of the body, feelings arising in the mind, and
as sparks in the fire,

1081. so are all created forms rooted in the One. When this
vision of unity is awakened, a man finds the ship of the
riches of Brahma [for crossing the ocean of life].

1082. Wherever he looks he sees only Brahma and enters into
the infinite bliss.

1083. So far, O Pārtha, the nature of spirit and matter has been
explained to thee step by step by means of experience.

1084. Thou shouldst value this experience as though it were a
handful of nectar or thou hadst come upon a hidden treasure.

1085. Besides this, O consort of Subhadrā, with this experience
thou canst build up the house of truth in thy mind; but
not yet, that will come later.

1086. Other deep truths will now be explained, so give me thy
earnest attention that thou mayest receive them.

1087. So said the Lord and began to speak further, while Arjuna listened with all his heart and soul.

1088. Know thou that this is the nature of the Supreme. It is like the sun which though reflected in water, does not become wet by contact with it.
1089. The sun existed before the water, O Kiriti, and will continue to exist after it. If its shape seems to be in the water, this is due to the vision of others.
1090. It is similarly untrue to say that the spirit exists in bodily form; it is, in fact everywhere.
1091. We say that a face is reflected in a mirror; the indwelling of the spirit in the body is like that.
1092. It is entirely false to say that spirit can contact a body, how could one say that wind and sand can mix together.
1093. How could a thread be made from fire and a feather? How could the sky be joined with a stone?
1094. Can a man setting out for the east meet another who has set out towards the west?
1095. The relationship between spirit and body is like that which exists between light and darkness, or living and dead.
1096. There is no more bond between them than between day and night or gold and cotton.
1097. The body is the product of the five elements, strung on the thread of action, and it spins around tied to the wheel of birth and death.
1098. Like a lump of butter it is thrown into the consuming fire of time and perishes as swiftly as a fly moves its wings.
1099. Should it fall into the fire it is at once reduced to ashes; if it is thrown to the dogs it becomes impure soil.
1100. If it escapes these two fates, it is consumed by worms. So vile is the end of it, O thou of the monkey banner.
1101. Such is the condition of the body; but as for the spirit, it is eternal, self-existent and without beginning.
1102. The spirit is neither divided nor whole, neither active nor inactive, neither slender nor gross; for it is without attributes.
1103. It is neither perceived nor unperceived, neither shining nor dark, neither small nor large; for it has no form.

1104. It is neither void nor full, neither with nor without possessions, neither with nor without form; for it is the void.

1105. It does not experience joy nor is it free from it, is neither
one nor many, neither free nor bound; for it is the Self.

1106. It is not measured by quantity, neither self-created or
created by another, it neither speaks nor is silent; for it
has no outward sign.

1107. It does not come into existence with the creation of the
universe, nor is it destroyed with its destruction; for it is
the final resting-place of being and not-being.

1108. It is immeasurable and indefinable, neither increasing nor
diminishing; it is imperishable and inexhaustible; for it
is without substance.

1109. Beloved Arjuna, those who declare that this Self is
confined in the body are like those who say that the ether
can be confined in the shape of a pot.

1110. O wise Arjuna, it neither assumes nor abandons bodily
shape; it is eternally the same.

1111. As day and night appear and vanish from the sky, so do
bodies come and go by the power of the spirit.

1112. So in the body it neither acts nor causes action, nor is it
the promoter of spontaneous events.

1113. Thus of itself it is not subject to the less or the more; it
may be present in the body yet is untouched by it.

> xxxiii. *As the all-pervading ether is not tainted, by rea
> son of its subtlety, even so the Self that is present in every
> body does not suffer any taint.*

1114. O Beloved, where is there not space? In what place is it
not present? Yet it remains unaffected by anything.

1115. So the spirit is present in all bodies at all times but it is
not contaminated by contact with them.

1116. Again and again this characteristic of the self is shown
clearly; thou shouldst realize that the knower of the field
is not involved with the field itself.

1117. A piece of iron is moved by contact with a magnet, but
the iron itself is not magnetic; there is the same difference
as this between the knower of the field and the field.

1118. The light of a lamp makes possible the activities within a
house; but there is a great difference between a lamp and
a house.

1119. Fire lies latent in a piece of wood, O Kiriti, but the fire is
not the wood. The Self should be regarded in this light.

1120. Thou shouldst consider this difference as the same as that
seen between the sky and clouds, between the sun and a
mirage.

> XXXIV. *As the one sun illumines this whole world, so
> does the Lord of the field illumine this entire field, O
> Bhārata [Arjuna].*

1121. Enough has been said! As from the heavens the sun alone
illuminates the whole earth from moment to moment,

1122. so, too, the knower of the field is the illuminator of all the
forms of the field. Do not ask any more than this; have no
doubt about it.

> XXXV. *Those who perceive thus by the eye of wisdom the
> distinction between the field and the knower of the field,
> and the deliverance of beings from nature [prakṛti], attain
> to the Supreme.*

1123. Thou who knowest the true meaning of words, the vision
by which the difference between the field and the knower
of the field is realized is the true wisdom.

1124. Men eager to understand this difference follow the wise
men acquainted with this truth.

1125. O wise one, for the sake of this knowledge, they seek the
riches of peace, and nourish in their homes the milch-
cows in the form of the scriptures.

1126. With this hope some eagerly scale the heights of the heaven of yoga.

1127. They regard their bodies and possessions as worthless
and with all their heart become the lowliest servants of
saintly men.

1128. Thus using all the different methods of gaining knowledge,
they become convinced within themselves.

1129. Let us then salute with knowledge the enlightenment of
these men who perceive this difference between the field
and the knower of the field.

1130. Those who understand the illusory nature of matter, dispersed in manifold forms and at various times among the
great elements,

1131. and who, though not caught up in this illusion like the

parrot frightened by a revolving bar, yet know that they
are so caught,

1132. who know that though a necklace may look like a serpent
it is in fact a necklace and the illusion about the serpent
is dispelled,

1133. who know that when the impression that a sea shell is
silver is destroyed, the shell is recognized for what it is,

1134. such men know in their hearts the truth that matter is
altogether different from spirit and thereby attain, I say,
to union with Brahma.

1135. Brahma is more pervasive than space; he is the further
shore of the unmanifest, where no confusion about difference remains.

1136. There all form disappears, all individuality ceases, duality
passes away and only the One remains.

1137. O Pārtha, they become united with Brahma, the highest
truth who are able to discriminate between the Self and
the Not-Self, as the royal swan [is able to separate milk
from water].

1138. Thus the Lord gave to his beloved Arjuna the full explanation of spirit and matter.

1139. He gave Himself to Arjuna as one would pour water from
one pot into another.

1140. Yet who gave to whom? For Arjuna is Man incarnate and
Krishna is Nārāyana; and Krishna had said that He was
Arjuna.

1141. But this is irrelevant; I am speaking without being asked.
In fact the Lord gave Arjuna all that He had.

1142. Yet Arjuna's mind was not satisfied and craved to know
more.

1143. The more a lamp is fed with oil the larger will be its flame;
so it was with Arjuna's heart as he listened.

1144. When a woman is an expert in cooking, liberal in serving,
and she has guests who are appreciative, all hands combine to make a good meal.

1145. So did Krishna feel, seeing the keenness of Arjuna's attention. His exposition became more and more eager.

1146. As favourable winds cause the rain-clouds to gather, as
the ocean tide rises with the full moon, so [a teacher] is
inspired by the eagerness of his listeners.

1147. Sanjaya said, O King, listen now to the words with which
the Lord will fill the whole universe with joy,

1148. and of which the sage Vyāsa with his great intellect has spoken in the Bhishma Parva of the Mahābhārata.

1149. I will now continue the story of the conversation between Krishna and Arjuna in refined Marāthi in the Ovi metre.

1150. This story will be told with the sentiment of tranquillity which is superior in beauty to the sentiment of love.

1151. It will be told in the beautiful Marāthi language which will be an ornament to literature, for it surpasses nectar in sweetness.

1152. In its cooling effect, it will rival the moon and by the beauty of its sentiment, it will even surpass the divine resonance.

1153. On hearing it, streams of purity will spring up even in the heart of an evil spirit; and a good man will experience the joy of spiritual trance.

1154. The eloquence of it will pour forth and will fill the whole world with the meaning of the Gitā, and a canopy of joy will be raised over all the universe.

1155. It will remove all that may be lacking in discrimination, the life of the ear and the mind will be renewed, and anyone who desires it will discover a mine of the knowledge of the Self.

1156. The eye will have vision of the highest truth, the festival of joy will dawn and the world will enter into the abundance of the knowledge of Brahma.

1157. As I am supported by my saintly guru Nivritti, all this will now come to pass and will be well spoken.

1158. So with words full of meaning and abundant similes and ornaments, I will clarify the meaning of the Gitā verse by verse.

1159. My revered guru has until now endowed me with all learning,

1160. and therefore through his grace, whatever I say will be acceptable and I will expound the Gitā to this assembly of saintly men.

1161. Moreover I have come here to sit at your feet, so that there is no barrier left between us.

1162. Sirs! The goddess of learning could not possibly give birth to a dumb child; the goddess of wealth could hardly be lacking in signs of good fortune!

1163. Then how could ignorance exist in your presence? I will therefore shower down upon you all the nine sentiments.

1164. But, my masters, grant me this opportunity! I will then
begin my explanation, said Jnānadeva.

*In the Unpanishad of the Bhagavadgitā, the science of the Absolute,
the scripture of Yoga and the dialogue between Shri Krishna and
Arjuna, this is the thirteenth chapter entitled The Yoga of the
Distinction between the Field and the Knower of the Field.*

NOTES

1. *Darshanas.*   These are the six systems of Hindu philosophy.
2. The reference here is to Buddhist, Jain and other sects.
3. *Kāma,* the god of love, visited Shiva while he was practising
penance, bringing him a message to persuade him to marry the
goddess Pārvati.
4. *the four brothers.*   These are the vital airs recognized in breathing in
yogic practice.
5. *Mahātattva.*   The 'great principle,' the intellect.
6. the *'treasure'.*   This is the created world.
7. *the Sacred centre.*   The brow, or forehead.
8. *the three calamities.*   See Ch. III, note 13.
9. *the boar.*   One of the incarnations of Vishnu.
10. *Shesha.*   See Ch. I, note 37.
11. *Garuda.*   See Ch. I, note 30. A mythical bird.
12. *the eleventh day.*   The eleventh day of the waxing and waning of the
moon is observed as a holy day.
Nāgapanchami.   The festival of the Snake, held on the fifth day of
the month of Shrāvan.
13. *Chāndi.*   A goddess who is worshipped on the ninth day of the
month.
Bhairava.   Another name of Shiva.
14. *Mula.*   One of the twenty-seven lunar mansions in astrology. It is
considered unlucky to look at someone born at this time.
15. *Kapila.*   The name of a great sage.
16. *thirty-six principles.*   This refers to the thirty-six evolutionary
factors of creation.

CHAPTER XIV

1. Hail to Thee O Preceptor, the greatest of all the gods, the sun of the rising of pure intellect, and the dawn of happiness.
2. O refuge of all, the delight of the realization of union with Brahma; thou art the ocean on which rise the waves of the various worlds.
3. Hear me, O brother of the afflicted, the ocean of eternal compassion, and consort of the bride of pure knowledge.
4. Thou revealest the whole universe to those from whose sight Thou art hidden, and Thou makest manifest to them all that is.
5. The juggler may bewitch the sight of the spectator, but the illusion by which Thou concealest Thyself is wonderful.
6. Thou alone art the whole universe, but while some have found true wisdom, others are still living in illusion; I salute Thee who hast this mysterious power.
7. We know that water on this earth has moisture, but it owes its quality of wetness to Thee; the earth derives from Thee its stability.
8. The discs of the sun and moon illumine the three worlds, but the light within them shines by the brilliance of Thy light.
9. It is through Thy divine power that the wind blows and the sky appears and withdraws within Thy being.
10. The great illusion and also knowledge are enlightened by Thee. But enough of description; for the Vedas have laboured to explain this.
11. They are skilful in describing Thee, so long as Thy form is not seen; when Thou art known, both they and we become silent.
12. In the final flood of the ocean of destruction, no single drop of water is visible; then how can the great rivers be distinguishable?

13. As at the rising of the sun the moon appears to be a mere firefly, so are both we men and the Vedas insignificant in Thy presence;

14. then the power of dualism comes to naught and the whole range of speech is helpless; how then can the tongues of men describe Thee?

15. So I cease praising Thee; it is better that I should prostrate myself silently at Thy feet.

16. I salute thee as thou art, O great Guru; be thou my source of wealth that my task in the exposition of the Gitā may flourish.

17. Give the riches of thy grace, and fill up the purse of my intelligence and strengthen me with this poem full of wisdom.

18. By this means I shall be able to make ear-rings for the saints and adorn them with the signs of discrimination.

19. Apply [to my intellect] the pigment [of thy love] so that my mind may be able to draw on the treasure of the Gitā.

20. Let the pure sun of thy compassion rise so that the eyes of my intellect may at once behold the world of speech.

21. O Thou who art the very crown of compassion, be thou my Spring, so that the creeper of my intelligence may bring forth the fruit of poetic composition.

22. Pour down generously showers of thy grace that the Ganges of my understanding may be flooded with the waters of great truths.

23. O thou who art the sole refuge of the universe, may the moon of thy kindness be as the full moon of my inspiration.

24. If thou so regardest me, in the ocean of my knowledge the full tide of the nine sentiments will rise to inspire me.

25. Then his guru, being pleased with these words said, We see that by expressing thy entreaty under the guise of praise, thou has fallen into dualism.

26. Leave now these irrelevant remarks. Explain to us clearly this book expounding the camphor-like knowledge contained in it, and do not let your hearers lose interest.

27. [Jnāneshvar said,] O honoured Master, I was in fact waiting until thou shouldst tell me to begin.

28. The roots of the durva grass are by nature immortal, and in addition to this a flood of nectar passes over its blades,[1]

29. so by the same grace I will expound the original text in skilful composition,

30. and in such a way that the boat of doubt within the heart may sink and the desire to listen will increase.
31. So as I come asking for alms at the door of the grace of my guru may true sweetness be expressed in my words.
32. In the thirteenth chapter Krishna explained to Arjuna this truth,
33. that this universe evolves from the union of the field and the knower of the field and how through contact with the qualities the Self enters upon worldly existence.
34. This contact with matter is the cause of the experience of pleasure and pain; apart from this the spirit is beyond all the qualities.
35. How can the free soul be in bondage? What is this union of the field and the knower of the field, and how can this spirit experience pleasure and pain?
36. What are these qualities and how many are they? How do they affect the Self? What are the characteristics of the Self that transcends these qualities?
37. The explanation of the meaning of all these is the subject of the fourteenth chapter.
38. Listen, therefore, to the teachings of the Lord of Vaikuntha on this subject.

The Blessed Lord said:

1. *I shall again declare that supreme wisdom, of all wisdom the best, by knowing which all sages have passed from this world to the highest perfection.*

39. Krishna said, O Arjuna, summoning all thy powers of attention, take a firm hold of this knowledge.
40. Already have I explained to thee in various ways all these theories, but thou has not fully understood them.
41. Therefore I will expound again to thee that knowledge which from time to time the Vedas call the Para—the highest.
42. This knowledge may be ours but, having found pleasure in this life and in the heaven world, it has become foreign to us.
43. For this reason I call this the best of knowledge; it is like fire before which all other forms of knowledge are as grass.
44. Other forms of knowledge teach men about earthly life and

life in heaven; they approve especially of sacrifice, and
through them duality is fully recognized.

45. All such forms of knowledge are as a dream when compared
with true knowledge, as gusts of wind are eventually
swallowed up by the sky;

46. or as the moon and other lesser lights are eclipsed by the
rising sun and the final deluge of the last day all rivers
disappear.

47. Similarly, O winner of wealth, when [true knowledge] is
awakened all forms of ignorance vanish and it is therefore
the highest.

48. It is through this knowledge, O son of Pāndu, that we are
able to find that liberation which was ours from the
beginning.

49. Owing to the realization of this knowledge all great
thinkers refuse to allow this earthly existence to overcome
them.

50. When by control of the mind it turns away from desire,
peace is attained and even while alive, their bodies have
no power over them.

51. Then they transcend all bodily limitations and in every
respect rise to an equal level with Me.

> II. *Having resorted to this wisdom and become of like
> nature to Me, they are not born at the time of creation; nor
> are they disturbed at the time of dissolution.*

52. O son of Pāndu, those who have entered into Me, the
Eternal, and are for ever endued with My fullness,

53. and are eternally joyful and filled with truth, as I am, and
are not separated from Me,

54. if they are as completely united to Me as the ether in a pot
is one with the surrounding ether when the pot is broken,

55. or as in a flaming light there may be many small flames that
appear to the eye to be one,

56. So, O Arjuna, when the activity of dualism ceases, they and
I live in one place, with one name.

57. For this reason there is no need for them to be reborn even
when all things are created.

58. How is it possible for such as are not, at the time of creation, subject to the bonds of the body, to die when all the
worlds are dissolved?

59. Therefore, O winner of wealth, those who have followed

the path of union with Me have transcended birth and death.

60. In such a manner did the Lord like to praise knowledge in order that Arjuna might be attracted towards it.

61. Then a change came over Arjuna and his whole body became a listening ear and he became full of rapt attention,

62. and as such affection as that of Krishna was being poured out upon him, [the marvel of] the exposition exceeded all bounds.

63. Then Krishna said, O consort of intelligence, today My oratory has surpassed itself in that it has met in thee a listener matching it in worth.

64. [Now will I explain to thee] how I, though one, have become entangled in the many nets of bodily life, trapped by the hunters in the form of the three qualities.

65. Listen as I tell thee how through contact with the field these worlds come into being,

66. and how matter is called the field because through the seed of contact with Me it brings forth all creatures.

   III. *Great Brahma [prakṛti] is My womb: in that I cast the seed and from it is the birth of all beings, O Bhārata [Arjuna].*

67. Matter is called the Great Brahma, for it is the dwelling-place of the great primal elements,

68. and, O Arjuna, because through it the whole vast extent of manifestation takes place; therefore it is called the Great Brahma.

69. By those who believe in non-manifestation it is called the unmanifest while according the Sānkhya belief it is matter.

70. O Prince of wisdom, the Vedāntists declare it to be illusion [māyā]; what need is there to quote any others? Matter is, indeed, ignorance.

71. It is called ignorance because through it arises that forgetfulness of our true nature as the Self, O conqueror of wealth.

72. Another characteristic of ignorance is that when discrimination is developed ignorance cannot be known, as a lamp is of no use for seeing darkness,

73. as when milk is undisturbed cream gathers on its surface but is not visible when the milk is shaken.

74. Similarly in deep sleep there is neither wakefulness nor
dream, neither is there awareness of form or position.

75. Before wind arises space is barren and void; ignorance is
indeed like this.

76. A man may be uncertain whether there is before him a
pillar or a man; he does not know what it is that he sees;

77. so [through this ignorance] an object does not appear as it
really is but is seen as something else.

78. As twilight is neither day nor night, but lies between the
two, so ignorance is neither perception of the Self nor the
opposite of that state.

79. This is the condition which is called ignorance, and the
insight hidden within it is called the knower of the field.

80. Thou shouldst understand that the property of the knower
of the field is that it increases ignorance while failing to
know its own true nature.

81. O beloved, know this to be the union of the knower of the
field with the field; it is the natural condition of existence.

82. The eternal Self sees itself as ignorance and does not know
of the many forms it assumes.

83. Some deluded wretch may say, see, here I come, the king;
another, in a swoon, [may think] he has gone to heaven.

84. In the same way, when insight fails, whatever a man perceives he believes to be the creation to which he himself
has given birth.

85. This complex matter I will explain later in various ways,
but in the meantime try to understand this in experience.

86. This ignorance is My wife eternal yet ever youthful and of
indescribable qualities.

87. But while I sleep she is awake and through union with My
existence she conceives.

88. Then in the womb of matter, the Great Brahma develops
the foetus of the eight common elements.

89. It is her nature to be without existence and yet her dwelling place is boundless; she draws near to those who sleep
[in ignorance] but remains remote from the awakened.

90. The union of these two first gives birth to intelligence
which then produces Mind.

91. The youthfulness of [the wife of] mind brings into being
consciousness of self; [out of this principle] arises the manifestation of the primal elements.

92. As these elements are naturally intermingled with the

senses and objects of sense, these also come into being at the same time.

93. When they are stirred into activity the three qualities arise, and they immediately enter the womb of desire.

94. The form of a tree lies within the seed, which sprouts at once when in contact with water.

95. In the same way, through contact with Me, ignorance begins to send forth shoots of many worlds.

96. O prince among virtuous men, hear how the form of that foetus then develops.[2]

97. Then the various species of egg-born, sweat-born, earth-born and those born from the womb appear.

98. The foetus nourished by the preponderance of ether and air develops into the egg-born.

99. With darkness and passion in the womb and fed abundantly with water and heat, the sweat-born are produced.

100. Arising from darkness with all the evil that pertains to it, and fed on water and earth, the immobile earth-born ones are formed.

101. Creatures endowed with the five motor and the five sensory organs, and possessing in addition mind and intelligence, are to be known as born of the womb.

102. Having these four species as hands and feet, gross matter as head,

103. worldly activity as the protruding belly, and cessation of action as the upright back, and the gods as the upper part of the body,

104. with the joyful heaven as his lofty neck, the realm of death as the middle trunk and the nether world as the fine hips,

105. such a child was born of matter and the three worlds are its growth.

106. The eighty-four lakhs of species are the joints of all its limbs and it increases in strength day by day.

107. Matter adorns with names, as with jewels, all the parts of its body and is perpetually nourished by the breast of delusion.

108. The various worlds are the fingers of its hands and the toes of its feet, on which are placed the rings of the pride of every species.

109. In this way, having given birth to this unique and mighty child in the form of the inconceivably beautiful universe, matter has greatly magnified itself.

110. For this child, Brahma is the dawn, Vishnu the noonday and Shiva the evening.

111. When its game is over it sleeps on the bed of the day of final dissolution and reawakens in its delusion when a new age begins.

112. O Arjuna, in such a way, in the house of false vision, this child prances with delight through the cycle of the four world ages.

113. Desire is his friend, egoism his playmate; he comes to an end when true knowledge appears.

114. In short, the great illusion gives birth to a universe and My power is fulfilled.

> IV. *Whatever forms are produced in any womb, O Son of Kuntī, great brahma is their womb and I am the Father who casts the seed.*

115. For this reason, O son of Pāndu, I am the father, Mahat-Brahma is the mother, and the child is the manifested universe.

116. Now seeing these innumerable bodies, do not let thy mind think in terms of diversity, for mind, intelligence and the other elements all are one.

117. Are there not different parts of the same body? In the same way thou shouldst see all this varying universe as one.

118. As from the same seed grow many and various branches, some high and others low,

119. so, too, I am related to everything. As a pitcher is a child of the earth and woven cloth the grandson of cotton,

120. as all waves are the offspring of the same ocean, so am I related to all living and inanimate things.

121. As fire and its flames are nothing but fire, so I am the whole universe and this relationship is a delusion.

122. If I am hidden under the form of this world, then who is manifested through its existence? Is a ruby hidden under its own lustre?

123. Is gold lost when it is made into ornaments? Or is a lotus not still a lotus when it is full-blown?

124. Tell me, O conqueror of wealth, is a body concealed by its own organs, or, are not the organs themselves the form of the body?

125. Is a grain of pulse lost when it grows into the full ear, or has it grown into more?

126. So then if this universe is drawn aside I shall be seen behind it. It is not different from Me; I am, in fact, all that is.
127. O warrior fix this great truth firmly in thy mind.
128. Thus though I manifest myself in different bodies and appear different, yet I seem to be bound by the same qualities of Nature.
129. O thou of the monkey banner, in a dream one may imagine his own death, and he must suffer the pain of it;
130. or when suffering from jaundice a man's eyes turn yellow, and all that he sees appears to be of that colour.
131. We see a cloud only when it is illuminated by the light of the sun; even when the sun is hidden by it, it is by the sun that it is visible to us.
132. A man may be frightened by the shadow which he himself casts; but is the shadow a thing apart from himself?
133. In the same way manifesting all this variety of bodies, I am different from them; yet it is I Myself who creates the impression that I am subject to the same bondage by the qualities as they are.
134. It is through ignorance that it is not known whether I am subject to this bondage or not.
135. Listen, O divine Arjuna, to the way in which I seem to subject Myself to this bondage.
136. First learn how many qualities there are, their names and nature, their forms and how they are produced.

> v. *The three modes [gunas] goodness [sattva], passion [rajas] and dullness [tamas] born of nature [prakṛti] bind down in the body, O Mighty-armed [Arjuna], the imperishable dweller in the body.*

137. These three qualities are called goodness, passion and darkness and they are born of nature.
138. Of these goodness is the best, passion is medium and darkness is the lowest.
139. These three qualities are inherent in the tendencies of mind as the three conditions of childhood, youth and old age are found in the same body.
140. The weight of gold is increased according to the amount of alloy mixed with it, but the value of the mixture is reduced even to half the same weight of gold.
141. When lassitude prevails over wakefulness one falls into a deep sleep.

142. In the same way the mood of the mind sucumbs to ignorance and darkness emerges out of goodness and passion.
143. Arjuna, thou shouldst know that these are the three qualities and I will now explain how they bring about bondage.
144. As soon as the Self enters the body as the knower of the
field, it becomes identified with the body.
145. At the moment when it commits itself to all the conditions
of the body from birth to death—
146. as happens with a fish when an angler pulls the hook with a
jerk as soon as it takes the bait in its mouth—

> VI. *Of these goodness [sattva] being pure, causes illumina-
> tion and health. It binds, O Blameless one, by attachment
> to happiness and by attachment to knowledge.*

147. the hunter in the form of goodness throws the net of happiness and knowledge over the Self and draws him in as a
hunter would trap a deer.
148. He becomes excited by his knowledge, destroying happiness, and ends by casting aside the joy of Self-realization.
149. He rejoices in learning, delights in honour shown to him,
and begins to boast that he has all that he wants.
150. He says to himself, 'How fortunate I am! My happiness is
unrivalled!' So he is puffed up with the various modifications of goodness.[3]
151. In addition to this he is in bondage to the evil spirit of the
pride of learning.
152. He feels no sorrow at having lost the realization that he is
the embodiment of spiritual illumination, and his knowledge of worldly affairs is as wide as the heavens.
153. A king in his dreams may fancy that he is a beggar wandering in the city and if he obtains a few grains of rice, he feels
as though he is Indra.
154. So also the bodiless Self enclosed in a body, O son of
Pāndu, gathers knowledge of the external world.
155. He masters all earthly knowledge, understands all about
sacrifices; he even knows what happens in heaven.
156. Then he begins to boast that none but he is learned and that
his mind is, as it were, the sky in which the moon of wisdom shines.
157. In this way goodness drives the individual self with the
reins of happiness and knowledge, as a mendicant leads
his bull.

158. I will now tell thee how this self is bound in the body by
passion: listen.

> VII. *Passion* [*rajas*], *know thou, is of the nature of
> attraction, springing from craving and attachment. It
> binds fast, O Son of Kuntī, the embodied one by attachment
> to action.*

159. Even if only slightly affected by it, the self seeks madly
after pleasure, and mounts the wind of anxious craving.
160. Passion is so called because it knows how to give the
greatest pleasure to the self and it is the eternal pleasure-
seeking youth.
161. When clarified butter is sprinkled on a flaming fire and it
blazes with lightning, can it be said that it is either more
or less?
162. So desire becomes excited, [sense objects though tinged]
with pain are felt as sweet, and even the glory of Indra
would be inadequate to satisfy it.
163. Then desire becomes intense that even the possession of
Mount Meru would urge him on to make further efforts to
satisfy it.
164. If he spends all that he has today he is concerned about
tomorrow, and so he enters on great undertakings.
165. Even for the smallest gain a man is ready to throw away
his life, and he considers that he has attained his goal if he
obtains a blade of grass.
166. He is anxious about what there may be to eat if he goes to
heaven and because of this fear he rushes to all kinds of
sacrifices.
167. He carries out one rite after another, on behalf of himself
and of others, but undertakes only what will bring him
personal gain.
168. O warrior, as at the end of the hot season the wind is never
still, so such a man does not cease working by day or night.
169. He is more restless than a fish or the glance of a woman in
love; even a flash of lightning does not move so swiftly.
170. He plunges with such speed into the fire of action in pursuit of earthly or heavenly profit.
171. [The self] in the physical body, though distinct from it,
puts on the chains of desire and bears round his neck the
burden of worldly affairs.
172. Such is the terrible bondage of passion fettering the self

incarnated in the body. Now listen to the account of the wiles of darkness.

VIII. *But dullness [tamas], know thou, is born of ignorance and deludes all embodied beings. It binds, O Bhārata, by [developing the qualities of] negligence, indolence and sleep.*

173. The veil of darkness by which the sight of earthly life is dulled is like the black clouds of the night of infatuation.
174. It is the very life of ignorance and it is through this alone that the world dances in its delusion.
175. Lack of discrimination is its magic charm; it is the cup of the wine of folly and acts as a stupefying weapon on the self.
176. O Pārtha, the nature of darkness is that it binds securely anyone who identifies the self with the body.
177. When this quality begins to grow within the form of all living and non-living creatures, nothing else can exist there.
178. The senses are dulled, stupidity enters his mind and sloth becomes firmly established.
179. The body deteriorates, there is little inclination for work, and the man yawns continuously.
180. O Kiriti, even with his eyes open he does not see, and without being addressed he will rise and call out.
181. As a fallen stone cannot turn itself over, he remains unable to change his posture.
182. Even were the earth to descend into the nether regions or the sky fall down on him it would not occur to him to rise.
183. Lying inert, with no thought of what is fitting or unfitting, his only inclination is to roll from side to side.
184. Resting his cheeks on his upturned hands, he places his head on his knees.
185. The one desire of his heart is for sleep and as he falls asleep even the bliss of heaven would give him less pleasure.
186. He would like to sleep for as long as the day of Brahma lasts, for he has no other desire.
187. If walking along a road he should lie down, he would not care even for nectar if only he could sleep.
188. Should he be compelled to work at any time he would set about it like a man enraged.
189. He does not know when and how to act, with whom and how to speak nor what he is able or unable to undertake.

190. Like a moth with the delusion that it could put out a whole forest fire with its wings,

191. he rashly and eagerly carries out improper actions, and delights in doing the wrong thing.

192. Thus darkness is that threefold force of lethargy, sloth and negligence which binds the originally pure and free individual self.

> IX. *Goodness attaches one to happiness, passion to action, O Bhārata, but dullness, veiling wisdom, attaches to negligence.*

> X. *Goodness prevails, overpowering passion and dullness, O Bhārata. Passion prevails, [overpowering] goodness and dullness and even so dullness prevails [overcoming] goodness and passion.*

193. As fire applied to wood appears to take in the form of the wood, as ether in a jar seems to take on the shape of the jar,

194. as the moon is reflected in the water of a lake, so does the self seem to be the qualities by which it is bound.

195. When bile, predominating over phlegm and wind, spreads through the body and increases the heat in it;

196. when the rains give way to the cold season, the whole sky looks chilled;

197. when both the waking condition and the state of dream are over, deep sleep follows and for a moment there is deep content;

198. so also, when goodness overcomes passion and darkness, goodness causes the self to say, Am I not now happy?

199. Further, when goodness and passion recede, darkness predominates and a man naturally falls into error.

200. Likewise when goodness and darkness are overcome by passion,

201. the spirit which dwells in the body thinks that there is nothing so beautiful as action.

> XI. *Greed, activity, the undertaking of actions, unrest and craving—these spring up, O Best of the Bhāratas [Arjuna], when rajas increases.*

> XII. *Unillumination, inactivity, negligence and mere delusion—these arise, O Joy of the Kurus, when dullness increases.*

XIII. *When the light of knowledge streams forth in all the gates of the body, then it may be known that goodness has increased.*

XIV. *When the embodied soul meets with dissolution, when goodness prevails, then it attains to the pure worlds of those who know the Highest.*

XV. *Meeting with dissolution when passion prevails, it is born among those attached to action; and if it is dissolved when dullness prevails, it is born in the wombs of the deluded.*

XVI. *The fruit of good action is said to be of the nature of 'goodness' and pure; while the fruit of passion is pain, the fruit of dullness is ignorance.*

202. When, overcoming passion and darkness, goodness increases, these are the signs by which this is known.
203. As in spring lotuses give out their fragrance, so knowledge, overflowing the mind, spreads beyond it.
204. Discrimination labours in the domain of the senses and the hands and feet even seem as if they were endowed with sight.
205. When a mixture of milk and water is placed before a royal swan, it separates one from the other with the tip of its beak.
206. So are the senses able to distinguish between right and wrong, with sense control, O Arjuna, as their willing helper.
207. The ears avoid whatever should not be heard, the eyes themselves shun what they should not see and the tongue refrains from uttering what should not be spoken.
208. As darkness is dispelled by a lamp, whatever is forbidden does not appear in the presence of the senses.
209. As a great river overflows its banks in the rainy season, the intellect of such a man ranges over all the sciences.
210. As moonlight spreads over the whole sky on the day of the full moon, the intellect easily grasps all knowledge.
211. Desire is concentrated [on Brahma], the activities of the mind subside and it feels no attraction towards pleasure.
212. Thus goodness increases and then if this is indicated and death should occur in such a state,
213. according to the wealth of the household and their generous tendencies, why should such a man not attain to glory and a place in heaven?

214. Then if it is a time of plenty, and a feast is held, the beloved ancestors from heaven would come to it.

215. O winner of wealth, in such favourable circumstances what other outcome could there be? Where else could a man of such purity go?

216. The man in whom goodness is supreme takes that quality with him, when he casts off his earthly tenement—the abode of worldly enjoyments.

217. Anyone who dies suddenly in this way is born again in goodness, or into a family of the wise.

218. Tell me, O wielder of the bow, would a reigning monarch be less regal if he retired to a hilltop?

219. O Pāndava, is not a lamp of this village still a lamp even if it is carried to a neighbouring village?

220. In the same way the purity of goodness grows with increase in knowledge and intellect floats on the surface of discrimination.

221. He then meditates, in sequence, on the nature of intellect and the other elements and ultimately becomes absorbed in Brahma.

222. He who is the thirty-seventh, beyond the thirty-sixth principles, the twenty-fifth, beyond the twenty-four elements, or the fourth, beyond the three qualities,[4]

223. this Brahma, the one who is all and is highest of all, is easily reached by such a man and he is born into a body that is beyond compare.

224. Now consider what happens when passion predominates over goodness and darkness.

225. When passion runs riot in the body, the following characteristics can be seen,

226. As a travelling whirlwind gathers up all manner of things in its sweep, so do the senses wander freely among the objects of sense.

227. Associating indiscriminately with women, he disregards prohibitions and behaves like a sheep that feeds on whatever it finds.

228. His greed is so unrestrained that only what is beyond his reach escapes his grasp.

229. O winner of wealth, he does not hesitate to undertake any enterprise which may come his way.

230. He conceives the boldest projects such as building a temple or performing the horse sacrifice.[5]

231. He desires to found cities, to plant great forests of trees or create reservoirs of water.

232. Such great designs does he undertake, while his desire for worldly and heavenly enjoyments is never satisfied.

233. His lusts are so overwhelming that even the ocean would overflow with them and fire be inadequate to consume them.

234. His eagerness runs ahead of thought, he competes in a race with desire and the whole universe is trodden underfoot.

235. These are some of the characteristics found in one in whom passion is dominant, and if he dies in this condition,

236. he will enter into another body accompanied by these traits, reborn in a human womb.

237. If a beggar were to reside in a palace, enjoying all its luxury, could he thereby become a king?

238. A bull feeds on straw; he would not be fed on anything else even if he were to pull a cart in the marriage procession of a rich man.

239. Such a man would be forced to live with those who are occupied without rest, by day or by night, with worldly undertakings.

240. Moreover one who dies submerged in the depths of passion may be born among those who are given to self-interested action.

241. On the other hand when darkness becomes the dominating influence, having overcome goodness and passion,

242. the characteristics that are to be found within the body and outside it will not be given. Listen with careful attention.

243. His mind becomes as dark as the sky, when on the night before the new moon neither sun nor moon are visible.

244. His heart also is altogether without inspiration and desolate, without trace of intelligent thought.

245. His intellect is heavier than a stone and his memory wanders aimlessly about.

246. Lack of discrimination takes possession of his whole body and only stupidity carries on any activity.

247. The signs of depravity are visible before the courtyard of his senses, and his evil deeds continue even after death.[6]

248. One can observe also that he delights in wrong-doing as an owl can see in the dark.

249. As for prohibited actions, he enjoys performing them and his sense organs run towards their objects.

250. His body sways though he may take no wine, he talks wildly though not delirious, and raves like a madman though not in love.

251. He may be bemused, not because he has reached emancipation but because he is possessed by infatuation.

252. In short, such are the signs of darkness, which increases by its own efforts.

253. and if death should occur in these circumstances, that man will be reborn with all the tendencies of darkness.

254. When a mustard plant dies, having passed on its essence in its seeds, can the seeds grow into anything other than mustard plants?

255. If a lamp is lit from a flame, will the flame be extinguished? Or does it not continue to exist in that to which it has been transmitted?

256. So then, a man who dies while his thoughts are burdened with darkness is reborn with this same quality.

257. What more need be said? When a man in whom darkness is dominant dies he may be reborn as a beast, a bird, a tree or an insect.

258. For this reason whatever arises from the quality of goodness is termed 'good action' by the Vedas.

259. The matchless fruit of happiness and knowledge which is born of pure good deeds is described as 'endowed with the quality of goodness'.

260. Action deriving from the quality of passion is like ripe Indravāni fruit, outwardly pleasing but bringing sorrow with it.

261. Such action is like the fruit of the neem tree, apparently sweet but bitter to the taste.

262. Action arising from darkness can bear only ignorance as its fruit, as poisonous shoots [can produce only] poison.

> XVII. *From goodness arises knowledge and from passion greed, negligence and error arise from dullness, as also ignorance.*

263. Therefore, O Arjuna, goodness awakens knowledge as the sun causes daylight.

264. Similarly passion is the source of greed as forgetfulness of self leads to non-duality.

265. O wise Arjuna, darkness is the root of the impure group of sins of infatuation, ignorance and negligence and so on.

266. Now I have shown to thy inner vision, in due order, the qualities [as clearly as one would see] an avala fruit in the palm of the hand.

267. It has been seen that passion and darkness lead to degradation, while only goodness leads to knowledge.

268. Therefore there are some who practice goodness all their lives; leaving aside all else they practise the fourth form of devotion through knowledge.

> XVIII. *Those who are established in goodness rise upwards; the passionate remain in the middle [regions]; the dull, steeped in the lower tendencies, sink downwards.*

269. Those who live and die in the excellent practice of goodness become the lords of heaven when they leave the physical body.

270. In the same way, those who live and die in passion are reborn as human beings in this mortal world.

271. Here they all eat from the same dish a mixture of pleasure and pain, and having fallen into the path of death they do not arise from it;

272. while those who, dominated by darkness, enjoy bodily pleasures inherit the land of hell.

273. In this way, O son of Pāndu, I have explained to thee the power of the one reality, Brahma, as being the cause of the existence of the three qualities.

274. The real lives entirely as reality, unchanging, but it manifests itself in accordance with the manner in which the qualities produce their effects.

275. As in a dream a king may see another king and think he is overcoming him, or is himself being defeated,

276. so the highest, the middle and the lowest states are but differences due to the activity of the qualities. When this impression is laid aside, only the pure Brahma is left.

277. Enough of this explanation; but do not think that this is irrelevant. Listen now as I tell thee of what has already been mentioned.

> XIX. *When the seer perceives no other agent than the modes, and knows also that which is beyond the modes, he attains to My being.*

278. Know that the three moods, each according to its power, naturally come into action owing to contact with the body.

279. As fire appears to take on the shape of the fuel it consumes, or as the watery element in the earth appears in the form of a tree,

280. as milk is changed into curds or as the quality of sweetness is manifested in the sugar-cane,

281. so the three qualities, with the interior organ of the heart make up the body, and they are the cause of bondage.

282. O wielder of the bow, it is a marvel that despite all these entanglements the state of liberation can still be attained.

283. Though the three qualities, according to their special properties affect the activities of the body, that which is beyond them is not diminished in power.

284. Now will I explain to thee why this liberation is natural; for indeed thou art the bee on the lotus of knowledge.

285. This is the principle that I have already expounded to thee, that the spirit, though involved with the qualities, is not of them.

286. This is perceived by the enlightened, O Pārtha, as a dream is realized as a dream by a man awakened from sleep.

287. If a man sees his reflection in water, watching from the shore it will seem to be in various pieces through the movement of the waves.

288. Again, an actor is not deceived by the role that he is playing. In the same way we should understand the qualities without being identified with them.

289. The three seasons are held by the sky, yet it preserves its separate existence.

290. So, too, when the self-born Brahma, beyond the qualities enters into the realm of the qualities, it maintains its identity in spite of being limited by individuality.

291. Regarding everything in this way, the individual self says, I am the observer, I am not the doer; it is the qualities which promote all activity.

292. The whole field of action arises from the three qualities of goodness, passion and darkness and actions are merely the modifications caused by them.

293. In them I am like spring in a forest, the cause of all its wealth of beauty.

294. All stars vanish, the sun-crystal gleams, the lotuses blossom and darkness is dispelled,

295. but the sun itself does not bring about all these changes. In

the same way I am in the body, not as the doer but only by
My presence.

296. Manifesting through Me, the qualities become evident;
they increase owing to Me and when they pass away what
remains is Myself.

297. He who has reached enlightenment, O winner of wealth,
rises above the qualities and proceeds on the upward path.

> xx. *When the embodied soul rises above these three modes
> that spring from the body, it is freed from birth, death, old
> age and pain and attains to life eternal.*

298. Then he knows without doubt that the one who is without
attributes is entirely different, for wisdom has taken up its
abode in him.

299. In short, O son of Pāndu, he attains to My Nature as a
river is absorbed into the ocean.

300. Like a parrot that has escaped from its perch and is sitting
on the branch of a tree, he is overcome by the consciousness of oneness with Brahma.

301. He is like a man who has been snoring in the deep sleep of
ignorance and suddenly awakes to the knowledge of his
real nature;

302. from his hand falls the mirror of delusion, O prince of
warriors, and he is freed from the reflected nature of life.

303. When the wind of concern with the body ceases to blow, O
warrior, the individual soul attains to union with Brahma
as the waves merge in the ocean.

304. Such a man immediately becomes one with Me; as the
clouds merge with the sky at the end of the rainy season,

305. he has indeed been united with Me, then although he remains in the body he is no longer at the mercy of those
qualities of which the body is born.

306. As the light of a lamp enclosed in a glass house is not
dimmed nor the fire in the centre of the ocean is not extinguished by the waters,

307. so his intelligence is not sullied by the coming and going
of the qualities; his life in the body is as the moon in the sky
reflected in water.

308. Even should the three qualities exercise their full play in
his body, he does not allow his consciousness to be aware
of them.

309. When he arrives at this state, with firm concentration in the heart, he is unaware of what his body is doing.

310. As a serpent, when it has shed its skin, retires beneath the earth and is no longer concerned with what will happen to it;

311. as when the fragrance of a lotus is sent forth and mingles with the air and does not return to the flower,

312. so such a man, having arrived at union with the self, does not concern himself with the nature or state of the body.

313. Thus the six conditions such as birth, old age and death affect only the body; they do not touch this man.

314. When the sherds of a broken pot are thrown aside, the air which was contained in the pot is absorbed by the ether,

315. and in the same way, when bodily awareness passes away, if a man remembers his true nature, he experiences nothing else but this union.

316. Therefore I say that such a man has transcended the qualities, having received this great illumination even while still in the body.

317. These words of the Lord pleased Arjuna greatly, like a peacock [hearing] the sound of a thundercloud.

Arjuna said:

> XXI. *By what marks is he characterized, O Lord, who has risen above the three modes? What is his way of life?*

318. Then the warrior, full of this joy, asked the Lord what the signs were of the man who had experienced this great enlightenment.

319. Having transcended the qualities how does he behave? In what way does he remain free from them? Thou art the abode of grace, let this be told.

320. Listen to how the Lord of the six great virtues will explain Arjuna's question.

321. The Lord said It is strange, O Arjuna, that thou shouldst ask such a question; it is like asking how a moving object can remain still.

322. He who has risen above the qualities cannot be subject to them; even should he come in contact with them, he can easily escape from their grasp.

323. How can one know whether he is bound by the qualities or not since he is entangled by them?

324. If this is the cause of thy doubt, thou shouldst ask Me
freely. Listen while I explain this.

The Blessed Lord said:

> XXII. *He, O Pāndava [Arjuna], who does not abhor illu-
> mination, activity and delusion when they arise nor longs
> for them when they cease.*

325. When under the power of passion the impulse to action is
awakened in the body and when he is enmeshed in it,
326. he [who has transcended the qualities] is not intoxicated
with pride that he is engaged in action nor is he despondent
if action fails.
327. When goodness predominates knowledge shines out
through all the senses, but his mind is not carried away by
[the thought of] his learning, nor is he despondent [if he
lacks knowledge].
328. When darkness increases in him he is not overcome by
delusion and infatuation, nor is he troubled by ignorance,
he does not accept it.
329. When confusion overtakes him he does not seek for knowledge; when he gains wisdom he disregards action, but he
feels no remorse if he finds himself engaged in action.
330. He is like the sun, which is in no way affected by the three
periods of the day, morning, midday and evening
331. Does he need any light from other sources, with which to
acquire wisdom? Is the ocean filled up by rain?
332. Does he consider himself as a man of action on account of
work undertaken? Do the Himālaya mountains tremble
under the snow [which lies on them]?
333. When infatuation comes to him, will he be annoyed? Can
he be consumed by the heat of the hot season?

> XXIII. *He who is seated like one unconcerned, unperturbed
> by the modes, who stands apart, without wavering, knowing
> that it is only the modes which act.*

334. Knowing that the qualities and their operation are all himself, he is not disturbed by the presence of one or the other.
335. Having this conviction, when he enters a body he is as a
man who on his journey encounters an obstacle.
336. He is like a field of battle that of itself neither gains a

victory nor suffers a defeat, in that he neither overcomes the qualities nor is overcome by them.

337. So therefore, O Pāndava, with the coming or going of the qualities he is not perturbed, as the waves of a mirage would not sway Mount Meru.

338. What more can be said? As the sky is not shaken by the wind, nor the sun swallowed up by darkness,

339. nor is he affected by the qualities, as a man who is awake is not deluded by a dream; understand this.

340. He is not influenced by them and sees them only from afar, as a well-informed man judging the merits and demerits of a puppet-show.

341. Good actions result from the quality of goodness, passion engages a man in the pleasure of the senses, while darkness promotes confusion and infatuation.

342. Thou shouldst understand clearly that it is by the power of such a man that the activities of the qualities come about, as the power of the sun [promotes the activities] of men in the world.

343. The tide of the ocean rises, the moon-stone oozes moisture and the moon-lotuses open their blossoms, yet the moon itself remains silent.

344. The wind may rise and subside, but the sky remains motionless; so is such a man undisturbed by the play of the qualities.

345. O Arjuna, by these signs one who has risen above the qualities can be recognized: now listen to the way he lives.

> XXIV. *He who regards pain and pleasure alike, who dwells in his own self, who looks upon a clod, a stone, a piece of gold as of equal worth, who remains the same amidst the pleasant and the unpleasant things, who is firm of mind, who regards both blame and praise as one,*

346. As a garment, O Kiriti, is nothing but threads throughout, that man likewise views the whole creation as infused with My form.

347. Whether he suffers pain or joy, his mind remains well-balanced, just as Hari gives gifts to his devotees and his enemies alike.

348. So long as he is like a fish in the waters of earthly existence, naturally he has to experience pleasure and pain;

349. nevertheless he disregards them both, being established in his true nature, as the seed is separated from the husks.

350. As the river Ganges, having run its course, merges itself in ocean and leaves behind its turbulent flow,

351. similarly, O winner of wealth, pain and pleasure are equally accepted in bodily life by him who has begun to dwell in the Self.

352. As night and day are the same to a pillar, so the pairs of opposites inherent in bodily life [do not exist for] the man who is one with the Self.

353. A sleeping man is indifferent to whether a snake or a heavenly maiden lies near him; similarly these opposites in the body do not affect the man who is united with Brahma.

354. For him cowdung does not differ from gold nor does he see a difference between a jewel and a stone.

355. His enjoyment of union with the Self never fades whether heaven enters his house or a tiger springs upon him.

356. As what is dead cannot come to life, what has been burnt cannot grow again, so the even balance of such a man's mind cannot be disturbed.

357. He cannot be praised as though he were Brahma, nor belittled as though lowborn, as ashes cannot be burned [as fuel].

358. Thus praise or blame are of no consequence to him as the sun is untouched by darkness or light.

> xxv. *He who is the same in honour and dishonour and the same to friends and foes, and who has given up all initiative of action, is said to have risen above the modes*

359. Whether he is worshipped as a divinity or shouted at as a thief; whether he is made a king or is surrounded by bulls and elephants,

360. whether friends approach him or enemies attack him, it is the same to him, as the light of the sun is indifferent to night or dawn.

361. The sky remains unaffected by whichever of the six seasons approaches; so the mind of such a man is unaware of differences.

362. He has yet another characteristic, that he seems detached from all action.

363. He remains separate from every undertaking, earthly

activity appears to have no existence for him and he himself is the fire in which the fruit of all action is consumed.

364. Such ideas as heaven or earth do not arise in his mind and
he enters naturally into whatever experience comes to him.

365. Unaffected by pleasure or fatigue, as if he were a stone,
his mind has abandoned all decision to act or not to act.

366. Why expand this further? He who acts thus indeed has
passed beyond the qualities.

367. The Lord Krishna said, Now listen to the means by which
this transcendence over the qualities can be achieved.

XXVI. *He who serves Me with unfailing devotion of love,
rises above the three modes; he too is fit to become Brahman.*

368. He who with unswerving mind serves Me through the path
of devotion is able to overcome the qualities.

369. I must explain to thee clearly who I am, what is devotion
and what is the mark of aberration.

370. Listen, O Pārtha, I am in this universe as the lustre is
inherent in a jewel.

371. Moisture is in water, space is in the sky, sweetness is in
sugar; in these there is no separation.

372. Flames and fire are one, lotus petals are one with the
flower, and the branches and the fruit of a tree are the tree
itself.

373. The snow which is drawn to the mountain becomes part of
it; curds are but curdled milk.

374. Similarly the entire universe is but Myself; there is no
purpose in stripping the moon; [one would find but the
moon itself].

375. Ghi is clarified butter, in spite of its solidity; though a
bracelet is not melted down, it is still gold.

376. Even if a garment is not unravelled, it is still nothing but
woven threads; one need not crush a pot to see that it is
but earth.

377. Therefore do not think that I can only be found through
the dissolving of the universe, for I Myself am all.

378. To realize Me this manner is called single-hearted devotion;
if any sense of difference appears, it is an aberration.

379. Thus laying aside all sense of dualism, with an undivided
mind, thou mayest know Me as one with thyself.

380. O Pārtha, as gold is one with the ornament made from it,

so thou shouldst not regard thyself as different from the Self.

381. A ray may be emitted by light, but the ray is the light itself; in such a way shouldst thou conceive of Me.

382. Like an atom of dust on the earth, or a particle of snow on a snowy mountain, so thou shouldst realize that thou art in Me.

383. However small a wave may be, it is not different from the ocean; nor is there any difference between Me and the Universal Self.

384. When the vision is illuminated by the experience of oneness, we say that this is devotion.

385. This vision is the excellence of knowledge and the whole essence of yoga.

386. O Warrior, this is as continuous a process as the flow of water between the raincloud and the ocean.

387. Such a man becomes united with the Supreme as there is no boundary between the air in the mouth of a well and the firmament above it.

388. This union of the self with Brahma is as the light of the sun which extends from its reflection in water right up to the sun itself.

389. Thus when this consciousness of union takes place, along with that experience even the sense of union itself is lost.

390. When a grain of salt has melted into the water of the ocean, O Pāndava, the process of melting ceases with it.

391. When fire has burnt up grass the fire itself burns out and awareness of duality is lost, not even the knowledge of it remains.

392. Any thought that I am beyond the qualities while My devotee is still subject to them passes away and the sense of timeless union becomes clear.

393. There is no more any meaning in saying that such a man overcomes the qualities, O Kiriti; rather, the bond of individuality is loosened.

394. In short, O wise one, this state is the nature of Brahma, and he who worships Me in this way attains to it.

395. For one who, possessing these attributes, is devoted to Me while in this world, this state of being Brahma is like being a devoted wife.

396. As when the turbulent waters of the Ganges flow onward they have no other end but oneness with the ocean,

397. so, O Kiriti, one who serves me with this enlightened vision is the crest jewel on the crown of the state of Brahma.

398. O Pārtha, this state is that of absorption into Brahma, known as the last of the four goals of man's existence.

399. Worship of Me is the ladder by which this state is reached; from this it may seem to thee that I am a means to that end,

400. but do not let this thought enter thy mind, for Brahma is not different from Me.

> XXVII. *For I am the abode of Brahman, the Immortal and the Imperishable, of eternal law and of absolute bliss.*

401. O wise one, the moon and its sphere are not different, nor am I separate from Brahma.

402. O Beloved, that Brahma is eternal, changeless, the essence of righteousness, limitless joy and one without a second.

403. I am that goal which is the end of the path of discrimination, the boundless essence of truth; I am indeed all this.

404. Thus the matchless friend of devotees spoke to Pārtha, the wielder of the bow. Hear, O King.

405. Then Dhritarāshtra said, O Sanjaya, why hast thou related all this to me unasked?

406. Remove my anxiety and tell me news of victory. Sanjaya said, Leave this matter aside.

407. Then Sanjaya, feeling surprised, sighed and said impatiently to himself, How far is the King separated from the divine!

408. May the gracious Lord have mercy on him, may he be filled with discrimination and be healed of this great sickness of confusion.

409. Reflecting thus and listening to the discussion between the Lord and Arjuna, great joy poured into the heart [of Sanjaya].

410. So with great delight he will continue to tell what the Lord said.

411. Jnānadeva, the disciple of Nivritti, says, Listen to me and I will impress on your mind the meaning of the Lord's words.

In the Upanishad of the Bhagavadgitā, the science of the Absolute, the scripture of Yoga and the dialogue between Shri Krishna and Arjuna, this is the fourteenth chapter entitled The Yoga of the Differentiation of the Three Modes.

NOTES

1. *Durva grass.* A special kind of grass, said to be immortal; couch-grass. Here it is used to express 'blessing upon blessing'.
2. *the foetus.* This term is here used to cover all forms of natal processes. Cf. Ch. VII, v. 23.
3. *The modifications of goodness.* The eight 'moods' which have an effect on the physical body.
4. *thirty-six principles.* Cf. Ch. XI, note 20.
5. *Ashvamedha.* The 'horse sacrifice', mainly performed by those of kingly rank.
6. *signs of depravity.* The reference here is to bones which lie about in the quarters of a village where outcastes live.

CHAPTER XV

---

1. Now on the pedestal of my heart I will place the feet of my Guru,
2. and pouring my senses as flowers into the cupped hands of the experience of union with the Supreme, I make the offering of a handful of these at his feet.
3. My desire, washed clean by the pure water of devotion, will be as sandal-wood ointment.
4. Making anklets of the pure gold of my love for him, I will adorn with them his beautiful feet.
5. My strong, pure and single-hearted devotion to him will be as a pair of rings for his two big toes.
6. I will place on them the bud of pure emotions, with the fragrance of bliss, the full-blown eight-petalled lotus.
7. Then I will burn before him the incense of egotism, wave round him the lamp of union with the Self and embrace him with the experience of oneness with Brahma.
8. I will put on his holy feet the two sandals of my body and my vital breath, and will wave around them the neem leaves of experience and liberation.
9. May I be worthy of the feet of the Guru by which I may attain all the goals of man's existence,
10. by which that clear knowledge will be gained which leads to the resting-place in Brahma and which transform speech into an ocean of nectar.
11. This good fortune brings forth such eloquence in all the words that thousands of full-moons should salute it.
12. As the sun, rising in the east, sheds its glorious rays of light over the earth, so does language become like a festival of the light of knowledge to the hearers.
13. Through this good fortune the eloquence is such that the divine resonance is diminished by it; the highest beatitude cannot compare with its beauty.

14. In the arbour of the joy of hearing, the world enjoys the spring time of wisdom and so the creeper of his speech blossoms forth.

15. Words then reveal the nature of that Divine Being which causes speech and mind to withdraw, failing to comprehend it. What marvel is this!

16. That Being which is beyond knowing, unattainable by meditation and not perceptible to the senses, is revealed in his words.

17. When the devotee receives the blessing in the form of the pollen falling from the lotus-like feet of the Guru there comes to him this wonderful power of speech.

18. Nothing further need be said. Jnānadeva says, This good fortune has come to none other than to me.

19. For I am as the tender child of my guru, who has no other Son, and his whole blessing is poured out on me.

20. As a cloud pours out its full showers for the chātaka bird, so my guru has done this for me.

21. So my untrained tongue has been set free and has been touched by the sweetness of the Gitā.

22. For a man of good fortune even sand is changed into jewels, and if a man is destined to remain alive, even one about to kill him will treat him with affection.

23. If the Lord wishes to save a hungry man, even sand boiled in water will turn into the sweetest rice.

24. So when the guru accepts a man as his own, this earthly existence becomes for him a life of liberation.

25. See how the Lord, the ancient one worshipped by the whole universe, removed all the short-comings of Arjuna.

26. Similarly my guru, Shri Nivrittirāja, has raised my ignorance to the state of knowledge.

27. But enough of this! My love for him grows more intense as I speak; where can be found the knowledge with which to describe the glory of the guru.

28. By his grace I will clasp the feet of you saintly men with my exposition of the Gitā.

29. The Lord of liberation has treated this subject at the end of the fourteenth chapter.

30. Only he who has found spiritual wisdom is able to reach liberation, as a man who performs a hundred sacrifices can ascend to heaven.

31. Only the man who throughout a hundred lives performs

Brāhmanic rites attains to the world of Brahma; none other can achieve this.

32. As it is only a man with sight who can enjoy the light of the sun, so is the sweetness of liberation tasted only through this wisdom.

33. When we consider who is worthy to attain to this knowledge we see that there is only one such man.

34. In order to discover treasures hidden in the earth, a special pigment must be applied [to the eyes], but even then the eyes must be those of a man born with his feet first.[1]

35. It is similarly true that knowledge will enable a man to gain liberation, but nevertheless his mind must be pure so that it will remain with him.

36. Without dispassion knowledge cannot endure; this truth has been established by the Lord after much thought.

37. Now the omniscient Hari has shown us the nature of that dispassion which takes possession of the mind.

38. If a man who is eating realizes that the food is poisoned, he will push away the dish;

39. so when a man realizes how transient this whole earthly existence is, he turns to dispassion.

40. In the parable of a tree the nature of impermanence will be explained by the Lord of the universe in the fifteenth chapter.

41. This tree of worldly existence is not an ordinary tree that falls down when it is uprooted and soon dries up.

42. And so by means of a simile the Lord removes [the necessity of] the cycle of birth and death.

43. The fifteenth chapter will show the deceptive nature of worldly existence and the way in which individuality may be merged in Brahma.

44. This is the essence of the teachings given in this chapter; I will expound them, I pray you to listen with all your heart.

45. The Lord of Dwārkā, the Ocean of the Highest joy, the Moon of the full-moon day, speaks thus:[2]

The Blessed Lord said:

   1. They speak of the imperishable ashvattham [pipal tree] as having its root above and branches below. Its leaves are the Vedas and he who knows this is the knower of the Vedas.

46. O son of Pāndu, that delusion of the universe, that hinders the seeker from reaching the home of Self-realization,

47. is to be thought of as a great tree, and not as earthly life in the form of an extended universe.

48. It is not like a common tree, having its roots in the earth and its branches pointing upwards, and for this reason none can describe it.

49. When fire or axe is applied to its trunk, however large it is, what will happen to its higher growth?

50. When its roots are torn up, it will fall with all its branches; but the tree of earthly existence is different; it is not so easily brought down.

51. O Arjuna, it is wonderful indeed that the growth of this tree is downwards.

52. No one knows how high the sun is, and yet its rays descend in every direction. This tree of earthly existence is the same, with its shoots growing downwards.

53. It penetrates all that is and is not, as the firmament will be submerged in the final deluge.

54. This tree pervades the whole of space as after sunset darkness night is filled with darkness.

55. There is neither fruit to taste nor flowers to give out fragrance; and yet, O son of Pāndu, the tree is all that is.

56. Though its roots point upwards, it is not uprooted, and moreover it is always green.

57. Though it is true to say that its roots are upwards it has also many roots which grow downwards.

58. Having roots which grow from its branches, like the pipal or banyan tree, it spreads vigorously in all directions.

59. In such a way, O conqueror of wealth, this tree of worldly existence not only has branches which grow downwards,

60. but in a strange way it has groups of well-developed branches which grow upwards.

61. It is as if space had grown into a creeper, or the wind itself had taken on the shape of a tree; as though the three conditions of waking, sleeping and dreaming had set in.

62. Thus the whole extent of the universe has taken on the form of a great tree with its roots extending upwards.

63. Now what is it that is upwards, what are the characteristics of the roots, and what is the nature of the downward growing branches?

64. Again, what are the roots of this tree below and the branches above?

65. Why has it been called the Ashvattha Tree, the name given to it by those who delight in the knowledge of Brahma?[3]

66. All this will I explain to thee in simple style that thy understanding may develop.

67. Therefore listen, O most fortunate one; thou art worthy to hear this; let thy body be all ears, listen with all thy heart.

68. When the Lord of the Yādavas had spoken these words, moved by his affection, Arjuna became the embodiment of attention.

69. What the Lord said seemed almost insignificant compared with Arjuna's eagerness to listen, as though the heaven were to be embraced by the ten directions.

70. He was like a second Agastya in that he strove to drink in one gulp the whole ocean of Krishna's explanation.[4]

71. When Krishna saw this overwhelming eagerness in Arjuna he encircled him with his own delight.

72. Then Krishna said, O Arjuna, Brahma is the upper part of this tree, and the quality of being uppermost is ascribed to it only in relation to the rest of the tree.

73. In reality there are no such distinctions as upper, lower or middle, for there is an indivisible unity in Brahma.

74. That which is the inaudible essence of all sounds, the fragrance of flowers imperceptible to the senses, that element in joy which is beyond the experience of sexual and other pleasures;

75. which is the same both near and far, in front and behind, which is the invisible witness of all and yet without sight,

76. and which becomes manifest in the world of name and form, still further affected by the limitation of illusion.

77. This is pure knowledge, yet without either the knower or the object of knowledge, the heaven filled with the pure quintessence of joy.

78. This Brahma is indeed the upper part of the tree and the roots of the tree sprout from this part in the following manner.

79. These shoots are known as Māyā; but in reality Māyā both is and is not and is as impossible to describe as the offspring of a barren woman.[5]

80. She neither exists nor does not exist, she cannot tolerate the idea of thought; this is her nature, and is thought of as eternal.

81. She is the seed of the tree of this earthly existence, the soil in which it is planted, and the lamp of all false knowledge.

82. She is the treasure-chest of all forces, the sky in which arises the cloud of the universe and the fold of the cloth of all that has form.

83. This Māyā abides in Brahma and therefore both is and is not; then only does the splendour of Brahma become manifest.

84. As a man who falls asleep loses consciousness, as the soot of a lamp dims its light,

85. as a young wife, sleeping beside her husband may suddenly waken him and even embrace him in a dream though not actually, and thus excite his passion,

86. so dies māyā arise in Brahma, O conqueror of wealth, and ignorance, the failure to recognize whence she comes is the first root of this tree.

87. This lack of awareness of Brahma, the Reality, is the root set deep in the upper part; in the Vedānta this is described as the existence of the seed.

88. The deep sleep of ignorance is called the seed-condition, while the dream state and the waking condition are the fruit.

89. This is the way in which it is explained in the Vedānta; but let this be, here we consider ignorance to be the root.

90. Above in the pure Spirit, roots sprout upwards and downwards, held in the strong grip of māyā.

91. Then the first innumerable forms of thought arise and their shoots grow downwards on all four sides.

92. Thus the tree of existence has its roots firmly established in the upper part and from those clusters of roots appear offshoots.

93. Then the first of the great elements, intellect, sprouts in consciousness and a tender leaf grows from it.

94. Out of this springs the three-leafed shoot, growing downwards as individual consciousness with its three qualities, goodness, passion and darkness.

95. From this again shoots forth the branch called reason, the sense of duality is developed from which grows naturally the branch called the mind.

96. Thus the root having gained strength from the sap of thought, from it grow four tender shoots which are the fourfold consciousness.[6]

97. After these grow up the straight stems of the five great elements, space, air, fire, water and earth.

98. From this fivefold stem the tender inner leaves of the five senses of hearing, sight, touch, taste and smell break out.

99. First appears sound, and the sense of hearing grows by reaching out eagerly towards it.

100. Then the creeper of the skin sends out the tendril of touch and from this arise all manner of new sensations.

101. Following this a leaf of form develops and the eye reaches out towards the enjoyment of it, spreading wide confusion.

102. As sprigs of taste grow apace leaves of many and various desires are excited in the tongue.

103. Then, through the sprouting of fragrance, shoots of the sense of smell grow strong and intense desire is aroused.

104. In this way from the great first principle, individuality, mind and the primal elements, the bonds of earthly life, are developed.

105. In short, though this tree expands throughout the eightfold division of nature, still in the same way as the apparent silver in a shell only seems to be silver on account of its base in the shell.

106. The waves of the ocean spread only as far as the ocean extends; so is Brahma manifested in the shape of this tree which is born of ignorance.

107. All this expanse [of the tree] is only the one Brahma in outward manifestation, as in a dream a man may become many persons though in reality he is but one.

108. This is enough. In this way does this strange tree grow and send down its shoots in the form of mahat and the other principles of matter.[7]

109. Now listen; I will explain why this tree is called Ashvattha by the wise.

110. [the 'shva' in]' ashvattha' means 'tomorrow', for it does not continue; there is no permanence in this tree of worldly life.[8]

111. As clouds in the sky change their colour every moment, as lightning is never still even for an instant,

112. as a drop of water on a trembling lotus petal cannot remain steady and the mind of a troubled man is restless,

113. so is the condition of this tree; it is in a constant state of degeneration and therefore it is said to be 'not remaining until tomorrow'.

114. Now Ashvattha is a name also applied to the pipal tree, but the Lord does not use it in this sense.

115. Though it is not inappropriate to call it the pipal tree, but let that be; we are not concerned here with popular usage.

116. Listen rather to the mystery of it. It is called Ashvattha because of its transitory nature.

117. Another important point is that it is also known as Avyaya, the imperishable one; the inner meaning of this is that,

118. since on the one hand the clouds draw their water from the ocean, and on the other the rivers replenish it,

119. there is neither increase nor decrease in its volume which seems to remain constant, but only as long as rivers and clouds work together in this way.

120. This tree is also popularly called Avyaya because its creation and passing away happen with a speed that is imperceptible.

121. Or again, as a charitable man appears to be saving even while he is spending, so in its constant destruction this tree seems to be indestructible.

122. Owing to their great speed the wheels of a coach seem not to be moving but to be stuck in the earth;

123. so as time passes, where branches of the tree wither and drop away, numberless other shoots break out;

124. and yet it is impossible to say when anyone disappears or when others sprout forth, like clouds in the sky during the month of Āshādha.[9]

125. Similarly at the end of a great age existing worlds pass away and multitudes of others spring up in their stead.

126. The fierce whirlwinds of the final dissolution destroy the trees of earthly life [of one cycle], and again thousands of trees [of the new cycle] spring up.

127. The era of one Manu follows that of another, races succeed each other, as in the sugar-cane plant one joint rises above another in the course of its growth.[10]

128. At the end of the Kali yuga the dry bark of the trees of the four ages falls off and at once the great trees of the Krita yuga begin to appear.[11]

129. As one year passes away, the next is called in; as one day follows another; yet one is hardly aware of it.

130. One cannot discern the point at which one breeze passes into another; nor can one tell how many branches of the tree fall and how many take their place.

131. As soon as one branch, in the form of a body, breaks off another grows, and this makes the tree of existence seem to be eternal.

132. A stream of water flows rapidly onwards and joins another stream; so, though unreal, this growth of the tree of existence is thought to be real.

133. Countless waves rise and fall on the ocean during the flick of an eyelid, but to one who does not know it seems like one continuous wave.

134. A crow has only one eye with a pupil, but when it moves its eyes cleverly in both directions, people are deluded into thinking that it has a pupil in both eyes.

135. When a top is spinning rapidly, it seems to be fixed to the ground; it is the great speed which gives this impression.

136. This is enough! When a burning torch is swung round in the dark it looks like a circle of fire;

137. so does this tree of earthly existence appear to the ignorant to be indestructible, though it is constantly being created and destroyed.

138. The man who recognizes that this is due to speed, however, and who knows that it is transitory, realizes that worlds arise and pass away innumerable times in a single moment,

139. who knows that it has no other source but ignorance, and that the existence of this decaying tree is an illusion,

140. is a wise man, O Son of Pāndu, and I the omniscient one say that he is to be revered as though he were the sacred teaching itself.

141. He alone is worthy to experience the fruit of all kinds of yoga; indeed, wisdom itself lives through him.

142. Enough has been said. Who can possibly describe the man who has realized the illusory nature of this tree of existence.

> 11. *Its branches extend below and above, nourished by the modes, with sense objects for its twigs and below, in the world of men, stretch forth the roots resulting in actions.*

143. Out of this tree of worldly existence with its branches growing downwards, there are also many branches growing straight upwards.

144. Those spreading downwards serve as roots and from their bases creepers and leaves sprout.

145. All this has been already explained at the beginning; but now listen while I explain it in simpler language.

146. Gathering up ignorance, the binding root, the power of the primary elements and the greatness of the Vedas,

147. from the trunk of the tree there spring four great branches, the four classes called sweat-born, womb-born, seed-born and egg-born.

148. From each of these shoots, eighty-four lakhs of smaller species come into being, and from them also grow innumerable shoots of individual lives.

149. These four straight branches also produce cross branches of creatures of various smaller classes.

150. Then appear clusters such as the divisions of man, woman, and creatures devoid of sex, with quivering bodies on account of the burden of their passions.

151. As the rainy season spreads throughout the sky in rain-clouds, so the creeper of all these forms spreads itself through ignorance.

152. Then, bending through the weight of the branches, they become entangled together, and this gives rise to the winds of excitement through the qualities.

153. So on account of the great struggle among the qualities, the upward-pointing roots grow in three directions.

154. When the wind of passion blows more strongly the small branches in the form of the human species thrive.

155. These do not shoot upwards nor downwards, but remain in the centre and grow as cross-branches of the four castes.

156. These branches then send out the tender foliage of prescribed and prohibited actions and the fresh leaves of the Vedic rules enhances their beauty.

157. From them arise the forests of desire and passion and the momentary pleasure derived from these.

158. Through the desire of māyā to expand, the shoots of good and evil deeds develop and innumerable offshoots of various activities appear.

159. Then as the human bodies, like decaying tree trunks, fall away, exhausted by past experiences, other sprouts of new bodies appear in their place.

160. And the beauty of the foliage of sense objects is constantly

renewed by the lovely tones of sound and the other senses.

161. In this way, with the strong wind of passion, the bowers of branches representing human life increases; this is known as the world of men.

162. As soon as the wind of passion dies down for a moment the hurricane of darkness begins to blow.

163. Then from those human branches base desires appear below, sending out shoots in the form of evil actions.

164. Twisted shoots of sloth break out and leaves and tendrils of error appear.

165. On the tips of the leaves of the precepts and prohibitions of the Rigveda, Yajurveda and Sāmaveda are heard humming.[12]

166. These produce the creeper of desire in the form of the precepts of the Atharvaveda, which teach about killing and incantation.

167. Meanwhile strong roots of evil actions are forming and branches of rebirth are increasing.

168. Deluded evildoers are trapped by the branches of all kinds of wickedness such as are committed by men of the lower castes.

169. Then there are the side growths of still lower species such as the beast, the bird, the pig, the tiger, the scorpion and the snake.

170. But, O Pāndava, branches grow out on all sides, of which the fruit is the perpetual experience of hell.

171. More and more shoots break out from recurring births due to evil deeds led by violence and sexual indulgence.

172. These in turn become trees, grass, iron, clods of earth or stone; such is the fruit of these branches.

173. Listen, O Arjuna, in this way the downward growth of the tree ranges from man to the inanimate world.

174. So therefore, the branches of humanity may be regarded as the downward growing roots by which the tree of worldly existence spreads.

175. On the other hand, O Pārtha, if we look at the chief root growing upwards we will find that the middle branch of humanity is the origin of it.

176. Between the downward and upward growing branches rise those produced by good and evil deeds resulting from the qualities of goodness and darkness.

177. Moreover, O Arjuna, the leaves of the three Vedas cannot grow elsewhere than here, as their precepts are not relevant to any beings except men.

178. So that though in terms of the human body these upward growing roots are branches, in terms of the development of action they are roots.

179. The roots of ordinary trees deepen as the branches grow, and the branches spread as the roots develop.

180. The same is true of the body, that so long as there is activity the body remains in the world and so long as there is a body there is activity. This cannot be denied.

181. It is for this reason that the Father of all men has said that the human body is the cause of all activity; there is no doubt about this.

182. At times when the fierce gale of darkness ceases the whirlwind of the quality of goodness rushes in.

183. Then this root of the human form produces blades of good desire, growing into sprouts of good action.

184. Through awakening knowledge and with the force of keen understanding, intellect immediately sends out abundant offshoots.

185. From this shining leaves of respect, pregnant with the sap of understanding, straight shoots of righteousness sprout.

186. Abundant shoots of good conduct spring from these and the sound of the Vedic hymns vibrates through them.

187. Such discipline as the Vedas prescribe and rites of sacrifices are some of the leaves which extend from these branches.

188. On the branches of self-restraint and control of the senses appear clusters of penance, spreading tenderly over the boughs of non-attachment.

189. Steady sharp pointed shoots of special vows rise upwards with the speed of creation.

190. Among these is the thick foliage of the Vedas which, while the strong wind of righteousness blows through it, resounds with right knowledge.

191. The branch of religious duty spreads out with the branch of life in the world, bearing on its cross branches the fruit of heavenly enjoyment.

192. Next to these the reddened branch of dispassion grows out and the branch of religion and liberation on which ever new tender leaves unfold.

193. In the extended transverse branches are the sun, moon and all the major planets, the ancestors, rishis and demi-gods.
194. Above these are the great branches of Indra and other gods, their stems laden with fruit.
195. Still higher are those of the sages Marichi, Kashyapa and others who reached the highest rank in penance and wisdom.
196. Thus the spread of the upward growing branches rises higher and higher, with small stems and pointed tips, bearing abundant fruit.
197. O Kiriti, from the fruit-laden bows which are above these upper branches come the tender shoots of Brahma and Shiva.
198. Weighed down by fruit the upper branches bend downwards so that they rest on the roots.
199. Trees are bent low towards their roots when the branches are laden with fruit,
200. with increasing knowledge this tree of Life is bowed down to rest on its own roots.
201. There is therefore no growth beyond Brahmā and Shiva for the individual soul, for above them there is only Brahma, the One Spirit.
202. Those branches cannot be compared with the root of Māyā from which this tree springs.
203. The topmost branches representing Sanaka and other sages rise upwards unimpeded, for they have already reached Brahma.
204. It should be understood therefore that this tree grows from its roots in humanity and extends upwards to the highest level in Brahma and other deities.
205. Thus humanity is that from which the highest Brahma evolves and therefore it is called the root.

III. *Its real form is not thus perceived here, nor its end nor beginning nor its foundation. Having cut off this firm-rooted Aśvattham [peepal tree] with the strong sword of non-attachment.*

206. So then I have described to thee this wonderful tree of worldly existence,
207. I have also fully explained to thee those roots which go

downwards. Now listen to the way this tree can be up-rooted.

208. Well mayest thou ask how it would be possible to uproot such a great tree.

209. How can it be that the highest branches reach up to Brahma [the deity] and yet the roots are above in the formless Spirit?

210. The lowest branches reach down into depths of inorganic while other roots in the form of humanity grow in the middle.

211. Who could destroy a tree of such thickness and breadth? But do not concern thyself with such an idle question.

212. If this tree is to be uprooted would any effort be needed? One does not have to rush here and there to save a child from [its fear of] a goblin!

213. Does one have to destroy castles in the clouds, break the horns of a hare or pluck a flower growing in the sky?

214. In the same way, O Warrior, there is no reality in this tree of existence, so why shouldst thou concern thyself anxiously with the uprooting of it?

215. My description of the spread of its roots and branches is like some one trying to describe a house full of the children of a barren woman.

216. Of what use are the words uttered in a dream when we waken? All talk of this tree is as meaningless as a fairy tale.

217. Therefore, O conqueror of wealth, the form of the tree as I have described it is an illusion; it would be like serving a king with ghi made from the milk of a tortoise.

218. Ignorance, the root of the tree, is unreal, so the effects of it can scarcely be real; how then can the tree itself really exist?

219. Some say that the tree has no end, and in one sense this is true.

220. If there were no waking there would be no end to sleep, nor would there be any dawn if night did not pass.

221. Similarly, O Pārtha, till discrimination is aroused, there will be no end to this tree of earthly existence.

222. Those who say that it has no beginning do not make a false statement.

223. Who can say who is the mother of an unborn child? How then can that which has no being have a beginning?

224. Why then consider the efforts of uprooting this tree, as it
has neither beginning, end, existence or form?

225. O Kiriti, it is on account of our ignorance that this illusory
tree thrives, so strike it down with the sword of self-
knowledge.

226. If thou do use any other means except self-knowledge
thou wilt become more deeply entangled in it.

227. How far then wilt thou wander through branch after
branch, upwards and downwards? Strike down ignorance
therefore, by means of true knowledge.

228. Otherwise thou wilt be like a man uselessly burdened with
sticks he has collected for beating a rope he has mistaken
for a serpent.

229. Indeed, it would be like a man drowning in a river while
he is running round a forest seeking a boat in which to
cross over the mirage of a river.

230. Similarly, O warrior, when a man strives after a way of
destroying this illusion of worldly life, his own true nature
is hidden and he is overcome by frustration.

231. O winner of wealth, waking up is the only remedy for a
wound felt in a dream, and in this case also, knowledge
is the only weapon with which ignorance can be destroyed.

232. In order that the sword of knowledge may be effective the
mind must be governed by strong and enduring dispassion.

233. When this dispassion is developed, [pleasures of] the three
worlds will be abandoned as a dog may vomit its food.

234. O Pārtha, dispassion must be so strong that there will be a
disgust for all worldly enjoyment.

235. Draw this sword from the scabbard of egoism it should
immediately be held in the hand of self-knowledge.

236. It should be sharpened on the stone of discrimination, and
a keen edge given to it by awareness of unity with Brahma
and polished with perfect understanding.

237. Holding it firmly in the grip of determination and observed
closely, let it be well tested in meditation.

238. When this sword of dispassion and consciousness of the
Self become united in constant meditation, there will be
nothing left to strike.

239. The sword of self-knowledge, strengthened by the radiance
of belief in non-duality, will not allow this tree of existence
to survive in any place.

240. Then this tree, with its upward growing branches and roots

and the network of branches extending downwards, will
disappear as a mirage vanishes in the moonlight.

241. Therefore, O lord among warriors, strike down the upper
roots of this tree of earthly existence with the sword of self-
knowledge.

> IV. *Then, that path must be sought from which those who
> have reached it never return, saying 'I seek refuge only in
> that Primal Person from whom has come forth this ancient
> current of the world' [this cosmic process].*

242. Then a sense of identity is realized in relation to things
which were formerly experienced as different from oneself,
and one becomes aware of one's true nature.

243. Do not become like fools who look at their faces in a mirror
and see two where there is only one.

244. In this way I am telling thee clearly how thou shouldst see
thyself from the point of view of non-duality.

245. That which is seen without seeing and known without
knowing is called Brahma, the primal being.

246. The Vedas take their stand on the limitations of Brahma
and strive to describe him in long drawn-out sentences,
speaking vainly of name and form.

247. It is he whom those who are weary of earthly and heavenly
pleasures and seek for liberation set out to find, resorting
to yogic practice and knowledge, with the purpose of not
returning to worldly existence.

248. Fleeing from attachment to worldly life in the boat of dispassion they reach the shore of the state of Brahma and
escape from the bonds of action.

249. Shaking off all moods such as egoism, the wise take as it
were a passport to their original home.

250. Ignorance of this Brahma has led to the false knowledge
which has spread throughout the world, giving rise to the
concept of duality.

251. From him there develops this expanding system of worlds
which is like the empty hope of an unlucky man.

252. O Pārtha, we should realize that this Brahma is our own
self, as though cold could shiver with its own coldness.

253. O winner of wealth, there is another sign by which this
state can be recognized; having once attained to it, there is
no return in rebirth.

254. Those who are filled with the knowledge of the Self as the fullness of the waters at the time of the final deluge, reach the state of Brahma.

> v. *Those, who are freed from pride and delusion, who have conquered the evil of attachment, who, all desires stilled, are ever devoted to the Supreme Spirit, who are liberated from the dualities of pleasure and pain and are undeluded, go to that eternal state.*

255. Those men who have freed their minds of all confusion as the clouds leave the sky at the end of the rainy season,

256. and who have thrown off the grip of passion as the family of a hard-hearted man is loathed by his family when he is poverty-stricken,

257. so, too, do those who earnestly seek for self-realization turn away from all action, as a plantain-tree falls when it has borne fruit.

258. All desires leave them, as birds will fly away from a tree that is on fire.

259. They are unaware even of the name of separateness, the soil from which sprout all manner of evil weeds.

260. Egoism and ignorance leave them as night flies at the rise of the sun.

261. As the body suddenly releases the lifeless soul, the ignorance of duality departs from them.

262. To them the sense of duality is as a famine; the touchstone brings destruction to iron, and the sun and darkness cannot exist together.

263. The pairs of opposites, such as pleasure and pain, which are experienced in physical life, cannot exist in their presence.

264. When a man is awake the kingdom that he possessed or the death he experienced in a dream do not bring him joy nor sorrow.

265. Such men cannot be caught up in the experience of pleasure and pain, which bring about the opposites of merit and demerit, as an eagle cannot be grasped by a snake.

266. They are like the royal swans, feeding on the milk of the knowledge of the Self, having separated it from the water of the non-self.

267. As the sun, having poured down its radiance on the earth, draws it back into itself through its rays,

268. so, also, the vision of the Self brings back into unity that One Spirit which, owing to confusion about its true nature, has seemed to be scattered in all directions [in the multiplicity of beings].

269. As the stream of a river merges into the ocean, so in these men discrimination is absorbed into the certainty of Self-realization.

270. Nothing is left to be desired by those who have realized that the one Self exists in all, as the sky has no need to move from one place to another.

271. Seed cannot germinate in a mountain of fire, nor can any feeling arise in their minds.

272. But why continue this any further? Objects of sense have no effect on them, as atoms of dust cannot remain steady before a strong wind.

273. They who have sacrificed every desire in the fire of wisdom are united with the fire, as gold unites with gold in one piece.

274. Shouldst thou ask where they go to, I tell thee that they go to the place where there is no loss.

275. It cannot be seen by the eye, it cannot be known, nor can it be described.

> VI. *The sun does not illumine That, nor the moon nor the fire. That is My supreme abode from which those who reach it never return.*

276. No flame of a lamp can lighten That, neither the beams of the moon or the brilliance of the sun.

277. All things are seen by this light which itself is not seen; the world is illuminated by its hidden light.

278. The more a shell is covered with silver the more it seems to be true silver rather than a shell; the more a rope is hidden beneath a snake, the more strongly it resembles a snake.

279. The light by which the sun and moon and great planets give forth their brightness, and even by whose darkness they shine,

280. that Brahma, is light itself, active in the spirit within all creatures and which shines also in the heart of the sun and moon.

281. Compared with That the light of the sun and moon is but darkness, and the brilliance of all lights is but the body of that Brahma.

282. In its light the whole universe with all the suns and moons vanish as the light of the moon and stars fades away when the sun rises.
283. In the same way the images in a dream pass away on waking and mirages disappear in the evening.
284. So know thou that in that invisible place of Brahma is My chief abode.
285. They who have gone to that place return no more, like the waters of rivers which flow down into the sea.
286. An elephant made of salt and put into the sea can never resume its form;
287. flames rising into the sky do not descend again, water in contact with hot iron ceases to exist as water.
288. So they who reach union with Me, through pure knowledge, can never return to this world.
289. [Hearing these words] that king of the world of understanding, Arjuna, said, O Lord, I have a question to ask; I entreat thee to listen with attention.
290. Are those who attain to union with Thee, and do not return separate from Thee or one with Thee?
291. It is inconsistent to say that those who were separate from Thee originally do not return. Do bees that enter flowers ever become flowers?
292. Arrows that are separate from a target hit it and then fall away; so, surely those [who reach Thee] will return.
293. If however they are one with Thee in their nature, who merges into whom? Can a weapon pierce itself?
294. It cannot be said therefore that the souls who are separate from thee are united with Thee or are separate from Thee. Are the limbs separate from the body?
295. And they who are eternally different from Thee can never become united with Thee; why therefore is there this confusion as to whether they return or do not return?
296. O Thou who dost face in all directions, explain to me who they are that, having been united with Thee, do not return.
297. On hearing Arjuna's question, the Lord, the highest jewel among the wise, was delighted, realizing the intelligence of his disciple.
298. Then the Lord said, O high-souled one, among those who reach Me and do not return, there are two kinds of men, those who are one with Me and those who are separate from Me.

299. Though, speaking superficially, they seem to be different from Me, deeper insight will show that they are one with Me.

300. Waves on the surface of the ocean seem to be different from it, but they are of the same clear water.

301. Gold in the shape of ornaments appears to be different from it, yet [when they are looked at] they are seen to be all gold.

302. So, O Kiriti, to the eye of wisdom all beings are one with Me, and yet this separateness arises from ignorance.

303. When considered with insight into reality, how can there be anything other than Me, the One? If there is, it arises from the dual operation of oneness and difference.

304. When the sun, swallowing up the whole of space, pervades the universe, how can its reflection of its rays be separately distinguished?

305. O winner of wealth, when the final deluge takes place at the end of an age, would it be possible to distinguish separate streams? In the same way can there be separate parts of Me, who am changeless?

306. Owing to the windings of its course the steady stream of a river appears to be bent; because of [its reflection in] water, the sun seems to be double.

307. Could one say that the firmament is either round or square yet it may be so when it is enclosed in a house or a jar.

308. Whilst asleep a man invests himself, in his dream, with royalty; does not he alone fill the whole world?

309. By mixing alloy with it gold loses some of its value though in itself still pure; in the same way, when I who am pure am surrounded by the illusion that I create,

310. then ignorance dominates all. Because of this, doubt arises as to who I am, and in men's thought I am identified with the body.

> VII. *A fragment of My own self, having become a living soul, eternal, in the world of life, draws to itself the senses, of which the mind is the sixth, that rest in nature.*

311. Thus when knowledge of the Self is limited to the body, then on account of this limitation it seems as though the Self is a part of Me.

312. When the sea, owing to the force of the wind, rises in waves, they appear to be small parts of it,

313. and in the same way, O son of Pāndu, I am thought to be, in this world, the individual soul giving life to the body and generating egoism.

314. All the outwardly perceptible activities promoted by consciousness are referred to as the world of living beings.

315. I regard the belief in the reality of the processes of birth and death as inherent in the world of living creatures.

316. Thou shouldst consider that in this world of life I am like the moon, which though reflected in water is unaffected by it.

317. O Pāndava, a piece of crystal lying on a red powder will seem to be red, but it is not really so.

318. In this way My eternal nature is not affected, nor is My state of changelessness disturbed, but through delusion I am regarded as the one who acts and experiences.

319. Briefly, the pure Spirit on coming into contact with Nature takes upon itself the qualities that belong to it.

320. Accepting as its own the mind and the other senses such as hearing and their activities, the individual soul enters into action.

321. As an ascetic, dreaming that he has a family, is carried away by the delusion and begins to engage in worldly activities,

322. so the self, forgetful of its real nature, imagines that it is nature and serves her accordingly.

323. Seated in the vehicle of the mind and passing through the gateway of the ear, it finds itself in a forest of words;

324. or taking the bridle of nature, it enters the dense jungle of touch through the pathway of the skin.

325. At times it goes out through the doors of the eyes and wanders over the hills of sense objects;

326. or, good warrior, it passes out along the path of the tongue and enters the valley of taste;

327. or this lord of the body strays away in the desert of fragrance by the gate of his nose.

328. Thus it enjoys sense objects, speech and the other senses, taking with it mind, the leader of all the senses.

> VIII. *When the lord takes up a body and when he leaves it, he takes these [the senses and mind] and goes even as the wind carries perfumes from their places.*

329. The self appears to engage in action and experience only when it enters into possession of a body.

330. O winner of wealth, as the way of life of a princely man are known only when he begins to live in a palace,

331. so it is only when the self enters into a body egoism and action increase, and the pleasures of sense run riot. Know this for certain.

332. When it relinquishes the body, it carries away with it all the assemblage of the senses,

333. as dishonouring a guest brings to nought the merit of host, or as puppets cease to act when their guiding strings are removed.

334. The vision of men is carried away by the setting sun and the fragrance of flowers is dispersed by the wind.

335. Similarly, O winner of wealth, the self on quitting the body takes with it the mind and the five senses.

> IX. *He who enjoys the objects of the senses, using the ear, the eye, the touch sense and the nose as also the mind,*

336. Whenever the Spirit may enter a body, in earthly life or in heaven, it becomes endowed with a mind and the five senses.

337. O Pāndava, when a lamp is extinguished it takes its light with it; when it is relit, it gives out its light again.

338. But it is only to the sight of the unenlightened that this process seems to take place, O Kiriti.

339. They believe that when the Spirit enters a body it experiences the pleasure of sense, and then it leaves the body.

340. In reality, birth, death, action, and enjoyment are functions of nature, not of the self.

> X. *When He departs or stays or experiences, in contact with the modes, the deluded do not see [the indwelling soul] but they who have the eye of wisdom [or whose eye is wisdom] see.*

> XI. *The sages also striving perceive Him as established in the Self, but the unintelligent, whose souls are undisciplined, though striving, do not find Him.*

341. As soon as a body is produced and is endowed with consciousness, they are deluded by this process into thinking that the self has entered the body.

342. Further, O Lord of Subhadrā, when the senses become active in their own ways, it is thought that this is the experience of the Self.

343. When the body loses its power of enjoyment and dies they declare that the Spirit is gone, because they cannot see it.

344. O Pāndava, could one say that wind blows only when a tree sways, and that when there is no tree there is no wind?

345. Should we think that we exist only when we see our reflection in a mirror, and that before then we did not?

346. Or, if we reverse it and the reflection is hidden, do we claim that we have ceased to be?

347. Sound is a property of space but thunder is attributed to the clouds; and the moon is held responsible for the swift movement of clouds.

348. Those who are blinded by lack of discrimination attribute the birth and death of the body to the changeless Spirit.

349. There are others, though, who recognize the individual soul as being of Brahma and the properties of bodily life as being of the body.

350. These, with the eye of wisdom, see beyond the sheath of the body and, like the fierce rays of the sun in the hot weather,

351. these wise ones are able to concentrate their thought on Brahma through the development of insight and to recognize the Spirit.

352. The firmament is full of numberless stars that are reflected in the waters of the sea; but this does not mean that it has fallen to pieces.

353. The sky is still the sky and it is the reflection that is unreal. In the same way these men perceive that the spirit is encased in the body.

354. The movement of a flowing stream is in the stream itself, and moonlight is steady within the moon;

355. whether a pool is dry or full, the sun is still the same. Similarly they recognize Me whether the body is born or dies.

356. Earthen jars and houses of men are created and destroyed, but the air that they enclose remains unchanged.

357. So the wise recognize clearly as the eternal spirit that which those blinded by ignorance identify with the body which comes and goes.

358. Through their clear recognition of the Self they know that

the Spirit neither grows nor diminishes, neither acts nor promotes action.

359. Now even if all knowledge is mastered, every particle is accounted for and all scriptures grasped,

360. unless dispassion is developed in the mind, I, the all pervading one, cannot be reached.

361. O holder of the bow, even if a man were filled with all knowledge he could never reach Me, the purest of all beings, so long as there was any desire for pleasure in his heart.

362. Can one free oneself from the entanglement of worldly life with the knowledge acquired in a dream? Is the mere handling of books a substitute for reading them?

363. Could the quality and value of pearls be detected by the sense of smell of a blindfolded man?

364. Similarly, so long as egoism remains in the heart, no one can reach Me, even by diligent study of the scriptures throughout numberless lives.

365. I am He who pervades all living creatures; listen while I explain to thee this manifestation [of Myself].

> XII. *That splendour of the sun which illumines this world, that which is in the moon, that which is in the fire, thou shouldst know as Mine.*

366. The brilliance of the sun that illumines the whole universe is eternally Mine.

367. O son of Pāndu, Mine is the light of the sun which dries up water and the light of the moon which again [gives out moisture].

368. Mine too is the heat of the limitless fire which gives men warmth and cooks their food.

> XIII. *And entering the earth, I support all vital beings by My energy; and becoming the sapful soma [moon], I nourish all plants.*

369. I have entered into the earth, and that is the reason why its clods do not melt in the waters of the ocean.

370. It is because I am in the earth sustaining it that it is able to support the whole of creation.

371. O son of Pāndu, I am, as it were, a moving lake of nectar in the sky in the form of the moon.

372. With the rays of that moon falling in limitless streams, I bring sustenance to all vegetation.

373. Thus are produced crops of all kinds of grain that bring
food for every kind of living creature.

XIV. *Becoming the fire of life in the bodies of living
creatures and mingling with the upward and downward
breaths, I digest the four kinds of food.*

374. How can the food thus created be digested, so that it may
satisfy those who partake of it?
375. For this purpose, O Kiriti, I have lit a fire in the circle
round the navel of each living being and I am that fire in
the belly.
376. Fanning this fire with the bellows of the ingoing and outgoing breaths, great quantities of food can be consumed
in the belly day and night.
377. Whether food is dry or succulent, well-cooked or burnt up,
it is I who digest the fourfold food,
378. I am thus all creatures, the very life supporting all creatures and I am the inner fire which is the chief means of life.
379. How is it possible adequately to describe the mystery of
My all-pervasiveness? Thou shouldst know that I am in
every place and except Myself there is nothing else anywhere.
380. Then how does it come about that some beings are always
happy and others afflicted with misery?
381. If in a whole city the evening is illuminated by only one
lamp, will there not be some who cannot see?
382. I will try to remove any such doubts that may arise in thy
mind.
383. Though I am in all and this cannot be otherwise, each
being realizes Me according to his own intelligence.
384. Thou art concerned about all this; listen, there is but one
sound in space, yet different instruments are played and
they produce different notes.
385. Though there is but one sun which rises, it serves many
different purposes as men go about their various activities.
386. Water is needed for the growth of plants in accordance
with the seed planted, so My form develops in different
ways in each creature.
387. A necklace of blue beads looks different to a man with
knowledge and a man without; it brings joy to the first,
while the second may take it to be a snake.

388. As the water in the Svāti cluster of stars becomes pearls
in a shell, but is poison to a serpent; in the same way I am
a joy to the wise and misery to the ignorant.[13]

xv. *And I am lodged in the hearts of all; from Me are
memory and knowledge as well as their loss. I am indeed
He who is to be known by all the Vedas. I indeed [am] the
author of the Vedānta and I too the knower of the Vedas.*

389. O Pārtha, I am verily that knowledge in the heart of each
human being by which he is perpetually aware of his
individuality;
390. but through association with saintly people, the practice of
yoga, the acquisition of knowledge, service of the spiritual
teacher and dispassion,
391. through such good practices ignorance passes away entirely, and the individual soul finds rest in Brahma.
392. When through Me, the Self, he sees that I am his Self, he is
for ever happy. Can this realization be attained through
anyone else?
393. O winner of wealth, when the sun rises it is seen by means
of its own light and, in the same way, it is through Me
Myself that I am known.
394. On the other hand, if men associate with seekers after
sense pleasures and listen only to the praises of worldly
life, with their egoism centred entirely in the body
395. chasing along the path of action after the enjoyments of
this life and of the next, they cannot but inherit a liberal
share of sorrow.
396. Nevertheless, O Arjuna, I Myself am the cause of this
ignorance, as a man when awake is the cause of his own
sleep and dreams.
397. That the day is darkened by clouds is known by means of
the daylight, so I am the cause of that ignorance in men
through which they are unaware of Me and perceive objects
of sense.
398. O winner of wealth, is it not the condition of being awake
that causes the awareness of sleep? So am I the root of
knowledge and also of ignorance of men.
399. O winner of wealth, the Vedas, not knowing Me as I am but
striving to learn about Me, have been divided into various
branches.

400. Nevertheless I, the pure one, am known in all three branches, as all rivers flowing either from east or west fall into the ocean.

401. The Vedas with all their words culminate in the highest truth, as fragrance borne upwards on the wind is lost in the sky.

402. When all the Vedas are lost in shame, then it is I who reveal the truth as it is.

403. I alone am the one who has the knowledge of the Self in which both the Vedas and the universe are finally absorbed.

404. If a man is awakened from sleep he knows that there is no one else in dreams apart from himself, but realizes his own oneness.

405. I also am aware of My oneness without duality, and I Myself am the one who brings about that awareness.

406. O Warrior, as when camphor is burnt there remains neither soot nor fire,

407. So when the knowledge that destroys ignorance is itself absorbed it is impossible to say whether there is anything or whether there is not.

408. Who can catch that thief who has stolen the universe leaving no trace? I am that pure state in which there is such a one.

409. While the Lord of heaven was explaining in this way to Arjuna how He pervades all things, He ended His discourse.

410. This teaching was reflected in Arjuna's heart as the image of the rising moon appears mirrored on the ocean.

411. As on a wall the picture opposite to it may be reflected on it so the teachings of the Lord Vaikuntha were reflected in Arjuna.

412. The more the knowledge of the Self is realized, the greater is the joy caused by it, and therefore Arjuna, the man of deep perception, said to Krishna,

413. O thou who art infinite, while explaining to me Thy universal immanence Thou has spoken from time to time of Thy nature which is without attributes,

414. I ask Thee now to explain this fully to me. Thereupon the Lord of Dwārkā replied, Thou has questioned Me well.[11]

415. O Arjuna, I am always delighted to explain this truth fully, but what can I do, for rarely do I find such an enquirer.

416. Now My desire has been fulfilled in meeting thee who hast come to Me with eager questions.

417. Thou hast helped me to experience that which is to be enjoyed beyond the sense of unity; thou indeed hast brought Me joy by asking [about My true nature].

418. When a mirror is placed before a man, he sees himself therein; in this way thou art the ideal partner in discussion.

419. O My friend, there is no formality in this; it is simply that thou dost ask what thou dost not know and I listen attentively.

420. With these words the Lord embraced Arjuna and regarding him graciously said to him,

421. Thy questioning and My responses are as complementary as the two lips which produce one speech or as the two feet which produce one gait.

422. Know that we two, thou who askest and I who respond, are to be considered as one.

423. Talking thus the Lord was overcome by His great affection for Arjuna and He stood embracing him; then He became afraid lest [expression of feeling] might be improper.

424. As the juice of sugarcane is spoiled by the addition of salt, so the joy of this conversation would be spoilt by this intimacy.

425. As Nara and Nārāyana there is no separation between us; but this emotion which I feel must be restrained.

426. With this thought in mind, the Lord said, O prince of warriors, what was thy question?

427. Arjuna who had been drawn into the Lord's consciousness, came to himself again and began to listen to the answers to his questions.

428. Overcome with feeling Arjuna said, My lord and master, I asked thee [to tell me] about Thy limitless nature.

429. At these words Krishna began to explain the condition of limitation in two ways.

430. If anyone were to wonder why, when He was asked about unconditioned existence, He spoke of conditional existence, [consider these examples].

431. When butter is to be extracted from milk, butter-milk must first be separated, when pure gold is required the alloy must first be removed.

432. When weeds are removed by the hand pure water appears; when clouds are blown away the sky is seen.

433. As soon as the husks are threshed and separated, the pure grain can be gathered.

434. So also, if one reflects on it, when that which is conditioned has been described, one need not ask any further about the unconditioned.

435. A young bride, asked to say her husband's name, will reject all other names; but she reveals it by her silence when the forbidden name is mentioned.

436. By speaking first of what can be described rather than of what cannot, Krishna explained unconditioned existence.

437. The branch of a tree is used to point out the phase of the moon on the day of the new year; similarly, here, conditioned existence must first be described.

> XVI. *There are two persons in this world, the perishable and the imperishable; the perishable is all these existences and the unchanging is the imperishable.*

438. The Lord continued, O left-handed archer, in this city of worldly life there are only two dwellers.

439. In the sky, day and night are the two occupants, so in the capital of this world also there are only two.

440. But there is still a third; but he cannot bear even the mention of the others' names. On his arrival he destroys them together with the whole capital.

441. Let us leave this till later; at present listen to the description of the first two who have come to live in the world-city.

442. The one is blinded by ignorance, deranged and crippled, and the other is sound in all its limbs, but they have come together by living in this city.

443. One of these is called the perishable and the other the imperishable, and these two possess the city of worldly existence.

444. Now I will explain clearly who is the perishable one and how the imperishable one is to be known.

445. O wielder of the bow, from the highest degree of self-consciousness down to the smallest blade of grass,

446. the large and the small, things movable and immovable, indeed everything that is perceived by mind and intelligence,

447. everything made of the five elements, all that has name and form, or that is under the control of the three qualities,

448. every form of living being which is a coin fashioned of gold and is used by time as a counter [in his game of dice];

449. all that is understood through false knowledge and all that is created and lost in one moment;

450. O Beloved, that which erects the whole structure of nature with the forest of illusion, in fact, all that is known as the universe;

451. that which has already been described in its eight-fold form as matter, and with its thirty-six divisions in the description of the field;

452. [but why repeat what has already been described here under the metaphor of the tree?]—

453. realizing that all these various forms are its abode, consciousness has entered into each of them.

454. As a lion, seeing the reflection of himself in a well is overcome with fury and impelled by his anger leaps down into the well;

455. or as the entire sky is reflected in water, which nevertheless originated from it, consciousness, from being non-dual becomes dual.

456. O Arjuna, in the same way the Spirit, in the sleep of forgetfulness, regards the city of forms as His dwelling place.

457. In the same way as a man may see a bed in his dream and lie down on it, so this city seems to the Spirit to be a bed.

458. Then in this deep sleep he snores, thinking he is happy or miserable, and absorbed in egoism he calls out loudly,

459. imagining that this man is his father, that is his mother, that he is fair, he is base or he is without blemish; or that he has a son, a wife, or wealth.

460. Carried away by these dreams and wandering through the jungle of earth and heaven, this aspect of consciousness, O Arjuna, is known as the perishable man.

461. Listen now to the description of that one that is referred to as the knower of the field, and the state which is the individual soul.

462. That Self which sets aside its own nature and takes on the form of living creatures is called the Perishable One.

463. In his real nature he is perfect and is called Purusha, who is endowed with personality; he is known thus also because he dwells, though asleep, in the city of the body.

464. Further, as he has taken on the limiting conditions of life
in the body, the quality of perishability has been falsely
imputed to him.

465. It is due to these same limitations that he appears to be
impermanent, as the moon appears to move when its
reflection is tossed about on the waves of the ocean.

466. As soon as the waves subside the reflection of the moon
disappears; so too this limited Self is no longer apparent
when the limiting conditions are destroyed.

467. Thus through these limitations the idea of impermanence
attaches to him and owing to this apparent defect He is
called the Perishable One.

468. Therefore all individual selves are called 'perishable' and I
will now explain clearly the nature of the Imperishable
One.

469. O winner of wealth, this other person, the Imperishable
Self, stands in the middle, as Mount Meru is central among
mountains.

470. Meru is the same throughout the three levels of earth, the
nether world and heaven; so knowledge and ignorance are
not separable.

471. He is not perceived through right knowledge nor by false
knowledge thought to be dual; therefore his true nature is
found in the absence of all knowing.

472. He is the middle state, as a clod of earth is neither the
original dust nor the vessels moulded from it.

473. When the waters of the sea are dried up there remain neither
water nor waves, and this Imperishable One exists thus in
a state which has no form.

474. O Pārtha, it is like the borderland of sleep, when a man is
neither awake nor dreaming.

475. The Imperishable One is like a state of non-perception, as
when the world passes away but realization of the Self
has not yet been awakened.

476. On the day of the new moon all the phases of the moon
have passed and yet the moon itself remains. The Imperishable can be thought of in this way.

477. As the life of a tree lies latent in the seed of the ripened
fruit, so this state of life emerges after the destruction of
all the limiting conditions.

478. Thus the state of life which infuses the conditioned existence of beings is called the Unmanifest.

479. This state is spoken of in the Vedānta system as the seed state, and it is in this that the Imperishable One dwells.

480. From this state false knowledge, spreading out into wakefulness and dream, enters the jungle multiplicity of forms.

481. O Kiriti, the Imperishable One is that from which the individual soul, creating the universe, is brought forth and is also that which causes them both to pass away.

482. The other, the Perishable One, is active in men in the states of wakefulness and dream, conditions to which he himself gave birth.

483. Again what is known as deep sleep in ignorance nevertheless falls short of the state of union with Brahma.

484. O warrior, if it were not so, and consciousness were not to return to the states of wakefulness and dream, this deep sleep could be identified with absorption in Brahma.

485. However, both Spirit and Matter are the clouds in the sky of deep sleep and the field and the knower of the field are but phenomena perceived in the dream state.

486. In short, the Imperishable One is the root of the tree of worldly existence with its downward growing branches.

487. He is called the Imperishable One because he lies in deep sleep in the city of illusion.

488. In this state there are no changing moods, no false knowledge, and therefore is it called deep sleep.

489. This condition does not pass away of itself, nor can it be destroyed without knowledge.

490. For this reason thou wilt find it referred to as Imperishable in the great philosophy of the Vedānta.

491. Thus thou shouldst know that this Imperishable One is the cause of individual life of which the characteristic is illusion.

492. Now the two states of false knowledge among men, wakefulness and dreaming, are absorbed in that dark ignorance.

493. That ignorance also becomes absorbed into true knowledge and this dies out just as fire, having consumed all the fuel, itself dies out.

494. In this way, when ignorance is removed by knowledge, and that knowledge ends in the realization of the One Reality, pure consciousness remains without any means of being perceived.

495. That is the highest state, the third of the group and different from the other two already described,
496. as the waking consciousness, O Arjuna, is different from the states of sleep or dream.
497. As the orb of the sun is different from its rays or the mirage [they cause], so is this highest state different from the others.
498. It is different from both the perishable and the imperishable as fire is different from the fuel which it consumes.
499. When the deluge takes place at the end of the world the oceans overflow their boundaries and all are merged in one great ocean.
500. As day and night are swallowed up in the blaze of the final conflagration, neither sleep, dream nor wakefulness exist.
501. Here it is not even known whether unity or duality exist or not and all perception is lost.
502. Such is this highest state, to be known as the Supreme Spirit;
503. O son of Pāndu, as there can be no union with him here, he is called by this name by the individual soul. As a man on the bank of a river speaking about another drowned in its waters,
504. so, O Kiriti, the Vedas, being the bank of thought, can speak both of what is near and what is distant.
505. On this side of spirit are the perishable and the imperishable states; what is beyond these is called the highest Self.
506. Thus, O Arjuna, thou shouldst know that Brahma and the Supreme Spirit are the same.
507. In other words, here all speech becomes silence, knowledge is but ignorance, existence and non-existence are one. Such is the One Reality.
508. Here even awareness of oneness with Brahma fades away, the speaker and what is spoken are merged together, and the object of vision is one with vision itself.
509. Though the light which is between the sun and its reflection is not perceived, one should not say that it does not exist.

510. One cannot deny that there is fragrance passing between a flower and the nose even though it is not visible.

511. So when both the seer and what is seen are lost, who can say what is or what is not? In this realization the nature of the Self can be known.

512. He is light yet not illuminated by another, he is the Lord of all and is controlled by none and fills all space with his own nature.

513. He is the sound which causes all other sounds, the essence of all taste and the delight with which all pleasure is experienced.

514. He is joy added to joy, the lustre in all that is lustrous, the great void in which all space is lost.

515. He is the culmination of all perfection, the supreme Person, the haven of rest of all that is peaceful.

516. He remains even after the universe has evolved and survives in his completeness after it has been swallowed up; he is greater than all things.

517. He is like the shell of pearl which though it is not silver seems to be so to those who do not know its nature.

518. Like the gold in ornaments which though not hidden is not recognized as gold, so though he is not the universe he sustains it.

519. As water and waves are not different from each other, so is he the existence and the light that penetrates the world.

520. O lord of warriors, his nature is the cause of both the restriction and expansion of the universe, as the moon appears in water to increase and decrease.

521. He does not come into being when the universe evolves nor perish when it passes away, as the sun is not different by day and by night.

522. In this way he can never fall short in comparison with anyone or by any measure; he is comparable only with himself.

> XVIII. *As I surpass the perishable and am higher even than the imperishable, I am celebrated as the Supreme Person in the world and in the Veda.*

523. O winner of wealth, what more can be said? He who is self-illuminated, and who is without a second,

524. that is, Myself, is beyond limitation, the supreme one beyond the perishable and the imperishable; therefore I am called in the Vedas the Supreme Person.

525. In short, O winner of wealth, the man in whom the sun of
knowledge has risen knows Me to be the Supreme Person.

526. When a man awakes from sleep, his dream vanishes; so too
when knowledge comes, the world is known to be illusion.

527. When a man takes a garland into his hands, the delusion
that it may be a serpent passes; in the same way a true
perception of Me destroys all illusion.

528. If one recognizes that ornaments are gold, one is not deluded by their shape as ornaments; similarly when I am
known the sense of duality passes away.

529. Then the man who knows himself to be one with Me, exclaims, I am the self-manifested one, I am he who is
existence, consciousness and bliss.

530. Even to say that he knows all that is would be inadequate
when the sense of duality has passed away.

531. So, O Arjuna, only such a man is worthy to worship Me,
as the sky alone can embrace the sky.

532. Only that which has the nature of the ocean of milk can
provide a feast for the ocean of milk; only nectar can mix
with nectar.

533. Only pure gold alone can properly be mixed with pure gold;
and so only when a man is united with Me is he fit to
worship Me.

534. If the Ganges were different from the ocean, how could its
waters merge in the sea? So how could one who is not
united with Me worship Me?

535. Hear, O Arjuna! A man who worships Me is not different
from Me, as waves are not different from the sea.

536. There is no difference between the sun and its brilliance;
by the same token the worship of such a man is to be
regarded as worthy.

xx. *Thus has this most secret doctrine been taught by Me,
O blameless one. By knowing this, a man will become wise
and will have fulfilled all his duties, O Bhārata [Arjuna].*

537. All that has been related from the beginning is like the
fragrance of the lotus-petals of the ten Upanishads, only
to be comprehended by the study of the scriptures.

538. This Gitā is the pure essence of the milk of the Vedas, churned out by me with the helping hand of the intellect of Shri Vyāsa;

539. is the Ganges of the nectar of wisdom, the seventeenth digit of the moon of bliss, and the new Lakshmi rising from the milky ocean in the form of thought.

540. Therefore, it cannot be known except through Me, who am its very life in each word, syllable and meaning.

541. These two, the Perishable One and the Imperishable One; approached this Lakshmi; but she rejected their manhood and gave all to Me as the Supreme Person.

542. So this Gitā which thou hast just heard is the devoted bride of Me, the Spirit, in this world.

543. Truly speaking it is not a learned science but a weapon wherewith to conquer this worldly existence, and its words are the mystic means by which it unveils the Spirit.

544. O Arjuna, the Gitā that I have taught thee is My hidden wealth and I have brought it out for thy sake.

545. O Pārtha, with thy devotion to Me thou hast become the sage Gautama, drawing out from My head, as from the Shiva of consciousness, the Ganges of My secret treasure.

546. O winner of wealth, thou hast made of Me a mirror in which thou canst clearly perceive thy whole nature before thee.

547. As the moon and the stars fill the sky and the ocean with their reflection, so hast thou drawn Me, with the Gitā, into thy heart.

548. O great warrior, having cleansed thyself from the threefold soil of sin, thou hast become a dwelling fit for Myself and the Gitā.

549. What more can be said? The Gitā is the blossoming creeper of My wisdom and he who knows it is freed from all deception.

550. O son of Pāndava, as the river of nectar takes away all the diseases of man and makes him immortal,

551. so not only will the Gitā, when understood, marvellously remove all delusion, but through self-realization, it brings about union with Me.

552. In this self-realization, the obligation incurred by [the fruit of] action is discharged and passes away for ever.

553. O thou who art the delight of heroes, when what has been

lost is found, the path [leading to it] ends; when knowledge is attained it rises to the pinnacle of the temple of action.

554. Therefore all action ceases for the enlightened man, said Krishna, the friend of the helpless.

555. The nectar of the words of Shri Krishna flooded the heart of Arjuna, and through the kindness of Vyāsa was received by Sanjaya.

556. Sanjaya gave this to Dhritarāshtra to drink so that at the end of his days he was not burdened [with confusion].

557. When he heard the Gitā he felt himself to be unworthy of it, but at the end he found enlightenment.

558. When a grapevine is watered with milk, it seems to be wasteful, but it causes the tree to bear abundant fruit.

559. The words spoken by Shri Krishna were told reverently to Dhritarāshtra by Sanjaya and in the end the blind king became happy.

560. With my limited understanding I have explained these things as clearly as possible in Marāthi composition.

561. When those without understanding see the Shevanti plant they think little of it; but the bee which sucks its honey knows its fragrance.

562. So you should accept whatever appeals to you, giving back to me what may be deficient, for ignorance is a natural characteristic of a child.

563. A child's parents delight in it endlessly and fondle it although it has no knowledge.

564. So you, O saints, are my parental home, and when I see you I should be treated with affection; accept this book as a token of my love for you.

565. Jnānadeva says, O Nivrittināth, my preceptor, soul of the universe, accept my worship in the form of these words.

In the Upanishad of the Bhagavadgitā, the science of the Absolute, the scripture of Yoga and the dialogue between Shri Krishna and Arjuna, this is the fifteenth chapter entitled The Yoga of the Supreme Person.

NOTES

1. A child born with its feet first is considered to be specially fortunate.
2. *Dvārkā.* The capital of the kingdom of Krishna.
3. *Ashvattha.* The Sanskrit name for the holy fig tree; in Marāthi called pipal.
4. *Agastya.* The name of a great sage, said to have been born in a pitcher.
5. *Māyā.* This word, here used as a name, is grammatically feminine in Sanskrit and Marāthi; hence the use of the feminine pronoun in the following verses.
6. *consciousness.* The four divisions of consciousness are mind, intellect, reason and individuality.
7. *mahat.* 'The great'. This is the term used to refer to the 'intellect', the first of the eight principles of matter in Hindu philosophy.
8. *derivation of Ashvattha.* The negative element in this derivation, not referred to here, is the prefix 'a-'.
9. *Ashādha.* The name of the month extending from mid-June to mid-July.
10. *Manu.* See Ch. IV, v. 16.
11. *Yuga.* One of the great ages of the world, of which there are four: the first is Krita, 1,728,000 years; the second Tretā, 1,296,000 years; the third, Dvāpara, 864,000 years; the fourth, Kali, 432,000 years.
12. *Vedas.* The Vedas referred to here are the three chief Vedas, Rig, Yajur and Sāma (Ch. X, v. 207); the fourth, Atharva, occurs in Ch. XIII, v. 827.
13. *Svāti.* An auspicious constellation.

CHAPTER XVI

1. Hail to that resplendent sun which has risen, dispelling the illusion of the universe and causing the lotus of non-duality to open its petals![1]
2. He swallows up the night of ignorance, removes the moonlight of the illusion of knowledge and ignorance and brings in the day of enlightenment for the wise.
3. At the dawning of the day the eyes of self-knowledge are opened and birds in the form of individual souls leave their nests of identification with the body.
4. At his rising the bee of consciousness, held in the lotus of the subtle body, gains its freedom.
5. On the opposite banks of the river of duality, which springs from the conflicting teachings of the scriptures, intellect and understanding cry out [like a pair of geese] in the distress of their separation.
6. For them this light of the world, set in the firmament of consciousness, brings about the comforting experience of union.
7. At the rising of this sun the dark night of thieves passes away and the travelling yogis set out on the path of spiritual experience.
8. Touched by its rays of discrimination, the sparks of the sun-crystal of intellect break into flames and burn up the forests of worldly existence.
9. The network of his scorching rays settles in the barren desert of the Self and the mirage of the flood of psychic powers arises.
10. When this sun reaches the height of knowledge of the Self and shines in the noontide of union with Brahma, it hides itself in the shadow of delusion about the nature of the personal self.
11. When the night of illusion has faded away who will take thought for the sleep of wrong perception, with its dreamlike delusion of the universe?

12. In this way in the city of perception of unity, the market is overstocked with the commodity of the great bliss, and then dealings in worldly joys fall off.

13. His light gives perpetual daylight for experience of the highest bliss of the auspicious day of one who is liberated.

14. As soon as this great monarch of the sky rises for ever, the processes of rising and setting and the four quarters of the earth disappear.

15. Appearance and disappearance vanish, and Brahma who is concealed beneath the outward forms is revealed. What more can be said? This dawn is beyond description.

16. Who can see that sun of knowledge, which is beyond day and night and which though illumined by none gives abundant light?

17. To that sun of consciousness, Nivritti, I bow down again and again, for spoken praise of him would suffer from the limitation of words.

18. When one considers the greatness of the deity, praise is excellent only if the one who praises is merged with it in him who is to be praised.

19. He is known only through not-knowing; he is described only by embracing silence, and can be brought to us only as we become nothing.

20. In praise of him pashyanti and madhyama, together with para and vaikhari, are powerless.[2]

21. I thy servant humbly adorn thee, who art thus described, with the ornament of my hymn of words; even inadequate as they are, accept them, O thou joy of union!

22. A beggar, finding a sea of nectar, does not realize what is suitable and hastens to offer to it of a meal of vegetables.

23. In that the offering of vegetables should be appreciated; but the eagerness with which it is given is the real value. When a man worships the sun with a tiny lamp, it is his intense devotion which we should consider.

24. If a child knew all that was right, what would childhood mean? But its mother delights in it [because of its childishness].

25. If the water from the streets were to fall into the Ganges would the river refuse to receive it?

26. How great an offence was committed by Brigu! Yet Krishna, the wielder of the Shārnga bow, accepted it gladly as a blessing.[3]

27. If the sky filled with clouds were to appear in the presence of the lord of the day, would he tell it to move away?

28. Bear with me, O Master, if in the language of duality I have weighed thee in the balance of comparison with sun,

29. thou whom the yogis perceive with the eye of meditation, and the Vedas praise with their speech! What thou hast suffered in this do thou make me also suffer.

30. Today I have delighted in extolling thy merits, so do not blame me, do what Thou wilt; I will not cease till I am fully satisfied with this feast [of praise].

31. It has been given to me to describe the sweet nectar of Thy grace in the form of the Gitā, and in this my good fortune has increased two-fold.

32. My tongue must have practised the penance of right speech through many lives, the fruit of which is that I have come into possession of this great island of the Gitā, O Lord.

33. I must have performed very special deeds of merit as a result of which I am set free from obligation by being allowed to describe Thy virtues.

34. Today the great adversity which, in the forest of this life, has caused me to be caught in the village of death, has totally disappeared.

35. It has been given to me to describe Thy fame which is known by the name of the Gitā and established by its victory over ignorance.

36. If great prosperity comes to dwell in the house of a poor man, should he be called poor?

37. If the sun were to enter by chance the house of darkness, would not that darkness be the light of the world?

38. The universe is but a speck compared with the greatness of God; but do not His devotees receive according to their devotion?

39. so my exposition of the Gitā is as if I tried to smell the fragrance of a sky-flower; but thou with thy power hast caused my desire to be fulfilled.

40. Jnānadeva says, O my master, therefore by thy grace I will explain clearly the deep verses of the Gitā.

41. In the fifteenth chapter Krishna expounded to Arjuna the whole doctrine of the Gitā.

42. As a good physician diagnoses a bodily sickness, so the Lord described the form of the whole world of conditioned life by the illustration of the Ashvattha tree.

43. The Imperishable, the highest Spirit, was spoken of as the Supreme Person and at the same time he showed how consciousness was connected with matter.

44. Afterwards the Lord explained the true nature of the Universal Spirit by speaking of it as the Supreme Person.

45. Then He spoke clearly of that strong inner wisdom, the means of the realization of the Spirit.

46. So in this chapter there remains no topic for discussion, but that love for each other, felt by the Teacher and his disciple.

47. This had been explained fully [to the wise] but seekers after liberation still search for understanding.

48. O wise Arjuna, he who through knowledge reaches Me, the Supreme Being, knows all things and is the very summit of devotion.

49. The Lord of the three worlds said this in a verse in the last chapter, and there He described knowledge at length and with great joy.

50. When the pleasures of this world have been renounced, the Supreme Spirit should be realized as soon as it is revealed and then the individual self will be set on the throne of Supreme Joy.

51. To arrive at this high station there is no other means, said the Lord, and right knowledge is the supreme method.

52. Now all the seekers after knowledge were delighted in their minds and reverently saluted it with their uplifted hearts.

53. It is in the nature of love that the object towards which it flows is constantly in mind.

54. Therefore until the wise among the seekers after knowledge have indeed experienced it, they are preoccupied with the question of how to obtain it and how to preserve it.

55. So they long know how to make this right knowledge their own and by what means it may be increased.

56. They also want to find out what prevents it from coming to them, or, when obtained, what leads it into the wrong path; or what works against this knowledge.

57. So everything that prevents the rise of it should be avoided, whilst all that promotes it must faithfully be kept in mind.

58. Now the Lord of Lakshmi will resume his explanation, so that the desire which all you seekers have in your minds may be fulfilled.

59. He will now describe the divine wealth which causes right knowledge to come to auspicious birth and how your peace may be increased.

60. The source of good and evil actions lies in these two forces. This matter has already been discussed in the ninth chapter.

61. Properly, the explanation should have been given there, but another subject intervened. The Lord will now proceed with this exposition.

62. Considering the arrangement of what has gone before, this chapter is now to be thought of as the sixteenth.

63. But enough has been said about that. These two forms of wealth are able to promote knowledge or to hinder it.

64. Now listen first to the description of that divine force which helps men along the path of the search after knowledge and which is the lamp of religious duty in the night of confusion.

65. When one thing assists another, and all meet together in a group, this is known among men as 'wealth'.

66. The force which produces spiritual happiness and supports the divine qualities is called divine wealth.

The Blessed Lord said:

1. *Fearlessness, purity of mind, steadfastness in knowledge and concentration, charity, self-control and sacrifice, study of the scriptures, austerity and uprightness—*

67. Now, of all these divine qualities, fearlessness holds the highest place. Listen to what it is.

68. One who does not leap into a flood can have no fear of being drowned, nor can one who lives a temperate life be in dread of illness.

69. So the man who does not allow egotism to arise in connection with good and evil deeds and abandons the anxieties of worldly life,

70. and through the realization of non-duality knows all others to be one with himself, casts out all fear.

71. When salt is thrown into water, it becomes one with it; so also he who realizes his unity with all destroys fear.

72. O Beloved, this is what is called fearlessness; thou shouldst know this to be the servant of true perception.

73. Now learn about purity of understanding which is known

by the following signs. Like embers that are neither burnt nor extinguished,

74. or, as the moon appears in a subtle form when the eve of the previous day passes into the first day of the new moon, so is this true perception.

75. As at the time when the rainy season is over and the hot season not yet begun, the form of a river becomes visible,

76. so in the same way, when the force of desire and doubt has ceased and the burden of passion and darkness removed, there remains only that understanding which loves to experience its own true nature.

77. Such an understanding remains undisturbed however much the sense organs may tempt it with pleasant or unpleasant objects.

78. When the husband of a devoted wife goes away from her she is troubled by the separation and takes little note of what gain or loss may come to her.

79. In the same way, the understanding which continuously delights in the Self is said to be in a state of purity; so said Krishna, slayer of Kansa.

80. Now with regard to the attainment of self-realization, devote all thy desire to it, whether thou dost choose the way of knowledge or the way of yoga.

81. Apply thy whole mind to this as a disinterested man will cast a full oblation into the sacrificial fire.

82. As a man of noble birth gives his daughter in marriage to another noble family, or when Lakshmi is settled as the bride of Mukunda,

83. so when, through absorption in union by means of yoga or knowledge one obtains one's goal, the third quality is known, said the Lord Krishna.

84. One who will never shun another in distress, even if he is an enemy, but will help him in word, deed and thought, and with all the resources of his wealth,

85. as a tree withholds nothing from a traveller, neither its flowers, fruit, shade, leaves nor roots, O winner of wealth,

86. such a man will go to the help of someone in affliction, when occasion arises, offering him everything from his heart to his worldly wealth.

87. This is called charity, the magic pigment that gives the vision of liberation. Now listen to the characteristics of self-control.

88. This quality destroys the union of sense organs with sense,
    separating them from each other as turbid water is made
    clear by alum.

89. [The man who is self-controlled] will not permit the wind of
    sense objects to blow through the gateways of his senses
    but binds them with self-restraint, handing them over to
    discipline.

90. Causing all tendencies to activity to turn back into the
    recesses of the mind, he lights the fire of dispassion at all the
    ten gates of the body.

91. Zealously practising many vows more severe than breath
    control, he performs them day and night yet is not satisfied.

92. This is known as self-control. Now I will explain briefly the
    meaning of sacrifice.

93. At the highest level are the Brāhmans and at the lowest
    are women and those of the Shudra caste; others lie in
    between, each caste with its own special status.

94. Each one should faithfully follow the form of worship
    prescribed for him, according to what is best for him.

95. As the brāhman performs the sixfold rites while the shudra
    salutes him, and thus they both reap the benefit of their
    respective forms of sacrifice,[4]

96. So in accordance with his own status each one performs
    sacrifice in his own way; but he should not have any desire
    for the fruit of it.

97. Moreover he should not allow the thought to enter his
    mind through the door of egosim, that he is the performer
    [of the sacrifice]; but he must be present and [the sacrifice
    carried out] according to the prescribed Vedic rites.

98. O Arjuna, thou shouldst know this to be the meaning of
    the word sacrifice. So said Krishna, master of the know-
    ledge of the way of salvation.

99. A ball is thrown to the ground for no other purpose than
    that it should return to the hand; seed is sown in a field
    with a view to reaping a crop.

100. A lamp is valued for seeing what is hidden; or the roots of a
    tree are watered that the tree may give forth branches and
    fruit.

101. A mirror in which we wish to see ourselves reflected must
    be often cleaned.

102. So in order to realize the deity constant study of the Vedas
    is necessary.

103. In order to reach the Supreme Spirit, the twice-born should study the Brahma-sutras while the rest may study hymns or repeat the names of the deity.[5]
104. This, O Pārtha, is what is understood by the study of the Vedas. Now listen while I explain the meaning of the word penance.
105. Charity means giving all one has; to keep one's wealth leads to death. A plant bears its fruit and then dies.
106. [Charity should be given as] incense is burnt up in fire, [as] impure gold loses weight on being heated, or as the moon wanes in the dark half of the month [when the spirits of] the ancestors feed on it.[6]
107. O warrior, when the vital airs, the senses and the body are mortified in order to attain to the Self, that state is called penance.
108. If there is any other form of penance, [it can be thought of as] the swan thrusting its beak into milk [to separate the water from it].
109. In the same way, one who differentiates the body from the Self as soon as he is born, and thus awakens discrimination in his heart; [this is known as penance.]
110. When a man looks inwards towards the Self, the activity of reason is restricted, in the same way that dreams vanish with sleep on waking.
111. O wielder of the bow, when discrimination is concentrated on the self, that is true penance.
112. Uprightness is kindness towards all that lives, as conscious-ness is inherent in all creatures and as the mother's milk is essential to all infants.

> II. *Non-violence, truth, freedom from anger, renunciation, tranquillity, aversion to fault-finding, compassion to living beings, freedom from covetousness, gentleness, modesty and steadiness [absence of fickleness].*

113. Harmlessness is shown in using one's own body, speech and mind for the good of the world.
114. A jasmin bud is sharp-pointed, yet it is soft; moonbeams give light though they are very cool.
115. There can be no medicine which, though able to cure disease, is not at the same time bitter to the taste; to what can it be compared?

116. Water is so soft that though it may touch the pupil of the eye it does not damage it; yet it can break up rocks.

117. So true speech is sharper than a sword in resolving doubts, but it brings sweetness to the sense of hearing.

118. When listening to it, the ear longs for mouths [with which to taste it]; yet by the power of its integrity it is able even to pierce Brahma.

119. However no one is deceived by its sweetness, nor really is hurt by it.

120. A hunter's music is pleasing to the ear; yet truly understood, it is a threat. Fire burns openly, but fie upon the kind of speech that hurts!

121. Speech which charms the ear while its sense wounds the heart of the hearer is not sweet, but devilish.

122. As it is the way of a mother to pretend to be angry when her children do wrong, but otherwise she is as tender as a flower,

123. so the resolute speech, which is able both to bring joy in hearing and to result in good conduct, is to be known as truth.

124. Now a stone will never send forth a shoot even though it may be well watered, nor can butter be produced by churning rice gruel.

125. Striking the head of a sloughed snake skin will not make it spread its hood, nor can spring flowers ever appear in the sky.

126. Passion was not awakened in Shuka even by Rambhā's beauty; nor can ashes rise in flames, even if ghi is poured on them.

127. Even if such man were to meet with such curses as would enrage young men, or for any other reason,

128. yet, O son of Pāndu, they would no more be filled with the waves of anger than a man whose life span is finished could be brought back to life even by falling at the feet of the Creator.

129. Such a state of mind is called freedom from anger, said Krishna.

130. A jar is destroyed by destroying the clay of which it is made, a piece of cloth by destroying the threads of which it is woven and a tree by destroying its seed.

131. A whole picture can be spoiled by ruining the canvas on which it is drawn; many dreams vanish when sleep passes away.

132. Waves disappear if water dries up and clouds pass away
when the rainy season is over; similarly all enjoyment
ceases with the abandonment of wealth.

133. In such a way wise men should give up all sense of individuality and then all attachment to worldly affairs can be
abandoned.

134. This is what is termed non-attachment, said He who is the
embodiment of sacrifice. Accepting this teaching the blessed
Arjuna then said,

135. Please explain clearly to me the characteristics of
tranquillity, and the Lord replied, Listen attentively to
Me.

136. Tranquillity is that state in which the object of knowledge
is attained and then both knowledge and the knower no
longer exist.

137. When the flood of the final deluge engulfs the whole universe, itself is the only thing that remains;

138. when neither rivers, their currents or the ocean into which
they flow, exist any longer in the world of separate activity,
who is even aware that all has become water?

139. Similarly, O Kiriti, when the object of knowledge is found
and the process of knowing ceases, the state that remains
is that of tranquillity.

140. When a patient is tormented by disease a good physician
is not concerned about whether he is a stranger until he is
restored to health.

141. When a cow is stuck in the mud one is disturbed by anxiety
for her, without considering whether she is giving milk or is
dry.

142. A man of compassion will save the life of another who is
drowning without first asking whether he is of high or low
caste.

143. A good man finding a woman in a forest stripped naked
does not look at her until he has clothed her.

144. So too, to those who are suffering from ignorance and error,
who are cursed with an evil fate or held down by every
kind of baseness,

145. such men give all that they have only to remove the distress that torments them.

146. They look on them only after they have cleansed them by
their own pure glance.

147. As a god should be seen only after due worship, as one must

sow his field before he goes to reap, and satisfy a guest before asking a blessing from him,

148. so these good men look upon such unfortunate ones only after they have removed all their faults by their own virtues.

149. Besides this, they will not hurt anyone's feelings or lead anybody into evil ways, nor will they call anyone by a name referring to his faults.

150. Also, they will raise up those who may have fallen but will not wound their hearts.

151. O Kiriti, they will not make comparisons between high and low, nor impute evil to any.

152. This, O Arjuna, is known as an absence of calumny and is an excellent way in which to seek liberation.

153. Now will I explain compassion. It is like the full moon that sends out her cooling rays on high and low without distinction.

154. A man of compassion takes no account of his higher or lower degree when with pity he relieves someone's distress.

155. He is in this world like water that pours itself out to save the life of vegetation dying from the lack of it.

156. Moved by compassion for those in distress he considers it a small thing to give himself to relieve it.

157. As water cannot flow on without filling the hollow [that lies in its way], he cannot pass by without refreshing a weary man [whom he may meet].

158. He is tormented by the sufferings of others as a man feels pain when a thorn has pierced his foot.

159. As when one's feet are cooled, the eyes too are refreshed, so he always rejoices in the happiness of others.

160. The purpose of water in this world is to quench thirst; so the purpose of his life is to succour the distressed.

161. Such a man, O prince of warriors, is kindness incarnate; I regard Myself as indebted to this man from whom springs all compassion.

162. A lotus faithfully responds to the sun, but the sun does not receive its fragrance.

163. In the course of spring all the wealth of the forest assembles like an army; but the season passes without taking any part in it.

164. Laksmi approaches with all her magic powers, but the great Vishnu disregards her.

165. Were all earthly and heavenly pleasures to be the servants of his desire, still his mind would not long for them.

166. In fact his heart has no desire for objects of sense; such a condition is called freedom from desire.

167. As the hive is a haven to the bee, as water to the animals that live in it, and as birds are free in the sky;

168. as the love of a mother is centred in her child, or the wind is soft to the touch in spring;

169. as the meeting with the beloved is dear to the eye, as the sight of a mother tortoise delights her brood, so [the desire-less man is] tender-hearted towards all creatures.

170. Camphor is soft to the touch, pleasant to taste, fragrant to smell and pure when applied to the body,

171. and if it were not harmful when taken in any quantity, one could compare with it this tenderness.

172. The tender-hearted man is like the sky, which holds all the elements in itself, and yet is contained in the smallest atom.

173. What can I say? he lives only for the creatures of the world; this is what I call tenderness of heart.

174. A king would be overcome with shame when he is defeated in battle, or a self-respecting man would be distressed if he committed a mean action.

175. An ascetic would feel humiliated if by chance he entered the house of an outcaste out of lust for woman.

176. Running away from the field of battle is an unbearable disgrace for a warrior, and a devoted wife would be distressed if she were addressed as though she were a widow.

177. A well-favoured man attacked by leprosy would feel it to be a reproach, and if a respectable man were slandered he would regard it as humiliation worse than death.

178. That a man should live like a corpse in a yard-long body and from time to time be born, die and be reborn,

179. being moulded into a body through all the processes of gestation and birth,

180. he thinks nothing is more shameful than having name and form in a human frame.

181. The pure-minded man, in these evil conditions, is disgusted with the body, but to the shameless it is a delight.

182. As a puppet cannot move when the strings controlling it are broken, when the control of breath fails the activity of the sense organs ceases.

183. Again, as at the setting of the sun its spreading rays are withdrawn, so when mental control is lost the organs of perception do not function.

184. In the same way if the mind and breath are under restraint, the activities of all the ten organs lose their power. This thou shouldst know as cessation of activity.

III. *Vigour, forgiveness, fortitude, purity, freedom from malice and excessive pride—these, O Pāṇḍava [Arjuna] are the endowments of him who is born with the divine nature.*

185. If some evil thing as bad as death itself should befall a widow about to mount her husband's funeral pyre, she would count it for nothing for the sake of her husband.

186. Similarly a man will hasten along the narrow path to the Absolute with great resolution, destroying the obstacles in the form of the poison of sense objects.

187. Prohibition of actions do not hinder him, nor does he pay regard to religious injunctions; nor do psychic powers have any attraction for him.

188. In such a way his mind turns naturally towards the Supreme; this is called spiritual light.

189. Now when pride in the greatness of being able to bear all things does not arise, as the body is not aware of carrying the hair that grows upon it, this is called patience.

190. Even if the force of the sense organs should be very powerful or if through fate disease attacks him, even though unpleasant things may happen to him and pleasant things be taken from him,

191. and all this should flood over him at one moment, he would face them with courage as though he were Agastya.

192. As a gentle breeze can easily disperse a great column of smoke rising into the sky,

193. so, O Pāndava, such a man easily overcomes all difficulties whether they arise from physical or spiritual sources or from destiny.

194. When in the midst of mental agitation a man remains courageous and undisturbed, that is called fortitude.

195. Purity is as a jar of pure refined gold filled with the holy waters of the Ganges.

196. When the activity of the body is without desire and true discrimination is in the heart, then there is present the whole image of purity.

197. As the Ganges removes the sin and distress of men and also nourishes the trees on its banks, eventually reaching the ocean,

198. as the sun sets out to encircle the earth, dispelling the world's darkness and opening up the whole temple of nature's wealth,

199. in the same way such a man will set free those who are in bondage, rescue the drowning, and remove the afflictions of the distressed.

200. In short, he works night and day for the happiness and welfare of humanity, attaining also his own goal.

201. Besides this, the thought of working for himself at the expense of the interest of others does not enter his mind.

202. This is called freedom from malice, O Kiriti, and I have explained it to thee in such a way that thou canst clearly discern it.

203. O Pārtha, as the Ganges on reaching the head of Shiva humbly withdrew, so the sense of shame when honour is bestowed on one,

204. is called humility, O wise one. This I have already explained to thee so is there any need to repeat it?

205. In this way spiritual wealth consists in the possession of these twenty-six virtues and is the royal reward of those who excel among the seekers after liberation.

206. This divine wealth is the holy Ganges of the liberated sons of Sagara, eternally renewed, surrounded by sacred places in the form of these virtues.[7]

207. Or they may be likened to a garland of flowers in the form of virtues that the bride of self-liberation hangs round the necks of all who are entirely free from worldly attachment.

208. These virtues are also as a lamp of twenty-four flames lit by the Gitā, [as the bride], which she waves in circles round the head of her bridegroom, the spiritual nature.

209. This wealth may be compared to a divine shell in the ocean of the Gitā which produces the pure pearls of all these virtues.

210. It is needless to enlarge upon this, for the various virtues which constitute this wealth have been described in such a way that they will reveal themselves.

211. In the course of this exposition, I must now describe demoniac wealth, which is the hidden creeper of sorrow and covered with the thorns of all the vices.

212. Though it should be cast out, in order to do so it must be known, even if it is worthless; so listen carefully with all thy capacity.

213. This demoniac wealth is the collection of all the dreadful vices that result in the terrible pains of hell.

214. Just as the [Kālakuta] poison is made up of all other poisons so is this wealth the combination of every vice.

IV. *Ostentation, arrogance, excessive pride, anger, as also harshness and ignorance, these, O Pārtha [Arjuna], are the endowments of him who is born with the demoniac nature.*

215. Among these demoniac qualities, O warrior, is ostentation, which is boasting of one's own greatness.

216. If a man were to bring shame to his mother before men, though she were as pure as a holy place, yet this would be a degradation.

217. If a man were to proclaim in public the knowledge which had been taught by his guru, this would be harmful even though the teaching in itself would be of value.

218. If a drowning man were to carry on his head the very boat which would quickly transport him to the other side, he would drown.

219. O son of Pāndu, food is the sustainer of life, but when taken in excess it can become poison.

220. Similarly if one were to proclaim one's religion, which is one's support in this world and the next, the very thing that brings salvation would become a cause of evil.

221. Thus the same religious life becomes in fact irreligious if it is openly spoken of in public; O warrior, this is the meaning of ostentation.

222. A fool gains a smattering of knowledge and is then unable to appreciate the learning of an assembly of brāhmans.

223. The well-trained horse of a horseman the size of an elephant is insignificant; to a chameleon on a thorny bush the heavens seem to be low.

224. A fire, fed by grass rises to the sky in flames, or a fish swimming in a pool might by comparison scorn the sea.

225. So may a man become vain about his wife, his wealth, his learning, his reputation or his standing among men; a beggar may be proud of the day's meal he obtains from the house of another.

226. An unfortunate man may pull down his house when he has the shadow of the clouds for shelter; or a fool, seeing a mirage, break down the wall of a tank.

227. Similarly when a man is full of conceit on account of worldly possession, this is arrogance. There is no need to say more.

228. The world believes in the Vedas, the Supreme Being is to be worshipped with faith; the sun is the only giver of light to the world.

229. The highest desire of a man is to rise to the throne of an emperor, and certainly all men desire freedom from death.

230. So if anyone were to praise God joyfully [for such gifts] the arrogant man would be filled with envy.

231. He would exclaim 'I will destroy God; as for the Vedas I will poison them'. In his pride he destroys his own power.

232. A moth dislikes a flame, the glow-worm cannot bear the sun, and to the titavi bird the ocean is an enemy.

233. So such a man, infatuated with the pride of egoism, cannot bear to hear even the name of God, and even claims to rival the Vedas.

234. He is inflated with conceit about his worthiness, full of arrogant pride, he is the established road to hell.

235. The sight of joy in others is cause enough for the poison of anger to arise in his mind.

236. Burning oil burns more fiercely when in contact with cold water, and a jackal becomes excited when it sees the moon.

237. The sinful owl is enraged when at dawn it sees the rising sun, which enlightens the life of the world.

238. Daybreak which is the joy of man is an evil worse than death to robbers; milk is poison to a snake.

239. The great sea fire, drinking [the waters of the sea], does not subside but burns more fiercely.

240. So when a man becomes more and more enraged at the good fortune of his fellowmen in learning, happiness and prosperity, this is called anger.

241. The mind of such a man is as a serpent's lair, his sight is like the shot of an arrow, his speech like a shower of live coals.

242. All his actions are like a sharp saw. In this way his whole nature is harsh.

243. He is the basest of men and the very embodiment of violence. Now listen to the characteristics of ignorance.

244. A stone is unable to distinguish between the touch of heat and cold, day and night are the same to a man born blind.

245. Fire rising into flames will consume without distinction everything that it touches; the touchstone cannot distinguish iron from gold.

246. A ladle may be put into various sauces but it cannot discern their taste.

247. The wind does not consider the direction in which it should blow; similarly baseness does not concern itself with good and evil deeds.

248. As a child puts into its mouth whatever it sees, without knowing whether it is clean or dirty,

249. so is the condition of an ignorant man who mingles at random sin and righteousness, not discerning in his mind the bitterness or sweetness of these two.

250. This is ignorance; there can be no other name for it; I have now told you the characteristics of the six vices.

251. Demoniac wealth is supported by these six vices, as a powerful poison may be in the small body of a serpent.

252. The triple conflagration of the day of doom seems to be insignificant, but the oblation of the whole world would not suffice to satisfy it.

253. The three bodily humours, [when in excess], will not fail to bring about death, even if one were to appeal to the Creator; but these six vices are twice as evil as they are.

254. This demoniac wealth is not inferior although this whole group consists of only six vices.

255. Even if all the harmful planets should be in conjunction in the same sign of the Zodiac, if every possible sin should assail a slanderer,

256. if many diseases should attack the man doomed to die, or if all unfavourable auguries should meet together at an inauspicious moment,

257. A man possessed by all these vices would be like a dying goat stung by a seven-tailed scorpion.

258. If one were to find that a man [whom one had trusted] was a thief, or if an exhausted man were thrown into a flood, that would be the effect of these vices.

259. If he were even to approach the road to liberation, he would cry out, 'I will not leave this world', and he would plunge into worldly affairs.

260. He descends into lower and lower births, O Kiriti, and eventually reaches the lowest order of inanimate beings.

261. Be that so. Together these six vices produce in a man what is called demoniac wealth.

262. Thus I have described to thee the two kinds of wealth, so well known among men, with their various signs.

> v. *The divine endowments are said to make for deliverance and the demoniac for bondage. Grieve not, O Pāṇḍava [Arjuna], thou art born with the divine endowments [for a divine destiny].*

263. Now the first of these two, which is known as divine, is the dawn of the joy of liberation.

264. The other, demoniacal, is the chain of greed and infatuation that binds the self.

265. But do not let these words fill thee with fear, does night fear the light of the moon?

266. O Conqueror of wealth, this demoniac wealth is bondage for him who resorts to these six vices.

267. But, O Pāndava, thou art fortunate in having been born endowed with all the divine qualities.

268. So that, O Pārtha, being the master of this divine wealth, thou mayest attain to the joy of final beatitude.

> vi. *There are two types of beings created in the world— the divine and the demoniacal. The divine have been described at length. Hear from Me, O Pārtha [Arjuna], about the demoniac.*

269. Men's endowment with either divine or demoniac wealth is eternally appointed.

270. Demons carry on their activities by night; human beings and other creatures should follow their proper occupations by day.

271. In the same way, O Kiriti, the two orders of created beings, divine and demoniac, carry on their activities according to their nature.

272. In an earlier part of the chapter, while describing knowledge, I have fully explained divine wealth.

273. Now I will describe for thee the nature of those endowed with demoniac wealth. Give Me thy full attention.

274. Without expressed sound there can be no word, as there can be no honey where there are no flowers.

275. So the demoniac nature cannot manifest itself unless it has recourse to a human body,

276. and as fire can be produced because it lies latent in wood, this nature manifests itself through the medium of a human body.

277. Then, as sugar cane gives more juice as it grows, [the demoniac nature increases] when it enters the form of a human being.

278. O conqueror of wealth, I will now describe to thee the characteristics of those men in whom this growth of demoniac forces takes place.

VII. *The demoniac do not know about the way of action or the way of reconciliation. Neither purity nor good conduct, nor truth is found in them.*

279. Their minds are the dark night in respect of knowing anything about tendencies towards good deeds and abstinence from evil deeds,

280. as a silkworm, preoccupied with weaving its cocoon, does not concern itself with the questions of entering or leaving it.

281. A fool will lend money to a thief, without considering whether his money will be repaid to him.

282. In the same way demoniacal men have no knowledge of the tendency towards good and abstention from evil and have no understanding of purity even in a dream.

283. Coal might lose its blackness, a crow might become white, or even a demon turn against animal food,

284. but, O conqueror of wealth, there can be no purity in a devilish man than there is holiness in a jar of liquor.

285. Such men cannot foster the desire for ritual acts, nor regard the way of life of their elders nor have any knowledge of right action.

286. Their actions are as random as the grazing of goats, the blowing of the wind, or the burning of fire.

287. Acting solely on impulse, they behave like demons and are always at enmity with truth.

288. They can no more speak truthfully than the tail of a scorpion could tickle the skin.

289. No truth can come to them any more than a sweet smell could come from the breath of the mouth.

290. Even though they do nothing, their very nature is evil.
Now I will tell you of their strange manner of speaking.
291. These devilish men are like the camel's body of which no
part is straight; listen to these things as they come.
292. Their speech is like the mouth of a chimney pouring out
columns of smoke. I will tell thee about this so that it can
be clearly understood.

> VIII. *They say that the world is unreal, without a basis,
> without a Lord, not brought about in regular causal
> sequence, caused by desire, in short*

293. This universe is eternal and is controlled by the Supreme
Being, and the Vedas decree, as in a public hall, what is
just and what is unjust.
294. They who are judged by them to be sinful suffer punish-
ment in Hell, while the just live happily in heaven.
295. Such is the eternal organization of this universe, nevertheless these people declare it all to be false.
296. They are fascinated by sacrifice and are deceived by it;
those who are over pious are deluded by the images that
they worship and those who wear the saffron robe of the
yogi, attracted by the experience of samādhi, are dis-
illusioned.
297. Is merit to be gained in any other way than through the
enjoyment of our worldly possessions?
298. If on account of physical weakness they are unable to accumulate possessions and are tormented by the lack of sense
pleasures, they regard this as sinful.
299. Taking the life of a rich man is certainly a sin, but if thereby one can possess oneself of the rich man's wealth, is not
that the reward of merit?
300. If it is a sin for the strong to destroy the weak, how is it
that fish are not exterminated?
301. If [among men], after examining the family heredity and
finding an auspicious moment for marriage, a maid is chosen
for the purpose of procreation,
302. then why has no similar procedure been established for
the mating of birds and beasts whose offspring is without
limit?
303. If stolen money comes into one's possession, does it turn to
poison? If a man commits adultery, does he therefore become a leper?

304. So, as the ruler of this universe, God causes men to experience both right and wrong, and according to a man's desire he will experience life in the hereafter.

305. But as neither God nor the hereafter can be seen and so they seem to be unreal and when a man dies and leaves no trace who is left to experience anything?

306. A mere worm can be as happy crawling in hell as Indra can be in heaven in the company of a heavenly maiden.

307. Therefore neither heaven nor hell is the result of merit or sin, for in both these places pleasure is the result of desire.

308. A man and a woman are brought together by desire, and from this the whole world is born.

309. Whatever a man covets for his own interest is nourished by desire; later, through mutual hatred desire destroys the world.

310. In such a manner do these devilish people claim that this world has no other basis than desire.

311. I will now leave this tiresome subject and not expand it further, for it is a waste of words.

IX. Holding fast to this view, these souls of feeble understanding, of cruel deeds rise up as the enemies of the world for its destruction.

312. Not only do they speak blasphemously about the Supreme Being, but they are convinced that he does not exist.

313. Their hearts are openly filled with heresy and the shafts of atheism are thrust deep into their souls,

314. and the feelings of respect for heaven and fear of hell have been burnt up in them.

315. O My friend, such men are imprisoned in the body and, like bubbles in impure water, they are sunk in the mire of sense pleasures.

316. When death draws near their bodies are attacked by disease, as fishermen approach the deep waters.

317. The rising of a comet augurs calamity in the world, and similarly they are born for the destruction of men.

318. As evil grows, so it thrusts out its shoots; and so these men are like walking memorials of sin.

319. As fire knows nothing else but to burn all that it meets, so they can only oppose all with whom they come into contact.

320. Krishna said to Arjuna, Now listen to the state of delusion
which prompts these acts.

> x. *Giving themselves up to insatiable desire, full of hypo-
> crisy, excessive pride and arrogance, holding wrong views
> through delusion, they act with impure resolves.*

321. A net cannot be filled with water, nor can a fire ever be
satisfied with fuel; these people are even more insatiable.
322. O Pāndava, harbouring desire in their hearts, they then
add to it deception and conceit.
323. As maddened elephants would become even more infuria-
ted if given intoxicating liquor, so with age they become
more and more arrogant.
324. Their obstinacy is equally strong, and aided by their folly,
how can any stable resolution be found in them?
325. Their actions distress others, and even cause the ruin of
those around them; these are the practices which they
constantly engage in.
326. They boast of their own actions, treat the whole world
with contempt, they spread the net of lust in every direction.
327. Through such acts they bring about great sins, as a cow
set free for religious purposes may dig up the crops at random.

> xi. *Obsessed with innumerable cares which would end
> only with [their] death, looking upon the gratification of
> desires as their highest aim, assured that this is all.*

328. Their sole object is to carry out their own intentions and
they are concerned with this even more than with their
lives.
329. They are deeper than hell and compared with their height
the heavens are small; even the universe is less than an
atom.
330. The endless anxiety in their hearts is like the ceaseless
exercise of yogic practices; [they cling to it] as a virtuous
woman refuses to leave her husband even in death
331. This anxiety continues to grow beyond all bounds while
they set their hearts on worthless objects of sense
332. They love to hear women sing, to enjoy the sight of their
form and to embrace them with all the pleasure of their
senses.

333. They are convinced that the company of wisdom is to be more highly valued than nectar.

334. To experience it they would hasten down to hell, ascend to heaven, or fly even beyond the boundaries of the earth.

> XII. *Bound by hundreds of ties of desire, given over to lust and anger, they strive to amass hoards of wealth, by unjust means, for the gratification of their desires. 'This day has been gained by me: this desire I shall attain',*

335. As a fish is likely to swallow the hook as well as the bait, so these men are caught up in the desire for pleasure.

336. They do not attain their desire and the seed of vain hopes multiplies like the silkworm.

337. This increasing lust remains unfulfilled and turns to hate and nothing remains as a purpose in life but lust and anger.

338. O Pāndava, as a watchman walks about all day and still has to be awake all night, he gets no rest either by day or by night,

339. so such a man, cast down from the heights by desire is dashed on to the rocks of anger below; yet because of his love of pleasure his anger and hate are beyond control.

340. He will harbour in his heart a craving for sense objects; but does it not need wealth to satisfy it?

341. In order therefore to obtain enough money to do so he plunders all and sundry.

342. Some he succeeds in killing, others he robs of all their possessions, for others he finds other methods of destruction.

343. As hunters setting out to hunt on the hills take with them nooses, sacks, snares, dogs, falcons, sticks and spears,

344. so in order to feed themselves these men kill many creatures and perform such evil deeds.

345. So by taking the lives of others they amass wealth; but having obtained it, how can they feel satisfied in their hearts?

> XIII. *This today has been gained by me; this desire I shall attain, this is mine and this wealth shall also be mine [in the future].*

346. 'Am I not blessed in that I have made my own the wealth that belonged to many people?'

347. Elated by such self-praise, his heart desires more and
     immediately he says, 'I will acquire still more of what
     belongs to others.
348. 'Through the means of what I have already gained I will be
     able to acquire all that is left in the world.
349. 'Then I will be the lord of all wealth and nothing within my
     sight will be allowed to remain.'

> xiv. *This foe is slain by me and others also shall I slay.
> I am the lord, I am the enjoyer, I am successful, mighty
> and happy.*

350. 'These are those whom I have destroyed, but they are too
     few, I will kill more so that I alone will remain in my great-
     ness.
351. 'I will destroy all, besides those who will serve me; in fact,
     I am the lord of all.
352. 'I am the king of the land of enjoyment, I am the centre of
     all pleasure, so compared with me even Indra will seem
     significant.
353. 'Whatever I do with mind, body or speech must be fulfilled,
     for who else is there but myself to command?
354. 'So long as my infinite power is not seen the god of death
     may seem to be mighty; in short I am indeed the whole
     mountain of happiness.'

> xv. *'I am rich and well-born. Who is there like unto me?
> I shall sacrifice, I shall give, I shall rejoice.' Thus they
> [say], deluded by ignorance.*

355. 'Kubera may be wealthy, but he does not know my enjoy-
     ment; even Vishnu himself is not worthy of my riches.
356. 'In comparison with my illustrious family and the extent
     of my kindred, Brahma is indeed of inferior descent.
357. 'They boast of such names as God and others; they cannot
     compare with me; who indeed is there who can?
358. 'Magical incantations have fallen out of use, but I will
     revive them and re-establish the sacrificial rites by which
     others are injured.
359. 'I will give whatever gifts they ask to those who sing songs
     in praise of me and to those who entertain me with dancing.
360. 'I will be the very embodiment of pleasure in the three
     worlds, indulging in highly seasoned food and intoxicating
     drink and consorting with young women.'

491

361. But enough has been said about this! All those who have become mad through their devilish nature are like people who try to smell the flowers of the sky.

> XVI. *Bewildered by many thoughts, entangled in the meshes of delusion and addicted to the gratification of desires, they fall into a foul hell.*

362. It is as if the dust of ignorance, caught up by the whirlwind of hope, were carried round and round in the sky of desire.

363. As a feverish man will talk wildly in delirium, they prattle about their desires.

364. Clouds of the month of Āshādha are massed together, waves rise incessantly on the surface of the ocean; in the same way these people desire endless pleasures.

365. Then there is formed in the being a thick cluster of creatures in the form of desires and the being is mutilated in the way that lotuses are when dragged over thorny bushes, or is broken in pieces.

366. O Pārtha, if a pitcher falls on top of a stone it will be broken into fragments; so are their hearts shattered.

367. As night passes darkness deepens; so does delusion develop in their hearts;

368. and as delusion increases, their desire for sense pleasures grows more intense and this leads to hell.

369. They heap up more and more sins so that even during their lives they experience the horrors of hell.

370. Therefore, O wise one, the devilish ones who entertain evil desires go down to live in hell.

371. In that awful place there are trees with leaves like swords, mountains of live coals and oceans of boiling oil.

372. Increasing agonies and ever new tortures imposed by the god of death pursue those of the demoniac nature who live in such a hell.

373. Yet the men who are doomed to inherit the infernal regions of hell continue, in their delusion, to perform sacrifices.

> XVII. *Self-conceited, obstinate, filled with the pride and arrogance of wealth, they perform sacrifices which are so only in name with ostentation and without regard to rules.*

374. Sacrificial rites, O conqueror of wealth, are of value, but these men render them fruitless because they perform them like actors in a play.

375. In the same way whores take to themselves lovers and enjoy [in imagination] the pleasures of married life.

376. They esteem themselves very highly and are inflated with unbounded pride.

377. They show no sign of humility but stand erect as a column of cast iron, or as a mountain which soars aloft in the sky.

378. So, rejoicing in their own superiority, they regard all others as being more worthless than grass.

379. Intoxicated in this way by the wine of wealth, O wielder of the bow, they are not concerned about good and evil actions.

380. Filled with these ideas, how can such men perform sacrifices? But such madmen will do anything.

381. At times they will pretend to perform sacrifices, intoxicated with stupidity.

382. They do not prepare a ground altar, or a shelter or sacrificial mound, or assemble the proper materials; and they reject all prescribed rules.

383. They will not brook even the mention of God or of brāhmans; so how can God or a brāhman attend at their sacrifices?

384. An experienced cowherd will place a stuffed calf near a cow, so as to be able to milk her,

385. and in the same way these men will invite people to be present at their sacrifices, and rob them of their possessions as sacrificial offerings.

386. Thus they sacrifice for the sake of their own profit, while desiring the destruction of everyone else.

> XVIII. *Given over to self-conceit, force and pride and also to lust and anger, these malicious people despise Me dwelling in the bodies of themselves and others.*

387. They proclaim their sacrificial skill to the world with drums and banners and vainly publish abroad their greatness.

388. Thus, as though smearing darkness with soot, these base men become even more swollen with pride on account of this fame.

389. Moreover their folly increases, their arrogance is doubled and egoism and lack of consideration is doubled.

390. Their strength grows more formidable as they strive to remove all trace of everyone else in the world,

391. so that selfishness and might combine and the ocean of arrogance swells beyond all limits.

392. Then with this upsurge of pride, lust turns into bile, and through the heat of this the fire of anger is lit.

393. As in summer a store of oil and clarified butter may be set on fire and a strong wind may arise,

394. so such people grow in egoism and arrogance is added to the combination of lust and anger.

395. Then, O prince of warriors, whom will they not seek to destroy in the pursuit of their own pleasure?

396. So, O wielder of the bow, they would not hesitate to sell their own flesh and blood for the sake of practising magic arts.

397. Thereby they burn us those very bodies in which I dwell, inflicting wounds on Me who am the Spirit.

398. And as I am the consciousness in all creatures, I suffer harm in all those others who art injured by the men who practise magic arts.

399. If any escape by chance from the danger of these arts, they hurl after him the stones of calumny.

400. On virtuous men and women, charitable men and priests, famous ascetics and recluses,

401. on devotees and great-souled ones in whom I dwell and who are purified by sacrifice, study of the Vedas and other practices,

402. these evil men sling sharp arrows of abuse smeared with the poison of hate.

403. Now listen to the way in which I deal with all sinners who in every way behave towards Me with enmity.

404. Those who are born into a human body, hating this world, I deprive of their human state and reduce to a lower condition.

405. I commit these evil ones to the state of the lowest order of life, that is, to the dunghill of trouble and the common of the city of worldly existence.

406. I transform them into tigers and wolves in a desert in which not even grass will grow for their sustenance.

407. There they are tormented by hunger and tear off their
flesh for food, and dying again and again are reborn to the
same condition.

408. Or they may be born as serpents confined in their holes
where, by the heat of their own poison, their skins are burnt
up.

409. O Arjuna, I do not grant to these wicked people rest even
for the time that it takes to breathe in and out.

410. I leave them in these torments for a period of time compared with which a million world ages would seem short.

411. Even this is only the first stage on the road they have to
travel; there are no experiences more terrible than those
which will come to them.

412. Listen now to the state of degradation to which those
possessed of demoniac wealth are brought.

413. Even birth in the darkest womb of such animals as the
tiger provide a slight relief through the support of a body,

414. but I deprive them of even this comfort, and then there is
continuous darkness in which even darkness itself would be
blackened.

415. Such darkness would arouse loathing in sin, hell would be
filled with terror, and in it is a weariness which would
cause even weariness to faint.

416. Through it impurities become more impure, heat is burnt
up, and the great terror is struck with fear.

417. O conqueror of wealth, those who are born into the wombs
of darkness have to undergo the most evil degradation in
the universe.

418. Speech would weep when describing this, the mind shrinks
from the memory of it. Alas, what hell have those fools
brought upon themselves!

419. Why do they encourage this demoniac wealth which has
brought about such a terrible fall?

420. O wielder of the bow, do not approach the place where
these demoniacal ones dwell.

421. It is not necessary to tell thee that thou shouldst avoid all
those in whom these six vices of hypocrisy and the rest.

XXI. *The gateway of this hell leading to the ruin of the soul is threefold, lust, anger and greed. Therefore one should abandon these three.*

422. Know that every evil thrives where the three vices of desire, anger and greed are grouped together.
423. O winner of wealth, all the sorrows have provided guides to show the way that leads to them.
424. They are among men the assemblage of all the sins whereby sinful men are cast down into hell.
425. So long as these three vices have not arisen in the heart, this hell is only heard of indirectly.[8]
426. They easily bring about harm and readily cause pain; and loss through them is not simply loss, for these three vices are the very incarnation of loss.
427. O great warrior, what more can I say? These are three spikes set on the threshold of the lowest hell which I have described.
428. He who associates with desire, anger and greed, in the assembly of the city of the underworld.
429. Therefore, O Kiriti, I tell thee again and again to rid thyself of these three vices which in every respect are most evil.

XXII. *The man who is released from these, the gates to darkness, O Son of Kuntī [Arjuna], does what is good for his soul and then reaches the highest state.*

430. Until a man has freed himself from the company of these, it is not possible to discuss any of the four goals of existence such as religious duty and others.
431. The Lord said, I cannot believe that anyone can find happiness as long as these three vices are active in his heart.
432. Anyone who has a regard for himself and fears the destruction of the Self should be careful to avoid them.
433. Swimming across the ocean with a stone tied to one's body, or living on meal of the Kālakuta poison,
434. would not be more impossible than attaining one's goal in company with desire, anger and greed; therefore wipe out every trace of them.
435. If ever one were able to break suddenly this threefold chain, he would go joyfully.

436. When a body is cleansed of the three humours, a city has
     been freed from the three forms of immorality, or a heart
     has been released from the three afflictions,
437. so when a man has freed himself from these vices, happi-
     ness is experienced in the world and the company of good
     men is found on the road leading to salvation.
438. Then he can pass through the dangerous forest of life and
     death supported by the company of the good and sustained
     by the scriptures.
439. Then he reaches the city of the grace of his spiritual tea-
     cher, where the joy of the Self lives forever.
440. There he will meet his mother, the Eternal Spirit, the sum-
     mit of all things desirable, and in a moment the clamour of
     worldly life will cease.
441. In short, he reaches the place where lust, anger and greed
     are utterly destroyed and he becomes the possessor of the
     great gift.

XXIII. *But he who discards the scriptural law and acts as
his desires prompt him, he does not attain either perfection
or happiness or the highest goal.*

442. One who does not care about these things and is obsessed
     with these vices is a traitor to the Self.
443. He who has disregarded the Vedas which are compassionate
     to all men and a light revealing good and evil,
444. one who pays no heed to prescribed actions and does not
     consider what is good for him, but indulges more and more
     in the pleasures of sense,
445. who refuses to give up attachment to lust, anger and greed,
     but remains faithful to them and resorts freely to the
     jungle of unrestrained conduct,
446. when the bonds of worldly life are removed, what will
     happen to him? He will not even experience the pleasures
     of earthly life.
447. He cannot approach the river of liberation near enough to
     drink its water; he cannot draw near to it even in a dream.
448. If a brāhman, in his desire for fish were to enter the tank
     [along with the fisherman] he would at once become an
     outcaste.
449. So a man who, for the sake of sense pleasure casts away
     the bliss of heaven, will be carried off by death.

450. In such a way, he obtains neither heavenly bliss nor earthly enjoyment of the senses; what possibility has he then of finding liberation?

451. Therefore he who, owing to his lust, desires to enjoy objects of sense, will have neither pleasure nor heaven; nor will he attain to liberation.

> XXIV. *Therefore let the scripture be thy authority for determining what should be done and what should not be done. Knowing what is declared by the rules of the scripture, thou shouldst do thy work in this world.*

452. Therefore, O My friend, he who seeks his own welfare should not disregard the commands of the scriptures.

453. A devoted wife will easily accomplish her own good if she follows the precepts of her husband.

454. A disciple will be able to enter the mansion of Self-realization if he gives heed to the teachings of his spiritual preceptor;

455. and a man will eagerly make use of a lamp when he wants to find his hoarded wealth.

456. In the same way, O Pārtha, a man who is anxious to realize all the aims of human existence, should revere the Vedas and the Smritis.

457. Whatever the scriptures tell us to give up [we should do so]; we should consider even a kingdom to be as worthless as grass. Whatever we are told to accept, we should take it without objection, even if it were poison.

458. O good warrior, the man who is thus entirely devoted to the Vedas cannot meet with misfortune.

459. The Vedas protect us from evil and bestow on us what is for our good; there is no better mother in the world than they.

460. They bring us to union with Brahma, so no one should disregard them. O Arjuna, thou also shouldst especially revere them.

461. O Arjuna, thou hast been born through the power of religious merit to fulfil the purposes of the sacred scriptures.

462. Being named the younger brother of righteousness, thou shouldst not behave otherwise than in accordance with that.

463. Let a man take the scriptures as his authority in discriminating between right and wrong and let him forsake all that is forbidden as evil.

464. Then thou shouldst carry out faithfully with all thy strength whatever is due to be done.

465. O thou wise one, the seal of universal authority has been given to thee and thou art supremely worthy to be the leader of men.

466. Thus did the Lord explain to Arjuna the nature of the demoniac qualities and how a man may escape from them.

467. Now listen with the ear of understanding to the way in which the son of Pāndu will earnestly question Him.

468. As under the direction of Vyāsa, Sanjaya entertained the king by narrating all this to him, so with the blessing of Nivritti I will continue this story.

469. If, O good men, you will favour me with your grace, I will fulfil your expectations.

470. Jnānadeva said, Do you, therefore, grant me the favour of your attention which will give me strength.

In the Unpanishad of the Bhagavadgitā, the science of the Absolute, the scripture of Yoga and the dialogue between Shri Krishna and Arjuna, this is the sixteenth chapter, entitled The Yoga of the Distinction between the Divine and the Demoniac Endowments.

NOTES

1. The reference here is to the guru of Jnāneshvar, often addressed as though he were a deity; here he is identified with the sun.
2. *the four divisions of speech.* See Ch. VI, v. 276.
3. *Brigu.* See Ch. IX, v. 477.
4. *the sixfold rites.* These rites are: personal sacrifice, sacrifice through the medium of another, study, teaching, charity and the acceptance of alms.
5. *Brahmasutras.* Aphorisms of the Vedānta philosophy, concerned mainly with Brahma.
6. *the waning moon.* This was a popular superstitition which accounted for the waning moon.
7. *Sagara.* A legendary king of the Solar race.
8. *Raurava.* This is the name of one of the various hells.

CHAPTER XVII

1. Salutation to my revered Guru, who is to me as the God Ganesha, through whose ritual gestures in deep meditation the universe is sent forth to blossom!
2. Shiva, as the Self, surrounded by the demon Tripura as the three cities of the qualities and confined the fortress of existence, was delivered by thee, as Ganesha, because thou didst remember him.
3. Compared with the god Shiva, therefore, thou art superior in greatness; yet, as a boat to carry us over the waters of this life of illusion, thou art light in weight.
4. Those who are ignorant about thee call thee the twisted-faced one but to the wise thou art seen to look straight ahead.[1]
5. Thy divine eyes seem to be small; but by opening and closing them thou dost bring about the creation and destruction of the world.
6. By the movement of thy ear [representing] activity, a breeze fragrant with the moisture emananting from thy temples blows and bees [in the form of] individual souls gather round as though worshipping thee with blue lotuses.
7. When thou movest thy other ear [representing] inactivity, the worship ceases; then the ornaments on thy body are displayed.
8. In the playful dance of thy consort who is the illusion of creation thou dost reveal the skill of thy movements.
9. Enough has been said, O thou creator of wonders, for those whom thou dost befriend are set free from the bonds of all relationships.
10. Thou art called Brother of all the world, for thou dost release all worldly bonds; therefore let us worship thee in this form.
11. O Lord, in that worship, one who taught himself to be

separate from thee finds that his separateness, perceived through dualism, no longer exists.

12. Thou dost remain far removed from those who regard thee as separate from them and seek after means [of finding thee].

13. Thou art not found in the hearts of those who try to reach thee by meditation, but thou lovest those who forget even meditation.

14. He who does not know thee truly but parades as all-knowing, is not accepted by thee even though his words may be as many as those of the Vedas.

15. Thy zodiacal name is Silence; why then should I seek to praise thee? How can I worship thee when all appearance is illusion?

16. Even if I desire to be thy servant, am I not thereby guilty of dualism? Therefore I should not enter into any relationship with thee.

17. When all these things have passed away, I will attain to union with thee; then I shall know thy inner meaning, O thou who art worthy of all worship.

18. When salt is put into water, no distinction is left; so is my salutation to thee. What more can I say?

19. An empty pitcher put into the sea overflows with water; when the wick of a lamp is lighted it becomes the lamp.

20. So by my salutation to thee I have become perfect in thee, O Shri Nivritti, and thereby I am enabled to expound the meaning of the Gitā.

21. In the last verse of the sixteenth chapter the Lord has given the following teaching in clear terms.

22. O Pārtha, in order to discriminate properly between right and wrong action the scriptures should be thy sole authority.

23. At this point Arjuna said to himself, How is it that for the performance of action there is no other source of permission than the scriptures?

24. How could one remove a jewel from the hood of a serpent, or pluck a hair from a lion's nose?

25. [Does it mean that] only he who can get the jewel and string it on the hair can have such an ornament, or his neck will go unadorned?

26. Who could bring together all the various teachings of the scriptures? And who would profit by this co-ordination?

27. If uniformity were brought about, would any man have the time to apply it? Would anyone live long enough to do so?

28. Even if someone were to have fourfold benefit of the texts, the means, time and place to study them, this would not be possible for all.

29. So in many respects it is impossible for all to follow the scriptures: therefore what will be the fate of those seekers after liberation who are ignorant?

30. The subject of the seventeenth chapter will be the inquiry concerning this matter made by Arjuna,

31. that Arjuna who is averse to all sense objects, skilled in all arts and a marvel even in the eyes of Krishna, [a second] Krishna in the person of Arjuna;

32. who is the support of all bravery, the ornament of the kingly line of the Lunar race and who delights in bestowing happiness and other benefits;

33. who was the beloved consort of pure intelligence, the repository of the knowledge of Brahma and faithful follower of the Lord.

Arjuna said:

> 1. *Those who, neglecting the ordinances of scriptures, offer sacrifices filled with faith, what is their position, O Kṛṣṇa? Is it one of goodness or of passion or of darkness?*

34. Then Arjuna said, O Krishna, Thou whose complexion is as dark as the tamal tree, who art Brahma in a form perceptible to our senses, Thy words leave me in doubt.

35. On what grounds did the Lord say that it is impossible for a man to attain liberation except according to the scriptures?

36. There might not be a place [where one could practise their teachings]; one might have no time or no one may be at hand to instruct.

37. All the aids to one's study may not be available at any time;

38. or former births may not provide sufficient merit, or intelligence may be inadequate; in such ways the scriptures may be beyond our reach.

39. In any of these circumstances, one may give up all consideration of the scriptures as one is unable to grasp their meaning.

40. There are those holy ones who, having understood the scriptures and followed their sacred injunctions now dwell in heaven,

41. and we desire earnestly to become like them and follow their example.

42. O Thou generous one, as a child copies out the letters of a lesson from a model, or as a man who is infirm sends a guide on in front of him,

43. so those who take [as their authority] the actions of a man learned in the scriptures follow after him in their faith.

44. They worship Shiva and other gods, make gifts of charity in land and in other ways, performing with devotion such rites as burning the sacrificial fire.

45. O Highest Lord, will thou tell me what the condition of such men will be, whether it will be of goodness, passion or darkness?

46. Then the Lord, the central emblem of the region of Vaikuntha, the very pollen of the lotus of the Vedas, to which the universe is as the shadow [to the body],

47. who art the vastness of time, mighty and beyond all conception, the invisible one without a second, full of joy.

48. Then out of His own mouth spoke Shri Krishna, He who is to be glorified, through whose power all that is exists.

The Blessed Lord said:

    II. *The faith of the embodied is of three kinds, born of their nature, good, passionate and dark. Hear now about it.*

49. O Pārtha, I understand thy contention that thou regardest the study of the scriptures as an obstacle,

50. O wise one, thou seekest to take by storm the highest state simply by faith; but that is not an easy matter.

51. O Kiriti, thou shouldst not rely on faith alone to reach this state, for if a brāhman has contact with an untouchable does he not become himself untouchable?

52. The water taken from the Ganges if poured into a wine vessel would not be accepted by anyone; consider this.

53. Sandalwood is a cool wood, yet when it is set on fire can it not burn the hand which holds it?

54. If gold falls into a vessel of inferior metal would not one be deceived if one took it as pure gold?

55. In the same way all forms of faith are pure in themselves;
but when a faith is held by men,

56. it is affected by the nature of men who are under the influence of eternal matter and conditioned by the three qualities.

57. In them two of the qualities are weakened and one pre-
domination; then the tendencies of the mind are affected
by this one quality.

58. Therefore, as tendency is, so is desire; as the desire is, so
men act; and according to a man's action is his birth into
another body after death.

59. Seed dies in growing into a tree, and the tree dies and is
carried on in the seed; this process continues eternally but
the species is never destroyed.

60. Similarly man passes through countless births, but the
action of the three qualities inherent in man never changes.

61. Therefore the faith with which men are endowed, thou
shouldst realize, is affected by these three qualities.

62. It may be that pure goodness is dominant in him and he
seeks knowledge, but the other two qualities are in opposition.

63. Faith that is sustained by goodness leads to the fruit of
liberation; then why do passion and darkness remain
inactive?

64. If passion breaks down the power of goodness and ascends
to great heights, then faith will become reduced to dust.

65. When the flames of darkness rise, faith is destroyed and is
ready to enjoy any undesirable pleasure.

> III. *The faith of every individual, O Bhārata [Arjuna], is
> in accordance with his nature. Man is of the nature of his
> faith: what his faith is, that, verily, he is.*

66. O wise one, there is no faith among human beings unaffected by goodness, passion and darkness.

67. Therefore faith is inevitably imbued with the three qualities and is therefore threefold, having the quality of either
goodness, passion or darkness.

68. As water is life-giving, but in contact with poison becomes
deadly; mixed with pepper it becomes pungent, or with
sugar-cane it becomes sweet,

69. so if a man is born and dies dominated by darkness, in him
faith will come to have that quality;

70. then as soot and black ink cannot be distinguished in colour, so his faith is identical with darkness.

71. In the case of a passionate man faith takes on nature, and when a man is good it is entirely good.

72. So therefore this whole world is moulded out of faith.

73. Under the influence of these three qualities faith is impressed with the stamp of this threefold nature; this thou shouldst understand.

74. As a tree is known by its flowers, as a man's mind is revealed by his speech, or as a man's actions in a previous birth are known by his experience in this life,

75. in the same way the threefold nature of faith can be recognized by the three characteristics which I will now describe to thee.

>IV. *Good men worship the gods, the passionate worship the demigods, and the demons and others [who are] the dull, worship the spirits and ghosts.*

76. Now the minds of those whose faith is solely pure are generally directed towards heavenly happiness.

77. They study all arts and sciences, they choose the proper sacrifices, and they reach heaven.

78. O warrior prince, those whose faith is passionate worship fiends and demons.

79. Those who offer up human sacrifices and after dark worship companies of evil spirits and corpses in the burning grounds,

80. are men created of the very essence of darkness and are the home of the faith that is dark.

81. These three are the signs of the three kinds of faith and I have described them to thee for this reason,

82. that the faith known as good should be held fast by men, O wise one, and the two which are opposed to it should be abandoned.

83. O conqueror of wealth, those whose mind is steadfast in the faith that is of goodness need not fear concerning ultimate bliss.

84. It does not matter if such a man does not study the Brahmasutras, master all the scriptures nor comprehend by his own insight philosophic doctrines.

85. But those elders who have become the very incarnation of the meaning of the Smritis and the Shrutis, giving it to the world by their practice of it,

86. these he follows in their conduct, walking in pure faith, and the same fruit is assured to him.

87. If with great efforts one man lights a lamp and another lights his lamp [from the first flame], would [the second man's lamp] be felt to be any less effective in giving light?

88. If someone were to build a mansion at great expense, would a temporary occupant not enjoy the pleasure of it?

89. Does a tank only quench the thirst of the one who builds it? Is not food prepared by a cook for others as well as for himself?

90. What more shall I say? Is the Ganges, [brought down by the sage] Gautāma, for him alone, and for all others a mere stream [must suffice]?

91. Even if a man is a fool, he will reach salvation if according to his ability he follows the conduct of those who are expert in the scriptures, provided that he has faith.

v. *Those men, vain and conceited and, impelled by the force of lust and passion, who perform violent austerities, which are not ordained by the scriptures,*

92. But there are other men who are unable even to utter the names of the scriptures and yet they will not allow one who is conversant with scripture to approach them.

93. They mock at the religious practices of their elders and snap their fingers at learned men.

94. Overwhelming in their power and proud of their riches they perform unauthorized penances.

95. Thrusting the knife into whatever lies before them they fill the sacrificial vessels with the blood and flesh.

96. They pour them into the flames of the sacrificial fires, offer them to evil spirits and even make oblations of little children for vows which they have made.

97. In an excess of zeal for some inferior deity they will fast for weeks on end.

98. In this way, O My friend, they sow the seed of injury to themselves and others in the field of darkness and later reap what they have sown.

99. O winner of wealth, they are like an armless man in the sea, who does not take to a boat;

100. or like a sick man who, angry with the physician, kicks away the medicine; how can he be cured of his illness?

101. Or they could be likened to a man, who out of envy for another who has sight, tears out his own eyes and is confined to his room [by blindness].

102. Those who have a demoniac nature are like these men, despising the teaching of the scriptures and wandering at random in the paths of infatuation.

103. They do whatever their lust dictates, kill any whom they are impelled by wrath to kill; indeed, they torment Me with the stones of suffering.

> VI. *Being foolish they oppress the group of elements in their body and Me also dwelling in the body. Know these to be demoniac in their resolves.*

104. Whatever pain they cause to their own bodies and those of others, it is I Myself who have to bear it.

105. One should not even have the contact of speaking with such sinners through a curtain; but I must mention them so that they may be avoided.

106. A corpse must be taken out of a house; one may have to speak with an untouchable; but then one must wash the stain from one's hands.

107. As for the sake of cleanliness one must not refuse to recognize dirt, so I must refer to these people so that they may be avoided.

108. O Arjuna, when thou dost see such men, remember Me, for there is no other means of cleansing this stain.

> VII. *Even the food which is liked by all is of three kinds. So are the sacrifices, austerities and gifts. Hear thou the distinction of these.*

109. Thou shouldst strive in every way to maintain thy pure faith,

110. thou shouldst associate with men whose company fosters goodness and eat food which will help to increase purity.

111. In fact, there is nothing so helpful towards the cultivation of a pure nature as suitable food.

112. O warrior, it is obvious that a man may, in full awareness, take an intoxicating drink and immediately become drunk.

113. If anyone takes even his natural food he may be overcome by the influence of wind and phlegm, or suffers from fever, will this be cured by drinking milk?

114. As immortality is won by drinking nectar and drinking poison will cause death,

115. so the state of a man's bodily humours vary according to the food he eats and these humours affect his inner nature.

116. Water heated in a jar becomes hot; in the same way one's moods are controlled by the humours of the body.

117. Therefore when pure food is eaten the quality of goodness is encouraged and when food of the nature of passion or darkness is eaten, the correspondong qualities are developed.

118. Now listen attentively and I will explain which food is pure and which leads to passion and darkness.

119. Now, O warrior, I will show thee clearly how there are three kinds of food that a man can eat.

120. Dishes are prepared according to the taste of the eater, and he is dominated by the three qualities.

121. The individual self who is the one who both experiences and acts and as he is affected by the qualities his nature and his actions are threefold.

122. Therefore his food is of three kinds, he performs sacrifices in these ways and his penances and his charitable gifts are also of three kinds.

123. First I will describe the different kinds of food, as I have said. I will make it quite clear.

> VIII. *The foods which promote life, vitality, strength, health, joy and cheerfulness, which are sweet, soft, nourishing and agreeable are dear to the good.*

124. Those fortunate ones who are endowed with the quality of goodness are attracted towards sweet foods,

125. those which in substance are juicy, sweet, succulent and ripe,

126. not too large, soft to the touch, pleasant to the tongue and tasty;

127. food which is full of juice and at the same time soft, moist and that cannot be spoiled by heating;

128. also that which is small in size, but, like the word of the teacher, powerful in their effect, so that even a small quantity will satisfy.

129. All foods that are not only sweet to the taste but also beneficial internally are liked by those who have the quality of goodness.

130. These are the properties of the foods which promote goodness and which are a protection and renewal of life.
131. When the clouds of such good food rain down into a man's
body, the river of his life flows more fully day by day.
132. This, O wise one, is the food which maintains goodness, as
the sun sustains the well-being of the day.
133. All these foods are a source of strength to both body and
mind; how then could there be any place for disease in
those who eat them?
134. When food of this kind is taken, the body is fortunate
enough to enjoy good health.
135. All the activities of the body result in prosperity and
happiness becomes a constant companion.
136. Such is the great effect of pure food on the body, bringing
happiness both within and without.
137. Now I will tell you in order of the foods which are liked by
those of passionate disposition.

> IX. *The foods that are bitter, sour, saltish, very hot, pun-*
> *gent, harsh and burning, producing pain, grief and disease*
> *are liked by the passionate.*

138. They like food which is more deadly and more bitter than
the Kalakuta poison, acid and burning more fiercely than
lime.
139. Filled with as much salt as the water needed to make
dough and with the same amount of other ingredients,
140. these extremely salt foods are much liked by a man of
passionate nature; while as for hot seasoning, eating such
food is like swallowing fire.
141. Such hot vapour is given out that a taper could be lit from
it; this is the kind of hot food that a passionate man desires.
142. A passionate man eats food so pungent that it could pierce
rocks, though it passes through him without causing any
injury.
143. He likes food that is altogether drier than ashes and he
enjoys the sting of it on his tongue.
144. He enjoys eating food that he has to grind between his
teeth.
145. The ingredients of this food are already pungent and
mustard is added to it so that when eating it hot vapour
passes through the mouth and nose.

146. The passionate man loves even more than his life such
     highly seasoned food that it would repel even the heat of
     fire.
147. Not being satisfied with this, his appetite runs riot and he
     would even consume flaming fire as a form of food.
148. As a result he is in a feverish heat and cannot rest either
     on the ground or in bed and the drinking vessel never
     leaves his mouth.
149. This is not food that he has eaten but rather a [stimulant] he
     has taken to arouse in him the sleeping serpents in the form
     of disease.
150. So disease and troubles arise at once in rivalry one with
     another; thus does the food of a passionate quality result
     in suffering.
151. O wielder of the bow, I have now described the food of a
     passionate kind and the nature of its many effects.
152. I will now tell thee the kind of food liked by those of the
     quality of darkness; do not let it fill thee with disgust.

*x. That which is spoiled, tasteless, putrid, stale, refuse and
unclean is the food liked by the dark ones.*

153. The man of a dark nature does not consider that eating
     decaying remains of food can do harm as a buffalo will
     eat mash.
154. One in whom darkness is present will eat in the afternoon
     food cooked in the morning, and even go so far as to eat it
     the next day.
155. He eats also what is half cooked, or altogether burnt, and
     what has no flavour.
156. He does not regard anything as food which is well cooked
     or succulent.
157. If he happens to get good food he will leave it as a tiger
     does, until it is putrid;
158. or he will take food that is several days old, that has lost
     its flavour, or is dried up, rotten or full of worms.
159. And this again is kneaded into a mass by his children's
     hands; or he sits down with his wife and family to eat from
     the same dish.[2]
160. When he has eaten such impure food he feels that he has
     had a good meal, but the sinner is not satisfied even with
     this.

161. Then see what happens! These substances which bear the
stigma of prohibition and are sinful and full of evil.

162. With impure water and unsuitable dishes, all serve to increase his eagerness for food of the quality of darkness.

163. O warrior, such are the tastes of these men of darkness,
and it is not long before their consequences are realized.

164. No sooner does [this unholy] food touch his lips than he
becomes liable to sin.

165. Moreover, what he eats cannot be called proper feeding,
for he is filling his belly with affliction.

166. Why should one seek to experience having one's head cut
off, or entering fire? Thou shouldst realize how this man
suffers.

167. The Lord said, O Arjuna, it is not necessary to describe the
various consequences of eating food of the quality of darkness.

168. Now hear how sacrifice is of three kinds, in the same way as
food is.

169. O thou highest among the eminent, listen to the essential
nature of the first form of sacrifice, of the quality of goodness.

> XI. *That sacrifice which is offered, according to the scrip-
> tural law, by those who expect no reward and believe firmly
> that it is their duty to offer sacrifice, is 'good'.*

170. A faithful wife does not allow her desire to go out to anyone
but her husband.

171. The Ganges does not flow beyond the ocean into which it
falls; the Vedas become silent when they perceive the Self.

172. So, too, they who devote their attention to their own welfare do not let themselves be egotistically concerned with
the fruits of action.

173. When water reaches the roots of a tree it does not turn
back but is absorbed into the tree.

174. In the same way they whose minds and bodies are absorbed
in the determination to perform sacrifices desire nothing,

175. and the sacrifice performed by those who have given up all
desire for reward and care for nothing but their duty is in
every way the best.

176. As a man can see his own face in a mirror and a jewel held
in the palm of the hand can be seen with a lamp,

177. as when the sun rises a road one wants to follow can be clearly seen; so these men, relying on the authority of the Vedas,

178. make receptacles for the fire, shelters and altars, and gather the requisite materials for the sacrifice in accordance with the prescribed rules.

179. As each limb of the body has its own suitable ornaments, they place all the materials in the correct arrangement.

180. How can I describe this in words? In this kind of sacrifice, richly adorned, is displayed the embodiment of the very art of all sacrifice.

181. Such a sacrifice is complete in every way, free from any desire for aggrandisement.

182. The tulsi plant is tended and watered, though it has neither fruit nor flower and gives no shade.

183. So thou mayest know that sacrifice carefully performed and without any desire for fruit is of the quality of goodness.

> XII. *But that which is offered in expectation of reward or for the sake of display, know, O Best of the Bhāratas [Arjuna], that sacrifice to be 'passionate'.*

184. O best of warriors, a similar form of sacrifice may be performed which is like inviting a king to a ceremony in honour of the ancestors.

185. If the king attends the ceremony it may be very profitable, for the ceremony will be carried but also fame will accrue to the host.

186. Entertaining such a desire, a man will perform such a sacrifice hoping thereby to reach heaven and to become famous as an expert in sacrificial rites.

187. O Pārtha, the performance of a sacrifice, for the sake of its fruits, and for acquiring fame in the world, is of the quality of passion.

> XIII. *The sacrifice which is not in conformity with the law, in which no food is distributed, no hymns are chanted and no fees paid, which is empty of faith, they declare to be 'dark'.*

188. As no priest but only the urge of instinct is required for the mating of birds and beasts, so desire is the basis of all sacrifices having quality of darkness.

189. As wind does not blow in a particular path, nor death seek
out an auspicious moment, and fire does not fear to consume what is prohibited,

190. so the conduct of a man of darkness is not restrained by
prescribed rites, and therefore, O wielder of the bow, it is
undisciplined.

191. He has no respect for proper rites, nor does he make use of
sacred chants; he is like a fly which eats any and every
kind of food.

192. He has an aversion to brāhmans, and so there is no question of gifts to them; like a hurricane to which fire is added,

193. he squanders all he has; he is quite devoid of faith as the
house of a man without an heir is despoiled.

194. Sacrifice performed thus in outward appearance only is the
sacrifice of darkness, said the consort of Lakshmi.

195. The water of the Ganges is one; but as it flows in different
streams, it may be polluted in one and remain pure in
another.

196. Penance, likewise, corresponding to the three qualities, is
threefold in its nature; the practice of one leads to sin,
practising the other brings salvation.

197. O wise one, if thou desirest to know why this is so, first
thou must understand what penance is.

198. First of all I will show thee the nature of penance, and then
speak of it as divided in accordance with the three qualities.

199. True penance, also, is threefold in kind; it is physical,
mental and verbal.

200. First listen to the explanation of physical penance, according to whether a man chooses to worship Shiva or Vishnu.

> XIV. *The worship of the gods, of the twice-born, of teachers
> and of the wise, purity, uprightness, continence and non-
> violence, this is said to be the penance of the body.*

201. His feet undertake the duty of walking day and night on
pilgrimages to the shrine of his chosen deity.

202. His hands are well used in beautifying the courtyard of the
temple and supplying the appropriate materials for the
worship.

203. As soon as he sees an emblem of Shiva or an image of
Vishnu, he prostrates himself at full length, like a pole.

204. He gives due service to brāhmans, the elders among men
on account of their virtues of learning and humility.

205. He brings relief to those who are worn out by travelling or afflicted by distress.

206. He offers up his body in the service of his parents whom he considers to be superior to all other holy places.

207. He serves his guru, the very sight of whom removes the sorrows of this terrible earthly existence and who is compassionate in the giving of knowledge.

208. O great warrior, in order to remove the soil of his physical egoism he pours it into the sacrificial fire of his own duty, covered with the repetition of sacred texts.

209. He salutes all creatures as imbued with the spirit, is zealous in doing good to others, and all times practises restraint with women.

210. His only contact with the body of a woman was at birth; since then he has always remained chaste.

211. He does not injure even a blade of grass, considering it to be among the living creatures; in fact he avoids all injury and all difference.

212. When all his physical behaviour is of this high quality, his penance may be called complete.

213. O Pārtha, as all this behaviour is principally the action of the body, I call it the penance of the body.

214. Thus I have described the nature of physical penance; now hear about the pure penance of speech.

> xv. *The utterance [of words] which gives no offence, which is truthful, pleasant and beneficial and the regular recitation of the Veda, this is said to be the penance of speech.*

215. The philosopher's stone transforms iron into gold without reducing its size or weight.

216. Such goodness is seen in the speech of one [who practises this penance] that he does not hurt his neighbour but gives pleasure to those around him.

217. As water is poured mainly for a tree, but at the same time keeps alive the grass, so if he speaks to one all others benefit.

218. If a man came upon a divine river of nectar he would become immortal, and by bathing in it all his sin and trouble would be removed; besides this, it is sweet to drink.

219. In the same way ignorance is dispelled by his speech, one's eternal nature is realized, and, like nectar, however much one listens to his speech one never grows weary of it.

220. Thus one who is practising the penance of speech speaks
whenever he is asked a question; otherwise he recites [the
Vedas] or repeats [the name of God].

221. He sets up in himself a temple in the form of his speech for
the three Vedas and his mouth is as a school of Brahma.

222. When the tongue is always occupied in uttering the name
of Shiva or Vishnu, this is known as the penance of speech.

223. I will now explain to thee mental penance; listen, said the
lord of all the gods of the three worlds.

> XVI. *Serenity of mind, gentleness, silence, self-control, the
> purity of mind—this is called the penance of the mind.*

224. As a lake with no ripples on its surface, the sky without a
cloud, a grove of sandalwood trees free from serpents,

225. the moon without changing phases, a king free from
anxiety or the milky ocean without the mountain Mandāra,

226. so, when the mind is freed from the meshes of doubt, it is at
rest in the Self.

227. The mind itself is like light without heat, food that is tasty
yet not heavy or the sky without hollowness,

228. for it knows that wherein lies its well-being, it escapes from
its natural tendencies, as though a chilled limb does not
allow itself to shiver.

229. Then the pure beauty of the mind is like the clear, un-
waning disc of the full moon.

230. The wounds inflicted by dispassion are healed, all disturb-
ing activities of the mind abate and the soul is prepared
for self-realization.

231. The tongue, usually active in thoughtful recitation of the
scriptures is released from its rein.

232. Then through the attainment of union with the Supreme
Spirit the mind ceases from carrying out its normal functions, as salt, at the touch of water, becomes one with it.

233. This being so, how can those moods arise in the mind which
drive it along the road of the senses until it reaches the
village of sense objects?

234. Thus the mind becomes cleansed from its normal tendencies
as the palm of the hand is free from hair.

235. O Arjuna, what need is there to say any more? When the
mind reaches this state it becomes fit for what is called
mental penance.

236. The Lord said, I have explained to thee fully the characteristics of mental penance,

237. and so have I told thee of penance in general and of its threefold division into that of the body, speech and mind.

238. Now listen, with all thy power of understanding, to the way in which this three-fold nature of penance arises from the three qualities.

> XVII. *This threefold penance, practised with utmost faith by men of balanced mind without the expectation of reward, they call 'good'.*

239. O wise one, thou shouldst practice in full faith the threefold penance which I have shown thee, foregoing any desire for the fruit of it.

240. When performed with a pure heart and with belief in the authority of the scriptures, the wise declare it to be of the quality of goodness.

> XVIII. *Penance which is performed in order to gain respect, honour and reverence and for the sake of show is said to be 'passionate'; it is unstable and not lasting.*

241. On the other hand penance that is performed in the spirit of duality to prove the performer's austerity and establish himself on the highest pinnacle of superiority,

242. so that the world may honour him and no other and give him the highest place at feasts,

243. that he may be worthy of the world's praises and that all men will make pilgrimages to him,

244. [penance practised in order] that he and none other should be the object of all forms of worship and that he should enjoy all the pleasures that accompany greatness,

245. putting on an appearance of penance in body and speech in order to win favour, as a whore adorns herself [to attract attention],

246. such penance, practised in the hope of gaining wealth and respect, is said to be of the quality of passion.

247. A cow which is diseased gives no milk after giving birth to a calf; if crops have been grazed when standing, there is nothing left for the harvest.

248. So that penance carried out with great effort in the hope of winning fame is completely devoid of fruit.

249. Besides being fruitless, O son of Pāndu, it is given up while
still unfinished; thus there is no stability in it.
250. Untimely clouds gathered in the sky may seem to shatter
the world with thunder; but how long do they stay?
251. So also this penance of a passionate nature is quite fruitless and has no continuity in practice.
252. Now when this penance is performed by the method per-
taining to the quality of darkness, a man loses both heavenly life and earthly renown.

> XIX. *That penance which is performed with a foolish
> obstinacy by means of self-torture or for causing injury
> to others is said to be 'dull'.*

253. O wielder of the bow, some, with the wind of folly in their
minds, regard their body as an enemy.
254. They set alight the five fires round their bodies so that it
may be burnt up as fuel.[3]
255. They burn balsam on their heads; they thrust hooks into
their backs and scorch their bodies with flaming wood.
256. They restrain their breath, perform unnecessary fasts, or
hanging head downwards [over a fire], swallow mouthfuls
of smoke.
257. They stand in cold water immersed up to the neck or sit on
the rocks or on a river bank where they tear their living
flesh.
258. In these and many other ways, O winner of wealth, they
inflict wounds on their bodies, performing penance in order
to do harm to others,
259. as a rock loosened by its own weight falls and shatters itself and at the same time crushes to powder anything that
comes in its way.
260. O Kiriti, these penances which are performed with such
skill in evil practices are of the quality of darkness
261. So also do these men inflict pain on themselves in their
desire to overcome others who are living in happiness.
262. In this way I have shown thee that there are three kinds of
penance, related to the three qualities.
263. Now the time has come for me to explain to thee the threefold nature of charity.
264. In correspondence with the three qualities, the giving of
gifts is also threefold. First listen to the giving which is of
the quality of goodness.

265. Whatever a man has received through performing his religious duties he should respectfully give [again to others].
266. This kind of charity is as rarely found as good seed and fertile soil are found at the same time.
267. One may come across a valuable jewel, but there may not be gold in which to set it, and even then there may be no one to wear it.
268. We are fortunate indeed if we meet with a festal day and at the time possess wealth and friends [to whom to give a feast].
269. When charity and the quality of goodness come together, the place, time, means and a deserving person will all be available.
270. In the first place, if possible one should be in Kurukshetra or Benares [when one offers gifts], or any other part of the world that is equally holy.
271. Secondly the time should be at the conjunction of the sun, moon and the planet Rāhu, or a similar propitious occasion.
272. Then at such a time and place there should be a person worthy to receive the gift, someone who is the incarnation of purity,
273. one who has become the very source of good conduct, the market for distributing Vedic knowledge, the purest jewel among brāhmans.
274. Then to such a person the gift should be given, renouncing all one's right to it, as a wife gives herself fully to her husband.
275. As one gives back to another what one has been keeping for him, or a king's servant [who carries] his box of spices offers it to him,
276. so, with the same absence of attachment and spirit of service one should offer gifts; in short, no desire should arise in the heart of the giver.
277. Further, one should see that he who receives the gift is in no way able to make any return for it.
278. If one shouts up into the sky there will be no echo; one sees nothing in a mirror from behind it;

279. a ball thrown on to the surface of the water will not rebound into the hand.

280. As a bull dedicated a temple makes no return for the food given to it, and an ungrateful man does not repay a benefit conferred on him;

281. so when a gift has been given to someone who cannot give anything in return, the giver should remain quite indifferent about it.

282. O prince of warriors, the giving of gifts in this excellent way, is the highest form of giving, called good,

283. for in it there is the combination of a right time, a right place, a proper recipient, a pure gift given with all propriety.

> XXI. *But that gift which is made with the hope of a return or with the expectation of future gain or when it hurts to give, is held to be 'passionate'.*

284. If a man feeds his cow that she may give him milk, or builds a storehouse and then goes out to sow the crop;

285. or if he invites his friends to a feast with a view to receiving gifts or sends presents to a friend who is observing a vow [and cannot accept them];

286. lend money to a neighbour after deducting the interest for it, or give medicine to a sufferer only after it has been paid for.

287. Gifts offered with such motives, in the hope that he will be able to enjoy life as a result of them, [are of the quality of passion].

288. O son of Pāndu, if a man should meet on the road a good brāhman, unable to give him anything in return,

289. and makes him a trifling gift, O Kiriti, so that in return the sins of his relatives may be forgiven,

290. he hopes to obtain thereby all manner of heavenly pleasure, although the alms would be insufficient to provide food for a single person.

291. Moreover, when the brāhman takes this offering, the giver is overcome with grief as though robbers had stripped him of all his possessions.

292. O Wise One, there is no need to say any more. Gifts given in this spirit are known in the world as passionate.

293. In places where infidels dwell, in forests inhabited by strange tribes, among the tent-dwellers and in the market squares of towns,

294. where people gather at dusk or at night and where ill-gotten gains are freely distributed,

295. to ballad-singers, jugglers, whores, gamblers and those who are under magic spells,

296. the sight of these givers is delighted with dances and their ears enchanted by hearing songs of their own praise.

297. Besides this, when they inhale the fragrance of balsam, they are bemused and behave like demons incarnate.

298. All such giving, I say, is of the quality of darkness; and there is yet another thing that by ill-fortune may happen.

299. As an insect may bore [holes in wood] and letters may be seen in its traces; or a crow may be caught by clapping the hands, a man of this quality may come upon an auspicious moment in some holy place.

300. There, seeing the giver of alms, a worthy recipient may ask him for alms; then he becomes confused with pride,

301. yet there is no faith in his heart, he does not bow his head, offer worship or show reverence, nor does he call on the other to do so.

302. He does not spread a seat for him or offer him red powder or rice grains; this is the behaviour of a man of passion.

303. He places a trifling sum in the hand [of a worthy brāhman] as though he were a creditor and dismisses him with disrespect.

304. He makes slighting remarks to him, as that he is not worthy of a greater gift and pushes him away with abusive language.

305. I will say no more; this kind of alms-giving is known everywhere as having the quality of darkness.

306. Now I have explained to thee the characteristics of all three kinds of giving; notice particularly those that have the qualities of passion and darkness.

307. I know, O wise one, that with thy clear mind thou wilt here raise a doubt,

308. that there is only one kind of action, that of goodness, which releases man from the bonds of earthly life; why shouldst thou speak of the opposite ones which are sinful?

309. One cannot obtain hidden treasure without first overcoming the evil spirit guarding it; a lamp cannot be lit without there being smoke.

310. So passion and darkness are doors barring the way to pure goodness; is it therefore wrong to remove them from the world?

311. Every act that derives from the virtues which I have described, from faith to charity, is under the domination of the three qualities.

312. But do not think that it was My desire to speak of all three; in order to explain goodness it was necessary to define the other two.

313. When two are set aside, the third is more clearly discerned, in the same way that between day and night the twilight is seen better.

314. So, by removing passion and darkness, the third quality remains and goodness stands out clearly.

315. Thus in order to show thee the quality of goodness, I have described passion and darkness, so that thou mayest avoid them and attain to goodness.

316. If thou dost perform sacrifices and all other duties in the spirit of pure goodness, thou wilt gain thy object in life as though in the palm of the hand.

317. What can escape our sight, if the sun shows us all that is? So if we do all in the spirit of goodness what fruit can we obtain?

318. Goodness has the means to satisfy all our desires. But as to what ensures the attainment of self-liberation,

319. that is a deeper matter and when we are helped to attain this we can enter into the state of liberation.

320. Though gold is worth fifteen rupees for a certain weight, without the royal seal it cannot be used as a coin.

321. Water may be clear, cool, sweet and pleasant, but its holiness depends upon its presence in sacred places.

322. A river may be large or small, but when it is received into the Ganges it is carried into the ocean.

323. So, O Kiriti, no obstacle can possibly fall in the way of a man once good works have led to liberation.

324. As soon as Arjuna heard these words, his heart could not
contain his eagerness [to know that this could be so] and he
exclaimed, O Lord, be pleased to tell me about this.

325. Then the lord of all compassion replied, Listen to the
nature of that by which a man can obtain the jewel of
liberation.[4]

> XXIII. *'Aum Tat Sat'—this is to be considered as the three-
> fold symbol of Brahman. By this were ordained of old the
> Brāhmans, the Vedas and the sacrifices.*

326. The eternal, Highest Spirit, the origin and abiding-place
of the universe, has one name, which is threefold.

327. Though he is beyond all name and class, yet in order that
man may recognize Him in the dark night of pride and
ignorance, the Veda has given Him a sign.

328. Men who are weighed down by the sorrows of this world
turn to God in supplication and the name to which He
answers is that sign.

329. The Vedas in their mercy have given a sacred word so that
Brahma, the One, may break His silence and meet duality.

330. When, by that one name, Brahma is entreated, that which
formerly was hidden is revealed.

331. However, only those who are worthy to sit with Brahma
in the city of the Upanishads on the mountain peak of the
Vedas know the meaning of this name.

332. Moreover the power of creation that lies in the Creator
emanates from this one name.

333. Before the creation of the world, O best of warriors,
Brahma was alone and in an undifferentiated state.

334. He was not conscious of Me, nor could He create, but this
name gave Him the power to do so.

335. When He meditated inwardly on the meaning of this name
and repeated the threefold word, He was endowed with the
power of creating the universe.

336. Then He created the brāhmans, gave them the Vedas to
direct them and established sacrifices and other rites as a
way of life.

337. After this He created innumerable living beings and gave
them the gift of the three worlds.

338. The Lord of Laksmi said, Hear now from Me the form of
that invocation which exalted the Creator, endowing Him
with the power to create—

339. Aum the prince of all invocations is the first syllable, Tat is the second and Sat is the third.

340. Thus these three, Aum, Tat and Sat make up the threefold name of Brahma; the Upanishads enjoy the fragrance of this flower!

341. When, uniting himself with this, a man performs deeds which are pure and good, then he lays hold of the final beatitude as a servant in his house.

342. A man may by good luck be given ornaments of camphor, but the difficulty is to know how to wear them;

343. similarly, good actions may be performed accompanied by the utterance of the threefold name of Brahma; yet if the secret of their use is not known,

344. it is as unprofitable as would be bringing into one's house numbers of sages if one does not know how properly to entertain them.

345. If a man were to tie up all his gold and jewels in a cloth and hang it round his neck,

346. it would be as fruitless as if a man were to perform good actions uttering the name of Brahma, but without knowing the proper method of doing so.

347. A hungry child will starve, even with food nearby, if it does not know how to feed itself.

348. O warrior, a man may have oil, wick and fire in his house, but there will not be light if he has no skill in handling them.

349. So when the moment arrives for an action and the invocation is remembered, all will be fruitless if it is not uttered in the correct way.

350. Therefore learn from Me the proper method of uttering this threefold name of Brahma.

> XXIV. *Therefore with the utterance of 'aum', the acts of sacrifice, gift and penance enjoined in the scriptures are always undertaken by the expounders of Brahman.*

351. So, the three letters of this name of Brahma should be uttered in three places, at the beginning, in the middle and at the end of an action.

352. O warrior, this is the method by which they who know Brahma receive the knowledge of Brahma.

353. Those who speak from the knowledge of the scriptures, in

their desire for union with Brahma, never omit the practice of sacrifice and other rites.

354. First by means of meditation they obtain a clear impression of Aum in their minds and then they utter the word;

355. and so meditating on it, expressing it in speech, they apply themselves to the performance of action.

356. As an unfailing light in darkness, as a strong companion in a forest, so is the utterance of the sacred Aum at the beginning of all undertakings.

357. Thus men offer up righteously obtained wealth in plenty, through the fire or through brāhmans, so that it may reach the deity for whom it is intended.

358. Also in the three fires, Āhavaniya, Garhapatya and Dakshina, they offer oblation in the form of renunciation, observing the proper ritual.

359. Performing various forms of sacrifice, they free themselves from all undesirable limitations.

360. At the proper time and place they offer to worthy recipients land and money that they have gained by rightful means.

361. They abstain from alternate meals, with great severity and eat and fast according to the waxing and waning of the moon, performing penances which dry up [the humours of] their bodies.

362. So that by the methods of sacrifice, charity and penance, usually thought of as forms of bondage, liberation is easily attained by them.

363. A boat drawn up on the shore is heavy, but launched it is possible to cross the sea in it; in the same way a man can free himself from the bondage of action by the proper use of this name.

364. Therefore all actions are effective when they are undertaken with the support of the utterance of Aum.

365. Again when they find they are entering into the fruit of their action they utter the word 'Tat'.

> xxv. *And with the utterance of the word 'tat' the acts of sacrifice and penance and the various acts of giving are performed by the seekers of salvation, without aiming at the reward.*

366. That which transcends the universe, which alone sees all and is beyond all, is referred to by the word Tat.

367. O wise Arjuna, meditating on Brahma as the primal source of all, they give expression to it in the word Tat.

368. Then they say, May all our actions and the fruit of them be dedicated to Brahma and may nothing be left for us to experience in this world.

369. So with the utterance of the word Tat, referring to Brahma, they offer all their acts to Him and saying, This is not mine, they cleanse themselves from the taint of action.

370. Therefore the action which is undertaken with the utterance of Aum and offered up with Tat is transformed into the nature of Brahma.

371. But although the act takes on the form of Brahma, it is not complete as long as the performer remains separate from Brahma.

372. Salt becomes one with water when mixed with it, and yet its quality of saltness remains; so, although the act has been merged in Brahma, duality [remains in the performer of it].

373. The more dualism grows the more the fear of earthly existence increases. So said the Lord, both here and through the Vedas.

374. In order that the sense of separateness with regard to Brahma may give way to a sense of unity, the Lord has given the reconciling word Sat.

375. If an action has become one with Brahma through the words Aum and Sat and praised as excellent,

376. the word Sat is applicable to it. I will now explain this to thee.

> XXVI. *The word 'sat' is employed in the sense of reality and goodness; and so also, O Pārtha [Arjuna], the word 'sat' is used for praiseworthy action.*

377. The meaning of the word Sat is that perfect nature of reality by which all unreality is deprived of any value, like a false coin.

378. This reality is unaffected by time and place and remains undivided in its own nature.

379. The whole world of form is unreality and once this is perceived one attains to union with Brahma.

380. It is owing to this that a worthy action becomes one with Brahma, and it should be seen in the light of consciousness of union [with Brahma].

381. Now an action which, through the use of the words Aum and Tat, has become one with Brahma, is immediately absorbed into the Supreme Spirit.

382. This is the very essence of the application of the word Sat. It is Krishna who says this, not I, Jnāneshvar.

383. If I were to say that it is I who speak thus, it would impute duality to Him and this would detract from His greatness. Therefore I say that these are the words of the Lord.

384. There is still another way in which to use the word 'Sat' that is helpful to one who performs good deeds.

385. If good deeds are performed in accordance with a man's status, but there is some defect in carrying it out,

386. then, as [the movements of] the whole body are impeded if one limb is defective, or if one part of a carriage is missing its movement is prevented.

387. Similarly if at the time a deed is performed there is one virtue missing, then a good deed loses its value;

388. but when the word Sat is spoken, following Aum and Tat, the utterance of this word rescues it from being worthless.

389. So the word Sat, owing to its power of purification, will nullify the defect in performing the action and its validity is restored.

390. As a divine medicine can cure a patient, or help be given to one who is overcome, so the word Sat can restore perfection to a deed carried out imperfectly.

391. An action may, by mistake, overstep the boundaries of what is forbidden,

392. like a traveller who loses his way, or an expert who is mistaken; do not such things happen in the world?

393. So when through lack of thought an action passes beyond the boundary and may be blamed as unrighteous,

394. then the use of the word, more powerful than the other two, makes the action a worthy one.

395. As the rubbing of iron with the philosopher's stone, the mingling of a stream with the waters of the Ganges, or a shower of nectar on a dead person,

396. so is the effect of the word Sat on an imperfect action, O king among warriors, such is the power of this name.

397. When thou hast understood the secret of it and dost consider this name, thou wilt know that it is indeed Brahma.

398. Thou shouldst know that the utterance of these three

words Aum, Tat and Sat, leads to that Brahma from which the whole visible world has become manifest.

399. This name is the hidden symbol of the absolute and purest Parabrahma.

400. This name is supported by Brahma as the sky is its own support; the name and the bearer of it are inseparable.

401. When the sun rises in the heavens it shines by its own light; so Brahma reveals this triple symbol.

XXVII. *Steadfastness in sacrifice, penance, gift is also called 'sat', and so also any action for such purposes is called 'sat'.*

402. This name is not only a triple symbol, but is Brahma Himself; know, therefore, that whatever action thou mayest undertake,

403. whether it be a sacrifice, a gift, or some severe penance, it may remain defective or remain incomplete,

404. but if it is offered to Brahma it is transformed into His nature; there is no question of the quality of the gold produced by contact with the philosopher's stone.

405. In Brahma the complete or the incomplete are no longer distinguishable, as rivers cannot be separated once they have flowed into the sea.

406. O Pārtha, who art full of insight, I have explained to thee the power of the name of Brahma,

407. and, O good warrior, I have also explained to thee the proper method of utterance of the syllables in this incantation.

408. Such is the greatness of this name of Brahma; O king, hast thou understood this mystery?

409. Therefore from now and at all times let thy faith increase in this name which will set thee free from all bonds.

410. Whatever action is accompanied by the proper use of this invocation can be considered as comparable with the whole recitation of the Vedas.

XXVIII. *Whatever offering or gift is made, whatever penance is performed, whatever rite is observed without faith, is called 'asat', O Pārtha [Arjuna]; it is of no account hereafter or here.*

411. If a man were to leave this path and lose the support of faith, letting the power of self-will increase in him,

412. then even if he performed innumerable horse-sacrifices, gave away alms that would fill the world with jewels, or performed thousands of penances upon one toe,

413. all these efforts would be as irrelevant as creating new oceans as reservoirs of water.

414. It would be as useless as showers of rain falling on rocky ground, pouring out oblations on to dead ashes, or embracing a shadow,

415. O Arjuna, such undertakings would be as ineffective from the beginning as trying to beat the sky with one's hands.

416. It would be like grinding stone in an oilmill, which would produce neither oil nor oilcake, but would lead only to poverty.

417. As a traveller who makes a bundle of potsherds [for food] would starve to death, for they would serve no purpose either in his own country or another,

418. so any action performed [without] faith brings no worldly happiness; how then could it give any hope for joy in heaven?

419. Therefore any action undertaken without faith in the name of Brahma would bring only weariness in this world and the world beyond.

420. So spoke Krishna, who is as a lion who destroys the elephant of sin, the dispeller of the darkness of the threefold misery, Shri Hari, the best of warriors.

421. So Arjuna was absorbed in the bliss of the Self, as if the moon were lost in its own light.

422. Now a battlefield may be thought of as a merchant who, with arrows as his tally, counts the lives of men as though they were pieces of flesh.

423. See how at this terrible time Arjuna experienced the bliss of union with the Self! Such matchless good fortune has never been known in any other.

424. Sanjaya said to the king of the Kauravas, One delights to see these virtues in the enemy, Arjuna, and he is a guru bringing us heavenly joy.

425. If Arjuna had not questioned Him, the Lord would not have revealed these mysteries; how then would we have been able to witness this experience of union with Brahma?

426. We should be groping in the darkness of ignorance on the cycle of births and deaths; but we have been brought into the temple of the light of the Spirit.

427. So great is the favour that he has bestowed upon us that in his power of teaching he is as a brother to the great Vyāsa.

428. At this point Sanjaya thought to himself that his praise of Arjuna would not please the king and that he was saying too much.

429. So he left this theme and began to speak of what Arjuna had asked Krishna.

430. Jnānadeva, the disciple of Nivritti says, I will now relate all this to you; be pleased to listen.

In the Upanishad of the Bhagavadgitā, the science of the Absolute, the scripture of Yoga and the dialogue between Shri Krishna and Arjuna, this is the seventeenth chapter entitled The Yoga of the Threefold Division of Faith.

NOTES

1. The face of the image of Ganesha, the elephant-headed god, is described as 'twisted' on account of the trunk, which falls to one side.

2. The actions described here are contrary to all dining customs among Hindus and would only occur in low caste or outcaste families.

3. *five fires.* The five external fires represented five internal mystic 'fires' which are said to be ignited by certain yogic practices. See note 5, below.

4. *Aum tat sat.* The mystic words given in XXIII below are the 'name' of Brahma; their meaning and the context in which they are used are given in the verses following XXIV to XXVI.

5. *three fires.* These are the names of certain sacrificial fires to be burned by brāhmans, kshatriyas and vaishyas: *gārhapatya*, the fire maintained perpetually by the householder and from which sacrificial fires are lit; *āhavaniya*, the consecrated fire lit from this and in which the oblations are placed; *dakshina*, the 'southern' fire, placed in the southward area of the site of the sacrifice. See also Ch. XVIII, note 6.

CHAPTER XVIII

---

1. Hail to Thee, O God, who art pure and ever merciful to Thy devotees; who like the storm wind dost dispel the net of the clouds of birth and old age![1]
2. Victory to Thee, O God, the mighty one, destroyer of all that is inauspicious, who art the fruit of the tree of the Vedas and also the giver of it.
3. Hail to Thee, O God, who art all in all; compassionate towards those who have freed themselves from worldly attachment, overcoming the relentless grasp of death, beyond all limitation.
4. Victory to Thee, O God, immutable, whose belly is swollen with feeding on those of fickle mind and who delightest in the constant play of the evolution of the universe.[2]
5. Hail to Thee, O God, the undivided one, who inspirest the fullness of joy, who destroyest for ever all sin and art the source of all creatures.
6. Victory to Thee, O God, the self-illuminating one, the sky which bears the world as a cloud, the pillar of support for the creation of the universe from its beginning and the destroyer of earthly existence.
7. Hail to Thee, O God, the pure one, ocean of mercy, the elephant in the garden of the dawn of knowledge, who by the practice of restraint dost destroy the passion of lust.
8. Victory to Thee, O God, one and indivisible, who hast overcome the power of the serpent of the god of love, who art the light in the house of Thy devotees, the remover of all trouble.
9. I salute Thee, who art without a second, sole object of the love of those who are mature in dispassion, worthy of the worship of those who have attained to Thee, beyond the reach of illusory matter.
10. Hail to Thee, O God and Teacher, who art as the tree of desire which is beyond the power of thought to imagine,

the soil in which grows the seed of the tree of self-knowledge.

11. O Thou who art supreme, how can I sing Thy praise with
all these various epithets?

12. I know that that form of Thine which I have described in
these words is invisible to us; therefore I am ashamed of
speaking of Thee thus.

13. It is known that the ocean keeps within its boundaries;
but this is only so as long as the moon does not rise.

14. The moonstone does not worship the moon by giving out
its own moisture; listen to this, it is the moon which
draws it out.

15. Who can tell what causes the trees to send out fresh foliage at the coming of spring? It is not in the power of the
tree to prevent this.

16. Does the lotus hesitate to open when it receives the rays of
the sun? Does not salt lose its form when touched by water?

17. So also, when I remember Thee, all thought of my own
individuality is lost. As a man who has eaten a full meal
cannot refrain from belching,

18. so Thou hast filled me with Thyself and I have lost all
consciousness of my self and my voice is wild with desire
to praise Thee.

19. On the other hand, if I were to praise thee in full consciousness, I would discriminate between Thee and Thy
qualities.

20. But Thou art the very image of oneness; how can I make a
distinction between Thyself and Thy qualities? If a pearl
is broken in two pieces, should the pieces be joined, or be
left as they are?

21. If I call myself a servant, would that not impute to Thee
the status of a master? Why should I use of Thee such
words implying separateness?

22. It would not be real praise to say that Thou art my father
or my mother; for this would imply wrongly the distinction of parent and child.

23. Were I to speak of Thee as the spirit pervading the universe, O Giver of all, that would suggest that Thou who
art within couldst also be outside.

24. Therefore it seems that there is no proper form of praise
in this world and that silence is the only ornament that
befits Thee.

25. Therefore silence is the only praise, absence of action is the only mode of worship, and cessation of separate existence is to be in Thee.

26. O my mother, accept my praise though it may be as the irresponsible words of one who is overcome by confusion.

27. I pray Thee place the blessed seal of the Gita on my exposition so that it may be acceptable to this gathering of saintly men.

28. Thereupon Shri Nivritti exclaimed, Do not go on repeating the same thing; how long must one go on rubbing a piece of iron with a touchstone?

29. Then Jnanadeva asked him to grant his blessing and listen to his discourse.

30. The Gita is like a jewelled temple and the meaning of it is the crowning jewel on its pinnacle; and this chapter is the guide to the revelation of it.

31. It is usually thought that as soon as the top of a temple is seen one has the vision of the god within it.

32. It is the same with this chapter, for when it is seen the meaning of the whole Gita is understood.

33. This is why I say that the eighteenth chapter is the pinnacle placed on the temple of the Gita by Shri Badarayana.[3]

34. In a temple nothing is added beyond the pinnacle; so this chapter is the completion of the Gita.

35. Shri Vyasa is a great craftsman, for on that mountain of jewels known as the Vedas he has marked out the site of the meaning of the Upanishads.

36. In the soil were found innumerable stones such as the threefold purpose of life, and with them he built a surrounding wall in the form of the Mahabharata.[4]

37. In the centre of this enclosure he fashioned many well carved stones in the form of knowledge of the Self which is wrought out of the dialogue between Arjuna and Krishna.

38. Then with the plumb-line of inaction and adding the essence of all the scriptures he erected the courtyard of liberation.

39. In this way he built a temple consisting of the first fifteen chapters, from the purifying of the ground to the top layer of the fifteenth chapter.

40. The sixteenth chapter is the dome over it, while the
seventeenth chapter is the base of its pinnacle.

41. The eighteenth chapter is the pinnacle which rises above it
and on which flies the banner of Vyāsa, author of the
Gitā and other sacred works.

42. Thus all the previous chapters are the layers rising one
above the other, while in this chapter is shown the completion of the work.

43. The pinnacle shows clearly that the work is indeed
finished and the eighteenth chapter reveals the whole
Gitā.

44. In this way the skilful Vyāsa erected the temple of the
Gitā, providing shelter for all creatures.

45. Some wander round it from a distance by means of its
daily repetition, some enjoy the shade it affords by hearing it recited.

46. Others making offerings of betel-leaves and money in the
form of complete attention and enter the inner temple of
the understanding of its meaning.

47. There, through self-illumination they at once meet with
the Lord Hari; but in the temple of liberation all men are
equal.

48. The Gitā is thus the temple of the followers of Vishnu
and the eighteenth chapter is its pinnacle; here I have
shown its special nature.

49. Now I will explain how, as I understand it, this chapter
arises from all the previous seventeen.

50. That the body is one and yet the two forms are not separate can be seen in the form of Shiva known as Ardha-
nāri-nateshvar.[5]

51. The Ganges and the Jamnā rivers are separate because
they flow in different courses; but because their streams
are of water, they are seen to be one.

52. In the bright half of the month the digits of the moon increase, but they do not appear as separate layers in the
moon.

53. So the four quarters of a verse seem to be separate
because they are divided into stanzas; similarly each
chapter [is separate only because of] the division into
chapters.

54. But in the continuity of meaning they are not separate,
as one thread holds together an ornament of jewels.

55. Pearls are strung together in a necklet, but in beauty of form they are as one.

56. The flowers in a garland can be seen separately, but the fragrance cannot be counted on the fingers; the verses and chapters may be regarded in this way.

57. There are seven hundred verses and eighteen chapters in the Gitā, but the Lord has taught but one truth and no other.

58. I have not departed from this method in expounding the Gitā. Now listen to the explanation of this chapter in the same manner.

59. At the end of chapter seventeen, in the closing verses, the Lord spoke thus:

60. O Arjuna, all works which are done without faith in the name of Brahma are worthless.

61. Hearing these words of the Lord Arjuna was pleased and said to himself, I think He has condemned all those who devote themselves to the life of action!

62. How can these poor people who, blinded by ignorance, do not see God, have any idea of the power of His name?

63. Without freedom from passion and darkness, faith is weak; how can it apprehend the name of Brahma?

64. As it is dangerous to grasp a spear, to run on a rope, or to play with the hood of a serpent,

65. so are works performed without faith harmful; they lead to rebirth and all kinds of evil lie in them.

66. Even if actions are properly performed, they only lead men as far as knowledge; otherwise they may lead to hell.

67. If the life of action is beset with so many difficulties, how can men who perform them hope to reach liberation?

68. So let us cast aside action, renounce all and resort to perfect non-attachment.

69. Then there would be no anxious concern about the evil effects of action and knowledge of the Self would be reached.

70. These are the mystic words which call forth knowledge, the good soil in which the crop of knowledge ripens and ropes by which it may be captured.

71. I would like to ask the Lord whether men would not be set free if they followed the way of renunciation and non-attachment.

72. With this thought in mind Arjuna asked Krishna to explain clearly the nature of these two.

73. The answer which Krishna gave is the subject of the eighteenth chapter.

74. Thus one chapter leads on to another as one generation gives birth to the next. Hear now how Arjuna asks Krishna about this.

75. When the son of Pāndu heard the concluding words of the Lord in the last chapter, his mind was distressed.

76. Though in reality he had thoroughly understood the teaching, he was troubled when Krishna remained silent.

77. When a cow has satisfied her calf she does not wander away; this is the nature of true affection.

78. Similarly, men long for the loved one to speak even without cause, and enjoy looking at each other again and again, increasing their delight.

79. This is the nature of true affection, and Pārtha was the embodiment of such love; he was, therefore, troubled at this silence.

80. Through the medium of discussion one may come to realize the [otherwise] unattainable Absolute, as one can see one's own image in a mirror;

81. but if the conversation comes to an end, the opportunity for this experience is lost. How could Arjuna, having already partaken of this joy, endure the loss of it?

82. So under the pretext of asking the Lord about renunciation and non-attachment, Arjuna reopened the subject of the Gītā, as one unrolls a piece of cloth.

83. This is not just an eighteenth chapter, it is the whole Gītā itself contained in one chapter. When a calf desires milk does not the cow respond at once?

84. So when the discussion of the Gītā was drawing to an end, Arjuna returned to the subject with which it deals. Can a master refuse to speak with his servant?

Arjuna said:

   1. *I desire, O Mighty-armed [Kṛṣṇa], to know the true nature of renunciation and of relinquishment, O Hṛṣikeśa [Kṛṣṇa], severally, O Keśinisūdana [Kṛṣṇa].*

85. I have said enough. Addressing his question to Krishna, Arjuna said, O Lord, listen to my request!

86. O Master, these two terms seem to have the same meaning,
as company and group are synonymous.

87. Similarly relinquishment also expresses renunciation; that
is how I understand them.

88. If there is any difference in what they imply wilt Thou
make it clear? Then Shri Mukunda said, They are certainly different.

89. Yet I agree with what you think, O Arjuna, these two
words have but one meaning.

90. Both these words do indeed mean relinquishment; but
this is the difference between them:

91. Renunciation means abandonment of all action, while
relinquishment implies abandonment of the fruit of
action.

92. I will now explain to thee when the fruit of an action
should be renounced and when the action itself should be
abandoned; pay heed to what I say.

93. In forests and on mountains trees grow in abundance, but
rice and garden shrubs do not grow naturally.

94. Grass grows freely without being sown; on the other hand
rice will not grow without cultivation.

95. The human body grows of itself, but the ornaments that
adorn it are made with skill; a river rises from its own
source, but a well is only made by digging.

96. In the same way daily actions and recurring ceremonies
take place naturally, but actions prompted by desire for
their results are not performed without this motive.

The Blessed Lord said:

    *11. The wise understand by 'renunciation' the giving up of
works prompted by desire; the abandonment of the fruit
of all works, the learned declare, is relinquishment.*

97. All acts performed with desire for their fruits such as the
horse sacrifice,

98. digging wells and tanks, planting gardens, donations of
land and large villages, and the carrying out of similar
kinds of vows,

99. in fact everything that is done for the sake of merit or
benefit, prompted only by desire, binds the doer of these
acts to the experience of their fruits.

100. O winner of wealth, when a man enters into the village of

this body, he cannot avoid the experiences of life and
death.

101. What is appointed by destiny cannot by any means be
evaded; a fair or dark complexion cannot be changed by
washing.

102. A man must experience the fruit of every act that he performs with desire as its motive; it is like a debt from which
one can never be freed except by payment.

103. O son of Pāndu, such an act might be suddenly committed
without the prompting of desire; even without fighting
one might be struck by an arrow shot by chance.

104. Sugar tastes sweet even if taken into the mouth unwittingly; a live coal would burn even if it were pressed in
the hand [in mistake for] ashes.

105. Similarly acts performed for the sake of their fruit have
an inherent power and therefore the man who seeks liberation should avoid them.

106. O Pārtha, a deed of this nature is like poison that must be
expelled from the stomach.

107. Abandonment of such actions as these is called in the
world renunciation. So spoke the Lord who sees into the
heart of every man.

108. As fear vanishes when wealth is given up, so when actions
prompted by desire are renounced all desire is rooted out.

109. The time of the conjunction of sun and moon is the
occasion for honouring the ancestors; the Shrāddha ceremonies are performed on the anniversary of the death of
father or mother.

110. When a guest arrives, certain things must be done. All
these rites are recurring duties.

111. In the season of rains the sky is filled with clouds; in the
spring [the beauty of] the forest is increased, and youth
adds beauty to the body.

112. The moonstone becomes moist under the moon and the
sun causes the lotuses to bloom. All this beauty emerges
from within; there is no outer agent.

113. So if all those acts which are performed daily are carried
out with proper observance, they are given the more
worthy name of recurring rites.

114. Also acts which are performed daily in the morning, at
noon and in the evening, are called daily actions. But as
the sight of the eyes is not superior to the eye itself,

115. as the power of walking is in the feet and not derived from elsewhere, or light lies potentially in a lamp,

116. as fragrance lies hidden in the sandalwood tree and is not given to it by another, so is the performance of an action inherent in it.

117. Thou mayest know, O Pārtha, that these acts are normally spoken of as daily actions; in this way I have explained to thee both daily acts and recurring rites.

118. Because both these kinds of action are performed of necessity, they are regarded by some as devoid of fruit.

119. Nevertheless, as surely as a man who takes his food is satisfied, and his hunger disappears, these daily and periodic duties produce their result.

120. If an alloy of gold is placed in the fire, the dross disappears and the pure gold is left, so also will such actions produce their corresponding fruit;

121. for when these actions are performed all sin is removed; then a man's own worthiness is increased and the state of liberation comes within his grasp.

122. So great is the fruit of daily acts and periodic rites; but it should be abandoned as one avoids a child born under the constellation Mula.

123. Creepers blossom and mango trees send out tender shoots, but as the season of spring passes away without even touching them,

124. so daily duties and periodic rites should be carried out with due attention and within the proper limits, and then the entire fruit be abandoned as though it were something vomited.

125. Wise men refer to the abandonment of the fruit of such actions as relinquishment and so I have expounded to thee both renunciation and relinquishment.

126. When renunciation is achieved, actions springing from desire cannot bind a man, for naturally everything that is prohibited is avoided;

127. and these actions become powerless when desire for them is a bandoned, in the same way that the whole body becomes lifeless if the head is cut off.

128. Then all action fades away, as a crop dies down after it has ripened, and self-knowledge is easily attained.

129. Thus through the practice of both these methods one is raised to the place of honour in self-knowledge.

130. If, however, one does not carry out this carefully and relinquishment is inadequately practised, this is no longer relinquishment and one falls into even greater entanglement.

131. Medicine taken without a proper diagnosis of the disease can be as harmful as poison; food eaten by a man who is not hungry may be a danger to him.

132. Therefore do not renounce that which should not be renounced and do not become attached to what should be renounced.

133. If relinquishment is carried out in the wrong way it becomes a burden; therefore dispassionate men struggle against forbidden actions.

134. Some men are unable to relinquish desire for the fruit of action and they say that all action is bondage; they are like naked men who regard others as quarrelsome because they call them naked.

135. A sick man who is greedy blames the food; a leper is not angry with his body but with the flies that settle on it.

136. So they who are incapable of relinquishing the fruit of action look upon all actions as evil and decide that they should be abandoned.

137. Others again declare that such acts as sacrifice must certainly be performed, for there is nothing else so purifying.

138. To attain a state of mental purity as quickly as possible, one should not be indolent in practising those acts which strengthen it.

139. If gold is to be purified one must not hesitate to put it in the fire; to keep a mirror clean dust must be collected for scouring it.

140. If one really wishes to have clean clothes, one must not despise the washerman's cauldron as dirty.

141. As one cannot have tender food except by cooking it, so, though actions are troublesome to perform, they should not be disregarded.

142. Arguing in this way some assert that action should never be abandoned; their relinquishment has become a subject of dispute.

143. Now give Me your attention; I will explain how this
conflict can be resolved and a decision on relinquishment
can be reached.

> IV. *Hear now from Me, O Best of the Bhāratas [Arjuna],
> the truth about relinquishment; relinquishment, O Best
> of men [Arjuna], has been explained as threefold.*

144. O son of Pāndu, know that relinquishment is of three kinds
of which I will now make the distinction.
145. Though I may make these three kinds of relinquishment
clear, thou shouldst know what is the essence of them all.
146. First thou shouldst listen to that confirmed opinion
which is abundantly clear to Me, the omniscient one.

> V. *Acts of sacrifice, gift and penance are not to be relin-
> quished but should be performed. For sacrifice, gift and
> penance are purifiers of the wise.*

147. This is a matter which must be understood completely by
every seeker who is alive to the importance of his own
liberation.
148. Sacrifice, charity and penance, and all such duties which
are considered obligatory, can no more be given up than a
traveller can avoid taking step after step.
149. The search for a lost object cannot be given up until it is
found, nor a dish of food be put aside till hunger is satisfied.
150. A boat cannot be left until the opposite bank is reached, a
plantain tree cut down till it has borne fruit, nor a lamp
set aside until the hidden object has been found.
151. So also a man should not be indifferent to the performance
of sacrifice and other duties as long as his determination
to gain self-knowledge is not firm.
152. On the contrary he should carry out sacrifice, charity and
penance again and again, according to his capacity.
153. The faster a man walks the sooner will he be able to rest;
so the more these duties are practised [the more rapidly
does he reach the state of] abandonment of action.
154. The more medicine a man takes the sooner will he be
free from disease.
155. Similarly, the more often a man performs such actions in
the proper way, the sooner passion and darkness will be
driven out.

156. When impure gold is placed again and again in a crucible with salt, the alloy is removed and the gold purified.

157. Similarly a deed performed with devotion casts out passion and darkness, and gives one the vision of pure goodness.

158. O conqueror of wealth, for those who desire purity of mind such actions are as effective as pilgrimages to holy places.

159. As if a stream of nectar were to come to a thirsty man in the desert, or the sun shine on the eyes of a blind man,

160. a river run to the rescue of a drowning man, the earth embrace a falling man or death prolong the life of one who is dying,

161. so, O son of Pāndu, good actions free the seeker from the bondage of actions. As a dying man can be saved by poison used as medicine,

162. so, O conqueror of wealth, if actions are expertly performed they are most effective in freeing a man from the bondage of action.

> VI. *But even these works ought to be performed, giving up attachment and desire for fruits. This, O Pārtha [Arjuna] is my decided and final view.*

163. Now, O Kiriti, I will explain to thee that expert procedure by which actions can annul the very results which they bring about.

164. When the five great sacrifices are performed in accordance with the rites, no pride in being the agent of them is left.[6]

165. A man who goes on a pilgrimage at the expense of another cannot rejoice or take a pride in the fact that he is making a pilgrimage.

166. A man who captures a king alone by the power of the royal seal cannot boast that he is a victor.

167. A man who crosses the water supported by another cannot claim that he is swimming; a priest distributing gifts for another is not displaying his own generosity.

168. In such a way one should carry out all actions at the proper time without taking to oneself the pride of having performed them.

169. Further, O Pāndava, once acts have been performed, do

not let any desire for the fruits they produce enter thy mind.

170. O conqueror of wealth, all desire for the fruit of actions should be given up before they are undertaken, as a nurse suckles the child of another woman.

171. One should perform actions with indifference towards their results, as one does not water a holy fig tree with the hope of getting its fruit.

172. A cowherd may gather the cows together without any longing for milk; one should have the same attitude towards the results of one's own deeds.

173. Whatever actions are carried out in this manner bring to the doer of them the blessing of self-knowledge.

174. Therefore My teaching is that a man should perform actions after renouncing all attachment to their fruit and to bodily desire.

175. I repeat that anyone who is weary of the bondage of earthly existence and longs to be freed from them should not depart from this teaching.

> VII. *Verily the renunciation of any duty that ought to be done is not right. The abandonment of it through ignorance is declared to be of the nature of 'dullness'.*

176. Avoiding prescribed duties from a hatred of activity would be like tearing out one's eyes because one is angry with darkness.

177. In my opinion such abandonment of action is of the quality of darkness, and it is like a man who cuts off his head because he has a headache.

178. If a road is difficult one can pass along it by walking; should one cut off one's feet on account of the fault of the road?

179. If a hungry man were to kick over a dish placed before him because the food was too hot, without considering that he would then have to go without it,

180. he would be like a man of the quality of darkness who, possessed by confusion, does not know that defects in the performance of actions are overcome by performing them in the proper way.

181. Should a man abandon actions that he should perform as a duty, he practises only that relinquishment which has the quality of darkness.

182. One should understand one's own capacity and recognize obligatory rites, yet realize the difficulty of performing them.
183. The beginning of an action appears at first sight to be difficult, as one may feel it is a burden to carry provisions for a journey.
184. As a neem leaf is bitter to taste, or the fruit of the Hirda is at first astringent, so before completion a duty may seem hard to perform.
185. Even the cow has horns which are harmful, and the Shevanti plant has a prickly stem; it is difficult to enjoy a meal if one has first to cook it.
186. In the same way the beginning of an action is difficult and therefore one feels that it will need effort to perform it.
187. Just as one may throw down a burning object, a man may begin an action because it is prescribed, but abandon it when it causes him trouble.
188. He may say to himself I have obtained this body as a result of my good fortune; why should I trouble myself with rites which sinful men perform?
189. I do not wish to enjoy later the fruits of action performed now; is it not better to enjoy what is already done?
190. O best of warriors, if a man abandons actions through fear of bodily suffering, such relinquishment is of the nature of passion.
191. Abandonment of works takes place in this case, but one does not obtain the real fruit of relinquishment; when some substance boils over on to the fire, this is not an oblation.
192. If a man loses his life by drowning, he cannot claim that he has offered up his life by submersion in water; he has merely suffered unnatural death.
193. So that the man who abandons an action through attachment to the body does not gain the fruit of real relinquishment.
194. In short, when self-knowledge arises in the mind, then as the dawn extinguishes the light of the stars,

195. so, O winner of wealth, all actions disappear with their cause; such relinquishment leads to liberation from the fruits of action.

196. O Arjuna, this liberation does not come through relinquishment born of ignorance. Thou shouldst not consider this as true relinquishment; it is born of passion.

> IX. *But the relinquishment of a man who performs a prescribed duty as a thing that ought to be done, renouncing all attachment and also the fruit of relinquishment, is regarded as one of 'goodness'.*

197. Listen now, while I tell thee in due course by what kind of relinquishment one can enter into liberation from the results of action.

198. A man who has the quality of goodness performs actions that have fallen naturally to his lot, in accordance with his own capacity carries them out with due respect [for the scriptures].

199. He renounces all claim to be the doer of actions and dismisses every hope for the results of what he does.

200. O Arjuna, should a man treat his mother with disrespect or have lustful thoughts about her, this would bring him to the deepest hell.

201. He should reject such impulses and worship her as his mother. Is a cow to be abandoned merely because its mouth is dirty?

202. Who would throw away his favourite fruit because there is no juice in the skin or the stone within it?

203. The pride of being the doer of actions and the desire for the fruit of them are the two fetters that bind a man [to the performance].

204. As a father does not behave in either of these ways towards his child, so [performed with relinquishment] no harm can come from prescribed actions.

205. Relinquishment is the greatest of all trees, for on it grows the fruit of liberation, and it is known throughout the world as having the quality of goodness.

206. As a tree is made barren if its seeds are burned, so by relinquishing the fruits of action, action itself is relinquished.

207. As soon as iron is touched by the alchemist's stone its

blackness is removed; so the impurities of passion and darkness disappear [when an action becomes pure].

208. Then through that pure quality of goodness the eyes of self-knowledge are opened, as the water of a mirage disappears in the evening,

209. and the illusion of the whole world of phenomena is no longer perceptible to the mind, as the space of heaven can nowhere be seen.

> x. *The wise man who renounces, whose doubts are dispelled, whose nature is of goodness, has no aversion to disagreeable action and no attachment to agreeable action.*

210. If on account of former births he has to perform both pleasant and unpleasant actions, they are to him as the clouds fade out of the sky.

211. For him, O Kiriti, all actions are equally pure, and therefore he is not affected by either pleasure or pain.

212. He knows which actions are auspicious but is he elated by them? Then will he shrink from what is inauspicious?

213. He is in no doubt about this, as a wakened man is not deluded by his dreams.

214. He has no conception of dualism between the doer and the action, O son of Pāndu; such relinquishment has the quality of goodness.

> xi. *It is indeed impossible for any embodied being to abstain from work altogether. But he who gives up the fruit of action is said to be the relinquisher.*

215. O Pārtha, actions given up in this way are truly renounced; abandoned in any other manner they bind the doer even more firmly.

216. O left-handed Archer, those who have become incarnate in a body yet are reluctant to perform actions are ignorant.

217. What would happen to a jar if it felt repugnance for earth? How can a garment rid itself of the threads of which it is woven?

218. Heat is the material property of fire; can it become weary of it? Can a lamp feel hatred for its own light?

219. If asaphoetida is repelled by its own unpleasant smell how can it acquire a sweet scent? What would be left if water cast away its own moisture?

220. So then as long as a man has to remain embodied in a
bodily form it is foolish to talk of giving up activity.

221. We ourselves place the religious mark on our forehead and
can remove and replace it at will; but can we do the same
with our forehead?

222. So we may renounce such actions as we ourselves have
undertaken, but can we give up that activity which is
inherent in bodily life?

223. Even during sleep we breathe in and out without any
effort on our part; other functions also continue without
our control.

224. On account of the life of the body activity is inevitable
and cannot cease either in life or after death.

225. There is only one way in which freedom from such activities can be obtained; that is, not to let oneself be overcome by desire for their results.

226. When a man offers up the fruit of his action to the
Supreme, illumination is attained by His grace; then he
loses all fear, as a man who recognizes a rope as a rope
ceases to fear that it might be a snake.

227. So through knowledge of the Self both ignorance and the
necessity for action are removed. O Pārtha, when relinquishment is made in this way it is true relinquishment.

228. When a man carries on activity in the world in this way, I
regard him as one who has made a true relinquishment;
otherwise he is like a sick man who mistakes a swoon for
taking a rest.

229. When a man is weary of one kind of activity, and seeks
respite in another, he is like one who is beaten with a stick
after a blow from the fist.

230. In short, one who has made activity ineffective through
giving up its fruit is truly a man of relinquishment in all
the three worlds.

> XII. *Pleasant, unpleasant and mixed—threefold is the
> fruit of action accruing after death to those who have not
> relinquished: there is none whatever for those who have
> renounced.*

231. On the other hand, O conqueror of wealth, a man who
does not make this relinquishment renders himself liable
to experience three kinds of result.

232. When a father to whom a daughter is born says that she

is not his and offers her in marriage to another, he withdraws [from responsibility] and the son-in-law is in a difficult position.

233. Anyone who plants a field of poisonous plants and sells the drug, lives on the profit; but those who buy the drug die from taking it.

234. So, whether a man performs actions with the idea that he is the doer, or whether he does them without this idea and with no desire for their fruit, there is no way of escaping activity.

235. The fruit of a tree on the roadside is for anyone who wants it; similarly the fruit of an action comes to him who performs it,

236. but he who even after performing an action relinquishes the fruit is not bound by the world, for the three worlds are but the result of activity.

237. The gods, humanity and inanimate creation make up the whole extent of the world, but they are the three aspects of the effect of activity.

238. Of this threefold fruit one is desirable, another is undesirable while the third combines both qualities.

239. All those who are addicted to worldly pleasures, and indulge in prohibited activity disregarding what is prescribed,

240. are reborn into forms of the lowest levels, insects, worms and clods of earth; this is called the undesirable fruit of actions.

241. Those who with respect for their own duty and regard for their proper capacity, perform good actions in accordance with sacred tradition

242. are reborn, O left-handed Archer, as Indra and other gods; this form of rebirth is known as the desirable fruit of action.

243. Now as when sweet and sour flavours are mingled a third taste is produced, different from the others and replacing them,

244. as in yogic practice the outgoing breath can be suspended by blocking the nasal passage, or as when truth and falsehood are blended in one, falsehood is vanquished,

245. so when sinful and meritorious deeds are in equal proportion, a man obtains rebirth into a human body; this is termed mixed fruit.

246. Thus there is in this world a threefold result of actions,
     and he who is caught up by the desire for pleasure does
     not relinquish the fruits of action.
247. So long as his tongue can taste a man will enjoy the pleas-
     ure of eating; but in the end he will surely die [from a sur-
     feit of food].
248. The company of robbers is not dangerous so long as one
     does not reach a forest; a whore is no threat so long as
     she is not touched.
249. So, if while performing actions with his body a man boasts
     of his importance, he will experience the fruit of them as
     soon as he dies.
250. As when a powerful usurer comes with the payment bill
     he will not be turned back, so is the experience of the
     fruit of one's actions inevitable.
251. When grains of wheat fall from the ear they will in turn
     produce new ears of wheat; 'this again falls and in turn
     produces more grain.
252. So when a man experiences the fruit of an action, this is
     the cause of further activity, as in walking one step takes
     the place of another.
253. As a ferry boat plies back and forth from one bank to the
     other, so there is no escape from the attraction of the
     enjoyment of the fruits [of activity].
254. In accordance with the goal and the means of reaching it
     experience of the fruit of action extends, so that those
     who renounce it are caught up in the toils of worldly
     existence.
255. As a jasmin flower begins to wither as soon as it opens,
     acts performed by those who renounce their fruit are as
     though they had not been performed.
256. If a farmer uses up all his seed in food he cannot cultivate
     any further crops; so also when the fruit of actions is
     renounced, there is no further desire for activity.
257. Such men, helped by their purified nature and by the
     shower of nectar which is the grace of their guru,
     remove the misery of duality by the prosperity of true
     knowledge.
258. Then that threefold fruit which brings into being the illu-
     sion of the universe is destroyed and both the experiences
     and the object of experience cease to exist,
259. O best of warriors, all those who, with wisdom as their

guide, make such renunciation, are delivered from the suffering of experiencing the fruit of their actions.

260. When through this renunciation a man attains to the vision of the Self, he does not see action as something separate from himself.

261. When a wall falls down the pictures painted on it are reduced to clay; when the dawn appears does the darkness of night remain?

262. When a man is no longer standing upright his body will not throw a shadow; without a mirror has a man's face any reflection?

263. Again, when a man awakes from sleep, what chance is there of dreaming? Then who can say whether his dreams are true or false?

264. So when renunciation has been made, the root of ignorance cannot live; who can then perform or renounce action which arises from it?

265. There can be no talk of action being performed when renunciation has been made; but so long as ignorance survives in a man

266. and he concerns himself with whether actions are auspicious or inauspicious, and, further, his mind is obsessed with duality,

267. then, O wise Arjuna, the Self is as widely separated from activity as the east from the west.

268. The sky and the clouds, or the sun and a mirage, are entirely different from each other, or the wind distinct from the earth.

269. The rocks in a river are covered by its waters, but thou knowest well that these two are completely different.

270. Weeds float on the surface of the water but they are very different from it; can lamp-black and light be considered as one because they are found together?

271. Though there are dark spots on the moon they are not identical with it; sight and the eyes are quite distinct from each other.

272. A path and the traveller who walks along it are as different as a river and the bed in which it flows; so too a mirror is in no way similar to the man who looks into it.

273. O Pārtha, in the same degree activity is quite separate from the Self; but it is certainly true that they are associated together through ignorance.

 O Mighty-armed [Arjuna], learn of Me these five factors, for the accomplishment of all actions, as stated in the Sānkhya doctrine.

274. By opening fully its blooms on the lake the lotus gives the impression that the sun has risen and at once the black bee feeds on the pollen.

275. Again I tell thee that the activity in which the Self appears to take part is derived from different causes. I will now explain these five causes.

276. Perhaps thou dost already know these five causes, for the scriptures have already described them openly.

277. In the royal city of the princely Vedas, in the palaces of Vedānta and Sānkhya they have been proclaimed to the accompaniment of drums.

278. They are the chief reason for the accomplishment of all actions in the world, but do not ascribe this cause to the majestic Self.

279. O Kiriti, they are widely known through this exposition and thou shouldst listen to them carefully.

280. Why shouldst thou trouble to learn about them from another when I, the Jewel of Wisdom, am at hand?

281. With a mirror placed in front of him why should a man ask another to tell him what is his true image?

282. I am here today as thy playmate, as when a devotee searches for something he always finds Me there within it.

283. While the Lord was speaking thus in the flow of His love for Arjuna, he forgot himself and Arjuna's heart melted with joy,

284. as in a flood of moonlight a mountain of moonstones would dissolve into a lake.

285. So, breaking through the barrier that separates joy from the experiencing of it, Arjuna's whole being was full of joy.

286. Then Krishna, being all-powerful, at once came to Himself and rescued Arjuna who was about to be overwhelmed.

287. The flood of ecstasy was so strong that even such a great soul as Arjuna, with all his wisdom, could have been submerged. So, lifting him out of it,

288. Krishna said, O Pārtha, come to thyself! Then Arjuna drew a deep breath and bowed his head.

289. O generous Lord, Thou knowest that, weary of the separateness of our individual existence, I was seeking to enter into union with Thee.
290. If in Thy love for me Thou dost wish to satisfy this urgent desire, why dost Thou raise this barrier of individuality between us?
291. Then Shri Krishna said, O foolish one, dost thou not yet know that there is no difference between us? Is there any separation between the moon and the moonlight?
292. I fear lest thou wilt be angry if I speak thus; but this only strengthens true affection.
293. The difference which lies between us enables us to recognize each other and live together; so speak no more of this.
294. O son of Pāndu, what were we discussing? Was I not telling thee of the separateness between activity and the Self?
295. Then Arjuna said, O Lord, thou hadst begun to satisfy my wish and explain this truth to me.
296. Thou didst promise to make clear to me the fivefold cause of activity,
297. and didst tell me that the Self was in no way connected with activity. I beg Thee to continue with this subject which I desire to understand.
298. The Lord of the universe, feeling much pleasure, said Where else could one find a man so persistent in his search?
299. O Arjuna, I will indeed explain to thee this inner meaning of our discussion; but I shall be even more indebted to thee for thy affection.
300. Arjuna then said, O Lord, hast Thou forgotten what Thou didst say earlier? Why dost Thou still say 'I' and 'thou' in the language of duality?
301. The Lord continued, Is that so? Now give thy full attention to what I am going to say.
302. O wielder of the bow, know it to be true that the whole structure of human activity results from five causes, quite separate from the Self.
303. Also the purpose from which the whole field of activity proceeds is clearly five-fold.
304. In this the Self remains indifferent; He is neither the purpose nor the material cause of the activity, nor does He support its accomplishment.

305. Good and evil activity originate in the same way that day
and night appear in the sky.
306. When water, heat and vapour combine with air, clouds
are seen in the sky, but the sky knows nothing of this.
307. When a boat made of wooden boards is rowed by a boat-
man and propelled by the wind; the water is no more than
a witness of its movement.
308. When a lump of earth is placed on a potter's wheel, it
becomes a pot through the turning of the wheel by a
handle.
309. The potter uses his skill; but consider, does it receive
anything from the earth except its support?
310. When at the rising of the sun the world begins its activity,
has the sun any part in this?
311. So when the five causes enter into combination the
creeper of activity is planted, quite apart from the Self.
312. Now will I describe these five severally and in detail, as
pearls are each separately weighed.

> XIV. *The seat of action and likewise the agent, the instru-
> ments of various sorts, the many kinds of efforts, and
> providence being the fifth.*

313. Now listen closely to the characteristics of these five
causes of action, of which I say that the first is the body.
314. It is termed the seat of action for this reason, that in it
there live both the experience and that which is to be
experienced.
315. Then the ten instruments of the organs of sense, active
day and night, are engaged in the activities which produce
pain and pleasure.
316. The body is called the seat of action because a man has no
other means of experiencing pleasure and pain.
317. It is the home of the group of twenty-four elements and it
is here that the entanglement of bondage and liberation
is unravelled.
318. Besides this, O winner of wealth, it is the basis from
which emerge the three states of consciousness in waking,
dreaming and sleeping, and this is why it is called the
body.
319. The second cause of action is to be known as the doer, the
reflection of consciousness.

320. When the water from the sky falls upon the earth it forms
pools and reflected in them the sky seems to have the
shape of a pool.
321. In a deep sleep a king forgets his kingship and dreams
that he is a beggar.
322. So also consciousness, forgetting its own true nature,
identifies itself with the body and takes on that form.
323. In this sense the universal consciousness is called the
individual self; and this self promises to remain attached
to the body in every respect.
324. It is matter that performs actions, but owing to delusion the individual self claims the credit for them; for this
reason he is called the doer.
325. There is but one sight looking through the hair of the
eyelashes; but it seems to be divided up as though by
the hairs of a fly-whisk.
326. A single lamp in a house appears to be many, because it is
seen through different windows;
327. so the one knowledge of the intellect seems to be distributed throughout the senses owing to the functioning of the
various sense organs.
328. The senses then, O Prince, are the third of the separate
causes of activity.
329. As rivers flowing from the east and the west fall into the
same ocean and their waters flow together,
330. as a single man portraying all the nine sentiments appears
to be many different persons,
331. so that force of action that resides in the inexhaustible
breath appears to be divided when manifested by the
various senses.
332. When expressed through the medium of the voice it is
speech; when through the hands it is the movement of a
giving and taking.
333. This is the moving force in the feet, and in the lower
organs of the body it is the passing of waste matter.
334. When it passes from the navel to the heart, uttering the
sacred syllable, it is called the vital breath in the body.
335. When this force rises towards the head it is called the
upward breath,
336. and when it flows through the lower passages, it is called
the downward breath. On account of its all pervading
nature it is called the diffused breath.

337. When with the essence of food it permeates the interior of the body, passing into every joint, including the navel,

338. and, O Kiriti, after it has carried out all these functions it is said to be evenly flowing throughout the body.

339. When it is manifested as yawning, sneezing and belching, it is called respectively by the names of 'serpent', tortoise' and 'lizard'.

340. O good warrior, in this manner the activity of the vital air in the body is one, though it seems to be many because it expresses itself in various ways.

341. This force, manifesting itself through different functions, is the fourth cause of activity.

342. The best of the seasons is Shārada, when the moon is at its best, and especially when the moon is full;

343. or the springtime when a garden is at its best and a man enjoys the company of his beloved, and all circumstances are favourable.

344. O Pāndava, lotuses are at the height of their beauty when in full bloom and their fragrance enhances it.

345. As poetic quality enhances speech, elegance of style increases this quality and the touch of the spirit inspires it.

346. so in the glorious company of activities intellect is the finest, and has incomparable beauty, superior to all other senses.

347. Pure intellect holds the place of honour in the company of the senses, for it represents the group of presiding deities.

348. For this reason the sun and other deities support with their favour each of the ten senses.

349. The Lord said, O Arjuna, this company of the ten deities is the fifth cause of activity.

350. So here I have explained to thee these five causes of activity in such terms that thou mayest easily understand them.

> xv. *Whatever action a man undertakes by his body, speech and mind, whether it is right or wrong, these five are its factors.*

351. Now I will explain how this group of five causes increases in its effect, giving rise to the whole sphere of actions.

352. If the season of spring suddenly sets in it causes new foliage to sprout; that produces flowers which in their turn form fruit.

353. The rainy season brings clouds, the clouds produce rain, and that leads to the joy of the harvest.

354. The east brings forth the dawn, the sunrise proceeds from the dawn, and gives light to the whole day.

355. So, O Pāndava, mind is the cause that gives rise to the thought of action, which then lights the lamp of speech.

356. That lamp of speech points out the path for all kinds of activity; then the doer enters into the performance of actions.

357. The whole bodily system supplies the motive for bodily actions, as iron goods are wrought from iron;

358. or, O wise one, as threads are interwoven in warp and woof and a piece of cloth is formed from them,

359. so the various functions of mind give rise to the actions of mind, speech and body, as a diamond is used to cut a diamond.

360. Now if someone were to ask how the body, for instance, can be both a cause and a motive. let him listen to the explanation.

361. For example, the sun itself is both the motive and the cause behind the sunlight, and one section of the sugar-cane plant is the cause of the growth of a succeeding section.

362. In order to praise the goddess of speech, speech itself must be used and to establish the Vedas, they themselves must be used.

363. So although it is well known that the body and its senses are both the cause of activity, it must be understood that they are also the motives.

364. Consequently when the body and its senses are both causes and motives, the whole world of activity is brought into existence.

365. O conqueror of wealth, if thou followest the path sanctioned by scripture, rightness itself is the motive of right conduct.

366. If a great volume of water were to fall on a rice field, it would serve a valuable purpose even though it would be absorbed by the earth.

367. If a man leaves his house in anger and finds himself by chance on the road to Dvārka, he may be weary but his steps will not have been in vain.

368. So that blind activity which owes its rise to the combination of cause and motive, through the insight given by the scriptures may be said to be right.

369. If milk boils over when it is needed for serving, it is lost, but not spent to any purpose.

370. So if an action carried out without the support of the scriptures is not to be regarded as useless, one would have to consider stolen money to be accounted as of equal value with a gift.

371. Is there any mystic verse which contains any letter beyond the fifty-two of the alphabet, O son of Pāndu? Or is there any human being who does not utter one of these fifty-two?

372. But, O holder of the bow, so long as a man does not understand the meaning of the verse the utterance of it will be fruitless.

373. Similarly the activity which arises at random from cause and motive does not adhere to the teaching of the scriptures.

374. It is action of a kind, but it is not effective and must be counted as sin arising from sinful causes.

> xvi. *Such being the cases, the man of perverse mind who, on account of his untrained understanding, looks upon himself as the sole agent, does not see [truly].*

375. In this way, O wise Arjuna, the five causes of action are also motives; consider now the part played in all this by the Self.

376. As the sun, not being a visible object, reveals objects to the eye, so the Self reveals action though it is not itself the doer.

377. O great warrior, one who looks in a mirror is neither the mirror nor the reflected image; but it is he who can account for both.

378. As the sun which is neither day nor night, causes them both to be, O son of Pāndu; so the Self, which is neither the doer nor the deed, is the evidence of activity.

379. If a man is deluded by the individuality of the body and identifies his mind with it, he is as blind to the Self as the darkness of midnight.

380. He who considers the boundless Spirit, God or Brahma in terms of the body, firmly believes that the Self is the doer,

381. He does not realize this about Me that I as the Self am beyond all action and am only the witness of it.

382. Therefore he measures the boundless Self by the limits of the body. Is this not strange? Does not an owl change day into night?

383. Would not a man who had never seen the sun in the sky take its reflection in a pool of water to be the sun itself?

384. He believes that the sun comes into being when the pool is there and vanishes when it is not, and trembles when the water ripples.

385. So long as a sleeping man does not wake he thinks that his dream is a reality; can one wonder that if a man does not recognize a rope he will fear it as a snake?

386. When a man's eyes are affected by jaundice, the moon will be seen to be yellow; is not a deer deceived by a mirage?

387. So this man will have nothing to do with the scriptures or with a teacher but lives his life in ignorance;

388. he casts the net of the body over Self through identification of the two, as a jackal projects onto the moon the movement of the clouds.

389. Owing to these false conceptions, O Kiriti, he becomes bound with the iron fetters of activity in the prison house of the body.

390. His condition is like that of the poor parrot which thinks it is bound to the revolving pipe and will not move its legs that are actually free.

391. Similarly anyone who attributes the workings of matter to the pure being of the Self remains confined within the limits of activity for endless sages.

> XVII. *He who is free from self-sense, whose understanding is not sullied, though he slay these people, he slays not nor is he bound [by his actions].*

392. Now the Self is always in activity but is untouched by it, in the same way that the waters of the ocean have no effect on the great sea-fire within them.

393. Now I will show thee how thou mayest know the man who remains separate from his actions.

394. When we realize the nature of a man who is liberated, we receive our own liberation, as we find a lost object when we look for it with a lamp.

395. When a mirror is cleaned we see our own image in it;
when salt is put into the water it is at once absorbed by the
water.

396. When a reflection in a mirror looks back at the original
form, then the act of seeing vanishes and only the real
form is left.

397. So when we wish to find our lost Self we should seek out
the saints [in whom we see ourselves]. For this reason
we should always praise the saints and listen to their
teaching.

398. He who, though living a life of activity, is untouched by
its good or evil effects, is like the sense of sight that is unaffected by the skin surrounding the eye.

399. I will now explain to thee with careful argument the
characteristic of the man who has been released from
activity.

400. O thou enlightened Arjuna, there was one who lay in the
deep sleep of ignorance and was occupied with a dream of
the whole activity of the universe.[7]

401. He was suddenly awakened by the Great Truth as though
by the hand of the guru striking his head.

402. All at once, O winner of wealth, being wakened from his
sleep and the illusion of his cosmic dream, he became
conscious of the bliss of union with Brahma.

403. The illusory flood of a mirage vanishes as soon as the
moon rises;

404. a phantom does not trouble one who is no longer a child,
and it is no longer possible to cook after the fire has burnt
out.

405. O Kiriti, a man [who has experienced this union loses] his
sense of individuality as after waking one does not see one's
dreams.

406. As the sun cannot find darkness even though it should
search for it in a cavern,

407. so when one who is filled with the consciousness of the
Self looks at visible objects, he recognizes them as forms
endowed with visibility.

408. Whatever is burnt by fire becomes one with it and then
the duality of the fire and the object disappears.

409. In the same way when the imputation to the Self of
responsibility for action, owing to the apparent separation between action and the Self, is withdrawn,

410. will the possessor of that state of consciousness which is left still identify himself with the body? Does the water of the great deluge consider itself a mere stream?

411. O son of Pāndu, can individuality be fulfilled in union through identification with the body? Can the sun be held by grasping its reflection?

412. When butter has been churned out of milk, can it again mix with buttermilk from which it has been separated?

413. O prince of warriors, when the fire has been removed from wood, can it be confined in a wooden box?

414. When the sun emerges from the womb of night does it know anything about the existence of night?

415. Likewise when a man once understands the relation between the knower and the thing to be known, how can he identify himself with the individuality of the body?

416. Wherever space extends it is filled with space, for it is all-pervading.

417. So also when a man sees himself in everything that he does, what actions is he responsible for as the doer?

418. The concept would be the same as that of there being no place apart from the sky, no current in the ocean or no fixed place for the polar star.

419. In this way his sense of individuality is transformed into enlightenment, yet so long as the body lives action con-tinues.

420. Even after the wind has ceased blowing trees may con-tinue to sway; the fragrance of camphor may remain in a casket even after the camphor has been used up.

421. Even when a gathering for song is over its moving effect remains; moisture lies on the ground long after water has been poured on it.

422. After the sun has set its light shines like a lamp on the background of the sky.

423. Even after an arrow is shot through a target it continues its flight until its momentum is lost.

424. When a potter removes from his wheel the vessel which he has made, the wheel continues revolving with the force of its spinning.

425. So, O conqueror of wealth, even when the sense of indi-viduality of the body comes to an end, its inherent acti-vity still promotes action.

426. A dream may arise without any previous thought, trees may grow in a forest without being planted and castles in the air may appear without being built.

427. So without the participation of the Self the five physical causes by their very nature initiate all kinds of activity.

428. Owing to the result of actions in past lives these five causes, with their accompanying motives, bring about manifold activities.

429. Whether that activity destroys the whole existing universe or brings another into being is of no consequence.

430. The sun does not observe how lotuses fade nor how others bloom.

431. The earth may be reduced to fragments by a stroke of lightning, or showers of rain may cause it to bring forth fresh grass,

432. but the sky knows nothing of this; such is the state of one who lives in the body but regards it as one detached from the body.

433. So he is unaware of bodily actions, whether they create or destroy the world, as a man on waking does not remember his dream.

434. On the other hand, those who see the body only with the physical eye believe it to be the originator of action.

435. A straw scarecrow set up on the border of a field is taken by a jackal to be the watchman of it.

436. Others have to take care that a madman is clothed and not left naked; the wounds of a dead soldier have to be counted by someone else.

437. A devoted widow [about to immolate herself] has no thought for the fire or her body or the people around her, while the onlookers look only at the ornaments she wears.

438. So also a man who has realized his true nature and is no longer aware of the duality of seer and what is seen, knows nothing of the activity of the organs of sense.

439. Though people on the shore may think that when small waves are hidden by large ones, one wave swallows another,

440. but we should look at this from the point of view of the water; what has been swallowed by what? So there is no one who can destroy the man who has no sense of duality.

441. If a golden image of Chandrikā kills a golden image of
Mahisha with a golden spear,[8]

442. a worshipper might well think that this represents a true
story; but the goddess, the spear and the demon are,
after all, nothing but gold.

443. Water and fire may be painted in a picture, but both
are only what appears to the eye; but applied to a piece
of cloth they can neither moisten nor burn.

444. In the same way the body of a man who has reached
liberation acts in accordance with the result of deeds in
past lives, while ignorant people consider that he himself
is the doer.

445. Even if the whole universe were to be destroyed by his
actions yet it could not be said that he had done this.

446. Could one say that first the sun sees the darkness and
then tries to dispel it? So to an enlightened man there
is nothing other than the Self; then whom can it
destroy?

447. His mind is unaffected by merit as by sin, as when a river
enters the Ganges its impurities are removed.

448. O conqueror of wealth, when two fires meet together does
one burn the other? Can a weapon strike itself?

449. What can pollute the pure intellect of a man who does
not think of activity as being separate from himself?

450. So he in whose mind action, the doer of action and the
performance of it are all one in the Self, is not bound by
action arising from the body and its senses.

451. The individual soul, which is the doer, skilfully digs five
furrows with a plough made from the ten instruments of
action.

452. Then, constructing a framework of prescribed and forbidden deeds, he erects in a moment of time the mansion
of activity.

453. The Self gives no help in this great work; thou shouldst
not even say that he plays a part in the beginning of it.

454. He is a mere witness, the essence of pure thought; can he
then permit himself to have any thought of promoting
action?

455. He takes no part in the activities which are such a labour
to ordinary men.

456. Therefore he who has realized that he is one with the pure
spirit is not in bondage to action.

457. Now when the picture of false knowledge appears on the
canvas of ignorance, it is known that the painter is the
threefold group.

458. This consists of knowledge, the knower and the thing to
be known. These three are the seed of this world, from
which all actions certainly spring.

459. I will now explain to thee, O conqueror of wealth, the
separate natures of these three.

460. The individual self is as it were the sun whose rays in the
form of the five senses spread out and force open the buds
of the lotuses of sense objects.

461. Or it is like a king mounting an unsaddled horse and with
the senses as his troops, plundering the lands of the objects
of sense pleasure.

462. Let [these images] be. The knowledge which works
through the senses and which gives the soul experience of
joy and sorrow becomes diminished in deep sleep.

463. This soul is the knower, and what I have just explained,
O son of Pāndu, is knowledge.

464. O Kiriti, it is born from the womb of ignorance, and immediately divides itself into three elements.

465. Putting the stone of the objects to be known in front of
its course, and placing behind it one's idea of oneself as
the doer,

466. between the knower and the object to be known stands
knowledge and they are related by mutual interaction.

467. When knowledge reaches the limit of the object to be
known, knowledge gives a name to all things.

468. That, undoubtedly, is what is called ordinary knowledge.
Now I will tell thee characteristics of the object of knowing.

469. Sound, touch, form, smell and taste are the five variations
of that which is to be known.

470. As the same mango is experienced differently by various
senses, through taste, colour, smell and touch,

471. so, though the object to be known is one, it is known
through the five senses and thus its nature is fivefold.

472. As the flow of a river ceases when it enters the ocean, as walking comes to an end when the destination is reached, and the plant dies when the grain has ripened,

473. so when the act of knowing, operating through the senses, ceases, O Kiriti, that goal is the object of knowledge.

474. Thus, O winner of wealth, I have explained to thee the characteristics of the knower, of knowledge and the object of knowledge. It is this threefold process which promotes action.

475. These five aspects of knowing, such as sound and the others, are either pleasant or unpleasant.

476. O winner of wealth, as soon as knowledge brings objects of knowledge to the knower, he is moved to accept or reject them.

477. A crane catching sight of a fish, a beggar discovering a treasure, or a lustful man seeing a woman, all these are impelled to pursue their object.

478. Water must rush down a slope, a bee flies towards a flower and a calf runs [towards the cow at the time of milking].

479. When men hear the heavenly nymph Urvashi, they try to set up a ladder of sacrifices in order to reach her.

480. O Kiriti, a pigeon soaring up in the sky drops with all the weight of its body at the sight of his mate.

481. A peacock hearing a peal of thunder will try to rise into the sky. All these are similar to the knower who is impelled towards the object of knowledge.

482. That is why, O son of Pāndu, this trinity of knower, knowledge and the object of knowing is the force which promotes all activity.

483. If the object is especially pleasing to the knower, he is unable to tolerate any delay in his enjoyment of it.

484. If, however, he happens to meet something unpleasant, he feels that it will take thousands of years to rid himself of it.

485. If he finds a snake he is immediately filled with fear, but is overcome with joy at the sight of a necklace.

486. He is affected in the same way when he encounters pleasant and unpleasant objects of knowing and is always occupied with accepting and rejecting.

487. A man who is a wrestler, even if he is the leader of an army, will descend from his chariot at the sight of another wrestler;

488. so he who is at first a knower, becomes a doer of action. Then, as a man who wishes to eat would cook himself some food,

489. or a bee might make for itself a garden of flowers; as a touchstone might go in search of metal or a god set out to build himself a temple,

490. so when, O Pāndava, through his passion for objects, the knower sets the senses into motion, he becomes the doer of actions.

491. Thus being himself the doer, his knowledge naturally comes to be the cause and naturally the object to be known becomes the effect.

492. In this way, O wise Arjuna, the process of knowing undergoes a change as the beauty of the eyes changes at night.

493. As the pleasure of a rich man diminishes when his fortune changes and the moon waves after it has reached fullness,

494. so, through the activity of the senses, the knower becomes involved in action. Now listen to the characteristics of this state.

495. The interior organ consists of the sound functions of intellect, mind, thought and consciousness of self.

496. The skin, the ear, the eye, the tongue and the nose represent the five exterior organs of sense.

497. The interior organ, the doer, considers what is to be done, and if it believes that such activity will result in pleasure,

498. it sets in motion all the ten exterior organs of sense,

499. and keeps them at work until the activity has brought about the desired result.

500. If the doer sees that this activity will result in pain, he diverts them all into the work of rejection,

501. and he will exercise his senses day and night until pain is relieved, as a king will keep his men at work day and night until the land-tax is paid.

502. In this way, when the knower directs the senses towards the experience of pleasure and the avoidance of sorrow, he is called the doer.

503. I speak of the senses as instruments for in all the actions of the doer their function is like that of a plough in farming,

504. and all the deeds performed by the doer by means of them go to make up a man's karma.

505. Ornaments are a token of the skill of the goldsmith, the
     rays of the moon spread out through the moonlight and a
     creeper is displayed by the extent of its growth.
506. Light is pervaded by its own radiance, the juice of sugar-
     cane is filled throughout with sweetness and the sky occu-
     pies the whole of space.
507. So, O winner of wealth, all that is comprised in the activ-
     ity of the doer is called karma; there is no other term.
508. In this manner, O prince among the wise, I have explained
     to thee the characteristics of the doer, the action and the
     instrument of action.

> XIX. *Knowledge, action and the agent are said, in the
> science of modes, to be of three kinds only, according to
> difference in the modes. Hear thou duly of these also.*

509. Thus knower, knowledge and object of knowledge to-
     gether produce the threefold stimulus of activity, while
     doer, action and instrument make up the whole process
     of activity.
510. As smoke is inherent in fire, a tree latent in the seed, or
     desire always dormant in the mind,
511. so the doer, the instrument and the action are the vital
     force in all activity, as gold is found in a gold mine.
512. Therefore, wherever there is a sense of oneself being the
     doer of action, even then, O son of Pāndu, the Self is far
     removed from all action.
513. O wise one, why should I repeat to thee that the Self is
     separated from action? Already thou knowest this well.
514. Knowledge, action and the doer of action which I have
     described, can be distinguished by their three separate
     qualities.
515. Therefore, O conqueror of wealth, do not put thy trust in
     this triad of knowledge, action or the doer of action, for
     two of them lead to bondage and only one to liberation.
516. I will explain to thee the difference in their qualities as
     it is expounded clearly in the Sānkhya philosophy, so that
     thou mayest understand this one, the quality of goodness.
517. In the matter of discrimination this philosophy is as the
     oceans of milk, in self-knowledge it is as the moon to the
     moon-lotus; O prince among men, it is the very eye of
     knowledge for all philosophy.

I*   565

518. It shows the difference between spirit and matter, which
are interwoven, as the sun enables us to distinguish day
from night.

519. It weighs up the vast mass of worldly life by the measure
of the twenty-four elements and brings men to the joy
of union with the Supreme.

520. O Arjuna, here now is the description of the distinctions
of quality as one reads them in the Sānkhya books.

521. These qualities have imprinted their threefold nature on
the whole visible creation.

522. So great is the power of the three qualities of goodness,
passion and darkness that they have divided into three
classes everything from the creation to the meanest
creature.

523. I will first of all explain that knowledge through which all
created things are seen to be divided into classes by the
distinction of these qualities.

524. Clear vision enables a man to see all things plainly, and
similarly with pure knowledge the true nature of things
understood.

525. Shri Krishna, the treasure-house of the highest bliss, said,
I will describe to thee that pure knowledge. Listen with
attention:

> xx. *The knowledge by which the One Imperishable Being
> is seen in all existence undivided in the divided, know
> that that knowledge is of 'Goodness'.*

526. O Arjuna, that knowledge is pure and of the quality of
goodness through the development of which the knower
and the object to be known are merged in one.

527. The sun can never see darkness, rivers are not known
separately by the ocean and no man can embrace his own
shadow.

528. So it is with this knowledge; for by it all creation, from the
highest gods to a blade of grass, is seen to be one.

529. A picture cannot be seen by feeling it; salt cannot be
washed with water and dreams do not occur after waking;

530. in a similar way, the knower, knowing and the object to be
known cease to exist separately when understood with the
help of this knowledge.

531. An intelligent man does not melt down gold ornaments

to see whether they are made of gold or strain waves to get water.

532. So that knowledge which is beyond the power to see differences in visible things is of the quality of goodness.

533. If one happens to look in a mirror one's image appears in it; in the same way when the knower knows himself the object of knowing disappears.

534. Again pure knowledge is the abode of the riches of liberation. Now I will explain the characteristics of knowledge of a passionate nature.

> XXI. *The knowledge which sees multiplicity of beings in the different creatures, by reason of their separateness, know that knowledge to be of the nature of 'Passion'.*

535. Listen, O Pārtha, the knowledge that is bound by the idea of separateness is passionate.

536. By this knowledge which attributes variety to all creatures we ourselves become separate parts of the whole, and even wise men are deceived by this.

537. As sleep draws the curtain of forgetfulness over the real form of things and sets in motion the activity of dreaming,

538. so when the domain of self-knowledge is surrounded by the network of false perceptions, the self is deluded by the play of the three states of consciousness.

539. As gold disguised in the form of ornaments is not recognized by a child, so owing to this kind of knowledge the inherent oneness is concealed in names and forms.

540. As an ignorant man will not recognize earth when it has been made into pots and jars, or as fire is not visible in a strong light;

541. as a foolish person does not distinguish threads if they are woven into cloth, or a dullard detest the canvas on which a picture is painted,

542. so, owing to knowledge which is passionate, created objects appear to be separate and the perception of unity is obscured.

543. Then as fire seems to be separate in several pieces of wood, fragrance distinct in several flowers and a separate moon reflected in each pool of water,

544. so knowledge which perceives a multiplicity in created things and distinguishes them as large and small has the quality of passion.

545. Now I will explain to thee knowledge that is of the quality of darkness, so that thou mayest know it and reject it as one avoids the house of an outcaste.

> XXII. *But that which clings to one single effect as if it were the whole, without concern for the cause, without grasping the real and narrow, is declared to be of the nature of 'dullness'.*

546. O Kiriti, this kind of knowledge wanders, as it were, naked, unclothed by the authority of the scriptures and turning its back on tradition;

547. other scriptures also cast it out and lest they should be defiled drive it away towards the distant hills of infidel faiths.

548. This knowledge, possessed by the evil spirit of darkness, spins round like a madman.

549. It regards no man as a friend nor any food as prohibited, like a dog let loose in a desert village,

550. which leaves on one side only what the mouth cannot reach, or what is hot enough to burn its tongue, eating all else.

551. It is like a rat which having stolen some gold cannot judge whether it is pure or alloyed, or a meat-eater who does not consider whether meat is dark or white.

552. It is like a forest fire that spares nothing or a fly which will settle on anything, alive or dead.

553. A crow does not choose between vomit and newly served food, or between what is fresh and what is putrid.

554. So this knowledge in its lust for sense pleasure is unaware that what is prohibited should be shunned and what is prescribed must be respected.

555. Whatever is perceived is grasped at for pleasure, be it relations with women or money for food.

556. Water may be holy or defiled, so long as it gives the pleasure of satisfying thirst;

557. and food may be sanctioned or forbidden, to be taken or rejected, but whatever is pleasing to the taste is regarded as pure.

558. This kind of knowledge causes a man to see women only as a means of sensual pleasure and seeks to associate with them.

559. It makes him look upon all those who serve his own interest as relatives and therefore consider them as of little consequence.

560. As everything is food for death, as all things are fuel for fire, so knowledge of the quality of darkness considers the whole world as its own possession.

561. It regards the world as an object of pleasure, and the nourishment of the body its sole purpose.

562. Its whole activity is directed towards the satisfaction of the body, as rain from the sky inevitably falls into the ocean.

563. The realization that heaven and hell arise from carrying out proper duties or neglecting them is like the dark night to a man with this kind of knowledge.

564. Its understanding cannot reach beyond the idea that the body is the Self and a stone image is the Supreme.

565. It believes that when the body dies the self with all its activities ceases to exist; then what material form is left to experience anything?

566. If it is claimed that God exists and causes us to experience [the fruit of action], then how is it that people live by selling images of gods?

567. If the stone gods in a village temple can punish men, why do the stones of the neighbouring hills remain silent?

568. Therefore if this kind of knowledge believes in a god at all it will regard the idol as a god, and the body as the spirit.

569. It considers merit and sin as false ideas and like a flame of fire devours all it finds to serve its ends.

570. All that is seen by the physical eyes and felt as pleasing to the senses is the only real experience.

571. O Pārtha, thou wilt see that this way of living grows as uselessly as a stream of smoke rising in the sky.

572. All this is as worthless as the bhanda tree, whether it is green or dry, increasing or withering.

573. The ears of the sugar-cane, a pasture of the prickly cactus plant and an impotent man are all equally useless.

574. The mind of a child, the hoarded wealth of a thief and the false teat on a goat's neck [serve no purpose].

575. Therefore I say that knowledge which is as empty and worthless as these things has the quality of darkness.

576. To call this knowledge would be as irrelevant as to say that the eyes of a man born blind are large,

577. that the ears of a deaf man are well shaped, or that what is
unfit for drinking is good drink; so knowledge that has
the quality of darkness is knowledge only in name.

578. But let this be. This is not to be seen as knowledge but
the very eyes of darkness.

579. So, Arjuna, the best of listeners, I have shown thee the
separate kinds of knowledge with its threefold characteristics.

> XXIII. *An action which is obligatory, which is performed
> without attachment, without love or hate, by one un-
> desirous of fruit, that is said to be of 'goodness'.*

580. Now, O wielder of the bow, the activities of the doer of
action can be clearly observed by the light of these three
kinds of knowledge.

581. Actions follow three directions, as water flows in the
channels made for it.

582. Governed by the threefold nature of knowledge, action
also is of three kinds. Hear now what actions have the
quality of goodness.

583. Such an act is one which is performed in accordance with
a man's status and duty, as proper to him as the embrace
of a faithful wife to a beloved husband.

584. A man's wrath is enhanced by daily duties as sandalwood
paste improves a dark complexion or black pigment increases the beauty of a young woman's eyes.

585. Such daily duty, supported by periodic rites, is good and
is like fragrance added to gold.

586. As a mother will devote all the strength of her body and
life to caring for her child without regard for her own
weariness,

587. so a good man will perform his duty whole-heartedly,
without a thought for the fruit of it, but offering the
whole of it to Brahma.

588. As a man gives hospitality without stint to a friend who
arrives at his house, so if the good man should be inter-
rupted in performing his duty by some profitable occasion,

589. he does not grieve because the act is unfulfilled, or give
way to resentment; nor does he become elated with joy
at its completion.

590. An action performed in this manner, O conqueror of wealth, is one which has the quality of goodness.

591. Now will I explain to thee the nature of an action which is passionate. Do not let thy attention wander.

592. As a fool who cannot speak a good word to his mother or father may treat all the rest of the world with respect,

593. or a man who will not sprinkle water on the sacred Tulsi plant even from a distance may pour milk on the roots of a vine,

594. so a man of passionate nature who cannot even make the effort of rising to perform the obligatory daily and periodic rites

595. would count it as nothing to spend his body and all that he possesses for the sake of actions which bring him pleasure.

596. As a man is never tired of lending money out at a high rate of interest, or a farmer is never satisfied however much he may sow his crops,

597. as one who has found a philosopher's stone does not consider himself prosperous until he has spent all he has on iron [for transmuting into gold].

598. With his mind set on the fruit of action he performs difficult acts which bring sensual pleasure, but is never satisfied.

599. So he will perform properly all those prescribed rites which will bring pleasurable results.

600. He boasts in public of having performed such rites and renders them valueless by constantly speaking of them.

601. Thus is he filled with pride about them and pays no respect to his father and his preceptor as a typhus fever yields to no medicine.

602. Therefore whatever is done reverently by a man, yet through egotism and the desire for the fruit of action,

603. and carried out with great exertion, is like the performance of an acrobat by which he earns a living.

604. It is like a rat burrowing through a whole mountain to find a single grain or a frog stirring up the ocean for a little moss;

605. or such a man is like a juggler who carries round a snake in order to earn more than he can get by begging. There are some who enjoy such toil.

606. The efforts which he makes for the sake of winning heavenly pleasure are like those of a white ant which penetrates down to hell in search of a particle of food.

607. Action prompted by desire, which is fraught with distress, is called passionate; now listen to the characteristics of action that has the quality of darkness.

> xxv. *The action which is undertaken through ignorance, without regard to consequences or to loss and injury and without regard to one's human capacity, that is said to be of 'Dullness'.*

608. Activity of the quality of darkness is as the dark house of censure and the birthplace of all that is prohibited.

609. Once it has been performed its result disappears from sight like a line drawn across water.

610. It is like churning gruel, blowing dead ashes, or grinding sand in an oil-press; there is nothing to show for it.

611. It is as useless as winnowing chaff, shooting into the sky or setting a snare to catch the wind.

612. All such action is worthless and after it is finished it is devoid of any result.

613. On the contrary, in performance the precious treasure of human life is expended and human happiness is destroyed by them.

614. If a net of thorns were dragged over a bed of lotus flowers the net itself would be spoiled and the lotuses destroyed.

615. A moth dazzled by a lamp not only has its body burnt but deprives one's sight of the light of the lamp.

616. Similarly action of this kind causes harm to others as well as being fruitless and hurting the body.

617. A fly, by letting itself be swallowed, causes a man to vomit; this conduct recalls such loathsome experiences.

618. A man of darkness does not consider whether he has the capacity to perform these actions, but continues to act blindly.

619. [He does not ask himself,] What powers have I? What opportunity is there? What will be the advantage of doing this?

620. Wiping out all such thoughts by treading the path of ignorance he completes all rites.

621. As fire spreads at random, burning up the very fuel which is its source, and as the ocean might rise and overflow its shores,

622. spreading in all directions without regard for any obstacles large or small,

623. so by such traits thou mayest recognize actions which have the quality of darkness; for they take no thought for what is proper or improper and do not distinguish between what is their own and what is another's.

624. O Arjuna, I have now explained to thee the nature and cause of the threefold distinction of action resulting from the three qualities.

> XXVI. *The doer who is free from attachment, who has no speech of egotism, full of resolution and zeal and who is unmoved by success or failure—he is said to be of the nature of 'goodness'.*

625. The individual selves who practise this activity, regarding themselves as the doer, are also of three kinds.

626. As a man appears to be fourfold according to the four stages of a man's life, so also the doers of actions are of three kinds because of these differences in activity.

627. Of these three I will first describe to thee the characteristics of the doer who has the quality of goodness. Listen carefully.

628. As the finest sandalwood tree grows straight branches without any hope of bearing fruit,

629. and the nāga creeper fulfils its purpose without yielding any fruit, so the man performs his daily and periodic duties.

630. These acts are not fruitless, though they seem to bear no fruit; O son of Pāndu, how can that, which in itself is fruit, bear fruit?

631. As he faithfully performs these duties no thought arises in his mind that he is the doer, as the clouds gather silently in the rainy season.

632. In order to perform all duties worthy of being offered to the Supreme,

633. he looks for an appropriate time, a proper place and determines all his actions in the light of scriptural teaching.

634. He brings together under control the mental tendencies
and the sense organs, refrains from any thought of the
fruit of action and accepts the bonds imposed by the
scriptures.
635. In order to carry out this discipline he bears within himself alertness and steady courage.
636. Moreover, from devotion to the Spirit, he renounces all
physical pleasure while he is carrying out his duties.
637. The more he deprives himself of sleep, endures hunger
and denies himself physical pleasures,
638. the more ardent he becomes, as gold loses weight but increases in value the more it is heated in the crucible.
639. Where there is true love one regards one's life as of little
worth; a devoted wife does not hesitate to immolate herself on her husband's pyre.
640. Similarly, O winner of wealth, if a man longs for such a
precious thing as self-realization, will he grieve on account of physical discomfort?
641. So the more detached he becomes from sensual pleasures,
the less regard does he have for the body, and the greater
joy he takes in performing his duty.
642. In this way he carries out what has to be done; but if the
occasion arises for refraining from action,
643. he is not affected by this interruption any more than a
wagon is concerned if it falls over a precipice.
644. If an action which he has undertaken is accomplished
without fault, he does not parade his success.
645. O son of Pāndu, the doer in whom these traits can be seen
while he is engaged in action, may be truly said to have the
quality of goodness.

646. Now as for the man of passion, he is known by this, that
he is a very storehouse of desire in the world.
647. As the dunghill is the place for depositing the refuse of a
village, and the burning ground for all that is impure,
648. so such a man is a receptacle for the greed of the whole
world, like a shed for washing the feet.

649. He applies himself resolutely to any undertaking that he sees to be profitable.

650. When he has obtained what he seeks he will not waste the merest trifle of it and is always ready to sacrifice his life to keep it.

651. He keeps as careful a watch on the possessions of others as a miser is concerned for his treasure and a crane is intent on catching fish.

652. If a man becomes entangled in a boru tree and struggles to free himself, he will be scratched by its branches and the taste of its fruit will burn his tongue;

653. so this kind of man acts with violence towards others in thought, word and deed, and though he may attain his own ends he has no consideration for others.

654. Moreover, if he has not the capacity or perseverance to carry out any action, he feels no dissatisfaction.

655. As the fruit of the thorn-apple tree can intoxicate with its juice while it is thorny without, he is devoid of any purity within or without.

656. O conqueror of wealth, if this man obtains the fruit of his actions, he laughs mockingly at the world in his joy.

657. On the other hand if he fails to get any result from what he undertakes, he is overcome with grief and curses all action.

658. In short, thou mayest know with certainty that, if such characteristics are revealed in his conduct, he is a man of passionate nature.

659. I will now describe to thee the doer who has the quality of darkness, the field in which evil deeds grow.

> XXVIII. *The doer who is unbalanced, vulgar, obstinate, deceitful, malicious, indolent, despondent and procrastinating, is said to be of the nature of 'darkness'.*

660. Fire has no realization that it will burn those things with which it comes into contact,

661. a weapon has no knowledge that its sharp edge can kill and poison is unaware of its effects;

662. so, O winner of wealth, the doer undertakes evil actions which will do harm to himself as well as to others.

663. When performing such actions he cares little what effect these may have, as a stormy wind blows at random.

664. O winner of wealth, there is no relation between the doer and his actions and he is more deranged than any madman.

665. He sustains his life on everything that sensual pleasures can provide, as a louse attaches itself to the hind quarters of a bullock,

666. and he acts on the impulse of the moment, as a child laughs and cries regardless of the occasion.

667. Controlled by his own nature, he is unable to discriminate between proper and improper actions and swells with satisfaction at whatever he does as a dunghill is built up of refuse.

668. He will not humble himself before those who should be reverenced, nor even before the Supreme and in obstinacy he is [more rigid than] a mountain.

669. His mind is deceitful, his conduct is dishonest and his look is like that of a whore.

670. In short, he is the very embodiment of deceit, and his life is like a gambling den.

671. His company is to be avoided, for is not his appearance like the village of a lustful tribesman?

672. If good is done to another it seems like hostility to himself, as salt put into milk makes it undrinkable.

673. Even if frozen fuel is put into a fire, it will immediately become fire in the flames;

674. and, O Kiriti, the most delicious food entering the body eventually becomes excrement;

675. so if such a man finds anything good in another, he begins at once to speak ill of him.

676. He turns all virtue into vice and nectar into poison, as milk given to a serpent becomes venom.

677. Even when opportunity arises for him to perform an action in this world which will benefit him in the next,

678. he falls into a natural sleep, whereas when he is engaged in evil deeds sleep deserts him like a woman sitting apart as unclean.

679. As the mouth of a crow turns sour with the juice of grapes or sugarcane, and an owl is blinded by daylight,

680. so when he has an opportunity of doing good he is slothful, but in the matter of careless performance, he does whatever he likes.

681. He is forever full of despair as the fire burns eternally in the heart of the ocean.

682. As a fire burning dung smoulders and the downgoing
breath in the body has an unpleasant smell, so at the end
of his life he is filled with depression.
683. O warrior, he engages in lustful actions which [he hopes]
will bear fruit for his enjoyment after myriads of years.
684. He is full of anxiety about life beyond this world, though
he is unlikely to obtain even the least fruit of his actions.
685. In such a man, the incarnation of all sins, thou wilt see
clearly the doer who has the quality of darkness.
686. Thus, O Prince among the virtuous, I have explained to
thee the threefold characteristics of these three, action,
doer and knowledge.

> XXIX. *Hear now the threefold distinction of understand-
> ing as also of steadiness, O Winner of wealth [Arjuna],
> according to the modes, to be set forth fully and separately.*

687. Dwelling in the town of ignorance, wearing the fire garment of illusion and decked with all the ornaments of
doubt,
688. the steady intellect, which mirrors truly the beauty of
self-realization, also has this threefold nature.
689. O Arjuna, consider, is there anything in this world which
is not thus distinguished by the three qualities?
690. O Kiriti, is there any piece of wood in which fire does not
lie latent? In the same way is there any perceptible object
in the world which has not this threefold aspect?
691. The intellect has also a threefold nature arising from these
qualities, and steadiness is similarly of three kinds.
692. Now I will begin to tell thee how they are severally distinguished by their characteristics.
693. O winner of wealth, of these two, intellect and steadiness,
I will first describe the different kinds of intellect.
694. O good warrior, for those beings which come into worldly
existence there are three ways of life, the best, the middle
grade and the lowest.
695. From the three well-known ways of prescribed action,
action with desire for the fruits of action, and prohibited
action, arises men's fear of worldly life.

> XXX. *The understanding which knows action and non-
> action, what ought to be done and what ought not to be
> done, what is to be feared and what is not to be feared,*

696. Daily duties are the only good actions of those prescribed by the scriptures, in accordance with a man's capacity.
697. In order to obtain the fruit of Self-realization, he should perform such actions as a man drinks water to quench his thirst.
698. By actions such as these a man is delivered from the terrible dread of earthly existence and it is easy for him to find liberation.
699. One who acts in this way does well, for he loses his fear of worldly existence and reaches the status of a seeker after liberation.
700. The man whose mind firmly believes in this path is as assured of attaining liberation as if he had already reached it.
701. Therefore should not such a one plunge into a life of activity which has exalted renunciation of the fruits of action and cast down activity that is performed for the sake of its fruits?
702. Water gives life to a thirsty man, a boat can save a man who is submerged in a flood and the sun's rays can help one who has fallen into a dark well;
703. if good medicine and proper diet is given a man recovers from a severe illness, and a fish will survive in water,
704. whereas it would die without it; so the man who carries out his duties cannot fail to obtain liberation.
705. The clear knowledge which enables a man to recognize which actions are right and which are not is to be known as good.
706. Those actions which are prompted by desire and which give rise to the fear of earthly life and are stained with unseemliness,
707. and undesirable actions which cause the recurrence of birth and death [have the same result]
708. as jumping into a furnace, plunging into deep waters or grasping a red hot weapon.
709. Seeing a hissing black snake one should not stretch out a hand to it, nor should one approach the den of a tiger.
710. This is the kind of wisdom which unfailingly inspires a man with fear at the sight of improper actions.

711. If one eats food cooked with poison, one must surely die; so this understanding recognizes the bondage inherent in all prohibited actions,

712. and being filled with fear of the bondage that is inseparable from such actions, it turns away from the practice of them.

713. This understanding is able to discriminate between actions that are proper and those which should be avoided, using the measure of activity and inactivity, as an expert can distinguish a true jewel from a false one.

714. The intellect which has this unlimited power of discrimination between desirable and undesirable actions, is said to be of the quality of goodness.

> XXXI. *That by which one knows in a mistaken way the right and wrong, what ought to be done and what ought not to be done—that understanding, O Pārtha [Arjuna], is of the nature of 'passion'.*

715. As cranes will drink a mixture of milk and water, [being unable to separate it], and a blind man cannot distinguish between day and night,

716. as the same bee which tastes the honey in flowers may then bore a hole in wood, though this is not inconsistent with the bee's nature,

717. so understanding of this kind is unable to discriminate right and wrong actions and duties.

718. If a man were to trade in pearls without a trained eye [for selecting them], he might by chance find one of value, but if not, he might as well not buy them.

719. Similarly if an unworthy action is not forced upon him, he may leave it aside; but he does in fact regard both good and evil as one.

720. Such understanding is clearly of the nature of passion and is like one who would invite guests to some celebration without regard to their suitability.

> XXXII. *That which, enveloped in darkness, conceives as right what is wrong and sees all things in a perverted way [contrary to the truth], that understanding, O Pārtha [Arjuna], is of the nature of 'darkness'.*

721. The royal highway is a dangerous road for a thief; day must become night for a demon to be able to see.

722. The treasure found by an unlucky man would be worth
no more to him than a heap of coal; though he possesses it,
it is no good to him.

723. In the same way understanding of this nature regards
righteous acts as evil and confuses the true with the false.

724. It turns into dross all that is of value and treats all virtue
as vice.

725. In short, whatever the scriptures have established is
interpreted by it as having the opposite meaning.

726. O son of Pāndu, that understanding is unquestionably of
the quality of darkness; what value is there in that which
is a night for religious actions?

727. Thus I have explained clearly the three different kinds of
understanding to thee, Arjuna, who art as the moon to
the lotus in the form of self-knowledge.

> XXXIII. *The unwavering steadiness by which, through
> concentration, one controls the activities of the mind, the
> life breath and the senses, is, O Pārtha, of the nature of
> 'goodness'.*

728. Now the resolution which supports the understanding by
which a man decides upon his course of action is also of
three kinds.

729. Listen attentively while the characteristics of the three
aspects of resolution are explained.

730. When the sun rises the darkness [necessary for] thieves
comes to an end, and a royal command will arrest evil
practices.

731. When the wind blows with all its force the clouds with
their thunder are dispersed.

732. At the sight of the Agastya star, the ocean becomes
tranquil; at the rise of the moon the sun lotuses begin to
close their blooms.

733. When an elephant is in rut he will be unable to put down
his raised foot if a roaring lion should be in his path.

734. So when resolution is firm in the mind, mental and other
activities cease.

735. O Kiriti, the knot that binds the senses to sense objects is
loosened with ease, and the ten senses return to the womb
of their mother, the mind.

736. The vital breath ceases in its upward and downward

course, and bound together with the remaining nine vital airs it plunges into the sushumna artery.

737. The mind strips itself of the garment of good and evil desires, and sits silently in its nudity behind the pure intellect.

738. That royal resolution dismisses all the activities of mind, the senses and the breath and their commerce with each other,

739. and with the skill of yogic practice confines them all within the inner chamber of meditation.

740. There, resisting all bribery, it holds them captive until it can deliver them into the hands of the great ruler who is the Self.

741. Krishna said to Arjuna, this is truly the resolution which has the quality of goodness.

742. While he is in a body a man dwells in both earth and heaven, satisfying his desires by three means.

> XXXIV. *The steadiness by which one holds fast duty, pleasure and wealth desiring the fruit of each on its occasion, is, O Pārtha, of the nature of 'passion'.*

743. Across the ocean of desires he sails in the boat of religious duty, wealth and passion, and with the help of resolution carries on the trade of action.

744. His resolution supports his intention of obtaining fourfold interest on the capital, in the form of the fruit of action, which he invests.

745. This kind of resolution has the quality of passion, O Pārtha; now hear about the third kind of resolution which has the quality of darkness.

> XXXV. *That steadiness by which a fool does not give up sleep, fear, grief, depression and arrogance, O Pārtha, is of the nature of 'darkness'.*

746. This kind of resolution is as full of the lowest quality as coal is of blackness.

747. Can one apply the term of quality to anything as vulgar and low as this? Yet is not Punyajana the name of a class of demons?[9]

748. Is not the fiery one among the planets called Mangala, the auspicious? So the word quality is not out of place here.

749. O great warrior, the man whose body is fashioned out of
     the quality of darkness is the home of all sin.
750. Being unduly given to idleness he takes every opportunity
     of sleeping and is never free from grief because he nou-
     rishes sin.
751. He is pursued by fear because he is attached to pleasure
     and wealth, as hardness cannot be separated from a
     stone.
752. He has always to live with sorrow, being bound by desire
     to objects of pleasure, as sin always accompanies an un-
     grateful man.
753. Day and night he is filled with discontent so that dejec-
     tion is his constant companion.
754. Garlic never loses its smell and a man who eats intem-
     perately is never free from disease; so depression follows
     him until the time of death.
755. Youth, wealth and desire increase his delusion and he
     becomes the very home of conceit.
756. Fire never loses its heat, viciousness is natural to a snake
     and fear is the perpetual enemy of mankind.
757. As death is at all times inevitable for the body, so infatua-
     tion is inseparable from the quality of darkness.
758. Indulgence in sleep and other faults are the faults of this
     quality and the resolution with which they hold a man
759. is known as the resolution of darkness, said the Lord of
     the universe.
760. Thus the threefold intelligence first determines the action
     to be done and resolution leads to its completion.
761. The sunlight makes a road visible and a man is then able
     to walk along it; but to do so he must have resolution.
762. In the same way intelligence directs activity and sets in
     motion the senses; but for all this resolution is needed.
763. Thus I have explained to thee the three kinds of resolu-
     tion which lead to the three kinds of action.

> XXXVI. *And now hear from Me, O Best of the Bhāratas,
> the three kinds of happiness; that in which a man comes
> to rejoice by long practice and in which he reaches the end
> of his sorrow.*

764. The fruit resulting from such activity, called happiness, is
     also threefold, owing to the influence of action.

765. I will now explain to thee in detail the three kinds of
happiness, the fruit of action, which are distinguished by
the three qualities.

766. But how can this be done? Thou wilt say, let us understand it through speaking, yet the means of hearing may
defile what is heard by the ear.

767. So listen with the inner ear of the heart; in this way thou
wilt be able] to disregard the external process of attention
[to what is spoken].

768. Saying this the Lord began the explanation of the three
kinds of happiness, on which I will now comment.

769. Now, O wise one, listen to the description of the three
kinds of happiness of which I have promised to speak.

770. O Kiriti, I will set out before thy vision that happiness
which is experienced when the individual soul meets the
Self.

771. A divine medicine is taken in a small dose at stated times,
and through the process of alchemy tin is transmuted into
silver.

772. Water is poured on to salt several times to make salt
water.

773. So even the least measure of such happiness experienced
by the self through training must wipe out sorrow.

774. This bliss of the Self is threefold in its nature and I will
describe these aspects in turn.

> XXXVII. *The happiness which is like poison at first and
> like nectar at the end, which springs from a clear under-
> standing of the Self, is said to be of the nature of 'good-
> ness'.*

775. The roots of a sandalwood tree are dangerous owing to
the presence of snakes and there are demons at the mouth
of a hole where treasure is hidden.

776. Laborious sacrifices must be made before reaching the
pleasures of heaven; the age of childhood is beset with
difficulties.

777. When lighting a lamp one has to endure its smoke, and
when one takes medicine it may be unpleasant for the
tongue.

778. So it is, O Pāndava, with this happiness which is obtained
through the difficult exercise of control of mind and senses.

779. When such indifference to worldly things is aroused, removing all desire, then the boundaries between heaven and earth are removed.

780. [For the sake of it] the intellect and other functions are deprived of their vitality by the rigorous discipline of listening to the teaching of true knowledge and the performance of exacting vows,

781. and the waves of vital breaths are absorbed into the sushumna artery; such are the initial difficulties which are encountered in attaining this happiness.

782. A pair of cranes [are distressed] by separation, a calf by being taken away from the cow's udder; and is not a beggar [also distressed] by being driven away from his meal?

783. A mother grieves when death takes her only child; a fish without water cannot survive.

784. In the same way a whole world age may be occupied in the separation of the senses from the objects of sense; yet such distress can be borne by dispassionate men.

785. This kind of happiness is attained only after great initial difficulty; but from the churning of the ocean of milk there came the reward of nectar.

786. When firm resolution, like that of the god Shiva, has swallowed the poison of dispassion, then will follow the feast of the nectar of knowledge.

787. Unripe grapes may sting the tongue like burning coals, but when ripe they are full of sweetness.

788. So when by the light of the Self dispassion is perfected, and with it ignorance in every form is destroyed,

789. then intellect becomes merged in the Self as the water of the Ganges flows into the ocean, the great store of the bliss of union is opened.

790. Therefore the happiness which is rooted in dispassion and leads to the experience of union is said to have the quality of goodness.

> XXXVIII. *The happiness which arises from the contact of the senses and their objects, and which is like nectar at first but like poison at the end, is recorded to be 'passionate'.*

791. When the senses and sense objects are united, O conqueror of wealth, this kind of happiness overflows its banks.

792. When a ruler visits a town a festival is held and money is
borrowed for the celebration of a marriage.

793. Sugar and plantains taste equally sweet to the tongue of a
sick man, and the poisonous bacnāga plant is pleasing to
look at.

794. As the friendship of knaves, the company of whores and
the strange feats of jugglers [are all attractive at first],

795. so the happiness of the self is fed by the sin of the union of
the senses with their objects; but [the result is the same
as that of] a swan dashing against a rocky place.

796. All such happiness comes to an end and even life may be
destroyed and all accumulated merit is wasted.

797. All the pleasures which have been enjoyed vanish like a
dream, leaving a man struck down by disaster.

798. Thus happiness of this kind brings about disaster in this
world and turns to poison in the next.

799. If sense pleasures are given full rein they burn up the field
of religious duty and enjoy a feast of sensual indulgence.

800. Sin becomes established and the sinner is cast into hell.
Therefore this kind of happiness is an obstacle to reaching
heaven.

801. There is a poison which by its name is sweet, but proves
deadly in its effects. Similarly [there is a joy] that is sweet
at first but in the end turns to bitterness.

802. O Pārtha, such is this happiness which is full of passion;
therefore thou shouldst avoid any contact with it.

> XXXIX. *That happiness which deludes the soul both at
> the beginning and at the end, and which arises from sleep,
> sloth and negligence, is declared to be of the nature of
> 'darkness'.*

803. The happiness which arises from indulgence in drink,
from eating undesirable food and in the company of loose
women,

804. from assault and robbery of others and from the praise of
bards,

805. that is fed by sloth and enjoyed in undue sleep and which
leaves a man always confused about the way he should
live,

806. such happiness, O Pārtha, is truly of the nature of darkness. I will not say much about it, for it can hardly be
experienced [as happiness].

807. So in accordance with the threefold nature of activity, happiness is also of three kinds. I have made this clear to thee here.
808. There is nothing in the world, either gross or subtle, that is not involved in this triplicity of doer, action and the fruit of action.
809. And, O Kiriti, this triplicity is woven into the nature of the qualities like the warp and woof of cloth.
810. There is no thing in the world of nature, the world of mortal men or in heaven, which is not dominated by the three qualities.
811. Could there be a blanket without wool, a lump of clay without earth or waves without water?
812. So there is no creature in the whole of nature into whose composition the three qualities do not enter.
813. Thou should know therefore that everything is fashioned from three qualities.
814. It is due to these qualities that there are the three gods, that the worlds are divided into three and that men belong to the four castes according to their various functions.

XLI. *Of Brāhmans, of Kṣātriyas, and Vaiśyas as also of Shūdras, O Conqueror of the foe, the activities are distinguished in accordance with the qualities born of their nature.*

815. Now shouldst thou ask which these four castes are, I will tell thee that the first and foremost is that of the Brāhmans.
816. Of the others the two, Kshatriyas and Vaishyas, are regarded equal to the Brāhmans, in that they are qualified to practise Vedic rites.
817. The fourth caste, the Shudras, O conqueror of wealth, have no relation to these rites, for they are bound to the service of the other three castes.
818. The Shudras are called the fourth class because of their close association with the Brāhmans and others.

819. When a rich man smells a garland of flowers, he smells also the string which holds them together; so through their association with the three twice-born castes the Shudras also are accepted by the Vedas.

820. O Pārtha, this is what is called the organization of mankind into the four castes, and I will now explain their respective functions.

821. By means of the three qualities the four castes can escape from the grip of the cycle of birth and death and reach the Supreme.

822. The three qualities born of the divine nature have allotted to each of the four castes their special functions.

823. A father divides his wealth among his children, the sun shows various paths to travellers and a master allots different duties to his servants;

824. so the three qualities, born of matter, have appointed duties for each of the four castes.

825. Their functions were assigned to the Brāhman and the Kshatriya castes by the greater and lesser degrees of the quality of goodness.

826. The Vaishya caste is established by the quality of passion with some quality of goodness, and the Shudra caste by passion mixed with darkness.

827. In this way, O wise one, the one human race consists of four different castes arising from the three qualities.

828. Thus the scriptures reveal the functions of the castes according to the difference of the qualities, as with the help of a lamp we may find something that is hidden.

829. Listen therefore, O thou who art endowed with the gift of hearing, while I tell thee how the appointed duties of the castes are known.

XLII. *Serenity, self-control, austerity, purity, forbearance and uprightness, wisdom, knowledge and faith in religion, these are the duties of the Brāhman born of his nature.*

830. When the intellect, gathering together the tendencies of all the senses, meets the Self, as a wife meets her husband in a quiet place,

831. this control is called tranquillity and it is the essential virtue of the beginning of all action.

832. Then, expelling all the outer senses with the rod of pres-

scribed duties and not allowing them to follow the path of
unrighteousness,

833. self-restraint, the helpmate of tranquillity, is the second
virtue, maintaining the proper execution of duties.

834. As on the sixth night after the birth of a child a lamp must
be kept burning, so a firm faith in God should be maintained.

835. This is called austerity and it is the third virtue. Then
comes sinless purity, which is of two kinds.

836. The mind should be filled with pure emotions and the
body adorned with right actions, and thus the whole life
is made gracious.

837. O Pārtha, this is called purity and it is the fourth virtue
in the performance of duties; and as the earth bears all
burdens,

838. so, O Pāndava, forbearance is the fifth virtue, as the fifth
note in the scale is the sweetest.

839. The Ganges, though her course may wind, flows straight
on [as a river]; sugarcane, though its joints may be
crooked, has the same sweetness throughout.

840. In the same way when a man is upright and straightfor-
ward even towards unpleasant people, this sixth virtue is
uprightness.

841. A gardener diligently pours water over the roots of trees
and sees the result in the fruit they bear.

842. Similarly it is wisdom through which a man obeys the
teaching of scripture and finds God.

843. This is the seventh virtue, needed in the performance of
action. Then comes knowledge, the nature of which we
will now see.

844. When true inner purity is attained, then certainly a man
can find the Supreme either by meditation or by study of
the scriptures.

845. This knowledge is good, and it is the eighth among these
virtues; the ninth is belief in the scriptures.

846. The people respect anyone who bears the royal insignia,
so the faithful following of those paths of conduct which
are accepted by the scriptures,

847. I say, is known as belief in the scriptures, the ninth of
these virtues make for right action.

848. The natural duty of a Brāhman consists of this group of
nine pure virtues, beginning from tranquillity.

849. He is the ocean of these virtues, a garland of these nine
jewels and is as inseparable from them as is light from the
sun.
850. As a champak tree is adorned by its flowers, as the moonlight adds to the brilliance of the moon, and the value of
sandalwood tree is enhanced by its fragrance;
851. so are these nine virtues the perfect ornament of the
Brāhman and they are inseparable from him.

> XLIII. *Heroism, vigour, steadiness, resourcefulness, not
> fleeing even in battle, generosity and leadership, these are
> the duties of a kṣatriya, born of his nature.*

852. Now, O conqueror of wealth, listen with full understanding to the explanation of the proper duties of a Kshatriya.
853. The sun gives its light without any need of help, and a
lion seeks no support from another,
854. so the courage which is strong and self-reliant, excelling
without being upheld by others, is the first and greatest
virtue of a Kshatriya.
855. In the light of the sun myriads of stars are eclipsed; the
sun is dimmed by them or by the moon.
856. So though the Kshatriya may astonish the world with his
valour, he himself should not be carried away by it.
857. Confidence in all that he does is the second virtue, and
steadfastness is the third.
858. Steadfastness is that courage through which a man would
not close the eye of clear perception even if the heavens
were to fall.
859. However deep the water may be, the lotus rises from the
bottom and opens its blooms, and the sky is able to rise
above all heights.
860. In the same way, O Pārtha, a Kshatriya should be able to
triumph in all circumstances and through his wisdom
perceive their results.
861. The ability to act in this way is the fourth virtue, and the
fifth is heroism in battle.
862. The Kshatriya should always face an enemy as the sun-
flower looks up at the sun.
863. He should never turn his back on an enemy on the battlefield as a woman avoids her husband at monthly periods.
864. This is the fifth of the great virtues which he should practice, as devotion is the chief of the four goals of existence.

865. The flowers and fruit of a tree are free [for all men] and a
lotus generously spreads its fragrance.
866. A man may enjoy as much moonlight as he wishes and
give to another according to his desire,
867. Such limitless generosity is the sixth virtue, as also encouraging obedience to commands.
868. When our limbs are properly nourished they will work
as we bid them; similarly when the Kshatriya protects
his people he is loved and served by them.
869. This is called leadership, embodying all power, the
seventh of the virtues and the ruler among them all.
870. A Kshatriya is adorned with these seven special virtues as
the sky is beautified by the constellation of the seven stars
of the Seven Sages.
871. The sacred duties carried out in the world by the Kshatriya through these seven virtues constitute the essential
quality of warriorship.
872. Indeed the Kshatriya is no ordinary man but is as Mount
Meru in the form of the gold of goodness and his duty is
that of supporting the heaven of these seven virtues.
873. His work is not ordinary action, but is like the earth
surrounded by these virtues as the seven oceans, which
the Kshatriya experiences.
874. Or the stream of these seven virtues are like the Ganges
in this world, giving delight to the ocean which receives it.
875. In fact, the duties arising from these virtues are the essential function of the Kshatriya caste.

> XLIV. *Agriculture, tending cattle and trade are the duties
> of a Vaiśya, born of his nature; work of the character of
> service is the duty of a Śūdra, born of his nature.*

876. O noble-minded Arjuna, listen now and I will tell thee the
proper functions of the Vaishya caste.
877. [They are:] earning interest on his wealth by means of
the land, ploughing and sowing,
878. living on the proceeds of agriculture and husbandry, and
buying goods at a low price to sell them at a higher
price.
879. The function of the Shudra caste is to serve the Brāhmans, Kshatriyas and Vaishyas, the three twice born
castes.

880. The Shudra has no other calling beyond the service of these castes. Now I have shown thee the duties of the four castes.

    XLV. *Devoted each to his own duty a man attains perfection. How one devoted to his duty attains to perfection, that do thou hear.*

881. O wise Arjuna, these are the proper duties of the various castes, as the ear and other senses have their related objects.
882. O son of Pāndu, as the proper destination of rain falling from the clouds is the river, and that of the river is the ocean,
883. so the natural duties according to his caste are proper to each man as fairness of skin is a natural property of the fair.
884. O best of warriors, let thy mind be firm in the resolve to perform thy caste duties as ordained by the scriptures.
885. One needs the help of an expert to determine the value of a jewel, and one must turn to the scriptures to know what is one's duty.
886. Though we possess sight, it cannot be used without light, and our feet are of no value if we do not know our road.
887. In the same way we should discover what are the duties proper to our caste through understanding the scriptures
888. Then, O Pāndava, as with the help of a lamp one has no difficulty in finding one's property in the dark,
889. the work that naturally falls to one's lot is confirmed by the scriptures. When the appointed duty is carried out,
890. abandoning sloth, having no thought for results, and devoting his whole body and mind to it,
891. then a man fulfils his function in an orderly way like a stream of water which flows steadily in one channel.
892. O Arjuna, one who performs his proper duties in this way reaches the further door of the entry into liberation.
893. Such a man is free from any dread of earthly existence as he never performs an unworthy action or one that is prohibited by the scriptures.
894. He is not tempted to turn towards any action prompted

by desire, as one would not willingly place one's legs in the
stocks even if they were made of sandalwood.

895. With regard to daily duties, he annuls the effect of them
by renouncing their fruit and so is he able to reach the
boundary of liberation.

896. Thus freed from good and evil actions in earthly life he
finds himself at the door of liberation in the form of dispassion.

897. To reach this dispassion is the height of good fortune, the
assurance of the attainment of liberation, and the end of
all striving.

898. It is the surety of the fruit of freedom, the flower of the
tree of merit on which, like a bee, the seeker after freedom
settles.

899. This dispassion is like the dawn that announces the
advent of the day of Self-realization.

900. It is like the magic pigment which, when applied to the
soul, gives the vision enabling one to find the treasure of
Self-knowledge.

901. O son of Pāndu, performing his own prescribed duties
makes a man worthy of attaining liberation.

902. Therefore, O Pāndava, these duties are our sole support
and to perform them is loving service which can be rendered to Me, the Supreme Spirit.

903. A devoted wife surrenders herself wholeheartedly to
pleasing her husband and in this way may be said to practise penance.

904. A mother is the sole support of her child, and therefore it
is the child's first duty to depend upon her.

905. A fish may regard the Ganges as only water, but by
remaining in it obtains the blessing of all sacred places.

906. So, too, there is no other way of salvation but the performance of one's duties without neglect; in this way the
burden is carried by the Lord of the world.

907. It is the purpose of the Supreme that each man should
have his appointed duty, and therefore in performing it he
surely attains to blessedness.

908. If a serving girl stands the test of a man's love, she may
become the wife of the master; the deed of one who risks
his life for his lord is written in the records.

909. So to be diligent in pleasing one's master, O Pāndava, is
indeed to serve him; all else is like the trade of a merchant.

910. When one performs one's duty it is not only that one has done that action, but one has carried out the purpose of Him from whom the whole creation proceeds.

911. This Creator has wrapped round the individual self, like a puppet, with the garment of ignorance and makes it dance on the string of egoism, woven from the three qualities.

912. He pervades the whole universe, within and without, as a lamp is filled with light.

913. When a man offers to this Supreme Spirit the flowers of his duty, O warrior, His joy is boundless,

914. and being gratified by such worship the Lord of the Spirit bestows on him as a [further] favour the attainment of dispassion.

915. When in this state of dispassion a man is overcome by his longing for the Supreme, he feels utter aversion towards all the things of this world.

916. As a wife separated from her husband feels her very life to be a burden, he regards all objects of pleasure as sources of misery.

917. As soon as true realization is awakened he becomes absorbed in the Spirit and acquires the worthiness to receive further teaching.

918. Therefore, he who is determined to attain liberation should apply himself diligently to the performance of his duty.

XLVII. *Better is one's own law though imperfectly carried out than the law of another carried out perfectly. One does not incur sin when one does the duty ordained by one's own nature.*

919. O Beloved, even though his appointed duty may be difficult to perform, a man should consider its ultimate reward.

920. O winner of wealth, if for one's own good it is necessary to take the juice of the neem tree, one should not be repelled by its bitterness.

921. One might be discouraged by the look of a plantain tree before it has borne fruit, but if one were to destroy it how would its sweet fruit be obtained?

922. Similarly if a man were to reject his duty because it was difficult, he would deprive himself of the joy of liberation.

923. A mother may be deformed, but the love by which her children live is not churlish.

924. Other women may be more beautiful than Rambhā but what does this matter to her children?

925. Clarified butter has qualities not found in water; but what would happen to a fish living in it?

926. What is poison to the whole world is like nectar to a worm, yet the juice of sugarcane [which is sweet] to the world, would cause its death.

927. Therefore a man's appointed duty which frees him from the bondage of life must be practised however difficult it may seem to be.

928. If one man were to undertake the duty of another, thinking it to be better, it would be like trying to walk on his head instead of his feet.

929. When a man thus performs the duty given to him according to his nature he overcomes the bondage of action.

930. It is unnecessary then to lay down the rule that a man ought to perform his own duty and leave that of another.

> XLVIII. *One should not give up the work suited to one's nature, O Son of Kuntī, [Arjuna], though it may be defective, for all enterprises are clouded by defects as fire by smoke.*

931. O Pāndava, until one has experienced the vision of the Spirit the performance of action does not cease, and where there is action there must first be effort.

932. If in the performance of duty others find initial difficulty, why should one consider that this is a fault in one's own?

933. If a man walks along a straight road his feet get just as tired as if he walked along a jungle track.

934. O winner of wealth, whether one carries [on a journey] stones or a bag of food, the burden is the same: he should therefore carry something that will be useful when he rests by the way.

935. The effort is the same whether one separates out grains or husks; it takes as long to cook food for a dog as to cook materials for a sacrifice.

936. If it is just as costly to support a wife as to keeps a mistress, why should a man bring censure upon himself?

937. O wise Arjuna, churning curds is as toilsome as it would be to churn water, and grinding sesamum needs as much effort as grinding sand.

938. As one cannot avoid death by a blow in the back, should one not face [the enemy] and receive it in front?

939. If a highborn woman is as likely to receive a beating in the house of another, there is no purpose in leaving her own husband.

940. If therefore a man cannot accomplish what he wishes without trouble, why should he consider his own duty to be burdensome?

941. O son of Pāndu, if by taking a little nectar a man could gain immortality, why should he not spend all that he has to obtain it?

942. Why should he spend his money to buy poison with which to commit suicide?

943. So if a man were to pass his whole life accumulating sin by the exercise of his senses, the only result would be sorrow.

944. Let him therefore perform his own duties, which will remove every burden and enable him to realize the supreme purpose of life.

945. For this reason, let no man neglect the practice of his duty, O Kiriti, as one would never forget a magic word that rescues one in difficulty.

946. A man should not let a boat [loose] at sea or [refuse to] take a potent remedy during an illness; this should be his attitude towards his duty.

> XLIX. *He whose understanding is unattached everywhere, who has subdued his self and from whom desire has fled, comes through renunciation to the supreme state transcending all work.*

947. Then, O Arjuna, bearer of the monkey banner, God, being pleased with the worship of the performance of one's duty, cleanses him from passion and darkness,

948. and leading his desire in the way of nectar-like purity shows him that earth and heaven are as deadly poison.

949. Thus he reaches his goal in that perfection which was earlier described as dispassion.

950. Now I will tell thee what he gains when he has reached this level [of perfect dispassion].

951. The dispassionate man cannot be entangled by physical existence or the conditions of worldly life, as the wind cannot be caught in a net.

952. His desire [for earthly things grows] weak, as when a fruit is ripe stem and fruit [no longer hold each other].

953. He becomes detached from his wife, his children and his wealth, not regarding them as his own, as no one would claim possession of poison.

954. His mind withdraws from sense pleasures as though it were burnt by their very touch, and he retires into inner silence.

955. His inner sense refrains from turning outwards and breaking its resolve to avoid sense pleasures, as a serving maid fears to disobey the command of her master.

956. O Kiriti, he places his mind securely within the grasp of union with the Self and drives it on with his longing for the Spirit.

957. Then every desire for worldly or heavenly enjoyment comes to an end, as smoke vanishes when a fire is extinguished with ashes.

958. With the mind under control desire dies away and he reaches the condition of self-restraint.

959. As a result of this false knowledge disappears, O Pāndava, and the self gains the power of true perception.

960. In the same way that stored water is gradually used up, his accumulated merit is expended and no new merit is acquired by further action.

961. O best of warriors, when a man has gained this state of perfect equilibrium in action, he will find his guru without difficulty.

962. When the four watches of the night are past we are able to see the sun, the destroyer of darkness.

963. When a plantain tree has borne fruit its growth ceases; so, having met his guru, the seeker is set free from the necessity of action.

964. Then by the grace of the guru, O best of warriors, he will reach perfection as the moon is made perfect on the day when it is full.

965. By means of that grace all ignorance is dispelled, as darkness passes away when night comes to an end,

966. With the death of ignorance all activity comes to an end, and this brings about complete renunciation.

967. With this total renunciation of ignorance, all visible nature disappears and the Self is all that remains to be known.

968. When a man wakes from sleep will he try to rescue himself from the deep river [in which he dreamt he was drowning]?

969. Then the dream in which he thought that he would eventually find knowledge disappears and he himself becomes that heaven in the form of knowledge in which there is neither knower nor object of knowledge.

970. O best of warriors, when a mirror that reflects one's image is taken away the reflection disappears and only the observer is left,

971. so when ignorance is removed knowledge also disappears and pure knowledge free from action remains.

972. O winner of wealth, because in such a state action is not possible, it is described as beyond action.

973. When the wind ceases blowing over the sea the waves [subside], and similarly when a man realizes that he is indeed the Self,

974. the sense of non-activity that is aroused is the perfect state of being beyond action and it is the highest attainment.

975. The pinnacle is the completion of a temple, its union with the sea is the supreme goal of the Ganges and one hundred per cent purity is the highest value of gold.

976. So the state in which knowledge dispels ignorance and then is itself dispelled,

977. is not surpassed by any other, and therefore it is regarded as the supreme attainment.

> L. *Hear from Me, in brief, O Son of Kuntī [Arjuna], how, having attained perfection, he attains to Brahman, that supreme consummation of wisdom.*

978. This realization is reached in time by one who is endowed with good fortune, through the grace of his guru.

979. When the sun rises darkness is lost in the light, when camphor is put into a flame it too is transformed into light;

980. when grains of salt are put into water, they melt immediately and seem to have become water.

981. When a man wakes his sleep vanishes together with all his dreams and he returns to his conscious self.

982. So too, when by good fortune a man hears the teaching of his guru, duality is overcome and his mind is at rest.

983. Then can it be said that there is any further need for
action? Is the sky concerned with coming and going?

984. Indeed, nothing further remains for him to do; but there
are some for whom it is not possible,

985. O Kiriti, to experience union with Brahma immediately
on hearing the words of the guru.

986. But first he must burn up passion and darkness in the fire
of his own duty, with the fuel of actions which are prohibited or prompted by desire.

987. Any desire for his son, his wealth or for heavenly life must
become as a servant in his house.

988. He must purify in the holy waters of restraint his senses
which are polluted by wandering among objects of sense.

989. He must offer up the fruit of his duties to the Supreme and
by this means he must remain firmly established in dispassion.

990. He must equip himself with all these means by which the
true perception is gained which leads to self-knowledge.

991. When this is accomplished he must find the guru who will
be sincere in his teaching.

992. When medicine is taken disease does not immediately
disappear; does noon follow the dawn of the day?

993. If good seed is sown in a well-watered field a good harvest
may be expected, but only in course of time.

994. Even if one finds an excellent road and one is in good
company, nevertheless it takes time to complete the
journey.

995. So when dispassion has been attained, the guru found
and the tender shoot of discrimination begins to grow in
the mind,

996. a man experiences with conviction the truth that there is
only the one Brahma and all else is delusion,

997. that Brahma is all pervading and the highest state and in
him even the work of liberation ceases.

998. The realization of these three states will continue to such
a pitch, O Kiriti, that even the oneness of union is no
longer felt as a separate experience,

999. and all bliss that is distinguishable as a mental perception
becomes merged in the Absolute, in Whom ends that
knowledge by which the triplicity of subject, object and
the link between them is lost in Absolute Union, and
nothing remains.

1000. The state of becoming one with Brahma is [then] experienced in due course.
1001. If a hungry man is served with the most delicious food he
becomes more and more satisfied with every mouthful.
1002. In the same way as when the lamp of the mind is fed with
the oil of dispassion, he is inspired by the wealth of the
Spirit.
1003. Then he becomes endowed with the worthiness to experience the full glory of Brahma.
1004. Now I will tell thee in order the steps by which union with
Brahma may be attained, and their inner meaning; listen
to this.

> LI. *Endowed with a pure understanding, firmly restrain-
> ing oneself, turning away from sound and other objects
> of sense and casting aside attraction and aversion.*

1005. Arriving at the holy place of discrimination, by means of
the road that has been shown by his guru, he cleanses his
mind from all stain.
1006. Then it is restored to its original purity like the light of
the moon when it is released from the grip of the demon
Rāhu.
1007. As a wife leaves the homes of both her mother and her
father-in-law and follows her husband, he renources the
world of duality and devotes himself to meditation.
1008. Then the various objects of sense which have been given
too much importance by all the sense organs, driving
away the helpful friend of wisdom,
1009. are deprived of their power, through restraint of the
senses, as a mirage is dispelled by the setting sun.
1010. As food taken inadvertently in the house of a low-born
man should be vomited, the senses and feelings of desire
must be detached from objects of sense.
1011. Their tendencies which are withdrawn from their objects
are then purified by penance as though by the waters of
the bank of the Ganges.
1012. Then the senses are cleansed by the practice of pure resolution and the mind perseveres in meditation.
1013. If in this condition of the mind he meets with pleasure or
pain as a result of past lives, he feels no resentment against
untoward experiences;

1014. nor does he allow desire to arise in his mind if pleasurable experiences come to him.

> LII. *Dwelling in solitude, eating but little, controlling speech, body and mind, and ever engaged in meditation and concentration and taking refuge in dispassion,*

1015. So, O Kiriti, renouncing both love of pleasure and hatred of what is undesirable, he withdraws to dwell in a cave or forest.

1016. He avoids all human activities and lives alone in a grove of the forest, with only himself for company.

1017. He practises control of the body and the mind, silence is his only converse and in meditation on the teachings of his guru he is unaware of time.

1018. Whether food will strengthen his body, satisfy his hunger or be pleasant to taste,

1019. these things he does not consider when taking food; he eats little, but there is no limit to his satisfaction.

1020. As the life force may be destroyed by feeding the inner fire, he eats only enough to sustain life;

1021. and as a wife of good family does not give up her body to the lust of another man, he does not yield to sleep or sloth.

1022. His body touches the ground only when he prostrates himself before his deity, but he does not lie down for the pleasure of sleeping.

1023. He uses his hands and feet only for the necessary movements of the body, thus he has complete self-control.

1024. He never allows desire to cross the threshold of his mind, O warrior, and therefore there is no opportunity for conversation.

1025. Having thus brought under control his body, his speech and his mind he then encompasses the further regions of meditation.

1026. As a man may look closely at himself in a mirror, he becomes firmly convinced of the wisdom which the teaching of the guru has impressed on him.

1027. Listen! Although he himself is the one meditating, in the practice of meditation the essence of the three elements is realized. This is the true method of meditation.

1028. O son of Pāndu, he continues his meditation until the meditation, the one who meditates and the object of meditation are all merged into one.

1029. So the seeker becomes expert in the attainment of knowledge of the Self and he resorts to the practice of yoga.

1030. O winner of wealth, he presses with his heel the lower organs of the body in the yogic posture.

1031. Contracting the lower part of the trunk and uniting three yogic postures he brings together three of the vital airs.

1032. He awakens Kundalini by opening the central passage and forces a way through from the lowest psychic centre to the highest.

1033. Now the cloud of the thousand petalled crown centre showers down a stream of nectar which flows through the body as far as the sacral centre.

1034. In the earthen bowl of the deity of consciousness, dancing on the holy mountain [of the crown centre], he serves a dish of the mixture of mind and vital airs.

1035. In this way the yogi thrusts forward a vanguard of yogic practices and behind it completes his meditation on the Self.

1036. Yet before these two, yoga and meditation, can enter into uninterrupted realization of the Self,

1037. he must first make a friend of dispassion and travel along the whole road in company with him.

1038. If a light is carried until the object sought for is found is there any delay in seeing it?

1039. Similarly as long as dispassion accompanies him a man who has experienced liberation cannot fail to reach union with Brahma.

1040. Thus the favoured man who has dispassion and the acquisition and practice of wisdom has become worthy of union with the Self.

1041. Therefore if a man wears the armour of renunciation, and mounts the steed of the highest yoga,

1042. if he holds in the hand of discrimination the sword of meditation and strikes down all obstacles great or small,

1043. he enters the battlefield of worldly life like the rising sun to win as a bride the glorious victory of liberation.

> LIII. *Casting aside self-sense, force, arrogance, desire, anger, possession, and is egoless and tranquil in mind, he becomes worthy of becoming one with Brahma.*

1044. There he defeats all the enemies in the form of vices which come in his path, the first of which is the sense of individuality associated with the body.

1045. This enemy will not set him free by killing him, having brought him in to life will not let him live, and imprisons him with the physical skeleton.

1046. O warrior, he captures the fortress of the body in which the enemy lives and then destroys his second enemy, power.

1047. This vice increases fourfold at the very mention of an object of pleasure, and reduces the world to a state of death.

1048. It is the deep source from which gushes the poison of the pleasures of sense and the king of all vices; but it cannot withstand a blow from the sword of meditation.

1049. It rejoices in the acquisition of all forms of sense pleasures and delights to surround the self with them as a garment.

1050. It causes a man to wander from the right path, leads him into the by-paths of evil and gives him into the power of the tiger of hell.

1051. He destroys that giver of false confidence, pride, which brings terror to the heart of those who practise penance,

1052. and anger, the greatest of vices, which becomes more empty the more it is fostered.

1053. He removes all trace of desire and with it anger is also destroyed,

1054. as when the roots of a tree are severed the branches will wither; when desire dies anger dies with it.

1055. So when the enemy called desire is killed in this battle, anger suffers the same fate.

1056. As a tyrant does not fail to make a criminal carry a load on his head even while his feet are shackled, so a man's burden increases with his possessions.

1057. It lays a burden upon a man's head, gives rise to many faults and places in his hand the staff of personal possession.

1058. It inveigles even a man who has become detached into establishing hermitages and yogic training for the pleasure of expounding the scriptures to disciples.

1059. Through it, sometimes, a man abandons his family, retires into the forest, and even there he becomes attached to the objects around him; it assails him even when he has abandoned clothing for the body.

1060. But the true seeker overcomes this powerful desire for possessions, and enjoys the experience of triumph over worldly life.

1061. Then humility and all the other great virtues of wisdom come out to meet him as princes of the land of highest bliss.

1062. They bestow on him the kingship of true knowledge and become the retinue which always accompanies him.

1063. As he walks along the high road of worldly activity, the three states of consciousness, as three maidens, wave around him at every step the protective leaves of happiness.

1064. Before him is carried the wand of enlightenment, discrimination moves aside the throng of the visible world and meditations accompany him waving their lamps.

1065. Companies of psychic powers gather together and he is covered with the flowers which they throw over him.

1066. When he approaches the kingdom of union with the Supreme Spirit, all the three worlds are filled with joy.

1067. Then, O winner of wealth, there is no sense of duality left by which he could call one man his friend and another his enemy.

1068. He has become so free from duality that he does not under any pretext claim anything as his own.

1069. O son of Pāndu, having thus brought the whole world under his rule, all sense of attachment to possessions is driven away.

1070. In this way he has overcome all his enemies and, having become one with the whole world, the steed of yogic practices is halted.

1071. He loosens for a while the tightly fitting armour of dispassion,

1072. and as that duality which he would kill with the sword of meditation is no longer before him, the hand of activity casts it away.

1073. Then he becomes like a medicine which, having had its effect, dies with the disease;

1074. or as a man stops running when he arrives at the end of his journey, he gives up his yogic practices, having reached Brahma.

1075. When a river flows into the ocean, the speed of its current
is lost; a wife is calmed in the presence of her husband.

1076. When a plantain tree has borne fruit its growth stops,
and the road comes to an end when it reaches a village;

1077. so when a man becomes aware of union with the Self he
gradually lays aside the various means [by which he
reached that state].

1078. Therefore, O winner of wealth, when union with Brahma
is attained the means of attaining it have no further purpose.

1079. When the sun of dispassion sets, knowledge reaches
maturity and the fruit of yoga ripens,

1080. the state of perfect peace is brought about, O fortunate
one, and a man is worthy to become Brahma.

1081. The moon on the fourteenth day is but little smaller than
it is on the day of the full moon; and the value of slightly
impure gold is but little less than that of pure gold.

1082. When a river reaches the ocean it remains a river so long
as it flows with a current; when the current disappears it
becomes the ocean.

1083. The difference that separates Brahma from a man who is
worthy to become Brahma is as slight as these other
differences, and by reaching the state of peace he very
soon becomes Brahma.

1084. He who realizes that he is Brahma in himself even before
he becomes Brahma, in this way is worthy of entering
into oneness with Him.

> LIV. *Having become one with Brahma, and being tranquil
> in spirit, he neither grieves nor desires. Regarding all
> beings as alike he attains supreme devotion to Me.*

1085. O son of Pāndu, the man who has reached this state of
worthiness attains the blessed condition of Self-realization.

1086. When the heat by which food is cooked cools, one can
enjoy it.

1087. The turbulent floods of the Ganges subside after the rainy
season; at the end of a song the accompanying drum dies
down.

1088. In the same way the stress and strain of striving after
Self-realization passes away [when its end is attained].

1089. This condition is known as the glory of realization of the Self. A great souled Arjuna, the man who is worthy of it enters into this experience.

1090. When complete equanimity is reached, there is no further sense of personality which can be subject to grief or desire.

1091. When the sun rises the light of all the stars is dimmed by its brilliance;

1092. so, O Pārtha, when a man has reached self-realization the sense of diversity in creatures is removed and he sees himself in all things.

1093. As letters written on a slate can be rubbed off with the hand, so in his sight all forms of difference disappear.

1094. With this disappearance the two states of consciousness, waking and dreaming, arising from false knowledge, are lost in ignorance,

1095. and ignorance also passes away as illumination increases and is absorbed in perfect Self-realization.

1096. As one walks along the distance of a journey grows less, and walking ceases at the end of it.

1097. As one eats a meal one's hunger decreases and when one is satisfied it passes away.

1098. In the same way when the waking consciousness becomes active sleep is overcome and when one is completely awake it is entirely lost.

1099. When the moon is full the phase of waxing ceases and the bright half of the month is over;

1100. so when knowledge overcomes all the objects to be known it is absorbed into Me, Brahma, and ignorance finally disappears.

1101. At the time of the final deluge the boundaries of all rivers and oceans break and the whole universe is filled with water.

1102. When all pots and all houses are destroyed, all space is one; when all fuel is burnt up only the fire is left for burning.

1103. When all ornaments are melted in a crucible only gold is left, and names and forms disappear.

1104. When a man awakes his dreams vanish and only the man himself is left,

1105. and when a man sees nothing but Me with him he has reached the fourth state of devotion.

1106. This is called the fourth form of devotion, the other three being practised by those who are afflicted, those in search of knowledge and those seeking wealth.

1107. Yet it is neither one of these three nor the fourth, it is not the first or the last; its true name is the devotion of oneness with Me.

1108. [That fourth form] illuminates ignorance about Me, which shows Me in a false light, and leads men to worship Me everywhere.

1109. It is that unbroken light which reveals everything, and by it each man sees an object according to his individual perception.

1110. It is the light by which the universe comes into being and is dissolved, as objects appear and disappear in a dream.

1111. O thou who hast the monkey banner, this inherent light in Me is therefore spoken of as devotion.

1112. For a man full of desire this devotion will take the form of desire, and he makes Me the object of his longing.

1113. O great warrior, for those who seek wisdom, it shows itself as the search for knowledge and I am the object of that search.

1114. For those who seek wealth, O Arjuna, it becomes the making of petitions, and by identifying Me with wealth attributes to Me that name.

1115. When devotion to Me is practised in this way, directed by ignorance, it makes of Me, the seer, that which is to be seen.

1116. It is true to say that [in a mirror] the face is seen by the face, but it is the mirror that gives the false impression of duality.

1117. A man perceives the moon with his eyes, but through defective sight he may see two moons where there is only one.

1118. In the same way I pervade all things through this devotion, but owing to man's ignorance there is the illusion that I can be seen.

1119. At the last this ignorance is dispelled, My apparent visibility and Myself become one as a reflection is united with the object reflected.

1120. Even when there is some alloy mixed with gold, the gold itself is pure, but when the impurity is removed only pure gold is left.

1121. Is not the moon complete in itself even before the day of the full moon? Yet on that day it seems to reach fullness.

1122. So through false knowledge I appear to be visible, though in various ways; but when this illusion of visibility is removed, I and My visible self are known to be one.

1123. For this reason, O Pārtha, the fourth kind of devotion transcends the other three in which I am thought to be visible.

1124. Thou knowest already that the devotee who has attained to union with Me through knowledge and devotion is indeed one with Me.

1125. O monkey-bannered warrior, in the seventh chapter I told thee, with hands upraised, that the wise man is My very spirit.

1126. At the beginning of the world I taught this to Brahmā the Creator, through the Bhāgavata, as the highest form of devotion.[10]

1127. The wise call it self-knowledge, the followers of Shiva say that it is energy, but I Myself call it the highest devotion.

1128. As soon as union with Me is reached through the way of action it bears fruit; [for such a yogi] the world is entirely pervaded by Me.

1129. Then discrimination and dispassion vanish, bondage and freedom pass away and the cycle of birth and death is released.

1130. As what is near is lost in what is more remote and as space envelops all the four elements,

1131. so he experiences only Me, the pure one, unlimited and beyond the distinction of the goal of life and the means of attaining it.

1132. As the waters of the Ganges still sparkle even after they have reached the sea, so is his enjoyment [of union with Me].

1133. His joy in Me is like the light reflected back and forth between two polished mirrors.

1134. A dream vanishes on waking, but then a man can experience his individual unity with no sense of duality.

1135. When a mirror is taken away the image in it disappears, all that one can experience is his own visibility.

1136. Some may hold the opinion that when union is reached there can be no experience of it; but one might as well ask how a word can be uttered by words.

1137. Does the sun shine in a village by means of a lamp? Do people erect a canopy to support the heavens?

1138. How can a man who is not a king enjoy sovereignty? How can darkness embrace the sun?

1139. Can anything that is not space understand the nature of space? Can a trinket lend beauty to a jewel?

1140. One who has not become united with Me cannot know where I am; therefore it cannot be said that he worships Me.

1141. Thus he who through the path of action becomes one with Me enjoys Me as a young woman delights in her youth.

1142. As waves delight in the embrace of the water, light rejoices in the sun and space wanders through the heavens,

1143. so when he is united with Me he worships Me without action, as gold ornaments do honour to the gold of which they are made.

1144. The fragrance of sandalwood could be said to offer its worship to the tree and the moonlight adores the moon with true joy.

1145. Similarly, though the thought of action is inconsistent with non-duality, yet there is a form of devotion in union; this cannot be described in words but only known in experience.

1146. Whatever such a man may say to Me, arising from the merit he has acquired in former lives, I respond to his appeal.

1147. Yet in this the speaker meets himself and there is no speech; this silence is the best form of praise.

1148. As soon as he speaks he meets Me, for I am the speaker; in this silence he truly worships Me.

1149. Similarly, O Kiriti, whatever he sees with his sight or perceives with his mind, the very seeing of it does away with it and only the seer remains.

1150. As a man in front of a mirror sees his own face, so his perception will see himself as the seer in everything seen.

1151. When the object to be seen seems to disappear and the

seer sees only himself, then their separateness ceases and also [the act of] seeing.

1152. If a man awakens and tries to grasp a woman seen in a dream they do not exist as man and wife and he alone remains.

1153. When fire is produced by rubbing together two pieces of wood, the two pieces are lost in the fire and they can no longer be called two.

1154. If the sun tried to grasp its own reflection in water, the sun would lose its power of being reflected.

1155. So when the man who is united with Me looks at any object neither the object nor the faculty of sight exist.

1156. When the sun illuminates darkness, it then exists no longer as the illuminator; so the power of being visible is no longer in the object because it has become Me.

1157. The state in which there is neither visibility nor invisibility is the true perception of Me.

1158. O Kiriti, perceiving Me in whatever he sees, a man experiences that vision which is beyond [the duality of] seer and object of seeing.

1159. As space is immovable because it pervades all space, so he is entirely filled with Me who am the Spirit.

1160. In the final deluge water is everywhere and therefore ceases to run in channels; in the same way he is wholly pervaded by Me, the Spirit.

1161. Can one foot climb upon another, fire burn fire water enter water or a river bathe in itself?

1162. When such a man has become one with Me, he neither comes nor goes; this is his pilgrimage towards Me, the One beyond duality.

1163. A wave on the surface of the water cannot cross the land however strongly it may flow,

1164. for whether it subsides or flows on, the movement which impels it lies, after all, in the persistent flux of water.

1165. Wherever it may go, O son of Pāndu, it never loses its oneness with the quality of water.

1166. So when such a man has become wholly united with Me he will always be My faithful pilgrim, though he may be assailed by the sense of individuality.

1167. If, however, owing to the nature of his body he is constrained to act in some way, I meet him through that very activity.

1168. For, O son of Pāndu, [the difference between] action and doer disappears and, seeing Me as the Spirit, he becomes one with Me.

1169. If one mirror is set in front of another, that would not produce the action of seeing, as gold overlaid with gold is not really hidden.

1170. If a lamp seems to illumine another lamp it cannot be said to give light to the other; so if action is performed by one who is one with Me, can it be regarded as action?

1171. When a man acts without any sense of being responsible for the action, it is as though he had not acted.

1172. Whatever act is performed by a man after union with Me is not action. This is true worship of Me.

1173. O warrior of the monkey-banner, even a carefully performed action is as no action, and such a man serves Me with the highest worship.

1174. Whatever he speaks is praise of Me, in whatever he sees there is a vision of Me and every movement is a step towards Me, the One.

1175. In whatever he does he worships Me, his every thought is the speaking of My name and whatever his condition he is absorbed in Me.

1176. As a gold bracelet is one with gold, so he is united with Me through his devotion.

1177. Cloth is one with its own woven threads, an earthen pot is made of earth; so too My devotee is one with Me.

1178. Waves are one with water, the fragrance of camphor is inseparable from it and the lustre of a jewel is inherent in the jewel.

1179. O wise Arjuna, by means of this single-minded devotion he recognizes Me as the Seer in all visible things.

1180. The whole phenomenal creation that is observed either in a manifest or an unmanifested state, that is perceived through the three modes of consciousness, and that is limited in the way of form or name, all in its entirety is I—the Seer.[11]

1181. O warrior, when this realization, [that I am the Seer,] comes to the devotee, he dances with [the joy of] this experience, as though at a wedding.

1182. A rope may be mistaken for a snake, but when it is clearly seen it is recognized as a rope.

1183. There is nothing but gold in an ornament, and this can be shown by melting it down.
1184. Waves consist only of water, and when this is realized one is not deceived by their form.
1185. If after waking one tries to measure the substance of a dream one finds that apart from oneself there is nothing.
1186. Such experience is similar to that of the man who realizes that I am the knower who inspires the desire to know all that is or is not.
1187. He will then know that I am beyond birth and age, imperishable and immortal, unprecedented and limitless joy.
1188. I am immutable, infallible, eternal, the one without a second, the origin of all and both manifest and unmanifest.
1189. I am the ruler and the ruled, without beginning, deathless, fearless, the support as well as that which is supported.
1190. I am the everlasting lord, self-originating and eternal; I am all, I pervade all and I transcend all.
1191. I am the ancient and the new, I am nothingness yet I am completion, I am both the particle and the mass; I am all that is.
1192. I am free from activity, without attachment and beyond grief; I am that which pervades and that which is pervaded; I am the Highest Spirit.
1193. I am beyond sound and hearing, without form or race, I am without variation or dependence; I am the Highest Brahma.
1194. Through this single-minded devotion I am known to be the One Spirit and he who knows this, knows Me.
1195. When a man awakens from sleep he realizes that only he as an individual remains.
1196. When the sun rises it is the illuminator and is not different from that which it illuminates.
1197. Likewise when objects of knowledge disappear, the knower alone is left, and he should realize this. When he does so,
1198. O winner of wealth, the knowledge by which he realizes this non-duality is none other than Myself.
1199. Then he knows that I am the Self, beyond both duality and non-duality, and he enters into the experience of full realization of this.

1200. When a man awakes from sleep he realizes that he is only
one, but when this perception is lost, can we know what
happens?

1201. When a man perceives with his eyes that ornaments are
made of gold, they are as it were reduced to gold without
being melted down.

1202. If salt is put into water it becomes mixed with the water,
the two elements merging; when the water dries up its
existence as salt comes to an end.

1203. In the same way the perception that he and I are one is
lost by being absorbed into the supreme joy of union with
Me.

1204. When he has no further sense of his own individuality,
how can he see Me as different from himself? Then both
he and I are merged in this union with Me.

1205. When camphor has been burnt up the fire also will disappear and then space which transcends them both will
be all that remains.

1206. As when one is deducted from one, zero is left, so only I
remain after being and non-being come to an end.

1207. Consequently such expressions as Brahma, the Self,
Lord, lose their meaning, nor is there any place for silence.

1208. Then one should speak only that which without speech
cannot be spoken, and know only that which is beyond
both knowing and not-knowing.

1209. [In this state of union,] knowledge is known through
knowledge, joy experienced through joy, and bliss
realized only through bliss.

1210. Profit is gained through profit, light embraced by light,
and wonder is lost in wonder.

1211. Even-mindedness is contained within itself, peace enters
into tranquillity and experience delights in experience.

1212. So by following the beautiful vine of the yoga of action a
man obtains the fruit of complete union with Me.

1213. O Kiriti, on the royal crown of this yoga I am the jewel of
pure consciousness and reciprocally he becomes My
[jewel].

1214. He is the space which surrounds the pinnacle of self-liberation on the temple of the yoga of action,

1215. and in the forest of this earthly existence [he is the
traveller who] by the road of the yoga of action reaches
the city of union with Me.

1216. On the current of the yoga of action he is like the Ganges
of devotion flowing swiftly to the ocean of blissful union
with Me.

1217. O wise one, such is the greatness of the yoga of action that
I constantly expound it to thee.

1218. I cannot be reached by any time, place or object; I am
by My own nature all in all to every man.

1219. The established method of reaching union with Me is
through the relationship of each disciple with his
guru.

1220. Therefore it requires no great effort to reach Me; this yoga
surely leads to Me.

1221. O Kiriti, treasures lie concealed in the earth, fire latent in
wood, milk is contained in the udders of a cow;

1222. but to obtain these things one must use the right methods
and I also am to be reached by certain means.

1223. If anyone should ask why the Lord is explaining the
means after having spoken of the result, I will tell you the
reason.

1224. The great teaching of the Gitā expounds fully the method
of attaining liberation, while no other scripture does this
with authority.

1225. The wind can drive the clouds from the sky [and reveal
the sun] but it cannot create the sun; the hand can remove
moss from the surface of water, but it cannot create the
water.

1226. In the same way other scriptures may remove the impurity of ignorance that obstructs the vision of Self-realization, but only I, the pure one, can reveal Myself.

1227. All other philosophies are capable of destroying ignorance,
but they have no power to bring about Self-realization,

1228. and when their validity is challenged, [the authority] to
which they turn is the Gitā.

1229. When the eastern sky is illuminated by the rising sun, all
other directions are aglow with light; so the Gitā, the
highest of all, gives support to all other scriptures.

1230. This great Gitā has already explained in detail the
methods by which the Self may be reached, as though
with the grasp of a hand.

1231. Thinking with compassion that Arjuna might not be able
at first to grasp them,

1232. Shri Krishna explains once more those principles, as